RAF Bomber Command Profiles

44 (Rhodesia) Squadron

RAF Bomber Command Profiles

44 (Rhodesia) Squadron

Chris Ward

www.bombercommandbooks.com

This edition first published 2021 by Mention the War Ltd., 25 Cromwell Street, Merthyr Tydfil, CF47 8RY.

Copyright 2021 © Chris Ward.

The right of Chris Ward to be identified as Author of this work is asserted by him in accordance with the Copyright, Designs and Patents Act 1988.

The original Operational Record Book of 44 (Rhodesia) Squadron and the Bomber Command Night Raid Reports are Crown Copyright and stored in microfiche and digital format by the National Archives. Material is reproduced under Open Licence v.2.0.

All rights reserved. No part of this publication may be reproduced, stored in a retrieval system, transmitted in any form or by any means, electronic, mechanical or photocopied, recorded or otherwise, without the written permission of the copyright owners.

This squadron profile has been researched, compiled and written by its author, who has made every effort to ensure the accuracy of the information contained in it. The author will not be liable for any damages caused, or alleged to be caused, by any information contained in this book. E. & O.E.

Cover design: Topics - The Creative Partnership www.topicsdesign.co.uk

Photos and captions: Clare Bennet.

A CIP catalogue reference for this book is available from the British Library.

ISBN 9781911255772

Also by Chris Ward from Bomber Command Books:

Casualty of War: Letters Home from Flight Lieutenant Bill Astell DFC

Dambuster Deering: The Life and Death of an Unsung Hero (with Clare Bennet)

Dambusters : The Complete WWII History of 617 Squadron
(with Andy Lee and Andreas Wachtel)

Other RAF Bomber Command Profiles:

10 Squadron (with Ian MacMillan)

35 Squadron

38 Squadron

50 Squadron

75(NZ) Squadron (with Chris Newey)

83 Squadron

101 Squadron

103 Squadron (with David Fell)

106 Squadron (with Herman Bijlard)

115 Squadron

138 Squadron (with Piotr Hodyra)

207 Squadron (with Raymond Glynne-Owen)

300 Squadron (with Grzegorz Korcz)

301, 304 and 305 Polish Squadrons (with Grzegorz Korcz)

467 Squadron RAAF

514 Squadron (with Simon Hepworth)

617 Squadron

619 Squadron

Contents

Introduction	11
Dedication	13
Narrative History	15
1939	15
1940 First Quarter	28
April 1940	30
May 1940	35
June 1940	43
July 1940	53
August 1940	62
September 1940	69
October 1940	77
November 1940	84
December 1940	90
January 1941	120
February 1941	124
March 1941	129
April 1941	135
May 1941	141
June 1941	146
July 1941	152
August 1941	160
September 1941	167
October 1941	174
November 1941	178
December 1941	182
January 1942	200
February 1942	202
March 1942	205
April 1942	209
May 1942	216
June 1942	221

July 1942	228
August 1942	233
September 1942	240
October 1942	246
November 1942	251
December 1942	255
January 1943	297
February 1943	302
March 1943	307
April 1943	312
May 1943	318
June 1943	322
July 1943	328
August 1943	334
September 1943	341
October 1943	346
November 1943	350
December 1943	355
January 1944	379
February 1944	385
March 1944	388
April 1944	394
May 1944	400
June 1944	408
July 1944	415
August 1944	422
September 1944	431
October 1944	438
November 1944	442
December 1944	447
January 1945	465
February 1945	469
March 1945	474

April 1945	480
Stations	489
Commanding Officers	489
Aircraft	489
Operational Record	490
Aircraft Histories	491
44 (Rhodesia) Squadron Roll of Honour	503
Key to Abbreviations	523

Introduction

RAF Bomber Command Squadron Profiles first appeared in the late nineties and proved to be very popular with enthusiasts of RAF Bomber Command during the Second World War. They became a useful research tool, particularly for those whose family members had served and were no longer around. The original purpose was to provide a point of reference for all of the gallant men and women who had fought the war, either in the air, or on the ground in a support capacity, and for whom no written history of their unit or station existed. I wanted to provide them with something they could hold up, point to and say, "this was my unit, this is what I did in the war". Many veterans were reticent to talk about their time on bombers, partly because of modesty, but perhaps mostly because the majority of those with whom they came into contact had no notion of what it was to be a "Bomber Boy", to face the prospect of death every time they took to the air, whether during training or on operations. Only those who shared the experience really understood what it was to go to war in bombers, which is why reunions were so important. As they approached the end of their lives, many veterans began to speak openly for the first time about their life in wartime Bomber Command, and most were hurt by the callous treatment they received at the hands of successive governments with regard to the lack of recognition of their contribution to victory. It is sad that this recognition in the form of a national memorial and the granting of a campaign medal came too late for the majority. Now this inspirational, noble generation, the like of which will probably never grace this earth again, has all but departed from us, and the world will be a poorer place as a result.

RAF Bomber Command Squadron Profiles are back. The basic format remains, but, where needed, additional information has been provided. Squadron Profiles do not claim to be comprehensive histories, but rather detailed overviews of the activities of the squadron. There is insufficient space to mention as many names as one would like, but all aircraft losses are accompanied by the name of the pilot. Fundamentally, the narrative section is an account of Bomber Command's war from the perspective of the bomber group under which the individual squadron served, and the deeds of the squadron are interwoven into this story. Information has been drawn from official records, such as group, squadron and station ORBs, and from the many, like me, amateur enthusiasts, who dedicate much of their time to researching individual units, and become unrivalled authorities on them. I am grateful for their generous contributions, and their names will appear in the appropriate Profiles. The statistics quoted in this series are taken from The Bomber Command War Diaries, that indispensable tome written by Martin Middlebrook and Chris Everitt, and I am indebted to Martin for his kind permission to use them.

Finally, let me apologize in advance for the inevitable errors, for no matter how hard I and other authors try to write "nothing but the truth", there is no such thing as a definitive account of history, and there will always be room for disagreement and debate. Official records are notoriously unreliable tools, and yet we have little choice but to put our faith in them. It is not my intention to misrepresent any person or Bomber Command unit, and I ask my readers to understand the enormity of the task I have undertaken. It is relatively easy to become an authority on single units or even a bomber group, but I chose to write about them all, idiot that I am, which means 128 squadrons serving operationally in Bomber Command at some time between the 3rd of September 1939 and the 8th of May 1945. I am dealing with eight bomber groups, in which some 120,000 airmen served, and I am juggling around 28,000 aircraft serial numbers, code letters and details of provenance and fate. I ask not for your sympathy, it was, after all, my choice, but rather your understanding if you should find something with which you disagree. My thanks to you, my readers, for making the original series of RAF Bomber Command Squadron Profiles so popular, and I hope you receive this new incarnation equally enthusiastically.

I am indebted to Christopher Dean at the RAF Waddington Heritage Centre for providing unlimited access to the photograph archive, to Kevin Lawry and the 44 (Rhodesia) Squadron Association for access to its photo album and Louise Bush for sharing the Lincolnshire Aviation Heritage Centre collection. My thanks are due, as always, to my gang members, Andreas Wachtel, Clare Bennett, Steve Smith and Greg Korcz for their unstinting support, without which my Profiles would be the poorer. Finally, my appreciation to my publisher, Simon Hepworth of Mention the War Publications, for his belief in my work, untiring efforts to promote it, and for the stress I put him through to bring my books to publication.

Chris Ward. Skegness, Lincolnshire. April 2021.

Dedication

This WWII history of 44 (Rhodesia) Squadron is dedicated to the memory of Warrant Officer Stan Dare, and to the other unsung heroes who served with the squadron in the air and on the ground at Waddington, Dunholme Lodge and Spilsby.

44 (RHODESIA) SQUADRON

Narrative History

1939

Although formed as a fighter squadron on the 24th of July 1917 to defend the London area, 44 Squadron would find fame as an offensive unit during the Second World War, flying bombers against the enemy wherever targets presented themselves, whether in its heartland, in the countries it occupied, or at sea. Following a period of disbandment from 1919, the squadron was resurrected at Wyton in March 1937, and having spent a brief spell at Andover, arrived at Waddington on the 16th of June. Located four miles south of the city of Lincoln, Waddington was an important WW1 airfield but after closing in January 1920, the buildings went into care and maintenance. However, the airfield reopened again in November 1926 as a fully equipped bomber station under the control of 5 Group, Bomber Command. It was chosen for expansion in 1935, and an entirely new complex was built in the north-western corner of the airfield, which is the present-day RAF Waddington. Having flirted briefly with Hinds, Blenheims and Ansons, the squadron received Handley Page Hampden twin-engine medium bombers in February 1939. Initially, it assumed a training role, converting 5 Group crews to twin-engine aircraft, until reverting to a front-line operational status from the 1st of June. It was in this form that the squadron faced the outbreak of war under the command of Wing Commander John Boothman, who had been appointed in April, and who, in September 1931, had won the Schneider Trophy outright for Britain in the famed Supermarine S6B.

On the day of the declaration of war, Sunday, the 3rd of September 1939, Bomber Command was represented by 3, 4 and 5 Groups as its main offensive arm, equipped respectively with Wellingtons, Whitleys and Hampdens, with 2 Group operating Blenheim light bombers. 1 Group had been sent to France with its Fairey Battles on the 1st and 2nd of September to operate as the Advanced Air Striking Force (AASF) and would remain there until the fall of France in June 1940. 5 Group, whose Air-Officer-Commanding was Air Commodore Callaway, organised its six front-line squadrons on three stations, 44 and 50 at Waddington, 49 and 83 at Scampton and 61 and 144 at Hemswell, and notification was received at the first-two mentioned at 17.50 to prepare to attack enemy warships, which were reported to have sailed from Wilhelmshaven at 14.30. Eighteen crews were briefed at Waddington and Scampton, nine representing 44 Squadron, and those selected for this momentous first offensive operation of the Second World War were the crews of W/C Boothman, F/L Weir, P/Os Penman, Robson, Sansome and Stuart, F/Sgt Cook and Sgts Farmer and Jeffrey. They departed Waddington between 18.15 and 18.30 to set course for the Schillig Roads on the north-western corner of Jade Bay, a distance of 350 miles, but arrived to encounter rain and generally unfavourable weather conditions, made more challenging by the gathering darkness. Having failed to make contact with the enemy vessels, all returned safely to Waddington for what would be an extended period of operational inactivity.

On the 14th, Air Commodore Callaway was posted to HQ 18 Group, and was succeeded by Air Vice Marshal Arthur Harris, who would become a household name in the ensuing years of war. On the 29th of September 5 Group sent eleven Hampdens from Hemswell in two sections to attack enemy warships in the Heligoland area, from which the 144 Squadron element of five failed to return. There would be a number of further small-scale forays by the group, and some of a larger scale by other groups, during which, the Command learned some expensive but valuable lessons about daylight unescorted incursions into enemy airspace. In 1919, Italian air-war strategist, General Giulio Douhet, had propounded the theory that future wars would be fought between giant armadas of self-defending bombers, flying directly over the front lines in daylight to target the economic centres of the enemy, and, thereby, destroy its will and capability to continue the fight. This theory would gain support in a number of countries, in Britain with Arthur Harris, in America with Billy Mitchell and in Germany with Walther Wever. Fortunately for the conduct of WWII, Wever would lose his life in a flying accident in 1936, and the development of the Luftwaffe be put in the hands of army minded strategists, who saw bombing as a tactical extension of artillery. This would prove to be an inspired decision in a short war, and Blitzkrieg was highly successful in rolling up France and the Low Countries. However, an extended conflict would require a strategic bomber force, and by the time Germany realized that fact, it would be too late to catch up. The main flaw in the Douhet theory concerned the suggested ability of bombers to get through in sufficient numbers in daylight to reach the target. During a shipping sweep in the Schillig Roads on the 14th of December, five of twelve Wellingtons would be lost, and twelve out of twenty-two on the 18th. This would force the air planners to take stock, and, ultimately, would lead to all but 2 Group becoming a largely nocturnal force.

There were, in fact, to be very few operational sorties by Hampdens until well into the following year, but the three 44 Squadron crews of F/O Dutton and P/Os Nicholson and Crossley took off at noon on the 20th of November, each with four 500 pounders in the bomb bay, to conduct a North Sea shipping search. They flew out over Skegness for some two hundred miles towards the north-east, before turning north-west for a further sixty miles, and returning to Skegness after a round trip of some five hundred miles and four hours duration. Nothing was sighted of the enemy, but they were fired upon by the Royal Navy over the mouth of the Humber. The squadron had to wait until the 4th of December before its next operational activity, a reconnaissance operation by three crews over the North Sea in search of enemy surface vessels. S/L Watts, P/O Eustace and Sgt Ennor and their crews departed Waddington at 12.10, each carrying four 500lb semi-armour-piercing (SAP) bombs and returned after four hours to report no contact. By the time that the squadron next ventured out in numbers, it would do so under a new commanding officer, W/C Boothman having been posted to the Air Ministry to be succeeded by W/C Ackerman, who arrived from HQ 40 Group on the 8th of December. Sgt Farmer and crew were dispatched at 07.50 on the 14th to join forces with eleven crews of 50 Squadron, which was operating for the first time. They flew out over Skegness as part of an overall 5 Group effort involving twenty-three Hampdens, flying as far as 7 degrees east, but it proved to be an uneventful exercise of some 750 miles in less-than-ideal weather conditions, and all returned safely after four-and-a-half hours aloft.

On the 21st, twelve 44 Squadron crews were briefed for an operation in company with a dozen others from Scampton and departed Waddington from 07.50 under the command of S/L Watts, before heading out over the Lincolnshire coast in search of the pocket battleship Deutschland, which had been reported to be off the Norwegian coast the previous day. Deutschland had actually been renamed Lützow, to avoid the risk of loss of national pride should she be lost in battle while bearing the nation's name. The original Lützow had been sold to the Russians even before her superstructure had been completed. The plan was to make landfall on the south-western corner of Norway at 10.30, and sweep north for a hundred miles, but having reached the limit of their range without sight of their quarry, the Hampdens turned for home and set course for Lossiemouth and Kinloss. Low cloud on the return flight separated the squadrons, and the Scampton element made landfall over the Northumberland coast to land, mostly, without incident. The Waddington contingent, however, having made an alteration in course, and unaware of their precise whereabouts, headed towards the Firth of Forth, an important naval base, where they were intercepted by RAF fighters from Drem. As a result, two of the squadron's Hampdens were shot down into the sea near Berwick by Spitfires of 602 Squadron. Fortunately, P/O Sansome and crew survived the incident in L4089, and were picked up by a fishing vessel, as were P/O Dingwall with two of his crew from L4090. Sadly, the fourth member of this crew, wireless operator, LAC Gibbin, did not survive, having been killed during the engagement, and his was the first name to be entered into what, by war's end, would be an extensive Roll of Honour. The other 44 Squadron crews were all safely on the ground at Drem by around 15.30 and were forced by unfavourable weather to remain there until the 24th.

Another uneventful shipping sweep by twelve Hampdens from 61 Squadron took place on Christmas Day, and this was the final activity of the year. During this final quarter of 1939, the squadron had undertaken five operations, generating twenty-eight sorties for the loss of two Hampdens to friendly fire and a single crewman.

44 Squadron Hampden JW-J L4098 at Waddington. This photograph was taken in July 1939 before 44 Squadron's code letters were changed to KM. The aircraft above landed with its undercarriage not fully locked at 16.15 on 2nd of May 1940 and was declared a write off. The figure in the foreground is Sergeant observer Percy D Nixon. He was killed on the 20th of July 1940 and buried in Denmark with Sgt R T Miller following a mining sortie in Hampden L4087.

Hampdens at their dispersals beside the A15 at Waddington on the day war was declared, Sunday 3rd of September 1939.

▶ *A young Jim Taylor of Smythe's Crew*

Sgt Jim Taylor in the W.Op/AG position.
Note - The increased fire power of two Vickers gas
operated machine guns and the Mk 1 reflector sight.

44 Sqn Air Gunners
L – R: Bill (Keith) Street DFM, (KIA 1942), Jim Taylor, 'Ginger' Bell (KIA 1940),
Jerry Preston (KIA 1941), Pete McLaren RNZAF, (KIA 1941)

P/O "Paddy" Stewart, P/O "Frankie" Eustace, F/L T C Weir.   October 1939.

The Dunston Pillar – a hazard to navigation at Waddington. The statue of George III on top was removed early in the war.

44 Sqn Hampdens at the outbreak of the war.

Cecil Mannix came from Rhodesia to join the RAF. He was a member of 44 Squadron ground crew while he waited for aircrew training. He became a pilot.

Cecil Mannix (Rhodesian) sitting on the nose of 'Dopey' of 44 Squadron at Waddington.

A royal Christmas message 1939.

Going to church in Waddington Village winter 1939/40. Gwen Stewart, Walter Lamb RN (transferred from 44 Sqn to Fleet air Arm), Paddy Stewart 44 Sqn.

W/C J H Boothman pictured in the British team, RAF High Speed Flight, for the Schneider Trophy race in 1931. He was 44 Sqn C.O. 24th of April 1939 to 8th of December 1939. He is third from right.

Waddington aircrew

One of the ground crew using a fine adjustment on an instrument panel.

L-R: F/O Bray. P/O Dutton, P/O Stewart, unknown, P/O Swayne (seated), unknown, P/O Jobson (glasses), P/O Moore, F/O Weir. Taken just before the war.

The Rhodesian element of 44 Sqn groundcrew during a visit by a Rhodesian government minister.

*F/O L G Johnson,
Squadron Gunner Leader*

44 Squadron ground crew. L-R: 'Shadow' Irwin, unknown, Cecil Mannix (became a pilot later in the war) Tommy Peacock, Pat.

Hampden take off

AVM J N Boothman
44 Squadron Commanding Officer 24th of April 1939 to 8th of December 1939.

1940 First Quarter

The winter of 1939/40 was particularly severe and seemed to deepen as the year progressed. This, and what the American pressed dubbed the "Phoney War", would restrict operational flying to an absolute minimum, and it would be towards the end of February before the icy conditions began to loosen their grip. During the first three months of the new year, reconnaissance and leaflet operations would occupy 5 Group squadrons, and a small detachment would also be sent on temporary duty to Coastal Command for anti-submarine patrols. On the 11th of January, the 5 Group Operational Instruction N°3 came into effect, and, that night, Waddington launched S/L Watts and a 50 Squadron counterpart at 17.00 to dispense 324,000 leaflets (nickels) each over Hamburg and Bremen respectively, both returning from uneventful sorties five hours and forty minutes later having fulfilled their briefs. On the following night, Sgt Smythe and crew took off at 17.45 to deliver a further 324,000 sheets of what Harris described as "toilet paper" over the Kiel area on the eastern seaboard of the Schleswig-Holstein peninsula, and this sortie, too, was completed without incident.

There was no further activity until the 26th, when 44 and 50 Squadrons sent six Hampdens each to Lossiemouth, led by S/Ls Watts and Good respectively, while twelve of 49 Squadron took up residence at Kinloss under the command of W/C Sheen. They were to provide defensive cover for large convoys from Norway, which might come under attack from German surface vessels. They stood-by for operations whenever convoys were at sea but were not called into action until the afternoon of the 8th of February, when six aircraft from 49 and 50 squadrons carried out a three-hour sweep of the North Sea, during which, no enemy surface vessels were encountered. It was the turn of 44 Squadron on the 10th, when its six Hampdens departed Lossiemouth at 12.35 in two sections of three, led by S/L Watts and F/L Dutton, to conduct a North Sea sweep, which ended after almost three hours with nothing to report. The two squadrons returned to Waddington on the 15th, and remained on stand-by, while the snow continued to fall, and the ground remained frozen.

During the course of the 16th and 17th, the armed German tanker/supply vessel, Altmark, had become cornered by elements of the Royal Navy in Jøssingfjord in south-western Norway, and had been fired upon and boarded in what the Germans correctly claimed were waters belonging to neutral Norway. Altmark had famously acted as the supply vessel for the Admiral Graf Spee pocket battleship, which sank nine merchant ships during its highly productive campaign in the South Atlantic between September and December 1939, before being trapped in the port of Montivideo following the Battle of the River Plate, and subsequently being scuttled. The crews of the merchantmen had been picked up by Graf Spee and transferred to Altmark, and the three hundred merchant sailors found on board were liberated. Eight German sailors were killed by small arms fire during the action, and the Germans denounced the episode as a gross violation of international law and Norwegian neutrality. The Waddington, Scampton and Hemswell squadrons were put on stand-by on the 17th to attack Altmark or any naval escorts, but, in the event, the thirty-six Hampdens were not called into action. On the 18th, German naval units were reported to be icebound in the Heligoland Bight, and 5 Group was put on stand-by to take advantage between the 19th and the 22nd, but, again, nothing became of it.

Heavy drizzle on the 22nd began a rapid thaw, which left Waddington wet, boggy and unserviceable, and sunshine on the following day melted the last vestiges of the white stuff. F/L Rogers and crew were selected for a nickelling sortie over Bremen on the 23rd and took off at 19.30 for what would be a flight duration of almost seven hours. On the 26th, P/O Crossley and crew took off at 18.20 for a nickelling sortie over Hamburg, to be followed into the air five minutes later by S/L Norris and crew on a security patrol over the Frisian islands of Norderney and Borkum, and Sylt, situated further north off the western coast of the Schleswig-Holstein peninsula. Both sorties were completed without incident until S/L Norris arrived at the Lincolnshire coast short of fuel, and force-landed L4253 three miles south of Grimsby at 02.50. The crew walked away, but the Hampden was declared a write-off. The final operations of the month in this leap year involved sorties by F/O Robson and F/L Dutton, who took off at 22.00 and 22.10 on the 29th. The former's brief was to deliver leaflets to Hamburg and conduct a security patrol over Borkum, while the latter checked out activity on Norderney, and both returned with nothing to report.

March began with 44 Squadron in action on the evening of the 1st, with the departure from Waddington of F/Sgt Cook and crew at 17.50 for a combined nickelling and security patrol sortie over Kiel. Seventy minutes later, F/O Taylor and crew took off to reconnoitre enemy seaplane bases on Sylt and other islands off Germany's north-western coast, and he was followed into the air by P/O Eustace and crew at 19.10. F/O Taylor's sortie lasted forty-five minutes and was ended by a generator issue, while the others completed theirs as briefed, and had nothing of value to pass on to the Intelligence Section at debriefing. On the following evening, Sgt Jeffrey and F/O Taylor and their crews departed Waddington at 17.30 and 18.30 respectively to conduct security patrols over Sylt and the west Frisian islands, comprising Texel, Vlieland, Terschelling and Ameland. They were on their way home by the time that Sgt Harbourne and S/L Watts and their crews took off at 22.15 and 22.35 under the same orders, and all returned safely, again with nothing to report. W/C D W Reid was appointed to succeed W/C Ackerman as commanding officer on the 12th of March, on the latter's posting to HQ 5 Group, a post he would take up in April. In contrast to that of his predecessors, W/C Reid's period of tenure would extend for more than twelve months. On the night of his appointment, F/L Rogers and crew set off at 18.30 to carry out a patrol over Sylt, and soon found themselves in extremely poor weather conditions, which would require five hours of instrument flying. They spent twenty-three minutes over the target area, and were held twice in searchlights, before returning safely, at last with something to report.

Similar adverse conditions were encountered by the crews of F/O Taylor, F/L Dutton, Sgt Smythe and F/Sgt Cook after they took off at 18.40, 20.30, 21.00 and 22.30 respectively on the 15th, all bound for security patrols over Sylt and the eastern Frisian islands of Norderney and Borkum. They also endured long periods of instrument flying and ran occasionally into searchlights, which they evaded with ease. At dusk on the 16th, fifteen enemy bombers carried out attacks on elements of the Royal Navy at Scapa Flow in the Orkneys, hitting HMS Norfolk and killing four of her officers. Bombs also fell close to Hatstone aerodrome and Bridge of Wraith on the road between Kirkwall and Stromness on the island of Hoy, and two cottages were damaged, leading to the death of one civilian and injury to seven others.

In retaliation for this, orders were issued on the 19th to carry out an attack on the seaplane base at Hörnum, located on the southern tip of the island of Sylt, off the western coast of the Schleswig-Holstein peninsula. 4 Group made ready thirty Whitleys, which were assigned a four-hour slot in which to carry out their attacks, to be followed by twenty 5 Group Hampdens from Waddington and Hemswell during a two-hour window later in the night. 44 and 50 Squadrons each made ready five Hampdens, which were loaded with four 500 pounders each, while the crews of S/L Watts, Sgts Harbourne and Jeffrey and P/Os Eustace and Crossley were being briefed. They departed Waddington between 23.00 and 23.45, for what, as events were to prove, was an undistinguished first deliberate attack on a German land target, during which only one succeeded in locating it. Sgt Harbourne and crew were still an hour from their destination when an engine began to lose power, and they turned back, for some reason, following a circuitous return route which took them via the Dutch and Belgian coasts to Manston in Kent, then Bircham Newton and finally Waddington. On the ground, they met P/O Crossley and crew, who had lost their heating system, and had turned back from a position some thirty minutes short of the target. They also found the crew of S/L Watts, who had been the only one from the squadron to reach and bomb the target. P/O Eustace and crew had located Sylt, but not the seaplane base, and Sgt Jeffrey and crew would have a similar story to tell when they returned from Drem on the following afternoon. The majority of returning 4 and 5 Group crews were enthusiastic about their part in the raid and were convinced that the base had been severely damaged, a claim that was splashed across the front pages of the dailies. 5 Group recorded that its aircraft had attacked between 23.45 and 01.50 from heights ranging from 1,000 to 10,000 feet and had delivered a total of sixteen 500 and forty-four 250 pounders along with 660 x 4lb incendiaries. The report added that the hangars had been hit several times and that direct hits had been observed on the living quarters and slipway. Two 82 Squadron Blenheims carried out a reconnaissance flight on the 21st, and their photos revealed only minor damage. Similarly optimistic claims would come back to haunt the Command eighteen months hence.

In the meantime, reconnaissance of Germany's north-western coastline continued on the 22nd, when the crews of P/O Eustace, S/L Norris and Sgt Williams and their crews were dispatched at 19.00, 19.25 and 20.10 respectively to the town of Wedel, situated on the North Bank of the Elbe some six miles west of Hamburg. P/O Eustace and crew saw nothing during their first pass, and continued on to Hamburg, where leaflets were dispensed from 14,000 feet. They then returned to Wedel, catching a glimpse of it through a gap in the cloud. On the way home, and a hundred miles from the English coast, a seagull smacked into the windscreen, causing slight injury to the pilot's face and considerably more damage to itself. An emergency landing was carried out at Digby, from where they returned to Waddington later in the day. The other two crews were denied a sight of the ground through the cloud and returned with nothing to report.

The focus remained on north-western Germany on the 25th when orders were received to prepare five Hampdens for security and reconnaissance operations that night. P/Os Homer and Mackintosh and their crews were to conduct a patrol over the Frisians, while F/L Dutton and Sgt Williams reconnoitred the Elbe estuary and Sgt Jeffrey Kieler Förde (Kiel Fjord), in the western Baltic approaches to the port. Cloud hampered the reconnaissance sorties, and, apart from the delivery of nickels to Cuxhaven by the Dutton crew, nothing was achieved. An S.O.S message was picked up from L4102 at 00.35, but nothing further was heard from Sgt Williams and crew, who were lost without trace in the North Sea. On the 28th, S/L Weir was posted across the tarmac from 50 Squadron and would assume the role of flight commander. During the course of the first quarter of 1940, 44 Squadron had carried out thirteen operations, and dispatched thirty-eight sorties for the loss of two Hampdens and one crew.

April 1940

The squadron was in action late on the 1st, dispatching P/O Mackintosh and crew at 23.10 to conduct a reconnaissance of Kiel Fjord, and they were followed into the air by F/O Robson and P/O Homer at 23.55 and 00.30 respectively, bound for the Elbe estuary. The latter encountered searchlight activity in the Brunsbüttel area at the western end of the Kiel Canal at its junction with the Elbe, but it was easily evaded, and all crews dispensed reading matter before returning safely to make their reports.

Orders came through on the 6th to prepare four Hampdens for further nickelling and reconnaissance sorties that night on either side of the Schleswig-Holstein peninsula. Three crews were assigned to areas in the western Baltic, with F/L Rogers and crew the first away at 19.35, bound for Kiel Fjord, while F/O Taylor and crew departed Waddington at 20.55 to head for the Kiel Canal, which stretched from the Baltic, all the way across the peninsula to the mouth of the Elbe, and was used by U-Boots to gain access to the Atlantic. F/O Robson and S/L Watts and their crews took off at 22.30, the former to reconnoitre the Elbe, and the latter, with the furthest of all to fly, the Baltic port of Swinemünde, situated some six hundred miles from Waddington. All completed their sorties without major incident, and only S/L Watts commented on heavy but inaccurate anti-aircraft fire over the Elbe.

On the 9th, Germany invaded Denmark and Norway, prompting a British and French response in the form of a naval assault on the area around the town of Narvik in the north. 5 Group responded by sending twenty-four Hampdens in search of enemy warships and troop transports off Bergen on that day, and, although twelve of the force were recalled, two of the remainder claimed hits on a cruiser. Insufficient cloud cover caused the abandonment of a similar operation by six Hampdens on the 11th, but, that night, twenty Hampdens joined a contingent of Whitleys in a shipping sweep from Kiel Bay to Oslo, and at least one ship was hit. Elements of the Royal Navy and the Kriegsmarine would come face-to-face on the 10th and 13th, and this would be followed by landings involving British, French and Polish troops, which linked up with Norwegian forces. Bomber Command was prevented by the extreme range from directly supporting the landings and would focus instead on attacking enemy supplies of men and equipment arriving by air at Oslo and Stavanger and by sea in the southern ports.

44 Squadron was not involved until the 11th, when squadrons across the Command were instructed to prepare for what would be the largest commitment of bombers since the war began. Eighty-three Wellingtons, Hampdens and Blenheims were assembled for the operation, which would take place on the following day, but, in the meantime, six Hampdens were sent to Kristiansand Bay in daylight on the 11th to search for shipping, including the Admiral Scheer, which was the third of the three Deutschland Class "pocket battleships", along with Graf Spee and Deutschland (Lützow). They were forced to turn back because of insufficient cloud cover, but, that night, P/O Smythe, F/L Dutton and S/L Weir and their crews departed Waddington at 23.05, 23.20 and 23.55 respectively to conduct a further reconnaissance of the region, which was identified in the squadron ORB as "gardening areas" "A" and "B". They all reached the target area to find clear weather conditions and good visibility, which yielded no sight of the Admiral Scheer, but Sgt Smythe aimed his four 500lb SAP bombs at a merchant ship, without observing any hits. The others saw nothing of interest, and returned safely, having been aloft for up to eight hours.

At 08.20 on the 12th, seven Hampdens from 44 Squadron followed five of 50 Squadron into the air to conduct a shipping search in Kristiansand harbour, after reports of the presence in the region of the heavy cruisers, Scharnhorst and Gneisenau. The Admiral Scheer was not mentioned specifically on this occasion but was almost certainly among the capital ships gathered near the port. The 44 Squadron crews were those of S/L Watts, P/O Eustace and P/O Cook, who would form the first of four sections of three aircraft each, F/L Rogers, P/O Homer and F/O Taylor making up section 2, F/O Robson with two 50 Squadron aircraft in section 3, and section 4 consisting of the three remaining 50 Squadron aircraft. They flew out over Skegness, before setting course for Lister Fjord, and being compelled by low cloud and bad weather to make the North Sea crossing at 300 feet. With the Norwegian coast on the horizon, the weather improved, and the profile of the land confirmed them to be on track. The latest intelligence suggested that Scharnhorst was at sea and making for Stavanger, while her consort,

Gneisenau, was on course for Kristiansand, further to the east near Norway's southern tip, and, it seems likely, that the Admiral Scheer was just one of a number of enemy warships reported to be at anchor off the harbour.

The appointed leader of the Waddington element was S/L Watts, who was persuaded by the weather conditions not to attempt to intercept Scharnhorst, but to concentrate instead on Gneisenau, and he set course for Kristiansand accordingly. The formation skirted the coast ten miles out and climbed to 8,000 feet before heading for the harbour, where two large cruisers, three transports and a smaller vessel were sighted. The target was approached from inland on a south-easterly heading with the sections in line astern at one-mile intervals and were flying at 180 m.p.h when they released their bombs, beginning at 12.15, in the face of intense anti-aircraft fire. S/L Watts reported attacking an enemy cruiser in Kristiansand Bay, but doubted that he had scored any hits, and then dived down to sea level at 210 m.p.h., followed by the others of his section. P/O Eustace had picked out two cruisers for attention but had been prevented by cloud from observing the results. He and his crew were chased away from the target area by BF109s, which attacked repeatedly, shooting off the starboard elevator control-rod and inflicting further non-critical damage, until one of them was shot down by crossfire from another Hampden. P/O Cook's navigator reported their bombs to have fallen between one and two hundred yards from a large vessel, after which, they managed to evade the fighter attacks. By the time that the second section came across the target, the flak batteries had found their range, and L4099 was hit and damaged. Although F/O Taylor also made for sea level, the Hampden fell behind the others, and was finished off by fighters to crash into the sea with the loss of all on board. P/O Homer's L4074 was attacked by a BF109 and hit by three cannon shells, one exploding in the starboard wing, another in the port-engine oil tank, and the third passing through the open astro-hatch and exiting the fuselage six inches above the pilot's head without exploding. The rear gunner responded with an accurate burst into the nose of the assailant, which was seen to head towards the sea with flames issuing from its engine, almost certainly to crash. The third section was pounced upon by fighters as it dived for the sea, and P1173 was set on fire by a BF109, before crashing with no survivors from the crew of F/O Robson. As far as can be determined, all twelve Waddington crews had delivered their four 500 pounders each, before becoming embroiled in the fight for life, and there would be four 50 Squadron crews absent from debriefing, one having ditched some 120 miles east of Newcastle-Upon-Tyne, sadly, to be lost. The failure to return of six Hampdens and three Wellingtons confirmed that daylight operations invited disaster and had dwindling fuel not compelled the BF109s to withdraw, the losses would surely have been substantially greater. This realisation prompted a further reappraisal of daylight operations, and, from this point on, they would become predominantly the preserve of the Blenheims of 2 Group, which would pay dearly for the privilege.

On the night of the 13/14th, 5 Group carried out the first mine-laying operation of the war, a task to which the Hampden was to prove itself eminently suited. This would represent the initial tentative steps in a new departure for Bomber Command operations, which would prove to be hugely successful, and, by war's end, would have sunk or damaged more enemy ships than the Royal Navy. The laying of parachute mines by air was given the code-name "gardening", and the entire enemy-held coastline from the Pyrenees in the south-west to the Baltic port of Königsberg in the north-east, and even the northern Italian coast, was divided into gardens, each with a horticultural or marine biological name. The process of delivery was known as planting, and the mines, themselves, were referred to as vegetables, and it would not be long before the other groups joined in to create a spiders' web of mines in chains across all of the sea-lanes employed by the enemy. There were no gardens allotted to the Kristiansand coastal region of south-western Norway, and the areas A and B, referred to earlier, were in what would become the Silverthorn and Hawthorn gardens off the east and west coasts respectively of Jutland on the routes from the major German ports. On this night, Waddington, Hemswell and Scampton provided fifteen Hampdens between them for mining duties in northern waters, which, for the three 44 Squadron participants, meant the Asparagus garden located in the western Baltic in the southern reaches of the Great Belt between the main Danish islands of Fyn and Sjælland. F/L Dutton, S/L Weir and P/O Smythe departed Waddington at 22.20, 22.35 and 22.55 respectively, and climbed away to cross the Lincolnshire coast and begin the North Sea crossing. They ran into very poor weather conditions of low cloud and driving rain, which persisted until they were within thirty miles of the German coast, forcing them to remain below 1,000 feet. They made landfall on the western coast of Jutland in the Esbjerg area after around three hours, before crossing the Schleswig-Holstein peninsula and identifying Odense on Fyn. In order to deliver the vegetables into the briefed location, it was necessary to establish a pinpoint on a landmark, from which to carry out a timed run to the drop zone, and the small island of Sprogo, at the mid-point between Fyn and Sjælland, probably fulfilled that function. Each dropped a single 1,500lb mine from around 600 feet, before returning safely after a six-and-a-half-hour round trip. *(In contrast to the detail provided by the 50 Squadron Operations Record Book, the 44 Squadron record is distinctly lacking.)*

On the 14th, all three 5 Group operational stations were notified of further mining operations that night off Denmark, for which twenty-eight Hampdens were made ready, seven of them at Waddington. The three 44 Squadron crews of Sgt Jeffrey, P/O Cook and S/L Watts took off at 19.10, 19.15 and 19.45 respectively, bound again for the Asparagus garden and exiting the English coast at Skegness, before setting a course for Fanø island to the south of Esbjerg. Based on 50 Squadron reports, this proved difficult to identify because of poor weather conditions and low cloud, but the 44 Squadron trio traversed the Schleswig-Holstein peninsula over ten-tenths cloud with a base at 1,000 feet, and, on reaching the target area, began their search for a pinpoint. Sgt Jeffrey and crew spent forty minutes in a vain attempt to establish a firm position, and eventually abandoned the quest and turned for home to land at Manston. P/O Cook and crew reported good visibility under a cloud base at 4,000 feet, while S/L Watts complained of poor weather conditions throughout, and both may have been assisted in their search by lights from Nyborg, Sprogo island and the main islands on either side of the Great Belt. They each descended to around 500 feet to plant their vegetable as briefed, before setting a course to pass some ten miles north of the Teschelling light, and join the Jeffrey crew on the ground at Manston

Thirty-three Hampdens were made ready for a return to the Asparagus garden on the 17th, Waddington responsible for eight of them, four from each squadron. The crews of F/L Rogers, P/O Smythe, S/L Weir and F/L Dutton took off ahead of their 50 Squadron counterparts between 22.00 and 22.25, before crossing the coast at Skegness and heading for Esbjerg at between 2,000 and 4,000 feet in excellent weather conditions and with moonlight to assist with navigation. It took around two-and-a-half-hours to reach Denmark's west coast, and a further hour to cross Jutland and locate the target area, where they planted their vegetables into the briefed locations at some time around 02.00. 5 Group sent out orders on the 20th for further mining operations that night, and twenty-three Hampdens were made ready, five of them by 44 Squadron, whose crews were briefed for the Eglantine garden, situated in the River Elbe estuary, an area familiar to crews from nickelling sorties. The crews of S/L Weir, P/Os Crossley and Eustace and Sgts Harbourne and Jeffrey departed Waddington between 00.35 and 01.00 on the 21st and began the North Sea crossing in the Skegness area, encountering poor visibility and rain until reaching the east Frisians, where the skies cleared to allow moonlight to assist with navigation. They were heading initially for Scharhörn, a small, Hamburg-owned uninhabited island situated some ten miles north-west of Cuxhaven near the mouth of the estuary, which they were to employ as the pinpoint for the timed run to the release-point. P/O Crossley and crew, who had been the last to take-off, failed to locate the target area in time to beat the approaching dawn, and turned for home, leaving the others to plant their vegetables in the briefed locations from between 500 and 800 feet, before returning safely to report many marine and shore-based lights, dubious weather conditions and no opposition.

Orders were received on the 5 Group operational stations later on the 21st, to prepare for another round of gardening operations that night, for which, thirty-six Hampdens were detailed. 44 Squadron briefed the crews of F/Ls Dutton and Rogers and P/Os Mackintosh and Smythe, who took off between 19.15 and 19.25 bound for the Daffodil garden, the stretch of water between Denmark's Sjælland island and Sweden's west coast, known locally as Øresund, and to the British as The Sound. They began the North Sea crossing at Skegness, maintaining around 7,000 feet, and followed the course of the Frisians, where P/O Mackintosh came under fire from Spiekeroog island. He reported four ships in a line at the mouth of the Elbe estuary as he passed over it on the way to making landfall on the German coast somewhere between the southern tip of Sylt and Husum on the mainland. Here, the moonlight was so bright, that it was possible to map-read all the way to the target area. The vegetables were planted according to brief from around 700 feet, and three crews returned to base after round-trips of up to seven-and-a-half hours' duration. F/L Dutton and crew were absent from debriefing, nothing having been heard from them since take-off. News eventually arrived from the Red Cross in Geneva, that L4088 had been terminally damaged by flak, possibly from a flak ship moored off Kiel, and had been force-landed on Danish territory, where the crew fell into enemy hands.

5 Group put up thirty Hampdens on the 23rd for gardening duties in the Baltic and to patrol seaplane bases on Norderney and Borkum in the eastern Frisians. 44 Squadron briefed the crews of S/L Weir, Sgt Jeffrey and P/O Crossley for the former and P/O Ashfield for the latter. In the act of taking-off for the patrol, P1331 sustained damage to its undercarriage, and returned immediately, only to be written off on landing, fortunately, without casualties among the crew of P/O Ashfield. S/L Weir had been assigned to the Daffodil garden when he took off at 19.20, to be followed into the air at 19.35 and 19.40 by the other two, who were bound for the Melon garden, situated in Eckernforde Bay, a dozen miles north-west of Kiel on the eastern side of the Schleswig-Holstein peninsula. The North Sea crossing was carried out under almost clear skies and bright moonlight, with landfall on the enemy coast in the area north of Sylt. From that point, S/L Weir climbed a little to cross Jutland and continued on across Fyn and Sjælland to reach The Sound, enabled by the conditions to map-read all the way. He ran into four searchlights, which were easily evaded, and delivered the vegetable as briefed. Meanwhile, Sgt Jeffrey and P/O Crossley and their crews had turned south-east across the German frontier with the lights of Flensburg as a guide, and, with navigation easy in the prevailing conditions, reduced height to below 1,000 feet as the target drew near. A number of searchlights flicked on at Eckernförde, which Sgt Jeffrey evaded through the appropriate action, and both established pinpoints from which to carry out a timed run and deliver the vegetables into the briefed locations.

The 25th brought further mining operations, for which 5 Group ordered twenty-eight Hampdens to be made ready. There was a new garden for the five 44 Squadron participants, Forget-me-not, which was located in the approaches to Kiel harbour. It was for this destination that the crews of P/Os Eustace, Homer and Mackintosh, F/L Rogers and Sgt Harbourne departed Waddington between 23.15 and 23.30. They began the North Sea crossing at Skegness, and soon ran into adverse weather conditions in the form of fog and ten-tenths cloud between sea level and 10,000 feet, which tested the crews' navigation skills as they made for the Terschelling light vessel at between 4,000 and 8,000 feet. P/O

Homer and crew were about two hours out when an engine issue persuaded them to turn back, leaving the others to press on to make landfall near the Westerhever light on the west coast of the Schleswig-Holstein peninsula, directly opposite Kiel on the eastern coast. Unable to break cloud even at 1,000 feet and having to rely on navigation based on dead-reckoning and e.t.a., it proved impossible to establish a pinpoint, and all abandoned their sorties, landing at Leuchars or Acklington with their mine still on board.

Poor weather over the UK and northern Germany curtailed operational activity over the ensuing days, and it was the 30th, before Waddington was alerted to prepare for an operation that night. The targets were aerodromes at Fornebu, near Oslo, and Sola, at Stavanger, both in Norway, and Aalborg in northern Denmark, for which a combined force of twenty-four Whitleys, sixteen Wellington and ten Hampdens was assembled. Waddington was to contribute five Hampdens for Fornebu, two representing 44 Squadron, while the Hemswell element of five targeted Aalborg. The 44 Squadron pair of P/O Smythe and S/L Watts took off at 20.30 and 20.40 respectively and set course from Skegness to Lindesnes on the southern tip of Norway. The North Sea crossing was conducted in good conditions, with five-tenths cloud lying well below at 5,000 feet, and landfall was made between Lindesnes and Kristiansand. Moonlight and an inefficient blackout aided map-reading, and, with Oslo fifty miles ahead, anti-aircraft fire could be seen, presumably having been stirred into action by the early arrivals. The target was identified from fifteen miles away by a large blaze, and, at around 01.00, S/L Watts dropped three 250 pounders into the centre of the aerodrome, while P/O Smythe delivered six into the north-eastern corner, both in the face of an intense searchlight and flak response.

During the course of the month, the squadron participated in twelve operations, and dispatched forty-seven sorties for the loss of four Hampdens and three crews.

May 1940

The squadron was in action immediately at the start of the new month, supporting an attack by six Hampdens on the aerodrome at Ålborg (Aalborg) in northern Denmark, and a mining effort by eleven in the Eglantine garden in the Elbe estuary. The crews of F/L Rogers and P/O Ashfield took off at 20.00 and 20.10 respectively carrying a 1,500lb parachute mine each, only for the latter to return seventy-five minutes later, because the wireless operator had forgotten to take the identification-signal card. One can only imagine the ensuing confrontation with the commanding officer. F/L Rogers also brought his vegetable home some six hours later after failing to locate the target area. P/Os Mackintosh and Homer and Sgt Harbourne and their crews remained on the ground at Waddington, until departing for Ålborg at 23.05, 23.20 and 23.42 respectively, each loaded with six 250 pounders with instant fuses. They flew out over a blanket of cloud, which dispersed some forty miles short of the Danish coast, enabling them to pinpoint their landfall on Nissum Fjord and the Lemvig lighthouse on the north-western coast of Jutland. They climbed then, and headed for the east coast, where P/O Homer, who had recently been awarded a DFC, turned 180 degrees to attack the target from east to west, descending to low level to deliver the bombs in a single stick in the face of intense searchlight and flak activity. The bombs were seen to explode close to the hangars on the western side of the aerodrome, and the gunners strafed the area as P/O Homer weaved them clear of the target area, with one small calibre shell hole for the ground crew to patch. Two Me110s approached but failed to establish contact with the Hampden at such a low altitude, and a safe return was made to Leuchars. P/O Mackintosh delivered his bombs in a stick from north to south, and observed bursts on the airfield perimeter, before setting a course for Kinloss, where he landed safely after six-and-a-half hours aloft. Sgt Harbourne and crew observed three bursts on the airfield, and also landed at Kinloss.

At some time during the 2nd, P/O Dingwall, who, it will be recalled, had been a victim of a "friendly fire" incident in December, wrote off L4098 on landing from a training sortie, after the undercarriage failed to lock down. Happily, on this occasion, the occupants walked away from the wreckage unscathed. 5 Group detailed twenty-six Hampdens to mine the waters of Kiel Bay (Forget-me-not) and Oslo Fjord (Onion) that night, and among them were five representing 44 Squadron. The crews of P/Os Lewis, Crossley and Ashfield were briefed for the former and P/O Eustace and Sgt Jeffrey for the latter, and all were safely airborne between 21.05 and 22.25. As was standard practice at the time, no strict time-on-target was laid down, and, consequently, operations could be spread over many hours. Similarly, it was left to each crew to determine the details of the sortie in terms of route and altitude, and, on this night, the optimum course to Oslo Fjord ran from Skegness to a point five miles east of Kristiansand, which was undertaken in good conditions over some low cloud. From there it was a direct course to the target, descending to between 500 and 800 feet for the delivery of the mine, which, in Oslo Fjord, required attackers to run the gauntlet of anti-aircraft fire from both banks. Neither 44 Squadron crew was successful on this night, Sgt Jeffrey failing to locate the release-point in the extreme darkness, and P/O Eustace running out of time to complete his brief before the approaching dawn revealed his presence. Meanwhile, those bound for Kiel Bay had made landfall somewhere near Husum and had crossed the Schleswig-Holstein peninsula to reach the target area in good conditions to plant their vegetables as briefed. They encountered searchlights and flak, but neither was troublesome, and P/O Crossley reported being fired at ineffectively by a BF109.

On the following night, 44 Squadron represented Waddington with three Hampdens in company with six others from Hemswell and Scampton. The destination again for the crews of S/L Watts, F/L Rogers and P/O Smythe was the Onion garden in Oslo Fjord, for which they took off between 20.00 and 20.10. The Rogers crew had to contend with an intercom issue, which delayed them sufficiently to prevent them from fulfilling their brief as they tried to fix the problem, but S/L Watts delivered his mine from 500 feet, and the rear gunner popped out three searchlights. P/O Smythe was also successful, and all three returned safely to Kinloss to make their reports.

As the gallant but doomed Allied efforts to gain a foothold in Norway faltered, 50 Squadron was stood down from operations for a week, unless anything of major importance were to take place, and there were no operations either for 44 Squadron between the 4th and the 8th. Orders were received at Waddington, Hemswell and Scampton on the 9th, to prepare for further mining operations that night in three gardens, Hollyhock, on the approaches to Lübeck at Travemünde, Jasmine, situated off the port of Warnemünde, also in the Baltic, and the familiar Eglantine in the Elbe estuary, for which twenty-nine Hampdens were detailed. Waddington put up eleven, six of which belonged to 44 Squadron, their crews assigned in pairs, with P/Os Ashfield and Mackintosh briefed for Jasmine, and taking off at 21.25 and 21.32 respectively, P/Os Eustace and Homer for Hollyhock, departing at 21.55 and 22.00, and, finally, the recently arrived S/L Gyll-Murray and P/O Siebert for Eglantine, lifting off at 22.45 and 23.00. They all flew out over Skegness to follow the same course as far as the Elbe estuary, flying over cloud, until reaching 5 degrees east, where it dispersed to leave generally good visibility but haze and extreme darkness at low level. It was this that thwarted the attempts of the 44 Squadron pair to locate the Eglantine garden, and neither was able to fulfil their brief. Those bound for the Jasmine garden had the furthest to travel, some 520 miles, and both crews ran into quite intense searchlight and flak activity as they bypassed the Kiel area, still some eighty miles short of their destination. They reached the target area after a three-and-a-half hour outward flight, and delivered their mines from 700 feet, before returning safely after seven hours aloft. P/O Eustace was the first to land, at 04.20, reporting intense searchlight activity and a few badly aimed "flaming Onion", presumably also from the Kiel defences, and a successful planting of his vegetable. P/O Homer was the last to return, at 05.15, with his mine still in the bomb bay, after spending fifty minutes searching in vain for a pinpoint.

The ill-fated Norwegian campaign was effectively over by the time that events closer to home grabbed the attention of the world. The storm broke at dawn on the 10th, when German forces began the invasion of Holland, Belgium, Luxembourg and France, and 5 Group was put on stand-by to attack communications targets to hinder their advance. It would signal the massacre of the Battle squadrons of the AASF in France, and also the Blenheim units of the England-based 2 Group, and, over the course of the ensuing five days, both types would be hacked out of the sky in alarming numbers in an unequal fight against murderous ground fire and marauding Luftwaffe fighters. It would fall to the so-called heavy bombers on the stations of eastern England to hinder the progress of the enemy forces by attacking bridges, roads and railways behind their lines. 5 Group was not called into action on that first night, but nineteen crews were summoned to briefing on the 11th to be told the details of that night's assault on road and rail targets at Mönchengladbach on the south-western edge of the industrial Ruhr Valley. This would be the first time that a German town had been intentionally targeted, and the crews of S/L Watts, F/L Rogers and Sgt Harbourne departed Waddington between 00.25 and 00.31, to play their part, each loaded with six 250 pounders, three with instant fuses and three with a six-hour delay. The weather conditions were perfect as they set out from Skegness on course for The Hague, but Sgt Harbourne and crew were forced by engine trouble to return at that point, leaving just two from the squadron to continue on, climbing to evade the intense searchlight welcome at the enemy coast. They turned south-east on track for the target, which was already on fire after being attacked by a Whitley element, and, together with the glare from the intense searchlight activity, this created challenging conditions in which to identify precise aiming points. S/L Watts and crew seemed to experience no difficulty and attacked from 8,000 feet in the face of what they described as "desultory" anti-aircraft fire, a sentiment echoed by the Rogers crew, who reported observing a single burst from their bombs.

Six Hemswell Hampdens represented 5 Group in attacks on roads and bridges in the Aachen-Maastricht-Eindhoven area on the night of the 13/14th, while six others, two from each station, were assigned to mining duties in the Lettuce garden, located at the eastern end of the Kiel Canal. S/L Watts and crew took off at 20.30 as the sole 44 Squadron participants and beat the deteriorating weather conditions to plant their vegetable centrally between the banks while under inaccurate machine-gun fire. This would prove to be the final operation with the squadron for S/L Watts, who was posted immediately to command 144 Squadron on the loss of W/C Luxmoore on the night of the 11/12th. He would be succeeded as a flight commander at 44 Squadron by S/L Johnson, sadly, for only a brief period.

The 5 Group and 44 Squadron ORBs are at variance concerning operations and losses on the night of the 14/15th and 15/16th and create confusion. According to the 5 Group record, twenty-two Hampdens were detailed on the 14th for mining duties in the Baltic region, specifically in the Quince garden, located off the southern tip of Langeland island, and Lettuce, the eastern end of the Kiel Canal. A further four from each station were to attack road and rail junctions at Breda and Roosendaal in southern Holland, which the 44 Squadron ORB recorded as taking place on the night of the 15/16th.

The 44 Squadron ORB assigned the crews of S/L Gyll-Murray and P/Os Homer, Lewis and Eustace to the Quince garden, and P/O Smythe to Lettuce on the 14th and made no mention of bombing operations. They took off from Waddington between 20.15 and 20.25, only for P/O Eustace to arrive back in the circuit within ninety minutes, to be joined thirty minutes later by P/O Lewis, both because of engine problems, and this left just two to fulfil their briefs unopposed. Meanwhile, P/O Smythe and crew planted their vegetable close to a wharf in the Kiel Canal, where three vessels were berthed, doing so in the face of searchlights and machine-gun and pom-pom fire. The 5 Group ORB recorded the failure to return of one Waddington Hampden on this night, 44 Squadron's P4286, which crashed at Oosterhout, five miles north-east of Breda, with no survivors from the crew of the recently promoted F/O Ashfield. The 44 Squadron ORB recorded this as occurring on the night of the 15/16th, when the squadron supposedly dispatched six crews to Ruhr targets between 20.55 and 22.10, and two, those of F/O Ashfield and Siebert to Breda after midnight. The 5 Group ORB, however, made no mention of a loss on this night, and it must be concluded that the 44 Squadron record is in error, and that the loss of the Ashfield crew did, indeed, occur on the night of the 14/15th.

After Rotterdam had been bombed by the enemy on the 15th, causing an outcry across the world, the War Cabinet finally sanctioned operations against Germany proper, thus prompting the start of the strategic offensive for which the Command had been prepared. That night, ninety-nine assorted aircraft took off to attack sixteen industrial and railway targets in the Ruhr, while twelve Wellington crews were briefed to bomb communications in Belgium, and this was the first time that a hundred aircraft had been despatched in one night. 5 Group detailed a dozen Hampdens from Hemswell, Scampton and Waddington, 44 and 50 Squadrons each making ready six. 44 Squadron briefed the crews of P/Os Crossley, Eustace, Lewis and Mackintosh, and Sgts Harbourne and Spencer for a number of targets, although the ORB does not signify which, if any, were alternatives or last-resort. They took off between 20.55 and 22.10, those bound for the northern Ruhr making landfall on the Dutch coast near Ijmuiden, and the others over the Scheldt estuary. Sgt Spencer and crew were soon contending with an engine issue, and jettisoned their bombs "live", before turning back after about ninety minutes. P/O Crossley and crew returned after barely four hours to report bombing at Cologne, possibly as an alternative target after being coned in searchlights, which they found difficult to evade. P/Os Eustace and Mackintosh found themselves over Kamen, a town situated on the north-eastern fringe of the Ruhr, which was home among others to a synthetic oil plant, but it was a nearby railway and a blast furnace that attracted their four 500 pounders each, the bursts from which were followed by fires. Ten miles to the south-west, meanwhile, P/O Lewis and crew found marshalling yards in Dortmund as a suitable recipient of their hardware, and ran immediately, thereafter, into searchlights, which, fortunately, were co-ordinating with inaccurate anti-aircraft fire. The last crew to return was that of Sgt Harbourne, who had carried out their attack on Mőnchengladbach, which suggests that they had searched in vain through the ever-present industrial haze for their primary target.

Preparations were put in hand on the 17th for another busy night of strategic operations involving more than a hundred aircraft. 5 Group detailed forty-eight Hampdens to attack oil-related targets in Hamburg, while twenty-four Whitleys of 4 Group were assigned to similar objectives in Bremen and a handful of 3 Group Wellingtons to railway installations in Cologne. While these raids were taking place over Germany, a force of forty-six Wellingtons and six Hampdens would conduct tactical operations against a road and railway junction in Belgium, through which enemy troop columns were passing on their way to the front. 44 Squadron made ready seven Hampdens to send against A10, which was the target code for the Rhenania oil refinery at Harburg, situated on the southern bank of the Elbe opposite Hamburg. One other Hampden was prepared for S/L Gyll-Murray and crew to take to Sedan on the French side of the Ardennes, to attack a canal crossing, a target, which, on the previous day, had cost the AASF more than forty Battles and Blenheims. The main element departed Waddington between 20.30 and 21.27 with W/C Reid the senior pilot on duty and flew out over Skegness on a night of unlimited visibility enhanced by an almost full moon. This would enable them to map-read to the enemy coast via the lightship at Terschelling and the lighthouses at Westerhever and Heligoland. They could expect an intense searchlight and flak defence as they followed the course of the River Elbe south-east into the heart of the docks and industrial districts, all surviving to deliver their 250 pounders and incendiaries into the target area, where bursts and fires were observed. P/O Lewis and crew reported the flames to be visible from the coast at Cuxhaven, some fifty miles away to the north-west. Meanwhile, S/L Gyll-Murray and crew had taken off at 22.25 for their target in France, exiting the Suffolk coast at Aldeburgh and heading towards a landfall over the Scheldt estuary. Low ten-tenths cloud hung over the region, forcing them down to clear air at around 4,000 feet, where they were engaged by light flak. The conditions and the defences combined to prevent them from locating the target, and they brought their payload home.

A similar pattern of operations against industrial targets in Germany and communications in Belgium and France would occupy the following two nights, and the need to provide tactical support for Allied ground forces would continue through to the fall of France in June. On the 18th, orders were received at Waddington and Hemswell to prepare six Hampdens each to attack road junctions and bridges in the battle area at Givet, located right on the Franco-Belgian frontier. 44 Squadron loaded three of its aircraft with six 250 pounders each, and sent them away at 21.00, 21.10 and 21.45 with F/L Eustace, F/O Siebert and Sgt Harbourne respectively at the controls. They crossed the enemy coast near Zeebrugge and made their way in perfect weather conditions to the target area via Ghent and Brussels, reducing height to below 10,000 feet to deliver their loads in bright moonlight and in the face of an intense searchlight and flak defence, the latter reported as inaccurate.

Twenty-four hours later, seventy-eight aircraft, including thirty-six Hampdens, were poised to carry out widespread attacks on German troop communications in France and Belgium and on railway and industrial targets in Germany. The 5 Group crews were briefed for a number of oil-related targets, those at Waddington learning that A21, a refinery at Salzbergen, was to be their target. Situated on the River Ems in the Münsterland, north of the Ruhr and ten miles from the Dutch border, this was, in fact, the oldest refinery in Germany, having been established in 1860, and belonged now to the Wintershall company, which operated refineries at a number of sites across Germany. The six 44 Squadron crews of S/L Gyll-Murray and P/Os Mackintosh and Smythe as section 1, and P/O Hattersley and Sgts Henderson and Spencer as section 2, departed Waddington between 21.15 and 21.28 intending to fly out in formation as far as the Dutch coast, before proceeding independently to the target. Bright moonlight glinted off the River Ems to aid navigation, and, by the time that the target hove into view, it was already on fire. In contrast to the experiences of the 50 Squadron crews, who arrived a few minutes later, and described intense searchlight and flak activity, the 44 Squadron crews reported no opposition to their presence, and all carried out their attacks as briefed, P/O Smythe and crew reporting one direct hit from 1,800 feet, the explosion from which, rocked the Hampden. The consensus at debriefing was of a successful operation, which left at least part of the target in flames.

The need to hinder the enemy advance continued to draw elements of the Command's resources from strategic to tactical bombing, including, on the 20th, ninety-two aircraft to attack troops and armour that were breaking into northern France. 5 Group detailed six Hampdens each from Waddington, Hemswell and Scampton to attack road bridges over the River Oise, the 44 Squadron element of W/C

Reid, S/L Johnson and P/O Lewis assigned to targets in the Cambrai region of north-eastern France at Le Cateau, Hirson, Vervins and Saint-Quentin. They took off at 21.10, and all reached the target area, where two carried out unsuccessful attacks in the face of an intense searchlight and flak defence. W/C Reid dropped illumination flares afterwards, which revealed that no damage had occurred, while P/O Lewis, although failing to locate his aiming point, observed that a bridge situated south-east of St-Quentin, had been destroyed.

The focus shifted to railways in Germany on the 21st, to attempt to stem the flow of troops and armour being fed into the battle area. 5 Group contributed twenty-five Hampdens to an overall force of 124 aircraft assigned to numerous aiming points on lines to the west of Cologne from Mönchengladbach in the north to Euskirchen in the south. The 5 Group effort was to be directed at a twenty-mile stretch of track between Cologne and Düren, situated to the south-west of the Rhineland Capital, and the order was to attack any trains encountered. The 44 Squadron crews were dispatched from Waddington in the wake of the 50 Squadron participants at twenty-minute intervals, beginning with F/O Crossley at 21.40, followed by Sgt Jeffrey, Sgt Henderson and the newly promoted F/L Siebert at 22.40. They set course for the Scheldt estuary, and all arrived in the target area within Cologne's western defence zone and carried out a reconnaissance that revealed no trains on the briefed stretch of line but prompted an intense and accurate searchlight and flak response. P/O Crossley and crew came across a stretch of track some six miles west of the city and reported four direct hits on what may have been the junction at Horrem, which would also be attacked an hour later by F/L Siebert and crew. Sgt Jeffrey and crew claimed one direct hit on track just to the north of Düren near Merzenich, and it was probably close by that Sgt Henderson scored another between a tunnel and a railway station.

It had been intended that the target for thirty-five Hampdens on the 22nd would be the oil refinery at distant Leuna, near Merseburg, one of many similar plants situated in an arc from north to south to the west of Leipzig. In the event, unfavourable weather conditions prompted a recall, which all but W/C Watts, now the commanding officer of 144 Squadron, picked up, and he went on alone to bomb and damage the target. Meanwhile, 5 Group contributed a dozen Hampdens from Waddington and Scampton to attacks on railway bridges and road targets in France, Belgium and Holland. The target for the six Waddington crews was road and rail communications at Binche, situated between Mons and Charleroi in Belgium, close to the frontier with France. The 44 Squadron trio of Sgts Jeffrey and Spencer and P/O Crossley departed Waddington at between 21.07 and 21.33 and crossed the North Sea in improving weather conditions to reach the Belgian coast at various points between Blankenberge and the Scheldt, before locating the target area without much difficulty. The crews of P/O Crossley and Sgt Spencer found the rail and road junction they were seeking, and bombed it with six 250 pounders each, but Sgt Jeffrey and crew were unable to locate it, and attacked roads in the Mormal forest as an alternative objective.

It was similar fare on the following night, when fifty Hampdens were among 122 aircraft sent to attack railway communications and trains in motion on either side of the Dutch/German frontier. 44 Squadron loaded nine Hampdens with four 250 pounders and a container of incendiaries each, and dispatched them between 21.05 and 21.17, with S/Ls Gyll-Murray and Johnson the senior pilots on duty. They flew out over Skegness in formation at between 4,000 and 6,000 feet, setting course for the Ijsselmeer above a thick layer of cloud, and, while the 50 Squadron element was fired on by a Whitley and some ships, those from 44 Squadron, at least, reached the enemy coast without incident. Once darkness closed in, the formations separated, and each crew proceeded independently to their respective targets in southern Holland, where cloud and poor visibility hindered the search for trains in motion. Railway stations, road and rail junctions, bridges and railway track were bombed at Eindhoven, Hedel, Helmond, Kempen and between Groesbeek and Nijmegen, and some results were observed, although Sgt Harbourne and crew were too busy evading intense flak from the Eindhoven area to notice the fall of their 250 pounders. Sgt Paskell and crew, who were undertaking their first sortie with the squadron, failed to locate their assigned target because of cloud and heavy rain, and reported bombing Borkum, a Frisian island off northern Holland near the mouth of the Ems, and a very long way from their squadron colleagues. S/L Johnson and crew were absent from debriefing, and it was learned eventually that L4171 had been hit by flak and had crashed near Aachen with the loss of all on board.

Fifty-nine aircraft were made ready on the 24th for a repeat of the previous night's operations against enemy communications between Germany and the advancing battle front. 5 Group contributed eighteen Hampdens, of which three represented 44 Squadron, and these, bearing the crews F/L Eustace and Sgts Henderson and Spencer, departed Waddington at 21.05, assigned to attack a railway junction at Bomal in eastern Belgium as the primary target, or the aerodrome at Flushing (Vlissingen) on the island of Walcheren at the mouth of the Scheldt. F/L Eustace and crew reached the primary target to carry out an attack, for which, typically, the squadron ORB provided no detail, other than to mention having to negotiate intense searchlight and flak activity. The other two crews attacked Flushing aerodrome, Sgt Henderson and crew returning after a little more than four hours to report bombing hangers and the tarmac. This suggests that they made directly for the secondary target, while Sgt Spencer and crew were airborne for eight hours, and, clearly, searched initially for the primary target, before bombing the secondary on the way home.

Now that the British Expeditionary Force had become trapped with its back to the Channel in a reducing pocket at Dunkerque, the relentless round of operations continued with further attacks on troop positions and communications on the 25th. 103 aircraft were involved, twenty-nine of them Hampdens, which, together with the Whitley element, would focus on road and railway links to the battle front between Düren and Aachen in Germany and near Liege in Belgium, while the Wellingtons targeted troop concentrations. The 44 Squadron quintet, consisting of the crews of P/Os Hattersley Lewis and Penman and Sgts Harbourne and Paskell, took off between 21.25 and 21.37, and followed corridor "G", the standard route for making landfall over the Scheldt estuary. Their primary targets were railways near Liege, towards which Sgt Harbourne and crew were proceeding when hit by flak, east of Antwerp, sustaining damage to the tail unit and losing the use of their hydraulics system. The bombs were dropped on railway installations at Diest, and a safe return completed. The others attacked the primary targets, P/O Hattersley doing so from 2,000 feet, but, like the others, observed nothing of the results.

The evening of the 26th brought the first evacuations from the Dunkerque beaches in a heroic campaign that would last until the 3rd of June and would result in the rescue of 338,000 British and French troops. Meanwhile, operations continued against enemy communications and airfields in France, Belgium, Holland and Germany, for which forty-three aircraft were detailed, twenty-one of them Hampdens. 44 Squadron briefed the crews of F/O Siebert, P/O Crossley and Sgt Jeffrey, and sent them on their way between 22.25 and 22.18 bound for two aerodromes, one at Flushing and the other referred to as Brasseneat, the location of which has not been traced. They climbed away into poor weather conditions, which, fortunately, began to improve over the North Sea, and F/L Siebert and Sgt Jeffrey delivered their loads onto Flushing aerodrome without observing the results. P/O Crossley and crew also located their assigned target, and all were safely back on the ground at Waddington by 03.10.

120 aircraft were detailed for a busy night of operations on the 27th, for which 5 Group assigned forty-nine Hampdens to a number of targets. Twenty-four crews were briefed to attack oil targets in Hamburg and Bremen, leaving twenty-five others to attend to communications behind enemy lines in Belgium and Germany. Eight 44 Squadron crews attended briefing, five of them to learn of their part in an attack on A10, the oil refinery in Harburg, while three others were to seek out trains in motion in an area to the west of Cologne. They departed Waddington between 22.15 and 23.17 with W/C Reid the senior pilot on duty, and S/L Gyll-Murray leading those bound for north-western Germany. Weather conditions over the whole of western Europe were less than favourable on this night, for what amounted to precision attacks on specific targets, and, while this would restrict success, it would also result in an absence of bomber casualties. S/L Gyll-Murray and crew ran into fog, searchlights and flak in the Harburg/Hamburg area, and, with no prospect of identifying the primary or even a last resort objective, brought their bombs home. F/L Siebert and crew, who, according to their recorded take-off time, were the last to set off, some twenty minutes after the last of the others, came upon the seaplane base on the Frisian island of Wangerooge, and delivered their load across the flare path. P/O Hattersley and crew reported that they located the primary target and carried out an attack without observing the results, while Sgt Spencer and crew found the aerodrome at Barge, some twenty miles south-east of Emden, and attacked it, also without observing bomb bursts. It is not known whether this crew was homebound, having failed to locate the primary target in the conditions, or had attacked the first target of opportunity in its path. Sgt Paskell and crew bombed a marshalling yard, the location of which was not recorded, and were confronted suddenly at point-blank range by a Ju88. The two rear gunners fired two hundred rounds each, and the enemy was last seen inverted at 500 feet, apparently with no chance of recovery, and would be claimed as destroyed. Meanwhile, more than two hundred miles to the south-west, W/C Reid and crew bombed a railway line at Barvaux, a dozen miles south of Liege, having been stalked by enemy night-fighters since their arrival over enemy territory. They would continue to be shadowed for much of the homeward journey, although without being engaged. Sgts Harbourne and Henderson were carrying out their own stalking, of trains travelling towards the battle area in the Brühl region to the west of Cologne, where the latter derailed one and bombed another, before patrolling parts of the Ruhr to force the local populace into air-raid-precaution measures to disrupt their sleep. The Harbourne crew dropped 250 pounders and incendiaries onto a stretch of track north of Brühl, while searchlights attempted in vain to latch onto them.

On the 30th, 5 Group detailed eighteen Hampdens for further operations against Germany's oil industry at Hamburg and Bremen. 44 Squadron prepared three Hampdens for use by the crews of F/L Eustace and P/Os Crossley and Smythe, who were assigned to one of the Harburg refineries, and took off between 21.51 and 22.07 to set a direct course for the target. Cloud over the North Sea extended up to 10,000 feet, but, over the target, the base was as low as 1,500 feet and was penetrated by searchlights and flak. It was impossible to locate the briefed aiming point, despite which, P/O Crossley and crew claimed a successful attack on A7, although observed no results. The other two crews were defeated by the conditions and brought their bombs home. During the course of the month the squadron took part in an impressive twenty-four operations and dispatched ninety-four sorties for the loss of three Hampdens and two crews.

June 1940

The Squadron was in action on the first night of the new month, when supporting 5 Group operations against oil targets and marshalling yards in Germany. Hemswell provided twelve Hampdens for the latter, while Waddington and Scampton put up twelve each to attack the previously targeted A7 plant in Harburg and A19, a refinery at Ostermoor, a location between the western end of the Kiel Canal, and the North Bank of the River Elbe. The six 44 Squadron crews of S/L Parker, F/L Siebert, P/Os Hattersley and Penman and Sgts Henderson and Spencer took off between 21.15 and 21.32, bound for A19, S/L Parker having been posted in to fill the vacancy for a flight commander created by the loss of S/L Johnson. In contrast to the flight deck configuration of the other bombers in service, the fighter-style single seat cockpit of the Hampden did not allow for a second pilot. It became standard practice, therefore, for the role of navigator/bomb-aimer to be performed by a qualified pilot, who would gain experience this way before captaining his own crew. On this night, P/O Penman's second pilot was P/O Dave Romans, who would experience an interesting, if brief, operational career before his untimely death. The weather conditions deteriorated as they crossed the North Sea, and low cloud and extreme darkness in the target area combined with accurate anti-aircraft fire to frustrate the efforts of both squadrons. Only S/L Parker and crew carried out an attack, during which they delivered three 500 pounders onto the target in the face of an intense flak defence.

The Dunkerque evacuations ended on the 3rd, and, that night, Bomber Command launched 142 sorties, the largest number in one night to date, targeting German industry, particularly oil, at various locations between Hamburg in the north and Frankfurt in the south. 5 Group committed forty-eight Hampdens to the fray, nine of them made ready by 44 Squadron, of which six were assigned to an oil depot in Frankfurt, two to an oil-related target in Emmerich, situated on the North Bank of the Rhine, north-west of the Ruhr, and one to a plant in Düsseldorf in the southern Ruhr. The crews bound for Frankfurt were those of S/Ls Gyll-Murray and Parker, F/L Eustace, P/O Hattersley and Sgts Jeffrey and Paskell, who departed Waddington between 21.18 and 21.35, before heading via corridor "G" to cross the enemy coast over the Scheldt estuary. From there, they would pass between Breda and Antwerp and Aachen and Cologne on a course to Coblenz, Wiesbaden and Mainz, where they would pick up the River Main south of Frankfurt. They selected their own heights for the North Sea crossing at between 6,000 and 14,000 feet, and, once over enemy territory, encountered searchlights and flak near the main population centres, although nothing of a troublesome nature. It is believed that P/O Penman and Sgt Spencer and their crews were assigned to Emmerich, for which they departed Waddington shortly before 22.30, leaving Sgt Henderson and crew as the last to get away, at 23.32, to head for the Ruhr. Four of the Frankfurt element located and attacked the primary target in the face of a spirited searchlight and flak defence, while Sgt Paskell and S/L Parker and their crews searched in vain for the aiming point. The former returned with the bomb load intact, but the latter flew north for 110 miles to the secondary target of Düsseldorf and left with an empty bomb bay. Sgt Henderson and crew had passed this way earlier to deliver an attack and were already at home by the time that the Parker crew began the North Sea crossing homebound. P/O Penman and crew landed at 03.10 to report fulfilling their brief at Emmerich, which, like all locations with oil installations to protect, they found to be bristling with searchlights, but less flak than anticipated. The return of P1340 with the crew of Sgt Spencer was awaited in vain, and it was a number of hours later before the first indication to their fate was received at group and then at Waddington. The Hampden had struck a barrage balloon cable near Harwich and had been abandoned by the crew to crash into the River Orwell. Sgt Spencer's cries for help were heard by a Royal Navy petty officer, who dived into the water to find him clinging to a buoy, sadly, as the sole survivor of his crew. On his return to the squadron, he was able to confirm carrying out the attack at Emmerich.

Later that day, an assessment by the government of Germany's oil industry suggested that a concerted effort against it could reduce its output by half a million tons over the summer period. In the light of the massive offensive by four-engine aircraft in 1944, this was a wildly optimistic view, and, although a sizeable proportion of the Command's effort would be directed against oil refineries and storage sites, the effect on Germany's war effort during this early stage of the war would be negligible. That night, twenty-four Hampdens were among fifty-eight aircraft returning to Germany, Scampton sending a dozen back to the Frankfurt oil depot, while Waddington and Hemswell provided six each for an oil production and storage plant at Mannheim. Three 44 Squadron crews took off between 21.45 and 21.50, although one, the identity of which the squadron scribe decided not to record, turned back almost immediately with an engine problem, leaving P/Os Smythe and Hynes to continue on to the Norfolk coast and beyond. The engine gremlins struck the Hynes crew over enemy territory, and an attempt was made to bomb a railway viaduct in Holland, without success. P/O Smythe crossed the North Sea over low cloud, which cleared shortly after entering enemy territory via the Scheldt estuary. There was no anti-aircraft fire during the outward flight, but searchlights awaited them over the target, which they reached at around 01.00, and left after delivering their load without observing the results.

5 Group stations were busy on the 5th preparing thirty-six Hampdens for an attack on A22, an oil refinery and storage facility at Schulau/Wedel, situated on the North Bank of the River Elbe a dozen miles downstream from Hamburg city centre. The Group would also be providing six Hampdens to resume the mining campaign, focussing on this night on the western Baltic. 44 Squadron made ready six Hampdens, which departed Waddington between 21.21 and 21.35 with F/Ls Eustace and Siebert the senior pilots on duty, supported by the crews of P/O Walker and Sgts Jeffrey, Henderson and "Kipper" Herring, who was undertaking his first sortie as crew captain. They made landfall shortly before midnight on Blauort, an island north of the Elbe Estuary, from where they picked up the Kiel Canal to follow to the Elbe. The outward flight thus far had been uneventful, but, once over enemy territory, they were subjected to an intense searchlight and flak defence as they made their way south to the aiming point. Five of the 44 Squadron crews attacked the primary target with four 250 pounders and a small bomb container (SBC) of incendiaries, some observing bursts and fires, while others were blinded to the results by searchlight dazzle. The sixth crew, which was not identified, failed to locate the primary target, and attacked instead the previously mentioned A19 site at nearby Ostermoor.

Harburg was the destination for eighteen Hampdens from Hemswell, Scampton and Waddington on the 6th, when the previously attacked oil refinery A7 was the target, while six other Hampdens sneaked into the Elbe to plant mines. The crews of P/O Hynes and Lewis and Sgt Harbourne were briefed and took off between 21.11 and 21.17 carrying four 250 pounders each and sixty 4lb incendiaries. They reached the target area to find haze and intense searchlight activity, the glare from which hampered their ability to identify the aiming point. P/O Hynes' effort overshot the target, but the other two observed their loads to fall across the aiming point, although they were blinded to the results.

The main battle for the next week would be the vain attempt to rescue France from impending occupation, as German ground forces consolidated their hold on the country and prepared for the assault on Paris. However, it was oil that continued to be the focus for 5 Group on the 7th, as the hectic start to the month continued. Twenty-four Hampdens were detailed to attack A17, the Deutsche Erdölraffinerie, also known as Deurag, a synthetic oil refinery at Misburg, situated east-north-east of

Hannover city centre. 44 Squadron was to represent Waddington with eight crews, while 50 Squadron attended to gardening duties in northern waters. They took off between 21.20 and 21.50 with S/L Gyll-Murray the senior pilot on duty and the last away, and flew out over Skegness to the target, making landfall on the Dutch coast in the region of Alkmaar. All made it to the target area with their loads of four 500 pounders, and F/L Eustace and crew delivered theirs across the aiming point, observing violent explosions and large chunks of flaming debris being hurled into the air. Sgt Jeffrey and P/O Hattersley and their crews also located the primary target to carry out an attack, but the remaining five were thwarted by what they described variously as haze, fog and low cloud. S/L Gyll-Murray and P/O Smythe bombed the aerodrome at Barge on the way home, and this may also have been the recipient of Sgt Herring's load, while F/L Siebert ran out of time to reach the primary target and bombed the Frisian island of Borkum as a last resort. P/O Walker found no suitable target for his bombs and returned them to store.

5 Group issued orders for a number of operations on the 8th, one of them by twelve crews from Scampton to attack enemy communications in the Amiens area of France, while other forces attended to industrial targets in Germany. Hemswell and Waddington detailed a dozen Hampdens between them to attack marshalling yards coded M408 at Euskirchen, situated some fifteen miles south-west of Cologne, and M405 at Aachen, 44 Squadron making ready four for the latter and one for France. P/O Lewis and crew took off first at 21.45 bound for the battle area but found that the extreme darkness prevented them from identifying the target, and a main road was bombed as a last resort. Those briefed for the marshalling yards, P/O Hynes, Sgts Harbourne and Paskell and S/L Parker, departed Waddington between 21.50 and 22.10, and set course via corridor "G" for the Scheldt, each carrying four 500 pounders. P/O Hynes and crew failed to locate the target but came upon a train in motion consisting of nine carriages and hit the track immediately behind it. The others encountered intense searchlight activity, and some bursts were observed, but no detail of damage emerged in their debriefing reports.

Forty-two Hampdens were detailed for operations on the 9th, thirty-six of them to continue the previous night's assault on marshalling yards in and around the Ruhr. Waddington was a hive of activity as 44 and 50 Squadrons each prepared eight Hampdens, while their crews were being briefed to attack one of three yards, at M116, Soest, situated north of the eastern end of the Ruhr close to the Mőhnesee, M470, Rheydt, south of Mönchengladbach, and M435, Duisburg, although the last-mentioned was actually the Wedau yards in Mülheim-an-der-Ruhr to the south-east of Duisburg. They took off between 21.40 and 22.07 with S/L Gyll-Murray the senior pilot on duty, three each briefed for Soest and Wedau and two for Rheydt, and set course for their respective targets, where they would encounter unfavourable weather conditions for navigation and target-finding. Only Sgt Jeffrey and crew located their primary target at Rheydt to carry out an attack, leaving the others to find alternative objectives for their bomb loads. Sgt Henderson and crew were defeated by haze and searchlight activity and bombed a landing ground ten miles north of Dinslaken and some sixteen miles north of Duisburg, and P/O Hattersley found a similar objective ten miles further north. F/L Eustace and crew were attracted by the glow of a blast furnace operating in Bochum in the central Ruhr, and dropped some of their bombs there, and the remainder on Flushing aerodrome as they crossed Walcheren on the way home. P/O Smythe also found the Bochum blast furnace, and another one at Mönchengladbach, before heading north to drop the last bomb on a landing ground at Wesel on the Rhine. P/O Walker and crew had been assigned to Rheydt, but having failed to locate it, bombed a stretch of railway track between Arsbeck and Wassenberg a few miles to the south-west. F/L Siebert came upon Lohausen aerodrome near Düsseldorf, and dropped his load there, leaving just S/L Gyll-Murray to bring his bombs home.

The priority on the 10th, the day on which Italy declared war on Britain and France, was to try to stem the tide of the German advance into Northern France. 5 Group committed twenty-nine Hampdens, the crews of which were briefed to attack railway yards and junctions, along with bridges over the River Meuse at Sedan. 50 Squadron would represent Waddington in this endeavour, while 44 Squadron made ready five Hampdens for the crews of S/L Parker, P/Os Hynes and Lewis and Sgts Harbourne and Paskell to take to the Wallflower garden, situated off the eastern bank of the estuary leading to the port of Kiel. They departed Waddington between 21.12 and 21.25, but P/O Hynes and crew turned back after ninety minutes having lost the use of their intercom. The others reached the target area to encounter low cloud and mist, which prevented P/O Lewis and Sgt Paskell from locating a suitable pinpoint from which to conduct a timed run, despite an extensive search. They brought their vegetable home, while S/L Parker delivered his from 600 feet and Sgt Harbourne from 1,000 feet shortly after midnight. Meanwhile, those engaged over France had encountered the most challenging weather conditions in the form of towering cloud with magnetic storms, rendering accurate navigation almost impossible and leading to the failure of the operation.

The need to slow the German advance demanded further attacks on communications targets in France, in response to which, 5 Group detailed thirty-six Hampdens for operations on the 11th, thirty-one of them to return to Sedan and five for mining duties. At the same time, eighteen Wellingtons of 3 Group were to attack the Black Forest in south-western Germany with incendiary devices known as "deckers" in an attempt to cause widespread fires, and thirty-six Whitleys would carry out the first attacks on Italy with a raid on Turin. Only nine would actually bomb at Turin, while the ill-conceived policy of setting fire to forests, which would be played out over the ensuing months, would prove to be a monumental waste of resources at a time when the Command had more important matters to focus on. 44 Squadron briefed seven crews to bomb railways and roads in the La Fére and Laon area in north-eastern France and dispatched them from Waddington between 21.59 and 22.11 with F/L Siebert the senior pilot on duty. They headed for corridor "G" to make landfall over the Belgian coast, but P/O Smythe and crew were back on the ground in a little over an hour having lost the use of their intercom. Sgt Henderson and crew were just twelve miles from the enemy coast, when engine problems ended their interest in proceedings, leaving the others to press on to their respective targets. P/Os Hattersley and Crossley located the German-occupied town of La Fére, the former delivering three bombs onto it and onto a road junction, observing fires to break out, and the latter observed two bursts among buildings. Continuing south, P/O Hattersley came upon a convoy of tanks between Laon and Soissons, which he also attacked. F/L Siebert was unable to locate his objective, so also sought out La Fére, which he bombed from 4,000 feet, while Sgt "Kipper" Herring attacked Laon from a lowly 1,500 feet. Nothing was heard from P1325 after take-off, and news eventually filtered through that it had crashed in the Pas-de-Calais area, with no survivors from the crew of Sgt Jeffrey. (Bomber Command Losses records F/Sgt Sumpster as the pilot.)

A reduced effort on the night of the 12th saw thirty Hampdens and eight 4 Group Whitleys detailed for a return to the same area of northern France, while five other Hampdens were assigned to gardening duties. 44 Squadron briefed six crews to attack road junctions and marshalling yards at Laon and Villers-Cotterets and sent them on their way between 21.45 and 21.55 with S/L Gyll-Murray the senior pilot on duty. They were to fly out over the Norfolk coast to cross the North Sea via corridor "G", where they ran into a thick bank of ten-tenths cloud. They found that this extended over the Scheldt estuary all the way to the target areas and prevented some crews from locating their briefed objective. P/O Lewis and crew turned back within an hour because of radio and intercom problems, while S/L

Gyll-Murray was defeated by an engine issue rather than the conditions and returned his bombs to store. The others pressed on through low cloud and rain, which defeated Sgt Paskell and crew, and they turned for home without having located a target worthy of their bombs. Searching for a target of opportunity, F/L Eustace came upon a railway junction at Soissons, onto which he dropped his 250 pounders and incendiaries, while some fifty miles to the north-east, P/O Hynes located the marshalling yards at Charleville-Mezieres, scoring direct hits on sheds and leaving them burning. Sgt Harbourne and crew were also unable to locate their briefed target, but chanced upon enemy columns at Soissons, which they attacked without observing results. The sad news was received that W/C Watts DSO, formerly of 44 Squadron, had collided with a barrage balloon over Suffolk on the way home, and had died with his crew.

163 aircraft were prepared for operations on the 13th, their crews briefed to attack a wide variety of communications targets in France, Belgium and Holland. 5 Group called for a maximum effort from its three operational stations at Scampton, Hemswell and Waddington, and sixty-four Hampdens answered the call, eleven of them provided by 44 Squadron. At briefing, the crews of S/L Parker, P/O Smythe and Sgts Harbourne and Paskell were assigned to a road junction at Beauvais, situated thirty miles north of Paris, while F/L Siebert, P/O Walker and Sgts Henderson and Herring were handed railway installations at Laon. This left W/C Reid, S/L Gyll-Murray and F/L Eustace to target a bridge over the River Seine at Pont-de-l'Arche some eight miles south of Rouen. They took off between 21.50 and 22.30, each loaded with four 500 pounders, and faced moderate weather conditions over the North Sea with six-tenths cloud, which would disperse over northern France to leave haze. This was particularly thick in the Laon region, where the visibility was down to around a thousand yards under six-tenths low cloud at 1,000 feet, and the moonlight became a hindrance by reflecting off the mist and preventing the crews of P/O Walker and Sgt Henderson from locating their aiming points. The former attacked a flak battery and a railway yard near Laon as an alternative, while the latter bombed a road and rail junction at Pouilly, ten miles to the north of the town. F/L Siebert located the junction and straddled it with his bombs but was denied observation of the results by the mist, and "Kipper" Herring and crew watched as two of their bombs hit a warehouse by the track, and two others fell close to the permanent way. Those with the town of Beauvais in their sights experienced no difficulty in identifying it, and dropped their bombs in the centre, after which, Sgt Paskell continued on to the north to hit a railway junction at Marseille-en-Beauvaises. On return, W/C Reid reported the closest of his 500 pounders to have burst twenty yards east of the bridge, while S/L Gyll-Murrays hit ground fifty yards to the west, but F/L Eustace claimed two direct hits, one on the centre and the other at the northern end.

Later, on the 13th, S/L Gyll-Murray was posted to Hemswell as successor to W/C Watts as commanding officer of 144 Squadron. He would remain in post until January 1941, and, after a period of screening, would return to the operational scene in July as commanding officer of 455 Squadron RAAF. While 4 Group prepared its Whitleys to continue the losing battle to save France from occupation on the 14th, Wellingtons and Hampdens from 3 and 5 Groups were detailed to attack targets in Germany. In fact, only five Hampdens were mobilized, three at Hemswell, one at Scampton and one from 50 Squadron to represent Waddington. There were no operations for 5 Group on the 15th, the day on which the battered remnants of the Advanced Air Striking Force arrived back from France with what remained of their Fairey Battles. 12 Squadron settled in at the 5 Group station at Finningley and 142 Squadron at Waddington, both temporarily, until they could become part of the newly reconstituted 1 Group, which, after continuing briefly with Battles, would convert to Wellingtons later in the year.

Adverse weather conditions on the 16th kept most of the Command on the ground that night, while 3 Group Wellingtons went to Italy, and Waddington detailed three Hampdens each from 44 and 50 Squadrons to carry out mining duties in the Radish garden in the Fehmarnbelt, between the Danish islands of Fehmarn and Lolland. The crews of S/L Parker and P/Os Crossley and Todd departed Waddington between 20.33 and 20.49, and set course for the Danish coast, encountering cloud at times, but clear skies over the western Baltic. Each planted a vegetable unopposed from either 500 or 600 feet shortly after midnight and returned safely.

Forty-six Hampdens were made ready for operations on the 17th, six from Scampton to continue the mining campaign, while a further twenty-one from there and nineteen from Waddington were assigned to attack the oil refineries coded A3, A7 and A10, respectively at Dollbergen, east of Hannover, and at Harburg on the South Bank of the Elbe and marshalling yards M107 and M434 at Coblenz and Hamm. 44 Squadron loaded ten of its own with either four 250 pounders and a container of incendiaries, or four 500 pounders each, and briefed five crews for Harburg and five for the marshalling yards at Hamm. The first element departed Waddington between 20.52 and 21.18 bound for north-western Germany with F/L Siebert the senior pilot on duty and flew out over the North Sea under a full moon and in good weather conditions with a few areas of cloud. All were subjected to intense heavy and light anti-aircraft fire as soon as they crossed the enemy coast but managed to deliver their bombs in the general target area, P/O Hynes and crew claiming one direct hit, while the others observed bursts but no detail through the searchlight glare. The second element took off between 22.00 and 22.11 led by S/L Macintyre, who had been posted in to fill the vacancy for a flight commander created by the departure of S/L Gyll-Murray. They crossed the Norfolk coast on course for landfall in the Alkmaar region of Holland, before traversing the Ijsselmeer and skirting the northern rim of the Ruhr on their way to Hamm, situated to the north of its eastern end. Sitting astride the River Lippe, it was a major railway centre serving Germany's industrial heartland and had a reputation as a flak "hotspot", ready to offer a hostile reception to any daring to come within range. On this night, that would not be of concern to Sgt Spencer and crew, whose wireless operator became indisposed, forcing them to turn back from a position over the Ijsselmeer. The others pressed on to reach the target and deliver their attacks, observing bomb bursts at various locations within the built-up area, but no claims of a direct hit on the marshalling yards.

5 Group's workload on the 18th was relatively light, with just eleven Hampdens detailed for gardening duties or to attack railway targets of opportunity on the approaches to the Ruhr. 44 Squadron briefed the crews of S/L Parker and P/Os Crossley and Todd for mining duties in the Eglantine garden in the Elbe estuary and sent them on their way between 21.30 and 21.35. All three reached the target area, and, benefitting from near perfect weather conditions, delivered their vegetables from 300 feet (P/O Crossley), 400 feet (P/O Todd) and 600 feet (S/L Parker), before returning safely from uneventful sorties.

5 Group would be out in force on the 19th, when contributing fifty-three Hampdens out of 112 aircraft operating that night against a variety of targets in Germany between Hamburg in the north and Mannheim in the south. Waddington was assigned to oil refineries, and roving commissions from Wesel to Coblenz to derail trains in motion, while Scampton focussed on marshalling yards at Aachen and Euskirchen, and Hemswell launched the first attack on the targets M25 and M25A, the twin aqueducts carrying the Dortmund-Ems Canal over the River Ems between Gittrup and Fuestrup north of Münster. 44 Squadron made ready nine aircraft to target the recently attacked Harburg oil plants,

A7 and A10, loading each with four 250 pounders, before dispatching them from Waddington between 20.58 and 21.41. P/O Lewis and crew had set off more than twenty minutes after the others and returned less than two hours later with a battery problem, to find P/O Hynes and crew already on the ground, after their sortie had been ended by an intercom issue. The others pressed on with S/L Macintyre the senior pilot on duty, and, after encountering ten-tenths low cloud over the North Sea and coastal region, enjoyed excellent conditions in the target area, where all delivered their attacks, some observing bursts and others not.

4 and 5 Groups were notified of operations in the Ruhr and in the Münsterland region to the north on the 20th, the latter responding with orders, among others, to Waddington and Scampton to prepare six Hampdens each to attack an aircraft park at Paderborn, situated some forty miles to the east of Hamm. 44 Squadron briefed six crews for mining duties in the Quince garden off the southern tip of Denmark's Langeland, and three others for bombing sorties, S/L Parker for Paderborn, and Sgts Farrands and P/O Todd to attack Schiphol aerodrome and trains in motion. They all took off together between 21.30 and 22.04, and, while the main element headed for the Danish coast, S/L Parker and crew set course from Skegness to cross the North Sea over ten-tenths low cloud. This cleared as they made their way eastwards over the Dutch/German frontier, and bright moonlight greeted their arrival in the target area, despite which, they were unable to locate the aerodrome at Paderborn and brought their bombs home. Sgt Farrands and crew were defeated by low cloud, and also returned with their bombs, while P/O Todd and crew came upon the marshalling yards at Lingen, situated in the Münsterland, north of the Ruhr, and dropped four 250 pounders onto track and rolling stock without observing the outcome. Meanwhile, the gardeners, among which F/L Siebert was the senior pilot on duty, had all located their pinpoints and carried out timed runs to release their vegetables into the briefed locations from between 400 and 700 feet.

On the following night, forty-two Hampdens were detailed to represent 5 Group as it and 3 and 4 Groups roamed far and wide over Germany from its central region to the north. The 5 Group targets were the Deurag oil refinery at Misburg, east of Hannover, and the Ruhrchemie A G plant at Sterkrade-Holten (Oberhausen) in the central Ruhr, moving trains and railway installations in and around the Ruhr, and an aircraft factory, F19, belonging to either Fieseler or Henschel at Kassel. 44 Squadron briefed six crews to target the railways and loaded their Hampdens with six 250 pounders each plus sixty 4lb incendiaries and dispatched them between 22.00 and 22.40 with no senior pilots on duty. They set course from Skegness via corridor "B" to make landfall north of The Hague and seek out targets in the flatlands of the Münsterland to the north of the Ruhr. P/O Walker and crew came upon a marshalling yard at Winterswijk, shortly before reaching the German frontier, and let their full load go in a single stick, observing four direct hits, before firing nine hundred rounds at an unidentified factory a mile to the south-west. P/O Smith, F/Sgt Clayton and Sgt Henderson and their crews arrived over the town of Lingen, situated on the banks of the River Ems and the Dortmund-Ems Canal close to the frontier with Holland, where they found two marshalling yards, a railway station and various communications targets. F/Sgt Clayton dropped two 250 pounders on the yard to the north of the town, and the bursts were followed by two terrific explosions. Continuing south, two more 250 pounders were aimed at a railway bridge over the river two miles south of the town, and the remaining two bombs and incendiaries were delivered onto a second marshalling yard nearby. Sgt Henderson dropped two 250 pounders in a salvo onto a railway line four hundred yards north-east of the town, and the rest of his load onto a stationary train in the station, observing hits and debris being flung into the air. P/O Smith and crew located a railway bridge three miles south-east of the town for two of their bombs and claimed direct hits on one end that resulted in damage. Ten miles to the east they came upon a goods train at Fűrstenau, which they derailed and wrecked with two well-aimed 250 pounders, before delivering the last two bombs and incendiaries on a goods train in a station at Ohrte six miles to the north, the explosion of which rocked the Hampden. Sgt Collins and crew, meanwhile, had dropped their entire load in a single stick across a marshalling yard one mile south of Bielefeld, observing four direct hits and two near-misses. Finally, Sgt Paskell and crew found themselves heading south towards the town of Lemförde, located just to the south of the Dümmer See, and spotted a goods train, at which they aimed two 250 pounders, only to miss by twenty-five yards. A mile further on they encountered a passenger and a goods train, which they attacked with two 250 pounders and the incendiaries, setting both on fire and sending one locomotive crashing into a crater. Not content with that, they fired five hundred rounds into the wreckage, before finding another train four miles south of the town, which they hit with their last two bombs and strafed with 1,500 rounds. All returned safely from what had been, perhaps, the squadron's most effective operation thus far.

For the first time since the start of the German offensive on the 10th of May, Bomber Command stayed at home on the 22nd. This was the day on which the French authorities signed the instrument of surrender at Compiegne, to leave Britain standing alone against a seemingly unconquerable enemy. Unfavourable weather conditions were to blame for the brief break in bombing operations, but orders were issued on the 23rd to resume the fight, and 5 Group detailed fifty-three Hampdens for that night, thirty-eight of them from Scampton and Waddington to attack the Horten aircraft factory at Wismar on the Baltic coast, and the Hamburger Flugzeugbau aircraft works belonging to Blohm & Voss at Wenzendorf, south-west of Hamburg. The nine crews from each of the Waddington squadrons were assigned to the latter, although, the 44 Squadron ORB listed only eight. The Hampdens were loaded with six 250 pounders and sixty 4lb incendiaries each and took off between 20.58 and 21.33 with S/L Macintyre the senior pilot on duty, leaving F/L Siebert and crew on the ground, delayed by an engine issue. They would eventually get away at 22.31, but have insufficient time to reach the primary target, and would fail to locate a suitable alternative objective. The others pressed on over the North Sea, flying either above or below the ten-tenths stratus cloud that contained icing conditions at 11,000 feet and electrical storms, which persuaded P/O Spencer and crew to jettison their load and head for home. Sgt Herring, P/O Crossley and S/L Macintyre and their crews were also defeated by the conditions, and returned some of their bombs to store, leaving five crews to press on to the target. P/Os Hynes and Todd crossed northern Holland, and, with Bremen ahead, decided to attack the Focke-Wulf aircraft factory and its aerodrome in the southern suburb of Hemelingen. Faced with intense anti-aircraft fire, the former ducked into cloud immediately after bombing, and were denied a sight of the result, while the latter observed explosions followed by large fires. P/O Lewis and the unnamed crew reached the primary target a dozen miles south-west of Hamburg, by which time, the cloud had diminished to six-tenths at 8,000 feet. The Lewis crew watched their stick fall towards heavily camouflaged buildings and observed two bombs strike home.

5 Group sent orders to Hemswell, Scampton and Waddington on the 24th to prepare for that night's attacks on marshalling yards at Hamm and Wanne-Eickel, on moving trains in the Ruhr and barges on the Mittelland and Dortmund-Ems Canals. According to the squadron ORB, six crews were briefed to seek out railway installations north of the Ruhr, close to the Rhine and the Dutch frontier, but only four were listed, the two unnamed crews apparently returning early with intercom issues. The crews of P/Os Smith and Walker, F/Sgt Clayton and Sgt Harbourne departed Waddington during a fifty-five-minute slot from 21.57, to begin the North Sea crossing at Skegness. They all reached the target area to find favourable weather conditions, with visibility aided by moonlight, which enabled P/O Smith and crew to spot a motorised convoy of some thirty lorries proceeding towards the south-west at

Drevenack, five miles east of Wesel. A salvo of three 250 pounders scored a direct hit, halting the convoy and setting off a dozen fires, after which, they followed the course of the River Lippe east towards Dorsten, and dropped the remaining four 250 pounders in a salvo onto a goods train of some thirty trucks a mile-and-a-half north of the town, reporting a near miss. F/Sgt Clayton and crew began their attacks at Wesel, where they dropped two 250 pounders onto the marshalling yards in the face of an intense searchlight response, which blinded them to the results. Afterwards, they headed north-east to Dűlmen, where they hit the railway station with two 250 pounders and sixty 4lb incendiaries, before continuing on to bomb a railway junction on the line between Westerberg and Műnster. P/O Walker and crew divested themselves of their entire load on a railway junction at Doetinchem in Holland, some six miles north of Emmerich, leaving Sgt Harbourne and crew to stray some distance from the others, and arrive on the approaches to the Hohenbudberg marshalling yards at Krefeld, at the western fringe of the Ruhr south-west of Duisburg. Six 250 pounders and sixty 4lb incendiaries fell along the line of track from west to east, and three fires were started.

Orders were received across the Command on the 25th to prepare for operations that night against twenty-one separate targets. 5 Group detailed eighteen Hampdens from Hemswell and Scampton to target oil refineries, marshalling yards and individual factories, while a 50 Squadron element from Waddington focussed on trains in motion in the Ruhr and barges in the Mittelland and Dortmund-Ems Canals. 44 Squadron was to take care of horticultural matters on this night, and dispatched the crews of P/Os Hattersley, Lewis, Spencer and Todd and Sgts Herring and Paskell either side of 21.30 to the Eglantine garden in the Elbe estuary. They enjoyed clear skies from Waddington to sixty miles out over the North Sea, where cloud built up to ten-tenths between 5,000 and 10,000 feet to cover the Dutch coastal region and the Frisian island chain. This had dispersed by the time that Germany lay beneath them, and a rising moon compensated to an extent for any haze lying over the estuary. P/O Todd and crew failed to locate their briefed pinpoint and headed for the island of Heligoland to attempt to cause some damage with their two 250lb wing bombs. They found an objective at the northern end of the island, which, based on the ferocity of the explosions, they assumed must have been an ammunition dump. They were intercepted by a BF109, which they shot down in flames to crash into the sea. The others all located their drop zones and delivered their vegetables from 500 to 600 feet, before seeking out suitable targets for their wing bombs. P/O Hattersley attacked a merchant ship steaming up the Elbe, P/O Lewis a slipway on the western side of Borkum island, Sgt Paskell a cargo ship at anchor in the estuary and P/O Spencer a hangar at the seaplane base at Hőrnum on the island of Sylt.

A force of over a hundred aircraft was made ready to send against various targets on the night of the 26/27th, 5 Group contributing thirty-four Hampdens to target marshalling yards, aerodromes, moving trains and canal barges in north-western Germany. 44 Squadron bombed up seven Hampdens, three with four 500 pounders and four with six 250 pounders and sixty 4lb incendiaries, before dispatching them from Waddington between 22.05 and 22.35 with S/L Macintyre the senior pilot on duty. Sgt Collins and crew were the last away, delayed by an accumulator issue, and they would ultimately return their bombs to store. The others flew out over Skegness, bound via corridor "B" for landfall between Rotterdam and Texel, before flying direct to their respective targets, which, for F/Sgt Clayton and crew, was Langenhagen aerodrome, situated five miles north of Hannover city centre. They encountered occasional thunderstorms over the North Sea and Holland, but conditions were good in the target area, where they were met by intense searchlight and anti-aircraft fire. The six 250 pounders and incendiaries were seen to burst among buildings and on tarmac, and large fires broke out. Meanwhile, two hundred miles to the west, S/L Macintyre and P/O Walker delivered their loads onto

Schiphol aerodrome near Amsterdam but saw nothing of the outcome because of low cloud and the need to evade intense ground fire. P/O Smith and Sgt Farrands located the marshalling yards at Soest, a town to the north of the one-day-to-be-famous Möhne reservoir and its dam. Six 250 pounders, four 500 pounders and sixty 4lb incendiaries were aimed at the track and rolling stock, and explosions were observed. On the way home, the Farrands crew loosed off four hundred rounds at Twente aerodrome in Holland, which had already been hit by four 500 pounders from P/O Price and crew, who reported direct hits on concrete runways and a hangar.

5 Group detailed twenty-three Hampdens for bombing and mining operations on the 27th, for which the Waddington squadrons were briefed to attack an oil-tankerage site at Nyborg on the eastern coast of Denmark's Fyn Island. 44 Squadron loaded eight of its own with either six 250 pounders with incendiaries or four 500 pounders and dispatched them between 21.07 and 21.49 with S/L Parker the senior pilot on duty. They made their way out over the North Sea in predominantly favourable conditions and visibility, which persisted all the way to the target area. On arrival, they encountered only desultory defensive activity, and all delivered their attacks accurately at around 00.30, observing large explosions and fires.

On the 28th, the Command committed 108 aircraft to the bombing of industrial targets in Germany, aerodromes in Holland and gardening activities in Kiel Bay. Ten aircraft each from Scampton and Waddington were assigned to the Bayer chemicals factory at Dormagen, situated in the southern Ruhr between Düsseldorf and Leverkusen, which was producing explosives and poison gas. *(The 44 Squadron ORB recorded the target incorrectly as a power station.)* 44 Squadron briefed the crews of P/Os Crossley, Price and Smith and Sgts Collins and Farrands for this operation, and W/C Reid and P/O Walker for mining duties in the Quince garden off the southern tip of Denmark's Langeland island. The latter took off first at 21.30 and 21.40, to be followed into the air between 22.35 and 22.49 by the bombing brigade, each of which was carrying four 500 pounders. They crossed the Norfolk coast to follow corridor "G" in favourable weather conditions, and, although the ORB makes no mention, once past the Rhine, they were forced to run the gauntlet of intense searchlights and flak of all calibres, which burst at the correct level but mostly behind. The 50 Squadron participants mostly failed to identify the target, blaming industrial haze, but the 44 Squadron crews all located it and carried out their attacks in the glare of searchlights, which blinded them to the results. Two large explosions were followed by a fire and a large, low, white blanket of cloud, possibly gas, and a column of black smoke was rising through 2,000 feet as they turned away. While this was in progress, the gardeners arrived at their destination three hundred miles to the north-east and delivered their vegetables into the briefed locations from 600 feet. W/C Reid dropped his two 250 pounder wing bombs onto a stationary motorboat, while P/O Walker let one go at buildings on Heligoland and the other at a bridge between Nordstrand and Hattstedt on the western edge of the Schleswig-Holstein peninsula.

5 Group notified Hemswell and Waddington on the 29th to prepare ten Hampdens each for an operation that night against a dynamite factory at Geesthacht, situated some ten miles south-east of Hamburg. 44 Squadron was to support the operation with seven Hampdens armed with a variety of bomb loads and took off between 21.51 and 22.17 with S/L Parker the senior pilot on duty. Thirty miles out over the North Sea they ran into a front, which stretched eastwards for 150 miles, and south from the Kiel Canal to cover the target area with ten-tenths cloud at between 2,000 and 7,000 feet. They ran immediately into searchlights and medium flak at 10,000 feet, which added to the difficulties caused by the poor visibility, despite which, the factory was somehow identified by the crews of F/L Siebert,

P/O Hynes and P/O Lewis in the face of intense opposition, which prevented them from observing the results. Sgt Harbourne and crew were defeated by the conditions, and brought their bombs home, while S/L Parker and P/O Spencer and their crews each attacked Barge aerodrome with eight 250 pounders after also failing to locate the primary objective. Finally, Sgt Paskell and crew bombed Schiphol aerodrome as a last resort target on the way home.

The last night of the month brought further operations by eighty-eight assorted aircraft against targets in Hamburg in the north to Darmstadt and Hanau in the south and the Ruhr in between. 5 Group would return to the previously targeted Harburg oil refineries coded A7 and A10, with a dozen Hampdens from Waddington, while twelve from Scampton went for an aerodrome near Dortmund and four from Hemswell attacked the marshalling yards at Osnabrück. 44 Squadron made ready six Hampdens, loading each with four 500 pounders, and dispatched them between 21.07 and 21.35 with P/Os Crossley, Price, Smith and Todd at the controls. They adopted the usual route via Skegness and the Frisian island chain to approach the target area over the Elbe Estuary, harried by searchlights and flak all the way south-east along the river to the target. The refineries, located on the South Bank, were reached at around midnight, and identified through cloud with a base at 3,000 feet, which added to the difficulties. The attacks were delivered from all points of the compass, south to north, east to west, west to east and north-west to south-east, but none observed the results of their efforts through the low cloud, ferocious anti-aircraft fire and searchlight dazzle. During the course of the month, the squadron carried out an impressive thirty operations, and dispatched 173 sorties for the loss of two Hampdens, one complete crew and three airmen.

July 1940

The new month began as the old one had ended, with operations on the 1st against industrial and communications targets in Germany and gardening. 5 Group detailed a dozen Hampdens from each of its operational stations, six of those from Waddington to conduct mining operations in the Endive garden in the Little Belt between the east coast of Jutland and Fyn Island, while six others attended to the marshalling yards at Osnabrück. 44 Squadron contributed three to each endeavour, and dispatched the gardeners, the crews of S/L Macintyre and P/Os Hattersley and Lewis, first, between 21.17 and 21.23, to be followed into the air between 21.50 and 22.00 by the bombing brigade consisting of the crews of Sgt Harbourne, P/O Hynes and one other, which returned early with W/T issues and was not identified. They began the North Sea crossing at Skegness, and found the marshalling yards with little difficulty, although had to face a hot reception from searchlights and heavy and medium calibre flak as they straddled the target with six 250 pounders and sixty 4lb incendiaries, each delivered in sticks from north-west to south-east. The Harbourne crew reported bursts and two brilliant green flashes, while P/O Hynes was unable to determine the result of his efforts because of haze and searchlight glare. Meanwhile, two hundred miles to the north-north-east, the gardeners had arrived over the western Baltic to encounter clear skies and excellent visibility, which enabled them to identify their target area without difficulty. The crews of P/Os Hattersley and Lewis delivered their vegetables into the briefed locations from 500 feet, the former then attacking a merchant ship with two wing-mounted 250 pounders, and the latter the aerodrome at Ribe on Denmark's western coast. S/L Macintyre released his mine from 700 feet but found no suitable target for his bombs.

On the 2nd, Hemswell and Waddington received orders to prepare ten Hampdens each to send to Hamburg, the former to attack the dynamite factory at Geesthacht, and the latter to take another swipe at the Harburg oil refinery, A10, while six others from Scampton took care of the gardening duties. In the event, the Hemswell element was cancelled, leaving the five 44 Squadron representatives from Waddington to take off between 21.15 and 21.44 with S/L Parker the senior pilot on duty, and make their way to north-western Germany with their 50 Squadron counterparts. They encountered dense cloud, haze and extreme darkness in the target area, which prevented S/L Parker, F/L Siebert and P/O Price from establishing their positions, despite the deployment by the Siebert crew of two illuminator flares. Sgt Paskell and crew located the target and delivered six 250 pounders and sixty 4lb incendiaries in a stick from 10,000 feet, observing no bursts, but a row of adjacent houses was set on fire by the incendiaries. Sgt Farrands and crew attacked from 15,000 feet flying west to east but could not determine the fall of their bombs.

5 Group detailed fifteen Hampdens for operations on the 3rd, when the marshalling yards at Osnabrück and the banks of the Dortmund-Ems Canal were the objectives for the bombing brigade, while six Waddington crews attended to gardening duties in the western Baltic. The three 44 Squadron crews of P/Os Crossley and Todd and Sgt Collins departed Waddington at 21.20 bound for the Quince garden, located off the southern tip of Langeland island in Kiel Bay. The outward flight was uneventful and undertaken in good conditions until reaching 5 degrees east, where the trio encountered eight to tentenths cloud with a base at 1,000 feet and visibility at no more than two miles. Despite the difficulties, the garden was identified, and the mines released by the Collins crew from 400 feet, and by the Crossley crew from 600 feet. They came under fire from two flak ships, which the former attacked with two wing-mounted 250 pounders from 1,500 feet, observing near misses. The latter came upon eight small, armed vessels in Tonning Bay, at which the 250 pounders were aimed from 1,500 feet, but no results were observed. It is believed that P/O Todd and crew fulfilled their brief before setting course for home, and a signal received from them at 01.03 revealed that they were returning on one engine. A fix on P4352 at 03.47 was the last contact, by which time the others had landed, and the fate of the Hampden and crew became clear only after a single body came ashore on the Danish coast sometime later.

It was at this point that the pace of operations slackened to a small degree, the fall of France having reduced the requirement to the extent that crews could expect to operate from now on every third rather than every other night. Hemswell and Scampton took the strain on the night of the 4/5th, when the target for sixteen Hampdens were a graving (dry) and a floating dock in the Krupp-Germania shipyard at Kiel, one of which was believed to be holding the under-repair cruiser Scharnhorst. There were no claims by returning crews, and a second attack was scheduled for the 5th, which would involve fifty-one aircraft, including a dozen Hampdens from Waddington. The six 44 Squadron participants took off between 21.16 and 21.30 with S/L Macintyre the senior pilot on duty and made their way across the North Sea in poor visibility with cumulus cloud between 4,000 and 10,000 feet. By the time that the target area drew near, the weather conditions had improved to good, with moderate visibility, but the crews had to endure the attentions of a hundred searchlights and all calibres of anti-aircraft fire as they made their approach. The crews of S/L Macintyre and P/Os Hattersley and Smythe adopted a south-south-west to north-north-east heading across the aiming point and delivered four 500 pounders each in sticks from 8,000 and 9,000 feet, observing a number of bursts and a large fire, while P/O Spencer and crew approached from the south-west at 9,500 feet, but saw nothing in the glare of searchlights and flak. P/O Lewis and crew preferred a glide approach from 11,000 down to 8,000 feet, but also failed to determine the bursts. P/O Hynes and crew carried out their attack on a reciprocal course from north-east to south-west at 10,000 feet, held for the entire time in a searchlight cone, despite taking evasive action, and they, too, failed to plot the fall of their bombs. Crews from 50

Squadron identified what they believed was a pocket battleship in N°6 graving dock, either the Lützow or Admiral Scheer, and Scharnhorst at the floating dock, but no hits were claimed.

Waddington was alerted on the 6th to provide a dozen Hampdens for gardening duties that night in the Quince region of Kiel Bay, for which 44 Squadron made ready six aircraft. They took off between 21.05 and 21.25 with P/Os Clark and Smith the senior pilots on duty and set course from Skegness to Esbjerg on the west coast of Jutland. They experienced adverse weather conditions of rain, sleet and occasional icing as they traversed the North Sea, where the cloud base was at 4,000 feet. They reached Denmark's western coast shortly before midnight and came under accurate fire from "pom-pom" batteries at Esbjerg as they turned inland for the forty-minute, one-hundred-mile crossing of the Schleswig-Holstein peninsula. On arrival over Kiel Bay, they found cloud at between 3,000 and 5,000 feet with visibility at up to six miles, enabling the drop zone to be identified without difficulty by all but Sgt Farrands and crew, who returned their mine to store. P/O Smith and crew carried out a timed run eastward from the southern tip of Langeland island, and planted their vegetable from 700 feet, before aiming their two wing-mounted 250 pounders at a medium-sized ship in Aabenraa Fjord. P/O Clark reported losing the starboard engine for four minutes between 00.01 and 00.05 as he passed close to the town of Schleswig but continued on to drop the mine into the briefed location from 500 feet. Sgts Paskell and Herring and F/Sgt Clayton chose the same altitude from which to complete the lethal chain of mines spreading out from Langeland's eastern seaboard, after which, the two last-mentioned found small armed vessels to attack with their 250 pounders.

All three 5 Group operational stations were to be in action on the 7th, Hemswell taking care of the gardening activities and a small-scale attack on the Dortmund-Ems Canal, while Scampton attended to an oil refinery at Offenbach, and Waddington to marshalling yards at Soest and Duisburg, and the Duisburg-Ruhrort inland docks complex situated on the East Bank of the Rhine south of the city centre. Sgt Collins and P/Os Price and Walker took off between 22.02 and 22.10, each carrying six 250 pounders and sixty 4lb incendiaries bound for Duisburg, and flew from Skegness to Texel in good conditions, before running into a fifty-mile-wide bank of cloud beginning twenty miles inland from the Dutch coast. They reached the target area to be greeted by an intense searchlight and flak response, through which P/O Price and Sgt Collins delivered their bombs in sticks onto the marshalling yards from 4,000 and 8,000 feet respectively, while flying east to west. The bursts were lost in the glare of searchlights, but they believed that fires resulted. P/O Walker approached the Ruhrort Rhine docks from the south at a perilously low 4,000 feet, and let his load go in a single stick, but, again, was blinded to the outcome.

50 Squadron was stood down from operations on the 8th while the move took place to a new home at Hatfield Woodhouse, located across the county line in Yorkshire, five miles north-east of Doncaster. This was a brand-new airfield, completed in June, and 50 Squadron would be its first resident unit. To prevent confusion with the Hatfield in Hertfordshire, which was home to the de Havilland aircraft factory, Hatfield Woodhouse would be renamed in August to become Lindholme, after a country house and hamlet on the eastern boundary of the airfield. This left 44 Squadron as the sole residents of Waddington until the arrival of 207 Squadron in November. On the 9th, P4393 ended a ferry flight by crashing on landing at Waddington, but F/Sgt Clayton and crew were able to walk away from the subsequent burn-out. That night, 5 Group dispatched fourteen Hampdens from Scampton and Hemswell to attack the battleship, Tirpitz, which had been reported to be at berth in Wilhelmshaven. While that operation was in progress, a dozen 44 Squadron crews were to sneak in to lay mines in the Yams garden in the Jade Bay approaches to the naval port. The latter departed Waddington between

22.10 and 22.35 with S/L Macintyre the senior pilot on duty and made their way via the Frisian island chain to Germany's north-western coast. Haze and extreme darkness created sufficiently poor visibility to prevent the crews of P/Os Spencer and Clark and Sgt Herring from establishing a pinpoint from which to carry out a timed run. The last-mentioned attacked a flak ship with two wing-mounted 250 pounders, while P/O Spencer found a similar target some twelve miles north of the uninhabited island of Scharhörn, and P/O Clark returned his vegetable to store. The remaining nine crews delivered their mines from between 500 and 1,000 feet into the briefed locations off Schillighörn, which no longer appears on a map, but was at the most north-westerly point of Jade Bay in what was once known as the Schillig Roads. With two 250 pounders each to aim at targets of opportunity, the newly promoted F/O Crossley and Sgt Paskell attempted to hit two lightships, while Sgt Farrands attacked a 4,000-ton cargo vessel five miles east of Wangerooge. P/Os Hattersley and Lewis and F/Sgt Clayton found flak ships, also off Wangerooge, and S/L Macintyre and Sgt Harbourne a flak battery on a concrete mole and a searchlight installation respectively. No results were observed, and no claims were filed during debriefing after all returned safely.

In preparation for a busy night of operations on the 9th, 5 Group notified all of its stations to make ready between them fifty-seven Hampdens for attacks on the Blohm & Voss shipyards in the Finkenwerder district of Hamburg (Scampton), the Dortmund-Ems Canal and gardening (Hemswell), the explosives works at Geestacht (Hatfield Woodhouse), and the Weser Flugzeugbau aircraft factory at Lemwerder (Waddington). 44 Squadron loaded a record fourteen Hampdens with either six 250 pounders and sixty 4lb incendiaries, or four 500 pounders, and sent them on their way to north-western Germany between 21.15 and 22.12 with S/L Parker the senior pilot on duty. Their objective, known in Germany as Weserflug, was a subsidiary of the Deschimag shipbuilding group of companies, and the fourth largest aircraft manufacturer in Germany with factories at Lemwerder, north-west of Bremen, Tempelhof in Berlin, and, later, at Liegnitz in Poland, where Junkers and Focke-Wulf aircraft were built. The Lemwerder plant had originally constructed the Ju86 bomber, which had been dropped by the Luftwaffe in favour of the Heinkel 111 and was now engaged in the development of vertical take-off-and-landing technology (VTOL) in the form of a rudimentary helicopter and was also working on a twin-engine amphibian aircraft. It may also have been building Ju87 Stuka airframes for the Berlin plant.

Aircraft heading for north-western Germany were often confronted by challenging weather conditions in the form of towering ice-bearing cumulonimbus cloud formations containing electrical storms, and this would severely affect this night's operations. All from Waddington reached the target area, where low cloud and poor visibility prevented the crews of F/L Siebert, F/O Crossley, P/O Spencer and Sgts Herring and Harbourne from locating either the primary target or a suitable alternative, three of them jettisoning their bombs into the sea on the way home. S/L Parker dropped his six 250 pounders and incendiaries onto the factory complex, observing direct hits on buildings, and P/O Smythe watched two from his similar load burst in the extreme south-east corner of the site. P/O Walker lost sight of the bursts of his four 500 pounders in the flashes from flak, while P/O Price and crew braved the defences to race across the target at 500 feet from east to west, but, even from that altitude, were denied the satisfaction of observing the bursts of their six 250 pounders and incendiaries. As they flew towards home near Borkum island, they spotted two Me110 night-fighters circling in preparation to land and shot one down in flames to crash into the sea. Sgt Farrands and P/O Clark each delivered a stick of four 500 pounders across a petrol storage facility at Nordenham on the West Bank of the Weser south of Bremerhaven but were too busy evading the searchlights and flak to admire the results of their work. P/O Smith and crew flew north to south over the aerodrome on the island of Norderney to dispense their load of 500 pounders, while Sgt Collins and F/Sgt Clayton attacked the aerodrome on Borkum with 250 pounders and incendiaries, the former claiming direct hits on buildings and the airfield and a large explosion.

While 44 Squadron remained at home on the 14th, a dozen Hampdens from Hemswell and Hatfield Woodhouse were sent to attack the Blohm & Voss aircraft factory at Wenzendorf near Hamburg, while Scampton took care of gardening. On the 15th, Scampton was detailed to provide nine Hampdens for a raid on the aircraft park at Paderborn, and Waddington a dozen 44 Squadron crews for the Deurag oil refinery at Misburg, Hannover, plus two for mining duties in the Verbena garden off Copenhagen in company with ten from Hatfield Woodhouse. F/L Eustace and S/L Parker took off at 20.35 and 20.48 respectively, bound for the Baltic, leaving the bombing element to depart between 21.20 and 21.48 carrying the two standard loads of either 500 or 250 pounders. P/O Price lost the use of his blind-flying instruments during the North Sea crossing, and turned back, while F/L Siebert, who was the senior pilot among the bombing brigade, was possibly persuaded by the low cloud and electrical storms over northern Germany to drop his 500 pounders inconclusively on the marshalling yards at Osnabrück, still some seventy-five miles short of the primary target. P/O Smith and crew came upon a flare path and hangar lights on the aerodrome at Hävern some thirty miles north-north-west of Hannover and observed a number of bursts from their 500 pounders. P/O Walker and crew spotted a moving train as they approached the Dümmer Lake and aimed two 250 pounders and two hundred rounds at it from 700 feet, bringing it to a standstill. Carrying on, they were almost on the target, when a factory and railway line in the eastern outskirts of Hannover attracted their attention, persuading them to release the remaining four 250 pounders and incendiaries, which straddled the track. P/O Smith and crew were defeated by the low cloud, storms and the failure of their intercom system, and jettisoned their bombs off Texel on the way home. This left P/O Spencer, Sgts Collins, Farrands, Harbourne and Herrings and F/Sgt Clayton to negotiate the conditions to reach the target and deliver their attacks through haze and a spirited defence, some observing bursts followed by fires.

The Command ordered attacks on six targets in Germany on the 18th, for which thirty-eight Hampdens and thirty 3 Group Wellingtons were detailed. Scampton was to launch eighteen aircraft, fifteen assigned to the Krupp works in Essen and three to marshalling yards in Cologne, while Hatfield Woodhouse sent ten to target the aircraft park at Paderborn and 44 Squadron nine to a similar objective at Eschwege, situated twenty miles east-south-east of Kassel. They departed Waddington between 21.30 and 21.58 with S/L Parker the senior pilot on duty and flew out via corridor "G" to make landfall over the Scheldt and skirt the northern rim of the Ruhr. F/L Eustace and crew were attracted by the glow of a blast furnace as they approached the town of Arnsberg at 5,000 feet, and dropped two of their 250 pounders onto buildings in the vicinity, before continuing on to the primary target. The remaining four 250 pounders and sixty 4lb incendiaries were released from 5,000 feet and were seen to straddle hangars and buildings in the southern corner of the airfield, causing explosions and fires. P/O Clark and crew braved the airfield defences to race from east to west across a line of hangars at 2,500 feet and watched as their stick of 250 pounders set off large fires, which were followed by violent explosions. S/L Parker and crew delivered their attack from just five hundred feet higher and observed the scene as one of their 500 pounders completely demolished a hangar. Sgt Collins and crew elected a loftier release point of 6,000 feet for their run from north-west to south-east, from where their six 250 pounders splashed in a stick across a runway. P/O Smith and crew were at the same height on the same heading as their four 500 pounders struck home across the flying field and turned for home satisfied by their night's work. F/O Crossley and crew were among the early arrivals back at Waddington, and they reported attacking the aerodrome on the Frisian island of Juist with six 250 pounders and incendiaries from 4,000 feet as they passed over from east to west. At debriefing, Sgt Harbourne and crew reported bombing marshalling yards at Münster from 8,000 feet and observing bursts and three fires, but no detail, while F/L Siebert and crew described carrying out a dive attack from 7,000 down to 2,000 feet to unload the contents of their bomb bay in a single salvo towards a blast furnace at Oberhausen in the central Ruhr.

When P1324 landed at 03.57, P/O Walker was extricated and rushed to Lincoln County Hospital with a severe head wound courtesy of a piece of shrapnel. As he fought for life, second pilot, P/O Dave Romans, and the other members of the crew, Sgts Logan and Wicker, attended debriefing to recount a harrowing tale. They had attacked Wunstorf aerodrome, ten miles north-west of Hannover, from 6,000 feet, and had observed some of the six 250 pounders burst on hangars, before they were hit by at least one piece of shrapnel from a bursting flak shell. P/O Romans was lying prone in the nose performing the roles of navigator, bomb-aimer and front gunner, as second pilots on Hampdens had to do in order to gain experience before being allowed to captain their own crew. The first indication that all was not well came when the nose of the Hampden pitched down, and Romans failed to elicit a response from his captain. He then had only seconds to act to save the aircraft and crew and gained access to the cockpit through the hatch behind the pilot's seat, where he found P/O Walker unconscious and slumped over the controls. The difficulty of changing pilots in the air in the narrow and cramped confines of the fighter-style cockpit of a Hampden cannot be overstated, and it was something that could be practiced safely only on the ground. He collapsed the seatback, allowing Walker's torso to lay flat, and manoeuvred himself astride him to place his feet above Walker's on the rudder bars. As he did so, the wireless operator pulled the pilot backwards, allowing Romans to gain full access to the controls and fly the aircraft home, while the wireless operator tended, as best as he could, to Walker's wounds. It took a Herculean effort by all involved to save the aircraft, but, sadly, P/O Walker never regained consciousness, and succumbed soon afterwards in hospital.

Waddington, Scampton and Hatfield Woodhouse were alerted on the 19th, and ordered to prepare for that night's gardening activity and attacks on the Admiral Scheer pocket battleship at Wilhelmshaven and the aircraft park at Paderborn. 44 Squadron made ready five Hampdens for mining duties in the western Baltic, three in the Undergrowth garden off Frederikshavn in northern Jutland, and two in the Pumpkin garden off Samsø island, and they took off between 20.42 and 20.48 with P/Os Price and Spencer, F/Sgt Clayton and Sgts Henderson and Farrands at the controls. All reached their target areas, where, it seems, visibility was sufficiently good to enable all to locate their assigned pinpoints and carry out timed runs to the release-points. P/Os Price and Spencer and Sgt Farrands were off north-eastern Jutland, where the first-two-mentioned planted their vegetables from 300 and 450 feet respectively, and, it is believed, that the Farrands crew had also fulfilled their brief before L4087 was hit by flak and crashed into the sea. Sgt Farrands and a gunner survived to fall into enemy hands, but the two remaining crew members were lost with the aircraft. Meanwhile, one hundred miles to the south, F/Sgt Clayton and crew let their mine go from 800 feet off Samsø island, before rocking a cargo vessel with two 250 pounder near-misses, while Sgt Henderson and crew planted their vegetable from 600 feet, and undershot a cargo vessel, possibly the same one, with their bombs by a mere fifteen feet.

On the 20th, orders were received to prepare for a number of operations to be conducted that night, for which Hemswell would provide fifteen Hampdens for an attack on the Tirpitz and Admiral Scheer at berth in Wilhelmshaven, while Scampton took care of gardening and 44 Squadron returned to the aircraft park at Eschwege aerodrome with eight aircraft. They departed Waddington between 21.18 and 22.10 with F/L Siebert the senior pilot on duty, and at least some, if not all, made landfall on the

Dutch coast near Alkmaar. For an undisclosed reason, F/O Crossley and crew elected to drop their six 250 pounders and sixty 4lb incendiaries from 5,000 feet onto the aerodrome at Nordhorn, just across the Dutch/German frontier, and observed five bursts and a fire among buildings. P/O Hattersley and crew penetrated deeper into Germany, as far as the central Ruhr, where they came upon an aerodrome near Gelsenkirchen, upon which they let go two 250 pounders from 8,000 feet, before continuing on towards the south, where they spotted a large, unidentified factory east of Essen city centre in the Steele district. This they attacked with three 250 pounders and the incendiaries in a dive from 8,000 down to 4,000 feet and reserved the final bomb for another factory two miles south-west of Steele. The others reached the primary target, where they would have to face an intense searchlight and flak defence, which, no doubt, had been beefed-up since the last attack. F/L Siebert dived from 6,000 to 2,000 feet to deliver his 250 pounders in a salvo onto buildings on the southern side of the aerodrome, where five bursts were followed by an equal number of fires. P/O Smythe and crew were carrying four 500 pounders, which they released at 1,500 feet after a stomach-churning dive from 10,000 feet from east to west across the target. Sgt Harbourne and crew chose a north-west to south-east heading and observed from 7,000 feet as their 500 pounders impacted the tarmac, while P/O Clark and crew kept the flak crews guessing by racing across the aiming point in a dive from west to east. Their 250 pounders set fire to a hangar, and many explosions could be seen inside it as they weaved their way out of danger. Sgts Collins and Paskell and their crews carried out equally effective attacks, and all returned safely to pass on the details to intelligence staff at debriefing.

On the following day, 5 Group detailed a total of twenty Hampdens from its four stations and briefed their crews for an attack on the important Dornier aircraft factory, located in the Hansastadt (ancient free-trade city) Wismar, on the Baltic coast. The 44 Squadron crews of S/L Macintyre, F/L Eustace, P/O Hynes and Sgt Herring departed Waddington between 21.30 and 22.07, each carrying six 250 pounders and sixty 4lb incendiaries, and set course for the one-thousand-mile round-trip in favourable weather conditions. All reached the target area, where they released their bombs in single sticks from between 3,000 and 10,000 feet on a variety of headings, and bursts, fires and explosion were observed, before cloud slid across the aiming point to obscure the ground. With France now out of the battle, and Prime Minister Churchill announcing that the Battle of Britain was about to begin, invasion fever gripped the nation, and the first operations were mounted on this night against the build-up of invasion barges and other craft in the occupied ports.

5 Group detailed twenty-three Hampdens for a variety of targets on the 22nd, a dozen of them representing 44 Squadron, eight assigned to the Nordstern (Gelsenberg A G) synthetic oil refinery in the Horst district of Gelsenkirchen in the Ruhr, and four to return to the aircraft park at Eschwege in company with a similar number from Hemswell. The latter, consisting of the crews of F/L Siebert, P/O Smythe, F/Sgt Clayton and Sgt Collins, took off first, between 21.22 and 21.28, and they were followed into the air between 22.00 and 22.14 by the others, carrying one or other of the two standard bomb loads. Not one of those bound for Eschwege reached the target, for which adverse weather conditions were probably responsible, but each found an alternative objective for their bombs. Sgt Collins dropped four 500 pounders in a stick from east to west across Schiphol aerodrome near Amsterdam but was blinded to the results by searchlight glare. F/Sgt Clayton and crew ran into thunderstorms and haze, and found an alternative target, coded H57, which they bombed with a stick of 500 pounders from west to east. Z57 was Schiphol aerodrome, and, as the Collins and Clayton crews had taken off two minutes apart and landed within six minutes of each other, it seems likely that they attacked the same target, and that the code H57 was a typographical error. F/L Siebert and crew were on course for their primary target when passing close to Münster aerodrome and chose to drop

their six 250 pounders and incendiaries there, doing so in the face of a hostile searchlight and flak defence, which prevented them from observing the results. It seems that P/O Smythe and crew opted to join in the main attack at Gelsenkirchen and delivered a stick of 250 pounders from north to south across the aiming point, observing three bursts and a large building on fire.

The Ruhr, fifty miles from west to east, and, if one includes the Cologne area, fifty miles from north to south, represented mostly a confusing region to bomb, containing more than twenty cities and towns with overlapping boundaries, all spewing out pollution from their myriad chimney stacks to create an impenetrable blanket of industrial haze. Even on a clear night, ground features were indistinct, and, when cloud-covered, it was anyone's guess as to where the bombs might fall. Gelsenkirchen lies slightly to the north of the central Ruhr, with its oil quarter in the north-western districts of Horst and Gladbeck, where the Nordstern and Scholven-Buer refineries were located. To reach it crews were required to enter the Ruhr defence zone, which, even this early in the war, was the most hostile region in Germany, tasked, as it was, with protecting the heart of war production. Sgt Harbourne and crew dropped their 250 pounders and incendiaries in a stick from south-east to north-west across E8, otherwise known as the Krupp complex, situated in Essen's north-western district of Borbeck, some ten miles south of the primary target, and observed five bursts straddling the southern reaches. P/O Hattersley and crew claimed to have bombed an aerodrome at Horst, delivering their bombs in a stick from east to west while dodging the searchlight beams. The remaining crews, however, all carried out attacks on the Nordstern plant, approaching from all points of the compass and delivering their 250 and 500 pounders and incendiaries in the face of an intense searchlight and flak defence. Some observed bursts and fires, but most were blinded to the results by the glare.

44 Squadron remained at home on the following two nights, while other elements of the group returned to the Blohm & Voss and Dornier aircraft factories at Wenzendorf (Hamburg) and Wismar respectively. A busy night of operations on the 25th would involve 166 aircraft, the crews of which were briefed to attack one of seven targets in the Ruhr and aerodromes in Holland. 5 Group detailed forty-one Hampdens to target oil refineries in the Ruhr, and eighteen from Scampton to attack a section of the Dortmund-Ems Canal at its junction with the River Ems. At Waddington, fifteen crews were called to briefing to learn that they had been assigned to the oil refinery at Castrop-Rauxel in company with five 50 Squadron crews, while others attended to a similar plant at Wanne-Eickel. Both production sites were employing the Bergius process to manufacture high-grade oil products, like aviation fuel, through the hydrogenation of highly volatile bituminous coal. The two refineries were east of Gelsenkirchen and situated on either side of the town of Herne, Wanne-Eickel to the west and Castrop-Rauxel to the east. The 44 Squadron element departed Waddington between 22.15 and 22.50 with S/L Macintyre the senior pilot on duty, and P/O Romans, now with a DFC to his credit, captaining his crew for the first time. All reached the Ruhr to encounter the expected industrial haze and hostile reception, with a scattering of cloud as an additional impediment to target locating, and only nine crews were able to identify the primary target. They delivered either six 250 pounders and incendiaries or four 500 pounders across the target, some observing bursts, while a number gained a more detailed impression of buildings receiving direct hits. Sgt Henderson and crew, who were among the last to arrive, braved the defences to conduct a reconnaissance of the target after bombing, and reported two large fires with smaller ones between, and assessed the entire middle of the target to be ablaze, the core of the conflagration emitting black smoke. Of those who failed to identify the primary target, Sgt Farmer and P/O Hynes bombed blast furnaces at nearby Sterkrade and Bottrop respectively, F/Ls Siebert and Eustace unidentified aerodromes, and Sgt Harbourne and P/O Clark the aerodrome at De Kooy, near Den Helder.

Scampton took care of 5 Group's business on the following night, when targeting oil plants in north-western France, while, on the 27th, it fell to Hemswell and Hatfield Woodhouse to carry the 5 Group flag into battle on mining operations and an attack on an oil refinery at Harburg. Orders were received at Waddington and Hatfield Woodhouse on the 28th to prepare twenty-four Hampdens between them for raids on oil-related targets in Hamburg and Bremen, and at Scampton to make ready for gardening duties. Sixteen 44 Squadron crews attended briefing, to learn that fifteen of them would be targeting the A10 and A19 oil refineries at Harburg and Ostermoor respectively, while Sgt Paskell and crew carried out a reconnaissance sortie over the Dortmund-Ems Canal at its crossing over the River Ems, north of Münster. It is not clear whether or not crews were specifically assigned to an objective, but the impression is that eight had the Harburg plant as their primary, and seven the Ostermoor site, situated on the North Bank of the Elbe estuary near its junction with the Kiel Canal. A total of eighty-nine aircraft would be roaming over Germany and the occupied countries on this night, including a number of 1 Group Fairey Battles to target invasion craft.

The 44 Squadron element departed Waddington between 21.20 and 21.55, with S/Ls Macintyre and Parker the senior pilots on duty. They began the North Sea crossing near Skegness, and, as they approached the enemy coast, they ran into a bank of cumulonimbus cloud between 3,000 and 12,000 feet, which combined with extreme darkness to prevent them from picking up pinpoints on the ground. These already challenging conditions for target-locating would become compounded by an intense searchlight and flak response, and some crews would be persuaded to seek out the briefed alternative targets. P/O Lewis and crew backtracked to H22, the seaplane base on the Frisian Island of Borkum, and dropped a stick of 250 pounders from north to south, observing bursts but no detail. Sgt Herring and crew followed suit, and observed two of their 500 pounders burst on the target, but, again, without being able to glean any detail. After their inability to locate the Ostermoor plant, P/O Hattersley and crew flew north to drop their four 500 pounders on the seaplane base at Hörnum, on the island of Sylt.

It seems that all but one of those assigned to the Harburg refinery, all of which were carrying six 250 pounders, were able to establish their position and carry out an attack, the exception, the crew of Sgt Harbourne, bringing their bombs home. As usual, and in contrast to the future "organised" format of an attack, crews ran across the target from all points of the compass at altitudes determined by themselves and delivered their bombs onto what they believed was the refinery. Some observed bursts and large fires, while others were more intent on evading the searchlights and flak than on making a precise observation. S/L Macintyre and crew selected an altitude of 8,000 feet for their run but failed to spot a barrage balloon cable in their path. P4375 struck it with great force, and three members of the crew managed to save themselves to fall into enemy hands, before the crash took the life of the pilot. This would be the only 5 Group loss of the night, and the remaining fifteen crews from Waddington landed between 02.30 and 05.15, before assembling in the debriefing room to make their reports. P/Os Romans and Smith and Sgt Farmer and their crews related their experiences over the Ostermoor plant but were able to provide the intelligence staff with no detail. P/O Clark and crew landed after seven hours aloft and reported that an engine issue had forced them to jettison their load. The fact that it was dropped "safe", suggested that they had been over occupied territory at the time. The last to touch down was the crew of Sgt Paskell, who had fulfilled their brief to reconnoitre the twin aqueducts of the Dortmund-Ems Canal, after which, they dropped six delayed-action 250 pounders on the nearby aerodrome at Münster and fired 250 rounds from the two rear gun positions at a Henkel 111, apparently, without effect.

On the last day of the month, 5 Group notified Hatfield Woodhouse to prepare for gardening duties that night in the western Baltic, and Waddington and Hemswell to make ready sixteen Hampdens to target the Deurag oil refinery at Misburg near Hannover. 44 Squadron was to provide a dozen aircraft for the main target, and two others to attack the marshalling yards at Osnabrück. They took off together between 21.15 and 22.15 with S/L Parker the senior pilot on duty and first away, and undertook the outward flight in poor weather conditions, which would severely compromise the crews' efforts to locate their targets. F/L Eustace and P/O Smith returned with their loads after failing to locate their primary or a suitable alternative target beneath the cloud cover. P/Os Hynes and Romans located the marshalling yards despite low cloud, and delivered their six 250 pounders each blindly, before heading home and dispensing nickels (leaflets) on the way. Most of the remaining crews would attack alternative and last-resort targets, P/O Lewis finding an aerodrome at Teuge in central Holland for his 250 pounders, while S/L Parker stuck to the oil theme and dropped his on a facility at Emmerich on the German side of the Rhine. F/L Siebert bombed a seaplane base at Amsterdam, Sgt Paskell another one between the Hague and Amsterdam, P/O Clark a concentration of some twenty small coastal vessels in the Waddenzee between Texel and the mainland, and Sgt Henderson the aerodrome on Texel. P/O Hattersley and crew picked out the aerodrome at Hesepe, situated two miles south-east of the German frontier town of Nordhorn, and left their calling card in the form of six 250 pounders aimed through haze. Sgt Herring and F/O Crossley and their crews were the only ones to reach Misburg, where they delivered four 500 pounders, the former in a stick from north to south. The return of Sgt Farmer and crew was awaited in vain, and it was later in the day when the news came through that L4085 had ditched at 06.30 off Aberystwyth in Cardigan Bay. The local lifeboat put to sea at 07.26 and recovered the body of the pilot, while a motorboat, Emerald Star, picked up two survivors and another body.

During the course of the month, the squadron took part in twenty-two operations and dispatched 152 sorties for the loss of four Hampdens, two complete crews, two pilots and another crew member.

August 1940

August's operations would follow a similar pattern to those of July as invasion fever increased, and 5 Group divided its effort on the 2nd between the oil refinery at Misburg for the Hemswell crews and mining for those from Scampton. On the following night, the Scampton element was sent in search of the cruiser Gneisenau at Kiel, while Hemswell went for the Dortmund-Ems Canal and Waddington took care of gardening duties. A dozen 44 Squadron Hampdens were loaded with a 1,500lb parachute mine each, while the crews were being briefed about the garden into which they were to be delivered. They were to target the main approaches to the naval port of Kiel in the Forget-me-not garden, while the attention of the defences was on the attack by the Scampton element and took off between 21.00 and 21.40 with F/Ls Eustace and Siebert the senior pilots on duty. All reached the target area to find favourable conditions, which enabled them to establish pinpoints from which to carry out their timed runs. The vegetables were released into the briefed locations from between 600 and 1,000 feet, leaving the crews free to search for suitable targets for their wing-mounted 250 pounders. F/L Eustace found an aerodrome east of Tonning on the Schleswig-Holstein peninsula, while P/Os Lewis, Hattersley and Spencer attacked the aerodrome at Husum on the west coast. Sgt Henderson went for the seaplane base at Hörnum on the southern tip of the island of Sylt, and Sgts Herring and Paskell the aerodrome in the centre of the island. F/Sgt Clayton and crew came upon six small cargo vessels anchored to the south of Husum and were fired upon by two flak ships for their trouble, sustaining extensive damage to the tail boom. P/O Hynes and crew spotted a flak ship in Kiel harbour, P/O Price searchlight installations in the Eckernförde Bucht (Bay) a dozen or so miles to the north-west, and Sgt Collins an aerodrome on the island of Amrum, south of Sylt.

44 Squadron remained at home on the night of the 5/6th, when Hemswell attended to the mining campaign and eighteen aircraft from Scampton and Hatfield Woodhouse went in search of the battleship Bismarck, which, it was believed, was at berth in Hamburg. The following night was devoted to gardening activities in the western Baltic undertaken by crews from Scampton, while 44 Squadron once more remained on the ground. Orders came through to Scampton on the 7th to continue the mining of northern waters, while Hemswell and Waddington were alerted to prepare for an attack on the cruiser, Gneisenau, at her moorings in the port of Kiel. Among those operating on this night was twenty-nine-year-old S/L Noel Challis "Hettie" Hyde, who had been selected as the prospective commanding officer of 207 Squadron, which was soon to be reformed at Waddington as the first to equip with the twin-engine Avro Manchester, one of the new generation of heavy bombers coming online towards the end of the year. He had been commissioned in September 1929, and, after serving as a pilot with 26 and 208 Squadrons, was posted to the Middle-East in 1935 for what turned out to be an eighteen-month tour of duty. On return to the UK in 1937, he became a test pilot at the A&AEE, and, having no operational experience thus far in the war, had been posted to Waddington to gain some with 44 Squadron, before taking up his new role.

He was the senior pilot on duty among the fourteen from 44 Squadron departing Waddington between 20.40 and 21.20, before climbing away to encounter unfavourable weather conditions in the form of ten-tenths cloud, electrical storms and barely moderate visibility. P/O Price and crew were soon contending with a loss of power in the port engine, and turned back after an hour, leaving the others to press on to complete the North Sea crossing and traverse the Schleswig-Holstein peninsula. They found the entire target area to be covered by thick, low cloud, and none was able to locate the target vessel, forcing them to bomb blind on estimated positions or seek alternative targets. The crews of S/L Hyde, F/L Eustace, P/Os Hattersley, Romans and Smith, and Sgts Henderson, Herring and Paskell delivered four 500 pounders each across the docks area, and Sgt Clayton and crew added their 2,000 pounder, most observing explosions, but all were denied a glimpse of the outcome. P/O Lewis dropped his 500 pounders in a stick from south to north over the aerodrome at Husum, and Sgt Collins and crew theirs in a run from east to west. F/O Crossley and crew failed to locate a suitable objective and jettisoned their load "safe" five miles off Amrum island, while F/L Siebert returned his to store.

Only Scampton operated on the 8th, to target an I G Farben oil refinery at Oppau, near Ludwigshafen, and the entire group remained on the ground on the 9th because of adverse weather conditions. On the 10th, nine Hampdens each from Hemswell and Hatfield Woodhouse operated against the Gewerkschaft Rheinpreussen A G Bergius-process oil refinery at Moers/Homberg, situated on the West Bank of the Rhine opposite Duisburg. Waddington and Scampton provided aircraft for operations on the 11th, the former nine for a mining operation in the Forget-me-not garden in Kiel Bay and the latter eighteen to attack an oil refinery at Dortmund in the Ruhr. The 44 Squadron element took off between 20.45 and 20.50 with F/L Siebert the senior pilot on duty, and, again, ran into less-than-helpful weather conditions, which would prevent four crews from establishing a pinpoint in the target area. F/L Siebert, P/Os Hattersley and Lewis and Sgt Henderson would bring their vegetables home, but P/O Hattersley and crew did, at least, find a target for their wing-mounted 250 pounders in the form of Hörnum aerodrome. Sgt Collins and crew delivered their mine from 900 feet, before attacking the aerodrome at List at the northern end of Sylt, and it was possibly here that F/O Crossley and crew bombed a flak battery after planting their vegetable into the briefed location from 800 feet. P/Os Romans and Price and F/Sgt Clayton fulfilled their briefs from 700, 900 and 800 feet respectively, before F/Sgt Clayton disposed of his two 250 pounders on the Danish port of Sønderborg.

The almost personal association between 5 Group and the Dortmund-Ems Canal, which would extend right to the end of the war, was continued on the night of the 12/13th by Hampdens of 49 and 83 Squadrons in a low-level attack on the older branch of the twin aqueduct section at its junction with the River Ems north of Műnster. Attacking last in the face of the most hostile searchlight and flak defence, and, after witnessing the loss of two 83 Squadron Hampdens, 49 Squadron's F/L Learoyd breached the channel, and made it home to become the first from Bomber Command to be awarded a Victoria Cross. Another operation on this night was conducted by an element from Hemswell against the previously targeted oil refinery at Salzbergen, while, at Waddington, the crews of F/O Ogilvie, P/O Hynes and Sgt Paskell took off for the Wallflower garden in Kiel Harbour. They delivered their vegetables into the briefed locations from between 500 and 700 feet, before Sgt Paskell unleashed two 250 pounders on Hörnum aerodrome.

On the 13th, all four operational stations were alerted to prepare for attacks that night on Junkers aircraft factories at Dessau and Bernburg, situated some twenty miles apart in east central Germany, south of Magdeburg. A force of thirty Hampdens was assembled, ten of them at Waddington, where take-off was completed without incident between 21.25 and 21.45 with F/L Siebert the senior pilot on duty. They set course from Skegness and flew all the way to Texel in cloud at 2,000 feet, before climbing to break into clear air at around 9,000 feet. There was some flak activity as they passed close to Hannover and then Braunschweig (Brunswick) but reached the target area to find a cloud base at between 1,500 and 7,000 feet, with haze and extreme darkness below. The distance caused a slight reduction in the weight of the bomb loads, and each Hampden was carrying either four 500 pounders or four 250 pounders and sixty 4lb incendiaries. Bombing runs were carried out from various points of the compass, and, while bursts were observed, only a few crews were able to determine any detail. Among these was that of P/O Hattersley, who dropped a stick of four 500 pounders from north-east to south-west and claimed hits on the assembly and jig and tool sheds and the destruction of the power-generating building. P/O Price and crew were unable to locate the primary target because of the low cloud and let their 500 pounders go over an aerodrome at Hildesheim, south of Hannover. The crew of P/O Clark was absent from debriefing, and, it was learned eventually via the Red Cross, or, possibly the Dutch Resistance, that P2077 had been brought down by flak and had crashed a dozen miles east-south-east of Alkmaar, and that the crew had been taken into captivity.

A change of focus on the 14th would pitch 5 Group against marshalling yards in Cologne and oil production and storage facilities at Pauillac, situated on the West Bank of the Gironde on the approach to Bordeaux in south-western France. 44 Squadron loaded six of its Hampdens with six 250 pounders and sixty 4lb incendiaries each, before dispatching the first section of three, containing the crews of the newly arrived S/L Gardner, P/O Ridpath and F/O Ogilvie between 20.55 and 21.10, and the second section of F/Sgt Clayton, and Sgts Harbourne and Paskell between 22.00 and 22.15. They were bound for the Eifeltor marshalling yards, situated south-west of Cologne city centre, and flew out via corridor "G" to make landfall over the Scheldt. They found the target area to be covered by cloud, which defeated P/O Ridpath and crew's efforts to locate the primary target or an alternative, and they brought their bombs home. F/Sgt Clayton and crew, it seems, also failed to locate the marshalling yards, but came upon the important Knapsack power station some three miles to the south-west and attacked it with a stick of bombs on a north-easterly heading, observing bursts but no detail as they dodged the flak response. The others attacked the primary target after running across it on a variety of headings, and only Sgt Harbourne and crew were able to report four fairly large fires, while the others saw only bomb bursts.

The 15th was the day selected by the Luftwaffe as "Adlertag", Eagle Day, and was intended to be the opening salvo in the destruction of the RAF's ability to defend Britain. It began the most intense four weeks of the Battle of Britain, the outcome of which might determine the course of the war. Scampton and Hemswell took care of 5 Group business that night, but Waddington and Hatfield Woodhouse were back in harness on the 16th, when a record seventeen 44 Squadron crews and eleven from 50 Squadron attended briefings. They learned that the I G Farben-owned oil refinery at Leuna, near Merseburg, was to be their target, which, as already mentioned, was one of many oil production and storage sites situated in an arc to the west of Leipzig from north of the city to the south. This would be an area of major interest to the Command from mid-1944 onwards, but that was in the distant future, when a thousand sorties might be launched in a single night, while on this night, the commitment of 150 sorties represented a major effort. The 44 Squadron element departed Waddington between 20.30 and 21.10 with W/C Reid and S/L Gardner the senior pilots on duty and disappeared into a fine night with gentle moonlight to illuminate their path. Once over enemy territory, however, low cloud slid between them and the ground, happily, to disperse as the target area drew near. Despite the clear skies and the brightness of the moonlight, some crews experienced great difficulty in identifying the well-camouflaged complex, and spent a long time searching, before either finding it or giving up. Somewhat optimistically, they had been briefed to aim for particular areas of the site, specifically the power generation and hydrogenation plants, and twelve crews reported attacking buildings with either four 500 pounders or four 250 pounders and sixty 4lb incendiaries. P/O Lewis and crew observed blue-green flames, while a number of others saw bursts, yellow and green flashes and fires, but most were too intent on evading the defences to take in the detail. F/O Crossley and crew were an exception and observed their bombs to burst near the base of chimneys and set off three explosions, followed by dense clouds of smoke and a fire that remained visible for seventy miles into the return flight. After all had returned safely from round trips of eight hours and more, P/O Hattersley and crew reported bombing a railway junction at Buttstädt, some twenty-five miles to the south-west of the target, while S/L Gardner, P/O Hynes and Sgt Collins attacked aerodromes, respectively, south-east of Münster, at Halle and at Nohra. W/C Reid and crew had been unable to find a target worthy of their bombs and jettisoned them in open country near Blankenberg.

On the 17th, Hatfield Woodhouse became Lindholme, and 44 Squadron stayed at home at Waddington, as it did on the 18th, and it was the 19th when it was next invited to take up arms. Orders were received to provide five aircraft for that night's mining duties in the Kraut garden off Aalborg in northern Jutland, while Hemswell and Scampton provided fourteen Hampdens between them for a return to the Bordeaux area to attack oil storage facilities at Bec-d'Ambes, situated on the West Bank of the Dordogne some ten miles north of the port. The 44 Squadron quintet took off between 20.35 and 20.55 with S/L Gardner the senior pilot on duty, and all covered the five-hundred-mile outward flight without incident, to deliver their vegetables into the briefed locations from between 500 and 800 feet. F/L Siebert and crew completed the round trip in five minutes short of seven hours, while the others followed them home over the ensuing sixty-five minutes to log flight times of up to eight hours and five minutes.

The dual targets for forty-four Hampdens on the 21st were a ship lift at the eastern end of the Mittelland Canal at its junction with the Elbe, and the Bergius-process Deutsche Erdöl A G synthetic oil refinery (hydrogenation plant), coded A78, both located in the same Rothensee district to the north of Magdeburg city centre. Also, on the target list was a second ship lift at Hohenwarthe, close by to the north-east, which, in reality, had not been built, and, as a result of the war, would not be. 44 Squadron made ready ten Hampdens for the refinery and dispatched them between 21.10 and 21.40 with S/L "Hettie" Hyde the senior pilot on duty. They began the North Sea crossing at Skegness, and made landfall on the Dutch coast near Alkmaar, running the usual gauntlet of flak from numerous hotspots on their way east, particularly when passing between Hannover and Celle either side of 23.00. That said, the poor weather conditions, which included thunderstorms and rain, provided a degree of protection, but also created challenges for target-locating. P/O Smith and crew took the decision to attack the Deurag refinery at Misburg, rather than risk the possibility of not finding the primary target in the prevailing conditions and dropped a stick of four 500 pounders towards it from north to south, observing two bursts and one to undershoot. The others pressed on to reach the primary target, where P/O Ridpath and Sgt Collins were thwarted by low cloud and rain, and backtracked to Misburg, which they attacked with 250 and 500 pounders respectively. Of those attacking A78, Sgt Paskell ran from west to east, P/O Romans from north to south, while the headings of P/Os Hattersley and Lewis were not recorded, but, together, they rained down a total of eight 250 and eight 500 pounders, some of which were seen to burst. Having failed to locate the refinery, S/L Hyde and crew flew north for ten miles, where they dispensed their four 250 pounders onto a section of the Mittelland Canal. On the way home with a full bomb bay, P/O Hynes came upon the marshalling yards at Osnabrück, and emptied it of the four 250 pounders, which were observed to burst. Some twenty-five miles to the north, F/O Ogilvie released four 500 pounders over Quackenbrück aerodrome,

Hemswell, Lindholme and Waddington received orders on the 22nd to prepare between them twenty-three Hampdens for an operation that night against an aircraft components factory (G82) in Frankfurt, while a dozen others from Scampton took care of the gardening duties. 44 Squadron loaded six of its own with either four 500 or six 250 pounders and dispatched them between 20.45 and 21.00 with S/L Gardner the senior pilot on duty. They made landfall over the Scheldt and traversed the length of Belgium before crossing the German frontier near St Vith. They found the target area to be concealed by cloud, which presented challenging conditions for target location, and only F/L Siebert and F/Sgt Clayton and their crews were able to carry out an attack with 250 pounders. Neither saw any results, and the likelihood is that the attacks were carried out on e.t.a., or on estimated positions based on dead-reckoning (DR) and missed the mark. The others headed north in search of alternative targets, and F/O Crossley and P/O Price located the Knapsack power station to the south-west of Cologne, which they attacked with four 500 pounders each without observing the results. F/L Rogers and crew were a little further north, and, with Duisburg on the port quarter, turned to run across the Ruhrort inland docks complex from north-east to south-west, releasing their four 500 pounders and observing bursts but no detail. This left just S/L Gardner and crew, who were further north still, well beyond the Ruhr, when they came upon an aerodrome at Lingen, near the Dutch border some forty miles north-west of Osnabrück, which they bombed from east to west, observing three bursts.

On the following night, 5 Group launched forty Hampdens to conduct mining sorties in the Jellyfish garden off the port of Brest. The 44 Squadron quartet departed Waddington between 23.40 and 23.45, before crossing the Dorset coast and heading for landfall on the French coast somewhere to the west of St-Malo. They arrived in the target area to find excellent conditions with bright moonlight, and the defences already stirred into action by earlier arrivals. The pinpoints for the timed runs were easily established, and the vegetables planted according to brief from between 400 and 800 feet. P/O Ridpath and crew then dropped their two 250 pounders onto docks to the north of the garden, while F/O Ogilvie attacked an aerodrome at Guipavas to the north-east and Sgt Harbourne a flak battery. On the following day, thirty-one Hampdens were detailed from Waddington, Hemswell and Lindholme for further mining operations that night in the Beech and Cinnamon gardens off the ports of St-Nazaire and La Rochelle respectively, which, along with Brest and Lorient, were havens for the Kriegsmarine's U-Boot fleet. It had been intended for 44 Squadron to provide eight aircraft, but two unnamed crews collided while taxiing, and their participation had to be scrubbed. This left six to take off between 22.40 and 22.50 bound for the Cinnamon garden with S/L Hyde the senior pilot on duty. They enjoyed an uneventful operation in favourable weather conditions and planted their vegetables into the briefed locations from between 500 and 700 feet, and, although they faced opposition in the form of light flak from various locations, it was inaccurate, and this encouraged some to drop their wing bombs onto suitable targets on the way home. P/Os Hynes and Smith picked out the coastal aerodrome at Les-Sables-d'Olonne, to the north-west of the port, and watched their 250 pounders burst among buildings. S/L Hyde bombed a merchant vessel anchored at the entrance to the Brest Canal, F/L Rogers a seaplane base at St-Nazaire, and P/O Price an aerodrome at Dinard, near the northern coast of Brittany.

In retaliation for the inadvertent bombing of London on the night of the 24/25th, the War Cabinet sanctioned the first raid of the war on Berlin to take place on the 25th. 5 Group responded with the preparation of forty-six Hampdens, thirty-four from Scampton, Waddington and Lindholme to attack an electrical power station, B57, one of five serving the city, while twelve from Hemswell targeted Tempelhof aerodrome to the south of the centre. During the day's air-tests in preparation, P4353 crashed soon after take-off and was damaged beyond repair, but the crew of P/O Quick walked away. The 44 Squadron element of six departed Waddington between 21.15 and 21.40 with S/L Gardner the senior pilot on duty and set course via the Lincolnshire coast for the target, six hundred miles away. The route would take them close to Hannover and Braunschweig, but a blanket of cloud stretching across northern Germany largely denied them a sight of the ground. The unfavourable conditions persisted in the target area, where the cloud base was down to 2,000 feet. S/L Gardner dropped a stick of four 500 pounders from south-east to north-west, F/L Siebert from east to west and P/O Ridpath from west to east, and all observed bursts without being able to determine the actual point of impact. F/O Hattersley provided no detail of his bombing run and saw nothing after his bombs had fallen away. F/O Ogilvie and crew were unable to locate the primary target, and joined in the attack on Tempelhof aerodrome, the briefed alternative. F/Sgt Clayton and crew failed to locate either objective, and found one for themselves in the form of the aerodrome at Johannisthal, in the city's south-eastern suburb of Treptow.

Another busy night of operations on the 26th saw the preparation of twenty Hampdens from Hemswell and two from Waddington to attack A77, the Leuna (Merseburg) oil refinery near Liepzig, while six others from Waddington were assigned to a gas production plant in the city itself. The 44 Squadron element took off between 20.30 and 21.10 with S/L Hyde the senior pilot on duty, and P/O Smith and Sgt Collins and their crews assigned to the oil plant. A seventh 44 Squadron crew was also dispatched to photograph repairs to the Dortmund-Ems Canal at its junction with the River Ems north of Münster but was not identified in the ORB. They were greeted at the target by ten-tenths cloud with a base at 5,000 feet, and, in the light of recent experiences, this was too low to go in alone at such a well-defended target. The weather conditions were equally unhelpful to the others as they passed between Münster and Osnabrück on their way to the Leipzig area, coming under heavy and accurate fire, and again, later on as they bypassed Celle. P/O Perkins and crew had to contend with engine problems once over enemy territory and bombed the marshalling yards at Osnabrück as an alternative target before returning home. P/O Price and crew were defeated by low cloud, which prevented them from locating any worthwhile objectives, and jettisoned their bombs off the Dutch coast. P/O Smith and crew ran across the Leuna refinery from north-east to south-west and watched their four 500 pounders burst across its centre, while Sgt Collins and crew followed up from east to west, neither crew gleaning any detail to pass on at debriefing. S/L Hyde and P/O Hynes and their crews delivered four 250 pounders and sixty 4lb incendiaries each over the gas plant, and F/L Rogers and Sgt Harbourne four 500 pounders each, and, on their return, they were able to report bursts, explosions and at least four fires.

Scampton took the strain on the 27th, looking after both the gardening duties and attacks on the oil plants at Bec-d'Ambes and Pauillac near Bordeaux, but all stations were in action on the 28th, preparing thirty Hampdens to send to Berlin to target the Siemens & Halske A G electrical engineering factory in the Siemensstadt district of Spandau, north-west of Berlin city centre. This site produced components for aero-engines and would be found after the war to have employed slave workers from concentration camps. 44 Squadron made ready six Hampdens, loading three with four 500 pounders and the others with four 250 pounders and sixty 4lb incendiaries, and they departed Waddington between 20.00 and 20.20 with F/L Rogers the senior pilot on duty. They all reached the target area to find the defences already stirred into action, and five of them carried out attacks on a variety of headings, observing their bombs to burst, while being unable to determine detail. F/O Hattersley and crew failed to locate the primary or briefed alternative targets and dropped their four 250 pounders onto an aerodrome two miles south-east of Magdeburg. On the way home, they passed over the aerodrome at Quakenbrück, thirty miles short of the Dutch frontier, and fired two hundred rounds at it from the lower rear gun.

On the 29th, Hemswell and Waddington dispatched twenty Hampdens between them to attack the Scholven-Buer synthetic oil refinery, situated north of Gelsenkirchen city centre and some two miles to the north-east of Gladbeck. 44 Squadron contributed six Hampdens, which took off between 20.15 and 20.30 with S/L Gardner the senior pilot on duty, and, although all reached the target area, only two were able to positively identify the primary target through the industrial haze. P/O Smith and crew dropped their four 500 pounders in a stick from north to south, and the second one caused a bright green flash, which lit up the cockpit, and this was followed by a large fire. S/L Gardner and crew were the others to locate the primary target but observed nothing of the outcome of their attack. Sgts Harbourne and Henderson attacked B26, which, it is believed, was a power station serving the refinery and other nearby factories, the latter claiming to have set off a large fire that was visible from twenty-five miles away. Sgt Collins and crew failed to locate either objective, and continued on towards the north-east, where they came upon the important marshalling yards in Hamm, an important hub linking the Ruhr with other parts of Germany. They delivered their four 500 pounders, observing them to detonate and fling pieces of track and rolling stock high into the air. P4372 did not return with the others, and the crew of P/O Hynes was duly posted missing. It was learned in time that the pilot and wireless operator/gunners had survived to be taken into captivity, but, that the second pilot, P/O Dunkels, had lost his life.

Elements from Scampton and Lindholme returned to the refinery on the following night, while fourteen other Scampton Hampdens flew further afield to the recently attacked hydrogenation plant at Magdeburg. 44 Squadron remained at home and was alerted on the 31st to the operations planned for that night, which included a return to the Magdeburg oil plant for fifteen crews from Scampton and Lindholme, the Bayerische Motoren Werke (BMW) aero-engine works at Spandau in Berlin for nine from Hemswell, while 44 Squadron was to provide five crews to attack Tempelhof aerodrome, also in

Berlin. The 44 Squadron element departed Waddington in a five-minute slot to 20.10, with F/L Rogers the senior pilot on duty, each Hampden loaded with four 250 pounders and up to seventy-two 4lb incendiaries. They reached the target area to find weather conditions that were moderate at best, with up to ten-tenths cloud that prevented a number of the 44 Squadron crews from locating their assigned objective. F/L Rogers and P/Os Hattersley and Romans were able to locate Tempelhof aerodrome, which they attacked from north-east to south-west, observing bursts but no detail. On the way home, P/O Hattersley and crew strafed Lembruch aerodrome, located on the eastern edge of Lake Dümmer, with three hundred rounds, causing the lights to be extinguished. P/O Ridpath and crew failed to locate the primary target, and attacked M499, which is believed to be a power station in Berlin, while P/O Burt and crew came upon an oil production site at Tegel, a north-western suburb of the Capital, and attacked it also on a south-westerly heading. P2123 ran out of fuel on return and had to be ditched at 05.35 by P/O Romans just off the beach at Cromer on the Norfolk coast, from where he and his crew paddled their way to the shore in the dinghy.

By this time, S/L Hyde had been posted away to familiarize himself with the new Avro Manchester, prior to his appointment to command the reforming 207 Squadron at Waddington in November. He had taken F/L Siebert with him as one of a number of highly experienced 5 Group pilots, who, once converted, would mentor the others recruited to introduce the type into operational service. In January, S/L Hyde's promotion to wing commander would be confirmed, and he would prove to be a popular and inspirational leader until failing to return from Kiel on the night of the 8/9th of April 1941, although he and his crew would survive as PoWs. During the course of the month, 44 Squadron carried out nineteen operations, including the photographic reconnaissance of M25, and dispatched 134 sorties for the loss of four Hampdens and two crews.

September 1940

While the Battle of Britain was reaching a crescendo overhead, and invasion fever gripped the nation, the overriding priority for the Command in September would be the destruction of the invasion craft assembling in ports along the Occupied coast. That said, the new month began for 5 Group with small-scale attacks on industrial targets in Germany, Hemswell providing six Hampdens to attack an aircraft components factory in Stuttgart, possibly the Hirth aero-engine plant in the northern suburb of Zuffenhausen, Scampton two for marshalling yards in Mannheim, and Waddington two for a hydrogenation plant at Ludwigshafen. The 44 Squadron pair, captained by S/L Gardner and Sgt Collins, departed Waddington at 20.05 and 20.15 respectively, but only the latter reached the target to carry out an inconclusive attack with four 500 pounders. They returned safely after a round trip of eight hours and thirty-five minutes to find that S/L Gardner and crew had landed almost two hours earlier after being airborne for five minutes under seven hours. They had abandoned their attempt to locate the primary target and had bombed the River Meuse (Maas) docks at Maastricht in south-eastern Holland as a last resort objective on the way home.

On the 2nd, P/O Price ferried P4374 to the Handley Page factory at Radlett in Hertfordshire, only to suffer an undercarriage collapse on landing and write-off the Hampden, happily, without injury to the occupants. During the afternoon, F/O Ogilvie and P/Os Perkins and Taunton were briefed for that night's operation against target A165, an oil plant in Mannheim, although the 5 Group ORB specified that they had been assigned to the aircraft components factory in Stuttgart mentioned in the paragraph above. Other 5 Group operations involved ten crews from Hemswell at an oil refinery in

Ludwigshafen, two pairs from Lindholme to attack marshalling yards at Hamm and the repairs to the Dortmund-Ems Canal, while Scampton put up a dozen aircraft in response to a report that six U-Boots were at berth in Lorient harbour. The 44 Squadron element departed Waddington at 20.00 and followed the course of the Franco/Belgian frontier, until crossing into Germany north of Strasbourg. All three reached the target area, where F/O Ogilvie and P/O Perkins delivered four 250 pounders and sixty 4lb incendiaries each onto the target, without observing the results. P/O Taunton and crew failed to locate either the primary or secondary targets, and, as a last resort, attacked an aerodrome at Böblingen, located ten miles south-west of Stuttgart and a considerable distance from Mannheim, which suggests that the 5 Group ORB was correct.

Eastern Germany would be the destination for 5 Group on the 3rd, Berlin to the north, where nine crews from Scampton and three from 44 Squadron were to attack the electrical power station coded B56, while five crews from Hemswell and four from 44 Squadron headed further south to target the Rothensee oil refinery at Magdeburg. The two elements departed Waddington together between 20.15 and 20.35, with F/L Rogers leading the Berlin-bound trio, and F/L Siebert the others. They adopted the standard route for these targets, crossing the Dutch coast over the Den Helder peninsula, and entering Germany near Meppen to pass between Bremen and Hannover, and it was shortly afterwards, at Braunschweig, that the routes diverged. All reached their respective targets, where intense searchlight dazzle, and, at Berlin, anti-aircraft fire, created challenging conditions for target locating. F/L Rogers and P/Os Hattersley and Ridpath each delivered four 500 pounders onto the target, but were blinded to the results, and returned with little of use to pass on to the Intelligence Section at debriefing. Meanwhile, F/L Siebert and Sgt Henderson and their crews had carried out their attacks on the oil refinery, again, without gaining a picture of the outcome, but Sgts Burt and Kneil had been unable to identify the primary target and sought alternatives. The former came upon the aerodrome at Magdeburg and aimed his high-explosives and incendiaries at the hangars, while the latter bombed a railway junction in the city, and all returned safely, Sgt Kneil and crew after being airborne for eight hours and twenty minutes.

On the 4th, a total of twenty-three Hampdens was detailed from all four operational stations and made ready for a long-range operation to an oil refinery at Stettin, almost certainly the Wintershall plant at Politz, some eight miles north of the city. Bircham Newton was to be used as a forward base for some, but it is believed, that the 44 Squadron crews of S/L Gardner and Sgt Collins took off from Waddington, doing so at 20.25, with full tanks for the twelve-hundred-mile round trip. They set course for Heligoland, to make landfall on the Danish coast north of Sylt, from where they were able to map-read their way across southern Jutland and the Baltic to the target area in favourable conditions that offered ten miles visibility. S/L Gardner and crew identified the target and attacked it from east to west with four 500 pounders, which were seen to burst, while Sgt Collins and crew ran across the aiming point from north to south and observed two bursts, followed by a large fire that remained visible for seventy miles into the return journey.

In view of the lack of information recorded in the 44 Squadron ORB, and in order to better describe the operation, the following passage has been constructed from the 50 Squadron ORB. *P/O Stenner and crew identified the target straight-away, and attacked it from 10,500 feet at 23.35, observing their four 500 pounders to burst along the southern edge of the site, although they were unable to determine the effects. F/O French and crew found the searchlight and anti-aircraft fire over Denmark to be both accurate and troublesome but came through unscathed to deliver their attack from 10,000 feet at 00.27, registering three direct hits that caused explosions and white fires visible for fifteen minutes and from fifty miles away. S/L Willan and crew spent thirty minutes searching for the target, before bombing it from 7,000 feet at 00.30, and observing their four 250 pounders and incendiaries to burst on buildings at the southern extremity of the site, causing fires with white flames that remained visible for twenty miles into the return flight. P/O Banker and crew bombed the target at the same time, having adopted a slightly different outward flight that made landfall first on Terschelling. They had found a thick haze lying over Denmark, which dispersed as they neared the target area, and, having identified the refinery, they carried out a dive attack from 7,000 to 3,000 feet. The four 500 pounders were seen to fall across the centre of the complex and cause three tall chimneys to collapse, the resultant large fires remaining visible for forty miles into the return journey.* The 5 Group ORB declared the operation to be a success and claimed that four tall chimneys had been brought down.

On the following day, Scampton, Hemswell and Waddington were alerted to a return to the same target that night, for which eighteen Hampdens were made ready, just two of them belonging to 44 Squadron. Hemswell was also to provide aircraft on this night for an attack on an oil refinery in Hamburg, and to disrupt and delay the repairs to the Dortmund-Ems Canal north of Münster. It was 20.05 and 20.35 when F/O Ogilvie and P/O Romans respectively set out on the long outward leg, and, true to form, the 44 Squadron ORB simply recorded, "Four 500lb bombs dropped on target A104", for each crew. It did, however, mention the fact that P4290 ran out of fuel as the Suffolk coast drew near, and P/O Romans carried out his second ditching in the space of a week, this time off Lowestoft, from where he and his crew were picked up by a passing patrol vessel, none the worse for their experience.

After orders came through to 5 Group stations on the 6th, Scampton and Hemswell found themselves preparing a dozen Hampdens between them to attack an oil refinery in Dortmund, while Waddington detailed nine to target marshalling yards at Krefeld, Hamm, Trier and Mannheim, and Lindholme took care of gardening duties in the Læsø Channel in the Kattegat, better known to the crews as the Yew Tree garden. The 44 Squadron ORB listed eight, not nine departures from Waddington between 19.40 and 20.30, with the crews of P/O Taunton, F/Sgt Clayton and Sgt Henderson bound for the Uerdingen marshalling yards at Krefeld on the western edge of the Ruhr, F/L Rogers and Sgt Burt for the Ehrang yards at Trier, situated in the Rhineland-Palatinate region close to the Luxembourg frontier, P/Os Perkins and Stewart for Mannheim and P/O Hattersley and one other for Hamm. The unnamed crew bombed the Hamm yards, but P/O Hattersley and crew failed to locate it and found a similar target at Münster for their six 250 pounders. At Trier, F/L Rogers delivered his six 250 pounders in a stick from south to north and observed five bursts on the western side of the target, but no detail. Sgt Burt and crew attacked from the opposite direction, also observing their bombs to burst on the western edge, and they dropped eight cans of "Razzle" incendiary devices into nearby wooded areas. The crews of P/Os Perkins and Stewart reached Mannheim to hit the railway yards with sticks of 250 pounders delivered from south-east to north-west, the latter observing three explosions followed by four large fires. Meanwhile, in the Ruhr, F/Sgt Clayton dropped four of his 250 pounders on the briefed target of the Krefeld marshalling yards, and two others on the aerodrome at Venlo in Holland on the way home, claiming large fires at the latter. Sgt Henderson let all six go in a stick over the yards from north-east to south-west but observed no results. P/O Taunton and crew, who had also been briefed for this target, were hit by flak at some point, and both wireless operator/gunners were killed when P2087 crashed near Münster. P/O Taunton and second pilot, P/O Vollmer, escaped with their lives to fall into enemy hands.

The first concerted effort to eliminate invasion barges in Channel ports was undertaken on the 7th, when 5 Group contributed twenty-nine Hampdens to attacks on concentrations at Ostend. 44 Squadron supported the operation with three aircraft containing the crews of W/C Reid, S/L Gardner and Sgt Collins, which departed Waddington between 19.55 and 20.00, each carrying eight 250 pounders. They set course via corridor "G" towards the mouth of the Scheldt, before turning to the west and running in on the target. A mist lay over the area, and light from a quarter moon reflected upon it to decrease visibility, but the main impediment to target identification and assessment of results was the hostility of the flak and searchlight defences. Although the searchlight glare blinded the attacking crews, the beams did, at least, provide an indication of the whereabouts of the target, which W/C Reid attacked with a stick from north to south, picking up in the process severe damage to the tail unit. S/L Gardner and crew observed their bombs to fall among a concentration of around sixty barges moored on the western side of the basin, while Sgt Collins and crew watched debris being flung into the air from the detonation of their bombs in the Bassin d'Evolution.

5 Group sent orders to all of its frontline stations on the 8th to prepare for a major operation that night against a section of the Blohm & Voss shipyards in the Altona district of Hamburg to the west of the city centre. The actual aiming point was recorded as lying five hundred yards south-east of the centre of the yards and was identified in the 44 Squadron ORB as D2, dockland installations, but may have been a capital ship, perhaps, Bismarck. Forty-nine Hampdens were made available, a dozen of them at Waddington, which took off between 21.15 and 22.55 with S/L Gardner the senior pilot on duty. The standard route to Germany's Second City involved skirting the chain of the Frisian Islands to make landfall on the Schleswig-Holstein peninsula, before running in from the north. An alternative was to pinpoint on Scharhörn island north of the mouth of the Elbe, thence to follow the river's course into the heart of the city, usually under the constant attention of searchlights and flak from both banks. Ten of the Waddington crews delivered either four 500 or six 250 pounders into the target area from all points of the compass, observing bursts and some fires, but no detail. One of two exceptions was P/O Hattersley and crew, who dropped four 250 pounders and ninety 4lb incendiaries on the primary target, and the rest on the aerodrome at Neumünster, thirty miles to the north. The other was S/L Gardner and crew, who took off too late to attack the primary, and, instead, bombed the harbour at Delfzijl on Holland's north-eastern coast with four 500 pounders.

Waddington was given the night off on the 9th, while twenty-one Hampdens were detailed to return to Hamburg for another shot at the special target in the Blohm & Voss shipyards. The weather on this occasion was excellent, with clear skies and a quarter moon to light the way and aid map-reading, but searchlight dazzle and gun flashes created challenges of their own. Returning crews were mostly confident that they had landed the bombs in the target area, but no confirmation was forthcoming. It was on this night that 106 Squadron launched its first three operational sorties from Finningley, having spent the war to date as the 5 Group pool training unit.

More than a hundred aircraft were in action on the 10th, eighteen of them 5 Group Hampdens assigned mostly to invasion barges at Ostend and Calais. 44 Squadron briefed the crews of W/C Reid, the newly arrived S/L Broad, F/L Rogers, P/O Penman and Sgt Burt for the latter, and dispatched them between 20.30 and 20.50 with a bomb load each of eight 250 pounders and incendiaries. They crossed the North Sea at around 7,000 feet to encounter seven to ten-tenths cloud in the target area, which severely hampered their attempts to establish a position. W/C Reid and crew observed one bomb to burst on the north-eastern edge of Basin 6, while the Penman crew saw flashes between Basins 2 and 3. Sgt Burt and crew watched one bomb hit a railway line south of Basin 6, and five others to fall among barges in that basin. P4371 failed to return after crashing into the sea, and it took with it to their deaths the crew of F/L Rogers, whose experience would be missed at Waddington.

For the third time in four nights, the Blohm & Voss shipyards was posted as the primary target on the 11th, and twenty-one Hampdens were made ready at Hemswell, Scampton and Lindholme. Over at Waddington, the crews of F/L Smythe, F/O Ogilvie, P/Os Perkins and Stewart and Sgt Collins were briefed to attack the two 50,000-ton ocean liners, Bremen and Europa, at their moorings in the commercial port of Bremerhaven. Sgt Collins was now the proud recipient of a coveted DFM, as was his second pilot/navigator/bomb-aimer, Sgt Ayton. F/L Smythe and P/Os Perkins and Stewart took off at 19.30, two hours ahead of F/O Ogilvie and Sgt Collins and flew out over the Lincolnshire coast on their way to the eastern side of Jade Bay. They found six to ten-tenths cloud over north-western Germany at between 3,000 and 12,000 feet, which hampered identification of landmarks, although the distinctive docks layout was identified without major difficulty. Each Hampden was carrying four 500 pounders, which P/O Perkins and crew delivered in a stick from south to north towards one of the vessels moored north-north-west of the dockyard. Sgt Collins and crew went for the same objective on a north-westerly heading, and saw their bombs burst close to the bows of the more northerly liner, while picking up a flak hole in the tailplane for their troubles. F/O Ogilvie and crew attacked from north-east to south-west, and their 500 pounders fell in a stick onto docks two-and-a-half miles north-west of D12. The crews of F/L Smythe DFC and P/O Stewart failed to return in P1338 and X2913 respectively, the latter having definitely crashed into the sea, and there were no survivors from either. The loss of three experienced crews in two days was a bitter blow to the squadron, but new crews would fill the gaps, and soon, memory of former colleagues and friends would fade.

The next four operations would be directed at invasion craft and shipping generally in the Occupied ports as the Battle of Britain approached its most critical moment. Orders were received at 5 Group stations on the 14th to prepare for that night's activity, and thirty Hampdens were made ready to send against Ostend, Dunkerque and Calais. 44 Squadron briefed the crews of S/L Gardner, F/O Booth, P/Os Penman and Perkins and Sgt Kneil for a return to Calais and sent them on their way between 20.30 and 20.45, each loaded with eight 250 pounders. They crossed the Channel in reasonable conditions to encounter patches of low cloud on the French side, but this was no impediment to target identification, and all were able to carry out an attack. S/L Gardner and crew observed a large explosion as six of their bombs burst among barges on the eastern side of Dock 6, and P/O Penman and crew reported a fire resulting from theirs, which remained visible for twenty miles into the return journey. P/O Perkins and crew saw their load burst among buildings on a wharf on the eastern side of Dock 6, while Sgt Kneil and crew watched their 250 pounders hit barges moored along the northern end of the north side, and also scored a direct hit on a 5,000-ton merchant vessel, from which dense clouds of smoke were seen to issue.

The 15th was the day on which the Battle of Britain reached its climax, and, by dusk, enemy losses had been sufficient to persuade Hitler to call off Operation Sealion, the invasion of Britain. This would not be apparent immediately to the British authorities, however, and anti-invasion operations would continue, as would the Battle of Britain at a reduced intensity for another six weeks. 44 Squadron prepared nine Hampdens for operations that night, six to send against invasion craft at Antwerp in company with twenty-six others from Scampton, and three for gardening duties in the Eglantine garden in the Elbe estuary. The horticultural trio of F/L Eustace, P/O Ridpath and F/Sgt Clayton departed Waddington between 19.40 and 19.55 and would be well into their return journey before the main element took off between 23.25 and 23.50. F/L Eustace and crew delivered their vegetable into the briefed location from 500 feet, before turning their attention upon a 7,000-ton tanker off the west coast of the island of Scharhörn some ten miles off Cuxhaven. They scored a direct hit with a wing-mounted

250 pounder and reported the vessel to have sunk. P/O Ridpath and F/Sgt Clayton planted their vegetables into the briefed locations from 800 feet, and the former then bombed a tanker of an estimated 6,000 tons, scoring one direct hit and a near-miss. Typically for the 44 Squadron ORB, the attack on the docks at Antwerp was dealt with in a most cursory manner, stating only that that each crew delivered either six or eight 250 pounders onto the docks and shipping, and bursts, flashes and explosions were observed. During this operation, 83 Squadron's wireless operator/gunner, Sgt Hannah, won the Command's second Victoria Cross, which meant that both had been awarded to Scampton recipients.

Following a night off for 44 Squadron, preparations were put in hand on the 17th for another major night of operations involving 174 aircraft, mostly in support of the campaign against invasion craft. 5 Group put up twenty-two Hampdens for a return to Antwerp, while Scampton provided fifteen for Flushing and Terneuzen, situated on opposite sides of the Western Schelde. The 44 Squadron crews of P/Os Lewis, Penman, Stockings and Sgts Henderson and Kneil were briefed for Antwerp, and departed Waddington between 22.20 and 23.00. Sgt Henderson and crew took off a full thirty minutes after the others, and, perhaps, this may have contributed to their subsequent loss. All reached the target area to encounter six-tenths patchy cloud at 8,000 feet that impeded their attempts to line up on the aiming point, but P/O Lewis managed to establish a bombing run and delivered four 500 pounders onto barges moored in Docks 15, 13 and 9, causing a medium-size explosion. P/O Penman and crew dropped their six 250 pounders and incendiaries in a stick from south to north onto barges in Docks 15 and 9, while Sgt Kneil chose a north-north-easterly heading for his run across the same three docks, and the incendiary element of the bomb load started a large fire on the quayside. P/O Stocking picked out Docks 12, 13 and 14 for a north-easterly pass, but was unable to observe the outcome. Sgt Henderson and crew arrived late on, after the defences had been stirred into action and the flak gunners had acquired their range, and P2121 was brought down in the target area, killing all on board. This was the fourth experienced crew to be lost to the squadron within a week.

Hemswell, Scampton and Waddington were alerted on the 18th to prepare aircraft for an operation that night against the docks and shipping at Le Havre. 44 Squadron made ready eight Hampdens, which took off between 19.45 and 20.10 with S/Ls Broad and Gardner the senior pilots on duty, five carrying six 250 pounders and three, eight. All reached the enemy coast, where six of the Waddington crews attacked the primary target, and two, those of S/L Broad and F/L Ogilvie, went for an alternative objective at Dieppe further east along the coast. S/L Broad and crew thought they might have hit an ammunition dump, based on continuing explosions and fires visible as they headed across the Channel homebound. F/L Ogilvie attacked an armed tanker with his two remaining 250 pounders, and his starboard mainplane was hit by return fire. At debriefing, the Le Havre crews reported hitting the docks and shipping and observing bursts, but no detail was forthcoming to enable an assessment of damage.

On the 19th, 5 Group detailed twenty-seven Hampdens to continue the anti-invasion campaign against the ports at Ostend and Flushing, while ten from Scampton returned to the now repaired Dortmund-Ems aqueduct. 44 Squadron was assigned to mining duties, and, according to the 5 Group ORB, detailed eight crews to carry out the task in the Deodar garden, the approaches to the port of Bordeaux at the mouth of the Gironde estuary. Situated towards the southern reaches of the Biscay coast, the port was home to a fleet of U-Boots, and oil storage facilities lined the banks of the estuary, which was the conduit for U-Boots and tankers sailing to and from the Atlantic. The 5 Group ORB recorded that only four were successful in the face of generally unfavourable weather conditions, and the squadron ORB listed only the crews of P/Os Penman, Romans and Stocking and Sgt Burt, who departed Waddington between 19.05 and 19.20 with on outward flight of some six hundred miles ahead of them. We are told only that the Penman crew planted their single 1,500lb vegetable from 500 feet, and the others from 600 feet, before returning safely after round trips of up to nine hours.

On the following day, the Command called on all groups to make ready for operations that night, which would be directed predominantly towards the anti-invasion campaign. In all, 172 aircraft were made available, of which forty Hampdens would represent 5 Group in a number of endeavours. Hemswell received orders to send eight aircraft to take care of gardening duties off St-Nazaire, while Scampton detailed six to attack the new aqueduct of the Dortmund-Ems Canal over the River Ems. This left twenty-six from Scampton, Hemswell and Waddington to target invasion barges at Dunkerque, Antwerp and Boulogne respectively. The 44 Squadron element of eight took off between 23.20 and 00.05 with S/L Broad the senior pilot on duty, and seven carried out an attack with either six or eight 250 pounders at the primary target, while Sgt Paskell and crew delivered their load onto the docks at Calais.

It was similar fare for ninety-two aircraft on the following night, when 5 Group had intended to send forty-five Hampdens to attack a variety of targets in Berlin. The threat of adverse weather forced a change of plans, however, and it was decided to commit fifteen aircraft from Scampton and Lindholme to the anti-invasion campaign. In the event, fog kept the Lindholme element on the ground, and Scampton operated alone. On the following day, ninety-five aircraft were made ready on 2, 3 and 5 Group stations to continue the assault on invasion craft in Channel ports, and 5 Group detailed thirty Hampdens from all but Finningley to target concentrations in the ports of Ostend, Boulogne, Le Havre, Flushing and Antwerp. Eight 44 Squadron crews were briefed for a return to Boulogne and took off between 02.20 and 02.50 on the 23rd with S/L Gardner the senior pilot on duty, and each carrying eight 250 pounders. They completed the Channel crossing in fine weather conditions, and found good visibility over the French coast, which enabled all to identify the primary target and carry out their attacks. As usual, there was no predetermined plan in place, and bombing runs were conducted from a variety of headings and heights, and bursts, explosions and fires were reported across Basins 3 to 7.

Ground crews were kept busy on all operational 5 Group stations on the 23rd, as forty-five Hampdens were made ready for that night's attack on an electrical power station, coded B59, located in Berlin's western district of Moabit. They were part of an overall force of 129 aircraft assigned to eighteen separate targets in the Capital, and the 50 Squadron ORB informs us that the five participants from Lindholme flew over to Bircham Newton as a forward base. The 44 Squadron element of ten took off from Waddington, between 20.45 and 21.40, with S/L Broad the senior pilot on duty and bomb loads of four 500 pounders and "Razzles". They probably flew out at high-level, in order to put themselves above a front that lay between the Dutch coast and a point 150 miles from Germany's Capital, but it may be that the crews of P/Os Ridpath and Smith and F/Sgt Clayton remained in cloud, as all failed to reach the primary target. P/O Smith came upon marshalling yards at Hannover, and observed three bursts on a section of track, P/O Ridpath and crew were homebound when they unloaded the contents of their bomb bay over the docks at Wesermünde (Bremerhaven) and observed two bursts, and F/Sgt Clayton and crew found a railway bridge further south at Bremen. The others were confronted by poor visibility as they approached the western extremities of Berlin and would have had to descend to gain a glimpse of the ground through the thick local ground haze. We are told only that they delivered their attacks from all points of the compass, observing bursts but no detail, and all returned safely.

44 Squadron remained at home on the 24th, while twenty-three Hampdens from the other four frontline stations took part in an operation against barge concentrations in the port of Calais. On the following day, plans were put in hand to send twenty-one Hampdens back to Berlin to attack a second electrical power station, this one coded B56. The Lindholme element of four proceeded to Bircham Newton as its launch pad, only to be delayed by late refuelling, and then be grounded by an air-raid Red Warning. This ended all hopes of taking off for Berlin and left seventeen others to attempt to fulfil their brief at the capital. 44 Squadron's eight participants departed Waddington between 21.15 and 22.10 with F/O Booth the senior pilot on duty and each Hampden carrying four 500 pounders. P/O Romans and crew had reached a position north of Hannover, when engine problems forced them to turn back, and they dispensed "Razzles" over wooded country on their way back over Germany, before bombing the Luftwaffe aerodrome at Leeuwarden in northern Holland. The others pressed on to reach the primary target, where they carried out their attacks and observed bursts and a few fires, but none was able to positively claim a direct hit on the power plant.

5 Group would divide its forces on the 26th, sending eight Hampdens from Hemswell and four from Waddington to attack the heavy cruiser, Scharnhorst, which was at berth in the Krupp-Germania shipyard in Kiel. This magnificent vessel, which entered service in January 1939, displaced 38,700 tons fully loaded, and boasted a length of 771 feet, with an armament of nine eleven-inch guns arranged in three triple turrets. During an engagement in June 1940, in which she sank the aircraft carrier, HMS Glorious, she was damaged by a torpedo from the sinking destroyer, HMS Acasta, and would spend the next six months at Kiel under repair. Another 5 Group effort on this night involved six more Hemswell crews taking another swipe at the Dortmund-Ems Canal north of Münster, while seven from Lindholme continued the anti-invasion campaign at Calais, and Finningley took care of gardening duties. The 44 Squadron crews of P/O Skinner and Sgts Ayton, Day and Burt took off between 20.45 and 21.10, each carrying four 500 pounders, and reached the target area via the Schleswig-Holstein peninsula to encounter intense searchlight and flak activity and patches of cloud, all of which created challenging conditions in which to bomb. P/O Skinner passed over the aiming point from east to west, delivering his bombs in a single stick, but ran immediately into cloud and saw nothing of the outcome. Sgt Day ran across the target from north-east to south-west and was denied a sight of the results by the intensity of the searchlights and flak. Sgt Ayton was one of the pilots flying as crew captain for the first time, and he claimed to have hit the target and set off a medium fire. Sgt Burt and crew attacked on a north-westerly heading, and observed two bursts but no detail, and there would be no confirmation of damage to Scharnhorst.

The anti-invasion campaign continued on the 27th, when twenty-five Hampden crews were briefed at Scampton, Hemswell and Lindholme to target barges, motor torpedo boats and U-boots at Lorient, which, early in the coming year, would be the site of a massive civil engineering project to construct three huge concrete U-Boot facilities. Having enjoyed the night off, 44 Squadron replaced 50 Squadron (Lindholme) on the Order of Battle on the 28th, when 5 Group was tasked with attacking the new Dortmund-Ems Canal viaduct over the River Ems (Scampton), invasion craft at Le Havre and Fécamp (Waddington and Scampton) and marshalling yards at Hamm and Mannheim (Scampton, Hemswell and Waddington). Nine 44 Squadron crew attended briefing to learn that seven of them would be involved in the anti-invasion campaign at Fécamp and Le Havre, while the crews of P/O Stockings and Sgt Kneil would be going alone to Mannheim in southern Germany. The latter, with much further to travel, took off first, at 23.35 and 23.50 respectively, and were well on their way to making landfall on the Belgian coast by the time that the main element departed Waddington between 01.10 and 01.45, led by S/L Broad. They encountered adverse weather conditions over the North Sea and Channel in the form of ten tenths low cloud, which combined with extreme darkness at the enemy coast to prevent some from locating the primary target. S/L Broad and crew attacked a "MOPA", (military objective previously attacked), which turned out to be the docks at Boulogne, upon which they unloaded their six 250 pounders and sixty 4lb incendiaries without observing the results. F/O Booth and crew arrived here also and dropped their eight 250 pounders and ten incendiaries across the northern side of the Bassin de Marée and Dock N°7, observing one large and two small fires. Sgts Ayton, Hartop and Smith found Le Havre, and delivered eight 250 pounders each, the Ayton crew claiming a direct hit on a merchant vessel. Sgt Day and crew attacked N°4 Dock at Fecamp from east to west, and P/O Mackintosh and crew from west to east across Docks 2, 3, 5 and 6, but no results were observed by either. Meanwhile, the Mannheim-bound duo had experienced more favourable conditions in their target area, identifying the railway yards without difficulty, before attacking from south-east to north-west and observing bursts but no detail.

Marshalling yards in Germany featured prominently again on the target list for the 29th, along with a Bosch electrical component factory at Stuttgart. Sixteen crews from Waddington, Hemswell and Lindholme were briefed for the last-mentioned, while nine others targeted the Cologne marshalling yards at Gremberg, situated to the east of the Rhine, and, possibly, Kalk, a mile or so to the north, and others at Hamm and Soest, both perched on the north-eastern edge of the Ruhr. 44 Squadron contributed the crews of P/Os Penman, Perkins and Skinner to the Stuttgart endeavour, and they departed Waddington at 22.55 loaded with four 500 pounders. The outward journey via corridor "G" was undertaken above the ice-bearing cloud, and it took a little over three hours to reach the highly industrialised city deep in south-western Germany, where nine-tenths cloud and intense darkness created challenging conditions. P/O Skinner and crew failed to identify the Bosch factory, and retraced their steps to the Belgian coast, where they unloaded the contents of their bomb bay onto the docks at Ostend. P/Os Penman and Perkins carried out their attacks at the primary target, the former attributing a large fire to his efforts, before climbing into cloud to escape the attentions of heavy flak.

Waddington was not called into action on the 30th, when an ambitious operation was mounted against the Chancellery building housing the German Air Ministry in central Berlin's Leipzigstrasse. Scampton, Hemswell and Lindholme put up seventeen crews between them, most of which were thwarted by cloud and extreme darkness. During the course of the month the squadron took part in twenty-six operations and dispatched 148 sorties for the loss of seven Hampdens and five crews.

October 1940

Waddington was in action immediately at the start of the new month, providing five crews to join thirteen from Scampton for an attack on the Synthetic oil refinery at Wesseling, situated on the West Bank of the Rhine in the southern reaches of Cologne. According to the 5 Group ORB, 44 Squadron also dispatched six crews for mining duties in the Deodar Garden in the Gironde estuary, while the squadron record named only the four that successfully fulfilled their brief. It was the latter element, consisting of the crews of S/L Broad (not listed), P/Os Mackintosh and Stocking and Sgts Kneil and Smith and one other unlisted, that departed Waddington first, between 18.30 and 18.50, to be followed into the air between 19.20 and 19.50 by the bombing quintet, with every man, apart from Sgt Ottaway's second pilot, P/O Kerr, wearing a sergeant's chevrons. The Ottaway crew failed to locate the primary target and turned their attention instead upon the Knapsack power station some five miles to the north-west, which they would claim at debriefing to have hit with four 500 pounders. X2965 failed to return with the crew of Sgt Day, and, after two bodies were washed ashore, the Hampden's fate became clear. Sgt Ayton and crew delivered six 250 pounders and incendiaries across the Wesseling site in a stick from south-east to north-west, observing flashes but no detail, while the Hartop crew carried out their pass in the opposite direction. Sgt Atkins and crew were carrying four 500 pounders, two of which were seen to burst, and they counted seven medium fires as they retreated to the west. Meanwhile, the four successful gardeners had planted their vegetables into the briefed locations from between 400 and 800 feet. Not among these, was the crew of S/L Broad, who had landed in P1324 at Brackley in Northamptonshire at 03.00, and suffered an undercarriage collapse, which condemned the Hampden to life as a ground instruction airframe but caused no damage to the crew.

The target for nineteen crews from Hemswell, Lindholme and Waddington on the 2nd was an oil refinery in Hamburg (A8), for which the six-strong 44 Squadron element took off between 23.35 and 23.55 with F/L Ogilvie the senior pilot on duty. As often was the case at this early stage of the war, an operation might be spread over an extended period, with individual squadrons deciding for themselves routes and timings. On this night, the arrival in the target area of the Waddington Hampdens would be some five hours after the Lindholme crews had attacked and two behind those from Hemswell. Barrage balloons were reported to be tethered at 6,000 feet over Wilhelmshaven, and this inconvenience had to be added to the eight to ten-tenths cloud with haze below, and the usual gauntlet of intense searchlight and flak activity on the route along the course of the Elbe south-east towards the heart of Germany's Second City. F/L Ogilvie, F/O Booth and P/O Skinner and their crews delivered four 500 pounders each while on a variety of headings across the aiming point but saw nothing of the impact. P/O Perkins and crew dropped six 250 pounders in a stick from east to west, also without observing the outcome, while Sgt Burt and P/O Penman sought out alternative targets. The former aimed four 250 pounders at the docks at Wilhelmshaven, while the latter dropped four over Bremerhaven and two onto the seaplane base on the Frisian island of Borkum.

There would be no further operations for 44 Squadron until the 8th, during which period, Air-Chief-Marshal Sir Charles Portal relinquished his post as Commander-in-Chief of Bomber Command on the 5th and took up his appointment as Chief of the Air Staff. He was succeeded at the helm of Bomber Command by ACM Sir Richard Peirse, whose tenure would be dogged by the inadequacies of the equipment available to him, and the increasing and often unrealistic demands of his superiors. That night, a dozen Scampton Hampdens were sent to bomb the Nordstern Oil refinery at Gelsenkirchen, while eight others from Lindholme targeted mostly marshalling yards at important locations north and south of the Ruhr and Hemswell attended to horticultural matters. On the 7th, Scampton took care of gardening duties off Lorient, while also supporting attacks on mostly the same marshalling yards as on the previous night in company with others from Hemswell and Lindholme.

Waddington was back in business on the 8th, when receiving orders for that night's attempt to hit the Bismarck-class Battleship Tirpitz, which was in the final stages of fitting-out at a floating dock in Wilhelmshaven. The Admiralty was acutely conscious of the threat posed by Germany's mighty battleships Bismarck and Tirpitz, and there was a constant pressure on Bomber Command to deal with them before they began their careers as surface raiders. Laid down in the Kriegsmarinewerft yards in 1936, Tirpitz had been launched in the spring of 1939, and, once ready for sea trials in early 1941, she would be two thousand tons heavier than her sister ship. Nine 44 Squadron crews and ten from 83 Squadron at Scampton attended briefings, before the former departed Waddington between 16.55 and 17.05 with S/L Broad the senior pilot on duty. Eight were carrying four 500 pounders each, while S/L Broad had two 500 and two 250 pounders in his bomb bay, all of which ordnance would find its way to the target. They were greeted over Wilhelmshaven by a curtain of anti-aircraft fire, but all from Waddington delivered an attack, and most saw bursts but no detail.

On the following night, while nineteen crews from Hemswell, Lindholme and Scampton attempted to hit the Krupp complex in Essen in the most unfavourable weather conditions, 44 Squadron dispatched the crews of S/L Gardner and Sgt Kneil at 18.00 to lay mines in the Artichoke garden off the port of Lorient. The standard route for gardening duties in the Jellyfish (Brest) Artichoke and Beech (St-Nazaire) gardens was via the Dorset coast to pass west of the Channel Islands and make landfall on the French coast in the region of Saint-Brieuc. After traversing the Brest peninsula, familiar landmarks would provide the starting point for a timed run to the point of release, and, in the Artichoke garden, the regular pinpoints were at Pont-Aven to the north and Ile-de-Groix off the mouth of the confluence of the Rivers Scorff and Blavet. Although the ORB does not favour us with the information, we can assume by the fact that Sgt Kneil and S/L Gardner planted their vegetables from 700 and 800 feet respectively, that they had established the appropriate pinpoints.

The promise of bright moonlight on the night of the 10/11th may have been a consideration in scheduling another assault on the battleship Tirpitz at Wilhelmshaven, for which thirteen Hampdens were made ready, nine at Waddington and four at Lindholme. A simultaneous operation would be conducted against Kiel dockyard by an element from Scampton, probably with the intention of hitting the heavy cruiser, Scharnhorst, while Hemswell attended to the mining of the Kiel Canal. The 44 Squadron element took off in widely separated waves of three, beginning with the crews of F/L Ogilvie, P/O Penman and S/L Broad between 18.20 and 18.50, P/Os Skinner, Ross and Stockings between 19.25 and 19.40, and, finally, Sgts Hartop, Ottaway and Atkins between 20.00 and 20.05. They began the North Sea crossing somewhere near Skegness, before following the course of the Frisian Islands to the target area, where they ran into an intense searchlight and flak defence. Moonlight glinted off the waterways in the dockyard to aid identification, and the crews made their bombing runs, mostly, from an easterly or north-easterly starting point, with flak shells bursting above and below at between 10,000 and 15,000 feet. S/L Broad was carrying a 2,000 pounder, and the others four 500lb semi-armour-piercing (SAP) bombs each, which they delivered onto dock installations without observing detail, and no sightings of Tirpitz were reported or claims of damage lodged. On their return, Sgt Atkins and crew claimed to have engaged an unidentified enemy aircraft, which they observed to crash into the sea.

44 Squadron remained on the ground on the 11th, as the pursuit of the Tirpitz continued at the hands of five Hampdens from Lindholme, while another one joined five from Hemswell to target the Blohm & Voss shipyards at Hamburg. Under cover of this, three Finningley crews would conduct mining sorties in the Eglantine garden at the mouth of the Elbe estuary. On the eastern side of the Schleswig-Holstein peninsula, a dozen Hemswell Hampdens were to attack Kiel dockyards, a few miles south of the Kiel Canal, where nine Scampton crews were to carry out mining duties in the Lettuce garden. Poor weather conditions hampered each operation, and few crews were able to carry out their brief.

On the following day, sixteen crews at Scampton and two at Hemswell were briefed for an operation that night against an aircraft components factory in the Herringen district of Hamm, while ten crews at Waddington were informed that they would be attacking the Krupp works at Essen, coded E8. The Krupp organisation had been the largest manufacturer of weapons in Europe since before the Great War and had a hand in all aspects of German war production from tanks to artillery and ship and U-Boot construction and was given a controlling share in all major heavy engineering companies in

Germany and the Occupied Countries. It also built manufacturing sites in other parts of Germany, many situated close to concentration camps, and employed vast numbers of forced workers in all of its factories. Once known as "Die Waffenschmiede des Reichs", the weapon-forge of the realm, its manufacturing sites in Essen included the Friedrich Krupp steelworks, the Friedrich Krupp locomotive and general engineering works, six coal mines and ten coke-oven plants, the Altenberg zinc works, the Presswerk plastics factory, and the Goldschmidt non-ferrous metals smelting plant, all situated either within or close to the four Borbeck districts, in a segment radiating out from near the city centre to the Rhine-Herne Canal on the north-western boundary on the banks of the Emscher River. The steel and engineering works alone employed in the region of eighty thousand people, and the company's sites covered an area of more than two thousand acres, of which three hundred acres were occupied by factories and workshops. All of that required massive rail and canal access in the form of marshalling yards and its own harbour, and energy from at least four nearby power stations.

Nine of the 44 Squadron crews departed Waddington between 18.10 and 18.40, with S/L Gardner the senior pilot on duty, leaving F/O Booth and crew on the ground until 19.50, for which no explanation was provided. They made their way via corridor "G" to make landfall over the Scheldt estuary carrying a variety of bomb loads, four 500 pounders for Sgts Kneil and Paskell, P/O Perkins, F/O Booth and F/L Mackintosh, a 1,000 pounder and two 250 pounders for Sgt Burt and P/O Romans, and six 250 pounders for Sgt Hartop, P/O Ross and S/L Gardner, most with an additional sixty 4lb incendiaries. Nine crews carried out an attack on the primary target, observing bursts and flashes, some specifying the recipients of their efforts as a railway line, a machine shop and a coke oven near a power station, but such was the vastness of the site, it would require a much larger force and heavier bombs to make an impact. P/O Perkins and crew bombed the Eifeltor marshalling yards at Cologne as an alternative target, P/O Romans' gunners fired two hundred rounds at buildings on Texel aerodrome, and Sgt Kneil's a hundred at Vught aerodrome in Holland.

The Admiralty continued to obsess about the Tirpitz, in response to which, 5 Group detailed thirty-five Hampdens from Hemswell, Lindholme, Scampton and Waddington on the 13th, and briefed their crews for a return to Wilhelmshaven. The eight Waddington participants took off between 19.55 and 20.35 with W/C Reid the senior pilot on duty, carrying this time a uniform load of four 500 pounders. Initially, they flew out over three-tenths cloud, but, ahead, beginning at the mid-point of the North Sea crossing, lay one of the enormous fronts that frequently barred the route into north-western Germany. Characterized by ice-bearing and storm-laden towering cumulonimbus cloud, they were a nightmare to negotiate, and too enormous to circumnavigate. The icing layer on this night extended from 6,000 to 12,000 feet, with rainstorms from 1,000 to 12,000 feet, which had crews climbing and descending in a vain search for clear air, before, in most cases, seeking an alternative target. Not one of the 44 Squadron crews identified the primary or alternative targets, Sgt Smith and crew coming closest, when bombing a flak battery somewhere in the Wilhelmshaven area. W/C Reid dropped his load on a flak position on Terschelling, and Sgt Ottaway and crew two ships five miles north-west of the same island, while the remainder returned their ordnance to store.

The group detailed twenty Hampdens on the 14th for another shot that night at the Air Ministry building in Berlin's Leipzigstrasse, on a night when cities in eastern Germany were targeted by fifty aircraft from other groups. The crews of P/O Ross and Sgts Burt, Hartop and Paskell departed Waddington between 22.35 and 23.00, and three are known to have reached the target area, where they encountered haze, which would have required them to spend time either circling or making dummy runs from a variety of directions in order to familiarize themselves with the lay of the land and to establish the best method of attack. They would have to face searchlight and flak activity, and some crews from other units also noticed a number of barrage balloons tethered at up to 15,000 feet. Over the target, P4285 was hit by shrapnel, which put the bomb-release circuitry out of action, and P/O Ross's second pilot/navigator released the four 500 pounders singly, manually, and in "safe" mode. Sgt Paskell and crew carried out their bombing run from east to west, and delivered a 1,000 pounder and two 250 pounders, observing bursts but no detail. Sgt Hartop and crew identified the aiming point and dropped four 500 pounders while on the same heading, believing them to have straddled the target, although observing no bursts. X2910 failed to return after falling victim to a night-fighter, and crashing near Röwitz, to the north-east of Wolfsburg, with only the second pilot surviving from the crew of Sgt Burt.

Oil targets featured prominently on the 15th, when 134 aircraft were detailed for wide-ranging targets in Germany and the Channel ports. 5 Group directed the bulk of its effort of thirty-three Hampdens against oil targets in Magdeburg, principally the Rothensee plant that they had attacked last in early September. 44 Squadron briefed the crews of F/O Booth, P/O Perkins and Sgt Ayton for the main event, and those of F/L Mackintosh and P/O Penman for mining duties in the Forget-me-not garden in Kiel Harbour. They took off between 18.10 and 18.35 to fly out over Skegness, before the bombing trio set course, it is believed, via corridor "G" to the mouth of the Scheldt, while the gardeners headed east to make landfall on the west coast of the Schleswig-Holstein peninsula. F/O Booth and crew did not reach the primary target and dropped their 1,000 and two 250 pounders onto a road, rail and canal junction at Hannover, observing bursts, followed by two large fires. A band of cloud lay over Magdeburg between 3,000 and 6,000 feet, despite which, P/O Perkins and crew claimed to have dropped their four 500 pounders and incendiaries onto the primary target but made no mention of the outcome. Sgt Ayton and crew aimed their 1,000 and two 250 pounders at a target coded A160, which is believed to be a second oil-related site within the Magdeburg area, and, although they saw the detonation of the large bomb, they were unable to determine the results. Meanwhile, 160 miles to the north, F/L Mackintosh had planted his vegetable into the briefed location from 800 feet and dropped his two wing-mounted 250 pounders onto the seaplane base at Hörnum, near the southern tip of the island of Sylt. P/O Penman planted his vegetable from 950 feet, before bombing a searchlight position at Eckernförde to the north-west of Kiel.

Twenty-four Hampdens were made ready at Hemswell and Waddington on the 16th for an operation that night against the oil refinery at Leuna, near Merseburg, west of Leipzig, while Scampton prepared a dozen to attack U-Boots in their base at Bordeaux. Lindholme was stood down because of adverse weather conditions, which would afflict returning crews to a major degree. Eight 44 Squadron aircraft had a variety of loads winched into their bomb bays, including "Razzles" to drop over the Harz Forest, located to the south of Braunschweig, and took off between 18.15 and 18.40 with S/Ls Broad and Gardner the senior pilots on duty. They reached the target area to find favourable weather conditions, but ground haze hindered the search for the aiming point, and P/O Smith and crew ultimately dropped their four 500 pounders onto a railway line in an unidentified town some twenty miles west of Leipzig. Sgt Kneil and crew found themselves a similar distance to the south of Leuna, where they came upon a factory with two chimneys in a wood near a small town and unloaded six 250 pounders and sixty 4lb incendiaries in its direction. The remaining six crews managed to locate the primary target, F/L Ogilvie releasing four 500 pounders in a stick from south-east to north-west, observing three bursts and a large explosion followed by a dull, red glow. S/L Broad attacked with four 500 pounders from the opposite direction, but saw only bursts and no detail, while Sgt Ottaway and crew watched as two fires developed after the burst of their similar load. S/L Gardner and P/O Stockings each had a 1,000 pounder and two 250 pounders beneath their feet, the latter observing a very large flash, and this left just P/O Romans and crew to deliver their six 250 pounders and incendiaries, which resulted in four red explosions. Returning crews were greeted by fog, which caused X2997 to collide with a disused hangar on landing at Waddington and cause sufficient damage to itself to be declared a write-off. S/L Broad sustained a broken leg and scalp wounds, and his second pilot, Sgt Hammond, injury to both knees, which required hospital treatment. Short of fuel, Sgt Kneil and crew force-landed P2142 close to St Mary's church to the west of Grantham town centre, and, according to the squadron ORB, walked away leaving the Hampden damaged beyond repair. However, talk of its demise were premature, and it would eventually find its way to 16 O.T.U.

There was little activity generally on the 18th, but 5 Group detailed nineteen Hampdens from Scampton and Lindholme to target the Bismarck at berth in Hamburg. They had to battle through ice-bearing cloud over the North Sea, and, on arrival over the Elbe estuary, they encountered eight to ten-tenths cloud that severely inhibited their attempts to locate the aiming point. Only eight crews were able to release their loads on estimated positions, and it was a typically indeterminate operation at this stage of the war.

Berlin was posted as the target for thirty-five Hampdens on the 20th, while more than a hundred other aircraft roamed far and wide, as far east as Pilsen in Czechoslovakia and as far south as Italy. The Lindholme element of five flew over to Bircham Newton as the forward launch pad, but, on a night of enemy intruder activity, a bomb was dropped onto the airfield, and all participation from there was cancelled. 44 Squadron made ready seven aircraft, the crews of which were briefed to attack the Air Ministry building in Berlin, a euphemistic cover for an area raid on the city centre in retaliation for German attacks on British cities. According to pre-war principles, it was still morally unacceptable to specifically target civilian areas, despite the fact that the Luftwaffe had bombed Warsaw and Rotterdam indiscriminately and was currently engaged in a fifty-seven-consecutive day and night assault on London. As far as the British public was concerned, the RAF was retaliating by attacking military and war-production targets, which, in reality, was beyond its capability, and it would be a further seventeen months before the pretence officially ended. They departed Waddington between 23.00 and 23.30 with F/O Booth the senior pilot on duty, and all reached the general target area, where favourable conditions prevailed. Five of the Hampdens were loaded with four 500 pounders each, while P/O Ross and crew were sitting on a 1,000 pounder and two of 250lbs and P/O Perkins and crew on six 250 pounders. Five crews would return to report bombing the primary target, coded H41, and claim bursts on and around the aiming point, while P/O Perkins and crew failed to locate it and dropped four 250 pounders onto the docks at Emden on the way home. News came through to Waddington that L4154 had been force-landed on Roman Way Camp in Colchester, Essex, after running out of fuel, and that Sgt Atkins and crew had walked away from the write-off unscathed. News of the fate of Sgt Hartop and crew took longer to arrive and confirmed that they had lost their lives after P2137 was brought down by flak at Hasenheide, a mile-and-a-half south of Berlin city centre.

5 Group airfields were largely fogbound over the ensuing two days, and the local watering holes did good business until the 23rd, when Lindholme, Waddington and Scampton were alerted to that night's operation against the Rothensee oil refinery in Magdeburg, while Hemswell targeted the Deurag plant at Misburg near Hannover. This would be the first of six consecutive nights of operations for 44 Squadron, whose six-strong element took off between 23.50 and 00.20 with, it is believed, S/L Tindall, the newly arrived replacement for the injured S/L Broad, the senior pilot on duty. The ORB listed P/O Perkins and crew twice in Hampdens P4310 and P4373, and, based on the fact that S/L Tindall and crew would be in the latter aircraft on the next operation, the assumption has been made that his was

the most likely crew to occupy it on this night. They headed out over the Lincolnshire coast on a direct course to the target area, encountering nine to ten-tenths cloud over the North Sea, which decreased slightly to seven-tenths over the Dutch/German frontier with a base at 6,000 feet. It seems that five reached the target area, where low cloud thwarted two crews' attempts to identify the aiming point, leaving S/L Tindall to attack the primary with six 250 pounders, two 20lb incendiaries and a hundred of the 4lb variety, P/O Perkins with four 500 pounders and two and forty respectively of the incendiaries, and Sgt Ayton with four 250 pounders and two and one hundred incendiaries. Some bursts and flashes were observed, but nothing of value to the Intelligence Section at debriefing. Sgt Smith and crew reported dropping two 250 pounders onto marshalling yards, M351, probably situated to the west or south of Berlin, and four on the aerodrome at de Kooy near Den Helder in Holland. Sgt Ottaway and crew were on their way home south of the Harz Mountains, when they came upon a railway station, believed to be in the town of Nordhausen, at which they aimed their four 500 pounders and incendiaries. P/O Ross and crew claimed to have bombed a railway junction and bridge and sidings at Wittenburg, a town some one hundred miles north of the primary target and forty miles east of Hamburg. If this is the case, the timings suggest that they abandoned their intention to reach Magdeburg early and began to seek alternatives after reaching the Hannover area. This is speculation forced by the paucity of information provided by the ORB.

Hemswell and Scampton provided twenty-two Hampdens to target the Misburg refinery on the 24th, while seven others from Waddington, Lindholme and Finningley took care of gardening duties off Brest (Jellyfish). The two 44 Squadron crews of P/O Robertson and S/L Tindall took off at 02.55 and 03.15 respectively and set course for the south coast to begin the Channel crossing near Start Point lighthouse. Reports of the weather conditions (by members of other squadrons) varied from poor to good, the 44 Squadron duo apparently experiencing little difficulty in identifying a pinpoint from which to carry out a timed run. Familiar landmarks for this garden were the island of Ushant and Saint-Mathieu on the headland to the north of the estuary leading past the port to the River L'Elorn. P/O Robertson and crew planted their vegetable from 750 feet, before attacking a medium-size merchant vessel with two wing-mounted 250 pounders. S/L Tindall released his mine at 900 feet and aimed his two bombs at a jetty at Saint-Mathieu.

The main focus on the 25th would be Germany's oil industry and shipbuilding, and 5 Group sent out orders to Hemswell, Lindholme and Scampton to prepare eighteen Hampdens to attack the Krupp-Germania shipyard at Kiel, while Waddington took care of the gardening requirements. The crews of F/O Booth and P/O Sandford were briefed for the Eglantine garden, the Elbe estuary, and P/O Ross and crew for Forget-me-not in Kiel Harbour. This would be P/O Sandford's first operation with the squadron, in what would be a long, but, ultimately, fatal association. They departed Waddington between 17.40 and 18.00, and adopted the same course, independently, as far as Cuxhaven, where the Booth and Sandford crews peeled off to starboard, leaving P/O Ross and crew to traverse the Schleswig-Holstein peninsula to reach the western Baltic. Under clear skies, P/O Sandford and crew delivered their 1,500lb parachute mine from 500 feet, and the Booth crew from 800 feet, before the latter dropped one 250 pounder on a bridge at Sankt-Peter-Ording on the headland, and the other on a flak battery close by to the west. Meanwhile, some seventy miles to the east, P/O Ross and crew planted their vegetable from 700 feet and dropped the two 250 pounders onto the docks at Kiel.

On the following night, when a total of eighty-four aircraft was committed to operations, 5 Group detailed seventeen Hampdens from Hemswell, Scampton and Waddington for what would be the night's largest raid, against the electrical power station in the Moabit district of north-western Berlin.

44 Squadron contributed just two crews, those of Sgt Smith and S/L Tindall, who took off at 23.10 and 23.15 respectively. They encountered a blanket of low cloud over northern Germany, which extended to the target area, and only six of the participants would reach it and identify the aiming point. Both 44 Squadron crews were among these, S/L Tindall dropping a 1,000 pounder and two 250 pounders, and Sgt Smith two 250 pounders and 120 x 4lb incendiaries.

On the 27th, Scampton, Lindholme and Waddington were ordered to prepare for an attack that night on the A10 Harburg oil plant situated on the southern bank of the Elbe. An attack by an enemy intruder on Lindholme reduced the 50 Squadron effort to three crews, along with nine from Scampton and four from Waddington. The crews of F/L Ogilvie and P/Os Perkins, Robertson and Sandford took off between 17.25 and 17.45, the first three-named carrying a 1,000 pounder and two 250 pounders and the Sandford crew four 500 and two 250 pounders plus twenty incendiaries. Searchlights sprang into action from Elmshorn on the North Bank, and the flak was fairly intense over Hamburg itself, for which a layer of cloud provided an element of protection but contributed to challenging conditions for target locating. The 44 Squadron crews attacked with sticks of bombs from north to south, west to east and south to north, before returning safely to reports bursts and a large fire visible from forty miles away, but no detail of damage.

Twenty-four hours later, Hamburg would host another visit from 5 Group, ten Hampdens from Hemswell and Lindholme assigned to the Harburg oil refinery, while ten others from Scampton and Waddington targeted dock installations. 44 Squadron contributed the crews of F/O Booth, P/O Ross and Sgt Ayton, who took off between 17.05 and 17.20 carrying a variety of bomb loads. They ran into eight to ten-tenths cloud at 3,000 to 6,000 feet over the North Sea, which persisted all the way to the enemy coast and made it difficult to establish a pinpoint. The early arrivals from other squadrons found Hamburg to be completely obscured, and some set course for alternative targets, while the cloud had dispersed somewhat by the time that those from Waddington began their approach to the docklands to the west of the city centre, running the gauntlet of searchlights and flak as they followed the course of the Elbe. P/O Ross and crew attacked from north to south with a stick of two 500 and two 250 pounders and 120 x 4lb incendiaries and claimed that the incendiaries caused two large fires. Sgt Ayton and crew had nothing to report from the delivery of their similar load, and nothing was observed of the bursts from F/O Booth's single 1,000 and two 250 pounders.

Waddington stood down on the 29th, while twenty Hampdens from Scampton, Hemswell and Lindholme battled the conditions in a largely failed attempt to reach Berlin. During the course of the month, the squadron carried out nineteen operations and dispatched ninety-nine sorties for the loss of four Hampdens and two crews.

November 1940

By the onset of November, the Battle of Britain had run its course, and the fear of invasion had been banished for the time being at least. Industrial Germany would now become the main focus of attention as the winter took hold, with oil related targets at the head of an impressive list drawn up by the Air Ministry in a new directive issued three weeks after the enthronement of C-in-C Sir Richard Peirse. 5 Group hoped soon to have a new weapon in its armoury in the form of the Avro Manchester, a twin-engine replacement for the Hampden, which would soon be delivered to Waddington. As already mentioned, the new type was to be introduced to operational service by 207 Squadron, which was reformed officially on this day under the command of W/C "Hettie" Hyde, who, it will be recalled, had spent August with 44 Squadron to gain operational experience. While the Manchester would prove to be hugely disappointing, its failure would force the development of its offspring, which would become the war's most successful bomber.

The trend of sending small forces to wide-ranging targets continued in November, and this diluting of the effort would render the operations ineffective and of little more than nuisance value. The first targets of the new month for 5 Group were two of Berlin's many electrical power stations, for which seventeen Hampdens were detailed from Hemswell, Lindholme and Waddington on the 1st, while Scampton and Finningley took care of gardening duties. Four aircraft were made ready by 44 Squadron to attack B57 in the hands of the crews of P/Os Penman, Perkins and Robertson and Sgt Atkins, who took off between 23.10 and 23.30 to head out over the North Sea. They ran into a bank of ice-bearing cloud before reaching the Dutch coast, and then found themselves in a one-hundred-mile-wide belt of rain, before closing on Berlin with five-tenths cloud beneath them at around 6,000 to 7,000 feet. Ground mist would add to any problems, but no hint of anything untoward found its way into the ORB as all from Waddington located the aiming point and delivered an attack. While most squadrons filled their bomb bays with a uniform load, which rendered the armourers' task routine, 44 Squadron continued to use mixed and individual loads, almost as if using up old stock. P/Os Penman and Robertson delivered four 500 pounders each, while Sgt Atkins's load consisted of a 1,000 pounder one 250 pounder and four 20lb incendiaries and P/O Perkins' two 250 and two 500 pounders. They ran across the target from various points of the compass, making no mention of the curtain of searchlights and flak, and P/O Perkins and crew claimed that their hardware set off a large fire, the glow from which remained visible for 150 miles into the return journey. The blaze and a lingering glow were confirmed by a number of 50 Squadron crews, but, in reality, it would take an entire city on fire to produce such a result, and, certainly, nothing of that magnitude occurred on this night.

The weather continued to challenge the raid planners, and most of the Command remained on the ground for the ensuing few nights. 5 Group sent ten Scampton Hampdens to Kiel on the night of the 3/4th, after cancelling the participation of the Lindholme and Hemswell elements, but it was the 5th before the other groups stirred into life again, detailing ninety-seven aircraft for operations over Germany, Italy and the occupied countries. The target for eighteen Hampdens was the Rothensee oil refinery at Magdeburg, while five others from Lindholme and Hemswell targeted a shipyard in Bremen and seven took care of gardening duties in the Willow garden off the Baltic port of Sassnitz on the island of Rügen. 44 Squadron made ready four Hampdens for Magdeburg and one for P/O Stocking and crew to take to the Baltic, and it was the last-mentioned that departed Waddington first, at 22.55, when weather conditions over eastern England were reasonably good. They reached the target area after an outward flight of more than four hours and circled above a blanket of ten-tenths cloud, before admitting defeat and turning for home. At around 04.30, a gap appeared in the cloud, which revealed them to be near Fehmarn Island in the Radish garden, and the vegetable was planted there. The bombing quartet had taken off between 00.15 and 01.00 with a one thousand mile round-trip ahead of them, and soon ran into ten-tenths cloud, which would deny them a sight of the ground until they returned. They were dogged by icing conditions and rain throughout their sorties, and none from Waddington elected to press on. The crew of the newly promoted F/O Penman came upon a flak battery on the eastern outskirts of Hannover, and let their bombs go, observing flashes but no details, while the others brought their loads home.

The prospects for decent weather conditions were again bleak twenty-four hours later, when 5 Group dispatched twenty-five Hampdens to the twin cities of Mannheim and Ludwigshafen. These major cities face each other from the East and West Banks respectively of the Rhine in south-central Germany, and, on this night, marshalling yards and or the Rhine docks were the intended targets. According to the recorded take-off times, 44 Squadron briefed the crews of S/L Gardner and Sgt Ayton for Mannheim, and those of S/L Tindall, P/O Sandford and Sgt Jones for an attack on the marshalling yards at Hamm, on the northern edge of the Ruhr. They had to wait until the early hours of the 7th before becoming airborne, the Mannheim duo with a greater distance to travel at 01.05 and 01.25, and those bound for the Ruhr between 02.15 and 02.30. The weather over France was unpleasant, but did, at least, relent to leave perfect conditions in the target area. This was of no interest to S/L Gardner and crew, who had lost the rear gunner's door, exposing him and the wireless operator to extreme cold and forcing the abandonment of the sortie. Sgt Ayton and crew pressed on to deliver a 1,000 pounder and two 500 pounders in a stick from south-east to north-west, observing a burst in the south-eastern corner of the target, before re-entering the foul weather conditions for the homeward journey. Severe icing afflicted the Ruhr-bound trio, and none reached the briefed target, P/O Sandford and crew alone finding a worthwhile last resort target in the form of a factory at Remscheid on the southern extremity of the region, which they straddled with their two 500 and two 250 pounders and 120 x 4lb incendiaries.

On the 7th, 2, 3 and 5 Groups combined to send sixty-three Blenheims, Wellingtons and Hampdens to attack the Krupp works at Essen in the heart of the Ruhr. 5 Group detailed thirty aircraft, seven of them made ready at Waddington, six of which took off between 20.20 and 20.40 with F/L Ogilvie the senior pilot on duty. P/O Robertson and crew remained on the ground for a further fifty-five minutes before getting away, possible to enable them to conduct a post-raid reconnaissance. All reached the target area after crossing the North Sea and Holland over cloud, and, although Essen also lay under a protective blanket, crews were able to pick up a distinctive bend in the Rhine to the south of the city and plot a course from there. It was at this point that P/O Cuthbert and crew ran into flak, and were hit in a fuel tank, which persuaded them to jettison their load and head for home. Most crews identified the target by the bursts of bombs and the intensity of the defences as they approached, weaving their way through accurate searchlight beams reaching to 17,000 feet. Although under fire from all calibres of flak, the 44 Squadron crews were very certain of their positions as they attacked, Sgt Ottaway and crew specifying machine shop N°9 as the objective for two of their 500 pounders. Sgt Atkins and crew mentioned the same building and a power station as recipients of their 1,000 and two 250 pounders, while the others were unable to be as precise and saw little of the impact of their assorted bomb loads.

On the 8th, 5 Group notified its four main stations of an operation that night against a marshalling yard in Munich, for which twenty-three Hampdens were made ready, two of them at Waddington for the crews of P/O Perkins and Sgt Smith. They took off at 17.35 with a thirteen-hundred-mile round trip ahead of them, and set course for the Scheldt estuary, to fly the length of Belgium until crossing into Germany south of the Eifel region. This leg was undertaken over unbroken cumulus cloud until some twenty miles from Frankfurt, where a tail wind sped them the remaining two hundred miles to the target. P/O Perkins delivered a 1,000 pounder, and Sgt Smith four 500 pounders across the aiming point from north-west to south-east, and both estimated that they had hit the yards, although saw nothing of the impacts.

Adverse weather conditions affected operations on the 9th and 10th, Waddington sitting out the former, and making ready three Hampdens on the latter in response to 5 Group orders to prepare twenty-eight of the type for a number of long-range operations that night, with destinations from Mannheim in the south to Danzig in the north-east and Merseburg, near Liepzig in the east. The crews of Sgt Ottaway,

P/O Stockings and Sgt Atkins learned at briefing that their destination was the distant Baltic port of Danzig, now Gdansk in Poland, for which they departed Waddington at 17.45, 18.00 and 18.55 respectively. They had ahead of them a round trip of some sixteen hundred miles, a somewhat ambitious undertaking for a winter's night in 1940, and Sgt Atkins and crew returned to base minus their bombs after four hours, having flown blind until recognising the futility of continuing. Sgt Ottaway and crew had reached the western Baltic, when it became clear that fuel was not flowing from the wing tanks. It was decided to unload two 250 pounders and 120 x 4lb incendiaries on Kiel docks, before attempting to reach home, which they accomplished after seven hours and forty minutes aloft. P/O Stocking and crew pressed on to the target area, where, in the face of poor visibility, they were unable to locate either the primary or alternative targets and jettisoned their load. They dispensed nickels (leaflets) over an area between Danzig and the River Vistula and touched down at Waddington twelve hours and ten minutes after leaving it.

The 5 Group targets for eighteen aircraft on the 12th were much closer to home and were oil refineries in the Ruhr located at Wanne-Eickel, north-east of Gelsenkirchen, and Dortmund further to the east. The Wanne-Eickel plant was another employing the Bergius process to produce high grade synthetic oil for aviation fuel, while, it is believed, that the Dortmund plant manufactured lower-grade diesel fuels through the Fischer-Tropsch process. Four Hampdens were made ready at Waddington and had to wait until the early hours of the 13th before departing for the latter between 02.10 and 02.35 with the crews of F/O Penman, P/Os Sandford and Skinner and Sgt Ayton on board. They ran into heavy cloud over the North Sea that extended beyond the target area, despite which, the crews of P/O Skinner and F/O Penman located the primary target and delivered their 500 and 250 pounders in sticks from west to east without observing the results. P/O Sandford located the target area, but not the precise aiming point, and they dropped two 250 pounders onto an unidentified railway junction close by. Sgt Ayton and crew failed to locate the primary target, and, on the way home, bombed an aerodrome, believed to be at Bottrop, situated to the north-east of Duisburg.

Seventy-two aircraft took off for various targets in Germany on the night of the 13/14th, twenty-five of them Hampdens detailed for operations over Hamburg. The Lindholme element of five had been cancelled by the station commander because of poor visibility, but four departed Waddington between 00.20 and 01.15, with Sgt Cuthbert and crew the last away. X2995 had reached 800 feet when it stalled and dived into the ground a mile east of the airfield, according to the 5 Group ORB, because of engine failure. The pilot and second pilot/navigator survived with severe injuries, to which the latter succumbed shortly afterwards, while the gunner/wireless operators died on impact. The crews of Sgt Jones and S/L Tindall were defeated by the weather conditions and abandoned their sorties when two hours into the outward leg. This left F/L Smales and crew to battle their way through the front over the North Sea, until making landfall on Germany's north-western coast, where they opted to drop their four 500 pounders onto the docks at Cuxhaven.

On the following night, the 14th, more than five hundred Luftwaffe bombers attacked the city of Coventry over a period of many hours and left the central districts in ruins and unrecognisable. While this was in progress, 5 Group dispatched seventeen Hampdens to target an oil refinery and the Blohm & Voss shipyards in Hamburg, and ten to attack an electrical power station in Berlin's south-western suburb of Wilmersdorf. The 44 Squadron crews of P/O Perkins and Sgts Ottaway and Smith took off between 22.40 and 22.55 bound for Germany's Capital, while F/L Ogilvie and P/Os Robertson and Skinner waited until fifteen minutes after midnight before following them into the air on their way to Germany's Second City. They began the North Sea crossing between Mablethorpe and Skegness, and, for a change, the weather conditions over north-western Germany were excellent, enabling crews to pick up the targets without difficulty. F/L Ogilvie and crew adopted a south-easterly heading to drop four 500 pounders in a stick over the refinery, A8, while P/O Skinner and crew flew west to east, and, although both saw bursts, they determined no detail. P/O Robertson and crew did not attack the primary target, delivering their four 500 pounders instead onto a flak battery at the southern end of Heligoland. Meanwhile, 160 miles to the east of Hamburg, Sgts Ottaway and Smith aimed what the ORB described as a landmine each onto the power station, B60, but observed nothing of the impact. As the 4,000lb blockbuster weapon, which would become known as a "cookie", had yet to be developed, one must assume that it was a 2,000 pounder. X2996 is believed to have exploded in mid-air over Berlin and crashed without survivors from among the crew of P/O Perkins. This was just one of ten failures to return from the night's operations, which represented the largest night loss of the war to date.

Hamburg was posted as the destination again for twenty-five Hampdens from Hemswell, Lindholme and Waddington on the 15th, this time to target the power station at Altona on the North Bank of the Elbe to the west of the city centre. 44 Squadron made ready four aircraft, which took off between 00.15 and 01.00 with F/L Booth the senior pilot on duty and flew out over Skegness to encounter difficult weather conditions over the North Sea in the form of heavy ice-bearing cloud between 1,500 and 11,000 feet and driving rain. The skies were clear over the target area, however, and this would offer the chance to attack from relatively high level, from where the massive docks area and Altona merged into a single entity. F/L Booth and F/O Penman specified the docks as the recipient of their 1,000 and 500 pounders plus incendiaries, while Sgts Jones and Ayton reported simply "Hamburg". The latter was intercepted by a BF109 some seven miles east of Bremerhaven, in response to which, the gunners fired off 240 rounds, and watched their assailant hit the ground in flames. P4414 apparently resembled a colander when it was handed back to the ground crew, but the aircrew strutted off without a scratch between them.

For the third night running, Hamburg would host a visit from 5 Group, but, on this occasion, only those among thirty-four Hampdens that managed to make it all the way on another night of hostile weather conditions. 44 Squadron made ready three Hampdens, whose crews had been among those briefed to attack the industrial areas of Veddel and Peute, located on the islands in the Elbe in the heart of the city. P/O Skinner, F/L Smales and P/O Stocking and their crews departed Waddington at five-minute intervals from 01.10 and headed into a weather front over the North Sea that contained all kinds of unpleasant surprises. In the face of low cloud and severe icing conditions, F/L Smales gave up the quest to reach the primary target, probably even before reaching mainland Germany, and dropped his four 500 pounders onto the Frisian island of Borkum. We are not told how close P/O Stockings and crew were to Hamburg when they, too, turned back, at which point, or soon after, they chanced upon three motor vessels of between 4,000 and 6,000 tons, which they attacked with four 500 pounders, scoring at least one near-miss. When P/O Skinner and crew landed at base at 07.15, they were able to report bombing the primary target, but observing nothing after their bombs fell away. Landing at night was an ever-present danger to crews returning tired after hours in the air, and survival was often a matter of luck. However, it must have been almost full daylight when P/O Stockings overshot his landing at Bircham Newton at 07.45, and, with his crew, walked away from the wreckage of X3008.

Adverse weather conditions at home and over Germany caused the cancellation of 5 Group operations on the following two nights, and, when orders were received on the frontline stations on the 19th, they contained details of that night's long-range operations by eight aircraft to the Skoda armaments works at Pilsen in Czechoslovakia, and by thirteen to a Bergius-process oil production site at Lützkendorf near Leipzig. 44 Squadron briefed four crews for the oil plant and that of Sgt Ayton for the Skoda works, the latter taking off first at 22.25 with a round trip of thirteen hundred miles to contemplate, while their colleagues, who took off between 00.50 and 01.25, had fewer than eleven hundred miles ahead of them. The weather conditions would prove to be too difficult for any of the Waddington crews to reach their assigned target, and the first to arrive back was that of Sgt Ottaway, who made landfall on the Norfolk coast to the south of Cromer. With the conditions still appallingly bad, X3023 came down almost immediately near the village of Southrepps at 06.30, killing the pilot and two others, and severely injuring the surviving gunner/wireless operator. To their credit, Sgt Ayton and crew had penetrated to within ten miles of the Czechoslovakian border when they turned back and bombed a factory in the town of Hof in northern-eastern Bavaria. Sgt Atkins and crew were defeated by the ten-tenths low cloud and arrived home with their bombs after more than seven hours aloft, recording the same landing time as S/L Tindall and crew, who had bombed railway installations at Osnabrück on the way home. Sgt Smith and crew were the last to land at 09.20, eight-and-a-half hours after they had taken off, having dropped their four 500 pounders onto an unidentified aerodrome near Halle, to the north-west of Leipzig.

The target posted on the 20th was much closer to home, requiring a trip to the East Bank of the Rhine at Duisburg in the Ruhr, where Germany's largest inland docks, Duisburg-Ruhrort, lay to the south of the city centre. 44 Squadron made ready three Hampdens for the crews of Sgt Hazelden, P/O Robertson and Sgt Jones, who departed Waddington at five-minute intervals from 22.55. They ran into the first outposts of the Ruhr defence zone some twenty minutes before reaching the target, but this was mostly searchlight activity, and they found clear skies, moonlight and excellent visibility to aid their search for the aiming point. Each adopted a north-easterly heading to release their four 500 pounders across the docks, observing bursts and a fire, but no details in the glare of what was now an intense searchlight and flak defence.

On the 22nd, AVM Sir Arthur Harris left 5 group on his appointment as second deputy to the Chief of the Air Staff, Sir Charles Portal, and he was succeeded by AVM Bottomley. Fifteen months hence, to the day, Harris would return to lead the Command and rescue it from the brink of disbandment. That night, 5 Group sent a small force back to Duisburg-Ruhrort and another to attack an aerodrome, almost certainly Merignac, near Bordeaux, the 5 Group ORB suggesting that 44 Squadron assigned two crews to each. However, the squadron Form 540 mentions three crews attacking M61, the Ruhrort docks, while the Form 541 lists three crews, two of which were assigned to Bordeaux. P/O Skinner and crew departed Waddington for Duisburg at 17.00 and returned five-and-a-half hours later to report aiming their four 500 pounders at a factory believed to be in the vicinity of the city. An hour after their return, Sgt Smith and F/O Penman took off for the long flight to the Bordeaux region, where the former attacked from south-west to north-east, and straddled hangars with a stick of six 250 pounders which set off a fire. F/O Penman and crew ran across the aiming point from west to east, with their three 250 pounders and 120 x 4lb incendiaries also observed to straddle the hangars, and both returned safely after round trips of nine hours thirty-five minutes and eight hours forty minutes respectively.

Twenty-four hours later, 5 Group sent ten Hampdens back to Duisburg-Ruhrort, while also assigning five to Gelsenkirchen. 44 Squadron sat out this night at home but was back on the Order of Battle on the 24th, to take care of gardening duties off the Biscay ports, while eleven others targeted the Blohm & Voss shipyards at Hamburg. It was actually the early hours of the 25th before the three 44 Squadron crews of S/L Tindall and F/Ls Ogilvie and Booth departed Waddington either side of 02.30 and set course for the Dorset coast for the Channel crossing. S/L Tindall and F/L Booth had been handed the Artichoke garden, off Lorient, and F/L Ogilvie Beech, further south off St-Nazaire, where they planted their vegetables according to brief from between 800 and 1,000 feet.

On the following night, Hemswell and Lindholme joined forces to send ten Hampdens to attack the Deutsche-Werke shipyard at Kiel, where the heavy cruiser, Gneisenau, had been built between 1935 and 1938. 44 Squadron remained on the ground until the 27th, when Cologne was posted as the destination for sixty-two aircraft, which would be allotted to five separate aiming points within the city, the ten 5 Group Hampden crews briefed to attack what was described as a "land armament factory". The 44 Squadrons crews of F/Ls Ogilvie and Booth were to be sent back to the Biscay coast, the former to mine the waters of the Beech garden off St-Nazaire and the latter the Jellyfish garden off Brest. They took off at 02.30 and 03.05 to follow the usual route across the Channel to make landfall on the French coast to the west of St-Malo. The most commonly employed pinpoints from which to carry out timed runs to the release points were Saint-Mathieu for Brest and La Calebasse Rocks for St-Nazaire, and both crews reported successfully fulfilling their brief from 800 and 600 feet respectively.

Hemswell and Lindholme were the stations called upon on the 28th to provide aircraft for operations against a naval store at Mannheim, and the inland port on the other side of the Rhine at Ludwigshafen. Six Hemswell crews were briefed for the former, and five from Lindholme for the latter, and 50 Squadron would also provide one crew to attack the Veddel and Peute industrial area in the heart of Hamburg. The 44 Squadron crews of Sgts Stammers and Hubbard departed Waddington at 17.15 and 17.25 bound for a naval store in the port of Le Havre, where each delivered four 500 pounders without observing the results. By the time that X2966 approached the Lincolnshire coast on return, it was running on fumes, and Sgt Hubbard put it down on the beach at Sutton-on-Sea, south of Mablethorpe, at 02.00, writing it off, but doing so without damage to the crew.

Le Havre was again the destination for six Hampdens on the 29th, two of them provided by 44 Squadron and containing the crews of P/O Robertson and Sergeant Jones. They departed Waddington at 16.55 and 17.45 respectively to target the docks and shipping, and both reached the target, where the former delivered four 500 pounders between Bassin de Makee and Bassin Bellot, and the latter across the centre of the docks. During the course of the month, the squadron took part in twenty-three operations, dispatching sixty-eight sorties for the loss of five Hampdens and three crews.

December 1940

At the 207 Squadron site at Waddington, F/O Lewis DFC arrived on posting from 44 Squadron, and he would be followed on the 6th by the former 44 Squadron stalwart, F/O Eustace DFC, who, since his screening, had been on the staff at station HQ Waddington. The new month began for 5 Group with the briefing of ten Scampton crews on the 1st, for an operation that night against shipbuilding yards at Wilhelmshaven, but adverse weather conditions reduced the number reaching and bombing the target to three. The weather continued to be unfavourable, and operations planned for the 2nd and 3rd were cancelled. The only sortie on the latter occasion was a patrol over Birmingham by S/L Ogilvie and crew, for which they departed Waddington just before midnight. They spent an hour over England's Second City at 12,000 feet, and, although they observed fires below from a Luftwaffe raid, they encountered no enemy aircraft.

It was the 4th, before orders were received to prepare for a raid on the Derendorf marshalling yards, situated just to the north of Düsseldorf city centre, for which Scampton and Lindholme detailed five Hampdens each. 44 Squadron dispatched the crew of Sgt Atkins at 03.10 on the 5th for mining duties in the Jellyfish garden off Brest, and they returned after six hours twenty minutes to report a successful delivery of their vegetable from 800 feet. On the 6th, ten Scampton Hampdens were sent on intruder sorties over Luftwaffe bomber aerodromes in the occupied countries, while twenty others from Scampton, Hemswell and Waddington pioneered a new role for the type, conducting offensive patrols over Bristol to seek out and destroy enemy bombers. The Waddington element of six took off between 21.30 and 21.55 with F/L Booth the senior pilot on duty, and soon lost the services of Sgt Smith and crew to instrument and communications issues. The others pressed on and failed to locate enemy aircraft but reported up to sixteen fires across the city. Lindholme and Hemswell received notification on the 7th to prepare to return to Düsseldorf that night for an attack on the Mannesman Rohrenwerke, which, it is believed, was manufacturing heavy gun barrels. They headed into an ice-bearing front over enemy territory, which would force a number of crews to jettison their loads in order to remain airborne, and only three would report bombing the target. Much later that night, in fact, shortly after 03.00, the crews of Sgts Hubbard and Stammers departed Waddington for the Jellyfish garden, and successfully planted a vegetable each into the briefed locations from 750 and 500 feet respectively.

On the 8th, Hemswell and Lindholme joined forces to send fourteen Hampdens to Düsseldorf to target the Mannesman steel works again, while 44 Squadron dispatched six crews between 18.45 and 19.10 to patrol the skies over Oxford, with S/L Smales the senior pilot on duty. They encountered very poor visibility, which restricted their ability to spot enemy aircraft or assess what was happening on the ground, and they returned with nothing to report. Two nights later, 5 Group sent orders to Scampton and Lindholme to prepare six Hampdens each to target the inland docks on the East Bank of the Rhine at Mannheim, while three 44 Squadron crews attended to mining duties in the Deodar garden in the Gironde estuary. The crews of S/L Tindall, F/L Ogilvie and P/O Sandford took off between 01.09 and 01.15 and headed for the south-west to begin the Channel crossing. As F/L Ogilvie and crew were landing at 09.00, a message was received from X3049 which read, "Ok. Down in France". It would be learned, eventually, that flak had ruptured a fuel tank, and that S/L Tindall and crew had joined the growing list of Bomber Command personnel on extended leave in German PoW camps. At debriefing, the Sandford and Ogilvie crews confirmed planting their vegetables successfully from 500 and 800 feet respectively, and, it was assumed, that the Tindall crew had also fulfilled their brief.

It was back to security patrols for six 44 Squadron crews on the evening of the 11th, when five took off between 18.15 and 18.40 bound for the Birmingham area. S/L Smales and crew remained on the ground until getting away at 21.45, and, for the first time during this type of operation, enemy aircraft were spotted, and attempts made to engage them. Sgt Hazelden and crew counted six enemy aircraft, one of them passing within fifty yards, which they chased but lost due to its superior speed. P/O Skinner and crew observed five "bandits" and dived onto one of them from 18,000 down to 14,000 feet, only to lose it from sight. Others caught brief glimpses of the enemy, but were unable to give chase, and an opinion was offered at debriefing, that a lower patrol height would have brought them into better contact with the enemy.

Berlin, Frankfurt and Kiel were the destinations for seventy-one aircraft on the night of the 15/16th, thirty of them Hampdens bound for Berlin to attack a number of targets. 44 Squadron briefed four crews to attack the Air Ministry building in the city centre, and five others for mining duties in the

Jellyfish and Artichoke gardens off Brest and Lorient. The bombing element departed Waddington first, between 23.40 and 00.05, with F/O Penman the senior pilot on duty and flew out over Skegness on a direct course for Berlin. They encountered nine-tenths cloud over the North Sea, which allowed them no sight of the ground until they reached the target, where they found around eight-tenths at 5,000 feet. This obscured the primary target, and it appears that F/O Penman and crew turned back in the hope of finding an alternative objective for their 500 pounders. This they found in the form of the marshalling yards at Soest, a town a few miles to the north of the Möhne reservoir at the eastern end of the Ruhr Valley. They claimed to have straddled the railway tracks but observed no bomb flashes in confirmation. The others reported delivering their high-explosives and incendiaries in the vicinity of the primary target in the face of a hostile searchlight and flak defence, but saw nothing of the impact, for which Sgt Ayton and crew blamed a thick smoke screen. They were on their way home by the time that the gardeners took off either side of 03.30, the crews of P/O Ross, F/Sgt Trickett and Sgt Hubbard bound for Jellyfish, and those of Sgts Dart and Stott for Artichoke. Sgt Dart and crew were discouraged by low cloud on the way out, and turned back, leaving the Stott crew to plant their vegetable in the briefed location from 700 feet. The three Jellyfish crews also succeeded in fulfilling their brief from 600 to 700 feet, after which, P/O Ross located a convoy of four ships as targets for the two wing-mounted 250 pounders. One struck home amidships of one vessel, flinging debris into the air, and the gunners expended six hundred rounds of .303 ammunition.

Orders came through from 5 Group on the 16th to prepare fifty-eight Hampdens to attack various targets in Mannheim that night in two waves. At briefings, crews learned that this was to be a major operation involving two hundred aircraft under the codename, Operation Abigail Rachel, launched in retaliation for recent devastating raids on English cities, particularly Coventry and Southampton. The plan called for eight of the most experienced 3 Group Wellington crews to open the attack on the centre of the city with all-incendiary loads, in order to start fires that would act as a beacon to those following behind. As the day drew on, it became clear that the weather conditions over the bomber stations might cause problems, and the force was cut to 134 aircraft. The first-wave crews, the "Abigail" element, took off either side of 21.00, and among them were twenty-nine Hampdens, the crews of which had been given the Motorenwerke Mannheim in the northern outskirts of the city as their aiming point. This is curious, as the purpose of the raid was to cause as much damage as possible to the central districts of the city in what was the first officially sanctioned area attack. The three 44 Squadron crews of F/L Booth and Sgts Atkins and Jones departed Waddington an hour later as part of the "Rachel" second wave, and they were to target Mannheim's Rhine docks. The weather conditions outbound persuaded perhaps a quarter of the force to turn back, but those reaching the target found largely clear skies and a full moon, with only a modest defence in operation. The three 44 Squadron participants identified their briefed aiming point, and delivered 500 pounders and incendiaries, F/L Booth and crew observing theirs to set off eight green explosions, followed by a large white one which shook the aircraft. On the way home, this crew dropped a single 500 pounder onto Haren aerodrome to the north-east of Brussels. Post-raid reconnaissance revealed that the operation had not produced the desired results, after the "Path Finder" element had missed the city centre and the subsequent bombing had been scattered. Even so, local reports provided a figure of 240 buildings either destroyed or seriously damaged, with more than a thousand people bombed out of their homes.

The weather kept 5 Group at home on the ensuing two nights, while very small forces returned to Mannheim. The teleprinters on 5 Group stations burst into life on the 19th to reveal plans to attack the Wesseling Bergius-process production plant, situated on the West Bank of the Rhine south of Cologne. Forty Hampdens were made ready across the group, four of them at Waddington, while eight others, five from Waddington and three from Finningley, would take care of mining duties in the Jellyfish and Artichoke gardens. The Wesseling force took off in the late afternoon, beginning around 16.25, as did the Waddington gardening element, between 16.25 and 16.45, however, the four crews of the 44 Squadron bombing section, those of S/L Smales, P/Os Ross and Smith and Sgt Hazelden, did not take off until much later. It was, in fact, long after the gardeners had landed, that they departed Waddington between 03.35 and 04.00, bound not for the Wesseling plant, but the nearby Knapsack power station. Sgt Hazelden and crew were defeated by severe icing conditions, and P/O Ross and crew failed to locate the aiming point, and neither carried out an attack, but S/L Smales and Sgt Smith and their crews delivered their four 500 pounders each without observing the results. Of the mining crews, all five successfully planted their vegetables as briefed in the Artichoke garden from 800 to 900 feet, and the crew of Sgt Dart dropped their two 250 pounders onto the port of Lorient.

The 20th would mark the resurgence of 1 Group, which had been reconstituted on return from its role as the major part of the AASF in France for the first nine months of the war. The Fairey Battles of 12, 103, 142 and 150 Squadrons had been replaced, and, with four squadrons of fanatical Poles added to its ranks and working towards operational status, this night would see the first six operational sorties in Wellingtons. 5 Group detailed a dozen Hampdens for Berlin and thirty-one for a return to the Wesseling plant at Cologne, and it was for the former, the Schlesischer Tor railway station, south-east of Berlin's city centre, that the three 44 Squadron crews of F/O Penman, P/O Stockings and Sgt Ayton departed Waddington at 00.10 and 00.15. Quite why they had been held back until then is unclear, particularly as the 83 Squadron element had departed Scampton either side of 17.00. The Lindholme and Waddington crews were under time pressure throughout, conscious that they would struggle to vacate enemy territory before the arrival of daylight, and this would prove to be the case for some. They exited the English coast at Skegness, and adopted a direct course for the target, which they reached at around 04.00. P/O Stockings and crew were on final approach for the bombing run when they were hit by a burst of heavy flak, which knocked out the hydraulics system, rudder control and the intercom. They immediately turned back towards the west, jettisoning the bombs "live" as they did so, the pilot fighting to maintain control of the Hampden. They would eventually reach base to land at 09.00 and find their colleagues already on the ground undergoing debriefing. F/O Penman and crew reported dropping two 500 pounders and 120 x 4lb incendiaries onto the railway station and watched them set off explosions and fires. Sgt Ayton and crew delivered a 1,000 pounder and observed it to explode in the centre of the station, and then expended 1,400 rounds of ammunition against searchlight and flak installations, inflicting casualties on their crews. As they returned near Alford, between Skegness and Mablethorpe, they encountered an enemy aircraft, which was engaged by groundfire and shot down.

5 Group detailed twenty-four Hampdens for operations on the following night, when an electrical power station at Halle, situated to the north-west of Leipzig, was to be the target. Waddington was not involved but briefed five crews for mining duties in the Forget-me-not garden in Kiel harbour, which took off between 23.00 and 23.40. They all reached the target area to plant their vegetables in the briefed locations from between 500 and 800 feet, after which, P/O Sandford and crew attacked a factory two miles south of Flensburg with their 250 pounders, the rear gunner confirming a direct hit. The others recrossed the Schleswig-Holstein peninsula before dropping their 250 pounders onto the aerodrome at Husum on the western coast, where P/O Skinner and crew observed a large blue explosion and a line of ten fires breaking out to the east of the airfield.

Waddington and its resident 44 Squadron would now enjoy a five-day break from operations, during which, the second wartime Christmas was observed in traditional style. In the meantime, Scampton and Finningley took care of 5 Group business on the 22nd, Hemswell on Boxing Day, before Hemswell, Scampton and Waddington were alerted on the 27th, for operations that night. Waddington would take care of mining duties, while the other stations sent ten Hampdens each to attack the aerodrome at Merignac near Bordeaux. The 44 Squadron crews of P/O Stockings and Sgts Ayton, Dart and Jones took off between 02.00 and 03.10 bound for the Lettuce garden in the Kiel Canal, but, in the event, only Sgt Jones and crew would identify the briefed release point and deliver their vegetable from 450 feet. They then turned their attention upon Target B, a searchlight concentration north of Rendsburg, a town some fifteen miles due west of Kiel. The attack was carried out with two 250 pounders from 2,000 feet, but no results were observed. P/O Stockings and crew failed to locate the briefed garden and planted their vegetable instead in Forget-me-not in Kiel harbour. They also then attacked a railway junction near Rendsburg from 2,000 feet, observing the bombs to fall alongside sheds, and the bursts to be followed by a dozen explosions. Sgt Ayton and crew released their mine over Forget-me-not after failing to locate Lettuce and dropped their two 250 pounders onto buildings at Pries, some six miles to the north of Kiel. Sgt Dart and crew carried out no attack.

On the following night, 5 Group operated for the final time during the year, when sending fifteen Hampdens from Hemswell and Scampton to target U-Boots in the docks at Lorient, where, as already mentioned, the Germans were about to embark on a massive U-Boot bunker building programme. While that was in progress, 44 Squadron sent four crews back to the Lettuce garden to try to redress the previous night's failure. The crews of Sgt Stammers, P/Os Skinner and Smith and Sgt Atkins departed Waddington between 16.35 and 17.10, only for P/O Skinner to be back on the ground after seventy-five minutes and Sgt Atkins after four hours twenty-five minutes, both for undisclosed reasons. P/O Smith failed to locate the elusive Lettuce garden and planted his mine in Kiel Fjord as an alternative. The two 250 pounders were aimed at a suspension bridge over the Schlei Fjord to the north of Rieseby, and a direct hit was observed on the railway track fifty yards south of the bridge. Sgt Stammers and crew alone located the briefed release point, and delivered their store from 900 feet, before, according to the ORB, bombing the docks at St Malo from 1,500 feet. It seems highly unlikely that they would attack a target on the Brittany coast, when there would have been many more convenient targets of opportunity, and, perhaps, this is an erroneous entry by the squadron scribe.

On the 29th, a new flight was formed under the temporary command of F/O Clayton to conduct proving trials of the Douglas A20 Havoc, known in Bomber Command as the Boston, a twin-engine bomber, which had first seen WWII service in French hands. Two examples of the type were taken on charge and had thirty-one hours of non-operational flying behind them. During the course of the month, the squadron took part in sixteen operations and dispatched sixty-two sorties for the loss of a single Hampden and crew.

It had been a backs-to-the-wall year, and one of presenting a defiant face to an as yet all conquering enemy. 1941 was not destined to bring more than a slight increase in effectiveness, and it would be a case of treading water for the foreseeable future. Some new aircraft were emerging to offer a degree of hope for the future, but the problems arising from pressing them too soon into service would result in a painfully slow development, and the existing types were to bear most of the burden for the next twelve months and even beyond.

The pilots who took part in Waddington's first mine-laying sortie of the war.
Back (L-R) – F/O Core (50 Sqn) and Sgt Smythe (44 Sqn).
Front (L-R) – F/L Dutton (44 Sqn), S/L Weir (44 Sqn), F/L Bennett DFC (50 Sqn)

Three Squadron Hampdens. Note the different camouflage patterns.

Formation of Squadron Hampdens

Three Squadron Hampdens carrying practice bomb carriers.

S/L 'Woggy' Watts (OC B Flt 44 Sqn), P/O Mike Lewis and S/L North (OC A Flt 44 Sqn).

King George VI presenting the DFC to F/O Mike Lewis at Waddington

F/O Mike Lewis. March 1940. A Canadian, he joined the RAF before the war.

*Mike and Bike
F/O W J Lewis DFC at Waddington*

W/O Frank Stott DFM

Believed to be Sgt Rowsell (Air Gunner)

Hampden KM-Z usually referred to as 'Zeke' was flown by P/O W J 'Mike' Lewis, a Canadian and Sgt 'Boozy' Kingston amongst others. Both these two later became POWs. The aircraft (as X2982) was lost in May 1941 when it crashed in Catterick, Yorkshire. The crew were unhurt.

W/O Frankie Stott and Sgt 'Pissy' Jones

Royal visit to Waddington 4th of April 1940. Station Commander G/C Anderson escorts HRH the Duke of Kent

W/C JN Boothman

P/O Dingwall pictured in the Officers' Mess at Waddington - March 1940
W/C Reid (OC 44 Sqn), Mike Lewis, Mike Homer, Mackintosh, Freddie Farrans, Dingwall, Dean Dutton, 'Smudger' Smith. Mike Homer was transferred to Fighter Command on medical grounds. He was shot down and killed during the Battle of Britain while flying a Hurricane with 242 Squadron.

Hampden L4088 KM-D
Airborne from Waddington on a mine-laying sortie in the Baltic Sound (Nasturtium Region) 21/22nd of April, 1940. Hit by fire from flak-ships near Kiel and crash-landed in Denmark. First complete Hampden crew to be captured. Crew: F/L F.G.Dutton, Sgt J.G.Slowey, Cpl W.P.J.Watson, Cpl W.R.Davidson.

Hampden P4098 May 1940.
The aircraft was written off when the undercarriage failed to lock down causing the aircraft to crash on landing. No injuries reported.

Remains of Hampden P4286, 14/15th of May 1940
Airborne from Waddington. Crashed at Oosterhout (Noord-Brabant), Holland after being coned by searchlights and hit by flak. All crew are buried in the Oosterhout Protestant Cemetery. Crew : F/O L.J.Ashfield, P/O C.D.Crawley, Sgt F.W.McKinlay, Cpl F.Preston.

Sgt Harry Moyles with Sgt Don Seager

Sgt Cyril Wood
KIA 2nd August 1940

Hampden L4085 Crew
On the 2nd of August 1940, L4085 of 44 Squadron, was returning from a raid on Misburg. It crossed England in thick fog and finally identified the Irish coast. The pilot turned to head back to base but ran out of fuel and landed in the sea off Aberystwyth at about 6 am. Sgt Seager was picked from the sea unharmed but lost a leg when an AA shell exploded on the platform at the railway station when he was returning from survivors' leave.

Hampden P2077, 13/14th August 1940
Airborne from Waddington. Hit by flak and crashed in Noord Holland. All crew became PoWs.
Crew: P/O H.P.Clarke, Sgt F.M.Wilkes, Sgt G.E.Harris, Sgt J.L.Brooks

44 Squadron Hampden KM-J, Summer 1940 crashed in fog at Waddington after night flying exercise. At the last minute, the pilot, Smythe, saw a lorry crossing the runway and pulled up at the edge of a cabbage field. The old hangars are in the background; the road on the right hand side is Mere Road.

(Aircrew Remembered)

S/L CE Johnson (Pilot) *Sgt H G Collins (Observer)*

Both KIA 24th of May 1940 when their Hampden L4161 was hit by flak and crashed near Aachen.

P/O Bernard Green flew his first mission with 44 Sqn on 20th of July 1940, in Hampden L4087, mine-laying in the Baltic. Hit by flak and crashing into the sea, Green swam to the Danish coast. He was picked up by the Danish police and handed over to the Germans. He was held in Stalag Luft III and was one of the Great Escapers. Recaptured, he was lucky not to have been chosen to be one of the fifty to be shot.

P/O Bernard Green

Hampden Cockpit

To get his injured captain out of the pilot seat, Dave Romans had to sit on his prone body (with the seat back down as here) while his wireless operator/gunner pulled the pilot out from under him.

Battle damage done to 44 Squadron Hampden AD982.

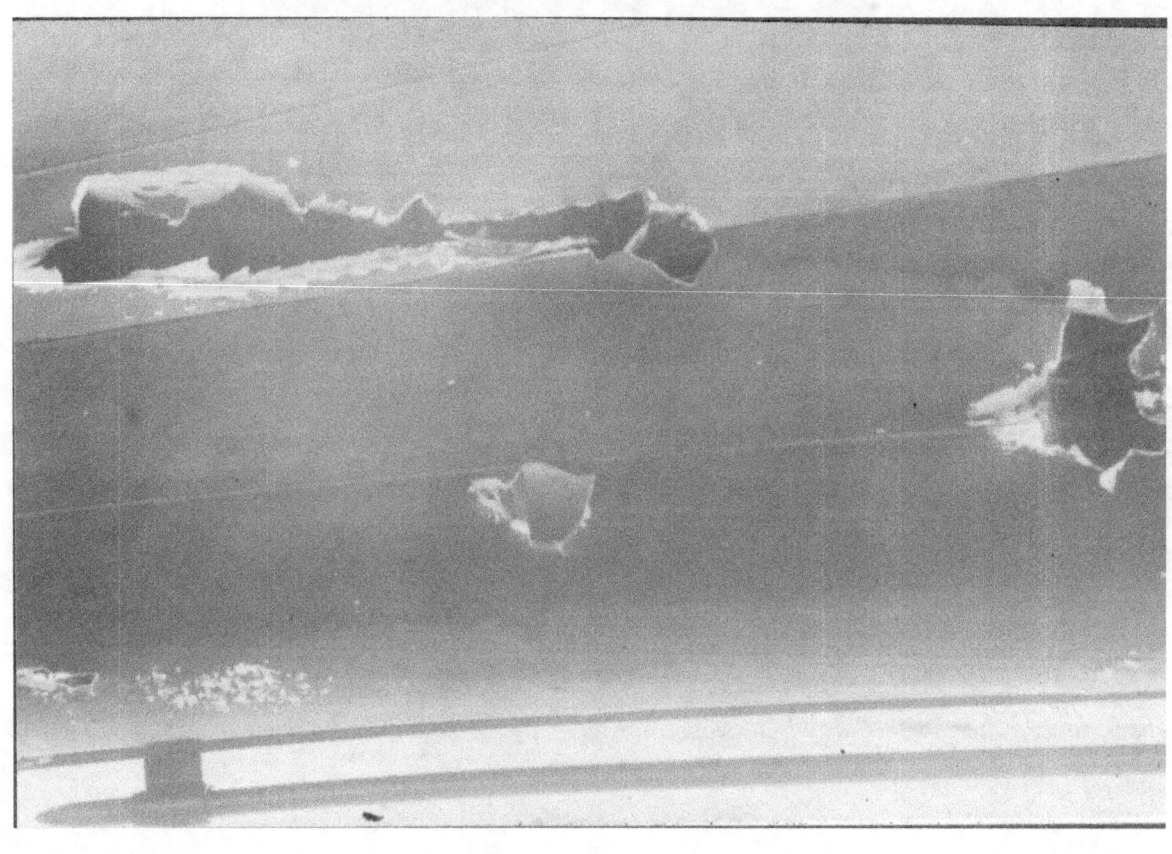

12/13th August 1940. The original shot of the destruction of the Dortmund-Ems Canal for which F/L R A B Learoyd was awarded the VC.

Modern views of the Dortmund Ems canal which was attacked by F/L Learoyd.

(Andreas Wachtel)
Present day parts of the Dortmund Ems Canal which had been attacked in 1940.

(Andreas Wachtel)

Above and below: Damage to 44 Sqn Hampden P4414 during an attack on the invasion barges at Ostend 7th of September 1940. The aircraft crew were W/C Reid DFC (Pilot), P/O Lowe (Nav), Sgt Jim Taylor (W.Op/AG), Sgt Keith Street (AG). They and the aircraft returned safely.

F/O Graham Ross of 44 Squadron at Waddington in 1940. The other figure could be his gunner Keith Street.

F/O Graham Ross and Sergeant Keith Street (RNZAF) after the awards of the DFC and DFM respectively.

Two Hampdens (L4171 and L4087) parked on the grass outside the Waddington Watch Office. The aircraft in the background is an Avro Anson.

Two Squadron Hampdens. Note the pilot's fixed machine gun in the nose section.

A group of 44 Sqn Air Gunners.

F/L Jeffcote
Gunnery Leader

Gunners – McGregor, Saville, Stacey and Tagg

Probably Hampden X2997 which crashed into one of the old hangars in fog on return from Merseburg on 16-17th of October 1940.

Damage to the Waddington hangar October 1940

German map of Waddington 1940

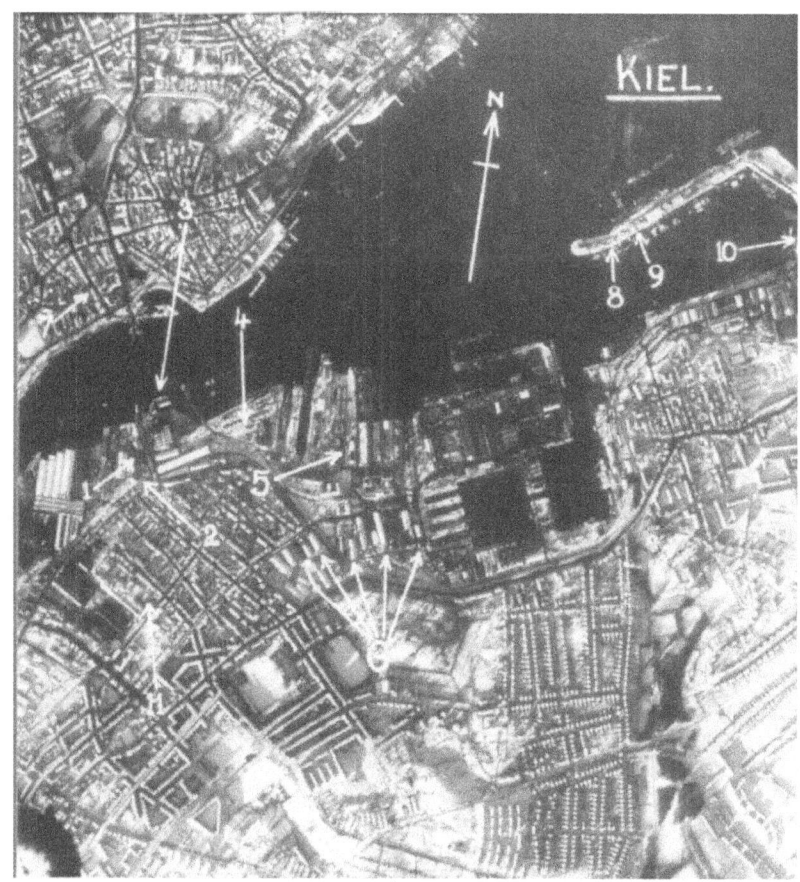

*A recce photo of Kiel docks 21st of December 1940 at 11.05GMT.
Used to brief 44 Sqn Lancaster crews on their target.*

The rear of a Manchester, a type used only by the 44 Sqn Conversion Flight.

F/O Peter Ball (right) pictured when a sergeant with his brother Leslie, who died in November 1940 while flying a Hampden with 49 Sqn. A third brother, Ken, was also a pilot killed in Bomber Command. Peter was killed in 1942.

F/O French and crew 11th of April 1940

Waddington 1940
L – R: P/O G E Grindley, Corr, P/O F E Eustace, Jill, F/O D J Penman

Jeff Jeffcote, Panda Ridpath, Ray Baker

Bombing up a Hampden (not 44 Sqn).

Drinking in a 'local' 23rd of October 1940.
L – R: F/L Dutton (PoW), unknown lady, P/O Dingwall, P/O A S Luxmoore (KIA 26th of June 1940), F/O Taylor (KIA 12 April 1940), P/O Dutton, /L Weir, P/O Homer DFC (KIA), Mrs Weir.

"The Drunks" - Unknown, P/O Robertson (Rhodesian), Ray Baker.

44 (Rhodesia) Squadron. A crew studying a map held by their Adjutant F/L Grummett.
L – R: F/Sgt Palmer, F/O Taylor, The Adjutant, W/O Smythe, Sgt Johnson. (Press photograph)

January 1941

A second successive severe winter restricted operations at the start of the year, when most of the effort was directed at French and German ports. The Command detailed 141 aircraft for operations on New Year's Night, with Bremen posted as the year's first target for 5 Group, which detailed ten Hampdens each from Scampton, Lindholme and Waddington. The briefings covered two targets, the Korff A G oil refinery, which the ORB suggested was also a depository for food stocks, and, it is believed, the Focke-Wulf aircraft factory in the south-eastern district of Hemelingen. The Waddington element of ten aircraft took off in unpromising weather conditions between 17.20 and 17.40 with S/L Smales the senior pilot on duty. As always, there would be contradictory reports concerning the weather during the outward journey, for which we have to rely on the testimony of crews from other squadrons. Some described the conditions as good, while others complained of a snowstorm over eastern England that extended as high as 11,000 feet, and severe icing as they climbed over the North Sea. A number of crews turned back, citing the weather, and this may have been the cause of the early return of Sgt Dart and crew after some three hours. The others reached the target area, where the cloud had built to between eight and ten-tenths, despite which, most crews located their aiming points without difficulty, aided in part by the intensity of the defences. It was, in fact, the flak and DR (dead-reckoning) that guided P/O Smith and crew to the approximate position of the refinery, but they were by no means certain of what lay beneath them as they released three bombs from 3,000 feet more in hope than expectation. On the way home over Holland, they came upon an aerodrome situated some twelve miles south-east of Amsterdam, at which they aimed two bombs from 7,000 feet, observing bursts close to buildings on the western edge. The 44 Squadron crews were carrying six 250 pounders plus two small bomb containers (SBCs) of 4lb incendiaries, and S/L Smales delivered a stick across the aiming point from 10,000 feet, observing nothing of the impact as he weaved his way through the intense flak. Sgt Atkins and crew dropped four 250 pounders in the target area from 9,000 feet, and two more from the same height on Delmenhorst aerodrome as they headed south-east towards the Dutch frontier. F/O Penman and crew described the target area as well ablaze as they arrived and watched from 11,000 feet as their stick fell short of the aiming point and burst in the adjoining docks area. The others carried out their attacks from 10,000 and 11,000 feet, observing many fires, the glow from which remained visible for eighty miles into the return journey. On arrival at the Lincolnshire coast, most crews responded to diversion orders because of a snowstorm and a cloud base as low as 600 feet. Crews were confident of an effective operation, which was partially confirmed by local reports of modest damage, citing the Focke-Wulf aircraft factory as among the industrial buildings hit, while fourteen apartment blocks had been destroyed, and three hundred others damaged.

5 Group returned to Bremen twenty-four hours later with eight Hampdens from Hemswell and Scampton, on a night of technical failures and wasted effort. On the 3rd, the new bomber station at Coningsby was declared open on a Care & Maintenance basis and would shortly welcome 106 Squadron as its first resident unit. Also, on this day, the decision was taken to draft all Rhodesian aircrew into 44 Squadron as they became available. This would lead, ultimately, to the adoption of the title, Rhodesia, to be inserted after the squadron number, once Rhodesian aircrew predominated. That night, Scampton sent fifteen Hampdens back to Bremen as part of an overall force of seventy-one aircraft, which benefitted from improved weather conditions and inflicted further damage that was confirmed by local sources.

Orders were received at Hemswell, Lindholme and Waddington on the 4th, to prepare thirty Hampdens between them for an operation that night against an unnamed Hipper class German cruiser in a dry dock at Brest. A process of elimination suggests that it was the Admiral Hipper herself, which had been raiding in the Atlantic following her part in the Norwegian campaign. Laid down in the Blohm & Voss shipyards in 1935, she had a length of 673 feet and displaced 18,500 tons, and was one of three of her design, including Prinz Eugen, which entered service in August 1940. The 5 Group contingent was part of an overall force of fifty-three aircraft, while others, four from Finningley and two from Waddington, were to take care of mining duties in the Artichoke garden off Lorient. S/L Fleming and P/O Broadhead and their crews were assigned to the latter, and took off at 16.50, leaving the six members of the bombing brigade on the ground until their departure between 18.05 and 18.20. Flying out over the Dorset coast at Chesil Beach in good conditions, they soon encountered a layer of eight-tenths cloud over the Channel at between 3,000 and 6,000 feet, which persisted all the way to the French coast and beyond. The target was easily identified on approach by the reflection of the searchlights in the cloud, and the volume of tracer breaking through it to reach 12,500 feet. Crews spent up to seventy-five minutes orbiting the target area and running across the estimated position of the aiming point, seeking one of the few gaps in the nine to ten-tenths cloud cover, but none from Waddington positively identified the target vessel. They bombed on estimated positions from between 2,000 and 6,000 feet in the face of an intense searchlight and flak defence but saw little of the results as they took evasive action. Sgt Jones and crew returned without carrying out an attack, and Sgt Stammers and crew walked away from L4042, which crashed on landing at Brackley, but was repairable. While the above was in progress, S/L Fleming and P/O Broadbent planted their vegetable each into the briefed locations from 500 and 600 feet.

On the 8th, S/L Stubbs arrived from 106 Squadron at Finningley to take command of the Boston Flight. However, his services would soon be required as temporary commanding officer of 144 Squadron, from where he would return to Waddington as a flight commander with 207 Squadron, before, ultimately, securing his first permanent command with 49 Squadron at Scampton. The naval shipbuilding yards at Wilhelmshaven were earmarked as the target for thirty-two aircraft that night, ten provided by 5 Group from Lindholme and Waddington, while sixteen other aircraft were assigned to Emden, some forty miles to the west. Nine further Hampdens were required for mining duties in the Eglantine garden in the Elbe estuary, and these were also provided by 44 and 50 Squadrons. The aiming point for the main element was the battleship Tirpitz, for which 44 Squadron briefed the crews of F/O Penman, P/Os Sandford and Stockings and F/Sgt Trickett, and they took off together with the gardeners, led by S/L Fleming, between 17.20 and 17.35. For a change, the weather conditions would act in their favour, although this was not immediately apparent as ten-tenths cloud blanketed the North Sea right up to the Dutch coast. It began to break up gradually, and, by the time the target area drew near, crews were able to map-read under clear skies and bright moonlight. F/O Penman attacked from east to west with four 500 pounders from 9,000 feet and saw one score a direct hit. As he climbed away to the west, he observed Jever aerodrome 11,000 feet below, and dropped his two remaining 250 pounders in its direction, without observing any impact. P/O Sandford ran in from the south to deliver four 500 and two 250 pounders from 10,000 feet, which, he believed, burst in the centre of the target, while F/Sgt Trickett found that the snow-covered ground and frozen water impeded identification. His bombs went down from 10,000 feet, and those of P/O Stockings from five hundred feet higher, but neither observed the results in the glare of an intense searchlight and flak defence. Meanwhile, the five gardeners had planted their vegetables into the briefed locations from between 600 and 900 feet, and P/O Broadhead and crew had followed up by aiming two 250 pounders from 1,200 feet at a merchantman of some two to three thousand tons anchored fifteen miles off Wilhelmshaven, narrowly missing it. P/O Robertson and crew came upon a similar "blacked out" vessel some two miles out in Jade Bay, the crew of which, had they been above deck, would have been showered by the splash from the near-miss.

The Commander-in-Chief, Sir Richard Peirse, had decided on launching one major raid each month on an important industrial city, for which Gelsenkirchen was selected on the 9th, and a force of 135 aircraft assembled. 5 Group detailed the Hemswell squadrons to take part, and the crews were briefed to aim for one of the synthetic oil plants, while four Finningley crews went mining in Kiel Bay. In the event, fewer than half of the force reached the assigned target area, and bombs were reported in parts of Gelsenkirchen and its environs. On the following night, thirty-five Hampdens and Wellingtons were detailed to go in search of the Tirpitz again at Wilhelmshaven, and the 5 Group ORB recorded that all sixteen of the former were provided by Scampton, completely ignoring the fact that nine of them actually belonged to 44 Squadron and departed Waddington between 02.20 and 02.55 on the 12th with S/L Smales the senior pilot on duty and last away. They had been preceded into the air between 01.35 and 02.15 by five crews bound for the Radish garden, which lay in Denmark's Baltic waters between Fehmarn and Lolland islands. As they approached the Schillig Roads area, Sgt Dart and crew began to experience a problem with the port engine and decided it unwise to press on to the western Baltic, choosing instead to plant their vegetable in the Eglantine garden in the Elbe estuary, where they found eight to nine-tenths cloud with a base at 1,300 to 1,500 feet and three miles visibility. Sgt Stott and crew had been the last of the gardening element to depart Waddington, and, by the time that they also arrived in the Eglantine area, believed they had insufficient time to reach their allotted garden on the other side of the Schleswig-Holstein peninsula. They too delivered their mine in an almost identical location from 500 feet, but, curiously, reported doing so under clear skies. The others identified the target area, which lay under five to six-tenths cloud, and delivered their mines from 500 and 800 feet, after which, P/O Broadhead and crew spotted a vessel of between two and three thousand tons steaming west and scored near misses with their two wing-mounted 250 pounders. P/O Carpenter and crew came upon a similar vessel moored off the coast, which they also narrowly missed with their bombs. Sgt Ayton and crew were on their way home and heading for the coast east-north-east of Kiel at 3,000 feet, when they spotted a small ship some six miles from the port, which they, too, missed by a hundred yards.

Meanwhile, on the western side of the Schleswig-Holstein peninsula, crews encountered ten-tenths cloud with a base at around 6,000 feet, below which, for those prepared to venture beneath it, visibility was ten miles. Only P/O Smith and crew of the 44 Squadron participants positively identified the primary target, which they attacked with four 500 pounders and 120 x 4lb incendiaries from 3,500 feet, observing three bursts in the centre of the target area. The remaining eight crews roamed over the coastal region at between 5,000 and 14,000 feet, occasionally finding a gap in the cloud, which enabled them to spot something at which to aim their bombs. Four let theirs go on estimated positions over Wilhelmshaven, while F/O Penman released his over what he believed to be Bremen, and P/O Skinner on a concentration of shipping twenty miles north of Emden. At least, all returned safely, from what was a typically ineffective operation for this period of the war.

During a period of inactivity for Waddington, Lindholme was notified on the 12th that it would be responsible for bombing operations that night, along with an element from Hemswell, when the target for the second time was the Hipper class cruiser at Brest. They took off into nine to ten-tenths cloud that persisted all the way out over the Dorset coast and the Channel, and it was only as the French coast drew near that the cloud began to disperse. By the time they reached Brest, the skies were empty and the target area clearly visible under the light of the moon. An intense searchlight and flak defence awaited them as they focussed on the dock layout, which could be identified, but none claimed to pick out the target vessel. 44 Squadron was not involved when a dozen 5 Group crews were briefed on the 13th for gardening sorties in the Jellyfish and Beech areas, respectively off the Biscay ports of Brest and St-Nazaire.

In a directive issued on the 15th, the Air Ministry had decided that an all-out assault against oil related targets would eventually take its toll on the German war effort, and operations from now on would reflect this. A list of seventeen sites was drawn up, the top nine of which represented 80% of Germany's synthetic oil production, but it was to be February before Peirse was able to comply. In the meantime, a force of ninety-six aircraft was assembled on the 15th to target the dockyards at Wilhelmshaven that night, and Hemswell provided the seventeen Hampdens. Returning crews claimed many fires in the town, and local sources confirmed damage to the head post office, main police station, army barracks, dock offices and seven commercial buildings.

Waddington and Scampton detailed a further fifteen Hampdens on the 16th to return to Wilhelmshaven to target Tirpitz as part of an overall force of eighty-one aircraft, on a night when the weather conditions would prove to be inhospitable. Seven 44 Squadron crews were briefed for this main event, while two others were to attend to mining duties in the Jellyfish garden off Brest. The latter took off first, F/O Carpenter and crew becoming airborne at 20.30, and, according to the 5 Group ORB, a second but unnamed crew came to grief during take-off, although without serious damage to aircraft or occupants. It would be more than six hours before the bombing element took to the air, by which time the Carpenter crew had returned to report a successful delivery of their mine from 600 feet. The 44 Squadron ORB listed only the departure of the crews of S/L Smales, P/O Sandford, P/O Robertson and Sgt Stott between 03.10 and 04.00, omitting three others, one of which returned early with technical problems, while two failed to locate the primary or alternative targets. It was extremely cold as they negotiated the North Sea crossing, and Germany's north-western coast was found to be concealed beneath ten-tenths cloud, which prevented a large number of crews from identifying the port. Only P/O Robertson and Sgt Stott of the Waddington element claimed to have found Tirpitz, or, at least, that section of the dockyard in which she was believed to be, and each released four 500lb SAP bombs and two 250 pounders from 9,000 and 10,000 feet respectively, without observing the results. S/L Smales failed to locate the primary target, but, through a gap in the cloud, spotted a railway station some fourteen miles north-east of Emden, probably at Aurich, which he attacked with a 1,000 pounder from 14,000 feet. The two 500 pounders hung up and were jettisoned "live" somewhere over German territory. P/O Sandford and crew followed a railway line south to the port of Emden, where they delivered a 1,000 pounder and two of 500lbs, which set off one large fire and three small ones some two hundred yards to the west of the docks.

Thereafter, twelve consecutive nights of operations were cancelled because of severe weather conditions, which rendered airfields frozen under a blanket of snow, and then left them waterlogged as a thaw set in. On the 27th, King George VI and Queen Elizabeth visited Waddington to conduct an investiture, in which W/C Reid, F/O Clayton and P/O Lewis received the DFC, F/O Scrutton was made an MBE, and the newly commissioned P/O Ayton was awarded a Bar to his DFM. Former squadron members, F/Os Eustace and Siebert, now with 207 Squadron, were also recipients of the DFC. After the ceremony, His Majesty carried out an inspection of the resident squadrons, while Her Majesty performed a similar duty among the WAAF ranks, before a brief visit to various sections and the viewing of a Hampden, a 207 Squadron Manchester and a Boston brought the tour to an end.

When operations finally resumed for 5 Group on the 29th, Wilhelmshaven, or more specifically, the Tirpitz, was posted as the target yet again, for a force this time of nine Hampdens from Lindholme and twenty-five Wellingtons. The Tirpitz remained elusive, and those locating the target area mostly bombed the town, inflicting, according to local sources, a degree of residential damage. During the course of the month, the squadron took part in nine operations, and dispatched fifty sorties without loss.

February 1941

February began as January had ended, with ports occupying the bulk of the Command's attention, although the accent shifted to those in France and Belgium. 5 Group dispatched a dozen Hampdens to attack warships in Brest on the night of the 2/3rd, and eleven more, all from Waddington, to lay mines in the Jellyfish and Artichoke gardens off Brest and Lorient twenty-four hours later. The 44 Squadron scribe chose only to record the names of the seven crews who delivered the contents of their bomb bays, while ignoring the four others. They had to wait until the early hours of the 4th before taking off between 03.25 and 03.45, and the fact that six of the successful crews had been assigned to Jellyfish, enables one to assume that the remaining five had been given Artichoke as their destination, and that, perhaps, the weather conditions over that area had defeated all but one. P/O Ross and crew offered no hint as to the conditions, recording only that they delivered their vegetable as briefed from 500 feet, observing the parachute to open and the weapon to splash down. Some fifty miles along the coast to the north-west, the others located the pinpoints from which to begin the timed runs and released their mines from 500 to 800 feet between 05.45 and 06.50, laying a lethal chain of high-explosives, hopefully to catch U-Boots on their way to their Atlantic feeding grounds. Only Sgt Atkins and crew found a target for their 250 pounders, and this was an aerodrome at Trequier, which they came upon as they crossed the French coast homebound at 2,300 feet at 05.40.

In a new departure for night raids, the Command assigned a specific target to each of 3, 4 and 5 Groups on the 4th, French ports for the first two-mentioned, and the Ruhr city of Düsseldorf for 5 Group. Thirty Hampdens were made ready at Scampton, Hemswell and Lindholme, while Waddington remained off the Order of Battle. It was a night when the moon was waxing towards full and clear weather conditions prevailed up to within about ten minutes of the target, when eight to ten-tenths cloud obscured the ground. However, an intense searchlight and flak defence left them in no doubt that they were over the target, whether or not they caught a glimpse of it through small gaps in the cloud. Bombs were dropped on estimated positions, and no details of the outcome emerged. The weather deteriorated again to keep 5 Group on the ground on the next two nights, but the Group Meteorological Section staff managed to find a window of acceptable weather across the Channel on the north-eastern coast of France on the 7th. This was sufficient to accommodate a dozen Scampton and fifteen Lindholme Hampdens, which carried out a raid on shipping and dock installations at Dunkerque.

On the 8th, Hemswell and Waddington were ordered to prepare nine and six Hampdens respectively for an operation that night against a specific target in Mannheim. Sadly, the 44 Squadron scribe listed only five crews taking off between 01.40 and 01.50, and they were those of F/O Robertson, P/O Ross, F/Sgt Trickett and Sgts Jones and Stammers. Most reached the target area after flying south-east across Belgium and entering Germany via Luxembourg, but two layers of cloud blotted out the ground, forcing crews to descend in an attempt to break into clear air to establish their whereabouts. In the event, all would be forced to bomb on e.t.a., on estimated positions, F/O Robertson and crew delivering their four 500 pounders from 3,500 feet at 04.20, and completely losing the bursts through the density of the cloud. Just five minutes behind, Sgt Jones and crew came down to 2,200 feet, but found themselves still enveloped in cloud, and climbed back to 4,000 feet to deliver their four 500 pounders, also failing to catch a glimpse of a burst. It was 04.50 by the time that P/O Ross and crew were sufficiently confident of their general location to risk two 250 pounders from 8,000 feet but decided to take the other two and 120 x 4lb incendiaries home. Sgt Stammers and crew had been first to arrive in the target area, but on finding ten-tenths cloud between 2,000 and 3,000 feet, headed north towards the Ruhr, and, at 04.10, dropped four 500 pounders and a single 250 pounder from 5,000 feet onto industrial buildings believed to be in Bonn. F/Sgt Trickett and crew realised as they crossed into Germany that the prospects for success were low, and they let their four 500 pounders go over the estimated position of Aachen from 3,500 feet, before landing at Hemswell after a trip of five minutes under five hours. In contrast, the Robertson crew did not land until 10.20, eight-and-a-half hours after their departure.

On the following day, twenty-three Hampdens were detailed at Hemswell and Scampton to be sent against the Tirpitz at Wilhelmshaven, but heavy cloud again ruined the operation, and only one crew claimed to have attacked the primary target. While 5 Group conducted the two above-mentioned operations, the rest of the Command had stayed on the ground, and C-in-C Peirse had not yet implemented the January directive against Germany's synthetic oil industry. First, he would launch his monthly "big" effort against a major industrial city, and orders went out across the Command on the 10th to prepare a force, which, at take-off time, would number 222 aircraft, a record for a single target. At briefings, the crews learned that the northern city of Hannover was to be their destination, and that they were assigned to attack one of a variety of aiming points in the industrial sector. The city was a major centre of war production, the home among others to the Accumulatoren-Fabrik A G, manufacturers of lead acid batteries for U-Boots and torpedoes, the Continental tyre and rubber factory at Limmer, the Deurag-Nerag synthetic oil refinery at Misburg, the VLW (Volkswagen) metalworks, and the Maschinenfabrik Niedersachsen Hannover and Hanomag factories, which were producing guns and tracked vehicles. A second operation was also planned for this night involving forty-three aircraft in an attack on oil storage tanks in Rotterdam, and, in a demonstration of the burgeoning power of the Command, the contribution by 3 Group of 119 aircraft would be the first time that any group had exceeded one hundred aircraft. Among them, as part of the Rotterdam force, would be the first three Stirling sorties.

5 Group notified all of its operational stations to prepare for the main event, and forty-six Hampdens were made ready, eleven of them at Waddington, where take-off was safely accomplished between 22.30 and 23.00, with S/Ls Fleming and Smales the senior pilots on duty. The weather conditions were ideal, with clear skies and bright moonlight to assist navigation and map-reading, and all of the 44 Squadron participants reached the target area, pinpointing, initially, on the Steinhuder Lake to the west, and then the Maschsee to the south of the city centre. Over the target itself, around three-tenths cloud was reported at 7,000 feet, but it would have no influence on the course of the raid, which attracted what appeared to be only a limited and inaccurate light flak defence. This emboldened crews to circle, if necessary, to establish their positions and decide on a method of attack, and, in a number of cases, to descend to a fairly low level. Some adopted a glide approach, while most favoured bombing from a higher-level between 10,000 and 14,000 feet. The 44 Squadron crews ran in on a variety of headings to deliver a mix of loads from between 2,000 and 11,000 feet, P/O Ross and crew responsible for the lower altitude. P/O Stockings and crew reported six colossal fires and around

twenty others, and all reports by returning crews confirmed many explosions and fires, with buildings standing out black against the background of flames. A fire in the north of the city remained visible for fifty miles into the return flight, until obscured by cloud, but no reports came out of Hannover to confirm or deny the success of the operation.

On the 11th, a force of seventy-one Hampdens, Wellingtons and Whitleys was made ready for Bremen that night, while eighteen Wellingtons and eleven Hampdens returned to Hannover. 44 Squadron briefed five crews for Bremen, which departed Waddington between 18.05 and 18.30 with S/L Smales the senior pilot on duty. They flew out over Skegness, crossing the North Sea over ten-tenths cloud, and arrived at the cloud-covered Dutch coast reliant upon dead-reckoning to take them to the target. When close to e.t.a., at Bremen, flares from other aircraft were observed, while black smoke puffs from exploding heavy flak shells and a few searchlights confirmed their close proximity to the primary target, which was hidden beneath eight to ten-tenths cloud with tops at around 6,000 feet. The flak was found to be intense and the heavy calibre particularly accurate as the Waddington crews carried out their attacks from between 8,000 and 10,500 feet, the results hidden by cloud. Fog over the bomber stations at home caused twenty-two aircraft to crash or be abandoned by their crews, three of them belonging to 5 Group, and one 83 Squadron crew died as a result.

The oil directive was finally implemented on the night of the 14/15th, when the Nordstern (Gelsenberg A G) refinery at Gelsenkirchen was attacked by Wellingtons, while Wellingtons and Blenheims tried their hand at a similar target at Homberg, situated on the West Bank of the Rhine opposite Duisburg. Both of these massively important plants were vital to the German war effort and employed the Bergius process to refine high-grade petroleum products such as aviation fuel. It was on this night that 207 Squadron had hoped to launch its maiden sorties, but the modifications to the Manchesters had taken twice the time planned for, and the aircraft had not been tested. On the following day, the DB7 (Boston) Flight was disbanded.

During the course of the 15th, seventy-three Wellingtons and Whitleys were made ready to attack the Sterkrade-Holten oil refinery located to the north of Oberhausen in the Ruhr, another Bergius-process plant. At the same time on 2 and 5 Group stations, thirty-seven Blenheims and thirty-three Hampdens were being prepared for an operation against the above-mentioned Homberg plant, ten of the latter at Waddington. *(The squadron ORB, never an easy document to negotiate, was somewhat chaotic during this period, and the Form 541 ran operations together without providing dates to separate one from another.)* They took off between 18.05 and 18.20 with S/Ls Fleming and Smales the senior pilots on duty, each carrying four 500 and two 250 pounders. They had no difficulty in locating the general target area, but cloud and haze combined with searchlight glare to confound many navigators and prevent identification of the primary target. Most crews simply followed the course of the Rhine, from either north or south, and only four of the Waddington crews released their bombs on estimated positions at Homberg, doing so from a perilously low 3,000 and 3,500 feet in the cases of Sgt Stott and P/O Ross respectively, and a more circumspect 11,000 feet by Sgt Dart and F/O Carpenter. The others selected Düsseldorf as an alternative target, which they attacked in the face of a hostile searchlight and flak defence from between 10,000 and 12,000 feet. Enemy intruders were operating over the bomber stations, and F/O Penman and crew reported being attacked over Lincoln, as a result of which, X2917 sustained some damage. S/L Smales lost his port engine to enemy fire in the Waddington circuit, but landed safely to report attempting to photograph the Homberg refinery before heading due south for ten miles to drop his bombs on Düsseldorf. F/Sgt Trickett and crew failed to locate a target and jettisoned their load "safe" somewhere over Holland.

On the 20th, Finningley was transferred out of 5 Group to be taken over by 7 Operational Training Group, and the evicted 106 Squadron moved south to take up residence at Coningsby. P/O Dave Romans had been screened after completing a first tour with 44 Squadron and was posted to 207 Squadron on this day to resume his operational career. He was joined in the posting by P/O Ayton DFM, the moves reflecting the high esteem in which both were held, which qualified them to be selected to participate in introducing the Manchester to operations. Romans would survive the brief period on Manchesters, sadly to lose his life in the coming September, after being recruited with others to pioneer operations on the Boeing B17 Fortress I with 2 Group's 90 Squadron.

5 Group would be out in force on the 21st when sending forty-two Hampdens to plant vegetables in the Jellyfish garden off the port of Brest. 44 Squadron was responsible for nine of them, and they departed Waddington between 18.00 and 18.20 with S/L Fleming the senior pilot on duty. They began the Channel crossing at the Dorset coast and set course for the target area in predominantly favourable conditions, encountering cloud over the sea, which had dispersed to five-tenths at 2,000 feet by the time that the target area drew near. F/O Carpenter and crew turned back with an intercom issue, leaving the others to establish pinpoints with ease in good visibility, particularly at Pointe-Saint-Mathieu on the headland west of the port, where searchlights ensnared some of the attackers and flak ships took pot-shots at them as they made their timed runs. Seven of the 44 Squadron crews successfully planted their vegetables in the briefed locations from between 600 and 800 feet, while Sgt Stammers and crew released theirs some three-and-a-half miles from the allotted spot.

5 Group would spend the next two nights on the ground, while a small force of Wellingtons targeted enemy warships at Brest on the 22nd and the docks at Boulogne twenty-four hours later. When orders arrived on 5 Group stations on the 24th, they signalled the introduction to operations of a new squadron and aircraft type. 207 Squadron had completed its working-up programme with the Manchester at Waddington and would contribute six of the type to this night's raid by fifty-seven aircraft on enemy warships at Brest. It had been a difficult gestation period for the squadron, and the coming operational career of the Manchester would be dogged by grounding orders caused largely by the unreliability of its Rolls-Royce Vulture engines. Despite this, and ignorant of the full extent of the problems that would occur, orders would be issued on the following day to reform 97 Squadron at Waddington as the second Manchester unit. Among those selected to launch 207 Squadron's new operational career were the former 44 Squadron members W/C Hyde, F/L Siebert, F/O Eustace and F/O Lewis. The Manchester would bring a massive increase in bomb-carrying capacity, and, on this night, each would carry a dozen 500 pounders to drop on the cruiser, Admiral Hipper, which was at berth at Brest. They were part of an overall force of fifty-seven aircraft, eighteen of them Hampdens, five of which belonged to 44 Squadron and departed Waddington between 18.05 and 18.25 loaded with four 500 and two 250 pounders each. They adopted the familiar route to the Brittany coast, passing to the west of the Channel Islands, and found the target to be under clear skies with good visibility, although searchlights and flak had advertised the whereabouts of the port from some distance away. The docks were identified clearly, but searchlight glare prevented any of the 44 Squadron element from glimpsing the enemy cruiser, and they were forced to run the gauntlet of intense flak of all calibres as they attacked from between 6,000 and 11,000 feet, most assessing the impact of their bombs to be in the vicinity of Dock 8.

Düsseldorf was posted as the target on the 25th, for which a force of eighty aircraft was assembled. Hemswell and Scampton provided the 5 Group contribution of twenty-two Hampdens, whose crews were briefed probably for oil-related targets. They encountered poor weather conditions and ten-tenths cloud over the target, and this resulted in only around seven bomb loads falling within the city. Briefings on the 26th revealed Cologne to be the target for a force of 126 aircraft, for which Hemswell, Lindholme and Scampton made ready twenty-eight Hampdens, while Waddington contributed five Manchesters. The crews were briefed to attack one of two specific aiming points in the city, but despite the claims of returning crews, the majority failed to find the mark, and bombs fell mostly on the city's western edge and in outlying communities. 44 Squadron was also active on this night, to conduct mining sorties in the Eglantine garden in the Elbe estuary, for which six crews took off between 18.35 and 18.55 with F/O Robertson the senior pilot on duty. They flew out over the Lincolnshire coast in favourable weather conditions to follow the chain of Frisian islands to the target area. Sgt Lauderdale and crew picked up a coded message, for which they did not have the appropriate code book, and, uncertain of the meaning, decided to turn back and plant the vegetable in one of the "free" mining areas. The others pressed on and delivered their stores into the allotted locations from between 600 and 900 feet without incident. On the way home, F/O Robertson spotted a group of bright lights on the eastern end of Norderney and bombed them from 3,000 feet with the two wing-mounted 250 pounders.

The Admiralty continued to maintain pressure on the Command to deal with the enemy's capital ships, and it was the Tirpitz at Wilhelmshaven that featured in briefings on the 28th. 116 aircraft were made ready across the groups, eleven of the Hampdens at Waddington, and they took off between 01.05 and 01.40 with S/L Smales the senior pilot on duty. Bomb loads were either two 2,000 pounders or four 500 and two 250 pounders, the majority of which would not reach the target in the face of severe icing conditions, ten-tenths cloud at heights up to 15,000 feet and extreme darkness. The newly promoted W/O Trickett and crew turned back with an engine issue at 02.10, when some forty miles west of Vlieland, while S/L Smales decided not to fight the conditions and bombed the aerodrome on Texel from 10,000 feet at 02.45. Sgt Stott and crew were experiencing severe tail-flutter as they approached the Dutch coast and dropped their load from 3,000 feet onto the well-lit Schellingwouder aerodrome near Amsterdam. Sgt Dart and crew found Bremerhaven rather than Wilhelmshaven fifteen miles to the west and bombed it at 03.35 from 10,000 feet without observing the results. F/O Carpenter and crew abandoned their attempt to locate the primary target at 03.50 and aimed their load from 8,000 feet at a flak battery on the southern extremity of Emden. P/O Sandford and crew made it all the way to Wilhelmshaven, where the town was distinguishable, but not the docks, and they attacked from 8,000 feet on a north-easterly heading. Sgt Atkins and crew risked life and limb in a dive attack on the primary target from 4,000 down to 3,000 feet at 03.20, releasing two 2,000 pounders, but failing to observe the bursts in the searchlight glare. P/O Hazelden and crew made landfall at Den Helder in reasonable conditions, which, by the time they reached the target, had deteriorated and left the coastal region concealed beneath ten-tenths cloud. They descended from 12,000 to 7,500 feet but could still not pick up the docks or an alternative target and returned their two 2,000 pounders to store. Sgt Stammers and crew were on their bombing run at 5,000 feet and were one mile west of the aiming point when the starboard engine cut at 03.00, persuading them to dump their two 2,000 pounders "live" immediately. Twenty minutes later, the recalcitrant engine picked up, and they returned safely to base without further incident. On e.t.a., at the primary target at 03.05, Sgt Skinner and crew dived through thunder cloud from 12,000 feet, only for the port engine to cut out for thirty seconds. They decided to go round again, but completely lost their bearings in the cloud, and abandoned the sortie. Sgt Lauderdale and crew identified the target area, but not the Tirpitz and Bauhafen, and delivered four 500 pounders in a pass from north to south at 8,500 feet without observing even the flash of a burst.

The irreconcilable dichotomy between Bomber Command claims and local reports would continue throughout the year and beyond and would culminate in a damning report in the coming August that would threaten the very existence of an independent bomber force. During the course of the month the squadron took part in nine operations and dispatched seventy-four sorties without loss.

March 1941

The new month began with a return to Cologne on the night of the 1/2nd by an initial force of 131 assorted aircraft, of which forty-four Hampdens were provided by 5 Group from its stations at Coningsby, Hemswell, Lindholme and Scampton. The crews enjoyed favourable weather conditions over the North Sea and were able to firmly establish their positions as they made landfall over the Scheldt estuary and headed across Holland. They arrived in the target area to find clear skies and easily identifiable ground features, predominantly the distinctive bends in the River Rhine, which provided most with the references they required to run in on the briefed aiming point. Bombs were delivered from a variety of altitudes up to 16,000 feet in the face of an intense defensive response, and returning crews claimed a successful operation. This was confirmed by local sources, which reported extensive damage in central districts, particularly in the docks areas on both banks of the Rhine.

The threat of adverse weather conditions caused a reduction in the 5 Group force briefed to attack the Admiral Hipper at Brest on the night of the 2/3rd, and, ultimately, it was left to eight crews from 44 Squadron to take off between 01.00 and 01.35 with F/O Carpenter the senior pilot on duty. According to the ORB, a ninth Hampden, with an unnamed crew on board, crashed during the take-off run, but there were no casualties. Although the weather conditions turned out to be better than anticipated, visibility over the port was insufficiently good to enable the crews to identify the vessel, and most bombed the general area of the docks from 1,500 to 11,000 feet between 04.20 and 05.30. It was P/O Sandford and crew who were responsible for the low-level attack, braving the defences in a shallow-dive approach from north-east to southwest to deliver five 500 pounders, a wing-mounted sixth having hung up. The fact that they attacked at 05.20 suggests that they had spent a considerable time in the target area, drawing a bead on the aiming point and working out the best method to hit it. On return, they were adamant that they had identified the correct basin but could not confirm the presence of the Admiral Hipper. Others reported bomb bursts in the town to the north of the docks, and Sgt Jones and crew described diving down to 1,500 feet after bombing, and strafing searchlights as they retreated. P/O Ross and crew saw two 500 pounders burst in railway yards, two among sheds to the west of the docks and two at the northern end of the docks but reported that it was too dark to identify the cruiser. They commented, that if it had been in the dock, it must have been hit.

A force of seventy-one aircraft was assembled later on the 3rd to send once more against Cologne, for which Coningsby and Scampton provided the 5 Group element, while Waddington made ready three Hampdens and two Manchesters for a return to the Admiral Hipper at Brest. The 44 Squadron trio, consisting of the crews of P/Os Hazelden and Skinner and Sgt Stammers, took off at 18.30, and encountered ten-tenths cloud and severe icing conditions, which caused P/O Hazelden and crew to abandon their sortie when thirty miles short of their destination. Over the target, the cloud base was down to between 500 and 1,000 feet, and heavy rain added to the difficulties experienced by P/O Skinner and crew, as they stooged around from 21.00 to 22.30 in search of the aiming point, before giving up and returning their six 500 pounders to store. Sgt Stammers and crew refused to be beaten, and eventually ran across the docks from west to east at 1,500 feet, with visibility at no more than two hundred yards at best. They identified dry docks 1 and 2 and delivered six 500 pounders in a stick, observing flashes but nothing else. They arrived home to discover that they alone had carried out an attack, after both 207 Squadron Manchesters had failed to locate the target.

Thereafter, the weather took a hand to keep most of the Command on the ground for the next week, and it was during this period, on the 9th, that the Air Ministry responded to the urgent and burgeoning threat posed by U-Boots, which were claiming a massive tonnage of shipping crossing the Atlantic in convoys with vital war supplies. A new Directive was issued, which would unleash a concerted campaign against this menace and its partner in crime, the Focke-Wulf Kondor long-range maritime reconnaissance bomber. These two threats were to be attacked where-ever they could be found, at sea, in their bases in the occupied ports, and at their point of manufacture in the shipyards and in the assembly and component factories. A new target list was drawn up, which was headed by Kiel, Hamburg and Vegesack (Bremen), all of which were home to U-Boot construction yards, and Bremen itself, which also boasted a Focke-Wulf aircraft factory in its south-eastern Hemelingen district. Other related targets included the diesel engine plants at Mannheim and Augsburg, aircraft factories at Dessau, and, of course, the U-Boot bases at Brest, Lorient and St Nazaire. Until otherwise instructed, this was to be the focus of Peirse's efforts, and, only occasionally, would he be able prosecute the oil campaign.

When 5 Group resumed operations on the 10th, only Hemswell and Waddington were involved in sending nineteen Hampdens back to Cologne. The nine-strong 44 Squadron element took off between 18.50 and 19.10 with S/L Smales and the newly promoted F/L Carpenter the senior pilots on duty, having been briefed to aim for specific targets in the heart of the city. They all arrived to find favourable weather conditions, which enabled them to identify the Hohenzollern bridge over the Rhine with the industrial and communications concentrations on the East Bank, and the Cathedral and main railway station close to the West Bank. They were carrying a mix of loads, but mostly four 500 pounders and 120 x 4lb incendiaries, which were delivered from all points of the compass from 6,000 to 10,000 feet between 21.30 and 22.08. Bursts were observed on the railway line at the western end of the Hohenzollern bridge and in other central areas, and crews were confident of a successful operation. The weather conditions had deteriorated by the time they reached the English coast, and seven were forced to land at Tangmere in Sussex. X2918 failed to return with the crew of P/O Stocking DFC, and news eventually arrived via the Red Cross to confirm that they were in enemy hands. They had been homebound over the Dutch/German frontier near Venlo, when intercepted and shot down at 22.18 by Hptm Werner Streib of I./NJG1.

The new directive would be implemented first on the night of the 12/13th, at the end of a day of hectic activity across the Command, as aircraft were made ready for three major raids to be conducted that night. Eighty-eight aircraft were to attack the Blohm & Voss shipyards at Hamburg, while eighty-six other crews were briefed for the Focke-Wulf factory and the city of Bremen, and, finally, seventy-two aircraft were prepared for the long slog to Berlin to target two aiming points. 5 Group was to support the first-mentioned with forty Hampdens and four Manchesters, and the last-mentioned with thirty Hampdens, and, with the addition of a single freshman crew on gardening duties, this represented the largest effort undertaken by 5 Group thus far in the war. The four Manchesters and three 4 Group Halifaxes at Hamburg would be the first of their type to operate over Germany. The 44 Squadron briefing was conducted by S/L Fleming as temporary commanding officer, following the posting to HQ Bomber Command of W/C Reid a year to the day after his appointment. As matters turned out, it would be the briefest of spells at the helm. The squadron was to be involved in both operations, briefing six crews for Germany's capital city and four for its second city, and it was the latter element of P/O Hazelden and Sgts Jones, Mercer and Stott which departed Waddington first, between 19.40 and 20.10, leaving the Berlin element on the ground until 22.00. They climbed away into largely clear skies, but Sgt Mercer and crew were soon contending with an engine issue, and they turned back before even reaching the Lincolnshire coast. The others pressed on and arrived in the target area to find what were described as perfect weather conditions, which allowed easy identification of the aiming point once they had run the usual gauntlet of intense searchlights and flak from both banks of the Elbe. Each was carrying a 1,000 pounder and two 250 pounders, which they delivered on north to south bombing runs at 10,000 to 12,000 feet between 23.40 and 00.30. Sgt Stott and crew reported a large fire with a deep orange/red glow that resulted from their effort and sent a large white puff ascending to 1,000 feet. Sgt Jones and crew saw nothing to report, while the Hazelden crew watched their 1,000 pounder fall into an existing small fire and increase its volume considerably.

The Berlin-bound element took off between 22.00 and 22,25 with S/L Smales the senior pilot on duty, having been briefed to attack the main railway station, and were enjoying the favourable conditions as they crossed northern Holland on course for the gap between Bremen and the Hannover/Braunschweig area. It was when approaching the German frontier that P/O Robertson noticed an oil pressure problem, which would prevent him from reaching the primary target. An aerodrome appeared below at 01.15, at which two 250 pounders were aimed from 10,000 feet and seen to detonate on tarmac and buildings. They pressed on towards Hannover, which they reached at 12,000 feet shortly after 03.00, and dropped the 1,900lb bomb onto a railway junction in the south-eastern outskirts. As a parting shot before retreating to the west, the rear gunners each fired four hundred rounds at barrage balloons, two of which were observed to fall in flames. S/L Smales and crew were at 12,000 feet between Hannover and Braunschweig, when they spotted a train travelling west at 02.20, which they attacked with a 250 pounder, observing it to detonate on an adjacent track. They were unable to locate the primary aiming point in Berlin, and, instead, attacked a railway junction in the Neukolln district to the south-east of the city centre at 03.25. Sgt Atkins and crew followed the course of the River Spree from the south-east, and released their bombs at 02.50 from 10,000 feet, at a point where the river intersected railway track. They watched them fall directly onto the station, before heading out of the target area and noticing four trains approaching a bridge eight miles east of Stendal. They released their incendiaries onto the bridge from 1,000 feet, forcing the trains to stop, and then dived to 700 feet to circle the bridge and fire two hundred rounds at the trains. F/L Carpenter and crew attacked the primary target from 14,000 feet at 02.52, but overshot on the northern side, while Sgt Dart and crew followed up from 11,000 feet at 03.01, after clearly identifying the aiming point. Sgt Stammers and crew failed to locate it, despite searching for twenty minutes, and were homebound when coming upon a railway junction believed to be at Hildesheim, which they attacked from 11,000 feet at 02.30. Local sources reported sixty buildings damaged in Berlin, mostly in southern districts, while, at Hamburg, twenty high-explosive bombs and up to four hundred incendiaries had inflicted significant damage on the Blohm & Voss U-Boot construction yards and four other shipyards. Meanwhile, Wellingtons had attacked the Focke-Wulf factory at Bremen, and a number of hits had been scored there also.

Weather conditions remained favourable as preparations were put in hand on the 13th to return to Hamburg that night with a force of 139 aircraft, including a contribution from 5 Group of thirty-four Hampdens and five Manchesters. After one day in charge, S/L Fleming was posted to 144 Squadron as a flight commander, and S/L Smales stepped into the breach pending the appointment of a permanent successor to W/C Reid. 44 Squadron made ready eight Hampdens and dispatched them from Waddington between 19.35 and 20.00 with no senior pilots on duty, but on a night of poor serviceability, not all would reach the primary target. They crossed the Lincolnshire coast in the region of Skegness, and made their way independently of each other, as was the practice at this stage of the war, towards the enemy coast. P/O Broadhead noticed falling oil pressure in the starboard engine, which began to overheat, and he decided to lighten the load by jettisoning two 500 pounders when sixty-five miles into the North Sea crossing. The intention then was to press on, at least, to drop the remainder on an enemy coastal target, however, having covered one hundred miles, it became necessary to jettison the rest of the load and turn for home. Sgt Mercer and crew had progressed a further ten miles when an engine issue forced them to turn back, while P/O Hazelden and crew lost the use of their TR9 radio equipment, and also abandoned their sortie after reaching enemy territory. For an undisclosed reason, Sgt Jones and crew did not reach the primary target, and bombed a SEMO (self-evident military objective) in the form of a railway junction in Germany from 7,000 feet at 22.50. The others continued on to the target, where moonlight helped with identification of the aiming point, and Sgt Lauderdale and crew suffered massive frustration as their bomb load failed to release. They decided to cause as much damage as they could anyway and strafed the target area with nine hundred rounds in a dive from 8,000 down to 200 feet. This left Sgt Stott and crew to attack from a northerly starting point from 8,000 feet at 23.20, and P/O Smith on a south-easterly heading from 10,000 feet at 23.45. On return, the Smith crew reported spotting a convoy of four merchant vessels as they approached the enemy coast outbound at 23.10, and dropping a single 250 pounder, which narrowly missed the lead ship. The general consensus was of an effective raid, which local sources and post-raid reconnaissance confirmed had inflicted further damage on the Blohm & Voss shipyards and caused 119 fires in Hamburg generally, thirty-five of them classed as large.

A raid on the Hydriewerk-Scholven synthetic oil refinery at Gelsenkirchen was briefed out to twenty-one Hampden crews on the 14th, as part of an overall force of 101 aircraft assigned to a number of similar targets in the city. Waddington was not involved in what turned out to be the most successful attack yet on this industry, after some sixteen bomb loads hit the oil plant. Hemswell, Lindholme and Waddington were notified of a return to the Ruhr on the 15th, this time to attack a specific target in Düsseldorf. 44 Squadron made ready six Hampdens and dispatched them between 19.25 and 19.40 with S/L Smales the senior pilot on duty. After experiencing haze over base, they enjoyed good visibility with cloud east of the Trent all the way to the Dutch coast, where the skies cleared. With ten miles to go they hit a wall of searchlights, but, surprisingly little flak, and then it was the industrial haze that hid ground detail from the eyes of the bomb-aimers high above. However, the moon had risen as the crews were outbound, and its light glinted off the Rhine to offset to some extent the effects of the industrial haze and provide a firm pinpoint for F/L Carpenter and crew, who were the first from 44 Squadron to reach and attack the target. They delivered one 1,000 pounder and two 500 pounders from 9,000 feet at 21.50, ten minutes ahead of F/O Robertson and crew, whose four 500 pounders and incendiaries went down from 10,000 feet. S/L Smales and crew also attacked from 10,000 feet at 22.08, and watched their two 500 pounders, single 250 pounder and 120 x 4lb incendiaries burst in the target area and set off a number of fires. The remaining three crews were defeated by the visibility, P/O Smith and crew led astray to drop their load from 13,000 feet onto Neuss, facing Düsseldorf from the opposite bank of the Rhine. It was only as they retreated westwards at 22.05 that they realised their error. After failing to locate the primary target, Sgt Stammers and crew headed towards the north-west, where they released two 500 pounders from 10,000 feet over a searchlight concentration near the Uerdingen railway yards at Krefeld at 21.44. Twenty-five minutes later, racing for the Belgian coast, they dropped their 1,000 pounder on an aerodrome believed to be at Antwerp. Sgt Jones and crew turned south to search for an alternative target and found a railway junction believed to be at Aachen, which they attacked from 12,000 feet at 21.43.

It fell to Scampton and Coningsby to provide eighteen Hampdens on the 17th for a force of fifty-seven aircraft targeting shipyards in Bremen. The raid took place in excellent conditions, and returning crews claimed a successful outcome. Thirty-eight Hampdens and two Manchesters were detailed by 5 Group on the 18th for an operation that night against the Deutsche Werke U-Boot yards at Kiel, which would also involve fifty-seven Wellingtons and Whitleys. 44 Squadron dispatched six Hampdens in two sections of three at 18.50 and 18.55, with the intention that they would fly out in formation until daylight faded, but W/O Trickett turned back immediately with a failed intercom. The others made their way out over the Lincolnshire coast to encounter ten-tenths cloud that persisted all the way to the target area, and this would prevent some members of the force from establishing a pinpoint on the enemy coast. Sgt Stott and crew were approaching the western Frisians, when X3150 began to vibrate violently, upon which, with the island of Wangerooge in sight, they located its aerodrome and emptied the contents of their bomb bay from 8,000 feet at 21.12. This left four 44 Squadron crews to press on to the target area, where thick ground mist hindered aiming point location, although the searchlight and flak activity alerted them to its general whereabouts. The bomb loads were delivered from 12,000 and 13,000 feet between 21.50 and 22.15, and returning crews reported a number of large fires that remained visible for thirty minutes into the return flight. Local reports would claim this to be the heaviest raid yet on Kiel, mentioning an increase in the number of incendiaries, and confirming damage to the U-Boot yards.

S/L Smales handed command of the squadron to W/C Misselbrook on the 20th, and, like his predecessor, he would enjoy a lengthy term of office before it was brought to a premature end. That night, 5 Group committed forty-two Hampdens to an extensive programme of mining off the Biscay ports of Brest, Lorient and St-Nazaire, while three Manchesters and twenty-one Whitleys turned their attention upon U-Boots at the base being built on the Keroman peninsula on the southern extremity of Lorient. The first phase of the massive construction project had begun just weeks earlier, and would continue until January 1942, by which time K1, K2 and K3 would be completed and capable of sheltering thirty vessels and their crews under cover. The complex would boast a revolutionary lift system, which could raise U-Boots from the water and transport them across the facility to repair and servicing bays. The thickness of the concrete would render the structure impervious to the bombs available to Bomber Command at the time, and attacks would be directed predominantly at the town and its approaches to prevent access by road and rail. The nine 44 Squadron participants in the night's activities had been assigned to the Beech garden off St-Nazaire and departed Waddington between 18.25 and 18.45 with S/L Smales the senior pilot on duty. They headed for the south coast to begin the Channel crossing in daylight, but instrument failure ended P/O Smith's sortie over Oxfordshire, and they landed at Upper Heyford. The others enjoyed a quiet outward flight, bypassing the Lorient area, where the port defences were in action against the bombing brigade. The skies over St-Nazaire were clear, with visibility at around five miles, which enabled the crews to establish their pinpoints, probably on the familiar landmarks of La Calebasse Rocks and Belle-Ile, before carrying out timed runs to the release points. The mines went down from 650 to 900 feet between 21.30 and 22.55, after which, a number of crews sought out targets for their 250lb wing-mounted bombs. Sgt Stott and crew had already deployed theirs on the way out, against two merchant vessels moored off Saint-Brieuc on the northern coast of Brittany, which they had attacked from 4,000 feet at 21.00. Sgt Lauderdale and crew bombed the aerodrome at Vannes-Meucon from 6,000 feet on the way home at 22.30, and others went for docks, an aerodrome at Saint-Brieuc and gun emplacements.

Twelve Hampdens returned to Lorient on the night of 21/22nd, and encountered poor visibility that led to scattered bombing, while a handful of others went mining in the Deodar garden in the Gironde Estuary on the approaches to Bordeaux. With the moon out of commission for a period, and weather conditions over northern Germany unfavourable, 5 Group sent thirty Hampdens to Kiel on the 23rd, while Berlin played host to a force of sixty-three Wellingtons and Whitleys. Five crews from 44 Squadron were also assigned to the Kiel region, but their task was to mine the waters of the Radish garden in the Fehmarn Belt. They took off between 19.25 and 19.40, and encountered heavy cloud over the North Sea, which persisted all the way to the Danish coast. P/O Smith and crew were unable to establish a pinpoint and assessed that they were opposite the island of Sylt when they decided to abandon their sortie. They spotted an aerodrome in the centre of Sylt, and bombed it from 12,000 feet at 22.10, before bringing their vegetable home. The cloud began to thin sufficiently over the Schleswig-Holstein peninsula to allow the others to identify pinpoints, and, by the time that they reached the western Baltic, the horizontal visibility was adequate for their purposes. The vegetables were planted from 600 to 800 feet between 22.25 and 22.58, after which, P/O Hazelden, W/O Trickett and Sgt Dart attacked Husum aerodrome from 10,000, 12,000 and 10,000 feet respectively between 23.10 and 23.20. Sgt Lauderdale and crew reported bombing an aerodrome at Glambek from 4,500 feet at 23.35, but its precise location has not been established.

Düsseldorf was posted as one of the targets on the 27th, for which a force of thirty-nine aircraft was made ready, consisting of twenty-two Hampdens from Hemswell, Scampton and Waddington, four 207 Squadron Manchesters, and thirteen Whitleys from 4 Group. The 44 Squadron element of six took off between 19.35 and 19.45 with W/C Misselbrook the senior pilot on duty and conducting his first operation with the squadron. They were carrying between them three 1,000, ten 500 and six 250 pounders, plus six SBCs of incendiaries, all of which made it to the target area, where they encountered the usual industrial haze. A number of small fires were already burning as they arrived shortly after 21.30 to begin their search for the specific, unnamed aiming point, and they were assisted in navigation by the distinctive reversed S-bend in the River Rhine to the west of the city centre. They carried out their attacks from 10,000 to 13,000 feet between 21.43 and 21.57, observing bomb flashes within the briefed aiming circle. No detailed assessment was possible, and an absence of post-raid reconnaissance and local reports left the crews uncertain as to the effectiveness of their work. The sad news soon made its way across the tarmac from 207 Squadron, that the former 44 Squadron stalwart, F/L Siebert, was missing with his crew. It would take time for the details to come through, that they had abandoned their Manchester over Holland, and, by the time that F/L Siebert had vacated the aircraft last, his parachute had insufficient time to deploy. His sacrifice allowed his six crew colleagues to survive, albeit in enemy hands for the duration.

On the 29th, the German cruisers Scharnhorst and Gneisenau were reported to be off Brest, and 50 Squadron was ordered to dispatch six Hampdens from Lindholme to carry out a cloud-cover daylight attack, a type of operation that would come to be known as "moling". The arrival of the vessels must have been expected, because Lindholme had been standing-by at two-hours readiness for seven days when the order was received. They flew out in two vics over the Lizard, until insufficient cloud cover over the Channel forced them to turn back. That night, twenty-five Hampdens were dispatched from Scampton, Waddington and Coningsby to mine the waters of the Jellyfish garden, the approaches to the port, the 44 Squadron element of eight taking off between 01.25 and 02.05 with S/Ls Collier and Smales the senior pilots on duty.

Twenty-five-year-old Devon-born Joe Collier had been posted to the squadron on the 11th to succeed S/L Fleming as A Flight commander. He was the holder of a DFC, awarded for a raid on oil storage facilities at Bordeaux on the 19th of August 1940, and had spent the previous six months convalescing from injuries sustained in a landing crash on return from his thirty-fifth sortie. He was already something of a legend in 5 Group after his tour with 83 Squadron as a contemporary of F/O Guy Gibson, who, himself, would gain fame two years hence as the leader of the Dambusters. In fact, both had been involved in the 5 Group operation launched on the first day of the war, the 3rd of September 1939, after which Collier completed a further thirty-four operations. His informal style of leadership would fit comfortably with the demeanour of the increasing number of Rhodesians joining the squadron, and he would soon learn their colloquialisms, like "Rooineks" their term for the English.

All eight 44 Squadron crews reached the target area, where they encountered low cloud with a base hovering at around 1,000 feet, and extreme darkness in which even the nearby coast was intermittently lost from sight. Sgt Stammers and crew failed to establish a positive pinpoint for their timed run and brought their mine and 250 pounders home. S/L Smales and crew experienced similar difficulties, and, ultimately, planted their vegetable more than three miles to the south-west of the allotted location. Seven mines were dropped from 500 to 800 feet between 04.05 and 04.42, most into the briefed locations, but only Sgt Atkins and crew found a target for their 250 pounders, a flak ship observed dimly through the mist by the navigator, moored in Douarnenez Bay. By the following day, the warships had taken up what amounted to a permanent residency, and their presence at Brest as a fleet-in-being would represent a constant distraction for the Command and necessitate the mounting of dozens of operations against the port and its lodgers over the next eleven months.

Hemswell and Lindholme joined forces on the 30th to send six Hampdens each on another daylight foray, but an absence of cloud cover again forced them to turn back. That night, fourteen Hampdens and four Manchesters returned to the port, while ten others from the group attended to gardening duties in the approaches. 44 Squadron assigned the crews of P/Os Baker and Curley and Sgt Sneeston to the latter and dispatched them from Waddington between 19.10 and 19.20. They returned between six and seven hours later to report uneventful sorties, during which they had delivered their mines into the allotted locations from 500 to 800 feet between 22.12 and 22.30. Seven crews took off at 07.00 on the 31st to detach to the Coastal Command station at St Eval in Cornwall, where they would stand-by for possible further operations against Brest. During the course of the month, the squadron undertook thirteen operations and dispatched eighty-one sorties for the loss of a single Hampden and crew.

April 1941

The first week of the new month was reserved exclusively for operations on and around Brest with the intention of disabling its lodgers. It began with 5 Group launching a dozen Hampdens from St Eval in Cornwall for a daylight attack on the 1st, when all but one turned back in the absence of cloud, and the one that continued on, failed to return. 49 and 83 Squadrons sent six Hampdens each from their Scampton base to St Eval for another attempt on the 3rd, with similar results. Ninety other aircraft were made ready on the 3rd to attack the German cruisers that night, and returning crews reported that it had proved difficult to identify them. While that raid was in progress, 5 Group Hampdens had conducted mining sorties in the waters off Brest (Jellyfish) and La Rochelle (Cinnamon).

On the 4th, Gneisenau entered a dry dock, which was to be drained on the following day for an inspection of the vessel, while, over at Waddington, 44 and 207 Squadrons were called into action to make ready three Hampdens and four Manchesters for yet another attempt on the enemy cruisers that night as part of a force of fifty-four aircraft. The 44 Squadron trio of F/L Carpenter, P/O Ross and Sgt Atkins took off between 19.25 and 19.45, two carrying four 500lb SAP bombs and P/O Ross a 1,900 pounder. Five of the eleven participating Hampdens carried out low-level attacks, and among these were P/O Ross and crew, who went in at 1,000 feet at 22.55 to score a direct hit on Scharnhorst, which was recognised in the flash as being in a dry dock precisely as depicted in the reconnaissance photos shown to the crews at briefing. The rear gunner confirmed the success, but it was impossible to determine which part of the vessel had been hit. Another of the low-level attackers was the 106 Squadron commanding officer, W/C Polglase, whose Hampden was seen to be shot down. Sgt Atkins and crew had been the first from the squadron to make an attack, gliding down from 8,000 to 6,000 feet to release their 500 pounders at 22.05, before weaving out of the target area to avoid the intense heavy flak. F/L Carpenter and crew preferred a higher-level approach from south-west to north-east at 11,000 feet, and released three 500 pounders at 22.21, the fourth hanging up. The Continental Hotel in the town was also struck by bombs just as dinner was being served, and a number of naval officers were killed. When Gneisenau's dry dock was drained on the following day, the 5th, a single unexploded 500lb bomb was found nestling at the bottom, and the ship's captain, Kapitän-zur-See Otto Fein, decided to move his vessel out into the harbour while it was dealt with. The dock was refilled to allow Gneisenau to vacate it, and she was spotted by a reconnaissance aircraft at some point, which led to an operation being planned by Coastal Command to be carried out at first light on the 6th.

In the meantime, still on the 5th, 44 and 50 Squadrons were ordered to prepare six Hampdens each for another daylight operation to be launched from St Eval. In the event, only four 44 Squadron crews took off at around noon, but, as the operation was launched from St Eval, no mention of it was made in the squadron ORB, and the 5 Group record mentioned only that the weather conditions were inhospitable, with ten-tenths low cloud, and, by the time that they had passed south of the Isles of Scilly, they were in rain at 500 feet. No 44 Squadron crews would reach even the Brittany coast, and one of the 50 Squadron aircraft crashed suddenly after falling out of formation. A number of the Lindholme crews reached the target, but only one carried out an attack on estimated position, with no hope of hitting anything of value.

The Coastal Command operation on the 6th took place in poor weather conditions, which led to the six Beauforts becoming separated while outbound, and F/O Kenneth Campbell and his crew alone pressed home an attack, which caused damage to Gneisenau that would require six months to repair. In the face of the most concentrated anti-aircraft fire, the Beaufort stood little chance of getting away with it and was shot down without survivors. F/O Campbell was posthumously awarded a Victoria Cross for his actions. That evening, fifteen Hampdens from Scampton were dispatched to the Jellyfish garden off Brest, while four others were sent to one of the three Nectarine gardens off the Frisians. Meanwhile, five Waddington crews had been assigned to the Beech garden off St-Nazaire, and four took off between 18.55 and 19.00, leaving P/O Smith and crew on the ground until 19.35. Although no mention was made, they may have been delayed by an engine issue, and, an hour after take-off, they landed at Weston-on-the-Hill before even crossing the English coast. The others reached the target area, where, beneath the ten-tenths cloud, visibility was adequate and enabled them to establish their positions and deliver their stores into the allotted locations from 400 to 900 feet between 21.59 and 22.30.

The naval port of Kiel was posted as the target for a major operation on the 7th, for which a force of 229 aircraft was assembled. 5 Group contributed sixty-one Hampdens, seven of which were made ready at Waddington. They took off between 20.05 and 20.35 with W/C Misselbrook and S/L Smales the senior pilots on duty, six crews sitting on two 500 and two 250 pounders, while W/C Misselbrook's feet rested on a 2,000 pounder. The crossed the English coast near Skegness, before setting course for Rømø Island on Denmark's western coast, where they would turn east to a position north of Flensburg to approach Kiel from the north. They encountered cloud at 6,000 feet for the first fifty miles of the North Sea crossing, but then clear skies for the remainder of the outward flight. S/L Smales noticed excessive fuel consumption, and, on reaching the enemy coast at 10,000 feet, delivered an attack from west to east across the aerodrome at Husum at 23.20. By the time that the remaining 44 Squadron crews arrived in the target area, the defences had already been stirred into action, but, at least, the bright moonlight helped to tone down the glare from dozens of searchlights. Medium calibre flak batteries were hosing shells up to 12,000 feet, with heavy flak reaching as high as 18,000 feet, and the light stuff awaiting any crew foolhardy enough to try to sneak in lower down. The Waddington Hampdens bombed from 7,000 to 12,000 between 23.20 and 00.05, noting many fires, which remained visible for up to eighty miles into the homeward leg. Returning crews were confident that the raid, which had taken place over a period of almost five hours, had struck a major blow against this important target, and this was confirmed by local reports of widespread damage to housing in the town, and to port facilities and the eastern docks area. The nightshift workers at the Germania Werft and Deutsche Werke U-Boot construction yards had been sent home, causing a number of days' loss of production.

A force of 160 aircraft was made ready during the following day to return to Kiel that night, and among them were twenty-nine Hampdens and twelve Manchesters, four of the latter belonging to 5 Group's latest addition, 97 Squadron, which would be operating for the first time. 44 Squadron was to send F/O Robertson and crew on this operation, and five others to conduct mining sorties in the Prawn garden off Calais. They took off between 19.45 and 21.25, the gardeners with a round-trip of just four hours ahead of them, and four delivered their mine into the briefed location from 700 to 900 feet between 21.25 and 23.06. Afterwards, Sgt Sneeston and crew climbed to 10,000 feet, from where they dropped their two 250 pounders onto the entrance to the main slipway at 22.08, while P/O Baker and crew let theirs go at 22.40 from 4,000 feet onto a building to the north-west of Bassin Carnot, which partially collapsed. AD899 failed to return after crashing some six miles south-west of Calais, killing P/O Curley and his crew. Meanwhile, the Kiel-bound F/O Robertson and crew had followed the same route as on the previous night, and, once again, had met a band of ice-bearing cloud between 3,000 and 6,000 feet extending from the coast. The cloud dispersed from 5 degrees east, to leave clear skies and bright moonlight that aided map-reading after landfall. They reached the target without incident, to run across the aiming point from east to west at 10,000 feet and deliver a 2,000 pounder at 23.50 onto the western U-Boot bunker, which had been marked on the target map with an X. A very large explosion was followed by a column of black smoke, and they described the target area as a mass of flames as they retreated to the west.

Eighty aircraft were made ready for Berlin on the 9th, among them twenty-four Hampdens, while a single Manchester was prepared at Waddington to join eight other aircraft for an attack on the shipbuilding yards at Vegesack, situated some eight miles downstream of the Weser to the north-west of Bremen city centre. 44 Squadron briefed four crews for the Capital, which took off between 20.25 and 20.40 with S/L Smales the senior pilot on duty. After being outbound for three hours, F/L Carpenter had reached the western coast of the Schleswig-Holstein peninsula and was concerned about excessive fuel consumption. With no prospect of reaching the primary target and returning, he turned back at 23.45, and, two minutes later, dropped his 2,000 pounder onto the aerodrome at Husum. The others pressed on to find Berlin under largely clear skies and almost perfect conditions for the accurate bombing of the briefed aiming point, the main railway station. F/L Broadhead and crew were the first to arrive at 00.58, and, from a height of 9,000 feet, delivered a 2,000 pounder into the north-western district of Wedding, claiming to actually hear the explosion and observing a number of fires. Five minutes later, Sgt Dart and crew released their 2,000 pounder from 12,000 feet, and so clear was the visibility, that they were able to track its fall almost to the point of impact on either a large warehouse or block of buildings. Immediately afterwards, a small fire broke out, which increased in intensity, and was still visible from one hundred miles into the return flight. It was at 01.24 when S/L Smales let his bomb go from 12,000 feet over the centre of the city, and observed a large yellow flash followed by a sizeable fire.

Orders were received on some 5 Group stations on the 10th to prepare for a joint 4 and 5 Group effort against Düsseldorf involving fifty-three aircraft, for which twenty-nine Hampdens were detailed. The other operation on this night was another assault on Brest and its guest enemy warships, for which fifty-three aircraft also were made ready, including five Manchesters of 97 Squadron to represent 5 Group. 44 Squadron sat out this night, while its 5 Group counterparts contended with thick industrial haze at Düsseldorf, which rendered their efforts largely ineffective. Meanwhile, at Brest, four bombs hit the under-repair Gneisenau on the starboard side of the forward superstructure, and, although only two detonated, seventy-two men were killed and ninety injured, sixteen of which would not survive.

It was the turn of Lindholme to stay at home on the 12th, while a dozen Hampdens and six Manchesters were detailed to represent 5 Group in a force of sixty-six aircraft continuing the campaign against the enemy warships at Brest. 44 Squadron made ready five Hampdens for Brest, and five others for a raid by fifteen Hampdens and Wellingtons on Merignac aerodrome near Bordeaux. With an additional three hundred miles to travel to reach the latter, the crews of F/L Carpenter, F/O Robertson and Sgts Lauderdale, Mercer and Stammers departed Waddington first, between 21.55 and 22.15, leaving the crews of S/L Smales, F/L Broadhead, P/O Baker and Sgts Dart and Sneeston to follow on between 00.50 and 01.30. When midway between Brest and the target, F/L Carpenter turned back after realising that he would have to cross the French coast homebound in broad daylight. The others reached the target to deliver four 500 pounders each from 2,200 to 8,000 feet between 02.10 and 02.45, some observing bursts in the vicinity of hangars, while others were too busy evading the searchlights and ground fire. At Brest, thick cloud prevented the crews from identifying the warships, and the two 2,000 and twelve 500 pounders were dropped on estimated positions from 7,000 to 11,500 feet between 03.20 and 04.15. On the way home, X2917 shed a propeller, and Sgt Dart landed the Hampden at Tangmere on the Sussex coast.

The Manchester's Rolls Royce Vulture engines were proving to be problematic, with overheating and component failures seriously affecting the squadrons' rate of serviceability. As a result, the first of a number of grounding orders was issued on the 13th, while investigations were carried out into the engine-bearing problem, and modifications put in hand. This meant that no further operations would be undertaken by the type during what remained of the month. That night, seventeen Hampdens were dispatched for mining duties in the Cinnamon garden off the port of La Rochelle, the crews having been briefed to drop their wing-mounted bombs on a hotel south of Quiberon, which, presumably, was home to U-Boot personnel. Waddington was not involved, and sat out the following night's activity also, when more than ninety aircraft, twenty-four of them Hampdens, returned to Brest on a night when cloud severely affected the outcome.

Kiel was posted as the target for ninety-six aircraft on the 15th, for which 44 Squadron contributed nine of the nineteen Hampdens, plus a tenth for Sgt Sanderson and crew to take to one of the Nectarine gardens off the Frisians. The bombing brigade departed Waddington between 23.00 and 23.45 with S/L Collier the senior pilot on duty and climbed away into cloud that would dissipate over the North Sea but return to largely conceal ground features inland of the enemy coast. Sgt Sanderson and crew were back on the ground after seventy-four minutes to report that the entrance hatch had blown open and could not be shut, and their mine was returned to store. It proved difficult for crews to establish pinpoints as they traversed the Schleswig-Holstein peninsula, and only five from the squadron would be among those reaching the port and its town. S/L Collier, F/L Carpenter, F/O Robertson, P/O Baker and Sgt Stammers carried out their attacks through cloud from 11,000 to 18,000 feet between 01.40 and 02.18, observing little of the outcome in the conditions. P/O Ross, who had just been awarded a DFC, dropped his bombs from 16,000 feet towards a flak battery on the island of Sylt at 02.05. Sgt Lauderdale attacked Westerland aerodrome on Sylt from 10,000 feet at 02.45, while Sgt Sneeston and crew, having spent fifty minutes searching for the primary target, turned to the north to attack the town of Flensburg from a lofty 19,000 feet at 02.59. Sgt Mercer bombed Emden town from 12,000 feet at 03.10 and returned safely along with the others. It had been impossible to assess the outcome of the operation, and local reports would suggest an ineffective raid that had caused little damage.

Berlin was posted as the target for 118 aircraft on the 17th, thirty-nine of them Hampdens, of which seven belonged to 44 Squadron. The Waddington crews were briefed to attack the telephone exchange, one of two aiming points, and took off between 20.05 and 20.30 with W/C Misselbrook the senior pilot on duty. They were routed out over Skegness and ran immediately into ten-tenths cloud at 12,000 feet until reaching Holland, where it began to disperse. Sgt Lauderdale and crew turned back with an engine issue before reaching the German coast and jettisoned their 1,900 pounder. There were clear skies over the border region between southern Denmark and Germany, but haze blotted out ground detail, and those reaching Berlin would find it difficult to locate the planned aiming points. F/O Robertson and crew were the first of three from the squadron to reach Berlin and delivered their 1,900 pounder from 14,000 feet on e.t.a., at 00.10, observing nothing of the impact because of the intense glare from searchlights. W/C Misselbrook was concerned about fuel consumption and dropped his 2,000 pounder from 11,000 feet at 00.58 onto the approximate position of Brandenburg, some twenty-five miles to the west of the capital. Sgt Mercer and crew reached Berlin shortly before 01.00, and attacked a SEMO at Neukolln, a south-eastern suburb, with a 1,900 pounder and two 250 pounders from 11,000 feet. P/Os Ross and Baker were also contending with excessive fuel consumption, the former turning back after reaching the Danish island of Langeland, before coming across a railway junction immediately south of Flensburg. The navigator/bomb-aimer released a 2,000 pounder towards it from 7,000 feet at 23.41, and a flash was observed as evidence of impact, but no detail could be determined. P/O Baker and crew attacked a railway station in Hamburg from 11,000 feet at 23.45, and they were rewarded also with a flash. Eight aircraft failed to return, and among them was X2999 containing the crew of F/Sgt Sneeston, and it was only after the body of the pilot washed ashore at Sheerness in Kent in early June, that their fate was confirmed.

While eleven Hampdens joined fifty others to raid Cologne on the 20th, a further nine were detailed for mining duties in the Jellyfish garden off Brest. 44 Squadron remained at home on this night, as did the entire group on the following night, and, when orders were received at Waddington on the 22nd, they revealed that 44 Squadron would be operating alone and taking care of mining duties in the Jellyfish garden off Brest. The six-strong element took off in a six-minute slot from 19.40 with F/L Carpenter the senior pilot on duty and set course for the south coast for the Channel crossing. Sgt Lauderdale turned back early again with an oil pressure problem, as did F/O Robertson and crew at about the same time because of compass and artificial horizon failure. The others pressed on to reach the target area where each delivered a mine as briefed, two from 500 feet and two from 700 feet, between 22.30 and 23.08. F/L Carpenter and crew proceeded then to Pointe-Saint-Mathieu and bombed a flak and searchlight battery from 1,500 feet at 22.55. Sgt Mercer and crew dropped their two 250 pounders onto the aerodrome at Morlaix as they passed over it at 5,000 feet at 23.00 on their way to the nearby Brittany coast.

Hemswell maintained the pressure on the German warships at Brest on the 23rd, when sending ten Hampdens, the crews of which failed to identify the location of the vessels and bombed on approximate positions. In addition, fourteen Hampdens were assigned to gardening duties and were divided equally between Quiberon Bay, off the Biscay coast, and the Frisians. The Nectarine region encompassed the entire Frisian chain, and was divided into three gardens, Nectarine I from Texel to the eastern tip of Ameland, Nectarine II, from east of Ameland to Memmert, and Nectarine III, Juist to Wangerooge. The 44 Squadron crews of P/O Tripp and Sgt Sanderson departed Waddington at 00.15 bound for one of these gardens, carrying only a single 1,500lb mine each, which they delivered into the briefed locations from between 500 and 550 feet at 03.10.

While ten Scampton crews set off for Kiel on the 24th, and six from Lindholme for the Daffodil garden in the southern straits of The Sound (Oresund) off Copenhagen, three 44 Squadron freshmen were briefed to join three more from Lindholme for an attack on the docks and shipping at Le Havre. The crews of Sgts Anderson, Jessop and Tyler departed Waddington between 20.05 and 20.20, and set course for the south coast to begin the Channel crossing. They reached the Normandy coast to find ten-tenths cloud in a layer between 5,000 and 10,000 feet, and searchlights providing the only clue to the location of the port. Sgt Tripp decided not to carry out an attack, and, on noticing a build-up of ice on his wings, jettisoned the four 500 pounders and headed for home. Sgt Anderson and crew spotted the glow of a fire estimated to be near Honfleur on the southern bank of the Seine estuary opposite Le Havre and dropped their bombs towards it from 14,000 feet at 21.55. Sgt Jessop and crew aimed at searchlights from 8,000 feet at 22.03 and returned with nothing useful to report at debriefing. Such operations provided a gentle introduction to an operational career, and useful experience in preparation for sorties over Germany.

Waddington was not called into action on the 25th, the day on which the awards of the DFC to P/O Ross and the DFM to his rear gunner, Sgt Street RNZAF, appeared in the London Gazette. The glowing citation recalled their low-level attack on the Scharnhorst at Brest on the 4th, describing the bombing run at 1,000 feet in the face of intense searchlight and flak activity, and the coolness of both as they carried out their respective duties.

Hamburg would be a frequent destination throughout the war and would receive its own mini campaign of six raids between the end of April and the middle of May. Twenty-eight Hampdens and twenty-two Wellingtons were prepared for an operation against it on the 26th, although, at this stage of the war, it is unlikely that they would have been over the target at the same time. Seven 44 Squadron crews were briefed to attack a specific area, probably the shipyards, and departed Waddington between 21.45 and 22.15 with S/L Collier the senior pilot on duty. The presence of ten-tenths cloud in the target area, with a base at around 6,000 feet, presented the usual problems for aiming point identification, and F/O Robertson abandoned the search before dropping his 500 pounders and incendiaries onto the aerodrome at Husum from 9,500 feet at 02.25. The others bombed on estimated positions from 9,000 to 17,000 feet between 01.20 and 01.46, observing flashes, bursts and a number of fires, but no detail. Sgt Lauderdale and crew lost their port engine shortly after crossing the English coast homebound, and force-landed at 05.30 in a field near West Raynham in Norfolk, where the wreckage of AD847 was declared to be beyond repair.

Mannheim was the destination for seventy-one aircraft on the 29th, fourteen of them Hampdens. In the face of adverse weather conditions, only around fifteen crews reported bombing in the area of the city, and local sources reported fairly minor damage. Meanwhile, a dozen 5 Group freshman crews were briefed to attack oil storage facilities in Rotterdam, a favourite target for the inexperienced, for which the 44 Squadron element of six departed Waddington between 20.30 and 21.00. The Dutch coast was concealed beneath ten-tenths cloud at 4,500 feet, which precluded any chance of identifying the target, and the crews of P/O Keartland, P/O Tripp and Sgt Tyler bombed a searchlight concentration to the south of the port from 4,000 to 9,000 feet between 22.50 and 23.16. The crews of Sgts Anderson, Jessop and Sanderson jettisoned their loads over the sea.

Kiel was posted as the primary target for ten Hampdens on the 30th, and Wilhelmshaven as the alternative. The five 44 Squadron crews of S/L Smales, F/L Broadhead, F/O Robertson and P/Os Baker and Trickett departed Waddington between 22.00 and 22.30 and headed out over the Lincolnshire coast to make landfall on the western coast of the Schleswig-Holstein peninsula. F/O Robertson's aircraft developed an engine issue over the North Sea, and he dropped two 500 and two 250 pounders plus two SBCs onto the island of Borkum from 8,000 feet at 01.05. F/L Broadhead failed to locate Kiel, and attacked a flak concentration at Meldorf, a dozen or so miles north of the mouth of the Elbe, on the way home. This left three crews to fulfil their brief at the primary target, where the attacks were delivered on estimated positions from 12,000 to 16,000 feet between 01.47 and 01.59, and a large fire was reported by P/O Baker and crew. During the course of the month, the squadron carried out eighteen operations, and dispatched eighty-one sorties for the loss of three Hampdens and two crews.

May 1941

The new month began with the posting of an operation to Hamburg on the 1st, but this was subsequently cancelled, only to be reinstated on the following day, for which a force of ninety-five aircraft was made ready. The grounding order on the Manchester had been lifted, and three of the type representing 207 Squadron would join nineteen Hampdens as the 5 Group contribution. 44 Squadron briefed the crews of Sgt Dart and P/O Tripp for the main event and dispatched them from Waddington either side of 22.00. They flew out over the Lincolnshire coast, and set course from there to Neumünster, a town situated some thirty-five miles to the north of Hamburg, from where the bombing run would begin. The weather for the outbound flight was fairly good with just a little low cloud, but this increased over Germany to eight-tenths to create poor visibility. Precisely where in the target area AD864 went down is not known, but there were no survivors from the crew of P/O Tripp, and the body of the second pilot/navigator, P/O Jeff, was not recovered for burial. Sgt Dart and crew attacked through cloud from 14,000 feet at 01.20 and observed their four 500 pounders burst along the North Bank of the Elbe south of the Binnen-Alster Lake. Local reports mentioned thirteen large fires, but no significant damage.

5 Group put up twenty-seven Hampdens and two Manchesters on the 3rd, in an overall force of 101 aircraft bound for Cologne, while a predominantly Wellington force of thirty-three continued the assault on Brest and its lodgers. 44 Squadron briefed nine crews and dispatched them from Waddington between 20.55 and 21.10 with S/Ls Collier and Smales the senior pilots on duty. They made landfall over the Scheldt and reached the target to find nine to ten-tenths cloud, through which very few crews would be able to establish a firm position, and most would bomb on e.t.a., or on the evidence of searchlights and flak penetrating the cloud tops. The 44 Squadron crews carried between them one 1,900 pounder, twenty-two 500 pounders, seventeen 250 pounders and six hundred 4lb incendiaries, which they deposited within the city boundaries from 9,000 to 15,000 feet between 23.38 and 00.07, observing bursts and fires, which could not be pinpointed.

5 Group contributed twenty-one Hampdens to the next attack on the cruisers at Brest, which took place in the absence of 44 Squadron on the night of the 4/5th and involved a force of ninety-seven aircraft. A number of returning crews claimed direct hits on the vessels, but these were not confirmed. The teleprinters on 1, 3, 4 and 5 Group stations began churning out the orders of the day on the 5th, to reveal that Mannheim was to be the destination for a force of 141 aircraft, of which 5 Group's contribution amounted to thirty-three Hampdens and four Manchesters. Eleven Hampdens and the four Manchesters were bombed and fuelled up at Waddington, and the 44 Squadron element took off between 21.55 and 22.30 with F/Ls Broadhead and Dugdale the senior pilots on duty. Sgt Sanderson and crew turned back at the enemy coast because of an engine problem and brought their bombs home, leaving the others to press on and become somewhat spread out as they flew across France over ten-tenths cloud. The ensuing attack became something of a lottery as crews struggled to establish their positions over the city, and the 44 Squadron crews bombed on estimated positions from 12,000 to 16,000 feet between 00.41 and 01.55. Although bursts and apparently large fires were observed by some, it was not possible to make a meaningful assessment of the results because of cloud and searchlight glare. A local report would suggest that approximately twenty-five bomb loads had hit the city, causing only light damage.

115 aircraft were detailed for an attack on the Blohm & Voss shipyards in Hamburg on the 6th, an operation supported by 5 Group with twenty-seven Hampdens and four Manchesters. In the event, cloud and poor visibility prevented any crews from identifying the aiming point, and bombs were dropped on estimated positions or on alternative targets. 44 Squadron sat this one out but was notified on the following morning of the intention to hit the German warships at Brest that night, for which a force of eighty-nine aircraft was assembled. Eighteen Hampdens were detailed, a reduced figure in the light of a forecast of adverse weather conditions, and the ten Waddington participants had to wait until 23.10 before F/L Broadhead led them away from Waddington, with F/O Robertson bringing up the rear at 00.20. The weather turned out to be more favourable than expected, and all from 44 Squadron reached the target area to find moonlight that enabled some to identify the dry dock occupied by one of the vessels. F/L Broadhead attacked from north-north-east to south-south-west and straddled the dock from 12,000 feet with his four 500 and two 250 pounders at 01.48, claiming at least one direct hit. The others delivered their mixed loads from 10,000 to 16,000 feet between 01.44 and 02.45, some observing bursts in the docks area, while others were blinded by searchlight glare. The claims of direct hits remained unconfirmed.

All 5 Group operational stations received orders on the following day to prepare aircraft for what would be a record-breaking night of activity involving 364 sorties. 188 aircraft were to attack

Hamburg, 119 of them assigned to the Blohm & Voss shipyards, and sixty-nine to target the city, while 133 Whitleys and Wellingtons attended to the A G Weser U-Boot construction yards in Bremen. 5 Group contributed a record seventy-eight Hampdens and nine Manchesters to the Hamburg forces, eleven of the former representing 44 Squadron, their crews briefed for Aiming Point B, which is believed to be the city. They departed Waddington between 23.15 and 23.30 with S/Ls Collier and Smales the senior pilots on duty and flew out over the Lincolnshire coast to pinpoint on Neumünster and approach the target from the north, with conditions promising to offer a reasonable chance of identifying the aiming point. Sgt Jessop and crew were almost two hours into the outward flight, when the intercom system failed, and, with no chance of co-ordinating an attack, brought their bombs home. The others found the target without difficulty in good visibility and described the defence as intense but inaccurate as they delivered their bombs from 14,000 to 18,000 feet between 02.05 and 02.45. Bomb bursts were observed in the general area of the briefed aiming point and in the docks, and fifty fires were counted by the rear gunner in P/O Caldwell's crew. Local sources confirmed that an accurate and effective raid had taken place, reporting eighty-three fires, thirty-eight of them large, ten apartment blocks demolished by a 4,000 pounder, and the highest death toll yet in a German city of 185 people.

The happy news was received on the 9th that His Majesty King George VI had approved the award of a DFC to B Flight commander, S/L Smales, and two further DFCs and three DFMs to former squadron members. During the course of the day, a force of 146 aircraft was assembled for that night's operation against the twin cities of Mannheim and Ludwigshafen, for which 5 Group would contribute twenty-four Hampdens and eleven Manchesters. The aiming point for the 5 Group element was the Badische Anilin & Soda-Fabrik (BASF) works in Ludwigshafen, which was part of the infamous I G Farben company, the largest manufacturer of chemicals and synthetic oil products in the world and major employer of slave workers. 44 Squadron dispatched the crews of Sgt Tyler and P/O Baker at 22.50, but neither made it even as far as the French coast as intercom and W/T transmitter failure ended their interest in proceedings. The rest of the force followed the same route as for the recent Mannheim operation, enjoying favourable conditions all the way into southern Germany, where they encountered a little low cloud in the target area, which may well have been smoke drifting across the Rhine from Mannheim. Local reports would confirm that some useful industrial damage had been inflicted on both cities, and more than 3,500 people had been left homeless.

Hamburg was posted to face its fourth major operation of the month on the 10th, for which a force of 119 aircraft was assembled and the crews briefed to aim for shipyards, the Altona power station (Tiefstack) and the general city area. 5 Group put up thirty-five Hampdens and a 97 Squadron Manchester for the main operation, and six Manchesters for Berlin as part of a force of twenty-three aircraft. 44 Squadron's eight crews were to target the electrical power station, situated south-east of the city centre north of the river, and departed Waddington between 22.40 and 23.00 with F/L Dugdale the senior pilot on duty. The freshman crew of P/O Tew remained on the ground until a minute before midnight, when they took off on a mining sortie to one of the Nectarine gardens off the Frisians. They would return after three hours forty minutes to confirm planting their vegetable into the allotted location from 700 feet at 01.46. This was at the same time as the spearhead of the Waddington element was closing in on Germany's second city, where the conditions were described as perfect for an effective attack. The 44 Squadron attack was spread over an hour, beginning with Sgt Anderson and crew at 01.50 and concluding with F/L Dugdale at 02.50, during which period the squadron delivered four 1,000, thirty 500 and a dozen 250 pounders from 12,000 to 20,000 feet. Sgt Lauderdale and crew reported what appeared to be a direct hit on an oil storage tank three miles west of the aiming point, followed by a jet of flame reaching 2,000 feet, while F/L Dugdale claimed a direct hit on the aiming point, which caused a large bluish-green flash and two tall chimneys to collapse. Returning crews were enthusiastic about the outcome, and local sources confirmed that 128 fires had broken out, forty-seven of them classed as large, with extensive damage resulting in the city centre.

There would be no respite for Germany's second city as plans were already in hand to send ninety-two aircraft back there twenty-four hours later, while eighty-one others, including thirty-one Hampdens and two Manchesters, sought out one of the Deutsche Schiff und Maschinenbau Aktiengesellschaft shipyards in Bremen. Abbreviated to Deschimag, this had been formed in the mid-twenties as a co-operation of eight shipyards to compete with the Blohm & Voss and Bremer Vulkan yards. The largest was the A G Weser company, which, after six of the others had fallen by the wayside before the outbreak of war, was partnered only by the Seebeckwerft, now as part of the Krupp empire, after that organisation was handed a controlling interest in 1941. 44 Squadron was not involved in this operation, which took place in favourable conditions, and was hailed as a success. Local reports confirmed that many bombs had fallen in the docks area, where a floating dock belonging to the A G Weser Company had been sunk. The main damage, however, was inflicted in the city, where housing was the principal victim. The Hamburg operation had also been effective, causing eighty-eight fires and damage mostly to residential property.

Mannheim and Ludwigshafen were posted again as the primary targets on the 12th, for which a force of 105 aircraft was divided 65/40 between the two cities and would involve forty-one Hampdens and four Manchesters. 44 Squadron briefed ten crews to attack the BASF plant and dispatched them from Waddington between 22.00 and 22.30 with F/L Broadhead the senior pilot on duty. They flew out across Belgium and reached the target area to find thick haze obscuring ground features, and this combined with intense searchlight and flak activity to prevent the crews of P/O Ross, P/O Trickett and Sgt Jessop from identifying the aiming point. They turned to the north-west to head the 120 miles to Cologne, where they dropped their 500 and 250 pounders in good visibility from around 15,000 feet between 01.26 and 01.48. They were not alone, as thirteen other crews would report bombing Cologne, where a number of industrial premises were damaged, and ninety-two soldiers were killed in an air raid shelter in a barracks. This left seven Waddington crews to fulfil their brief at Ludwigshafen, and they carried out their attacks from 12,000 to 18,000 feet between 01.10 and 01.55, observing bursts but little else through the poor vertical visibility. Local sources estimated that around ten bomb loads had fallen within the target area, causing only minor damage.

The weather precluded operations on the following two nights, and it was the 15th when the northern city of Hannover was posted as the target for 101 aircraft, for which 5 Group detailed twenty-seven Hampdens, while a simultaneous raid on Berlin involved eight Manchesters and six Stirlings. The briefed aiming point for the latter was the main post office and telephone exchange, which, in reality, identified this as an area attack. 44 Squadron did not take part in this night's activities, or in the following night's main event at Cologne, which involved ninety-three aircraft, twenty-four of them Hampdens, and was ruined by adverse weather conditions. However, the freshman crews of P/Os Caldwell and Tew took off at 02.00 on the 17th bound for the Nectarine I garden to lay a mine each off Terschelling. They fulfilled their brief from 700 feet at 03.25, before returning safely from uneventful sorties. They were probably still in bed when the teleprinters spewed out the details of that night's return to Cologne by a force of ninety-five aircraft, including twenty-three Hampdens, of which 44 Squadron would provide eleven. An order, issued earlier in the day, forced the withdrawal of Manchesters from operational activity, while intensive testing was carried out to identify and solve persistent problems, particularly with regard to the unreliable Rolls-Royce Vulture engines. The 44

Squadron element departed Waddington between 22.20 and 22.50 with S/L Smales the senior pilot on duty and headed for the Scheldt estuary on a moonless night in which extreme darkness would become a problem over the target. All from Waddington reached the target area, F/O Ridpath and crew arriving first and bombing from 11,000 feet at 00.55 on e.t.a., and on fires already burning. The others followed up from 11,000 to 16,000 feet between 01.12 and 01.58 but were mostly blinded to the results by searchlight glare. According to local sources, bombs were widely scattered across the city, resulting in some damage to housing and public and commercial buildings, mostly in districts south of the city centre.

44 Squadron would not be required for operations again until the 23rd, during which period, seventy aircraft, including eighteen Hampdens, were sent to attack Kiel's shipyards on the 18th. The weather kept the Command on the ground during the ensuing four nights, while Blenheims carried out daylight "Circus" operations and shipping sweeps. On the 22nd, ten 44 Squadron crews were put on stand-by for a possible operation against German surface raiders, which, although not named, were the battleship Bismarck and heavy cruiser Prinz Eugen. They had put to sea on operation "Rheinübung", which for Bismarck, would be its first offensive action, and were being shadowed by Coastal Command aircraft as they slipped out of Bergen, heading for the Denmark Straits, between Greenland and Iceland. In the event, the Waddington crews were not required, and a dozen of them were notified on the 23rd of a return to Cologne that night as part of 5 Group contribution of twenty-four in an overall force of fifty-one aircraft. The ORB listed only eleven departures from Waddington between 22.40 and 23.10 with F/Ls Broadhead and Dugdale the senior pilots on duty, and they headed via corridor "G" for landfall over the Scheldt estuary. The visibility was poor as they crossed Belgium, and the timings suggest that a number of crews decided early on that they would seek an alternative target. Sgt Sanderson and crew came upon Eindhoven aerodrome in southern Holland, and attacked it from 12,000 feet at 00.40, observing the bursts of their 1,000 and two 500 pounders to the north of the flare-path. P/O Trickett and crew found a railway junction at Aachen on the border and dropped a stick of four 500 and two 250 pounders across it in a north-westerly direction from 16,000 feet at 01.30. P/O Caldwell and crew attacked Schiphol aerodrome from 14,000 feet at the same time, and saw flashes followed by two explosions with a red glow. The remaining nine crews reached the primary target, where ten-tenths cloud largely obscured the ground, forcing them to bomb on estimated positions from 12,000 to 17,000 feet between 01.00 and 01.47. Uncertain of his precise position over Cologne, Sgt Lauderdale had delivered only two 250 pounders, and retained his four 500 pounders in case of spotting a suitable target on the way home. He found one in the form of Bickendorf aerodrome, some fifty miles south of Cologne, and a goodly distance from a direct return route across Belgium. As far as the main operation was concerned, local sources reported only a few bombs falling within the city and causing damage to twenty-five houses.

5 Group operated alone on the 25th, committing forty-eight Hampdens to mine the approaches to Brest and St-Nazaire, (Jellyfish and Beech gardens), the former, in particular, anticipating the arrival of the Bismarck, which, it was correctly believed, was racing for sanctuary with the Royal Navy snapping at its heels, determined to avenge the shocking sinking of HMS Hood on the 24th. Waddington and Lindholme were left off the Order of Battle on this night, when the cloud base was found to be down to around 600 feet, and only half of the force located the target area. In fact, the Bismarck's rudder would be crippled by a Fleet Air Arm torpedo during the 26th, rendering the vessel unable to manoeuvre, and restricted to a top speed of ten knots.

Later that night, 5 Group sent thirty-eight Hampdens to continue mining the approaches to Brest, and, among them this time were twelve representing 44 Squadron. They took off between 22.40 and 23.15 with S/L Smales the senior pilot on duty, and flew out via Chesil Beach, before crossing the Brest peninsula to pick up their pinpoints for the timed runs. Once again, the weather conditions were unhelpful, with a layer of five to eight-tenths cloud at between 1,000 and 8,000 feet dispensing hail and rain. Despite this, all but one of the Waddington crews located the garden, some assisted by shore-based searchlights, and after spending a considerable time searching. The vegetables were planted from 400 to 1,000 feet between 01.25 and 02.50, and nine crews brought their wing-mounted 250 pounders home after failing to find a suitable target. Sgt Mercer and crew had been the last to take off, and the last to return after more than seven hours aloft, clearly having searched diligently in vain. F/O Clayton dropped his bombs on a coastal flak battery at Pointe-de-Creac'h Meur, F/O Robertson on a flak ship two miles off Pointe-Saint-Mathieu, while Sgt Tyler and crew claimed a direct hit on a 2,000 tonner off L'Anse-de-Berthaume, causing three flashes, the third a particularly violent one that rocked the Hampden 15,000 feet above. In the event, the pride of the Germany navy would never come within range of Brest. At first light on the 27th, multiple units of the Royal Navy closed in on the helpless ship, and, from 08.47, engaged her with guns and torpedoes until she slipped beneath the waves at 10.39. This left her consort, Prinz Eugen, at large, and the mining at Brest would continue over the succeeding nights in case she put in an appearance.

On the night of the 27th, 5 Group continued the mining of the Jellyfish and Beech gardens with thirty-six Hampdens, while Waddington remained inactive, and had now concluded its offensive activity for the month, in which it had operated on thirteen occasions and dispatched 111 sorties for the loss of a single Hampden and crew.

June 1941

June began for 5 Group with an operation against Düsseldorf on the night of the 2/3rd, for which forty-three Hampdens were detailed in an overall force of 150 aircraft. Bombing took place on estimated positions through cloud and in the face of considerable searchlight and flak activity, and returning crews were able to report fires in the centre of the target area, but no detail. Thereafter, 5 Group, and, in fact, most of the Command, was kept on the ground by an unprecedented period of adverse weather conditions during the best part of the moon period. This was a source of monotony and massive frustration, until, finally, on the 10th, Brest was posted as the target for thirty-nine Hampdens in company with sixty-five Wellingtons and Whitleys, which would not have been over the target at the same time. Until the advent of the bomber-stream system introduced by Harris in 1942, groups, squadrons, and even, sometimes, crews, continued to determine for themselves the details of an operation with regard to timings, routes and attacking height, and, the likelihood is, that each group on this night attacked individually.

The Scharnhorst and Gneisenau had been joined at Brest by Bismarck's former consort, Prinz Eugen, which had spent the previous two weeks evading British attempts to locate her and bestow upon her a similar fate to that of Bismarck. 44 Squadron made ready thirteen Hampdens for the main event and four others for freshman crews to take to the Gorse garden in Quiberon Bay between Lorient to the north and St-Nazaire to the south. They would not take off until late, and, in the meantime on this day, a third, or C Flight, was formed under the command of F/L Burton-Gyles DFC, a highly experienced officer and pioneer of Manchester operations, who was posted across the tarmac from 207 Squadron.

It was 23.10 before S/L Collier lifted off the Waddington runway, to be followed over the ensuing thirty-five minutes by the sixteen other participants in the night's activities. The senior pilot on duty was W/C Misselbrook, while, among the gardening quartet was a young P/O Henry Maudslay, whose fame and untimely demise lay almost two years hence. All of the bombing element reached the target area, where the Germans had activated a smoke screen, through which, in the early stages at least, the various docks and jetties could be identified and bombed from 9,000 to 16,000 feet between 01.41 (S/L Collier) and 02.31 (P/O Trickett). F/L Broadhead released his four 500 pounders and a single 250 pounder during his third pass from the north-north-east, the rear gunner confirming two flashes close to a dry dock occupied by one of the vessels. In actual fact, not one crew positively identified any of the target vessels, which had been expertly camouflaged, and a claim by F/O Ridpath and crew to have scored a direct hit remained unconfirmed and doubtful. While this operation was in progress, the gardening element was some eighty miles to the south seeking out their release points, which P/O Salazar and crew failed to do. Having crossed the English coast in cloud, they had not been able to establish a firm position and landed at base after seven hours aloft with their mine still on board. The others completed their sorties successfully from 500 or 600 feet between 02.18 and 02.50. P/O Bell and crew were running short of fuel, and, after landing at West Malling in Kent, found just twelve gallons left in the tanks.

Düsseldorf and Duisburg were posted as the primary targets on the 11th, for which forces of ninety-eight and eighty aircraft respectively were made ready. 5 Group supported the latter with thirty-five Hampdens, although none representing 44 Squadron, and they flew out over Skegness, climbing through five tenths ice-bearing cloud in a layer between 5,000 and 9,000 feet. Once over enemy territory, they found themselves racing a sheet of ten-tenths low cloud to reach the target first. Those ahead of the eastern edge of the front enjoyed the benefits of good visibility and bright moonlight to assist their map-reading and found the target with ease by the fires already burning. The others, beaten to the target by the cloud, bombed on estimated positions, and returning crews reported fires, and that the new 2,000 pounders exploded with a large orange flash. There was no information from Duisburg, but Cologne reported extensive damage to its main railway station, the docks area and 173 houses.

The following night was devoted predominantly to attacks on railway yards at four locations in Germany to the east and north of the Ruhr, with 5 Group committing most of its available Hampden force, amounting to ninety-one aircraft, to attack the important hub at Soest. 4 Group was to target the yards at Schwerte, south of Dortmund, while 1 and 3 Groups were handed those at Hamm and Osnabrück, and a small Halifax element was assigned to the "Buna" works, a chemicals and synthetic rubber plant at Marl-Hüls on the north-eastern fringe of the Ruhr. 44 Squadron made ready seventeen Hampdens, a new squadron record for a single target, and they departed Waddington between 22.45 and 23.30 with S/L Smales the senior pilot on duty and F/L Burton-Gyles leading a C Flight element. They were routed out over Skegness, where large stretches of medium cloud were encountered, extending from 5,000 to 12,000 feet over the North Sea. There was only one early return among the Waddington crews, Sgt Hall and crew experiencing an engine problem as they crossed the North Sea, and they bombed De Kooy aerodrome at Den Helder. The others all reached the target area, some pinpointing on the Möhne Lake a few miles to the south, while others were guided by fires already burning at Soest and at nearby Hamm. Only ten positively identified the primary target in poor visibility, and five were drawn to Hamm, where attacks were carried out from heights ranging from 1,000 to 15,000 feet between 01.00 and 02.30. P/O Baker and crew delivered bundles of reading matter from 14,000 feet at 00.45, intended for the residents north of the Ruhr, before descending to 1,000 feet to race across the marshalling yards at 1,000 feet at 01.30, straddling track and adjacent buildings with two 500 and two 250 pounders. The bursts were followed immediately by a line of explosions lasting around fifteen minutes, as if the trucks of an ammunition train were going up one-by-one. Their report suggested that they returned thirty minutes later to drop a 2,000 pounder from 8,000 feet, but this may have been a confused entry by the squadron scribe. What was not in doubt, was their claim of a Me110 shot down over Enschede in Holland. Debriefings revealed that only forty-one crews reported bombing the primary target, and two Hampdens had failed to return. Both belonged to 44 Squadron, P4310 crashing somewhere in the Ruhr with no survivors from the crew of F/Sgt Mercer, and AE127 coming down in the sea on the way home. F/L Shaughnessy DFC and two members of his crew survived and were rescued by the enemy to become PoWs.

A major assault on the enemy warships at Brest was notified across 1, 3 and 5 Group stations on the 13th, and resulted in the assembling of a force of 110 aircraft, of which, thirty-seven were Hampdens. 44 Squadron made ready thirteen of its own, and three others for freshman crews to take mining in one of the Nectarine gardens, and all departed Waddington together between 23.00 and 23.30 with the former commanding officer and incumbent Waddington station commander, G/C Boothman, guesting, and S/L Collier the senior 44 Squadron pilot on duty. Sgt Saunders and crew were among the mining trio and were returning with a technical problem when AE129 crashed at Southrey, midway between Horncastle and Lincoln, at 00.50, killing all on board. Sgts Gammon and Wilson located their drop zones and delivered one vegetable each into the briefed locations from 700 and 600 feet at 01.43 and 01.54 respectively. Meanwhile, some six hundred miles to the south-west, the bombing brigade located their target area, and encountered no low cloud, but thin layers at 14,000 to 16,000 feet. There appeared to be no smoke screen at first, but the searchlight and flak defence was as hostile as ever as the bombing took place from 8,000 to 16,000 feet between 01.30 and 02.30. Crews ran in from all points of the compass and clearly identified the docks, but as always seemed to happen, not one could positively locate the target vessels. F/L Burton-Gyles and crew observed what they thought was a cruiser close to the torpedo-boat station, and, following their attack, saw a large volume of white smoke emanating from the western end towards the east, of which the funnel was definitely not the source.

Twenty-nine Hampdens were detailed on the 14th for a 5 Group operation that night, which was the first of four raids on consecutive nights against Cologne, a city that would continue to be a popular destination throughout the month. 44 Squadron was not involved in what turned out to be an indeterminate raid delivered through ten-tenths cloud, which caused only minor damage. The rest of the month would be devoted largely to eight simultaneous raids on Cologne and Düsseldorf, the first of which was posted on the 15th, and involved forces of ninety-one and fifty-nine aircraft respectively. 5 Group contributed forty-two Hampdens to the night's operations, the dozen 44 Squadron crews briefed for Düsseldorf, and they took off between 22.50 and 23.20 with S/L Collier the senior pilot on duty. Among them were the freshman crews of P/Os Biggane and Salazar and Sgt Gammon, who were bound for one of the Nectarine gardens off the Frisians. They crossed the North Sea in, under or over ten-tenths cloud, and F/O Ridpath and crew were eighteen minutes from landfall on the Dutch coast when engine trouble forced them to turn back. Sgt Hall and crew lost their intercom, and selected Rotterdam's Waalhaven aerodrome as a last resort target, leaving ten crews to press on to the Ruhr. On arrival, it became clear that the prospects of fulfilling their brief through dense cloud between 3,000 and 8,000 feet were nil, and most headed south down the Rhine to join their 5 Group colleagues at Cologne. They found conditions to be no better, and bombing took place on estimated positions over and in the vicinity of the city, guided to an extent by the flak coming up through the cloud. Attacks were carried out from 4,000 (F/L Burton-Gyles) to 15,000 feet between 01.17 and 02.15, with none observing bomb bursts, and no assessment of results was possible. Rather than head south, S/L Collier turned to the north towards Essen, where he aimed two 500 pounders, one 250 pounder and 120 x 4lb incendiaries at a flak position from 11,000 feet at 01.50. Meanwhile, Sgt Gammon and P/O Biggane and their crews had planted a vegetable each into the briefed locations from 600 and 700 feet at 01.32 and 01.35 respectively.

Cologne and Düsseldorf were the principal targets again on the following night, for which 5 Group put up forty-seven Hampdens in an overall force of 105 bound for the former. Waddington was not involved as the 5 Group element set course initially for Brussels, some meeting intense searchlights and flak at the Belgian coast, while others remained unmolested until near the target. The ground was obscured by thick haze and perhaps fog, despite which, a few crews were able to establish their position and home in on the aiming point on the eastern side of the Rhine, probably the Kalk marshalling yards. At debriefing, some crews reported fires and many explosions, while the local authorities claimed scattered damage but nothing of significance.

Forty-three Hampdens and thirty-three Whitleys took off to return to Cologne on the 17th, while fifty-seven Wellingtons were dispatched to Düsseldorf. 44 Squadron made ready thirteen Hampdens for the main event, and three for the freshman crews of P/Os Sauvage and Biggane and Sgt Gammon to deliver a mine each into the Nectarine II garden off the central Frisians. The two elements departed Waddington together between 22.55 and 23.45 with F/L Dugdale the senior pilot on duty, and the bombing brigade carrying between them five 1,000, thirty-four 500 and fifteen 250 pounder plus 360 x 4lb incendiaries. Poor visibility, caused by thick ground haze, prevented most crews from locating their respective targets, although all from Waddington reached the Cologne area to deliver their loads in sticks on a variety of headings from 9,000 to 17,000 feet between 01.37 and 02.20, most observing bursts through the haze and a fire or two, but no detail. While this was in progress, 180 miles to the north, the gardeners dropped their mines into the allotted locations off Schiermonnikoog from 600 to 800 feet between 01.17 and 01.45, before returning safely to make their reports. The Cologne authorities made light of the raid, claiming insignificant damage from a relatively few bomb loads falling within the city.

An unspecified aiming point in Bremen was posted as the target for a hundred aircraft on the 18th, for which 5 Group made a contribution of thirty-nine Hampdens, although, none representing 44 Squadron. Low cloud hindered attempts to locate the target, and returning crews reported a ring of dummy fires up to twenty miles outside of Bremen, and the employment also of dummy flares to draw the bombing away from the city. It was another inconclusive raid, typical of the period, and cost six aircraft and crews. On the following morning, P/O Lauderdale and Sgt Greig were sent to Ternhill in Shropshire to collect Hampdens AD747 and AD904 respectively from 24 Maintenance Unit (MU). Shortly after taking off, the former lost an engine and had to be force-landed at 12.10 two miles east of Market Drayton, where it immediately burst into flames. The incident was observed from above by Sgt Greig, who became distracted while circling, lost control of his aircraft, and dived into the ground with fatal consequences for himself and the two other occupants. P/O Lauderdale and his passengers, which included a member of ground crew, escaped with their lives, but were badly burned around the face and hands, and P/O Lauderdale sustained a fracture to his lower spine. They were taken to RAF Hospital Cosford for treatment.

The country was now basking in a spell of very hot weather, which began on the 19th, and would continue through the 23rd. 115 aircraft set off for Kiel on the 20th in search of the battleship Tirpitz, and among them were twenty-four Hampdens, ten of which represented 44 Squadron. They departed

Waddington in a ten-minute slot either side of 22.30 with F/Os Ridpath and Robertson the most senior pilots on duty and flew out over the Lincolnshire coast on course for landfall on the western coast of the Schleswig-Holstein peninsula. F/O Ridpath and crew were approaching the southern Frisians when engine trouble ended their interest in proceedings, and, on spotting a 6,000-ton tanker some ten miles north of Terschelling, attacked it with a 2,000 pounder from 2,500 feet at 00.30, but saw no result. Ten-tenths cloud completely obscured the ground in the target area, preventing any hope of locating Tirpitz, and attention was turned instead upon the general area of the town. P/O Maudslay descended to 1,500 feet without breaking through the cloud base, before climbing back to 6,000 feet to bomb on estimated position at 01.50. The other Waddington crews also attacked on estimated positions from 8,000 to 16,000 feet between 01.30 and 02.01 and had no clue as to the fall of their bombs. P/O Salazar and crew abandoned their search and dropped their four 500 and two 250 pounders from 3,000 feet on e.t.a., over Husum aerodrome.

It was not until the 21st that the Manchester was once more declared fit for operations after almost five weeks on the side lines. During the course of the day, a record number of eighteen was made ready to target the docks at Boulogne, and this figure included a contribution from 61 Squadron, which would be blooding the type for the first time. The main operations on this night were against Cologne and Düsseldorf, the former the target for sixty-eight Wellingtons, while twenty-eight Hampdens and an equal number of Whitleys attended to the latter. The crews reached the target area after flying through the protective belt of searchlights and flak, but experienced difficulty in establishing their position, and even the Rhine proved to be elusive in the hazy conditions. Fires provided the best reference, and bombing was carried out with the aid of flares, although, without observing the results. Returning crews reported many fires, while local sources barely noticed that a raid had taken place and mentioned only broken windows.

Bremen was the destination for twenty-five Hampdens in company with Wellingtons on the night of the 22/23rd, and this operation was another abject failure. Kiel, Cologne and Düsseldorf were posted as the targets for modest forces on the following night, the last-mentioned for a 5 Group effort against railway yards involving thirty Hampdens and eleven Manchesters. 44 Squadron made ready ten Hampdens for the main event, and two others for the crews of Sgt Dart and P/O Baker to take on what the ORB referred to as "Boom" operations against special targets at Hannover and Bremen respectively. Sgt Dart and crew took off ahead of the main element at 22.35, leaving the rest to follow them into the air between 22.50 and 23.20 with S/L Burton-Gyles and S/L Smales the senior pilots on duty. Sgt Gammon's wireless operator became indisposed shortly after crossing the coast outbound, and they had to turn back, and they were joined on the ground ninety minutes later by Sgt Hall and crew, whose sortie had been curtailed by engine issues. Sgt Tyler and crew also experience engine problems, but having reached enemy territory, bombed the docks at Ostend from 10,000 feet at 01.42 and observed a fire to break out. Sgt Robertson (not to be confused with F/O Robertson) and crew were at 15,000 feet and within striking distance of Gilze-Rijen aerodrome in southern Holland, when electrical failure forced a rethink, and, although the bomb-release system had been compromised, they managed to let go one 500 pounder and one of 250lbs towards the airfield.

The poor serviceability on this night left just five crews to continue on to the primary target, where thick haze blotted out ground detail, and they bombed the general city area from 11,000 to 16,000 feet between 01.20 and 02.20. After failing to identify the aiming point, S/L Burton-Gyles headed south to attack Cologne from 8,000 feet with four 500 and two 250 pounders at 02.24. P/O Baker had noticed his engines overheating, and, to lighten the load, jettisoned the two 250lb wing bombs over an aerodrome at Huntlosen, a dozen miles south of Oldenburg, at which point, he was intercepted by a Me110, which he evaded. As he closed on Bremen from the south-west, he was caught in searchlights and attacked by a further two Me110s, which he also evaded after jettisoning the remainder of his bomb load. Sgt Dart and crew dropped their wing bombs on Langenhagen aerodrome five miles north of Hannover from 12,000 feet at 01.25, before attacking their briefed target within the city from the same height five minutes later.

5 Group assigned a force of twenty-five Hampdens to the docks at Kiel on the 24th, while the Manchester brigade tried its hand at Düsseldorf. 44 Squadron remained on the ground, but made ready two Hampdens on the 25th, as part of a thirty-strong 5 Group force to return to Kiel that night to target the Deutsche Werke shipyard. P/O Biggane and S/L Collier departed Waddington at 22.55 and 23.00, before exiting the English coast near Skegness and setting course for Rømø island on the western coast of South Jutland. From there they flew eastwards to the Baltic to approach the target from the north, and, despite thick haze and intense searchlight and flak activity, found it without major difficulty, P/O Biggane and crew carrying out their attack from 8,000 feet at 02.15, but observing nothing of the outcome. S/L Collier had dropped his two 500 pounders, two 250 pounders and 120 x 4lb incendiaries a minute earlier from a more circumspect 14,000 feet and watched them fall in a stick across the south-eastern corner of the target.

Yet again, Kiel, Cologne and Düsseldorf were selected as the targets on the 26th, and, on this occasion, it was for the important naval stronghold on the eastern side of the Schleswig-Holstein peninsula that eighteen Manchester crews were briefed, while thirty Hampden crews learned of their part in the operation against marshalling yards at Düsseldorf. The Manchester crews were told that they would have fifteen Stirlings and eight Halifaxes for company, although, not necessarily over the target at the same time, and the Hampden crews would share their target with 1 Group Wellingtons. 44 Squadron made ready nine aircraft for the main event, and another for P/O Thompson to take to one of the Nectarine gardens off the Frisians. They departed Waddington together between 23.00 and 23.20 with no senior pilots on duty, on a night when cloud, snow, electrical storms and icing conditions would persuade many crews to turn back or seek out alternative targets. P/O Bell and crew turned back from a position seven miles south-east of Skegness, blaming an engine issue, and Sgt Robertson would return with his bomb load intact after being defeated by ten-tenths cloud and icing conditions as high as 16,000 feet. Of the others, Sgt Jessop and crew wasted their wing bombs on a dummy town six miles south of the target from 8,000 feet at 01.35, and, realising their error, headed north to drop the rest on the estimated position of the intended target. Sgt Anderson and crew were the only others from 44 Squadron to attempt to hit the estimated position of Düsseldorf, aiming at the flashes from a flak concentration from 9,000 feet at 01.15. The rest returned to report attacking searchlight and flak positions, along with aerodromes in Holland and Belgium as last resort targets, and P/O Thompson confirmed the successful planting of his vegetable from 500 feet at 01.10. The only loss from Düsseldorf was a 1 Group Wellington, but two Manchesters failed to return from Kiel, one each from 61 and 97 Squadrons, neither with a survivor, and the latter contained the crew of the former 44 and 207 Squadron stalwart, F/O Eustace DFC.

Earlier in the day, F/L John Dering Nettleton had been posted in from 185 Squadron, a group pool training unit at Cottesmore in Rutland, which prepared new crews to join 5 Group's operational squadrons. He had arrived in England with his mother in the autumn of 1938, having travelled for a holiday from his home in the South African province of Natal, and, despite the family tradition of serving in the Royal Navy, for which he had passed the necessary exams, he decided to join the RAF.

He gained his wings in July 1939 and joined 207 Squadron, at the time a training unit, from where he was posted to 98 Squadron, a Fairey Battle unit that remained in the UK when the others moved to France as part of the Advanced Air Striking Force. He remained in the flying training system with a posting to 185 Squadron, until being posted to 44 Squadron to begin an operational career, which would bring him celebrity, a Victoria Cross, but, sadly also, an untimely end.

Bremen was chosen to be in the firing line again on the 29th, when thirty Hampdens were detailed to join seventy-six other aircraft, while six of the group's Manchesters took part in a small raid on Hamburg. 44 Squadron made ready fifteen Hampdens, a dozen for the main event to be directed at the Deschimag shipyards, and a further three for the crews of F/L Nettleton, P/O Thompson and Sgt Atkinson to take on mining sorties to the Nectarine II garden around the central Frisians. They took off together between 22.55 and 23.30 with W/C Misselbrook and S/L Burton-Gyles the senior pilots on duty and crossed the Lincolnshire coast to encounter cloud over the North Sea. The target area was largely free of cloud, but ground haze created challenging conditions for navigation and target location, and this was the principal cause of W/C Misselbrook's inability to establish the position of the aiming point. He bombed the city area instead with four 500 and two 250 pounders from 12,000 feet at 01.40, observing bursts but no detail. P/O Maudslay was another to be thwarted by the poor vertical visibility, and eventually headed for the port of Emden, where the docks were identified by a river junction and bombed from 12,000 feet at 02.40. A navigational error caused P/O Biggane and crew to overshoot Bremen, and they had all but reached Hamburg before realising, and joined in the attack there from 15,000 feet at 02.45. This left nine crews to fulfil their brief at the primary target, which they attacked from 10,000 to 18,000 feet between 01.45 and 02.30, some observing bursts and a few fires, but nothing of value for the Intelligence Section at debriefing. The mining trio ran into difficult conditions but planted a vegetable each in or close to the briefed locations from 500 and 600 feet between 01.35 and 01.40. It emerged at debriefings that the 50 Squadron crews at Lindholme had been provided with incorrect navigational information, which resulted in them attacking Kiel rather than Bremen.

Following a spate of engine failures, particularly some afflicting 61 Squadron aircraft, another Manchester grounding order was issued on the 30th. A conference was held at 5 Group HQ on this day, when it was decided that each Manchester squadron would select four aircraft for intensive flight testing. During the course of the month, 44 Squadron took part in seventeen operations and dispatched 130 sorties for the loss of five Hampdens and four crews.

July 1941

Having been prominent during the final few days of June, it fell to Bremen to open the Command's July account on the night of the 2/3rd, while smaller forces targeted Cologne and Duisburg. The last-mentioned was an all-Hampden affair, for which 44 Squadron provided eleven aircraft in an overall force of thirty-nine. They were briefed to aim for the marshalling yards and were given Cologne and Düsseldorf as alternative targets before departing Waddington between 22.55 and 23.35, with F/L Dugdale the senior pilot on duty. The briefed route took them out over Skegness to make landfall on the Den Helder peninsula, where they turned to the south-east to run across Holland and the Rhine to the target area. They were greeted by seven-tenths cloud hanging over the Ruhr at 6,000 feet, with thick industrial haze lurking beneath, and this left the crews with no prospect of identifying the briefed aiming point. Searches were carried out, some aided by flares, but it was a futile exercise, and only the crews of P/O Bell and Sgt Wilson would claim to have bombed the estimated location of Duisburg.

The former carried out two passes, the first at 12,000 feet at 01.32, and the second at 11,000 feet at 01.45, delivering part of the load on each occasion, while the latter let theirs go in a single stick from 12,000 feet at 02.05. The others went in search of alternative objectives, and found themselves over Essen, Düsseldorf and Cologne at heights ranging from 12,000 to 16,000 feet between 01.35 and 02.10.

Scampton and Hemswell combined on the following night to send thirty-nine Hampdens to join Wellingtons in attacking shipyards at Bremen, while ninety Wellingtons and Whitleys attempted to hit the Krupp armaments works and railway installations at Essen. 44 Squadron stayed at home, and, thereby, had rested crews to respond on the 4th to the order to attack U-Boots at Lorient, where construction of the major new concrete structure was well under way on the Keroman peninsula. 5 Group put up twenty-five Hampdens, ten of which were loaded with four 500 and two 250 pounders each at Waddington and dispatched between 22.50 and 23.45 with F/L Dugdale the senior pilot on duty. Taking off among them were the crews of P/O Anekstein and Sgts Atkinson and Rea, who were bound for one of the Nectarine gardens off the Frisians, P/O Anekstein operating as crew captain for the first time. While the latter headed for the Lincolnshire coast, the bombing element pointed their snouts to the south-west to begin the Channel crossing at Chesil Beach in Dorset. They benefitted from ideal weather conditions with an almost full moon shining down from a cloud-free south-western sky, and they were able to identify the Brittany coast from many miles away. They all reached the target area, where no U-Boots were evident, and the heavy flak was bursting at up to 18,000 feet as they aimed their bombs at the general dockyard from 8,000 to 16,000 feet between 01.50 and 02.30. For any of the force prepared to brave the light flak at lower levels, there lurked another danger in the form of barrage balloons tethered at between 4,000 and 8,000 feet. Returning crews reported bomb bursts along the edge of the docks, in the dry dock adjacent to the Naval Fusiliers School, on the oiling jetty, naval barracks and a frigate, but there was no confirmation of specific damage. The gardeners, meanwhile, planted their single vegetable each from 500 and 600 feet between 01.15 and 01.20, and returned safely to report uneventful sorties.

Waddington and Lindholme sat out a 5 Group attack on marshalling yards at the garrison town of Osnabrück on the night of the 5/6th, and then 44 Squadron made ready a record nineteen Hampdens on the 6th to contribute to a 5 Group force of eighty-eight of the type for a raid on the German warships at Brest. Fourteen were to be occupied by its own crews, while five were lent to fellow Waddington residents, 207 Squadron, whose crews had become frustrated by the latest grounding of the Manchester. As the situation dragged on, they would continue to borrow from 44, until receiving six Hampdens of their own as a stopgap measure. The two squadron elements took off together between 22.50 and 23.35 with S/L Smales the senior 44 Squadron pilot on duty, and all reached the target area to encounter perfect weather conditions, and the usual intense searchlights and flak defence providing a barrier between the attackers and the targets. Initially at least, the smoke generators were not active, allowing those arriving in the vanguard a clear run, but, for most from 44 Squadron, the smoke screen proved to be highly effective and completely obscured Scharnhorst and Gneisenau. The squadron carried in its bomb bays sixteen 2,000, thirty-two 500 and sixteen 250 pounders, which fell into the general target area from 10,000 to 17,000 feet between 01.48 and 02.15, producing bursts but little evidence of any damage. P/O Salazar and crew carried out their first pass at 17,000 feet at 02.05 and dropped two 500 pounders and one of 250lbs on the estimated positions of the cruisers, before spotting a liner-class vessel of some 10,000 tons at moorings to the east of the Rue-de-la-Rade jetty. They sneaked back in twenty minutes later at 150 feet to drop two more 500 pounders and one of the 250 pounder wing bombs, and observed a flash on the vessel's stern, although could not positively attribute that to their own bombs. Despite arriving in the latter stages of the Waddington presence over the target, F/O Clayton and crew saw nothing of the smoke screen as they attacked the clearly visible docks from 15,000 feet but could not identify the location of the cruisers through the searchlight glare. In all, 5 Group delivered over three hundred high explosive, armour-piercing and semi-armour piercing bombs into the target area, and returning crews reported fires in the town centre, in the northern outskirts and near the seaplane base. A number also reported an aircraft being hit at around 3,000 feet and crashing into the sea in flames, and this was probably the single 5 Group casualty, a 144 Squadron Hampden. Despite the best efforts, the warships remained a threat as a "fleet in being", and the strategists at Bomber Command HQ continued to seek a solution.

Four main targets were posted on stations across the Command on the 7th, Cologne, Osnabrück and Münster for Wellingtons and or Whitleys, while forty Hampdens were to target marshalling yards in the town of Mönchengladbach on the south-western rim of the Ruhr. 44 Squadron made ready nine Hampdens, four for the crews of P/Os Biggane, Clayton and Maudslay and Sgt Anderson, and five for 207 Squadron, before sending them on their way between 23.00 and 23.15. In accordance with the practice of the day, some adopted the northerly route via Skegness and Enkhuizen, while others preferred Orfordness and the Scheldt. Whichever, the outward flight took place under clear skies with a full moon to aid map-reading in coastal areas, until thick ground haze blotted out detail over land, and, ultimately, only four crews would find the target area. A number of lakes to the north-west of the town were of benefit to those approaching from the north, as were the railway lines running into the town, and Sgt Anderson and crew located it with ease despite the presence of ground haze. They dropped a 2,000 pounder from 15,000 feet at 01.24 but lost its burst in the searchlight glare. They had followed in the wake of the Clayton crew, who had identified the railway station and bombed it with their 2,000 pounder from 14,000 feet at 01.20, also without tracking its fall. P/O Maudslay and crew picked up the target from 8,000 feet in the light of a flare some thirty minutes later, only to lose it again and bomb on the estimated position of the town centre. P/O Biggane came upon a railway junction near Grevenbroich, south-east of the target, and attacked it from 12,000 feet at 01.52. Debriefings revealed that most crews had turned their attention upon alternative targets at Düsseldorf, Neuss and Duisburg.

5 Group was handed marshalling yards again on the 8th, when forty-five Hampdens were detailed at Scampton, Waddington and Lindholme to target the northern half of those at Hamm, while twenty-eight Whitleys attended to the southern half. 44 Squadron made ready eleven aircraft, which took off between 23.00 and 23.15 with F/L Nettleton the senior pilot on duty and set course from Skegness to Enkhuizen on the eastern shore of the Den Helder peninsula. They encountered cloud over the North Sea, which dispersed as they skirted the northern rim of the Ruhr, but thick ground haze rendered target identification something of a challenge. Those from the squadron able to identify the yards attacked from 2,000 to 14,000 feet between 01.25 and 02.00, the low figure that of P/O Anekstein and crew, who raced in from the south-south-west and watched their 1,000 and two 500 pounders impact a large warehouse on the eastern side of the tracks. It burst into flames and remained visible for some minutes, but they were too low to gain an impression of the bigger picture. Sgt Jessop and crew were blinded by a large number of searchlight beams and found an alternative target in the form of a large factory with six chimneys on the eastern edge of the town. They ran in at 1,000 feet and watched their four 500 and two 250 pounders burst on the building, one at the base of a chimney, but were too low for a more detailed assessment. P/O Thompson and crew observed their bombs to burst on the southern outskirts of the town, before taking violent evasive action as they were pounced upon by five Me110s. Having shaken off their assailants, they were intercepted again by two BF109s over the Zuider Zee

(Ijsselmeer) and shot one down. AD840 and AE153 failed to return, the former crashing in Germany, killing Sgt Wilson and his crew, and the latter disappearing into the sea with the crew of F/Sgt Tyler.

A new Air Ministry directive was issued on the 9th, which alluded to the German transportation system and the morale of its civilian population as the enemy's weakest points. The C-in-C, Sir Richard Peirse, was, consequently, ordered to concentrate his main effort in these areas, which meant that from now on during the moon periods, he was to target the main railway centres ringing the Ruhr, to isolate it from the other regions of Germany, thus preventing the movement in of raw materials and the export of finished goods. On dark nights, the Rhine cities of Cologne, Duisburg and Düsseldorf would be easier to locate for area attacks, and, when unfavourable weather conditions prevailed, operations were to be mounted against more distant urban centres in northern, eastern and southern Germany. 44 Squadron remained at home on that night, while thirty-nine Hampdens joined forces with forty-three Whitleys and Wellingtons to target the Nazi Party HQ at Aachen, the first time that Germany's most westerly city had faced a major attack. This choice of aiming point meant, in reality, that it was intended as an area raid, which took place in favourable weather conditions and resulted in much destruction to housing, particularly in central districts.

On the following night, 5 Group detailed thirty-two Hampdens to join ninety-eight Wellingtons in attacking a number of aiming points in Cologne. One of the 5 Group targets was the Klöckner-Humboldt mechanical engineering works in the Deutz district, situated on the East Bank of the Rhine in the city centre. They found the target largely hidden beneath eight-tenths cloud and thick haze extending up to 12,000 feet, which forced them to search for a pinpoint. Barely half of the force would claim to have bombed in the general target area, and local sources reported only a handful of bombs falling. 44 Squadron sat out this operation and was at full strength to respond to orders on the 11th to prepare six aircraft for that night's 5 Group raid by thirty-six Hampdens from Coningsby, Hemswell and Waddington against the main railway station in the naval port of Wilhelmshaven. Two additional Hampdens were lent to 207 Squadron, which took four of its own on charge on this day, to begin the process of preparing them for operations in anticipation of the Manchester remaining grounded for some time. They were all airborne and on their way by 23.15, and reached the port to find generally favourable conditions, but haze to inhibit the vertical visibility. Attacks were carried out from 12,000 to 16,000 feet between 01.45 and 02.25, and it was estimated that most of the bombs fell within the target area, although the searchlight and flak defence prevented a detailed assessment. P/O Salazar and crew had been the first from 44 Squadron to bomb, approaching from the north to deliver four 500 pounders. They returned forty minutes later at a perilously low 150 feet to drop two 250 pounders, and survived to return home with the others, two of which bore the scars of shrapnel hits. Thirty-three Hampdens and twenty-eight Wellingtons were sent to Bremen on the night of the 12/13th, but this operation did not involve Waddington, and no report is available concerning the outcome.

Four 207 Squadron crews joined seven from 44 Squadron for briefing on the 14th, to learn of that night's operation to the northern city of Hannover, where the railway station and main post office building were designated as the aiming points for a force of eighty-five aircraft, forty-four of them provided by 5 Group from Coningsby, Hemswell and Waddington. Based on past performances, the choice of aiming points was somewhat optimistic, and, in reality, disguised the actual intention to destroy the city centre. The 44 Squadron element departed Waddington between 22.55 and 23.05 with F/L Dugdale the senior pilot on duty and headed for the Lincolnshire coast to begin the hour-long crossing of the North Sea. Once at the other side, they had to traverse northern Holland, before passing south of Bremen to reach the target, where conditions were reasonably good, but visibility was impaired by ground haze. Some ground detail was revealed by the light of flares, and the bombing was carried out from 10,000 to 18,000 feet between 02.00 and 02.25, but only P/O Anekstein and crew observed their 1,000 and two 500 pounders burst among buildings. Returning crews reported many fires, but few reports came out of Hannover, and it was not possible to establish the level of damage, if any.

Hamburg was posted as the target for 107 aircraft on the 16th, of which thirty-two Hampdens represented 5 Group. 44 Squadron was not involved, and the participation from Waddington of 207 Squadron's own four Hampdens was cancelled because of doubtful weather conditions. In the event, poor visibility persuaded half of the force to seek out alternative targets, and the operation became yet another disappointment. On the following day, the 17th, S/L Burton-Gyles, six aircrew and a maintenance party of ten proceeded to Boscombe Down to familiarise themselves with an Avro Lancaster, before returning with it to Waddington for evaluation trials. This was a momentous day for Bomber Command in general and 5 Group in particular, whose struggles with the Manchester had led to the development of the four-engine Lancaster, a type which would change the face of bombing, and, ultimately, contribute massively to victory. That night, the weather intervened again, causing the 44 Squadron contribution to a raid on the Gereon marshalling yards to the west of Cologne city centre to be reduced from ten to three Hampdens containing the experienced crews of F/L Dugdale, P/O Bell and Sgt Jessop. This left twenty-five Hampdens to join fifty Wellingtons in a late take-off, the Waddington trio departing between 23.00 and 23.15 and flying out over Orfordness to adopt corridor "G" to the Scheldt estuary and Brussels. They reached the target to encounter cloud and generally unfavourable conditions along with a hostile searchlight and flak defence and bombed from 11,000 to 14,000 feet between 01.35 and 02.09. They had little clue as to the outcome, and local sources would suggest that, perhaps, ten bomb loads had fallen within the city, causing little damage and no casualties.

5 Group issued orders to North Luffenham and Waddington on the 19th, to prepare for mining operations that night in the Eglantine and Yams gardens, respectively in the Elbe and Weser estuaries, which provided passage for shipping and U-Boots from the Hamburg and Bremen shipyards. 44 Squadron loaded sixteen Hampdens with a single 1,500lb mine accordingly, fifteen for its own crews and the other to supplement 207 Squadron's five and sent them on their way between 22.35 and 22.55 with S/Ls Collier and Nettleton the senior pilots on duty. The side-lining of S/L Burton-Gyles had created a vacancy for a flight commander, which Nettleton's promotion filled. The Waddington element had been briefed for the Eglantine garden, which they reached to find favourable conditions that enabled them to plant their vegetables into the allotted locations from 400 to 600 feet between 00.58 and 02.22. Afterwards, S/L Collier bombed the aerodrome on Langeoog from 10,000 feet, while F/L Ridpath attacked a 2,000-ton merchantman and an E-Boot in the Elbe, and others went for Norderney town and the island's aerodrome. P/O Thompson and crew reported an engagement with an enemy fighter, assumed to be a BF109, which Sgt Dyer shot down in flames from the upper rear gun position. Earlier in the day it had been announced that W/C Misselbrook had been awarded a DSO, S/L Burton-Gyles a Bar to his DFC, and there was a DFC for P/O Smith and DFMs for Sgts Stammers and Stott.

Waddington was not called into action on the 20th to support a force of 113 aircraft assembled to target marshalling yards in Cologne. Thirty-nine 5 Group Hampdens took part, and, despite poor weather conditions of cloud and haze during the outward flight, all reached the target area to find seven to nine-tenths cloud with tops at 7,000 feet accompanied by haze. Glimpses of the Rhine provided an approximate reference, but there was no possibility of identifying the marshalling yards, and the bombing, carried out on estimated positions, produced little damage.

Frankfurt and Mannheim were named as the targets for a mini-campaign on three consecutive nights from the 21/22nd, and it would be the former's first taste of a major Bomber Command assault. Thirty-seven Wellingtons and thirty-four Hampdens were made ready, the latter at Coningsby, North Luffenham and Waddington, while thirty-six Wellingtons and eight Halifaxes were prepared to attack Mannheim city centre some forty-five miles to the south. At 5 Group briefings, crews were instructed to aim for the post office and main telephone exchange building, for which the 44 Squadron element of nine, led by F/L Dugdale, and seven from 207 Squadron, took off between 22.30 and 23.15, accompanied by the 44 Squadron crews of Sgts Armstrong and Bruce, who were bound for the Nectarine I garden off the Frisian island of Terschelling. With a shorter distance to travel, the latter would complete their sorties well ahead of the bombing brigade, and the Armstrong crew returned at 04.38 to report delivering their store into the briefed location from 550 feet at 00.56. The tragic news arrived soon afterwards that AD983 had crashed at 04.00 onto a hall of residence building for Lindum Hall School for Girls in Lincoln, killing Sgt Bruce and his crew, and causing the death of the senior French mistress, Miss Fowler.

Meanwhile, in a demonstration of the remarkable reliability of the Hampden, the entire sixteen-strong Waddington-based element had reached the Frankfurt area, which they identified after picking up the River Rhine and following it towards the south until coming upon the River Main. They delivered their loads, consisting either of two 500 and two 250 pounders and 120 x 4lb incendiaries or one 1,000 and two 500 pounders, into the city from 6,000 to 12,000 feet between 01.25 and 02.00 in the face of an accurate searchlight and flak defence, the glare from which largely concealed the results. A number of bursts were observed along with fires, but the local reports spoke of minor damage, and the fact that the city of Darmstadt, situated some ten miles to the south, had sustained a greater level of destruction.

On the following night, while Waddington remained off the Order of Battle, thirty-four Hampdens were joined by twenty-nine Whitleys and Wellingtons in a return to Frankfurt, while a small force of Wellingtons attended to Mannheim. In the face of eight-tenths cloud, and, with no prospect of identifying the briefed aiming point, the main post office and telephone exchange, bombing was carried out on estimated positions and another inconclusive raid ensued. The final raid of the series on Frankfurt involved thirty-two Hampdens from Scampton and Swinderby, 50 Squadron's new home, for the all-5 Group show, while fifty Wellingtons tried their hand at Mannheim. They encountered a small amount of cloud, but thick haze blotted out ground detail, and bombing had to be carried out on estimated positions, a number of bursts offering some evidence that a few incendiaries and high-explosive bombs had fallen within the city.

Preparations and formation flying training had been ongoing for a number of weeks to carry out an audacious attack by daylight on the German warships at Brest under the codename Operation Sunrise. Scheduled for the 24th, it was discovered at the last minute that Scharnhorst had slipped away to La Pallice, some two hundred miles further south, and this required an adjustment to the original complex plan of attack. The intention had been to send three 90 Squadron Fortress Is in to bomb from 30,000 feet to draw up enemy fighters, while 5 Group Hampdens performed a similar function at a less rarefied altitude under the umbrella of a Spitfire escort. While this distraction was in progress, it was hoped that Halifaxes and Wellington from 1, 3 and 4 Groups could sneak in unopposed to target the ships. Now that Scharnhorst had moved, it was decided to send the Halifax element to deal with her, while the rest of the original plan went ahead at Brest. 5 Group detailed six Hampdens each from Waddington, Coningsby and North Luffenham, whose crews had congregated at Coningsby on the previous day for the briefing, before taking off at 10.45 to proceed to Predannack in three boxes with Coningsby leading. The 44 Squadron crews of S/Ls Collier and Nettleton, F/L Ridpath, F/O Clayton, P/O Tew and Sgt Gammon became airborne at 11.00, and, together with the rest of the 5 Group formation, collected the Spitfire escort provided by 10 Group over Cornwall. They were shepherded all the way to the target, which they reached at 14.15, seven minutes after the Fortresses had bombed.

Five of the 44 Squadron participants returned to relate their experiences at debriefing, and to tell what they knew about the absentee crew of F/O Clayton DFM in AD962. The enemy defence had been more fierce than anticipated, and the Hampdens had found themselves in a hornet's nest of single and twin-engine fighters. S/L Collier and crew watched F/O Clayton's Hampden come under attack by a BF109 to port, and the gunners swung their barrels round to lend support. It was already too late for the Clayton crew, and the enemy continued straight on to bear down upon S/L Collier's AD975 from the port quarter, eliciting a response from F/Sgt Williams in the upper gun position. He opened fire from fifty yards range and was joined from the lower gun position, both of them loosing off two hundred rounds. The enemy fighter was observed to turn onto its back and dive vertically into the ground to be claimed as destroyed. F/L Ridpath's gunners were also attempting to support a colleague under attack from two BF109s, when one turned its attention upon them and came at them from astern above tail level, which prevented the lower gunner from bringing his guns to bear. The upper gunner engaged at fifty yards range, firing seventy-five rounds from each gun, upon which this assailant stalled, before also diving vertically into the ground to be claimed as destroyed.

S/L Nettleton's gunners noticed a BF109 approaching from astern, slightly below and to port, apparently fixated on a Hampden flying above them. Upper gunner, Sgt Bain, allowed the range to diminish to two hundred yards, before firing seventy-five rounds from each gun, causing the fighter to flip onto its back and fall away to starboard. He emptied his magazine into it and both under gunners fired off a hundred rounds, observing smoke to pour from the enemy's engine as it continued to spin down to impact the ground and burst into flames. P/O Tew and crew came under attack from a BF109 at 150 yards range, in response to which, the under gunner returned fire, forcing the enemy to swerve to starboard and become lost to view. A second BF109 came in from the starboard quarter high and was fired upon by the upper gunner at two hundred yards range, persuading its pilot also to swerve away to starboard, followed by a continuing stream of fire from Sgt Bull's guns. Reappearing on the port quarter, the enemy seemed to stall and lose control, emitting black smoke and falling away still under heavy fire from the Hampden. The crew was convinced that it had crashed, but their attention had been drawn to more immediate concerns and they could claim it only as "damaged, probably destroyed". AD933 had been lagging behind the formation unable to make up the gap and was soon stalked by a BF109 from astern and slightly above. The upper gunner had been watching the area of the sun and failed to notice the enemy fighter until it had closed to 150 yards range. Sgt Slater opened up with a short burst at the same time as the fighter fired, and the 109 appeared to throttle back, before coming in again and hitting the Hampden with a number of rounds. The upper gunner emptied his magazine into the enemy, which turned onto its back with grey smoke issuing from the engine, and dived past the under gunner, who fired two hundred rounds into it and watched it crash into the ground on the coast.

Ten of the seventy-nine Wellingtons had been shot down by flak and fighters, along with two Hampdens, in return for six unconfirmed hits on the Gneisenau. News eventually arrived via the Red

Cross that F/O Clayton and the two gunners had parachuted to safety and were in enemy hands, but the second pilot, P/O Grant RCAF, had gone down with AD962. The Halifaxes had also suffered the loss of five aircraft at La Pallice, and the ten survivors had all sustained damage to some extent, while scoring five confirmed hits on Scharnhorst to necessitate her return to Brest, where superior repair facilities existed.

Kiel was posted as the primary target for that night, for which a force of thirty-four Wellingtons and thirty Hampdens was made ready, the latter on the stations at Coningsby, North Luffenham and Waddington. 44 Squadron prepared eight Hampdens for its own crews, four for 207 Squadron, and two others for the crews of Sgt Armstrong and P/O Bayley to take mining in one of the Nectarine gardens. The Rhodesians took off between 22.30 and 22.45 with F/L Dugdale the senior pilot on duty, and all reached the target area, where the Deutsche Werke and Krupp Germania shipyards were the aiming points. The weather conditions were favourable, and the visibility clear enough for ground features to be identified during the run in as they ran the gauntlet of an intense searchlight and flak barrage. Bombing was carried out from 10,000 to 18,000 feet between 01.28 and 02.10, and some crews were able to observe the fall of their all-high explosive loads in the shipyards and the town, while others were blinded by searchlight dazzle. Meanwhile, Sgt Armstrong and crew had planted their vegetable from clear skies into the briefed location from 500 feet at 00.39, five minutes ahead of the Bayley crew, who dropped theirs from 600 feet. Despite the enthusiastic claims of some crews, the bombing was scattered, and inaccurate, and local authorities reported only a few bombs falling in the shipyards or the town.

Orders were received at Scampton and Swinderby on the 25th to provide thirty Hampdens to join forces with twenty-five Whitleys for an attack on Hannover. The crews were briefed to aim for the main railway station and post office, which meant that it was to be an area raid to target the city centre. Whether or not they succeeded will never be known, as the crews themselves failed to observe the results and no local report was forthcoming. The teleprinters at Waddington and Coningsby spewed out the details of the forthcoming night's activities on the 27th, revealing them to relate to mining operations in the Artichoke garden off Lorient for the former and the Beech garden off St-Nazaire for the latter. 44 Squadron made ready fourteen aircraft for its own crews and two for 207 Squadron, and they took off between 22.30 and 23.15 with S/L Nettleton the senior pilot on duty. P/O Salazar and crew turned back before crossing the English coast because of intercom failure, leaving the remainder to all reach the target area to deliver their single mine each into the allotted location from 400 to 700 feet between 01.40 and 02.45. The U-Boot base was well-defended, and most crews reported intense searchlight and light flak coming at them from the coast and Groix island out in the bay. F/L Dugdale and crew observed an aircraft become ensnared in a searchlight cone from the two locations and fall victim to flak before crashing in flames into the sea. It became clear later, that they had witnessed the demise of P4406 and the crew of Sgt Gammon, from which none survived.

On the following night the gardens were in the western Baltic, Radish, Forget-me-not and Quince, (Kiel Harbour, Kiel Bay and the Fehmarn Belt), for which forty-two Hampdens were detailed on the stations at Scampton and Swinderby. Unfavourable weather conditions hampered attempts to identify pinpoints from which to time the runs, and only twenty-five vegetables were planted in the allotted locations, while another was dropped in an alternative garden.

A force of 116 aircraft was made ready to unleash on Cologne on the night of the 30/31st, 5 Group contributing forty-two Hampdens from North Luffenham and Waddington. 44 Squadron detailed thirteen of its own, which taxied towards the runway threshold either side of 23.30, only for P/O Sauvage to collide with a ground object and have to scrub his sortie. The remaining twelve, only nine of which were recorded in the ORB, took off between 23.40 and midnight with W/C Misselbrook the senior pilot on duty, and S/L Burton-Gyles back in the fold following his detachment to Boscombe Down. They exited the English coast at Orfordness on their way to the Belgian coast, intending to approach the target from the west, but ran into thunderstorms, heavy rain and icing conditions, which would persuade many crews to seek alternative targets. Sgt Armstrong and crew were soon contending with an engine problem that forced them to turn back, and their sortie ended at 01.15 with a crash-landing in a field at Carlton-le-Moorland, some four miles south-south-west of Waddington. Fortunately, the crew members were able to extricate themselves and scrambled clear unhurt, before AD755 was consumed by fire. W/C Misselbrook and crew ran into a severe electrical storm at the Belgian coast and turned away to seek an alternative route into Fortress Europe. Failing to find one, they headed for home and jettisoned their 1,000 pounder and two 500 pounders into the sea. Aachen lay close to the planned track to Cologne and proved to be a popular alternative target for crews recognising the futility of pressing on, and they had to base their attacks on searchlights and the flashes from flak batteries. Those reaching the primary target encountered nine to ten-tenths cloud at 4,000 feet, and not one made a positive identification of the city. F/L Dugdale, P/O Anekstein and Sgt Robertson bombed it on estimated positions from 12,000 to 15,000 feet between 02.10 and 02.30, and local reports confirmed that a few high explosive bombs and incendiaries had hit the city, causing minor damage and no casualties.

During the course of the month the squadron carried out sixteen operations and dispatched 134 sorties for the loss of six Hampdens and five crews. It had also claimed six enemy fighters destroyed, and another almost certainly destroyed.

August 1941

August got off to a bad start for 44 Squadron on the 1st, when AD966 crashed at 17.10 near Bracebridge Heath on Lincoln's southern outskirts during an air-test, killing all five occupants. The pilot, Sgt Le Blanc Smith, was Rhodesian, and one of the two men listed as of aircraftsman 1 (a/c1) rank, was recorded as a wireless operator under pilot training. 5 Group opened its August account on the night of the 2/3rd, when sending fifty Hampdens from Coningsby and Scampton to attack the town of Kiel and its shipyards, while larger forces attended to Hamburg and Berlin. An incomplete report from Kiel sources confirmed a failed operation, and mentioned a single house damaged, but did not refer to possible hits in the docks and shipyards.

44 Squadron remained at home until the 5th, when orders were received to prepare aircraft for that night's operations over southern Germany. Mannheim would be the destination for sixty-five Wellingtons and thirty-three Hampdens, while ninety-seven aircraft, including fifty Hampdens, targeted railway installations at Karlsruhe, and sixty-eight Wellingtons and Whitleys focussed on Frankfurt. 44 Squadron briefed eleven crews for Karlsruhe, where railway workshops provided the aiming point, and three for the main railway station at Mannheim, but, sadly, the squadron ORB is frustratingly confused and substituted the details of a raid on Kiel for Karlsruhe and failed to list the Mannheim trio. What seems to be clear, is that they departed Waddington between 22.10 and 22.40 with W/C Misselbrook and S/Ls Burton-Gyles and Collier the senior pilots on duty, but lost AE218 to an engine issue immediately after take-off, forcing Sgt Robertson to put it down at Bassingham Fen,

some three miles to the south-west of the airfield. This act would elicit complimentary comments from his commanding officer for his skill, coolness and clear thinking, which prevented the Hampden from being written-off. Both elements were routed out over Orfordness with orders to fly direct to their respective destinations after making landfall over the Scheldt, and flew the length of Belgium over cloud with a bright, full moon to light their way. P/Os Anekstein and Thompson mistook a recall signal to a Scampton crew to be a general recall and landed back at Waddington some three hours after taking off. The others reached Karlsruhe to find that the cloud extended over the target area, and, whilst this prevented them from identifying the railway workshops, they were able to hit the town, W/C Misselbrook doing so from a lowly 4,500 feet at 01.40, estimating his 1,900 pounder and two 250 pounders to have fallen into the southern part of the target area. S/L Collier had already attacked from 10,000 at 01.00, and these were the only reports from those of the squadron to reach the primary target, although we know that S/L Burton-Gyles, P/Os Tew, Bell and Salazar and Sgt Atkins also delivered their bombs there. P/O Maudslay and crew overshot Karlsruhe without realising, and ended up over Heilbronn, which they bombed with 500 and 250 pounders and 120 x 4lb incendiaries from 9,000 feet at 01.30. The Mannheim-bound force encountered five to ten-tenths cloud over the city in a band between 14,000 and 18,000 feet, but excellent visibility below, and most identified the city with ease although not necessarily the briefed aiming point. Local sources confirmed some destruction in the western side of Karlsruhe and in the Rhine harbour, while several areas of Mannheim and northern Ludwigshafen sustained severe damage.

It was decided to repeat the Mannheim and Karlsruhe operations on the following night, along with another to railway yards at Frankfurt. A 5 Group force of thirty-eight Hampdens from North-Luffenham and Swinderby was handed the Karlsruhe job, which was to be launched from North Luffenham in Rutland. The force encountered nine-tenths cloud over the target, which prevented the crews from identifying the railway workshops, and they mostly deposited their bombs and incendiaries on the town. Meanwhile, 5 Group dispatched twenty-one freshman crews from North Luffenham, Scampton and Waddington to bomb the docks and shipping at Calais. The eight-strong 44 Squadron element contained the first six pilots to be trained in Rhodesia and took off between 22.15 and 22.35 under strict orders to bring their bombs home if they could not identify the aiming point. An indistinct distress signal was picked up from Sgt Bradbury and crew at around 23.30, a matter of minutes before X2917 clipped trees and crashed onto Barton Bendish airfield in Norfolk, a satellite of Marham. There were no survivors, and the Accident Investigations Branch was tasked with uncovering the cause of the early return and subsequent fatal incident, which took place in poor weather conditions. Shortly afterwards, the others reached the French coast to find eight to ten-tenths cloud in layers between 4,000 and 10,000 feet, which severely compromised target location. Sgt Nicholson descended from 14,000 to 8,000 feet, from where the town was just visible, but not the docks, and they complied with the briefing to bring their bombs home. In the event, only the crews of Sgts De Brath, Dedman, Musgrave and Redfern carried out attacks, from 8,000 to 10,000 feet between 23.40 and 01.25, the last-mentioned, Sgt Redfern, clearly having spent a considerable time searching.

The troublesome operational career of the Manchesters got under way again on the night of the 7/8th, when three from 207 Squadron and fifty-four Hampdens were made ready to join forces with forty-nine other aircraft to attack the mighty Krupp munitions complex in Essen. 44 Squadron was called upon to provide just two crews for the main event and five others for mining duties in the western Baltic. The latter departed Waddington first at 22.00, with P/O Thompson bound for the Asparagus garden (Great Belt south), P/O Sauvage for Broccoli (Great Belt south), P/O Bayley for Carrot (Little Belt), P/O Bell for Quince (Kiel Bay) and P/O Anekstein for Pumpkin (Great Belt north), leaving Sgts

Atkinson and Dobbs to take off for the Ruhr at 00.35. The weather conditions in the latter's target area were favourable with good horizontal visibility, but the main problem, as always over the Ruhr, was the blanket of industrial haze, and, while some crews were able to establish their position by the Rhine, picking out individual buildings was a different matter. The density of Krupp buildings in the Borbeck district should have guaranteed that some would be hit, if only the crews could pinpoint on that segment of the city, but neither of the 44 Squadron crews was able to locate the aiming point. Sgt Atkinson and crew dropped a 1,000 pounder and two 500 pounders from 15,000 feet at 02.30, and Sgt Dobbs a similar payload from 13,000 feet thirty minutes later, but neither could plot the fall. Local sources reported no more than forty high explosive bombs and two hundred incendiaries falling within the city, which destroyed a bakery but caused little other damage, and it would be a further eighteen months before the means were to hand to defeat the industrial haze.

Meanwhile, some 270 miles to the north, P/O Bayley and crew dropped their store from 500 feet at 01.10, five minutes before attacking a merchant vessel from 3,500 feet and missing by eighty yards. P/O Bell and crew planted their vegetable also at 01.10, from 700 feet, and, four minutes later, bombed a 5,000-ton merchantman, claiming a near miss, before, as a parting gift, firing off two hundred rounds. P/O Anekstein and crew delivered their mine as briefed from 600 feet at 01.15, and also found a target for their 250 pounders in the form of a two-funnel merchant vessel of around 3,000 tons in a fourteen-ship convoy. They bombed it from 1,000 feet, setting off a fire on board, which remained visible for fifty miles into the return flight. P/O Thompson and crew delivered their mine from 500 feet at 01.17, before spotting a convoy of about eight ships steaming north, which they attacked with the two wing-mounted 250 pounders from 1,500 feet at 01.25. They claimed one direct hit and a near miss on a 1,000 tonner and spent a further thirty minutes strafing the other vessels, one from mast height, without opposition, by which time they were able to report the bomb-damaged vessel to be listing with the appearance of going down. P/O Sauvage and crew also fulfilled their brief from 500 feet at 01.30, but found no suitable target for their wing bombs, which they brought home.

With another daylight operation in the planning stage, the crews of W/C Misselbrook, S/Ls Burton-Gyles and Nettleton and P/Os Maudslay, Salazar and Tew, with F/L Marshall as a reserve, took part in practice formation flying on the 8th. That night, fifty Hampdens from North Luffenham, Swinderby and Coningsby were launched for a raid on the U-Boot construction yards at Kiel in company with four Whitleys, and, in keeping with the level of performance established thus far during the year, little damage resulted. Poor weather kept 5 Group on the ground for the next two nights, and it was the 11th when the next batch of orders was received, detailing an operation against marshalling yards in the Ruhr city of Krefeld for twenty Hampdens from North Luffenham, and Rotterdam docks for thirty freshman crews. The five 44 Squadron crews of Sgts De Brath, Harvey, Knight, Nicholson and Redfern were undertaking only their second sortie, and departed Waddington between 01.15 and 01.45, each carrying four 500 and two 250 pounders. (The squadron ORB recorded Calais as the target). They found the Dutch coast to be concealed beneath nine to ten-tenths cloud with tops at 9,000 feet and a base estimated to be below 3,000 feet, and only Sgts Harvey and Knight were able to carry out an attack. The latter broke into clear air at 2,800 feet, and delivered his load onto dock buildings at 03.00, but cloud slid across to block his view of the outcome. Sgt Harvey and crew delivered their load on estimated position from 11,000 feet two minutes later, leaving the others to search in vain until the approaching dawn persuaded them to give up and go home.

The daylight operation mentioned above turned out to be an attack on Longueness aerodrome at St-Omer in support of a 2 Group raid on Cologne's power stations at Knapsack and Quadrath on the 12th.

Coningsby sent a similar number to Gosnay power station, also in France, and both 5 Group sections would be protected by a fighter escort. The intention was to support the beleaguered Russians by persuading the Luftwaffe to withdraw fighters from the Russian front to protect economic targets in the west. The Waddington element of six took off at 08.55 and reached the target area to encounter ten-tenths cloud with tops at 8,000 feet, which thwarted any hope of identifying the briefed target. W/C Misselbrook led the formation to a section of railway line some two-and-a-half miles south of St-Omer, where all twenty-four 500 pounders were dropped from 11,000 feet at 10.42. Cloud prevented an observation of the results, but it was believed that the bombs had straddled the track.

The night of the 12/13th was to be a busy one for the Command, and, throughout the day, aircraft were made ready for attacks on Berlin, Hannover, Magdeburg and Essen. 5 Group detailed thirteen Hampdens to join sixty-five Wellingtons for Hannover, and thirty-six to operate on their own at Magdeburg, while a force of seventy aircraft assigned to the Capital included nine Manchesters. Together with minor operations, the night's activities involved a total of 234 aircraft. Hannover lay on the route to both Magdeburg and Berlin, and the three forces would fly out together until reaching it, at which point the Berlin element would continue straight on for the 150 additional miles, while the Magdeburg section peeled off to the south-east with eighty miles still ahead of it. Eleven Hampdens were made ready at Waddington for Magdeburg, and an additional five for freshman crews to take to Calais, but, as they climbed away shortly after 21.00, they were recalled because of the threat of adverse weather conditions. F/L Ridpath and crew got away at 21.15, and, having failed to pick up the signal, continued on to reach German airspace over ten-tenths cloud, by which time they had noticed excessive fuel consumption. They decided to join in on the Hannover raid, to which they were attracted by bomb bursts, and delivered their own 1,900 pounder and two 250 pounders towards the middle of the built-up area from 12,000 feet at 00.10.

Orders were received across the Command on the 14th to prepare for operations that night against railway targets in three major cities in northern Germany to the north of the Harz mountains, Hannover the most westerly, Magdeburg the most easterly and Braunschweig (Brunswick) in-between. 5 Group detailed eighty-one Hampdens to operate alone against the main railway station in Braunschweig, while seven Manchester crews were briefed for Magdeburg as part of an overall force of fifty-two aircraft. Twelve 44 Squadron crews attended briefing, ten to learn of their part in the main event, while F/L Marshall and Sgt Dorehill were told that they would be mining in one of the Nectarine gardens off the Frisians. The bombing brigade departed Waddington between 21.00 and 21.15 with S/L Collier the senior pilot on duty but lost the services of Sgt Dedman and crew within an hour because of engine trouble. The gardeners took off at 21.40, for what would be roughly a four-hour round trip, and Sgt Dorehill and crew delivered their mine into the allotted position from 500 feet at 23.33, F/L Marshall and crew following suit from one hundred feet higher at 23.56. The bombing brigade pressed on to reach northern Germany over a blanket of medium-level cloud, which prevented all from identifying the aiming point and led to five crews bombing the Braunschweig city area generally from 7,500 to 14,500 feet between 23.49 and 00.45. The remaining four crews tracked back to Hannover, where they joined in the ongoing raid, and delivered their loads from 4,000 to 15,000 feet between 23.50 and 00.30. Returning crews reported bursts at both locations but had no genuine idea as to where their bombs impacted, and nothing was forthcoming from local sources.

Railway objectives featured again on the 16th, when orders went out to stations across the Command to prepare for attacks on installations in the Ruhr cities of Düsseldorf and Duisburg, and Cologne to the south. Düsseldorf was to be a 5 Group show involving fifty-two Hampdens and six Manchesters, sixteen of the former provided by 44 Squadron. They took off between 22.30 and 23.15 with S/L Nettleton the senior pilot on duty, leaving F/L Marshall and crew on the ground pending their departure at 01.40 to bomb the docks and shipping at Ostend. Sgt Dobbs and crew turned back after an hour with intercom, instrument and flaps problems, while a number of engine issues persuaded F/L Ridpath and crew to divert to Haamstede aerodrome on Schouwen in the Scheldt estuary, which they bombed from 10,000 feet at 00.37. The others reached the target area to be welcomed by cloud and industrial haze, penetrated by intense searchlight and flak activity. They carried out their attacks from 12,000 to 16,000 feet between 00.59 and 02.01, mostly on estimated positions over the general city area. Sgt Nicholson and crew were defeated by the poor visibility, and bombed Neuss, on the other side of the Rhine, from 17,000 feet at 01.40, just as F/L Marshall and crew were setting off for their appointment at the Belgian coast. They delivered their four 500 pounders from 12,000 feet at 03.26 and estimated them to have straddled the quayside south-east of the new tidal harbour. AE239 failed to return with the crew of Sgt Armstrong and is known to have come down in the North Sea without survivors.

Waddington was not involved in the 5 Group operation on the 17th, for which thirty-nine Hampden crews were briefed to attack the main goods railway station in Bremen, while twenty 4 Group Whitleys targeted the city's Focke-Wulf factory. It was another inconclusive attack in the face of extreme darkness and haze, and no results were observed by the 5 Group crews, while a number of those from 4 Group claimed hits on the aircraft factory.

Unknown to the crews, the operations during June and July had been monitored in order to provide an assessment for the War Cabinet of the effectiveness of the strategic bombing campaign. The project was initiated by Churchill's chief scientific advisor, Professor Lindemann, otherwise known as Lord Cherwell, who handed the responsibility to David M Bensusan-Butt, a civil-servant assistant to Cherwell working in the War Cabinet Secretariat. What became known as The Butt Report was released on the 18th, and its disclosures sent shock waves reverberating around the Cabinet Room and the Air Ministry. Having studied around four thousand photographs taken during night operations, he concluded that only a small fraction of bombs had fallen within miles of their intended targets. This swept away at a stroke any notion, that the Command was reducing the enemy's capacity and will to continue the fight. It also demonstrated the claims of the crews to be wildly optimistic, and unjustly blighted forever the period of tenure as Commander-in-Chief of Sir Richard Peirse. In his defence, the focus of operations changed frequently, the demands and expectations of his superiors were not realistic and the crews, though doing their best, were ill-equipped for the tasks required of them.

While the report was being digested that evening, 5 Group sent forty-two Hampdens from North Luffenham and Coningsby to attack the West Station at Cologne in company with twenty Whitleys and Wellingtons. Returning crews reported many fires on the western side of the Rhine, but local reports of nothing more than superficial damage suggested that a decoy fire site had attracted the main weight of bombs. It was to be a similar story on the following night, when forty-one Hampdens from Scampton and Waddington joined sixty-seven other aircraft to attempt to hit a railway junction in Kiel. 44 Squadron made ready sixteen of its own and dispatched all but one of them between 20.50 and 21.10, with S/L Collier the senior pilot on duty. Sgt Nicholson and crew took off a little later and would be the last over the target. They all encountered unhelpful weather conditions in the target area in the form of nine to ten-tenths cloud with tops at around 8,000 feet and a base below 5,000 feet in places. Attacks were carried out on estimated positions from 6,000 to 17,000 feet between 23.21 and 00.25, but S/L Collier and F/L Ridpath suffered the frustration of their bomb doors refusing to open and having to bring their loads home. P/Os Maudslay and Tew also returned with their bombs still on board after failing to identify the target. They were not alone, and local sources reported that no bombs had fallen into the town.

A series of three operations against Mannheim began on the night of the 22/23rd, for which 5 Group provided forty-one Hampdens from Coningsby, Syerston and Waddington, which were to join forces with fifty-six Wellingtons. Three aiming points included the main railway station, for which the fifteen 44 Squadron crews were briefed before taking off between 21.30 and 22.05 with S/Ls Burton-Gyles and Nettleton the senior pilots on duty. Sgt Dobbs and crew crossed the Belgian coast at Veurne, between Ostend and Dunkerque, and penetrated fifteen miles inland before falling oil pressure persuaded them to turn back and land at Manston. The others pressed on along the line of the Franco/Belgian frontier until crossing into Germany and reaching the target area by following the Rhine, only to find haze impairing the view of the ground. The visibility proved to be no impediment to the searchlight batteries, which ensnared Sgt Nicholson and crew and held them in a cone of blue beams while a box barrage of flak shells exploded all around them. They escaped by diving steeply from 17,000 feet and jettisoning their load, leaving the others to deliver their bombs from 9,000 to 16,000 feet between 00.15 and 01.00. Returning crews reported bomb bursts and fires, but local sources claimed that only one house had been destroyed and five others lightly damaged.

It was left to Scampton to provide a dozen Hampdens to represent 5 Group at Düsseldorf on the 24th, when 4 Group Whitleys and Halifaxes completed the force of forty-four aircraft. Six additional Hampdens were assigned to searchlight suppression duties in the Wesel defensive belt, their task to attack with small bombs and guns any battery holding a bomber in its beams. This activity turned out to be more effective than the raid on Düsseldorf and caused the beams either to become erratic or to be extinguished altogether. A 5 Group attack on Mannheim by thirty-eight Hampdens and seven Manchesters was briefed out on all stations on the 25th, when the main post office was specified as the aiming point for an area raid. 44 Squadron remained at home, while 207 Squadron represented Waddington in what turned out to be another inconclusive affair. Cologne was posted as the target on the 26th, and a force of ninety-nine aircraft made ready, which included twenty-nine Hampdens and a single Manchester from Coningsby, Scampton and Syerston, while six other Hampdens were to carry out flak suppression sorties to the west of the city. Waddington was not involved in what became another highly unsatisfactory performance that deposited no more than 15% of the bomb loads into eastern districts.

Orders arriving on the 27th revealed a return to Mannheim for ninety-one aircraft, including thirty-five Hampdens from North Luffenham, Waddington and Swinderby, whose crews were to attack the main railway station, while elements of 1, 3 and 4 Groups focussed on other aiming points within the city. Meanwhile, seventeen Hampdens would be mining the waters of the Nectarines gardens around the Frisians, and 44 Squadron would be represented in both undertakings. The eight gardening crews, which were all-NCO, departed Waddington first, between 20.00 and 20.20, to be followed into the air between 21.40 and 22.10 by the ten members of the bombing brigade, of which S/Ls Burton-Gyles and Nettleton were the senior pilots on duty. Before the last one climbed away, the first of the gardeners had reached its destination off the island of Borkum in the Nectarine II garden to find five to ten-tenths cloud with a base at around 2,000 feet. Sgt Knight and crew delivered their vegetable from 500 feet at 22.05, and the others arrived soon afterwards to plant their single mine each from 600 to 800 by 22.33, before returning home, mostly to land at Horsham-St-Faith in Norfolk. The bombing element found clear skies but extreme darkness and haze, and many were prevented by searchlight glare from identifying the aiming point, forcing them to bomb the built-up area generally. The attacks were carried out from 9,000 to 15,000 feet between 00.34 and 01.30, and some bursts and fires were observed. S/L Nettleton had been forced to turn back with an engine issue when over Belgium and dropped his bombs onto an aerodrome between Brussels and Ghent at 00.20. There was some optimism concerning the effectiveness of the raid, but local sources reported no significant damage. On the following morning, Sgt Johnson and crew set off from Horsham-St-Faith to return to base but crashed while attempting to land at a Q Site at Potter Hanworth, five miles east of Waddington. AD917 was written off, and two members of the crew lost their lives.

44 Squadron sat out the following night's operation to attack marshalling yards in Duisburg, for which 5 Group put up thirty Hampdens and six Manchesters in an overall force of 118 aircraft, and six further Hampdens for searchlight suppression duties. Returning crews claimed a successful raid, but, again, this was disputed by local reports, which suggested that only around a dozen bomb loads had hit the city. The final raid of the Mannheim series was posted on Wellington stations on the 29th, while Frankfurt was notified as the destination for a 4 and 5 Group force of 143 aircraft. This would be the first time that this city had faced an attack by a hundred-plus aircraft, the crews of which had been briefed to use the inland docks as the aiming point. 5 Group would be contributing seventy-three Hampdens and three 207 Squadron Manchesters, 44 Squadron providing a dozen of the former, which departed Waddington between 21.50 and 22.15 with S/Ls Collier and Nettleton the senior pilots on duty. Sgt De Brath and crew were soon back on the ground because of an engine issue, leaving the others to adopt the briefed route from Orfordness to Namur in Belgium, while some opted to fly directly to the target from the English coast, which meant landfall over the Scheldt estuary and skirting northern Belgium to pass south of Cologne. Cloud lay over most of the route, and icing became a problem for some, but all of the remaining 44 Squadron crews reached the target area, where seven to nine-tenths cloud prevented many from identifying the planned aiming point. However, some were able to pick out the river and docks by running in from below 10,000 feet, and bombing was carried out on largely estimated positions from 7,500 to 13,000 feet between 00.40 and 01.10. Some crews observed bursts in the built-up area but no detail, and Sgt Harvey and crew, having searched in vain for the primary target, set course for home, and, at 03.14 released their 1,000 pounder and two 250 pounders from 13,000 feet onto a searchlight concentration estimated to be at Aachen. Local reports from Frankfurt described scattered and insignificant damage, and, certainly, nothing commensurate with the size of the force and the effort expended.

A non-operational crash accounted for AD939 on the final day of the month, while it was being flown by P/O Owen. He was providing fighter affiliation instruction for a student pilot, when a collision occurred with a Canadian Spitfire from Digby, which resulted in the Hampden crashing near Waddington at 12.10, killing the three occupants. That night would bring an attack on railway targets in Cologne involving a force of 103 aircraft. 5 Group put up thirty-nine Hampdens and six Manchesters for the main event, and five further Manchesters to perform a flak suppression role. The 44 Squadron element of ten departed Waddington between 20.15 and 20.45 with F/O Sauvage the senior pilot on duty and the only officer among thirty-nine NCO airmen. They were routed out over southern Holland and would have to run the gauntlet of searchlights and flak in the Roermond area, where the ground on this occasion was concealed by ten-tenths cloud, but bright moonlight above provided ideal conditions for night-fighters. This was of no interest to Sgts De Brath and Dorehill and their crews, who were forced to turn back early with engine issues. F/O Sauvage and crew were intercepted by a BF109 as they closed on the target and dropped their 1,000 pounder and two 500 pounders hastily onto the western suburbs from 13,000 feet at 22.15 as they took evasive action. AD975 was hit in the tailplane and rudder, and the rudder controls were rendered almost ineffective. They struggled back to base, where the airframe was found to be riddled with holes, some in the oil and fuel tanks, and both propellers were damaged. Sgt Dedman and crew failed to locate the primary target through the ten-tenths cloud but spotted a flarepath on the aerodrome at Geilenkirchen as they approached the Dutch frontier homebound at 14,000 feet. They dropped a mix of high-explosives and incendiaries at 23.05 and observed a large fire result immediately. The others carried out their attacks at Cologne from 8,500 to 16,000 feet between 22.40 and 23.25, and all but Sgt Harvey returned home to make their reports. It was established eventually, that AD726 had crashed into the North Sea some twenty-five miles east of Harwich without survivors, and the remains of two occupants were washed ashore sometime later on the Belgian coast.

During the course of the month, the squadron participated in eighteen operations and dispatched 157 sorties, including fourteen recalled, for the loss of five Hampdens and seventeen crew members.

September 1941

With the impending, but highly secret, conversion of 44 Squadron to the new Lancaster, a large number of aircrew personnel would arrive at Waddington during the month, the new type, like its forerunner, the Manchester, requiring a crew complement of seven, rather than the four routinely squashed into a Hampden. The influx began in the first week with the posting-in of F/L Wood from 16 O.T.U and F/L De Mestre from 6 BAT, although the latter would be posted to Scampton in mid-month to join 49 Squadron. 5 Group was in action on the first night of the new month, when twenty Hampdens joined forces with Wellingtons to attack Cologne in what turned out to be favourable weather conditions. Despite this, few bombs found the mark, and the fires reported by returning crews were probably from decoy sites. Briefings took place across the Command on the 2nd for two operations to be carried out that night, both supported by 5 Group. The main operation would be conducted by 126 aircraft, including eleven Hampdens, against the inland docks at Frankfurt, while a force of forty-nine aircraft was to target the central railway station in Berlin, some 260 miles to the north-east. The bulk of the latter force, thirty-two Hampdens and four Manchesters, was provided by 5 Group, with a handful of 3 Group Stirlings and 4 Group Halifaxes in attendance. 44 Squadron would support both operations, sending nine Hampdens to Germany's capital city led by S/Ls Burton-Gyles and Nettleton, while four all-NCO crews were briefed for Frankfurt, and they departed Waddington together between 20.25 and 20.45.

Sgt Dorehill and crew were the first from the squadron to arrive at Frankfurt, having crossed France over varying amounts of cloud between two and eight-tenths. They attacked with four 500 pounders from 13,000 feet at 23.27 and estimated the bursts to have occurred in the centre of the target. Sgt Knight and crew were thirteen minutes behind and bombed from the same altitude, immediately after which, the port engine cut. They would negotiate the four-hundred-mile return journey from the target to the county of Surrey, where the starboard engine failed at 5,000 feet. The Hampden pitched into a dive, forcing the crew to take to their parachutes, and, as AD913 crashed near Dorking at 02.45, the pilot, second pilot/navigator and a gunner drifted down to land safely. The body of the fourth crew member was found close by, and it was assumed that he had failed to leave the aircraft. Sgt Musgrave and crew were the last to reach Frankfurt, which they bombed from 11,000 feet at 23.55, observing bursts but no detail, and then came to grief on landing at North-Luffenham, although, without injury to the crew or serious damage to the Hampden. AE313 failed to return after crashing in Germany, killing Sgt de Brath and his second pilot, and delivering the two survivors into enemy hands.

The Berlin element had set a course from the Lincolnshire coast to the east Frisians, and Sgt Dobbs and crew were some twenty miles east of Norderney when attacked by a Me110, which inflicted heavy damage on AD982 and wounded two of the crew. The gunners returned fire and claimed hits on their assailant before both aircraft retreated to return to their respective bases. F/L Ridpath ran into the five to ten-tenths cloud that lay over the whole of northern Germany at between 6,000 and 8,000 feet, and, determining that there was little prospect of establishing a firm pinpoint on the ground, back-tracked to Hamburg, which he bombed from 10,000 feet at 00.21. At the same time, 160 miles to the east, S/L Burton-Gyles and crew were at 10,000 feet assessing the impact of their 1,900 pounder, with P/O Anekstein and S/L Nettleton hot on their heels to deliver their loads from 14,000 and 15,000 feet at 00.20 and 00.22 respectively. P/O Bell and crew arrived at 00.40 to carry out their attack from 15,000 feet, while P/O Tew and crew chose a lofty 20,000 feet for theirs at 00.55, before all returned safely to Wittering, Cottesmore and Linton-on-Ouse. It would prove to be an expensive night for 44 Squadron, which would have a number of empty dispersal pans to contemplate in the cold light of dawn. Two of them should have been occupied by AE152 and AE254 with the crews of P/O Thompson and Sgt Robertson respectively. The former is presumed to have gone into the sea, probably having fallen victim to a night-fighter, as the body of the pilot eventually came ashore for burial on the Frisian island of Ameland. The latter crashed at Wittenberg, some fifty miles south-west of Berlin, and, again, there were no survivors. At 03.20, a 50 Squadron Hampden landed at Waddington on return from a mining sortie, and collided with 44 Squadron's X3025, writing off both aircraft. Returning crews from the two main targets reported many fires, but local sources suggested that ineffective raids had taken place.

The enemy warships at Brest returned to the spotlight on the 3rd after a respite in recent weeks, and a force of 140 aircraft was made ready. 5 Group contributed thirty Hampdens and two 207 Squadron Manchesters, which took off, only for a recall signal to bring them home shortly afterwards, along with those from 1 and 4 Groups, because of deteriorating weather conditions. In the event, 3 Group and four other aircraft that had failed to pick up the signal, carried on and bombed on estimated positions through a smoke screen. On the 6th, 5 Group detailed eighteen Hampdens from Coningsby to join with sixty-eight other aircraft to target the I G Farben-controlled chemicals/synthetic rubber factory at Marl-Hüls on the north-eastern edge of the Ruhr. It was known locally as the Buna works, after the Butadiene and Natrium (Sodium) chemicals employed in the manufacturing process of synthetic rubber for tyres. *(In previous books I have mistakenly located this factory in the Hüls district of Krefeld in the western Ruhr).* Earlier in the day, thirty-four additional Hampdens had been sent to Kinloss and Lossiemouth as forward launching pads for mining operations that night in the Onion garden off Oslo. Among these were ten representing 44 Squadron, but, in the event, insufficient refuelling facilities allowed only six of them to take off from Lossiemouth between 21.20 and 22.15 led by S/L Collier. They all reached the target area to find clear skies and perfect conditions and delivered a single mine each from 400 to 700 feet between 01.25 and 02.01. S/L Collier had already dropped his 250lb wing bombs on an aerodrome, and Sgt Musgrove found a similar target for his, while F/L Ridpath and Sgt Dobbs attacked merchant vessels from 7,000 and 2,000 feet respectively. AD930 sustained damage from the burst of a flak shell, but S/L Collier brought the Hampden back to a safe landing at Lossiemouth, and, later in the day, to Waddington.

Berlin was posted as the night's main target on the 7th, for which a force of 197 aircraft was made ready, while the Deutsche Werke U-Boot yards and the town of Kiel would occupy a further fifty-one aircraft. 5 Group supported both operations, with eighteen Hampdens for the latter and forty-three

Hampdens and four 207 Squadron Manchesters for the Capital. 44 Squadron made ready five Hampdens for Kiel and four for mining sorties in the Nectarine II garden off the central Frisians. The latter departed Waddington first between 21.00 and 21.30, but, two minutes after X2921 lifted off the runway at 21.15, it crashed on Branston Hall Farm, causing the mine to detonate on impact and kill Rhodesian pilot, Sgt Watt, and his crew. The others pressed on to the target area, where they encountered six-tenths cloud but good visibility. They planted their vegetables from 550 to 700 feet between 23.24 and 23.42, Sgt Hackney and P/O Budd respectively also bombing buildings on Schiermonnikoog and an aerodrome on Borkum. The all-NCO bombing element had taken off between 22.15 and 22.25 and arrived in the target area to find favourable conditions with up to three-tenths cloud, which they exploited to carry out their attacks from 14,000 to 18,000 feet between 01.48 and 02.25. They were able mostly to plot the fall of their bombs, and, while no claims were made of direct hits on the shipyard, local sources reported damage in a number of locations to warehouses and housing, and to two passenger vessels.

On the morning of the 8th, four Fortresses of 90 Squadron were sent to attack the German battleship, Admiral Scheer, at anchor in Oslo, and two of them, including the one captained by the former 44 and 207 Squadron pilot, F/O Dave Romans, were shot down from 25,000 feet without survivors, and another crashed at home. It was sad news for Waddington, where Romans had been a popular young man, who, in 1940, had survived a number of ditchings and earned a DFC. The first large Bomber Command attack on the city of Kassel was briefed to crews of all groups that afternoon, and would involve ninety-five aircraft, including twenty-seven Hampdens. There were to be two aiming points, both of them belonging to the Henschel Company, the presence of whose numerous manufacturing sites dominated the city and employed eight thousand workers in addition to a large number of slaves. Aside from building the Dornier Do17Z bomber under license, Henschel was the main producer of the Panzer III tank and the Tiger I and II, as well as narrow-gauge locomotives. The force was to be divided, sixty-eight aircraft assigned to the tank works, and twenty-seven to the locomotive workshops, with the ten 44 Squadron participants assigned to the latter. They departed Waddington between 19.50 and 20.15 with S/L Burton-Gyles the senior pilot on duty and adopted the briefed route from Orfordness to Dinant in Belgium, benefitting throughout from the fine weather conditions, which aided them in their search for the target. Kassel lay beneath clear skies, the excellent visibility enhanced by bright moonlight, which the crews exploited to bomb from 8,000 to 16,000 feet between 23.23 and 00.05. The squadron delivered a total of nine 1,000 and eighteen 500 pounders onto the target area, and the later arrivals reported at least a dozen fires among sheds in the locomotive works, with flames reaching a hundred feet and smoke rising through 5,000 feet. Crews from other squadrons observed bursts and fires, and a particularly large conflagration at the main railway station to the west of the aiming point. S/L Burton-Gyles mistook the town of Korbach, situated some twenty-five miles to the west of Kassel and a little to the north of the Eder reservoir, for the primary target, and bombed its centre from 2,000 feet at 23.25. On return at 03.50, and with failing engines, P4285 struck trees while trying to land at Coningsby, but P/O Anekstein and one other walked away from the ensuing crash, while their two colleagues sustained injuries. Local sources in Kassel reported serious damage to two industrial concerns and the destruction of eleven houses with more than seventy others requiring repair, which was a poor return for the size of the force operating in favourable conditions. On a positive note, at least, no aircraft had been lost.

Orders were received on the 11th to prepare for an attack on the A G Neptun shipyards at Rostock, while the rest of the force targeted the nearby Heinkel factory and the town itself. A total force of fifty-six aircraft consisted of thirty-nine Hampdens and five 207 Squadron Manchesters from Coningsby,

North Luffenham and Waddington, and a dozen Wellingtons. This was one of three Baltic coast targets for the night, the others, at Kiel and Warnemünde, having been assigned to Wellingtons and Whitleys respectively. Other operations on this night involved eight freshman crews to attack the docks and shipping at Boulogne, and twenty Hampdens mining off the Frisians, Heligoland and Warnemünde. The crews of P/O Budd and Sgt Hackney were the first to depart Waddington, at 20.25 and 20.50 respectively, bound for the French coast, and they were followed into the air between 21.40 and 22.00 by the five crews briefed for Rostock. There should have been six for this target, but P/O Salazar had been involved in a collision of some sort while taxiing to the runway and was unable to continue. The gardeners were the last to leave Waddington behind them, between 23.35 and 23.50, by which time Sgt Hackney and P/O Budd and their crews had bombed Boulogne on estimated positions through cloud from 12,000 and 13,000 feet respectively at 22.30. The bombing element flew out over ten-tenths cloud, each carrying a 1,000 pounder and two of 500lbs, and, as Sgt McBarnett and crew approached the Danish coast, the fuel gauges suggested insufficient petrol to take them all the way and back. They turned towards the Island of Sylt and bombed its northern end from 15,000 feet at 01.20, leaving the others to press on across southern Jutland to reach the western Baltic. The cloud began to thin to eight-tenths by the time that the target area drew near, and ground features could be identified by some through a large gap at around 8,000 feet. There were no searchlights and only a small amount of light flak as they carried out their bombing runs from around 14,000 feet either side of 01.30, and, while crews from other squadrons reported bursts and fires across the harbour area, the 44 Squadron ORB offered scant detail. Sgt Dedman and crew were within twenty miles of the Kent coast on return, when the starboard engine of AD981 cut and caught fire. The petrol feed was switched off, and the propeller fell away soon afterwards. The port wing tank was running short, and with no means available to transfer fuel from the starboard side, a ditching became inevitable. Fortunately, a convoy with two escort vessels was sighted, and Sgt Dedman pulled off a ditching alongside, enabling the crew to be picked up thirty-five minutes later by the destroyer, HMS Garth, which landed them at Sheerness on the 13th. The gardeners, meanwhile, had planted their vegetables off the Frisians as briefed from 500 and 600 feet between 01.13 and 02.09, and returned safely.

On the 12th, the squadron was notified that it was now to be known as 44 (Rhodesia) Squadron, and it would carry its new title into battle for the first time that night against marshalling yards in Frankfurt. 5 Group detailed thirty-one Hampdens to contribute to an overall force of 130 aircraft, and 44 (Rhodesia) Squadron made ready nine of its own, loading each with a 1,000 pounder and two of 500lbs. The first six took off between 22.30 and 23.00 led by S/L Collier, before a Luftwaffe attack on the airfield prevented the last three from getting away. They headed out over Orfordness for the North Sea crossing to the Scheldt estuary and set course then for Namur in Belgium. They encountered cloud over the sea and for most of the outward flight, until it thinned to some extent, but as was usually the case, opinions varied as to the state of the conditions. The cloud density ranged between six and ten-tenths in the target area at around 6,000 feet, and some crews also mentioned moonlight filtering through gaps to provide a glimpse of the ground. The visibility was described as both good and poor with searchlight dazzle cited as a major impediment to aiming point identification, but, as far as the Waddington crews were concerned, they saw nothing of the ground through the cloud as they bombed from 8,500 to 14,500 feet between 01.18 and 02.00 and observed only the flash of bomb bursts. Returning crews reported large fires, and local sources confirmed that thirty-eight blazes had to be dealt with, and most of the damage had been in residential districts.

It was time for another attempt on the German warships at Brest on the 13th, for which a force of 147 aircraft of six different types was assembled across the Command. 5 Group contributed thirty-eight

Hampdens and four Manchesters from North Luffenham, Coningsby and Waddington, all of which, like the rest of the participants, were thwarted by the smoke screen that engulfed the vessels and hid them from view. 44 (Rhodesia) Squadron remained at home on this night and would do so until the 15th, when Hamburg would provide the focus for a force of 169 aircraft of six different types. 5 Group detailed fifty Hampdens to target the city's Blohm & Voss shipyards in company with more than a hundred others, while four Manchesters attacked a railway junction. 44 (Rhodesia) Squadron made ready nine Hampdens for the main event and four for freshman crews who were to attack the docks and shipping at Le Havre. As the former were taxiing to the runway, a 207 Squadron Manchester in transit arrived in the Waddington circuit at 18.10, and dived suddenly into the ground at South Hykeham, five miles to the west of the airfield, killing all four aircrew and the six members of groundcrew on board. As the bombing element departed Waddington between 18.15 and 18.35 with F/L Wood the senior pilot on duty, they would have seen the smoke and flames from the burning wreck but may not then have understood the significance. The freshmen followed them into the air an hour later, by which time, F/L Wood and crew had turned back with an engine issue shortly after crossing the coast near Mablethorpe, and Sgt McBarnett and crew, who were contending with starboard engine problem, followed them home after reaching a point some 130 miles from base.

A layer of ten-tenths stratus cloud at 5,000 feet hid the North Sea from view, but it had dispersed sufficiently to allow sight of the Elbe Estuary, from which point, the force would have to run the gauntlet of searchlights and flak all the way to the aiming points. The skies over the city were clear, but searchlight glare proved to be a serious impediment to aiming point identification and bombing by the few 44 (Rhodesian) Squadron crews to attack as briefed was carried out from 9,500 to 15,000 feet between 21.55 and 22.20. Light flak was reaching 10,000 feet, with searchlights co-operating with night-fighters to create the usual hostile environment for the attackers, and it was this that deflected P/O Budd and crew from their bombing run. They picked up some shrapnel damage as they unloaded their high explosives and incendiaries indiscriminately over the built-up area, but not enough to prevent their safe return. Sgt Nicholson and crew were beaten back by the defences and turned their attention upon the port of Cuxhaven instead, while Sgt Tetley and crew ran into a nest of searchlights co-operating with intense flak some ten miles west of the town of Schleswig. They dropped their load from 8,000 feet at 22.00 with no clue as to what was beneath them. On return at 03.17, AD930 crashed near Harmston after flying into trees while trying to land, and two members of Sgt Musgrave's crew perished, while he and the second pilot sustained injuries.

The freshmen had an easier time over Le Havre, where P/O Firth and Sgts Moss and Scatchard and their crews bombed from 7,000 to 12,000 feet between 21.25 and 21.57. Sgt Owen and crew had been contending with a gradually developing engine problem since leaving the English coast and dropped their four 500 pounders from 8,000 feet at 21.30 onto what they believed was Veulettes-sur-Mer aerodrome to the west of Dieppe. Crews returning from Hamburg reported the glow of fires visible for eighty miles, and a post-raid analysis and local reports confirmed that Hamburg had sustained quite severe damage in various residential districts. Seven large fires had erupted, and more than fourteen hundred people had been bombed out of their homes, while a 4,000lb blockbuster had destroyed a block of flats in Wandsbek, killing sixty-six residents.

The 16th was a momentous day in the history and fortunes of Bomber Command, with the arrival at Waddington of the first prototype Lancaster, BT308, for crew familiarization, in preparation for 44 (Rhodesia) Squadron to introduce the type into squadron service. This early Lancaster retained the narrow and three-fin configuration tailplane common to the Manchester, but, in time, would be replaced with the iconic two large fins, some of which would also be fitted to modified Manchesters. That was for the future, however, and, in the meantime, operations would continue with the magnificent and trusty, but, increasingly obsolete, Hampden.

Bad weather conditions began to play a part in proceedings at this stage, and the squadron was put on stand-by for a number of operations that were subsequently cancelled. This happened on the 18th, but a freshman operation to Le Havre was allowed to go ahead that night, and three crews from 44 (Rhodesia) Squadron joined forces with eight aircraft from 3 Group. Sgts Moss and Scatchard and P/O Firth departed Waddington at 18.55, and all reached the target to deliver four 500 and two 250 pounders from 10,000 and 12,000 feet between 20.58 and 21.25, estimating them to have fallen across the docks, although few bursts were observed and no fires.

Orders were received at North Luffenham, Swinderby and Waddington on the 20th to prepare for operations that night against Berlin and Frankfurt, and it was the crews of F/O Sandford and Sgts Dedman, Dorehill and Tetley who departed Waddington first, between 19.15 and 19.30, bound for the latter. There would be more than an element of chaos surrounding the Berlin endeavour, when the force of seventy-four aircraft was recalled because of deteriorating weather conditions. 5 Group had sent thirty-six Hampdens to forward bases at Horsham-St-Faith and Swanton Morley, but ten of these were cancelled when they could not be refuelled in time. 44 (Rhodesia) Squadron's ten Hampdens took off from Swanton Morley between 19.50 and 20.45 with S/Ls Burton-Gyles and Nettleton the senior pilots on duty, and were spread from the western coast of Denmark to the eastern side of the Schleswig-Holstein peninsula by the time that the recall came through via W/T. The two flight commanders and F/O Sauvage and Sgt Knight failed to pick up the signal and carried on to Berlin, where they found clear skies, but intense darkness and a hostile searchlight and flak defence. S/L Nettleton bombed a railway near Wiltenau, eight miles north-west of the Capital, from 14,000 feet at 23.37, while the others attacked the city from 8,000 to 16,000 feet between 23.45 and 00.15. F/L Ridpath and Sgt Redfern dropped their loads on Hamburg, P/O Maudslay on Sylt aerodrome and P/O Salazar on Heine aerodrome, north of Bremen, leaving P/O Anekstein and Sgt Nicholson to bring their loads back. The chaos continued as the crews made their way home to encounter challenging conditions of fog and mist, which resulted in diversion to a variety of stations in Lincolnshire and Yorkshire. Most made it onto terra-firma with dwindling reserves of fuel, but a number of 44 (Rhodesia) Squadron crews were involved in incidents on the ground. P/O Salazar landed at Middleton-St-George, whereupon the tail wheel collapsed, leaving AE242 immobile and sufficiently close to the runway for P/O Anekstein's AE106 to run into it. Neither was severely damaged, and no crew casualties resulted. Sgt Knight was over Pocklington when an engine cut through fuel starvation, and he overshot the runway to end up in a field, but, again, with minimal damage to AE352 and its crew.

While all of the above was taking place, three of the those assigned to Frankfurt carried out their attacks with a 1,000 pounder and two of 500lbs each from 8,000 and 15,000 feet between 22.35 and 23.01, while Sgt Tetley and crew were thwarted by engine trouble after crossing the enemy coast and jettisoned their bombs near the Belgian city of Charleroi from 7,000 feet at 21.20.

Among awards published in the London Gazette on the 23rd was a Bar to his DFC for S/L Collier, which was recorded in the ORB on the 27th. After eight days away from the operational scene because of adverse weather conditions, 5 Group detailed forty-eight Hampdens from Coningsby, Scampton, Swinderby and Waddington on the 28th for an attack that night on the main railway station at Frankfurt.

However, continuing bad weather caused the withdrawal of the less experienced crews, and, together with accidents and incidents, this reduced the numbers to thirty Hampdens from Scampton, Coningsby and Waddington. 44 (Rhodesia) Squadron dispatched the crews of F/O Sandford and P/Os Budd, Maudslay and Salazar in a ten-minute slot from 22.30, and they made their way to the target area over ten-tenths cloud, that thinned to an extent over the target to be replaced by thick haze, which was equally efficient at concealing the aiming point. P/O Maudslay abandoned his search, and, on spotting lights at a bend of the Rhine twenty miles south-west of the city, dropped two 250 pounders and 360 x 4lb incendiaries from 10,000 feet at 03.15. The others attacked the general city area from 9,500 to 16,000 feet between 03.00 and 03.15, observing a few bursts, while F/O Sandford reported fires burning in many parts of the town.

On the 29th, five 44 (Rhodesia) Squadron crews were called to briefing to be told that a force of eighty-nine aircraft was being assembled to attack the Hamburger Flugzeugbau aircraft factory, a subsidiary of the Blohm & Voss company, situated in Hamburg's Finkenwerde district on the southern bank of the Elbe to the west of the city centre. 5 Group's contribution would be thirty-eight Hampdens and four Manchesters, while ten others, including S/L Burton-Gyles, attempted to hit the Admiral Scheer pocket battleship moored nearby. The all-NCO crews of Sgts Johnson, Nicholson, Owen, Redfern and Tetley departed Waddington between 17.55 and 18.05 each carrying a 1,000 pounder and two of 500lbs and were followed into the air five minutes later by S/L Burton-Gyles and crew, who were sitting on a single 2,000 pounder. Sgt Johnson was closing on the enemy coast when a port engine issue forced him to abandon thoughts of pressing on to Germany's second city, and he dropped his 1,000 pounder onto the Frisian island of Borkum from 9,000 feet at 20.24. Sgt Owen and crew were caught in a searchlight cone as they flew at 17,000 feet over Neumünster, thirty miles north of Hamburg, and decided to drop their load there at 20.50 to lighten the Hampden for evasive action. Conditions over Hamburg were hazy, which made identification something of a challenge, and accurate searchlight and flak activity added to the difficulties. There was also some moonlight, but it was insufficient to allow a positive identification of the aircraft factory, and, after the three remaining 44 (Rhodesia) Squadron crews had carried out their attacks from 11,000 to 16,000 feet between 21.00 and 21.25, they estimated their bombs to have fallen about a mile, two miles and four miles from the intended aiming point. S/L Burton-Gyles and crew identified the battleship, and attacked it from 11,000 feet at 21.12, claiming a near-miss. Local reports confirmed nine fires within the city, but no damage worthy of particular mention.

Hamburg was posted as the destination again on the last night of the month, this time for eighty-two aircraft again targeting the Blohm & Voss aircraft factory after the previous night's failure. 5 Group put up forty-eight Hampdens from Coningsby, Scampton, North Luffenham, Syerston and Swinderby, while sixteen freshman crews were briefed to bomb the docks and shipping at Cherbourg. The three 44 (Rhodesia) Squadron freshman crews of P/O Holland and Sgts Gruber and Nonett took off at 19.40, and all reached the target to find small amounts of medium-level cloud and good visibility. They delivered their four 500 pounders each from 12,000 to 14,000 feet between 21.15 and 21.38, estimating them to have fallen across the docks area, and a number of fires were burning as they turned away.

Earlier in the day, W/C Misselbrook had led a formation in low-level training for an intended upcoming operation. During the course of the month the squadron carried out seventeen operations and dispatched ninety-four sorties for the loss of nine Hampdens, five complete crews and three individual airmen.

October 1941

The adverse weather conditions would continue to disrupt operations at the start of the new month, and the forty-four Hampdens dispatched to Karlsruhe on the night of the 1/2nd were recalled because of the risk of fog at the time of their return. Among these were four all-NCO crews from 44 (Rhodesia) Squadron, who had taken off at 19.40, and arrived back on diversion airfields between 00.05 and 00.50. F/L Avis was posted in from Syerston on the 2nd, and he was an officer, who, late in 1944, would achieve squadron commander status with 150 Squadron. There were no operations for 5 Group and most other elements of the Command between the 2nd and 9th as the weather took a hand, and this would pave the way for a busy and record-breaking night of operations on the 12th.

In the meantime, on the 10th, an overall force of seventy-eight aircraft was assembled for an operation against the Krupp complex in the Borbeck district of Essen, while sixty-nine others were assigned to attack Cologne, thirty-five miles away to the south. 5 Group detailed forty-six Hampdens and ten Manchesters for Essen, and six Hampdens for searchlight suppression duties in the Bocholt-Borken area on the northern approaches to the Ruhr. 44 (Rhodesia) Squadron made ready ten Hampdens for the main event and six for a freshman raid on the docks and shipping at Dunkerque, and it was the latter which departed Waddington first, between 18.45 and 19.00. It was a short round trip to the French coast, from which some would return before the Ruhr bound element even took off. They all reached the target area to find small amounts of medium-level cloud, through which four reported delivering their four 500 pounders from 11,000 to 12,500 feet between 20.07 and 20.35, observing bursts but no detail amongst the flashes from flak and searchlights. Sgt Marston and crew were uncertain of their position after a two-star cartridge caused the searchlights and flak to shut down, and they brought their bombs home. AE382 obtained a fix off Lowestoft at 21.37, and nothing more was heard of Rhodesian Sgt Bonett and his crew, until the Red Cross confirmed that they were on extended leave as guests of the Reich.

The main element took off between 23.50 and 00.25 with F/L Wood the senior pilot on duty and set course via the Lincolnshire coast to cross Holland and approach the target from the north. Sgt Johnson and crew ran into intense searchlight and flak activity shortly after entering Germany, and jettisoned their load near Münster, leaving the others to reach the central Ruhr, where five to ten-tenths cloud and haze created challenging conditions for target location. The Krupp complex occupied many square miles in a north-western segment of the city, and seven crews managed to locate it by following the River Ruhr and the canal system. They carried out their attacks from 6,000 to 17,000 feet between 02.10 and 03.30 and could only estimate the fall of their bombs. Sgt Knight bombed the built-up area, while Sgt Moss aimed his at lights to the north of the city, and all ten participants returned safely between 06.40 and 08.40.

The first major night of operations in the month was notified across the Command on the 12th, when a number of targets were posted in northern and southern Germany and the Ruhr in-between, which would require the highest number of sorties yet in a single night. The largest effort, for which 152 aircraft were detailed from 1, 3 and 4 Groups, would be the first major assault of the war on the southern city of Nuremberg, the site of massive Nazi rallies during the thirties. The other targets were the Deutsche Schiff shipbuilding yards at Bremen, for which ninety-nine aircraft were detailed, including twenty-two Hampdens, and the Buna works at Marl-Hüls on the north-eastern rim of the Ruhr, which was to be a 5 Group show involving seventy-nine Hampdens and eleven Manchesters.

The total number of sorties for the night was 373, which included eight Hampdens to carry out an intruder role in the searchlight belt in the Bocholt area. 44 (Rhodesia) Squadron made ready eight aircraft for Marl-Hüls, two for Bremen and two for intruder duties, and proceedings got underway at Waddington at 19.35, when S/L Collier and Sgt Moss and their crews took off for Bremen. Sgt Moss and crew were forced to curtail their sortie because of an overheating port engine and attacked the island of Heligoland with a 1,000 pounder and two 500 pounders from 12,000 feet at 22.18. S/L Collier and crew pressed on to the target to encounter ten-tenths cloud at around 5,000 feet with occasional gaps and bombed on e.t.a., and flak bursts from 9,000 feet at 23.24. The rear gunner, Sgt Bott, picked up a shrapnel wound in the left arm.

W/C Misselbrook led the Ruhr-bound element and the intruder duo away between 00.55 and 01.25, beginning the North Sea crossing under clear skies and a half moon, en-route for Enkhuizen on the eastern side of the Den Helder peninsula. They reached the Dutch coast to find nine to ten-tenths cloud at 7,000 to 10,000 feet, which extended all the way to the target and tested the crews' ability to establish their positions. P/O Maudslay and crew were unable to locate the chemicals factory or even Essen in the conditions, and, on returning via the French coast, bombed a military camp at Ambleteuse near Cap Gris Nez. F/O Sauvage and crew bombed the general area of Hüls from 14,000 feet at 03.55 on e.t.a., and DR, before dropping two 250 pounders onto the aerodrome at Hertogenbosch in Holland from 12,000 feet at 04.30. Sgt Hackney and crew returned their bombs to store after also failing to locate the primary target, and this left seven crews to carry out attacks from 10,000 to 16,000 feet between 03.23 and 04.15. Meanwhile, Sgts McBarnett and P/O Salazar and their crews were seeking targets of opportunity in their assigned beats, but the former found nothing worthy of attack and returned the bombs to store. P/O Salazar roamed further afield and found searchlight and flak batteries ten miles south of Rotterdam, which he attacked twice at 02.50 and 04.40, and an aerodrome at Vught, a few miles south of Hertogenbosch, in-between at 04.00.

Thirty Hampdens and nine Manchesters eventually made their way to take-off from 5 Group stations in the early hours of the 14th, after a number had been withdrawn for technical reasons. The Manchesters all represented 207 Squadron, which had to share the runway with six Hampdens from 44 (Rhodesia) Squadron, the latter becoming airborne between 01.10 and 01.40 with S/L Burton-Gyles the senior pilot on duty. The target for this 5 Group operation was the main railway station in Cologne, situated in the shadow of the cathedral on the West Bank of the Rhine. Twenty miles to the north, elements of 1 and 3 Groups would be attending to Düsseldorf, and the close proximity of the two operations would guarantee an intense searchlight and flak response. Once the sound of the departing bombing element had receded, a further six Hampdens trundled to the threshold, and took off between 02.20 and 03.00 bound for the Nectarine III garden off the eastern Frisians. The bombers crossed the English coast at Orfordness and headed for the Scheldt Estuary in good weather conditions, which held firm all the way to Cologne. Once in the target area, however, haze and searchlight glare combined with accurate flak, to render identification of the aiming point impossible. F/L Wood was hit suddenly by oxygen starvation when more than ninety minutes out, and the bombs were jettisoned as he descended to denser air. Only S/L Burton-Gyles and P/O Salazar positively identified the target and attacked it from 10,000 and 12,000 feet at 03.45 and 04.25 respectively, believing their bombs and incendiaries to have impacted the general area. Of the others, Sgt Tetley and crew delivered their 1,000 pounder and two 500 pounders onto unidentified Ruhr towns from 12,000 feet at 03.45, while Sgt Knight bombed an aerodrome about a mile to the south of the city from 15,000 feet at 04.00. Sgt Owen and crew failed to return in AD975, after being intercepted by Oblt Roderer of 1./NJG1 while outbound over Belgium and crashing without survivors four miles east-north-east of Lokeren in northern Belgium at 03.39. The gardeners, meanwhile, had located their respective drop zones under eight-to ten tenths thin cloud, and planted the vegetables in the briefed locations from 500 to 650 feet between 04.04 and 04.30.

A new basis of operations was introduced for 44 (Rhodesia) Squadron on the 16th, which allowed for it to operate on every third night, and for operational training to occupy those in-between as the Lancaster era loomed. That night, 5 Group contributed twenty-six Hampdens from Scampton and Syerston to a force of eighty-one aircraft sent to attack railway yards at Duisburg, when cloud cover forced all to bomb on estimated positions. The weather intervened to keep the bomber force on the ground on the following three nights, until orders came through at all but 4 Group stations on the 20th to prepare for a major raid on Bremen that night. The force of 153 aircraft included a 5 Group contribution of eighty-two Hampdens and eight Manchesters, but the only departures from Waddington were of 207 Squadron Manchesters for the main event and gardening duties.

Bremen was posted as the destination again on the 21st for a force of 136 aircraft, the aiming point for which was the shipyards. This operation signalled a return to the fray for 44 (Rhodesia) Squadron after a week at home, as 5 Group detailed eighteen Hampdens and two Manchesters, fifteen of the former provided by the Rhodesians, and they took off between 18.07 and 18.40 with F/L Avis the senior pilot on duty. Ten minutes later, Sgts Dando and Gruber and their crews departed Waddington bound for the docks at Boulogne, and, although both reached the French coast, Sgt Gruber failed to identify the target through the nine-tenths cloud and returned his bombs to store. Sgt Dando's second pilot/bomb-aimer had the town in his sights as he unloaded four 500 pounders from 12,000 feet at 20.25. Many miles to the north-east, Sgt Calcutt and crew were struggling to climb through the bank of cloud that lay over the North Sea with a base at 5,000 and the tops somewhere beyond the 13,000 feet maximum height that AD968 could achieve. They were uncertain of their position in relation to the Frisians, and brought their bombs home, leaving the others to reach the target area, where eight-tenths cumulus cloud and haze hid the target from their prying eyes. They established that they were over Bremen, but only three identified the target, the first of them, that of Sgt Moss, bombing from 15,000 feet at 20.40. Sgt Day attacked twenty minutes later from 9,200 feet, and F/O Sandford from 13,000 feet at 21.15, delivering between them one 1,000 pounder, eight 500 pounders and four 250 pounders, along with 180 x 4lb incendiaries. Five crews bombed the general city area, and the others either brought their payload home or bombed targets of opportunity. Sixteen Hampdens returned safely, leaving AE257 as the sole absentee, and it would be established in time that it had crashed into the sea off the German coast with no survivors from the crew of P/O Budd.

As an extension of the squadron's training programme now in force, it was decided that crews with no or limited operational experience would operate against freshman targets on any night of favourable weather conditions. This would give the new arrivals from the training units the opportunity to learn their trade before becoming members of a Lancaster crew. The system would also ensure a maximum effort against main targets by fully experienced crews. The main operation on the night of the 23/24th was a two-wave attack on the shipyards in Kiel involving 114 aircraft, including thirty-eight Hampdens from Swinderby and Coningsby and six Manchesters from 97 Squadron. The two waves were widely separated, and it was the second one that gained some success by hitting the Deutsche Werke U-Boot yards. Among the minor operations on this night was one by thirteen aircraft against the docks and shipping at Le Havre, for which 44 (Rhodesia) Squadron put up nine Hampdens crewed by freshmen. They departed Waddington between 03.25 and 04.10 with F/L Avis the senior pilot on duty, and, it is believed, all reached the Normandy coast, where seven crews seemed to experience no difficulty in establishing their positions and identifying the aiming point. Bombing was carried out from 9,000 to 15,000 feet between 05.15 and 05.50, and the bursts of their 500 and 250 pounders could be observed across the docks area. Unaccountably, P/O Holland and crew failed to locate the target through what they reported as ten-tenths cumulus cloud, and, finding similar conditions at the briefed alternative, brought their load home. AE290 failed to return and was lost without trace with the crew of Rhodesian, Sgt Bell.

Orders were received across the Command on the 24th to prepare for that night's operation against railway workshops and marshalling yards in Frankfurt-am-Main, which would involve a force of seventy aircraft. 44 (Rhodesia) Squadron made ready eleven Hampdens and dispatched them in daylight between 18.10 and 18.30 with S/L Burton-Gyles the senior pilot on duty. They ran into ten-tenths cloud at around 8,000 feet shortly after crossing the enemy coast, and this persisted all the way to the target, which was located by just a fraction of the crews taking part. Only Sgt Nicholson and crew from 44 (Rhodesia) Squadron could claim to be among them, dropping a 1,000 pounder and two 500 pounders from 11,000 feet at 22.30, and, although they failed to observe the bursts, the glow of a fire became visible through the clouds some three minutes afterwards. The newly promoted F/L Sandford and Sgts Day, Dorehill and Johnson bombed the built-up area, while S/L Burton-Gyles attacked an aerodrome some thirty miles south-south-east of Cologne and P/O Maudslay a railway junction, leaving the others to return their ordnance to store. The dismal failure of the operation was typical for the period, a situation that was heaping frustration on C-in-C, Sir Richard Peirse.

Hamburg was posted as the target for 115 aircraft on the 26th, for which 5 Group contributed an unknown number of Hampdens and six Manchesters, briefing the crews of the former to aim for the Blohm & Voss shipyards, and the latter the main railway station. Those reaching the target area found good bombing conditions under moonlight and delivered a sharp and effective attack. 44 (Rhodesia) Squadron sat this one out, and, apart from three mining sorties on the last night of the month, had concluded operations for the month. Following two nights on the ground because of continuing adverse weather conditions, 5 Group detailed forty Hampdens and five Manchesters on the 29th to target the aerodrome at Schiphol, situated to the south-west of Amsterdam. It became another operation beset by the most difficult conditions of ten-tenths thick cloud and rain, and only six crews would report locating and bombing the primary target. While this operation was in progress, W/C Misselbrook led a formation of seven Hampdens with experienced crews in a low-level bombing exercise in co-operation with searchlight batteries.

The month ended with a return to the Blohm & Voss shipyards at Hamburg on the 31st, for which a force of 123 aircraft was assembled. 5 Group called upon the services of Syerston, Coningsby and Swinderby to prepare forty-two Hampdens and five Manchesters, while a further eighteen Hampdens and a single Manchester were assigned to gardening duties in northern waters, in the Forget-me-not garden in Kiel Harbour and Nectarine II, off the central Frisians. Sgt Grober and P/Os Sturgess and Southgate flew over to Coningsby, which they departed at five-minute intervals from 17.50, and they reached the target area to find favourable conditions of four-tenths cloud at 2,000 feet. They pinpointed on Juist, before making timed runs to the drop zones, where the vegetables were planted from 800 feet between 20.02 and 20.45. During the course of the month, the squadron undertook thirteen operations and dispatched eighty-four sorties, including those recalled, for the loss of four Hampdens and crews.

November 1941

The new month began for 44 (Rhodesia) Squadron with another massive influx of flying personnel, many of them officer pilots, with others following over the ensuing two weeks, by which time, fourteen pilots would have arrived, some soon to find themselves detached to Boscombe Down for Lancaster training. On the 1st, preparations were put in hand to send a force of 132 aircraft to attack harbour installations at Kiel. Thirty-two Hampdens were detailed from Scampton, North Luffenham and Waddington, while nine further Hampdens and two Manchesters conducted mining and anti-shipping sorties. 44 (Rhodesia) Squadron made ready ten Hampdens and sent them on their way between 17.40 and 18.40 with F/Ls Avis and Sandford the senior pilots on duty. Sgt Nicholson and crew were some fifty miles out from the Humber estuary when a port engine issue curtailed their sortie, while F/L Avis was about 130 miles out over the North Sea when severe weather and icing conditions persuaded him to turn back also and jettison his load. Sgt Knight and crew had reached a point some fifteen miles west of Rømø island off the Danish coast, when intercom failure ruined any chance of a co-ordinated bombing run, and they also abandoned their sortie. The others pressed on across the Schleswig-Holstein peninsula to find the target area concealed beneath ten-tenths cloud, and only F/L Sandford, P/O Maclagen and Sgts Dorehill, Marston and Tetley were able to drop their bombs in the approximate target area, doing so from 10,000 to 17,400 feet between 21.35 and 22.38, and observing nothing but the glow of a single fire. P/O Holland flew north from the Kiel area, and bombed the estimated position of Flensburg from 15,000 feet at 22.30, while, ten minutes later and on the western side of the peninsula, Sgt Day and crew attacked the north-east corner of the island of Sylt from 10,000 feet.

The weather kept most aircraft on the ground on the 2nd, and only minor operations were mounted on the following day, among them an anti-shipping patrol by six Hampdens off the Frisians, for which S/L Burton-Gyles and P/O Maudslay and their crews departed Waddington at 18.00. S/L Burton-Gyles returned with his load intact after encountering very poor weather conditions and flying for an hour at 1,000 feet as far as 4 degrees east. P/O Maudslay and crew came upon two stationary trawlers in the Waddenzee between the western end of Terschelling and the Dutch mainland and attacked them with four 500 and two 250 pounders from 300 to 1,000 feet, claiming two near misses. Continuing eastwards along the channel between the islands and the mainland, they then spotted four vessels of around 500 tons heading westwards at ten knots, towards which they unloaded their last 500 pounder. The result was lost in the barrage of light flak issuing from batteries on the decks, but some of these were silenced by return fire from the Hampden's rear guns.

A busy night awaited 5 Group on the 5th, the programme of operations involving six Hampden "sneakers", five on anti-shipping sorties, twenty-four gardeners and twenty-two to bomb the docks at Cherbourg. 44 (Rhodesia) Squadron remained at home on this night and until shortly after midnight on the 6th, when the crews of S/L Burton-Gyles, F/O Sauvage and Sgts Hackney and Moss taxied out to the runway at Waddington to take off between 00.10 and 00.35 bound for the Forget-me-not garden in Kiel Harbour. As three of them were arriving over the western Baltic, 450 miles to the east-south-east, six freshman crews took off to join sixteen other Hampdens and two Manchesters for an attack on the docks and shipping at Cherbourg. For an undisclosed reason, Sgt Moss and crew failed to reach their assigned target area and planted their vegetable in one of the Frisian's Nectarine gardens from 600 feet at 03.44. The others encountered seven-tenths cloud at 3,000 feet, and delivered their mines as briefed from 400, 500 and 600 feet between 03.25 and 03.45, but found no suitable target for their two wing bombs each. P/O Sturgess and crew had been outbound for Cherbourg for no more than thirty minutes before intercom failure ended their sortie, leaving the others to reach the French coast, where five to nine-tenths low cloud partially hid the target. Visibility, otherwise, was good as four released their four 500 pounders each from 13,000 to 15,000 feet between 05.56 and 06.20, while P/O Frost and crew sneaked in at 3,500 feet at 06.15. Bursts were observed, but the cloud prevented an accurate assessment of the outcome.

No doubt still frustrated by his inability to deliver a telling blow on Germany during the extended period of unfavourable weather, and almost certainly eager to rescue the besmirched reputation of the Command after the damning Butt Report, Peirse planned a major night of operations for the night of the 7/8th. The original intention was to send over two hundred aircraft to Berlin, but continuing doubts about the weather prompted the 5 Group A-O-C, AVM Slessor, to question the wisdom of going ahead, and he was allowed to withdraw his force and send it instead to Cologne. A third operation involving fifty-three Wellingtons and two Stirlings from 1 and 3 Groups was also to take place with Mannheim as the target. 169 aircraft eventually took off for the Capital, while sixty-one Hampdens and fourteen Manchesters set off for the Rhineland Capital. In addition to these operations, a further thirty-four Hampdens and four Manchesters were to carry out mining, intruder and small-scale bombing sorties. 44 (Rhodesia) Squadron made ready thirteen Hampdens, four for the crews of W/C Misselbrook, S/L Nettleton, F/L Sandford and F/O Sauvage, who were to attack the Knapsack Power Station to the south-west of the city, while the remainder focussed on the main railway station in the city centre on the West Bank of the Rhine.

They departed Waddington between 18.55 and 19.25, and all but one reached Cologne to find it lying beneath thick haze and six to eight-tenths cloud in a band between 6,000 and 11,000 feet. Sgt Marston and crew had lost their starboard engine on approach and jettisoned their load before heading for home. The conditions prevented all of the Waddington element from identifying their briefed aiming points and left them with the rest of the giant city to drop their bombs into. This they did from 3,000 (W/C Misselbrook) to 16,000 feet between 21.20 and 22.52 but saw nothing of the outcome and had little to report on their return. Sgt Dando and crew retained their bombs after failing to identify Cologne but jettisoned them five miles off Skegness because of concerns over fuel. Returning crews from other squadrons claimed to have observed the flashes as their bombs hit home and evidence of many fires, but local reports mentioned just eight high-explosive bombs and sixty incendiaries falling into the city, causing minor housing and no industrial damage. The only positive from this was the absence of casualties from among the 5 Group participants on a night when a new record loss would be established.

There was a similar story of failure at Mannheim, where local authorities recorded no bombs falling on this night, at a cost to the attackers of seven Wellingtons. Fewer than half of the Berlin crews reported bombing within the target area, and twenty-one aircraft failed to return, which, when added to the losses from the night's main and minor operations, provided an overall casualty figure of thirty-seven aircraft, more than twice the previous highest for a single night. This was the final straw for the War Cabinet and the Air Ministry, and AM Peirse was summoned to an uncomfortable meeting with Churchill to make his explanations. On the 13th, he would be ordered to restrict further operational activity, while the future of an independent bomber force was considered at the highest level, and this shackle would remain in place for the next three months. With loud voices calling for the redeployment of bomber aircraft to combat U-Boots in the Atlantic and to redress reversals in the Middle East, the very existence of an independent bomber force hung in the balance.

In the meantime, on the 8th, 5 Group detailed twenty Hampdens for an attack on the Krupp works at Essen in company with thirty-four other aircraft, and ten Hampdens and five Manchesters for freshman sorties over Dunkerque. 44 (Rhodesia) Squadron briefed the freshman crews of P/Os Frost, Mackay and Sturgess and Sgt Rowan-Parry for Dunkerque and sent them on their way between 17.30 and 18.00, each carrying four 500 pounders. Sgt Rowan-Parry and crew were just approaching the Suffolk coast outbound when their W/T transmitter failed to end their sortie, and, sometime during the operation, AE377 disappeared into the sea and took with it the crew of P/O Frost. The remaining two found clear skies and good visibility in the target area but had already identified the port by the searchlight and flak activity from its defenders. They carried out their attacks from 10,000 and 15,000 feet at 19.07 and 19.40 but were unable to plot the fall of the bombs, and P/O Mackay and crew were uncertain as to whether or not they had attacked the assigned target.

Hamburg was posted as the main target on the 9th, the aiming point for which was the Blohm & Voss shipyards. A force of 103 aircraft was assembled, thirty Hampdens and six Manchesters provided by 5 Group, of which six were made ready by 44 (Rhodesia) Squadron for the main event and a further five for mining duties in the Eglantine and Yams gardens, respectively in the Elbe estuary and Jade Bay/Weser estuary. The two elements took off together between 17.10 and 17.40 with S/L Collier leading the bombers and F/L Sandford the gardeners. They were to adopt the same course as far as Jade Bay, where the Yams duo would peel off soon afterwards to be followed by the Eglantine trio, while the bombers flew on to a position north of Hamburg. Despite generally clear skies over north-western Germany, the visibility in the coastal region was very poor, probably due to sea mist, and the gardeners experienced great difficulty in establishing their positions. Sgt Calcutt and crew accidentally released their wing bombs, believing that the mine had left at the same time, and were surprised to find it still aboard after they landed. Sgt Tetley and crew found their allotted drop zone and delivered their store from 600 feet at 20.23 and were the only ones to fulfil their brief. F/L Sandford and F/O Sauvage located the Eglantine garden, but not the precise drop zone and planted elsewhere within it, while Sgt Johnson dropped his in the Nectarine III garden somewhere off the eastern Frisians.

Meanwhile, Hamburg-bound F/L Avis had turned back with an engine problem, and Sgt McBarnett followed suit later after dropping his load onto Wilhelmshaven as a last resort target. The others found Germany's second city to be basking under clear skies and bright starlight, despite which, only S/L Collier and Sgt Marston identified the shipyards and attacked them from 17,000 and 16,000 feet at 20.30 and 20.15 respectively. This left the crews of Sgts Nicholson and Dando to bomb the general area of the city, after being blinded by searchlight glare, and they released their 1,900 pounder each from 11,000 and 15,000 feet at 20.15 and 20.45 respectively. According to local sources, the operation achieved only modest success, and just three large fires had to be dealt with.

Adverse weather conditions kept 5 Group on the ground for the ensuing six nights, and it was during this period, on the 12th, that F/O "Kipper" Herring was posted back to 44 (Rhodesia) Squadron from 207 Squadron to participate in the start of the Lancaster era. 207 Squadron was about to be relocated to a new home at the just-completed Bottesford, located on Lincolnshire's border with Leicestershire, and within spitting distance also of Nottinghamshire. The advance party left Waddington to begin the moving process at 09.45 on the 15th, leaving the main body to pack up the squadron's goods and chattels.

Meanwhile, 5 Group detailed eleven Hampdens and six Manchesters as its contribution to a force of forty-nine aircraft targeting the port of Emden. 44 (Rhodesia) Squadron was not invited to take part, but, among minor operations taking place was one by freshman crews to Boulogne, which was not mentioned in the 5 Group ORB and appears to be an erroneous entry. According to the 5 Group ORB, there was a mining operation in one of the Nectarine gardens, for which Waddington detailed a single Hampden, and it is believed that the four crews listed in the squadron ORB on this night must have been involved in that. They took off for their respective destinations between 17.15 and 17.40, but P/O Mackay and crew turned back because of oxygen failure, and Sgt Rowan-Parry with an engine issue. P/O Sturgess and crew climbed through 8,000 feet of ice-bearing cloud before reaching clear air and continued on over ten-tenths cloud until coming within range of flak when some forty-five minutes short of the target. This suggested that they were south of track and persuaded them to fly north for fifteen minutes until resuming the original course for thirty minutes. The map reference provided by the crew has them close to the Danish coast, which suggests that they may have gone astray while participating in the Emden raid, by which time, anyway, an engine issue and regular flak prompted the decision to turn back. Only P/O Rail and crew completed their sortie as briefed, delivering a mine into the Nectarine garden from 700 feet at 20.00.

At 10.00 on the 17th, the 207 Squadron air party took off from Waddington, while the main body proceeded by road at 13.45, and the entire relocation was completed by 16.00. Adverse weather kept the Command almost entirely on the ground, with 3 Group mounting just one small Stirling attack on the warships at Brest on the 18th. It was the 23rd before orders were received on all 5 Group stations to make ready fifty-one Hampdens and two Manchesters for an all-5 Group attack on the docks and U-Boots at Lorient, while 3 Group focussed on Dunkerque. The crews of P/O Mackay and Sgt Rowan-Parry took off at 16.35 and 16.50 respectively, leaving P/O Sturgess and crew on the ground for some reason until 17.20, only for them to be recalled by Group at 18.36 because of anticipated deteriorating weather conditions at base and the lateness of their departure. The weather conditions in the target area were found to be favourable with little or no cloud and good visibility, and this enabled the second pilots for P/O Mackay and Sgt Rowan-Parry to draw a bead on the aiming point from their bomb-aiming positions. They released their four 500 and two 250 pounders each from 15,000 feet at 19.35 and 20.15 respectively and observed them to burst within the target confines.

On the 24th, His Majesty King George VI approved the 44 (Rhodesia) Squadron badge, "On a mount an elephant", and the motto, "Fulmina Regis Iusta". Scampton and Coningsby provided twenty Hampdens between them for an operation to Emden on the 26th, the day on which 50 Squadron moved from Swinderby to a new station at Skellingthorpe situated on the western outskirts of Lincoln. The squadron was still settling in at its new home on the 27th, when other 5 Group stations were alerted to make ready for a raid that night on marshalling yards in Düsseldorf. Thirty-four Hampdens and six Manchesters were made ready, ten of the former at Waddington, and they would be joined in the operation by forty-six 3 Group aircraft. The 44 (Rhodesia) Squadron element took off between 16.55 and 17.10 and lost the services of Sgt Knight and crew to a broken wireless aerial even before they had left the circuit. Sgt McBarnett and crew turned back when thirty miles south-east of Yarmouth because of a port engine issue, while Sgt Dedman and crew were also compromised by an engine problem, but did, at least, reach the Belgian coast to drop their bombs on Ostend docks. By the time that P/O Maclagan and crew had pinpointed on the Rhine, they were behind schedule, and bombed Cologne from 15,000 feet at 20.20 as an alternative target. The southern Ruhr was largely cloud-free, although some crews would report up to eight-tenths of the white stuff, but the usual blanket of industrial haze created poor vertical visibility. Sgt Dorehill and crew were uncertain as to their exact position and dropped their 1,000 pounder and two 500 pounders from 14,000 feet onto the town of Neuss on the West Bank of the Rhine. Five crews returned to report bombing the Düsseldorf city area from 6,000 to 16,000 feet between 20.00 and 20.35 and claims of large fires in the railway yards were not confirmed by local reports, while the Cologne authorities recorded damage to 119 houses. Running out of fuel, Sgt Moss had to crash-land AD933 at 00.10 in a field near Honeybourne railway station, five miles east of Evesham, and, although the Hampden was written off, the crew emerged unscathed. Not so Sgt Day's navigator, who had to be removed to hospital in a serious condition after sustaining a shrapnel wound to his leg.

50 Squadron was ready to go to war again by the last night of the month, when a major raid was planned for Hamburg. A force of 181 aircraft included forty-eight Hampdens and four Manchesters, whose crews had been briefed to aim for the Blohm & Voss shipyards. 44 (Rhodesia) Squadron was not to be involved in the main event, but detailed P/O Sturgess and crew to take part in a raid by fifty aircraft on the port of Emden, only three of which would be representing 5 Group. They departed Waddington at 17.10, and two hours and twenty minutes later, dropped four 500 and two 250 pounders from 16,500 feet, observing them to fall in the target area. During the course of the month, the squadron carried out eleven operations and dispatched sixty-two sorties for the loss of two Hampdens and one crew.

December 1941

The dominant theme during December would be the continuing presence at Brest of Scharnhorst, Gneisenau and, sometimes, Prinz Eugen, and no less than fifteen operations of varying sizes would be mounted against the port and its guests during the month, some by daylight. The weather kept the entire Command on the ground for the first six nights of the new month, and it was not until the 7th that a posted operation would actually go ahead. The target for a force of 130 aircraft was Aachen, Germany's most westerly city, perched on the frontiers with both Holland and Belgium. The briefed aiming point was the Nazi Party HQ, which had no special significance other than the fact that it was situated in the city centre, at a time when it was still not admitted publicly that population centres were being bombed. 5 Group detailed fifty Hampdens and a dozen Manchesters, seven of the former provided by 44 (Rhodesia) Squadron, which departed Waddington between 02.00 and 02.15 with W/C Misselbrook the senior pilot on duty. Sgt Dedman and crew were back in the circuit within ninety minutes with a failed a.s.i., leaving the others to undertake the outward flight, initially, in fair weather conditions with isolated clouds. However, this built up to nine to ten-tenths cloud with tops at 15,000 feet, through which Sgt McBarnett was unable to coax the aged L4091. At 12,000 feet, with ice beginning to coat the wings and make the controls sluggish, he decided to turn back. Sgt Knight became ill during the sea crossing towards the Scheldt estuary and bombed the docks at Boulogne from 9,000 feet at 04.44, before also heading for home. Sgt Dorehill and crew were within thirty miles of the target when the starboard engine began to behave in a threatening manner, persuading them to jettison the bombs and abandon the sortie. This left three 44 (Rhodesia) Squadron crews to attack the primary target, where poor visibility made identification a challenge, and the best option was to follow railway lines towards the Aachen-West marshalling yards. W/C Misselbrook attacked with bombs and incendiaries from 9,000 feet at 04.40, five minutes ahead of F/O Sauvage and crew, who carried out their bombing run at 11,500 feet. P/O Salazar and crew approached at 10,000 feet guided by searchlights and flak but found the visibility so poor that they went round again and came in at a plucky 2,000 feet, which afforded them a plan view of the roads and railways. Searchlight glare prevented them from identifying the briefed aiming point, but they spotted a large factory on fire on the north-western edge of the city, although too late to attack it. Going round yet again, they released their 2,000 pounder from 2,500 feet at 04.55 and claimed a near miss. Flak punctured a fuel tank, and they lost an engine shortly after crossing the English coast but reached home safely.

Daylight operations were a matter of course for 2 Group squadrons, and some, known as "Circus", had the purpose of tempting enemy fighters into the air to face RAF Spitfires in a war of attrition. These were, however, very different from the unescorted daylight operations known as "moling", conducted by the other groups, which relied on cloud and surprise to protect the crews. It was utter madness to put crews' lives at risk for a very small potential gain, but 5 Group ordered six crews into the air on the 10th to target ports and aerodromes in Germany and Holland. It was similar fare for six 5 Group crews on the 11th, Sgts Marston and Day drawing the short straws at 44 (Rhodesia) Squadron and departing Waddington at 12.05 and 12.15 respectively bound for the port of Emden. Sgt Day and crew reached the target at 14.00 and dropped four 500 pounders from 200 feet, observing them to burst along the wharves and cause a large column of black smoke to form. Sgt Marston found an unidentified town west of Borkum at 15.30 and released a stick of 500 pounders from 1,500 feet, observing them mostly to overshoot the south-eastern edge of the built-up area. This was not the end of operations for the day, as orders were received to prepare for an attack on the main railway station in Cologne, for which sixty aircraft were detailed, while thirty-four freshmen cut their teeth on the docks and shipping at Le Havre. 5 Group would provide fourteen Hampdens for the main event, four of them representing 44 (Rhodesia) Squadron, which took off between 17.15 and 17.40 bearing the crews of S/L Burton-Gyles and Sgts Hackney, Knight and Moss. Sgt Hackney and crew turned back with engine trouble when thirty miles south of Orfordness, leaving the others to press on in deteriorating weather conditions to encounter eight to ten-tenths cloud in a band between 2,000 and 5,000 feet. Sgt Moss attacked the city suburbs from 15,000 feet at 19.40, and Sgt Knight an unidentified part of the built-up area from 12,000 feet at 20.00. Defeated by the poor visibility, S/L Burton-Gyles flew north to the Ruhr and dropped his load indiscriminately from 4,000 feet at 20.06.

Daylight operations continued on the 12th and 13th, and the consequences of such stupidity on the part of the raid planners was about to impact massively on 44 (Rhodesia) Squadron. Six 408 Squadron Hampdens were dispatched to Brest on the latter occasion but turned back twenty miles short of the Brittany coast because of insufficient cloud cover. At Waddington, W/C Misselbrook, S/L Burton-Gyles and Sgt Hackney and their crews took off at 13.00 to lay mines in the Jellyfish garden off Brest, and, by the time that the Hackney crew had reached Pointe-Saint-Mathieu, on the headland to the north of the mouth of the estuary, the cloud had diminished, and its base was at 2,000 feet, leaving them exposed to the shore batteries, which opened fire. The decision was taken to plant the vegetable at that point, some seven miles west of the allotted location, and it was seen to enter the water. S/L Burton-Gyles bravely pushed on to the briefed drop zone, where the mine was released from 400 feet at 16.46 in the face of heavy and light flak. They were then pounced upon by an enemy fighter, believed to be a BF109, whose cannon fire caused an extensive catalogue of damage, but failed to bring the Hampden down. They made it back to a forced-landing at Boscombe Down, where S/L Burton-Gyles spoke highly of the conduct of his crew. The return of W/C Misselbrook DSO was awaited in vain, and no trace of AE196 and its occupants was ever found, thus depriving 44 (Rhodesia) Squadron and Bomber Command of an outstanding commanding officer, who, recognising the perils of operating near a well-defended target in daylight, had put himself and a flight commander on the Order of Battle. His loss prompted a message from G/C "Gus" Walker, the former 50 squadron commanding officer and now station commander at North Luffenham. It read; *"On behalf of all ranks on this station, I should like to express great sympathy in the loss of W/C S.T. Misselbrook DSO. The failure of this very able officer to return from operations leaves a gap which will be very hard to fill. His loss, a very temporary one we hope, will be keenly felt throughout the Service, and especially throughout Nº5 Group, wherein he was held in great respect by all ranks, as a very fine and gallant officer. It is a loss which this country can ill afford at this juncture."*

S/L Collier stepped temporarily into the breach, but he would move to pastures new within a week. He presided over his first operation as commanding officer on the 14th, when Scampton, Syerston and Waddington made ready twenty-two Hampdens for Brest to attack Scharnhorst and Gneisenau, which had been dubbed by the British press as "Salmon and Glückstein" in a tongue-in-cheek reference to the famous London tobacconists with the same initials. With the senior crews currently absent under training at Boscombe Down, 44 (Rhodesia) Squadron prepared a dozen aircraft for NCO crews and those captained by junior officers and dispatched them between 00.01 and 00.20 on a night of extremely unfavourable weather conditions. Heading towards the south-west for the Channel crossing, Sgt Dedman and crew landed at an airfield south of Banbury after experiencing engine trouble, while the remainder pressed on to encounter a band of ten-tenths ice-bearing cloud at between 1,500 and 3,500 feet over the sea, which would force most to turn back after reaching a position west of the Channel Islands. All but one returned to base with their bombs still aboard, and only Sgt Moss and crew would claim to have reached the target, believing their bombs to have fallen into the sea.

Waddington remained inactive on the 15th, when twelve Hampdens targeted the docks at Ostend, and 44 (Rhodesia) Squadron stayed at home also when Scampton represented the group at Wilhelmshaven on the night of the 16/17th, while eighteen from Coningsby took care of gardening duties. Another major assault on Brest was notified across the Command on the 17th, for which a force of 121 aircraft was assembled, among them twenty-five Hampdens from Waddington, Scampton and Syerston. 44 (Rhodesia) Squadron made ready thirteen, loading each with four 500 and two 250 pounders, and dispatched them between 18.20 and 18.35. P/O Mackay and crew were contending with wireless failure as they approached the Dorset coast and began the Channel crossing in the hope that the wireless operator would be able to fix the problem. Despite a gallant effort, he failed, and the sortie was abandoned when some thirty miles south-west of Weymouth, leaving the others to press on towards the northern coast of Brittany. Sgt Marston and crew crossed the English coast at 2,000 feet over Seaton in east Devon, and climbed to 12,000 feet over the Channel, before making landfall, but skirted the coast rather than traverse the Finistere peninsula. Sgt Day reported searchlights between Ile-de-Batz in the east and Ile-Vierge to the west, which appeared to be attempting to force the intruders out to sea and were co-operating with night-fighters. Three to seven-tenths cloud lay over the target area, and the good vertical visibility was marred only by extreme darkness and then, later, the effects of smoke generators. Light flak was reaching 10,000 feet as they ran in on the aiming point and formed only part of a hostile defence as the attacks took place from 9,000 to 12,000 feet between 20.20 and 21.25. Evasive action and searchlight glare prevented most from observing the results of their efforts other than bursts, and none could claim to have hit the target vessels, which, according to the squadron ORB, included Prinz Eugen. P/O Maclagan and crew actually reported their bombs detonating close to that particular vessel, and, once all of the crew reports had been collated, the squadron could claim to have delivered 25,000lbs of high explosives during the operation. AD868 failed to return with the crew of Rhodesian pilot, P/O Kaschula, whose body was recovered eventually for burial at Camaret-sur-Mer, on the southern headland of the estuary, confirming that the Hampden had gone into the sea. This was the final loss of a Hampden in 44 (Rhodesia) Squadron service.

Eleven Manchesters took part in the next attempt on Brest, by daylight on the 18th, when claims were made of at least one hit on Gneisenau. On the 19th, S/L Roderick Learoyd VC was posted to the squadron from 14 O.T.U., to assume command, and was detached immediately to Boscombe Down. His previous experience of command had been with 83 Squadron between February and June. This was the day also on which 420 (Snowy Owl) Squadron RCAF was formed at Waddington under the command of W/C Bradshaw, and S/L Collier now became attached to help with the workload of establishing a new unit. Nine days hence, on his promotion to temporary wing commander rank, Collier would succeed Bradshaw as squadron commander, and set about the process of preparing his new charges for operations in the New Year.

A dozen daylight intruder sorties by Hampdens over north-western Germany on the 21st came to nothing, after insufficient cloud presented itself to protect them. Scampton, Syerston and Waddington were alerted on the 23rd to prepare twenty Hampdens for an operation by sixty-eight aircraft on Cologne, while they and other stations provided a further seventeen for gardening duties off the Frisians and in Kiel Harbour. 44 (Rhodesia) Squadron made ready six aircraft for the main event and one for mining and sent them on their way between 17.15 and 18.05 on what would be the squadron's final operations as a Hampden unit. P/O Holland and crew turned back from a position south of Wisbech after the intercom became unserviceable, but the others reached the target area, where ten-tenths cloud lay across the city with a base at 3,000 feet, and bombing took place on estimated positions from 10,000 to 12,000 feet between 19.39 and 20.17. In the event, fewer than half of the force claimed to have bombed the city, which, according to local reports, recorded no bombs falling. Meanwhile, P/O Rail and crew had planted their vegetable in the allotted location from 500 feet at 19.00. When Sgt Day and crew touched down at Waddington at 00.35, they brought the Hampden era to an end after two years and four months in the firing line. Despite that, six were made ready on the 24th for a possible operation, which did not materialise.

The ORB announced on the 24th that 44 (Rhodesia) Squadron was re-equipping with Lancaster aircraft, and the first three, L7530, L7537 and L7538, were taken on charge, while pilots, Sgts Dedman, Johnson, Knight, Moss and Rowan-Parry, were sent to Finningley to begin their conversion training. The six Hampden crews remained on stand-by on Christmas Day, the third of the war, but were not called into action, and, on Boxing Day, which also passed without the call to arms, the squadron was informed that no further Hampden sorties would be flown. 50 Squadron supported the epic and successful raid by commandos on Vaagso island off the Norwegian coast on the 27th, before Düsseldorf was posted as the target for 132 aircraft later that night. 5 Group contributed thirty Hampdens and seven Manchesters, whose crews were briefed to aim for the main marshalling yards, in what turned out to be another ineffective attack on a Ruhr target, which caused little damage at a cost of seven aircraft and crews. The two main operations on the 28th involved eighty-six Wellingtons at Wilhelmshaven, while eighty-one Hampdens returned to the synthetic rubber factory at Marl-Hüls on the north-eastern edge of the Ruhr. The raid took place in excellent visibility under bright moonlight, and returning crews claimed good bombing results, although, no report came out of the target to confirm or deny.

On the 28th, Lancasters L7532, L7533, L7536 and L7539 were taken on charge, along with a number of Manchesters for the Conversion Flight, and, on the 30th, the twenty-two Hampdens were transferred to 420 Squadron RCAF, although, 44 (Rhodesia) Squadron ground crews would continue to service them until the Canadians had their own qualified personnel. W/C Learoyd departed the squadron temporarily on detachment to Bomber Command HQ, and S/L Nettleton stepped into the breach to oversee crew conversion until his return. During the course of the month the squadron undertook eight operations and dispatched forty-eight sorties for the loss of two Hampdens and crews.

It had been a disappointing year for the Command, and despite the best efforts of the crews, one of under-achievement, with little to show in terms of an advance on the performance of 1940. The new aircraft types, the Stirling, Halifax and Manchester, introduced into operational service early in the year, had each failed to meet the requirements expected of them, and had undergone long periods of grounding while essential modifications were carried out. 1942 would bring changes, however, chief among which were the arrival on the operational scene of the war-winning Lancaster, and a new Commander-in-Chief, who would know how to exploit it.

F/Sgt J N Sneeston

Pilot of Hampden X2999. Airborne 20.15, 17th of April 1941 from Waddington. Lost over the North Sea. The body of F/S Sneeston was washed ashore 6th of June 1941 at Sheerness, Kent, but his crew have never been found and are commemorated on the Runnymede Memorial.

Hampden AD983 crashed on Lindum Hill girls' school staff accommodation in Lincoln when returning from a mining (gardening) sortie over the Friesian islands on the 22nd of July 1941. All four crew members were killed in the crash - Sgt D.M.Bruce, Sgt W.R.B.Relyea RCAF, Sgt J.A.Connolly and Sgt P.J.Lynch. Senior French mistress Miss Edith Fowle was also killed.

RAF Waddington Watch Office – Posed for the media.
L – R: F/L Hobson FCO, W/C Burton-Gyles, OC 44 Sqn, W/C Lewis.

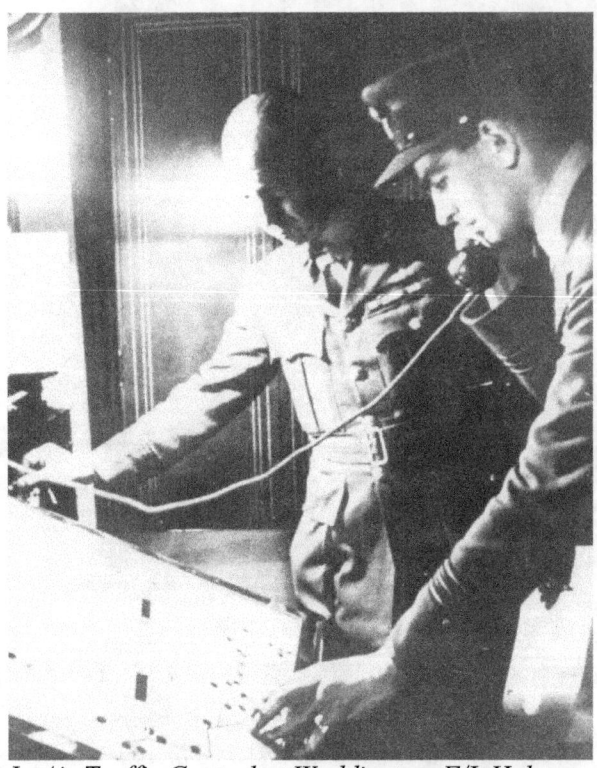

In Air Traffic Control at Waddington. F/L Hobson the FCO and W/C Burton-Gyles.

S/L Burton-Gyles Flight Commander when first Lancaster arrived.

Target Düsseldorf 17th of June 1941

RAF Waddington

W/C S T Misselbrook CO 44 Sqn March 1941 – December 1941
KIA 13th December 1941

W/C Roderick 'Babe' Learoyd VC. CO 44 Sqn December 1941 – May 1942.

Waddington 1940. The NAAFI before the bomb hit it.

The airmen's mess and NAAFI at Waddington on the 9th of May 1941, the morning after the air raid. The building to the right is the Catering Squadron headquarters. The building was quickly repaired and has been in use ever since. It is now called the Raven club after the manageress who died in the air raid.

On 9th of May 1941, Waddington village came under heavy bombing which destroyed the local church, the RAF station NAAFI, and many individual homes. This was the scene in the aftermath of the raid which the Echo described as utter devastation.

At the Predannack emergency aerodrome, Cornwall after the attack against the Scharnhorst at Brest on the 24th of July 1941. 18 Hampdens took part - 44 Squadron S/L Joe Collier, 106 Squadron W/C R D Allen, 144 Squadron, S/L J J Bennett. The attack was carried out by three boxes of aircraft starting at 13,000 feet and bombing at 10,000 feet.

Mr Lannigan O'Keefe, the High Commissioner for Southern Rhodesia on his visit to 44 (Rhodesia) Squadron on 28th of August 1941.

44 Sqn aircrew in front of Hampden 'K' for Kitty (P1322). This aircraft swung on take-off from Balderton on August 1941 and was categorised Cat R (b) – beyond base repair. L – R: Sgt J C Macgregor DFM (KIA), F/Sgt R V C Oliver DFM, (PoW), Sgt M J Dacey, Sgt G H Gregory DFM (KIA on the Dams raid in John Hopgood's crew).

Watch belonging to 26 year old pilot Sgt Archibald Watt.
On the 7th of September 1941, he was tasked, along with several Hampdens from Waddington, to attack Kiel submarine yard and also minelaying. On his first operation, his Hampden, X2921 KM-Z failed to climb after take off and crashed in a field at nearby Branston. The bomb exploded and the fuel laden aircraft was destroyed, also killing Sergeants J.R.Newcombe, A.D.Wimbush and E.S.Cox. The watch was recovered in 2012.

Bombing up for minelaying and an attack on Kiel submarine yard, 7th of September 1941.

P/O W H Budd with his crew and groundcrew of Hampden AE257 KM-X.
All crew lost 21/22nd of October 1941, P/O W.H.Budd, P/O D.Schafheitlin RCAF, Sgt W.E.Austin Sgt M J Hughes.

Visit to Waddington of King George VI in January 1941.

F/O D A A Romans DFC
KIA 8th of September 1941 aged 21 while with 90 Sqn.

Dave Romans and crew returning from the first raid on Berlin.

44 Squadron Christmas party in the Assembly Rooms, 1941.

44 Sqn Air Gunners

The Prototype Lancaster BT308

On the 12th of September 1941, the Air Ministry gave authority for the Squadron to be known as. No.44 (Rhodesia) Squadron to mark the generosity of the people of that country in donating money towards the war effort. This was particularly appropriate as approximately 1/4 of the Squadron's personnel were, by this time, Rhodesian. In November, His Majesty King George VI, graciously approved the squadron crest, described as "On a mount an elephant" with the motto,'Fulmina Regis Iusta' (the King's thunderbolts are righteous). The elephant symbolises the weight and heaviness of attacks.

44 Squadron at dusk

January 1942

As far as most crews were concerned, the New Year would look and feel exactly like the outgoing one, and, still under the restrictions of the November directive, the Command's activities reflected the continuing obsession with the German raiders at Brest, against which a further eleven operations would take place during January. While 44 (Rhodesia) Squadron watched from the side-lines, 5 Group detailed a dozen Manchesters for a raid on St-Nazaire on the 2nd, and thirty-six Hampdens for gardening duties off the Biscay ports and the Frisians. Small-scale mining operations occupied elements of the group on the 3rd, and daylight "moling" operations on the 4th. Twenty-seven Hampdens and twelve Manchesters took off on the evening of the 5th as part of a force of 154 aircraft targeting the Scharnhorst and Gneisenau at Brest and the naval docks area. An effective smoke screen prevented accurate bombing, but many fires were claimed. Nineteen Hampdens were committed to "scuttle" sorties over northern Germany on the 6th, which were roving commissions against targets of opportunity at specific locations. They appear to differ from "moling", only by relying on the cover of darkness rather than cloud. Brest was posted as the target for a force of 151 aircraft on the 8th, reconnaissance having revealed that Scharnhorst and Gneisenau had been joined by Prinz Eugen. 5 Group contributed thirty-seven Hampdens and ten Manchesters for this attack, for which take-off took place in the early hours of the 9th. A force of eighty-two aircraft was assembled for a return to Brest on the night of the 9/10th, for which 5 Group put up twenty-seven Hampdens and six Manchesters. It turned into another inconclusive raid, from which eleven Hampden crews brought their bombs home after failing to identify the target. Thirty-four Hampdens and nine Manchesters were detailed by 5 Group on the 10th to contribute to an overall force of 124 aircraft bound for Wilhelmshaven that night for what turned out to be another wasted effort.

As the month progressed, Lancasters continued to arrive from the Avro assembly factory at Woodford in Stockport, and, when the weather allowed, the crews began a programme of intensive training both in the air and on the ground in lectures. On the 9th, one Lancaster was transferred to 97 Squadron at Coningsby, which had been selected to be the second recipient of the type. 97 Squadron had a sprinkling of Rhodesians among its number, and exchanges would take place between the squadrons, to continue to make 44 as Rhodesian as possible. It would create a spirit of friendly rivalry between the two units, which would continue into the future through joint operations. The focus remained on north-western Germany for the next two operations, both of which were to be directed at Hamburg. Thirty-two Hampdens and eleven Manchesters were made ready on the 14th, and their crews briefed to aim for the Blohm & Voss shipyards, situated on the Kuhwerder Island opposite the Sankt Pauli district to the west of the city centre. They were to be part of an overall force of ninety-five aircraft, and those reaching the target were challenged by extreme darkness and thick ground haze, which created difficult conditions for aiming point identification. That said, crews could always rely on the searchlight and flak batteries to guide them into the heart of the city, where large ground features like the Binnen and Aussen-Alster Lakes on the north-western edge of the centre were a good guide for non-precision bombing. Half of the crews involved in this operation claimed to have bombed within the city, and local authorities confirmed damage to the Altona railway station, situated on the North Bank of the Elbe to the west of Sankt Pauli. Hamburg was "on" again twenty-four hours later, for which a force of ninety-six aircraft was assembled. 5 Group's contribution amounted to twenty-seven Hampdens and ten Manchesters, whose crews had been briefed to attack the city centre, but the raid proved to be another in the long line of disappointments since the start of the autumn. According to local sources, the emergency services dealt with thirty-six fires, only three of them classed as large, and there had been no major incidents.

Having been selected as the third Lancaster unit, 207 Squadron set up a Conversion Flight on the 16th in preparation for the arrival of its first example of the type. The flight would be equipped, initially, with two Manchesters, the type it had introduced into squadron service and had struggled with for more than a year. Once the first Lancaster arrived on the 25th, the conversion programme would begin with selected second pilots and crews from the squadron.

Attention remained on north-western Germany on the 17th, when Bremen was posted as the target for eighty-three aircraft, including twenty Hampdens and six Manchesters. In the event, only eight returning crews claimed to have attacked the primary target, while others went for alternatives, including Hamburg, where eleven fires were reported. Emden had also been a regular destination for small forces since the 10th, sometimes with a contribution from 5 Group, and five Hampdens joined twenty Wellingtons there on the 20th, after snow and severe frost had kept aircraft on the ground for two nights. Bremen and Emden shared the Command's attention on the night of the 21/22nd, when eleven Hampdens joined in a raid by fifty aircraft on the former, while twelve Hampdens and three Manchesters plied their trade at the latter in an overall force of thirty-eight aircraft. The garrison town of Münster was posted as the destination for forty-seven aircraft on the 22nd, for what would be the first attack on a target in inland Germany since late December. 5 Group detailed twenty-two Hampdens and five Manchesters in an overall force of forty-seven aircraft, which found the many canals and rivers in this region of Germany, north of the Ruhr, standing out as dark lines in the snow-covered landscape, making navigation a simple task in cloud-free skies and under bright moonlight. There was no post-raid reconnaissance to assess the outcome, and a cursory local report mentioned five fatalities but no details of damage.

The battleship Tirpitz had been sent to Trondheimsfjord to act as a "fleet in being" and a deterrent to an Allied invasion. 44 (Rhodesia) Squadron's initial training on the Lancaster would be biased towards the mining of the sea areas into which she was likely to stray, although the crews were not aware of this. Three Lancasters were put on stand-by to carry out the operation from a forward base at Wick in northern Scotland, but bad weather caused the plans to be abandoned, and this allowed an opportunity for a number of 44 (Rhodesia) Squadron crews to assist 97 Squadron in its conversion onto Lancasters. The seemingly interminable campaign against the enemy warships at Brest continued on the night of the 25/26th, for which a force of sixty-one aircraft was made ready. 5 Group put up thirty-five Hampdens and fifteen Manchesters, which made their way to the Cornish coast, where small amounts of cloud were encountered, but this increased during the Channel crossing to three to eight-tenths in the target area. The crews had a clear view of the coastline as they approached and were also guided to the aiming point by searchlights, flares and the heavy and accurate flak defence. Another inconclusive and frustrating raid ensued, however, from which returning crews were unable to offer any indication of the results. Hannover was posted as the primary target on the following night, for which a force of seventy-one aircraft was dispatched, nine of them Hampdens belonging to 50 Squadron as the entire 5 Group contribution. Returning crews described many fires but reports rarely came out of this city to confirm or deny, and the likelihood is that decoy sites were operating.

The next attack on Brest was mounted on the 27th, and involved thirty-two Hampdens and three Manchesters from Scampton, Syerston, North Luffenham and Bottesford. *(The Bomber Command War Diaries does not record any operations taking place on this night)*. It was reported that Prinz

Eugen was also "still in town" as an added attraction for the force that arrived in the target area under a half moon and two to ten-tenths cloud with a base at 3,000 feet. Haze, or a smoke-screen, further obscured the docks area, and it was not possible to identify the warships, which escaped damage yet again. Orders were received on the 28th to prepare for a return to Münster, for which a force of fifty-five Wellingtons and twenty-nine Hampdens was prepared, while a second force consisting of four Hampdens, seven Manchesters and thirty-seven other aircraft was assembled for a freshman operation against the docks at Boulogne. On the last night of the month, a force of seventy-one aircraft took off for another tilt at Brest, and among them were forty-one Hampdens and eleven Manchesters representing 5 Group. The Brittany coastline was clearly visible in the bright moonlight, and intense flak and searchlights pointed the way to the docks area, but this made the run-in to bomb an uncomfortable experience, and 61 Squadron lost three Manchesters in return for another inconclusive raid.

February 1942

There were no operations for 5 Group during the first few days of the new month, and all available personnel were press-ganged into snow-clearing duties. Although the impending breakout from Brest by the three enemy warships would take the Royal Navy and the RAF by complete surprise in what would be a most humiliating episode for the government and the nation, there was clearly some advance warning, as three Manchesters were put on stand-by for daylight operations at Bottesford on the 4th in preparation for precisely that event, and six more on the 5th. 5 Group notified its stations on the 6th to prepare for daylight mining operations in the Nectarine I garden off the western Frisians, and between them they raised a force of thirty-three Hampdens and thirteen Manchesters. Conditions in the target area were generally favourable, and the drop zone, off the island of Terschelling, was easily located, mostly by an approach from the south via Vlieland, some finding cloud to mask their approach and others not. Those finding cloud cover were able to make timed runs to their briefed release points, while the remainder planted their vegetables as close as possible in known sea-lanes. That night, 3 Group sent fifty-seven Wellingtons and three Stirlings to continue the assault on Brest, but only a third of the crews reported bombing through thick cloud.

The inevitable first loss of a Lancaster came via a training accident on the afternoon of the 7th, when F/Sgt Nicholson misjudged his landing at Skellingthorpe, and ended up in a bank of snow with a collapsed undercarriage. The crew walked away, leaving L7542 to be declared beyond economical repair. The squadron was actually in the process of dispersing its Lancasters to Skellingthorpe, and this would continue over the ensuing days. The daylight gardening operation in the Frisians was repeated on the following day employing thirty-two Hampdens, when the target area on this occasion was further north, in the Nectarine III garden off the island of Wangerooge in the Waddensee, where cloud was very thin and provided little cover. They attracted some moderately accurate heavy flak from the western end of the island, and German fighters were seen to be operating, which, it is highly probable, were responsible for the loss of three Hampdens. 5 Group was not called into action again until the 10th, when nineteen Hampdens and a handful of Manchesters were assigned to attack the main railway station in Bremen. It became another shambles of an operation, carried out by a few crews through complete cloud cover, while most attacked alternative targets, jettisoned their bombs or returned them to store. Orders were received at Bottesford, Coningsby and Swinderby on the 11th to prepare a dozen Hampdens and six Manchesters between them for an operation that night against a railway station at Mannheim. They were part of an overall force of forty-nine aircraft, which enjoyed favourable conditions that enabled them to identify the target and release their bombs unopposed by flak in the vicinity of the briefed aiming point.

Among other small-scale operations on this night was one against Brest by eighteen Wellingtons, the crews of which would have been unaware that they were the last to engage in this seemingly endless saga. As the sound of their engines receded into the eastern cloud-filled skies, Vice-Admiral Otto Cilliax, the Brest Group commander, whose flag was on Scharnhorst, put Operation Cerberus into action at 21.14, and Scharnhorst, Gneisenau and Prinz Eugen slipped anchor, before heading into the English Channel under an escort of destroyers and E-Boats. It was an audacious bid for freedom, covered by bad weather, widespread jamming and meticulously planned support by the Kriegsmarine and the Luftwaffe, all of which had been rehearsed extensively during January. The planning, and a little good fortune, allowed the fleet to make undetected progress until spotted off Le Touquet by two Spitfires piloted by G/C Victor Beamish, the commanding officer of Kenley, and W/C Finlay Boyd, both of whom maintained radio silence, and did not report their find until landing at 10.42 on the morning of the 12th.

The British authorities had prepared a plan in advance for precisely this eventuality, under the codename, Operation Fuller, but so secret was it, that few, it seemed, either knew of its full requirements or even of its existence. Once the enemy fleet was spotted in the late morning, hectic efforts were made to get Coastal and Bomber Command aircraft away, but only 5 Group was standing by at four hours readiness. It was 13.30 hours before the first sorties were launched, and the 5 Group stations worked frantically to get sixty-four Hampdens and fifteen Manchesters into the air. They were part of the largest commitment of aircraft by daylight in the war to date, amounting to 242 sorties, and were given a search area off the Hague, where rainstorms and squally conditions compounded the difficulties and prevented most crews from locating the enemy fleet. Despite the heroic effort and sacrifice of the Bomber Command, Coastal Command and Fleet Air Arm crews, the enemy fleet made good its escape into open sea, although, its own trials and tribulations were not yet over. Scharnhorst struck a mine in the late afternoon and began to fall back, and, at 19.55, a magnetic mine detonated close enough to Gneisenau, when off Teschelling, to open a small hole in the starboard side, and, temporarily, slow her progress also. Later still, at 21.34, when passing through the same stretch of water, Scharnhorst hit another mine which stopped both engines and damaged steering and fire control. The vessel got under way again at 22.23 using its starboard engines and making twelve knots, while carrying an additional one thousand tons of seawater. The day's activities were not yet over for 5 Group, and the crews of twelve Hampdens and nine Manchesters were briefed to lay mines in the Nectarines garden off the Frisians through which the enemy fleet would have to pass to reach safety.

Gneisenau and Prinz Eugen reached the Elbe Estuary at 07.00 on the 13th, and tied up at Brunsbüttel North Locks at 09.30, while Scharnhorst arrived at Wilhelmshaven at 10.00 with three months-worth of damage to repair. The mines had been laid almost certainly by 5 Group Hampdens over the preceding nights and demonstrated the remarkable effectiveness of this war-long campaign. The entire episode was a major embarrassment to the government and the nation, but, worse still, cost the Command a further fifteen aircraft and crews on top of all of those sacrificed to this endeavour over the past eleven months. 5 Group alone posted missing nine Hampdens and crews, all lost in the North Sea, six of them without trace. On a positive note, this annoying and distracting itch had been scratched for the last time, and the Command could now concentrate its forces against the strategic targets for which it was best suited.

Among awards announced on the 13th was a DSO for S/L Burton-Gyles, and a DFC for F/Os Sauvage and Maudslay and P/O Salazar. A new Air Ministry directive, issued on the 14th, was to change the emphasis of bomber operations from that point until the end of the war. Lengthy consideration having been given to the Butt Report and the future of an independent bomber force, the new policy authorized the blatant area bombing of Germany's industrial towns and cities in a direct assault on the morale of the civilian population, particularly its workers. This had, of course, been going on since the summer of 1940, but no longer would there be the pretence of claiming to be attacking industrial and military targets. Waiting in the wings, in fact, at this very moment, four days into his voyage from the United States in the armed merchantman, Alcantara, was a new leader, a man well-known to 5 Group, who would not only pursue this policy with a will, but also possessed the self-belief, arrogance and stubbornness to fight his corner against all-comers on behalf of his beleaguered Bomber Command.

That night, a force of ninety-eight aircraft took off to employ the main post office and railway station as the aiming points for an area attack on Mannheim, to which 5 Group contributed twenty-five Hampdens and nine Manchesters. Crews were guided to the city by the searchlight and flak activity and encountered four to ten-tenths cloud at between 2,000 and 12,000 feet, with fair visibility above and ground haze below. Such weather conditions proved to be unhelpful, and, despite the claims of sixty-seven crews to have bombed the city, local reports spoke of two buildings destroyed and fifteen damaged. 5 Group detailed thirty-seven Hampdens and twelve Manchesters on the 16th to carry out gardening duties in the Nectarine I garden off Terschelling and Nectarine III garden, encompassing the east Frisian islands of Wangerooge, Juist and Borkum. Conditions were challenging, but fourteen Hampden and seven Manchester crews succeeded in fulfilling their brief.

A similar accident to that of F/Sgt Nicholl on the 7th, accounted for the second loss of a Lancaster on the afternoon of the 20th, when Sgt Rowan-Parry landed too fast and ran out of runway. L7538 came to a halt in a ditch with a collapsed undercarriage, but, again, the crew walked away. On the 21st, twenty-two Wellingtons and twenty Hampdens were detailed to carry out "scuttle", or roving commission sorties over many regions of Germany, while five Manchesters attacked Sola aerodrome at Stavanger and six others went mining in the Yams garden off Wilhelmshaven.

Air Chief Marshal Sir Arthur Harris took up his post as the new Commander-in-Chief of Bomber Command on the 22nd. He was a man well-known to 5 Group, having served as its A-O-C until November 1940, when he became second deputy to Sir Charles Portal, the Chief-of-the-Air-Staff. Harris arrived at the helm with firm ideas already in place on how to win the war by bombing alone, a pre-war theory, which no commander had yet had an opportunity to put into practice. It was obvious to him, that the small-scale raids on multiple targets conducted under his predecessor, served only to dilute the effort, and that such pin-prick attacks could not hurt Germany's war effort. He recognized the need to overwhelm the defences and emergency services, by pushing the maximum number of aircraft across the aiming point in the shortest possible time, and this would signal the birth of the bomber stream, and an end to the former practice, whereby squadrons or even crews determined for themselves the details of their sorties. He knew also that urban areas are most efficiently destroyed by fire, rather than blast, and it would not be long before the bomb loads carried in his aircraft reflected this thinking. In the meantime, while he developed his ideas, he would continue with the fairly small-scale attacks on German ports favoured by his predecessor, and, later on the evening of his appointment, he sent thirty-one Wellingtons and nineteen Hampdens to Wilhelmshaven to attack the floating dock likely to be employed during repairs to Scharnhorst and Gneisenau. Sadly, the target area was covered by dense cloud and the bombing that took place on estimated positions missed the target altogether.

On the night of the 23/24th, 5 Group detailed twenty-three Hampdens for mining duties in the Rosemary and Yams gardens in the Heligoland Bight and Schillig Roads respectively, and forty-two Hampdens and nine Manchesters on the 24/25th to return to the same gardens. On the 25th, 5 Group detailed a dozen Manchesters to target the Gneisenau, now believed to be at Kiel, while eighteen Hampdens and a Manchester took care of gardening duties in the Nectarine I and II, Yams and Rosemary gardens. Scampton and North-Luffenham dispatched ten Hampdens between them on the 26th to join Wellingtons and Halifaxes in targeting the floating dock at Kiel, and the operation, which took place under clear skies, threw up one of the war's great ironies. A high explosive bomb struck the bows of Gneisenau, now supposedly in a safe haven after enduring eleven months of constant bombardment at Brest, and not only did it kill 116 of her crew, it also ended her sea-going career for good. Her main armament was removed for use in coastal defence, and she was towed to Gdynia, where she remained unrepaired for the rest of the war. The British authorities were unaware of the success, however, and sent another raid of sixty-eight aircraft on the 27th, which included eighteen Hampdens and seventeen Manchesters. They encountered bright moonlight above the ten-tenths cloud in the target area, but poor visibility below, which offered no chance of identifying the floating dock, and most bombed the general area of the town, guided by the flashes of searchlights and flak. Throughout the month, the 44 (Rhodesia) Squadron crews had been learning the ways of the Lancaster, which, they found, had few vices, and they now stood on the threshold of launching it against the enemy for the first time.

March 1942

Adverse weather conditions welcomed in the new month and kept the bomber force on the ground on the 1st. It was the same on the 2nd, and it was the 3rd before orders were received across the Command to prepare for an operation, which, in its bold conception, was a clear indication of what was to come. Bomber Command's evolution to war-winning capability was to be long, arduous and gradual, but the first signs of a new hand on the tiller came early on in Harris's reign with this meticulously planned attack on the Renault lorry factory, which was located in a loop of the Seine in the district of Billancourt to the south-west of central Paris. The plant was capable of producing 18,000 lorries per year, which was a massive boon to the German war effort, and the attempt to destroy it came in response to an Air Ministry request. The operation would be conducted in three waves, led by experienced crews, and would involve extensive use of flares to provide illumination. In the face of what was expected to be scant defence, crews were also encouraged to attack from as low a level as practicable, both for the sake of accuracy, and in an attempt to avoid civilian casualties. In time, such operations would be led by Gee-equipped aircraft, but the 3 Group squadrons already employing the device were forbidden from taking part on this occasion, lest one be lost over enemy territory and its secrets revealed. A force of 235 aircraft was assembled, a new record for a single target, and among them were forty-eight Hampdens and twenty-six Manchesters representing 5 Group. Bright moonlight aided target location, and most crews picked up the River Seine in good time to enable them to plan their bombing runs. 223 crews reported successful sorties, many describing the factory buildings as being well alight as they turned away, and post-raid reconnaissance confirmed the operation to have been an outstanding success for the loss of just one aircraft. 40% of the factory's buildings had been destroyed, and production was halted for four weeks, costing the Germans around 2,300 lorries, although, sadly, not all of the bombs had fallen precisely where intended. Inevitably, adjacent workers' housing had been hit by stray bombs, killing 367 French civilians and severely injuring 341 others, some of whom would die. At the time, this was more than twice the heaviest death toll inflicted on a German target. It was somewhat paradoxical, that, as a champion of area bombing, Harris should gain his first major victory by way of a precision target.

While the above was in progress, some 330 miles to the north, S/L Nettleton, F/L Sandford and W/Os Crum and Lamb were taxiing Lancasters L7546, L7568, L7549 and L7547 to the runway under the eyes of the 5 Group A-O-C, AVM Slessor, each carrying four mines for delivery to the Yams and Rosemary gardens in the Schillig Roads and Heligoland Bight area respectively off north-western Germany. They became airborne in the minutes from 18.15, S/L Nettleton and F/L Sandford bound for Yams and W/Os Crum and Lamb for Rosemary, further to the north-west. They encountered favourable weather conditions with no low cloud and planted their vegetables into the allotted positions from 600 and 700 feet between 20.20 and 20.56, before returning home safely to make their reports. It was a low key beginning for an aircraft type that would be dominant among bombers and contribute more than any other to the destruction of Germany and the winning of the war.

It rained all day on the 4th, and snowed all day on the 5th, and it was the 7th before orders came through from 5 Group to make ready seventeen Hampdens for gardening duties in the Artichoke garden, in the approaches to the port of Lorient, an operation not recorded in the 5 Group ORB. 44 (Rhodesia) Squadron put eight Lancasters and crews on stand-by and warned them to be prepared for a briefing at 06.00 on the following morning, Sunday, the 8th. At 12.45, seven Lancasters departed Waddington for Lossiemouth, from where an operation was possibly to be launched, but W/O Beckett remained behind because of a problem with the heating system. During the course of the day, Lancasters L7576, L7578, R5484, R5491, R5492, R5493 and R5494 were delivered from Woodford, while three went in the opposite direction for wing modifications.

Essen was to feature prominently in Harris's future plans, and a series of raids was planned against this massively important industrial powerhouse of a city, beginning with the first of three on consecutive nights from the 8/9th. A force of 211 aircraft was put together during the course of the 8th, of which thirty-seven Hampdens and twenty-two Manchesters were to represent 5 Group. The leading aircraft, belonging to 3 Group, would be those equipped with the new Gee navigation device, which carried the great hope that it could solve the problem of blind target locating. They arrived over the Ruhr to find fine weather conditions, and, also, the ever-present industrial haze, which obscured ground detail, including the assigned aiming point "B", the Krupp complex, and few crews were able to make a positive identification after pinpointing on the Rhine. Most crews bombed the general city area, some observing bursts and others not, and, while few of them had useful information to pass on at debriefing, local reports described a light raid with a little housing damage in southern districts.

The Krupp works was back on twenty-four hours later as one of two aiming points at Essen, and a force of 187 aircraft made ready, which included a 5 Group contribution of fifteen Hampdens and ten Manchesters. This figure had originally been higher, but adverse weather conditions, technical difficulties and one unidentified Manchester becoming bogged down on the way to take-off at Bottesford, reduced the numbers significantly. Some crews claimed to be able to see the flares over Essen even before reaching the Dutch coast, which confirmed that the horizontal visibility was reasonable, while vertical visibility at the target would be compromised by industrial haze. The bombing was scattered over twenty-four other Ruhr towns and cities, with Hamborn and Duisburg the chief beneficiaries, and the Essen authorities reported the destruction of two buildings, with seventy-two others damaged.

F/Sgt Warren-Smith and crew returned from Lossiemouth on the 10th for undercarriage retraction tests to be conducted on L7549 KM-Q, and they would re-join their six fellow crews in Scotland on the 12th. Essen was posted as the primary target again on the 10th, for which a force of 126 aircraft was made ready to attack two aiming points, the Krupp sector and the main square. 5 Group provided almost half of the force in the form of forty-three Hampdens, thirteen Manchesters and, for the first time over Germany, two 44 Squadron Lancasters, which would be employing TR1335 (Gee) for the first time. F/Os Ball and Wilkins took off at 19.50 and 20.05 respectively, their bomb bays loaded with fourteen small bomb containers (SBCs), each of which contained 90 x 4lb incendiaries. They reached the target area to find two to eight-tenths cloud at between 3,000 and 8,000 feet, extreme darkness and poor visibility, made worse by the glare from searchlights and flares and the attentions of intense and accurate flak. F/O Ball, who was flying with a second pilot on board, carried out his bombing run at 18,000 feet, at which altitude the defences were initially ineffective, and released his load at 21.48 south-east of what he described as the "blitz" area, which is believed to have been the city centre. F/O Wilkins and crew followed up eight minutes later from 15,000 feet, a height within range of the defences, at which evasive action became necessary, and they could only estimate the fall of their incendiaries to be somewhere between the aiming point and two miles to the east. Unable to identify either the Krupp sector or the main square, most others bombed the built-up area generally, before turning for home to report observing some bursts and fires but no detail. Local sources claimed damage to a railway line and the destruction of one house.

The Deutsche Werke U-Boot construction yards at Kiel was the target for a force of sixty-eight Wellingtons on the night of the 12/13th, while forty Wellingtons and Whitleys, probably crewed by freshmen, attended to Emden. 5 Group committed twenty-six Hampdens and a lone Manchester to gardening duties in the Yams, Hawthorn and Rosemary regions off Germany's North Sea coast. Six of the Lossiemouth contingent returned to Waddington in the early evening of the 13th, leaving F/L Barlow behind with an unserviceable Lancaster. As they landed, Sgt Rhodes and crew were preparing to take part in an operation against Cologne, for which a force of 135 aircraft of six different types had been assembled. They took off at 19.27 with a second pilot on board and fourteen SBCs of incendiaries under their feet, but lost the use of their Gee-box, and had to rely on the navigator to guide them to the target area by pinpointing on bends in the Rhine. They found the visibility to be good through the partial cover of three to five-tenths cloud lying over the Rhineland Capital at between 8,000 and 12,000 feet and had to run the gauntlet of intense searchlight and flak to reach the aiming point. Flares provided effective illumination, and Sgt Rhodes and crew delivered their attack from 16,000 feet at 22.15, observing at least three fires and a fourth to develop following the impact of their incendiaries. On return, Sgt Rhodes overshot his landing and L7548 sustained AC category damage, which meant that it was beyond the scope of Waddington fitters to effect repairs. A post-raid assessment revealed that some useful industrial damage had resulted, mainly in the Nippes district, to the north of the city centre, west of the river, which was also the location of a major marshalling yard with railway workshops. In addition to this, 1,500 houses had been hit in what proved to be the first genuinely successful Gee-led raid.

During the following week, operations were posted and cancelled, and it was the 20th before 5 Group next stirred into action to send nineteen Manchesters and Lancasters on a daylight mining operation in the waters off the Frisians. The four 44 (Rhodesia) Squadron Lancaster sorties were cancelled because of poor weather conditions over Waddington, but, further to the east at Coningsby, six 97 Squadron Lancasters were able to take off on the squadron's maiden Lancaster operation. One of these grazed a house roof with a wingtip, and was crash-landed on a beach near Boston, where it was written off by the incoming tide, and became the first Lancaster to be lost on operations.

On the 23rd, twelve Hampdens and two Manchesters were detailed for mining duties in the Artichoke garden off the port of Lorient, and this was repeated twenty-four hours later by twenty-three Hampdens three Manchesters and two Lancasters of 44 (Rhodesia) Squadron. R5484 departed Waddington at 19.22 containing the eight-man crew of W/O Osborn, and they were followed into the air at 19.50 by the crew of F/Sgt Warren-Smith in R5493, which also included a second pilot. Each Lancaster was carrying five assorted vegetables, and they arrived in the target area a little over two hours later to take advantage of the moonlight and good visibility to pinpoint on Quiberon and the Ile-de-Croix, from where the Osborn crew carried out a timed run to deliver three of their mines into the briefed location. They returned alone fifteen minutes before midnight, and, it soon became clear, that the inevitable first operational failure to return of a Lancaster had taken the Warren-Smith crew. A 420 Squadron Hampden crew reported an unidentified aircraft being heavily engaged by flak over Lorient, while a sea-plot signal was picked up before fading at 23.28 at a position in the Channel some forty miles north-north-east of Brest. Ultimately, no trace of the Lancaster and its crew was ever found, and the conclusion was that they had fallen victim to coastal flak in the target area and crashed into the sea.

Harris resumed his campaign against Essen on the night of the 25/26th, when sending the largest force yet to a single target of 254 aircraft. 5 Group played its part by contributing twenty Manchesters, nine Hampdens and seven Lancasters, three of the last-mentioned representing 44 (Rhodesia) Squadron. F/L Barlow and F/Sgt Jones and their crews departed Waddington at 19.45 and 19.54 respectively, carrying a full load of incendiaries, and F/Sgt Nicholson and crew followed on an hour later, only to abandon their sortie over the Wash because of an unserviceable rear turret. F/Sgt Jones and crew crossed the enemy coast at 19,000 feet, untroubled by the defences, and approached the target in a shallow descent to 16,500 feet, but, despite clear skies and good visibility, thick industrial haze thwarted the attempts of all crews to identify Essen. The Jones crew relied on a Gee-fix supported by visual clues before dropping their load from 16,500 feet at 21.35, and then circled to check on the results. F/L Barlow and crew were aware of an urban sprawl beneath them when they released their load in the light of flares from 15,500 feet at 22.00. On return, they would comment that some of the Wellington-laid flares were burning at 18,000 feet, which was of no benefit in terms of illuminating ground features. The promise of Gee demonstrated in the recent attack on Cologne was not repeated, and much of the effort was wasted on a decoy site at Rheinberg, some eighteen miles away. It was a bad night for 5 Group, which posted missing six aircraft, two-thirds of the overall casualty figure, and among them were five of the twenty Manchesters dispatched, a loss rate of 25%.

On the 26th, instructions were received to ground Lancasters as far as operations were concerned, and that training flights should be restricted to a fuel load not exceeding 580 gallons in inner tanks only, and absolutely no bombs to be carried. This resulted from an incident of wingtip rippling and loose rivets, and it brought an end to operations for 44 and 97 Squadrons for the remainder of the month. That night, a force of 115 Wellingtons and Stirlings returned to Essen, while 5 Group detailed thirty Hampdens and fifteen Manchesters to conduct mining operations in the Yams, Nectarines and Deodar gardens, respectively in Jade Bay and the Weser estuary, off the Frisians and the Gironde estuary leading to the port of Bordeaux in south-western France.

These operations preceded another foretaste of things to come, when Harris launched a major assault on the historic Hansastadt (free-trade) city of Lübeck on the north German coast, believing, that, if he could provide his crews with the means to locate a target, they would hit it. Coastlines offered the most distinctive features for the purpose of identification, hence, Lübeck, which not only lay on the Baltic coast to the east of Kiel, but also represented the perfect target for destruction by fire because of the narrow streets and half-timbered buildings in its old centre. The operation, to be carried out on the night of the 28/29th, was to be conducted along the same lines as the highly successful attack on the Renault factory at the start of the month, and a force of 234 aircraft was assembled, 5 Group represented by forty-one Hampdens and twenty-one Manchesters. Those reaching the target area had found excellent visibility during the outward flight, that allowed them to map-read their way across the Schleswig-Holstein peninsula to gain the western Baltic. Many fires were seen to develop, and returning crews reported the burning city to be visible from seventy miles into the homeward flight. Post-raid reconnaissance and local sources confirmed the operation to have been a major success, which destroyed almost fifteen hundred houses and seriously damaged almost two thousand more in a 190-acre area of devastation representing some 30% of the city's built-up area. It was the first major success for area bombing, and another sign of what was in store for the residents of Germany's towns and cities. There was an outcry following this unexpected attack on Lübeck, which was a city of culture and a vital port for the Red Cross. An agreement was struck that ensured its future protection from bombing, and apart from a few isolated incidents, would be adhered to.

Eighteen Hampdens and eight Manchesters were made ready for further gardening operations on the 29th, all but two assigned to the Nectarine gardens, while two of the Manchesters ventured as far as the Bottle garden, off Haugesund on Norway's western coast. A return to the madness of daylight "moling" cloud cover operations on the 31st involved eleven Hampdens and six Wellingtons, whose crews had been briefed to seek out railway targets in north-western Germany. They flew out over Skegness over ten-tenths cloud, which began to disperse as they crossed Holland to within ten miles of the German frontier, where it ran out altogether, forcing most of them to turn back. During the course of the month, the squadron took part in five operations and dispatched twelve sorties for the loss of a single Lancaster and its crew.

April 1942

The new month began for 5 Group with operations on the 1st in company with Wellingtons, although not operating together. Twenty-two Hampden crews were briefed to take part in a raid on the docks area and shipping at Le Havre, while fourteen others were to be sent to carry out low-level attacks on railway targets in north-western Germany in the Meppen and Lingen region just over the frontier from Holland. It turned into a disastrous night for 3 Group, whose railway targets were at Hanau and Lohr to the east of Frankfurt, from which five out of twelve 57 Squadron Wellingtons failed to return and seven of fourteen belonging to 214 Squadron. This caused a rethink by those responsible for planning operations, despite which, a similar disaster awaited 5 Group in December. On the following night, twenty-three Hampdens were detailed for mining duties in the Gorse garden in Quiberon Bay, situated on the western coast of Brittany, north-west of St-Nazaire. The operation took place in ideal, moonlit conditions, in which the crews established their positions without difficulty, pinpointing on Quiberon Point or Ile-d'Houat, from where they carried out their timed runs to deliver the vegetables into the allotted locations. A daylight mining operation in one of the Nectarine gardens was planned for the late afternoon of the 4th, when crews would have to rely on cloud cover over the Frisians to provide protection. When this failed to materialize, the operation was abandoned, and all crews returned home with their stores.

The first major operation of the new month was directed at Cologne on the night of the 5/6th and involved a new record force of 263 aircraft, which included a 5 Group contribution of forty-four Hampdens and eleven Manchesters. The aiming point was the Klöckner-Humboldt engineering works in the Deutz district on the East Bank of the Rhine in the city centre, which manufactured a wide range of commercial and military vehicles. Over the target, bright moonlight penetrated the nine-tenths cloud to glint off an S-bend in the Rhine to the south of the city centre, and this assisted with the accurate establishing of positions for the bombing runs. Despite the advantages, many crews scattered their loads right across the built-up area, destroying or seriously damaging ninety houses but nothing of industrial significance. On the following night, Harris turned his attention back upon Essen, with the first of three raids against it in six nights, to which 5 Group contributed eighteen Hampdens and ten Manchesters. Only a third of the crews reported bombing the target, which escaped with minor damage at a cost to the Command of five aircraft, three of them belonging to 5 Group.

Hamburg was posted as the target on the 8th, and yet another record force, this time of 272 aircraft, was made ready. 5 Group stepped up with thirty-two Hampdens and thirteen Manchesters assigned to the Blohm & Voss shipyards located to the west of the city centre, while the seven Lancasters and nine further Hampdens were to attack aiming point C, the industrial centre of the city. 44 (Rhodesia) Squadron detailed five Lancasters, which departed Waddington between 21.38 and 22.00 bearing aloft the crews of F/O Garwell, the newly commissioned P/O Nicholson and W/Os Beckett, Lamb and Stott, each of which had beneath their feet 112 x 30lb incendiaries. They had to fly through or round one of the towering electrical storms with icing conditions that frequently built up over the North Sea to bar the approaches to north-western Germany, and, on this night, not all who set out would reach their intended destination. In fact, only 188 crews would report bombing the general area of Hamburg through ten-tenths cloud, among them four of the 44 (Rhodesia) Squadron element on estimated positions from 19,000 and 20,000 feet between 23.48 and 00.13. F/O Garwell failed to identify the primary target and headed towards the south-west to bomb Bremen as a last resort from 17,000 feet at 00.08. The result was another poor performance, which deposited no more than the equivalent of fourteen bomb loads in the city and caused eight fires.

It was back to Essen for 254 aircraft on the 10th, an operation supported by 5 Group with forty-three Hampdens, ten Manchesters and eight Lancasters. 44 (Rhodesia) Squadron loaded five Lancasters with 30lb incendiaries and one or two of the new 250lb "oil" bombs for what the ORB labelled a "shaker" operation and dispatched them from Waddington between 21.45 and 22.01 with F/L Sandford the senior pilot on duty. Shaker was the codename given to the dropping of target illuminator flares by 3 Group aircraft employing Gee as a rudimentary form of pathfinding. On this night, the 44 (Rhodesia) Squadron crews navigated to the target area also guided by TR (Gee) and were expecting to find the clear skies forecast at briefing, but, instead, were confronted by a layer of eight-tenths cloud across the central Ruhr at between 5,000 and 8,000 feet. The route in was described by F/L Sandford as "hot", with scores of searchlights from all sides working in conjunction with light and heavy flak. W/O Crum, who was undertaking his first ever sortie over the Ruhr and his first over enemy territory for a year, lost the use of TR three minutes before reaching the briefed aiming point, but maintained track for the short distance to bomb release. On return, he would express himself to be amazed by the visual experience of searchlights and flak. F/O Ball was the other to attack the briefed aiming point, while F/L Sandford, F/O Garwell and Sgt Rhodes were unable to identify the main square and bombed the general city area instead. They carried out their attacks from 16,000 to 20,000 feet between 23.54 and 00.05, observing some bursts and the glow of fires beneath the cloud, but little of use to the Intelligence Section at debriefing. Local reports confirmed the operation to have been another dismal failure, which destroyed only twelve houses and caused no industrial damage.

On the 11th, the squadron was instructed to detail six Lancasters to carry out formation flying in two sections of three in order to gather data on the endurance of the Lancaster under formation flying conditions. Orders were received across the Command on the 12th to prepare another large force to return to Essen that night, and 251 aircraft were made ready accordingly, 5 Group responding with thirty-one Hampdens and nine Manchesters. 44 (Rhodesia) Squadron was not to be involved and sent F/O Maclagan and crew to join a handful of other 5 Group freshmen to drop reading matter to the residents of Paris. They took off at 21.16 and delivered more than two hundred bundles of assorted nickels from 11,000 feet at 23.23, before landing at 01.54 to report the lights of Paris to be clearly visible. The Essen raid turned out to be another disappointing affair, which caused a fire and some useful damage to the Krupp works, and destroyed or seriously damaged eighty houses, but it was a poor return for the size of the force. Harris took stock, thereafter, and the statistics made uncomfortable reading. During eight heavy attacks on the city since the 8/9th of March, 1,555 sorties had been launched, of which 1,006 crews had claimed to have bombed, at a cost to the Command of sixty-four aircraft. Only twenty-two bombing photos had shown ground detail within five miles of Essen, demonstrating in the eyes of the critics, that there had been no improvement in the effectiveness of operations since the Butt Report.

There was much speculation at Waddington and Woodhall Spa, the home of 97 Squadron, concerning the low-level training, and the fact that the two squadrons had been taken off other duties. Amidst the greatest secrecy, the speculation increased on the 14th, when elements from both units carried out a long-range practice flight, which culminated in a simulated attack on the city of Inverness in northern Scotland. Meanwhile, Dortmund was posted as the target for a force of 208 aircraft that night, by far the largest effort yet against this industrial giant situated at the eastern end of the Ruhr. 5 Group made a contribution to the operation of thirty-four Hampdens and four Manchesters, which, like the rest of the force, had to run the gauntlet of intense searchlight and flak activity as they traversed the most heavily defended region of Germany. Clear skies enabled them to map-read their way by river and railway features to the aiming point, where they dropped their loads from around 8,000 feet, while attempting to dodge some eighty searchlights in cones. It would be established later that the bombing had been scattered over a forty-mile stretch of the region, with no significant damage to the intended target.

A reduced force of 152 aircraft was assembled for the same target twenty-four hours later, this time supported by 5 Group with nineteen Hampdens and seven Manchesters. The crews had to contend with severe icing conditions on the southern approaches to the Ruhr, only then to run into intense searchlight and flak activity over the target, where two-tenths low cloud combined with the industrial haze to muddy the vertical visibility. Despite the effort and the courage, this raid was another dismal failure that scattered bombs over a wide area and caused only the slightest damage in the target city. Minor operations occupied the night of the 16/17th, for which 5 Group contributed ten Hampdens and two Manchesters for gardening duties and five Hampdens and two Manchesters for nickelling activities over Lille in north-eastern France.

At noon on the 17th, the crews of S/L Nettleton, F/L Sandford, F/O Garwell, W/Os Beckett and Crum and Sgt Rhodes filed into the briefing room to be enlightened as to their immediate future. They were incredulous to learn that they were soon to embark on Operation Margin, an epic low-level deep-penetration flight to Augsburg in Bavaria, to attack the diesel engine assembly shop in the middle of a large factory complex belonging to the Maschinen Fabrik Augsburg Nürnburg Aktien Gesellschaft, otherwise known as the M.A.N. works, situated on the outskirts of the beautiful and historic city. This particular shop was, strategically, the most important part of the factory as it assembled the diesel engines that provided U-Boots with motive power while on the surface. It was believed to be the bottleneck in the entire U-Boot industry at a time when the Battle of the Atlantic was the main preoccupation of both Britain and the United States. The operation had been planned meticulously and required the crews to fly in formation at the lowest possible level, both to evade enemy radar and to provide protection from fighters and flak. There would be no fighter escort, but a large-scale diversion was arranged to attract the attention of the defences as the Lancasters crossed the enemy coast and made their way across France. This was to be provided by Bostons of 2 Group, which were to carry out a number of attacks in the Calais-Cherbourg-Rouen area under a strong fighter escort. The two sections of six Lancasters, formed into vics of three, were routed out over Selsey Bill to begin the Channel crossing within sight of each other, and make landfall at Villers-sur-Mer on the Normandy coast. They would then pass south of Paris on course for Sens and thence make for Lake Constance on the Swiss frontier for the final run in to the target as dusk approached. The return flight was to be made under the cover of darkness.

The two Waddington vics took off at 15.12 and 15.14, with, ahead of them, a 1,250-mile round trip, and, on arriving at the French coast at 16.45, descended to 25 to 30 feet, following the contour of the terrain as they had in practice flights over Scotland. The two vics were in line astern and half a mile or so apart, sometimes climbing to avoid trees and other ground obstacles, and made good progress across Normandy until reaching the Bernay region some thirty miles inland at around 16.50. Here, they were spotted by two formations of BF109s of II./JG2 Richthofen, which numbered thirty plus and were about to land at their base at Beaumont-le-Roger, having been scrambled to meet one of the Boston diversionary raids. At first, S/L Nettleton noticed only two or three fighters a thousand feet above him, but then, they were swarming all round and attacked him from astern at such low level that he watched cannon shells impact buildings ahead. The rear gunner provided a running commentary as he witnessed the destruction of the rear vic, which was under a relentless attack with nowhere to hide. The first to attract the fighters' attention was W/O Beckett's L7565, which had an unserviceable rear turret, and was on fire from stem to stern as it sank into the ground and exploded in a clump of trees, ten miles west-north-west of Evreux, with no survivors. L7548 was the next to go, and, with its port wing in flames, W/O Crum ordered the bomb load to be jettisoned, before, in a masterly display of airmanship, bringing the stricken Lancaster down on its belly in a meadow without injury to the crew. They would retain their freedom for fourteen days and reach Vichy France before being captured. Shortly thereafter, R5506 ploughed in with all four engines ablaze, killing F/L Sandford and his crew.

Now that the rear vic had been wiped out, the fighters advanced on the remaining three Lancasters, focusing first on L7536 which, in its death throes, reared upwards before stalling and diving in at 16.55, taking with it to their deaths Sgt Rhodes and his crew. Nettleton and Garwell came under repeated attack and sustained damage, before a lack of fuel and ammunition forced the fighters to withdraw. The Lancasters still faced a flight of almost three hours before even reaching the target, and continued on, mercifully, without further interference from the enemy. To airmen accustomed to flying in darkness at high level, the close proximity to the ground in broad daylight offered a new experience of scattering livestock, German officers out riding and the patchwork of rural France rolling beneath them at great speed. Augsburg lay hidden behind a hill, and only came into view as Nettleton crested it and followed its slope down the other side with the city laid out ahead of him and the factory complex positioned exactly as on the maps and photos at briefing. They ran into a hail of light flak that threatened to shred the Lancasters, but Nettleton was focussed on the engine assembly sheds, which he picked out as he flew between two towering chimneys to deliver his four 1,000lb eleven-second-delayed-action bombs at 19.56. Garwell's Lancaster was hit by light flak, but he released his bombs on the target, and, with fire having taken hold and no prospect of keeping R5510 aloft, he carried out a forced-landing two miles west of the city, which he and three of his crew survived to fall into enemy hands.

Nettleton turned to watch the bombs detonate, throwing dust and debris high into the air, and then headed westwards into the twilight, remaining low until darkness arrived to cloak his presence, at which point, he climbed to standard operational altitude. At half past midnight, with fuel running low, the crew's distress call was answered, locating them over the North Sea, and they were directed to Squires Gate at Blackpool, where a landing was made at 00.50, almost ten hours after take-off. Back at Waddington, those awaiting the return of the force waved off that afternoon, were in sombre mood, until news came through of Nettleton's landing. The 97 Squadron element had seen the 44 Squadron attack as they closed on the target, and lost the crews of the leader, S/L Sherwood, and W/O Mycock during the attack, Sherwood alone miraculously living to tell the tale after being catapulted through the shattered windscreen on impact, still strapped to his seat. Some damage was inflicted on the M.A.N. factory, but not in proportion to the losses incurred, and a substantial number of the bombs had failed to explode. In recognition of his epic flight, Nettleton was awarded the Victoria Cross, and he would become something of a celebrity over the ensuing months, speaking in a radio broadcast about the operation, and paying a visit to a Lancaster factory, something which was later shown on Pathé newsreel in cinemas. Among many messages of congratulations was one by the Prime Minister, which Harris passed on. It read; *"We must plainly regard the attack of the Lancasters on the U-Boat Engine Factory at Augsburg as an outstanding achievement of the Royal Air Force. Undeterred by heavy losses at the outset, 44 and 97 Squadrons pierced in broad daylight into the heart of Germany and struck a vital point with deadly precision. Pray, convey the thanks of His Majesty's Government to the officers and men who accomplished this memorable feat of arms, in which no life was lost in vain."*

While S/L Nettleton and crew were nearing the end of their homeward flight, 173 aircraft took off for an operation against Hamburg, for which 5 Group contributed five Manchesters. Germany's second city was found to be under clear skies but shrouded in haze and protected by the usual intense searchlight and flak barrage from both banks of the Elbe. The city-centre aiming point could not be identified, and most crews bombed the built-up area generally, setting off seventy-five fires, thirty-three of which were classed locally as large, but, even so, fewer than a third of the bomb loads had actually found the mark. There would be no further operations for 44 (Rhodesia) Squadron for ten days, and, in the meantime, 5 Group detailed twenty-five Hampdens, ten Manchesters and two Lancasters for gardening duties in one of the Nectarine regions around the Frisians on the 19th. On the 21st, P/O McLaren led a party of seventy-three ground personnel to Lossiemouth by rail, in anticipation of the arrival of a Lancaster striking force from 44 and 97 Squadrons. On the following day, W/C Learoyd set off by road to command them, and they were joined by the 44 Squadron Lancasters on the 23rd, which contained the crews of F/L Barlow, P/O Nicholson, W/Os Lamb, Stott and Wright and F/Sgt Jones.

The first attempt to employ Gee as a blind bombing aid took place on the night of the 22/23rd, when Cologne was the target for a 3 Group force of sixty-four Wellingtons and five Stirlings. Fewer than 20% of the bomb loads fell into the city, and some landed up to ten miles away, proving that Gee was capable of guiding a force to a general area, but lacked the precision necessary to deliver a telling blow on an urban target. While this operation was in progress, 5 Group dispatched twenty-two Hampdens and a dozen Manchesters on gardening duties on both sides of the Schleswig-Holstein peninsula in Forget-me-not (Kiel Harbour), Quince (Kiel Bay), Radish (Fehmarn Belt) and Rosemary (Heligoland Bight). They encountered clear skies and good visibility over the western Baltic and pinpointed on the southern tip of Denmark's Langeland Island and on the German mainland north-east of Kiel, before making their timed runs and dropping their mines into the briefed locations.

In an attempt to repeat the success gained at Lübeck, Rostock, also on the Baltic coast, was earmarked for a series of four raids on consecutive nights from the 23/24th, with the old town and the Heinkel aircraft factory on its southern outskirts the specific aiming points. A force of 161 aircraft was assembled, 143 of them assigned to the town and eighteen to the factory, and 5 Group managed to put up eleven Hampdens, six Manchesters and a single Lancaster. Despite favourable weather conditions and good visibility, the majority of crews failed to find the mark at either aiming point, and the bombing fell between two and six miles away. The 5 Group element for round two at Rostock amounted to thirty-four aircraft, including four Lancasters from the newly-converted 207 Squadron at Bottesford, and all were assigned to the Heinkel factory, while ninety-one aircraft from the other groups focussed on the old town. Those reaching the target area were drawn on from many miles away by the fires already burning. Bright moonlight illuminated the Unterwarnow River running south from the coast to the heart of the town and provided excellent visibility for the low-level attacks. The town seemed to be ablaze as they crossed over it to reach the Heinkel factory, which most attacked on existing fires, while trying to evade the attentions of the many searchlights co-operating with light flak. According to the observations of returning crews, the Heinkel factory and adjacent aerodrome had been hit by many bombs and were left burning, and, while post-raid reconnaissance revealed extensive damage within the town, the factory buildings were revealed to be still intact, demonstrating that the impressions gained by crews in the heat of battle could be somewhat unreliable.

Meanwhile, on the 24th and 330 miles away in northern Scotland, a briefing was held at Lossiemouth, attended by the 4 Group A-O-C, AVM Roddy Carr, at which the target was revealed to be Tirpitz at her mooring at Aavikennet in the Foetten Fjord, the most southerly inlet of Aasen Fjord, approximately eighteen miles east-north-east of Trondheim. Should Tirpitz have been moved, or could not be located, alternative targets were the Admiral Scheer and Prinz Eugen in Lo Fjord, where a Hipper class vessel was also believed to be at berth. The briefing went on to describe the Tirpitz, her location and defences, and predicted that she would be difficult to identify in conditions other than good visibility and moonlight. The attack would take place in two phases, covered by a diversionary operation by Beaufighters, beginning with six Lancasters each from 44 and 97 Squadron and a dozen 76 Squadron Halifaxes carrying special 4,000lb bombs. They were to approach at 6,000 feet and to attack in as great a concentration as possible, before turning their attention upon the searchlight and flak defences with 500 pounders, while nineteen Halifaxes of 10 and 35 Squadrons released special mines from 200 feet or lower. A further briefing was held at 15.00 on the 25th, with a take-off planned for 20.15, but ten-tenths cloud forced a postponement, and all crews were released until 10.00 on Sunday the 26th. Back at Waddington, the news was received of the award of the Victoria Cross to S/L Nettleton, the DFC to the three commissioned members of his crew and the DFM to the four NCO members of what had been an eight-man crew.

The third Rostock raid was launched on the night of the 25/26th, and involved 110 aircraft assigned to the town, while eighteen from 5 Group targeted the Heinkel factory, led by 106 Squadron's commanding officer, W/C Guy Gibson. Ideal weather conditions again prevailed, and post-raid reconnaissance revealed that the factory had, at last, been hit, and that the town had suffered severe damage without loss to the attackers. A force of 106 aircraft was detailed for the final raid of the series on the 26th, which included a contribution from 5 Group of nineteen Hampdens, nine Manchesters and a single Lancaster. Those reaching the target area found moonlight, excellent visibility and existing fires to aid target location, and another successful raid ensued. An analysis of the Rostock campaign revealed it to have been highly successful, destroying 1,765 buildings and seriously damaging five hundred more, which represented 60% of the town's built-up area. In his diaries, Propaganda Minister Goebbels used the phrase "Terrorangriff", terror raid, for the first time.

The weather conditions for the Tirpitz operation remained unfavourable on the night of the 26/27th, and it was 20.12 on the 27th when F/L Barlow and crew led the 44 Squadron element into the air, to be followed by those from 97 Squadron and, finally, the Halifax brigade. W/O Wright turned back immediately with an unserviceable rear turret, and W/O Osborn and crew took off at 20.25 in the reserve aircraft to fill the gap, only for F/Sgt Jones to lose his port-outer engine as he climbed out and have to abandon his sortie. The Lancasters identified Tirpitz with ease in excellent visibility under clear skies and bright moonlight and delivered their 4,000 pounders from 6,000 to 8,000 feet between 00.06 and 00.28, believing they had done so accurately. They were clear of the target area by the stipulated time of 00.35, when the 4 Group attack was scheduled to begin. One 97 Squadron Lancaster was shot down along with four Halifaxes, one of the latter containing the 10 Squadron commanding officer and future A-O-C of the Path Finder Force, W/C Don Bennett, who would evade capture and return to his post within six weeks. A few bombing photos were taken, revealing no apparent damage to Tirpitz, and this was confirmed by further photos taken by the Photographic Reconnaissance Unit (PRU) on the 28th.

The operation had to be repeated that night, and, prior to take-off, a message of encouragement was received from the prime Minister. The 44 (Rhodesia) Squadron sextet departed Lossiemouth between 20.49 and 20.55, to be followed by the five-strong 97 Squadron element and arrived some three-and-a-half hours later to be greeted once more by good visibility, which enabled the crews to map read their way from the Norwegian coast to the target. Five of the 44 (Rhodesia) Squadron element attacked from 7,000 to 8,500 feet between 00.25 and 00.35, while P/O Nicholson apparently made two runs at 14,000 feet, the second one at 00.36. Again, the belief was that the bombing had been accurate and had, at least, scored a number of near-misses, but, despite claims of direct hits by other units, no damage was confirmed and two Halifaxes were lost. While the above was in progress, ten Hampdens took part in a raid on the shipyards at Kiel and contributed to damage to three of them. The month ended for 5 Group with a raid by nine 420 Squadron Hampdens on the 29th against the Gnome & Rhóne aero engine factory at Gennevilliers in Paris. During the course of the month, 44 Squadron took part in six operations, and dispatched twenty-nine sorties for the loss of five Lancasters and crews.

May 1942

The weather kept the Command on the ground on the night of the 1/2nd, but it had relented sufficiently on the following day for ninety-six aircraft from 3 and 5 Groups to be detailed for mining operations that night. 5 Group provided twenty-one Lancasters, eight Manchesters and twelve Hampdens for gardens in the Baltic and off the Biscay coast, and nine Manchesters for nickelling duties in the Rennes area of north-western France. 44 (Rhodesia) Squadron made ready five Lancasters for the Deodar garden in the Gironde estuary, and another for the Endive garden in the Little Belt in the western Baltic. The former took off from Waddington between 22.16 and 22.27 with S/L Weston the senior pilot on duty, leaving P/O Maclagan and crew on the ground until their departure at 00.26, all six Lancasters carrying a crew of eight and six assorted mines. The flight to south-western France took three hours in excellent conditions under clear skies and bright moonlight, and all mines were delivered in or close to the assigned locations from 500 to 1,000 feet between 01.20 and 01.38. The flight to a point north of Brandsø island took the Maclagan crew two hours and forty minutes, also in excellent conditions, under which they delivered their stores in two passes from 500 feet at 03.04, before returning safely to describe a "very pleasant trip".

Hamburg was posted as the primary target for a force of eighty-one aircraft on the 3rd, the numbers somewhat reduced in the face of a forecast of poor weather conditions. 5 Group contributed just five Hampdens from 420 Squadron RCAF, while other elements from the group were occupied by minor endeavours elsewhere. Orders were received on the 4th to make ready for the first of what would be a "Rostock-style" sustained assault on the important industrial city of Stuttgart over three consecutive nights. A force of 121 aircraft included a contribution from 5 Group of nineteen Hampdens and fourteen Lancasters, the crews of the former briefed to aim for the highly important Robert Bosch factory, which was engaged in the manufacture of dynamos, injection pumps and magnetos. The Lancaster crews were briefed to attack military barracks, and the five 44 (Rhodesia) Squadron participants departed Waddington between 22.23 and 22.40 with F/L Barlow the senior pilot on duty, each carrying a full load of incendiaries. At the end of their five-hundred-mile outward flight, with a rising moon to light the way, they found all of their good intentions thwarted by ten-tenths cloud at around 6,000 feet over the series of deep valleys occupied by the sprawling city. It proved impossible to pick out ground features by which to establish a position, and the bombing was carried out on DR and evidence of flak from 9,000 to 15,000 feet between 01.16 and 01.30. Very little was observed of the results, and all but one returning 5 Group crew reported bombing fires and red flares through the cloud, with just one Hampden crew claiming to have bombed the primary target. Local reports confirmed that the operation had scattered bombs over a wide area and onto a decoy site at Lauffen, fifteen miles to the north of the city, which was "defended" by thirty-five searchlights and fifty flak guns. It was a clever ruse that would lure away many bomb loads during the course of the war, that might otherwise have caused damage in Stuttgart.

5 Group contributed four 97 Squadron Lancasters to the same target on the following night, and they again bombed the town rather than the Bosch factory to which they had been assigned. Despite clear skies, ground detail was obscured by haze, and no bombs fell in the city. 44 (Rhodesia) Squadron dispatched the freshman Lancaster crew of P/O Hackney at 22.10 to dispense reading matter to the residents of Paris, and, under clear skies, they dropped 188 bundles from 14,000 feet at 23.58. W/C Lynch-Blosse arrived from 25 O.T.U on the 6th, pending his appointment as successor to W/C Learoyd two days hence, as the latter went in the opposite direction. It was Stuttgart again that night, for which

5 Group detailed ten Hampdens and ten Lancasters in an overall force of ninety-seven aircraft. 44 (Rhodesia) Squadron loaded six of its own with 112 x 30lb incendiaries and sent them on their way from Waddington between 21.50 and 21.56 with F/L Barlow the senior pilot on duty. They exited the English coast at Orfordness, from where P/O Maclagan and crew were forced to turn back with turret malfunctions. The others flew out across Belgium, and, after an outward flight lasting almost three hours, reached the target area to find largely clear skies, but haze again making target identification difficult. Most picked out a built-up area on e.t.a., backed up by evidence of searchlights, flak and burning incendiaries from other aircraft, and scattered their bombs over a wide area. The Waddington crews carried out their attacks from 10,000 to 14,000 feet between 00.45 and 01.05, by which time, W/O Stott and crew had bombed what they believed was Saarbrücken as an alternative target after losing their port-outer engine. The port-inner also cut but restarted when the fuel feed was changed. When some twenty to forty miles from the coast homebound, they were attacked by a BF109, which they shot down in flames. The operation was another massively ineffective affair, which again failed to land a single bomb in Stuttgart, but did hit 150 buildings in Heilbronn, a large town situated five miles from the Lauffen decoy site and twenty miles from Stuttgart.

On the 8th, W/C Learoyd concluded his tour as commanding officer, and handed over to his successor, for what would prove to be the briefest possible term of office. Lord Trenchard visited Waddington that day and met with S/L Nettleton and his crew, conversing with them about the Augsburg raid and assuring them that Bomber Command was having a material effect on the German war effort. The recent successes at Lübeck and Rostock may have encouraged the posting of another Baltic coast target on the 8th, this time, Warnemünde, situated on the West Bank of the estuary ten miles north of Rostock. The docks were the site of U-Boot crew training, and also supplied German forces on the Russian front, but, equally important was the Heinkel aircraft factory, the destruction of which was handed to 5 Group. An initial force of more than two hundred aircraft was detailed, among which 5 Group put up twenty-one Lancasters, nine Manchesters and nineteen Hampdens, the last-mentioned representing the two Canadian squadrons, 408 and 420, the only units still equipped with the type. An elaborate plan called for a three-phase operation, beginning at zero hour with eighteen aircraft delivering high-explosives in a five-minute slot, followed by phase two, which involved 104 aircraft attacking with general purpose (GP) bombs, and phase three, six 44 (Rhodesia) Squadron Lancasters and a dozen aircraft from other groups targeting the Heinkel factory at low level to ensure its destruction. As this was ongoing, sixty-two 1 Group crews were to drop incendiaries, while others carried out low-level attacks on searchlight and flak batteries. In the event, 193 aircraft took off, which would reduce slightly the aircraft available for each phase.

W/O Wright and crew had been assigned to the second phase attack, and took off from Waddington at 22.30, leaving W/C Lynch-Blosse, P/Os Maclagan and Nicholson, and W/Os Jones, Lambert and Osborn on the ground until their departure for phase three between 23.17 and 23.25. From the eastern coast of Jutland, W/O Wright's navigator, P/O Evans, could see a veritable forest of searchlights seventy miles distant at the target, which they reached soon afterwards under clear skies at 11,000 feet. They were completely blinded to the actual aiming point by the glare from the searchlights, into which they delivered their six 1,000 pounders at 01.44, observing a large unidentified aircraft to crash in flames in the target area, another closer to the coast and a third over Denmark. W/O Osborn and crew arrived thirty minutes later as a member of the low-level force, and dived down to 700 feet, only to be blinded by the searchlight dazzle. They retained their bombs and climbed back up to 8,000 feet to draw a bead on the target, before diving on the aiming point again through intense light flak and releasing their bombs from 2,500 feet onto a large fire, which they assessed to be at aiming point B or

C. The rear gunner observed them to burst some fifty yards short of the fire and reported a large block of buildings to be burning fiercely. It was 02.45, thirty minutes after the Osborn attack, that P/O Nicholson and crew arrived on scene at a perilously low 70 feet, from which altitude, the target was obscured by rising ground. Only after they crested this could they see a large fire ahead but were on top of it before establishing what it was and gained nothing more than an impression as four 1,000 pounders fell away, and two others hung up. The three above-mentioned crews touched down at Waddington at between 04.20 and 05.46 and waited to be joined by the remaining four eight-man crews, whom they had last seen just a few hours earlier. Sadly, they would be among nineteen failures to return, eight of which belonged to 5 Group. W/C Lynch-Blosse, who was undertaking his first operation as commanding officer, died with the other seven men on board R5555, when it was shot down to crash at Lambrechtshagen, some four miles west-north-west of Rostock, and this was close to where R5568 came down, killing F/O Maclagan and all but his rear gunner, who fell into enemy hands. This was the first all-Rhodesian Lancaster crew to be lost in Bomber Command service. L7533 and R5557 went missing without trace with the crews of W/O Lamb and W/O Jones respectively. S/L Weston stepped briefly into the breach, pending the return to the squadron from 14 O.T.U of the now W/C Smales on the 10th to become the squadron's seventh commanding officer since the outbreak of war.

Losses were a fact of life in Bomber Command and could not be allowed to interfere with the process of war. A team from the Committee of Adjustment would descend upon the billets of the missing men and remove all trace of them to prepare the way for the next occupants. Such was the size of a bomber squadron, and the constant turnover of arrivals and departures, that close friendships beyond one's own crew were discouraged. Perhaps it was different among officers, who were fewer, and were more frequently in each other's company in the officers' mess, but, generally, the faces of the missing soon faded from memory, and those returning within a matter of months after evading capture, were often shocked to discover how few faces they recognised. The squadron scribe commented on the fact, that the loss of four such experienced crews would severely handicap the squadron's operational capacity, and that strength now stood at eight fully experienced and two freshman crews, and five others under training with the Conversion Flight. It was suggested that the squadron should be stood-down for a month to allow intensive training, but, instead, it was to be reformed into an operational and a training flight, the latter to merge with the Conversion Flight under S/L "Kipper" Herring. Furthermore, it was made clear that the operational flight would not be called upon to operate beyond its capacity. On the 11th, changes were made to the make-up of a crew, which removed second pilots, second navigators and second wireless operators. From this point on, a standard crew would consist of a pilot (captain), flight engineer (pilot's mate), navigator, bomb-aimer, wireless operator/gunner and mid-upper and rear gunners.

On the 12th, W/C Smales was detached to 97 Squadron at Woodhall Spa to learn the ways of the Lancaster and would be away for six days. The weather kept the Command on the ground for the next few nights, and it was the 15th before four 44 (Rhodesia) Squadron crews were called to briefing to learn of their part in that night's mining operations involving fifty aircraft in the western Baltic, of which sixteen Hampdens and six Lancasters would represent 5 Group. The Waddington crews of F/L Barlow and W/Os Osborn and Wright were assigned to the Yew Tree garden, located in the Læsø Channel of the Kattegat, while W/O Stott would ply his trade in the Pumpkin garden in the northern reaches of the Great Belt. They took off between 22.57 and 23.28, but F/L Barlow's port-outer engine began to show signs of distress within minutes, and he was forced to abandon his sortie. The others reached their respective gardens to encounter clear skies and generally good conditions, but W/O Stott was unable to locate the allotted drop zone because of sea mist, and recrossed southern Jutland to deposit his five assorted mines into one of the Hawthorn gardens off Esbjerg from 900 feet at 02.43. W/Os Wright and Osborn found perfect visibility off Læ island and planted their vegetables from 500 and 600 feet at 02.02 and 02.20 respectively. On the following day, Harris passed on a message from the Chief of Naval Staff, Sir Dudley Pound, in which he expressed his congratulations on the Augsburg raid.

Mannheim was posted as the primary target on the 19th, and a force of 193 aircraft made ready, which included a 5 Group contribution of fifteen Hampdens, thirteen Lancasters and four Manchesters. Four of the Lancasters departed Waddington between 22.20 and 22.45 bearing aloft the crews of W/Os Osborn, Stott and Wright and P/O Nicholson, but W/O Stott had barely left the circuit before complete instrument failure forced him to turn back. The others pressed on to the French coast and continued south until crossing into Germany south of Luxembourg, where they had to run the gauntlet of masses of searchlights before finding the target area under clear skies. However, the absence of a moon created extreme darkness, which combined with haze to blot out all ground features. Most crews identified the city by means of a Gee-fix and the River Rhine but picking out the main post office aiming point was beyond them, and the 44 Squadron crews delivered their 4,000 pounder and 720 x 4lb incendiaries each onto existing fires from 14,000 to 18,000 feet between 01.05 and 01.35. Local reports claimed that only around ten bomb loads landed in the city, and this was after the force was heard overhead for an extended period, as if searching for it. Also, in action on this night was the crew of P/O Hackney, who took off at 22.06 bound for Vichy to deliver leaflets. Having picked up the River Loire, they followed its course, and, on e.t.a., dropped a flare, which failed to ignite. Assuming that they were over the correct target, they dropped 288 bundles, and it was only later that the navigator realised that they had probably provided the residents of the town of Moulins with an unexpected supply of toilet paper. L7581 was written off on the afternoon of the 20th, when the leading edge of the port wing failed before it had left the ground. The Lancaster veered off the runway and collided with two 420 Squadron Hampdens, but the crew of W/O Wright walked away, apparently unscathed.

There now followed another lull in major operations as Harris prepared for his master stroke. At the time of his appointment as C-in-C, the figure of four thousand bombers had been bandied around as the number required to wrap up the war. Whilst there was not the slightest chance of procuring them, Harris, with a dark cloud still hanging over the existence of an independent bomber force, needed to ensure that those earmarked for him were not spirited away to what he considered to be less-deserving causes. The Command had not yet achieved sufficient success to silence the detractors, and the Admiralty was still calling for bomber aircraft to be diverted to the U-Boot campaign, while others demanded support for the North Africa campaign. Harris was in need of a major victory, and, perhaps, a dose of symbolism to make his point, and, out of this was born the Thousand Plan, Operation Millennium, the launching of a thousand aircraft in one night against a major German city, for which Hamburg had been pencilled in. Harris did not have a thousand front-line aircraft and required the support of other Commands to make up the numbers. This was forthcoming from Coastal and Flying Training Commands, and, in the case of the former, a letter to Harris on the 22nd promised 250 aircraft. However, following an intervention from the Admiralty, the offer was withdrawn, and most of the Flying Training Command aircraft were found to be not up to the task, leaving the Millennium force well short of the magic figure. Undaunted, Harris, or more probably his able deputy, AM Sir Robert Saundby, scraped together every airframe capable of controlled flight, or something resembling it, and pulled in the screened crews from their instructional duties. He also pressed into service aircraft and crews from within the Command's own training establishment, 91 Group. Come the night, not only would the thousand mark be achieved, but it would also be comfortably surpassed.

During the final week of the month, the arrival on bomber stations from Yorkshire to East Anglia of a motley collection of aircraft from training units gave rise to much speculation among crews and ground staff alike, but, as usual, only the NAAFI staff and the local civilians knew what was really afoot. The most pressing remaining question was the weather, and, as the days ticked by inexorably towards the end of May, this was showing no signs of complying. Harris was aware of the genuine danger, that the giant force might draw attention to itself, and thereby compromise security, and the point was fast approaching when the operation would have to take place or be abandoned for the time being. Harris released some of the pressure by sanctioning operations on the night of the 29/30th, for which the Gnome & Rhone aero-engine and Goodrich tyre factories at Gennevilliers in Paris were the main targets. A force of seventy-seven aircraft included a contribution from 5 Group of fourteen Lancasters and three Hampdens, three of the former provided by 44 (Rhodesia) Squadron, while W/O Stott and crew were assigned to mining duties in the Nasturtium garden at the northern end of Oresund (The Sound) between Denmark and Sweden. They took off at 22.31, only to be thwarted by ten-tenths low cloud in the target area that prevented them from establishing a pinpoint, and they brought their stores back home. F/L Barlow, F/O Ball and P/O Nicholson departed Waddington at 00.32 and reached the target area to find bright moonlight above partial cloud, which allowed crews to pick out the distinctive Y-shaped inland docks and plan their low-level bombing runs. The searchlights were described by some to be ineffective, but the light flak was intense and accurate as F/L Barlow went in at 1,500 feet to deliver six 1,000 pounders at 02.52. This was some twenty-five minutes after P/O Nicholson and crew had attacked in a shallow dive from 5,000 down to 3,500 feet, and seven minutes after F/O Ball and crew had delivered their load from 4,300 feet. It proved difficult to gain an accurate picture of the outcome, and, in spite of claims of a successful operation, the only damage caused was to eighty-seven houses, in which thirty-four people were killed and 167 injured.

It was in an atmosphere of frustration and hopeful expectation, that "morning prayers" began at Harris's High Wycombe HQ on the 30th, with all eyes turned upon the civilian chief meteorological adviser, Magnus Spence. After careful deliberation, he was able to give a qualified assurance of clear skies over the Rhineland, while north-western Germany and Hamburg would be concealed under buckets of cloud. Thus, did the fickle fates decree that Cologne would bear the dubious honour of hosting the first one thousand bomber raid in history. At briefings, crews were told that the enormous force was to be pushed across the aiming point in just ninety minutes. This was unprecedented and gave rise to the question of collisions as hundreds of aircraft funnelled towards the aiming point. The answer, according to the experts, was to observe timings and flight levels, and they calculated also that just two aircraft would collide over the target. It is said that a wag in every briefing room asked, "do they know which two?"

5 Group had seventy-three Lancasters, forty-six Manchesters and thirty-four Hampdens bombed up and ready to go, and, at Waddington, fourteen Hampdens of 420 Squadron RCAF and ten Lancasters of 44 (Rhodesia) Squadron with two Manchesters of the Conversion Flight awaited the arrival of their crews, who had been briefed to attack aiming point Y, one of three areas spanning the city centre from north to south, and bordering the western and southern extremities of the city centre on the West Bank. The 44 (Rhodesia) Squadron order of Battle comprised the Lancaster crews of W/C Smales in R5846 KM-X, S/L Weston in L7541 KM-U, F/L Barlow in L7568 KM-W, F/L Halls in R5516 KM-F, F/O Ball in R5603 KM-D, P/O Hackney in R5554 KM-Q, P/O Nicholson in L7584 KM-S, P/O Stephens

in R5624 KM P, W/O Stott in L7537 KM-L, F/Sgt Taylor in L7576 KM-E Bar, and the Manchester crews of S/L Herring in L7480 KM-A Bar and F/O Maudslay in L7430 KM-N Bar. Late that evening, the first of an eventual 1,047 aircraft took off to deliver the now familiar three-wave-format attack on the Rhineland Capital, the older training hacks struggling somewhat reluctantly into the air, lifted more by the enthusiasm of their crews than by the power of their engines, and some of these, unable to climb to a respectable height, would fall easy prey to the defences, or would simply drop from the sky through mechanical breakdown. The 44 (Rhodesia) Squadron element departed Waddington between 23.59 and 00.51, the Lancasters carrying a 4,000lb "cookie" and 720 x 4lb incendiaries, while the Manchesters were loaded with ninety-six 30lb incendiaries each. W/O Stott's starboard-inner engine began to show signs of distress as they headed for the Scheldt estuary, and he decided to bomb the aerodrome at Haamstede on Schouwen island as a last resort target, doing so from 14,000 feet at 02.00, before turning for home. The remainder pressed on across Belgium, drawn on for the last seventy miles by the glow of the already burning city, and were greeted at the target by precisely the weather conditions of clear skies and bright moonlight predicted by Magnus Spence. Bombing took place from 6,800 (F/O Maudslay) to 18,000 feet between 01.54 and 02.20, but the volume and intensity of the fires prevented any from plotting the fall of their bombs. As they turned away, columns of black smoke were drifting up through 10,000 feet, and no one was in any doubt, that they had taken part in a successful operation.

Returning crews described a city on fire from end to end, and never-before-witnessed scenes. Post-raid reconnaissance confirmed that the operation had, by any standards, been an outstanding success, and had destroyed more than 3,300 buildings, while inflicting serious damage to two thousand others. Although the loss of forty-one aircraft represented a new record high, the conditions had favoured both attackers and defenders alike, and, in the context of the scale of success and the numbers dispatched, it could not be considered an inordinately high figure. 5 Group registered a loss of four Manchesters, one Lancaster and one Hampden, but it was the training units that sustained the greatest losses amounting to twenty-one aircraft. During the course of the month, the squadron took part in eleven operations and dispatched forty-eight Lancaster and two Manchester sorties for the loss of five Lancasters and four crews.

June 1942

S/L Nettleton VC was posted to Station Headquarters Waddington on the 1st at the conclusion of his tour, pending a permanent posting, but would return to the squadron in time. While the Millennium force remained assembled, Harris wanted to exploit its potential again immediately, and was no doubt excited about the prospect of visiting upon the old enemy of Essen a similar ordeal to that just experienced by Cologne. A force of 956 aircraft was the best that could be achieved during the 1st, 5 Group managing seventy-three Lancasters, thirty-three Manchesters and twenty-six Hampdens, with 44 (Rhodesia) Squadron contributing eleven Lancasters and a single Manchester, while lending two of its Conversion Flight Manchesters to 50 Squadron. The Lancasters were loaded with a cookie each and eight SBCs of incendiaries, and F/O Maudslay's Manchester with a dozen SBCs, and they departed Waddington between 23.11 and 23.42 with S/L Weston the senior pilot on duty. They had been briefed to employ the sprawl of the Borbeck-located Krupp sector as the aiming point and flew out under favourable weather conditions that promised the possibility of actually being able to identify ground detail. P/O Tomkins turned back at the enemy coast with an unserviceable rear turret, and W/O Dainty was forced to abandon his sortie from a similar position because of an airscrew issue, leaving the others to run into five to ten-tenths cloud at 4,000 to 6,000 feet. This combined with industrial haze and smoke drifting over from Cologne to muddy the vertical visibility, and bombing took place largely on TR (Gee) supported by occasional visual references on waterways. P/O Stephens and crew picked up a canal to the north of Hamborn, a district of Duisburg, and, it seems, dropped their load there from 12,000 feet at 01.11, while flares were igniting above them. The others benefitted from the unusually inactive defences as they closed on the target by Gee-fix and attacked what they estimated to be either the Borbeck district or the city generally. The Waddington Lancasters attacked from 8,000 (F/O Maudslay) to 20,500 feet between 00.49 and 01.38, F/O Ball and crew having spent thirty minutes circling to try to establish a pinpoint. An accurate assessment of results was not possible, and crews returned with reports of many fires, some identified as dummies, but no detail. They would have to wait for post-raid reconnaissance to assess what had happened on the ground, and, in the meantime, a counting of the cost revealed the loss of thirty-one aircraft. Sadly, there would be no major success to mitigate the scale of the loss, local reports confirming that only eleven houses had been destroyed in Essen, and fewer than two hundred others damaged, mostly in southern districts, and more bomb loads had actually fallen on Oberhausen, Duisburg and Mülheim-an-der-Ruhr.

A follow-up raid was planned for twenty-four hours later, and a much-reduced force of 197 aircraft made ready, with 5 Group providing twenty-seven Lancasters and a dozen Hampdens. 44 (Rhodesia) Squadron briefed five crews and sent them on their way between 23.51 and 23.57 with F/O Ball the senior pilot on duty on a night of cloudless skies over the Ruhr, with the usual industrial haze and a low moon providing some illumination. Most crews would describe the visibility as good, and reported being further aided by flares, which highlighted the Rhine over to the west. Those equipped with Gee confirmed their positions over what they believed to be the Krupp works aiming point and delivered their cookie and incendiaries from 13,000 to 18,000 feet between 01.29 and 01.40. Despite the apparent confidence of the crews that they had attacked Essen, local authorities reported just three high explosive bombs and three hundred incendiaries falling in the city to cause only minor damage. Such was the density of the Ruhr, with overlapping town and city boundaries, it was difficult not to hit something urban, but concentration was the key to success, and the scattering of bombs over a wide area was never going to achieve a knock-out blow. Harris was stubborn and would keep trying, but it would be a further nine months before the means were to hand to make a genuine impact.

For the next operation, on the 3rd, Harris turned his attention upon Bremen, which, along with Essen and Emden would share the Command's attention for the remainder of the month. A force of 170 aircraft was made ready for the first major attack on the port-city since the previous October, fifteen Lancasters, nine Hampdens and six Manchesters provided by 5 Group. 44 (Rhodesia) Squadron was not called into action for the main event but briefed the crews of W/O Dainty and P/O Tomkins for mining duties in the Deodar garden in the mouth of the River Gironde, through which U-Boots from Bordeaux would have to pass to reach the Atlantic. They took off at 00.05 and 00.20 respectively and arrived three hours later to find good visibility with a little sea haze. W/O Dainty and crew crossed the Gironde while seeking a pinpoint and attracted the attention of intense light flak from eight ships and both shores, which drove them off to consider their options. They came in for a second time but were forced to plot a course to the drop zone a little to the west of where they wanted to be and delivered their five mines close to the western shoreline from 200 feet at 03.18. P/O Tomkins and crew seemed to avoid any unwanted attention, and delivered their mines from 500 feet at 03.24, the pilot praising the map-reading skills of Sgt Wrigley, who was occupying the front turret. Crews returning from Bremen lacked confidence in the effectiveness of the raid, but local reports told a story of heavy damage to housing in six streets and to harbour installations, and there were also hits on U-Boot construction yards and the Focke-Wulf aircraft factory, although, any loss of production was slight.

180 aircraft were prepared for the next intended assault on Essen on the 5th, for which 5 Group put up thirteen Lancasters and eleven Hampdens. 44 (Rhodesia) Squadron briefed the crews of F/Ls Barlow and Halls, P/O Stephens and F/Sgt Taylor, and sent them on their way between 23.29 and 23.33. The force flew out over Belgium, and some identified a bend in the River Ruhr to the south-east of the target, while others relied on a TR-fix, flares or evidence of searchlight and flak concentrations to establish their positions in conditions of poor vertical visibility. F/Sgt Taylor lost his starboard-outer engine on the way out, and, after a vain ten-minute attempt to rectify the problem, decided to bomb the town of Goch, a short hop from the Dutch frontier, which he did from 17,000 feet at 01.12. His squadron colleagues were over the general area of Essen within five minutes and released their loads from 12,000 and 15,000 feet at 01.17 and 01.20. There was no report from F/L Halls and crew, who failed to return in R5516, and the eventual recovery of three bodies on the Dutch coast told its own story. Local sources again confirmed an ineffective and wasteful raid, which caused only minor damage in Essen at a cost of twelve aircraft and crews. Also missing from this night's operations was the 44 (Rhodesia) Squadron Manchester, R5833, which had been loaned to 50 Squadron for the "Thousand" raids and had also found a watery grave while on gardening duties. Some of the crews not involved in the operation took part in night training, during which, P/O Tomkins ran out of runway after landing too fast at 03.35, and wrote off R5515, fortunately without injury to the occupants.

The first of four attacks during the month on the naval port of Emden was posted on the 6th, and a force of 233 aircraft made ready. 5 Group contributed twenty Lancasters, fifteen Hampdens and seven Manchesters, 44 (Rhodesia) Squadron providing four of the Lancasters and briefing the crews of F/O Ball, P/Os Nicholson and Stephens and W/O Wright. They departed Waddington between 23.34 and 00.02 carrying the standard city-busting payload of a cookie and 720 x 4lb incendiaries but lost the services of W/O Wright and crew to immersion pump failure and fluctuating engine revs. The others found the skies over the coast of north-western Germany to be clear of cloud and the visibility to be good, which enabled those dropping flares to illuminate the docks area for the bomb-aimers. F/O Ball and crew arrived at 01.18 and carried out a dummy run based on TR and ground references, before a second pass along the length of the docks in a shallow dive from 16,000 to release the bombs from 13,000 feet at 01.25. P/O Stephens attacked from 15,000 feet at 01.24, three minutes after and a thousand feet lower than P/O Nicholson, but neither saw anything of the results among the fires already burning. Smoke was rising through 8,000 feet as they retreated, and the glow from the port remained visible for up to eighty miles into the return journey. Photographic reconnaissance and local reports confirmed that the raid had been responsible for the destruction of some three hundred houses, with a further two hundred severely damaged in return for the loss of nine aircraft.

The following night was devoted to mining operations in the Nectarine I garden off the western Frisians, for which 5 Group detailed nine Lancasters and two Hampdens. 44 (Rhodesia) Squadron chose W/O Dainty and crew for this task, but the first to take off from Waddington on this night at 00.21 was the crew of P/O Dorehill, who were bound for Angers in north-western France with reading matter for the populace. They arrived to find clear skies and extreme darkness and released 312 bundles from 16,000 feet at 02.17 at a position some thirty miles to the west of the target. W/O Dainty and crew took off at 01.08 and reached their pinpoint a little over an hour later to encounter seven-tenths cloud with a base at 4,500 feet. They released the six mines at five-second intervals from 2,800 feet at 02.28, while flying at a speed of 170 m.p.h on a north-easterly heading.

The Command entered a period of gardening and minor operations, thereafter, punctuated by two further attacks on Essen. The first of these, by an initial force of 170 aircraft, took place on the night of the 8/9th, and was supported by 5 Group with thirteen Lancasters and nine Hampdens. It was another disappointing and widely scattered raid, which caused only minor housing damage. Mining operations in northern waters were posted on the 9th, for which the crew of P/O Nicholson took off at 22.05, to be followed at 22.25 by a delayed W/O Stott in the spare aircraft. It was still daylight, and the order was to turn back if the forecast cloud cover failed to materialize before darkness enveloped them. Their destination was the distant Geranium garden off the naval port of Swinemünde, situated some eighty miles to the east of Rostock, and it was not an absence of cloud that defeated W/O Stott and crew, but rather an abundance of it. They had crossed the North Sea and southern Denmark over ten-tenths cloud with tops at around 10,000 feet and failed to establish a pinpoint at the coast on reaching the Baltic. This and their delayed take-off persuaded them to turn back and return their mines to store. P/O Nicholson and crew pressed on to the target area, where they, too, encountered thick, ice-bearing cloud with tops at 3,000 feet and a base at sea-level, and, with no prospect of establishing a pinpoint, turned back and jettisoned their payload to the east of Rügen island.

On the 10th, the squadron was instructed to detach six Lancasters with air and ground crews to Nutts Corner in Northern Ireland to carry out convoy patrols on behalf of Coastal Command. F/L Barlow and a ground party of seventy personnel left Lincoln by train that evening bound for Stranraer for the sea crossing and were followed on the morning of the 11th by the air party consisting of the crews of S/L Weston, F/O Ball, P/Os Hackney and Nicholson and W/Os Dainty and Wright, whose Lancasters were loaded with ground crew, stores and tool kits. W/C Smales joined them in another Lancaster, presumably to oversee their settling-in and liaise with the senior Coastal Command officers. The first sortie, a U-Boot patrol, was to be conducted by F/O Ball and crew in R5603 on the 12th, and, as this was the first time that a Lancaster had been employed in this kind of operation, it would also act as a fuel consumption test. They took off at 11.00 and returned seven hours and forty-five minutes later to report poor weather, low cloud, and nothing observed other than friendly shipping.

The same Lancaster was pressed into duty on the 13th and took off at 10.05 in the hands of F/L Barlow and crew, who picked up a convoy at 13.20, and carried out an anti-submarine patrol on a heading of 300 degrees. Nothing was found, and they left the convoy at 16.00, eventually clocking up an eleven-hour sortie in fair weather conditions and without incident. On the 14th, P/O Nicholson and crew took off at 09.05 in R5858, with two members of 220 Squadron on board, and headed into the western Atlantic to pick up a convoy. Almost eight hours later, when some two hundred miles west of Lough Erne, both port engines failed, and the Lancaster had to be ditched, fortunately, when close to the convoy. The crew was picked up safe and sound and was next heard of in Africa. On the following day, F/O Ball and crew spent three hours searching for their convoy, which they eventually found, and also spotted a U-Boot on the surface five miles away. Having seen the Lancaster bearing down upon it, the enemy vessel crash-dived some fifteen seconds before six depth charges were released from 50 feet. A shortage of fuel forced F/O Ball to leave the scene immediately and warn the convoy of the U-Boot's presence, before heading back to base after ten hours and twenty minutes aloft. S/L Stewart was posted to the squadron from 25 O.T.U on the 14th and would assume the role of flight commander.

F/L Barlow and crew took off in L7568 at 08.25 on the 15th and headed into the western Atlantic to pick up their convoy. While searching over a calm sea at 12.41, they observed a U-Boot on the surface some three miles ahead and raced towards it to find it already ten feet below the surface by the time that they delivered six depth charges from 70 feet. A large oil patch formed on the sea, and the U-Boot resurfaced at 13.25, before sinking again within five seconds. A 250lb anti-submarine bomb was dropped from 860 feet into the swirl and oil slick some twenty seconds later, but nothing more was seen. W/O Dainty and crew took off at noon, but wireless failure ended their sortie soon afterwards. W/O Dainty and P/O Hackney and their crews were on duty for evening convoy escort duties on the 16th, but the former lost their starboard-outer engine after around two hours, while the latter had not located its convoy by the time that darkness forced them to abandon the search.

After spending four nights on the ground because of adverse weather conditions, the Command stirred itself on the 16th at Harris's behest to have another crack at Essen, for which 106 aircraft were made ready, 5 Group contributing fifteen Lancasters. All crews had been briefed to employ TR to locate the target and bomb blindly based on that, which, under the conditions of up to eight-tenths cloud on a moonless night with visibility down to three miles, was the best that could be expected. It emerged at debriefing that only sixteen crews claimed to have bombed the primary target, while fifty-six others had found alternatives, mostly the city of Bonn. This concluded a series of five raids on Essen in sixteen nights, during which 1,607 sorties had been dispatched and eighty-four aircraft lost. The city had sustained no industrial damage, and a few wrecked houses was all that Bomber Command had to show for the massive effort expended.

Across the Irish Sea, F/L Barlow and crew were back in the air at 08.40 on the 17th but failed to find the convoy in the briefed position. They carried out a creeping line-ahead search, and, despite more than twenty changes of course over a seven-hour and thirty-minute patrol, plotting their positions by DR alone without landmarks as a reference, they were only twelve miles off track and five minutes out in e.t.a., which represented an amazing feat of navigation.

Having hosted an effective attack earlier in the month, Emden became the focus for three raids in the space of four nights, beginning on the 19th, for which a force of 194 aircraft was assembled. 44 (Rhodesia) Squadron remained at home while nine Lancasters and eleven Hampdens from other units represented 5 Group, their crews having been briefed to switch to Osnabrück, eighty miles to the south, if the weather conditions over the coastal region became troublesome. Part of the flare force did, indeed, initiate an attack on Osnabrück by twenty-nine aircraft, leaving 131 others to claim that they had bombed the primary target. Despite the numbers, the Emden authorities reported only a handful of high-explosive bombs falling and a few hundred incendiaries. 185 aircraft were made ready to return to the port on the following night, and, this time, 44 (Rhodesia) Squadron contributed the crew of P/O Dorehill to the twenty-four Lancaster and dozen Hampden crews provided by 5 Group. They departed Waddington at 23.31 and reached the target area shortly after 01.00 to be greeted by five to eight tenths cloud and generally poor visibility. The docks were the briefed aiming point and the town the alternative, and positions were established by TR-fix and glimpses of the coastline. The Dorehill crew was among the first to arrive before any flares went down and attacked with a cookie and 720 x 4lb incendiaries from 17,500 feet at 01.07, observing nothing other than the burst of their cookie. Local reports confirmed that only a proportion of the force had located the target, and around a hundred houses had been damaged.

In Northern Ireland, there was a 05.00 take-off for F/O Ball and crew on the 22nd, and they met their convoy on the first leg of the search, before patrolling for four-and-three-quarter hours and exchanging messages with the convoy by Aldis Lamp. The remainder of the nine-hour and thirty-minute sortie proved to be uneventful, and, probably, somewhat tedious, but the work they were undertaking was important and vital. That night, a force of 227 aircraft took off for the third raid of the series on Emden, for which 5 Group contributed eleven Lancasters and eight Hampdens. Most crews established their approach to the target by identifying the coastline and confirming it via a TR-fix backed up by flak and fires, before running in on the aiming point in good visibility under moonlight. Some returning crews had been able to distinguish between genuine and decoy fires, but the latter succeeded in drawing off many loads, and those finding the target destroyed fifty houses and damaged a hundred more.

P/O Stephens and crew carried out their first patrol on the 23rd, taking off at 05.05 and meeting the convoy at 08.50 after flying through a cold front with its associated weather conditions. They escorted the convoy for three-and-a-half hours, and had to contend with a burst hydraulic pipe, which meant that they had to use a bottle to deploy the landing gear. That night, the freshman crew of P/O Wakeford took off at 23.40 to resupply the residents of the Angers region of north-western France with toilet paper in the form of 288 bundles of leaflets delivered from 10,500 feet at 02.04.

The time had now arrived for the final deployment of the Thousand Force, and, indeed, for the Manchester in operational service. A force of 960 aircraft was assembled, 142 provided by 5 Group in the form of ninety-six Lancasters, twenty-six Hampdens and twenty Manchesters. It was an indication of the failure of the Manchester, that the aircraft it had been intended to replace, the Hampden, would continue to serve 5 Group in small numbers until mid-September. To the above numbers were added five aircraft from Army Co-operation Command and 102 aircraft from Coastal Command, which had been ordered by Churchill himself to take part, although, its contribution was to be deemed a separate operation. However, the 1,067 aircraft from all sources would represent a larger combined force than that sent to Cologne at the end of May. 44 (Rhodesia) Squadron was able to call on the services of eleven crews, plus one from 49 Squadron, which departed Waddington between 23.29 and 23.57 with W/C Smales the senior pilot on duty, supported by the two new flight commanders, S/Ls Stewart and Penman, the latter formerly of 97 Squadron and a veteran of the Augsburg raid. Their briefed aiming point was the Focke-Wulf aircraft factory in the south-eastern district of Hemelingen on the East Bank of the Weser, which W/O Stott and crew would not reach after a number of malfunctions forced them to turn back from thirty miles east of Skegness. The others pressed on, and, above the ten-tenths cloud that persisted all the way from the English coast to the target area, the sky was extremely bright, courtesy of a full moon and the Northern Lights. A band of nine to ten-tenths cloud lay over Bremen at between 3,000 and 5,000 feet, completely obscuring ground detail, which precluded any chance of picking up the Focke-Wulf aircraft factory, and positions were established by TR-fix, the glow of fires on the ground and the volume of flak coming up through the cloud. The 44 (Rhodesia) Squadron crews carried out their attacks from 13,500 to 20,000 feet between 01.23 and 01.45, while the recently promoted F/L Maudslay and crew were contending with bomb doors that refused to open. The Lancaster had been hit by flak when a dozen miles south-west of Oldenburg at 01.31, still some twenty-five miles short of Bremen, and sustained extensive damage, despite which, they had continued on, only to find that their load could not be released. The doors finally opened over the sea off Borkum, by which time they were coated with hydraulic fluid, and the six 1,000 pounders and incendiaries were jettisoned safe off the island.

Returning crews could only estimate that they had hit the city, and reported several areas of fire, but none of the 696 crews claiming to have attacked the primary target had any real clue as to the outcome. Local sources confirmed a number of hits on the Focke-Wulf aircraft factory and some shipyards, along with the destruction of 572 houses, and damage to more than six thousand others, mostly in southern and eastern districts, but estimated the size of the bomber force to be around eighty. The level of success fell well short of that achieved at Cologne, but surpassed by far the failure at Essen, albeit at a new record loss of forty-eight aircraft, which represented 5% of those dispatched. The O.T.Us of 91 Group suffered the highest casualty rate of 11.6%, largely because they were employing tired, old Whitleys, Wellingtons and Hampdens, which were not up to the task, while 5 Group lost one Lancaster and one Manchester.

The first of a number of follow-up operations against Bremen was mounted on the night of the 27/28th, and involved 144 aircraft, including twenty-four Lancasters from 5 Group. Weather conditions were very much as those of two nights earlier, with ten-tenths cloud up to around 4,000 feet and decreasing amounts thereafter as high as 15,000 feet. The sky above the cloud was as bright as day under a large moon, even though the Northern Lights, on this occasion, were masked by high cloud. Most located the target area by TR-fix, and crews could only estimate that they were over the target. Local reports confirmed hits on the previously damaged Atlas Werke shipyard and the Korff refinery, but further details were scant and of little value. On the following night, 44 (Rhodesia) Squadron dispatched the freshman crew of P/O Chrystal to plant vegetables in the Deodar garden in the Gironde estuary. They took off at 22.54, and had reached the Normandy coast, when the starboard-outer engine failed and forced them to abandon their sortie.

It was Bremen again on the 29th, for which a force of 253 aircraft was assembled, including sixty-four Lancasters as the 5 Group contribution. 44 (Rhodesia) Squadron loaded five Lancasters with a cookie and incendiaries and launched them into the air between 23.25 and 23.54 with S/L Stewart the senior pilot on duty. It was not to be a good night generally for the squadron, and W/O Stott, who had experienced more than his fair share of technical failures, was a victim again, this time of electrical failure when twenty miles east of Skegness. P/O Dorehill and crew were about to cross the Dutch coast near Haarlem, when a starboard engine failed, while P/O Wakeford and crew had just crossed the Dutch/German frontier near Nordhorn in the Bentheim region, when the wireless operator misread a message from group to jettison bombs. They were, at least, fused, and the flash of their detonation was observed beneath the cloud from 18,000 feet at 01.05. S/L Stewart and W/O Wright and their crews had flown out over six to ten-tenths cloud at between 3,000 and 5,000 feet, with excellent visibility above, and found around seven to ten-tenths cloud in layers up to 16,000 feet in the target area, with large gaps that afforded some a glimpse of the ground. They delivered their loads from 15,000 and 16,000 feet at 01.24 and 01.27 respectively, and, in keeping with other returning crews, could provide only impressions of the raid. Local reports, however, spoke of extensive damage to the Focke-Wulf factory, the A G Weser U-Boot construction yard and three other important war-industry premises, along with the local gas works and some limited destruction of housing.

Over at Nutts Corner, the web-footed brigade had been kicking their heels for a week by the end of the month and would continue to do so for a few days into July. During the course of the month, the squadron took part in thirteen Bomber Command operations and dispatched forty-nine Lancaster sorties and one by a Manchester, in addition to eight sorties on behalf of Coastal Command, all for the loss of two Lancasters without crew casualties, and a Manchester in the hands of a 50 Squadron crew.

July 1942

A gentle start to the new month had 5 Group operating alone on the night of the 1/2nd, when sending two Lancasters each from 97 and 106 Squadrons to mine the waters of the Great Belt in the western Baltic. The campaign against Bremen continued on the 2nd, with the preparation of a force of 325 aircraft, more than half of which were Wellingtons. 5 Group squadrons contributed fifty-three Lancasters and twenty-eight Hampdens, five of the former provided by 44 (Rhodesia) Squadron, which departed Waddington between 23.27 and 23.45, each loaded with a cookie and 720 x 4lb incendiaries. P/O Wakeford and crew were experiencing problems with their oxygen system as they crossed the North Sea and turned back at the Dutch coast near The Hague. The others pressed on to find the target in favourable weather conditions, with excellent visibility, no low cloud, high cirrus at around 22,000 feet, and only a little haze to spoil the view below. Positions were established by TR-fix confirmed by a visual check, but searchlight glare created great difficulty for the bomb-aimers trying to identify the Focke-Wulf aircraft factory aiming point, and most would settle for estimating the fall of their bombs. The 44 (Rhodesia) Squadron crews carried out their attacks from 15,200 to 19,000 feet between 01.29 and 01.43 and returned safely to add their reports to those from other units and groups, W/O Stott and crew claiming to have shot down three enemy aircraft. A large fire was reported on the aerodrome attached to the Focke-Wulf factory, and another at Delmenhorst to the south-west, and the consensus was of an effective operation. Local reports spoke of a thousand houses damaged, along with four small industrial premises, while three cranes and seven ships were hit in the port, one of the vessels sinking and becoming a danger to navigation. The likelihood is, however, that much of the effort was wasted beyond the city's southern boundary.

The remainder of the first half of the month would be low-key, with mining operations occupying much of the night-time activity. Sgt Knight and F/Sgt Rowan-Parry took off at noon on the 3rd to join others in a sea search for downed crews and spent seven hours flying at between 500 and 1,500 feet, sadly, without success. That night, 5 Group sent six Lancasters to lay mines in the Great Belt, but there was no operational activity at Waddington. F/O Ball and crew conducted a patrol from Nutts Corner on the 5th, picking up their convoy after just ten minutes, and continuing until darkness fell. F/L Barlow and crew took the next patrol from the late afternoon of the 6th, which would prove to be the last, while, over at Waddington, mining operations involved five 44 (Rhodesia) Squadron crews, which took off between 22.48 and 23.13 with S/L Stewart the senior pilot on duty. They were bound for the Deodar garden in the Gironde estuary, and, having departed fifteen minutes late, F/Sgt Taylor and crew were within forty miles of it at 02.12 when determining that there was insufficient time to complete the sortie before the arrival of daylight. They jettisoned their payload and turned back, leaving the others to establish pinpoints on Cordouan island under largely clear skies and starlight, and carry out timed runs to the release point. Unaccountably, W/O Stott and crew were unable to find a reference despite a thirty-minute search, and also jettisoned their five mines from 5,000 feet. The remaining three crews delivered their mines unopposed into the briefed locations from 750 to 1,000 feet between 02.03 and 02.10 and returned safely.

The detachment to Coastal Command ended at about this time, and the crews returned to Waddington. 5 Group detailed fifty-two Lancasters and twenty-four Hampdens on the 8th to attack Wilhelmshaven as part of an overall force of 285 aircraft. 44 (Rhodesia) Squadron briefed the crews of S/L Stewart, P/O Chrystal, W/O Wright and F/Sgt Taylor, and sent them on their way from Waddington between 23.58 and 00.15, each carrying a cookie and six 500 pounders for use against the U-Boot construction yards. W/O Wright and crew had reached the mid-point of the North Sea crossing when a malfunctioning fuel pump ended their interest in proceedings at 01.10, but the others continued on to the target to find around three-tenths thin cloud at 10,000 feet and haze below. This made it almost impossible for most to identify ground detail, including the docks and shipyard aiming points, and positions were established on e.t.a., and by TR-fix, some backed up through a visual check assisted by the use of flares. The 44 (Rhodesia) Squadron crews attacked from 16,000 to 19,000 feet between 01.40 and 01.52, observing bursts among buildings and dummy fires. Local reports confirmed some damage in Wilhelmshaven, but post-raid reconnaissance revealed that much of the bombing had missed the town to the west. S/L Burnett was posted in from 25 O.T.U on the 9th, and he would assume flight commander duties.

The first daylight foray deep into enemy territory by Lancasters, the previously mentioned raid on the M.A.N diesel engine factory at Augsburg in April, had cost seven of the twelve aircraft dispatched, and Harris, never an enthusiast of such operations, particularly at low level, had not been eager to repeat the exercise. Despite this, he sanctioned a similar plan by 5 Group for an attack on the U-Boot construction yards in the distant port of Danzig on the 11th. The forty-four Lancasters of 61, 83, 97, 106 and 207 Squadrons were to fly out in formation at low level, before splitting up to cross Denmark and the Baltic independently, and then climb to bombing altitude and make their own individual approaches to the target. The attack was to be carried out in the fading light, to allow a withdrawal to take place under the cover of darkness, and the 1,500-mile round-trip would be the longest yet attempted by the Command. An unanticipated band of ten-tenths ice-bearing cloud was encountered over the North Sea extending from 1,000 to 14,000 feet, and this ruined the plan as aircraft lost contact with each other, forcing the individual crews to break formation and make their way independently to the target. This would have a detrimental effect on the raid and cause some crews to abandon their sorties or arrive late when darkness had already settled over the area to make identification a challenge. Twenty-six aircraft bombed either the ship-building wharfs or the town, and two of them were shot down by flak.

On the 12th, after three nights of inactivity, 44 (Rhodesia) Squadron briefed the crew of F/Sgt Rowan-Parry for a nickelling trip to the Angers region, and those of P/Os Chrystal and Dorehill, W/O Wright, F/Sgt Taylor and Sgt Knight for mining duties in the Nectarine II garden off the central Frisians. The leafleteers took off at 00.59 and headed south, while the gardeners followed them into the air between 01.24 and 01.32 and pointed their snouts towards Skegness on the Lincolnshire coast. The Frisians lay beneath a blanket of ten-tenths cloud at between 1,500 and 3,000 feet, and not wishing to descend below the cloud base, positions were established by TR and the mines delivered from 1,500 to 2,800 feet between 03.16 and 03.56. Meanwhile, 280 bundles of leaflets had been dropped from 10,000 feet from a position twenty-four miles west of Angers at 03.15.

The first of a series of five operations over a four-week period against Duisburg was mounted on the night of the 13/14th, and involved 194 aircraft, including thirteen Lancasters from the 5 Group stations of Bottesford and Coningsby. The operation failed to find the mark in adverse weather conditions consisting of electrical storms and heavy cloud, and the bombing became widely scattered and ineffective. Low-key operations continued for 44 (Rhodesia) Squadron on the 14th, when F/Sgt Rowan-Parry and crew were briefed for mining duties in the Nectarine I garden, and the crews of F/Sgts Day and Tetley for nickelling in the Tours region of France, some forty miles east of Angers. The latter took off at 00.50, and, between them delivered 444 bundles from 10,000 feet, F/Sgt Day and crew theirs over the briefed area and F/Sgt Tetley and crew over Chartres to the south-west of

Paris, after a discrepancy arose between the TR and DR estimates of position. The Rowan-Parry crew took off at 01.40 and ran into five to eight-tenths cloud at 1,000 feet in the target area, where, as a result of the failure of their TR-box, they came down to 800 feet, and dropped five mines at 178 m.p.h., indicated air speed, into the allotted location at 03.21.

The madness of "moling" reared its ugly head again on the 18th, under the guise this time of a "porpoise" operation, when ten Lancasters, including those of F/Sgt Taylor and P/O Chrystal, and their crews, were detailed to present themselves over the Krupp district of Essen in broad daylight, one of the most ferociously defended areas in the whole of Germany, protected only by cloud. The 44 (Rhodesia) Squadron pair departed Waddington at 10.44 and 11.39 respectively and flew out over the North Sea with ten-tenths cloud below them at 5,000 feet, until it began to diminish as they neared the enemy coast. F/Sgt Taylor turned back from a position five miles off Schouwen in the Scheldt estuary, and P/O Chrystal may have pressed on beyond the Dutch coast, had his TR equipment not failed, and the presence of two BF109s become a strong motivation to turn back. A number of attacks were directed at the Lancaster, whose rear gunner sustained a foot wound, but he and his colleague in the mid-upper turret claimed hits on one of the assailants, and they managed to evade further attention.

A force of ninety-nine four-engine types was assembled on the 19th to send that night against the Vulkan U-Boot construction yards at Vegesack, situated on the River Weser a few miles to the north-west of Bremen city centre. 5 Group contributed twenty-eight Lancasters to the attack, of which six belonged to 44 (Rhodesia) Squadron, and they took off from Waddington between 00.07 and 00.27 with W/C Smales the senior pilot on duty and each carrying six 1,000 pounders. They all arrived in the target area to encounter up to ten-tenths cloud with tops at 10,000 to 12,000 feet and delivered their attacks on the basis of a Gee-fix (TR) from 14,500 and 18,000 feet between 02.10 and 02.40. They gained an impression that a lot was going on beneath the cloud, but, in reality, the raid had completely missed the target, confirming the fact that Gee was useful as a guide to navigation, but was not precise enough to employ as a blind-bombing device.

A force of 291 aircraft was assembled on the 21st for the second raid of the series on Duisburg, and this number included twenty-nine Lancasters and seventeen Hampdens representing 5 Group. 44 (Rhodesia) Squadron put up eight Lancasters for the main event, and two others for P/O Day and F/Sgt Tetley to take on mining sorties to the Trefoil garden, which covered the Marsdiep from the southern end of Texel and the northern region of the Den Helder peninsula. The two elements took off together between 23.55 and 00.47 with S/L Stewart the senior pilot on duty, and the gardeners reached their destination in a little over an hour to deliver six mines each into the allotted positions from 700 and 1,000 feet at 01.23 and 01.24. It was a moonless night, and, despite the presence of clear skies over the target, extreme darkness and the usual industrial haze took their toll on vertical visibility, the effects of which, it was hoped, would be negated by flares dropped from the leading aircraft by TR. However, these proved to be not entirely accurate, and some illuminated an area of open country on the West Bank of the Rhine. The 44 (Rhodesia) Squadron crews had been briefed to attack aiming point D, the identity of which was not revealed, and seven of them located it by TR backed up by visual reference. They dropped their all-incendiary loads from 14,500 to 19,000 feet between 01.31 and 01.43, observing little of the outcome. The departure from Waddington of W/O Dainty and crew had been delayed, and, as they flew eastwards, their Lancaster performed sluggishly, putting them further behind schedule, and it was 02.23 before they emptied the contents of their bomb bay from 18,000 feet onto the general area of Duisburg. On their way home, S/L Stewart and F/O Ball were fired upon by a convoy, which ignored the colours of the day, and light flak shells passed close by the wingtips.

Returning crews could offer no useful information to the Intelligence Section at debriefing, but local reports confirmed extensive damage in residential districts, with ninety-four apartment buildings destroyed and 256 seriously damaged, and there was also mention of damage to the Thyssen steel works and to two other important war-industry factories.

A reduced force of 215 aircraft was made ready to continue the assault on Duisburg on the 23rd, and forty-five of these were Lancasters, eleven of them representing 44 (Rhodesia) Squadron. The Waddington element took off between 00.59 and 00.28 with no senior pilots on duty, and lost the services of Sgt Knight and crew, who had both starboard engines fail over the North Sea. The remainder reached the target to encounter seven to ten-tenths cloud with tops as high as 12,000 feet in places, and a large gap that afforded some crews a sight of the ground. Despite that, for many, there was little chance of locating the briefed aiming point, which was probably the Thyssen steel works. The Gee-based (TR) flares were again scattered and largely ineffective, leaving most crews to carry out their attacks on their own TR-fix. The 44 (Rhodesia) Squadron crews delivered their high-explosive loads from 11,000 to 19,200 feet between 02.27 and 02.51, P/O Dorehill and crew making two passes, one with the searchlight radar jamming switch on and the other with it off. P/O Day brought back a heavily damaged R5729 courtesy of flak near the target and a night-fighter over the Dutch town of Deventer on the way home and reported that the night-fighter had paid for its affrontery by being shot down during its third attack. Returning crews were confident that they had hit the city's built-up area, many claiming to have identified specific ground features, and the outcome of the raid was similar to the previous one, with residential property sustaining the bulk of the damage.

The fourth raid on Duisburg was posted on the 25th, for which the largest force yet of the series was assembled. Among the 313 aircraft were 177 Wellingtons and fourteen Hampdens, with the four-engine types making up the numbers. The thirty-three Lancasters included nine representing 44 (Rhodesia) Squadron, each of which was loaded with fourteen SBCs containing either 90 x 4lb incendiaries or eight of 30lbs. They departed Waddington between 00.15 and 00.26 with F/O Ball the senior pilot on duty, and lost P/O Stephens and crew to TR failure on the way out. The others pushed on to find around seven-tenths cloud over the target, with fair visibility, which enable a visual confirmation of the TR-based approach, but not the briefed aiming point D. The extensive and distinctive Ruhrort inland docks complex provided a solid reference point to bomb the built-up area generally for those unable to identify the briefed aiming point, among which was the crew of W/O Dainty, who released their load from 17,000 feet at 01.49. Sgt Knight and crew were on their third pass over the target when hit in the bomb doors by flak at 14,000 feet, and this persuaded them to release their SBCs from 13,000 feet seconds later at 01.58. They were held in a box-barrage for eight minutes, which knocked out their starboard-inner engine, and left them with just one serviceable gun turret. To compound their difficulties, they found that the damaged bomb doors would not close, and this condemned them to a return flight at 150 m.p.h., which ended at Wittering at 05.08. The others carried out their attacks from 15,500 and 19,000 feet between 01.48 and 02.05, and a number of bursts and fires were observed. It was left to local reports to confirm further damage to residential property, but less extensive than in the two previous attacks.

A maximum effort was planned on the 26th for the annual last-week-of-July attack on Germany's second city, Hamburg, and 404 aircraft answered the call, among them seventy-seven Lancasters and thirty-three Hampdens. 44 (Rhodesia) Squadron made ready eleven Lancasters, which departed Waddington between 22.47 and 23.19 with S/Ls Burnett and Stewart the senior pilots on duty. They flew out over the Lincolnshire coast, and, over the North Sea, had to negotiate the frequently met conditions on this route of towering cloud, electrical storms and severe icing. The skies over the target were clear, however, and the visibility excellent, which allowed the crews to confirm their positions by visual reference, with the docks area standing out particularly clearly in the bright moonlight. The 44 (Rhodesia) Squadron crews had been handed aiming point D, which was probably the shipbuilding yards to the west of the city centre, but they found smoke already drifting across the city to obscure some ground detail. Eight of the squadron's Lancasters were carrying a cookie, six 500 and two 250 pounders, and three all-incendiary loads, and ten crews would claim on their return that they had bombed the primary target from 12,000 to 19,000 feet between 00.57 and 01.32, while F/Sgt Rowan-Parry and crew attacked the city generally from 18,000 feet at 01.20. The glow from the resultant fires remained visible for around seventy miles into the homeward journey, and returning crews reported bomb bursts and thirty to forty fires seeming to merge into one single conflagration. The effectiveness of the raid was borne out by local reports, which spoke of eight hundred fires, more than five hundred of which were classed as large, and it seems that the residential and semi-commercial districts bore the brunt of the raid. When the flames had died down and the smoke cleared, 823 houses were found to have been reduced to ruins, with five thousand others damaged to some extent. It was a highly successful raid for the period, which the Command hoped to build on forty-eight hours later until the weather took a hand to reduce the number of aircraft available.

Another maximum effort was called for on the 28th, and a force well in excess of four hundred aircraft was assembled for the return to Hamburg that night, 256 of them provided by 3 Group and the operational training units. In the event, these would take off alone, after the weather conditions over the 1, 4 and 5 Group stations prompted the withdrawal of their contributions to the operation, and, as conditions worsened over the North Sea, the O.T.U aircraft were recalled. Many of the 3 Group crews turned back also, and only sixty-eight would claim to have attacked the primary target, where fifteen large fires and forty smaller ones were reported. This modicum of success was gained at the high cost of twenty-five aircraft, 15% of those dispatched, and four O.T.U Wellingtons also failed to return, while a fifth, a Whitley, ditched, and its crew was picked up safely.

Saarbrücken was posted as the target on the 29th, and a force of 291 aircraft assembled, which would be the largest raid by far on this major industrial and coal-producing Saarland capital city, situated right on the frontier with France in south-western Germany. 5 Group contributed sixty-nine Lancasters and seventeen Hampdens, eleven of the former representing 44 (Rhodesia) Squadron and departing Waddington between 23.36 and 23.52 with S/L Burnett the senior pilot on duty. They had been briefed to attack aiming point C, and, in the expected absence of a strong searchlight and flak defence, the intention was to attack from a lower level than customary for the period. Eight crews were sitting on a cookie and incendiaries, while three supplemented their cookie with six 500 and two 250 pounders, and all completed the sea crossing to make landfall on the French coast, before following the frontier with Belgium and entering Germany south of Luxembourg. At the target, they encountered a layer of four to eight-tenths low cloud at between 2,000 and 9,000 feet, below which the visibility was good, and this enabled crews to confirm their TR positions by visual references on ground features like the River Saar. The 44 (Rhodesia) Squadron crews bombed either the primary target, by coming below the 7,000-foot cloud base, or the city generally from 4,300 to 14,000 feet between 01.40 and 02.03, and observed many fires, some large and emitting black smoke. F/O Ball and crew arrived at the target with their central fuel tank gauges registering just 170 gallons, and those for the inner tanks zero, which would not get them home. They set course for Dover at 01.43, and, when only twenty gallons showed in each central tank, F/O Ball warned his crew to prepare to abandon the aircraft. They were forty miles short of the French coast when the gauges registered empty, but, still, the Merlins purred, carrying them across the Channel and over the English coast, and it was at this point, that the second pilot switched the gauges off and back on, whereupon the needle flicked up to 450 gallons. Returning crews were confident that their bombs had found the mark, and this was confirmed by local reports of severe damage in central and north-western districts, where almost four hundred buildings had been destroyed in return for the loss of nine aircraft.

The month ended with a major assault on the Ruhr city of Düsseldorf, for which a force of 630 aircraft was assembled, the numbers bolstered by a large contribution from the training units. 5 Group offered 113 Lancasters, the first time that the one hundred figure had been reached, and they would be accompanied by twenty-four Hampdens belonging to the two Canadian squadrons, 408 and 420. The fifteen Waddington Lancasters took off between 00.14 and 00.56 with W/C Smales the senior pilot on duty, carrying either a cookie and 720 x 4lb incendiaries or a cookie and 500 and 250 pounders. P/O Wakeford and crew turned back from the Dutch coast with a malfunctioning oxygen system, leaving the others to press on to the southern Ruhr, where bright moonlight, clear skies and good visibility enabled the crews to confirm their TR-fixed positions visually by an S-bend in the River Rhine. They carried out their attacks from 14,000 to 19,000 feet between 02.00 and 02.50 in the face of an intense and accurate searchlight and flak defence, and most crews were confident in the quality of their work, some commenting on a column of black smoke rising through 10,000 feet as they turned away. More than nine hundred tons of bombs were dropped, some wasted in open country, but the remainder had been scattered across all parts of the city and the neighbouring city of Neuss on the opposite bank of the Rhine. Local sources confirmed the destruction of 453 buildings, with varying degrees of damage to fifteen thousand more, and sixty-seven large fires had to be dealt with. The success came at the cost of twenty-nine aircraft, including five Hampdens and two Lancasters, and the O.T.U.s were again hit disproportionately hard, losing fifteen of their number. F/Sgt Rowan-Parry and crew reported an aircraft shot down in flames near Mönchengladbach, and this turned out to be 44 (Rhodesia) Squadron's L7537, in which South African F/Sgt Tetley and his crew lost their lives.

During the course of a busy month, the squadron carried out seventeen offensive operations involving ninety-eight sorties, two convoy patrols and a sea search, all for the loss of a single Lancaster and its crew.

August 1942

A gentle start to the new month saw the heavy brigade remain at home because of unfavourable weather on the first two nights, before 5 Group sent out orders to Swinderby and Woodhall Spa on the 3rd to prepare small numbers of Lancasters for mining duties in the Forget-me-not and Radish gardens, respectively Kiel Harbour and the Fehmarn Belt in the western Baltic. On the following night, 5 Group contributed a handful of Lancasters and Hampdens for mining duties around the Frisians and off the Biscay coast. Meanwhile, ten Lancasters from 44 (Rhodesia) and 97 (Straits Settlements) Squadrons had been briefed to join twenty-eight other aircraft in a blind attack on Essen employing Gee. The 44 (Rhodesia) Squadron crews of F/L Barlow, F/O Ball, P/Os Day and Dorehill and W/O Wright departed Waddington between 01.27 and 01.32, and, over enemy territory found in their path a towering, ice-bearing front with electrical storms, which topped out at 22,000 feet and extended over the Ruhr. W/O wright and P/O Day were among many who opted not to press on to the primary target and dropped their bombs from 19,000 and 21,000 feet at 03.06 and 03.08 respectively onto the German town of Geldern, situated just five miles east of the Dutch frontier. F/L Barlow was enveloped in ten-tenths cloud as he delivered his load from 21,000 feet at 03.04, while P/O Dorehill was two thousand feet lower when his bomb-aimer pressed the tit at 03.25. They were among eighteen crews who claimed to have attacked Essen based on TR readings, and it was deemed necessary to repeat the exercise twenty-four hours later. The return of F/O Ball DFM and his crew was awaited in vain, and no trace of them and Lancaster R5603 was ever found. It was always a blow to lose experienced crews, and this was the second to go missing within five nights.

5 Group detailed eight Lancasters for the return to Essen on the 5th, for which P/O Stephens and W/O Stott were briefed, while the crews of S/L Burnett, F/L Barlow and P/Os Dorehill and Wakeford were assigned to mining duties in the Deodar garden in the Gironde estuary. The bombing duo departed Waddington first, shortly before 23.00, and they had crossed the Dutch coast via the Scheldt estuary by the time that the gardeners took off between 00.09 and 00.20. W/O Stott turned back at this point, strangely citing lack of cloud cover as the reason for abandoning his sortie and jettisoning his bombs. P/O Stephens and crew also failed to reach Essen, after their TR became unserviceable as they passed south of Cologne. They sought out an alternative target, which was recorded as possibly Münster, but this seems highly unlikely, as they would have had to traverse the Ruhr from south to north and pass very close to Essen anyway. Meanwhile, the gardeners had reached their target area under clear skies, but haze and extreme darkness thwarted S/L Burnett's attempts to establish a pinpoint, and he eventually abandoned the search and brought his stores home. The others delivered their five mines each into the allotted locations from 500 and 800 feet between 03.05 and 03.12, before returning safely, two to report uneventful sorties, while F/L Barlow attracted the attention of inaccurate searchlights from the shore and flak ships in the target area, at which the rear gunner fired back.

5 Group's contribution to the fifth and final operation of the three-week campaign against the Ruhr industrial giant of Duisburg amounted to forty-seven Lancasters and ten Hampdens, which were part of an overall force of 216 aircraft assembled on the 6th. 44 (Rhodesia) Squadron made ready six Lancasters, loading four with a cookie and incendiaries and two with a cookie, six 500 pounders and two of 250lbs. They took off between 01.03 and 01.21, among them the crew of P/O Nicholson, who, it will be recalled, had ditched during a convoy patrol, and, after rescue, had been forced to continue on to Africa, from where they had just returned. All reached the target area, where cloud was reported at between zero and ten-tenths with tops at 10,000 feet and barrage balloons tethered as high as 12,000 feet. Positions had to be established by TR-fix confirmed by visual reference aided by fires, flak and flares, and the bombs were delivered by the Waddington crews from 14,000 to 21,000 feet without their fall being plotted. According to local reports, eighteen buildings were destroyed and sixty-six seriously damaged, giving a sum total over the five raids of 212 houses destroyed, 741 seriously damaged, and significant industrial damage resulting from just one raid. In return for this modest gain, Bomber Command had lost forty-three aircraft.

Earlier on the 6th, 420 Squadron had vacated Waddington on transfer to 4 Group, where it would convert to Wellingtons, and, on the 7th, 9 Squadron arrived from 3 Group to begin conversion to the Lancaster as the replacement for 83 Squadron, which was about to leave 5 Group for pastures new. The garrison town of Osnabrück was posted as the target on the 9th, and a force of 192 aircraft assembled accordingly. 5 Group contributed forty-two Lancasters, eight of them made ready by 44 (Rhodesia) Squadron, and they departed Waddington between 00.17 and 00.34 with a specific "special" aiming point in mind, which neither the 5 Group nor squadron ORBs identified. On a night of poor serviceability for the squadron, W/O Dainty and crew lost a port engine shortly after crossing the English coast at Skegness, and the same happened to P/O Stephens and crew at the mid-point of the North Sea crossing. S/L Burnett and crew had traversed the Den Helder peninsula, when a starboard flame damper bracket broke, causing the engine to emit excessive flame and forcing them to turn back also. Some forty miles ahead of them, over central Holland, W/O Wright and crew suffered the exact same malfunction, and also abandoned their sortie. There were clear skies over the Münsterland region of Germany to the north of the Ruhr, but haze contributed to the poor visibility that awaited the approaching bombers. They all found that they were unable to establish their positions by TR after it was jammed by the enemy on crossing the Dutch coast. Flares were dropped to illuminate the area, and some crews picked out railway lines and the River Hase, but it was mainly the fires, searchlights and flak that pointed the way to the aiming point. Bombing was carried out by the remaining 44 (Rhodesia) Squadron crews from 13,000 to 17,000 feet between 02.16 and 02.31, and some observed the burst of their cookie. The resulting fires remained visible for eighty to a hundred miles into the return flight, and TR functioned again once the Dutch coast had been crossed homebound. Local sources confirmed an effective raid, which destroyed 206 houses and a military building, and damaged a number of industrial premises along with four thousand other buildings, mostly lightly.

The night of the 10/11th was devoted to mining operations in northern waters, and would occupy fifty-two aircraft, including a contribution from 5 Group of seventeen Lancasters. 44 (Rhodesia) Squadron briefed the crews of F/Sgt Taylor and F/O Chrystal for the Quince Garden in Kiel Bay and P/Os Dorehill and Nicholson for Forget-me-not in Kiel Harbour. They took off at 23.35, and lost F/Sgt Taylor and crew almost immediately to port-outer engine failure, and F/O Chrystal to gun turret and compass issues when a hundred miles out over the North Sea. The remaining two also turned back after running into increasing amounts of dense, low cloud, and failing to establish a pinpoint on the Danish coast.

The main operation on the night of the 11/12th was the first of two on consecutive nights against the city of Mainz, situated to the south-west of Frankfurt-am-Main, for which 154 aircraft were made ready. The number included a contribution from 5 Group of thirty-three Lancasters, for what would be the first large-scale raid on this target. 44 (Rhodesia) Squadron made ready seven Lancasters, which departed Waddington between 22.55 and 23.19, but, as only three were listed on Form 541, this may be slightly incorrect. F/Sgt Taylor and crew were in R5732, which had let them down on the previous night, and did so again, with, apparently, the same problem of port engine failure. They jettisoned the cookie and incendiaries, and crashed on landing, writing off the Lancaster, happily, without crew casualties. P/O Stephens and crew mistook Coblenz for Mainz, but their sortie was omitted from the ORB, along with those of S/L Burnett, P/O Hackney and F/Sgt Rowan-Parry. P/O Wakeford attacked the primary target with four 2,000 pounders from 10,500 feet at 01.05, and W/O Dainty from 9,000 feet at 01.25. The raid was highly successful, and caused major destruction in the central districts, where many historic and cultural buildings were damaged or destroyed. In the excellent tome, Bomber Command War Diaries by Martin Middlebrook and Chris Everitt, the losses from this operation are put at six aircraft, but the actual number failing to return was fourteen, while four others were lost in crashes at home.

The ordeal was not yet over for Mainz, which was posted as the primary target again on the following day, and a force of 138 aircraft made ready, to which 5 Group contributed thirty-three Lancasters and ten Hampdens. This time, 44 (Rhodesia) Squadron prepared six Lancasters for the main event and another for the freshman crew of Sgt Beattie to use for a nickelling sortie over Chalons-sur-Marne in north-eastern France. They took off first, shortly after 22.00, and were followed into the air between

22.33 and 23.03 by the bombing brigade in the absence of a senior pilot. They all reached the target area, where they found eight to ten-tenths cloud between 3,000 and 12,000 feet and generally poor visibility, but some still managed to identify the aiming point visually by islands in the River Rhine north and north-west of the city centre and the fires already burning. The cookies, 2,000 pounders and incendiaries were released unopposed from 5,000 (F/Sgt Rowan-Parry) to 14,000 feet onto the centre of the built-up area between 0.53 and 01.25, and many fires were reported by returning crews. Post-raid reconnaissance and local reports confirmed further heavy damage in central and industrial areas, and the main railway station was also a casualty. Meanwhile, Sgt Beattie and crew had fulfilled their brief by delivering reading matter to the assigned populace from 10,000 feet at 23.49 but had lost 140 gallons of fuel after an electrical discharge in cumulonimbus cloud caused a leak.

On the 13th, 5 Group issued orders to Waddington and Swinderby to prepare a dozen Lancasters between them for gardening duties in the Geranium, Willow and Radish gardens in the Baltic. 44 (Rhodesia) Squadron briefed the crews of S/L Burnett, P/O Stephens and F/Sgt Taylor for the Willow garden situated off the port of Sassnitz on Rügen island, and the crew of P/O Wakeford for Radish, in Denmark's Fehmarn Belt. The former departed Waddington between 22.26 and 22.38 with a round-trip ahead of them of 1,160 miles if they flew directly there and back, which rarely happened, and a track over the Danish half of the Schleswig-Holstein peninsula would add at least another one hundred miles to the journey. When P/O Wakeford and crew took off at 23.20 to follow an identical course, they had a mere 970 miles plus the detour distance over southern Jutland to negotiate, before Lincoln Cathedral hove once more into view. The outward flight was uneventful for all, and clear skies greeted their arrival in the target area, where F/Sgt Taylor pinpointed first on Jasmund and then on a lighthouse, from which a timed run was carried out to the release point. S/L Burnett pinpointed on the stretch of water in the bay known as Tromper Wiek, which led them to the garden, while P/O Stephens and crew, having lost the use of their DR compass, strayed off track, and found themselves over the brightly lit towns of western Sweden, where warning flak sent them on their way. Having established a firm fix on Tralleborg, they were able to locate the garden without further difficulty. The fifteen assorted mines were delivered from 600 to 1,000 feet between 01.40 and 03.11, while P/O Wakeford and crew dropped their five under seven-tenths cloud from 800 feet at 01.59.

A new era for Bomber Command began on the 15th, with the formation of the Path Finder Force, and the arrival at their new homes in Huntingdonshire and Cambridgeshire of the four founder heavy squadrons. 83 Squadron moved into Wyton, the Path Finder HQ, as the 5 Group representative operating Lancasters, and it would be the responsibility of 5 Group's front-line units to provide a steady supply of their most promising crews. The other founder members were 35 (Madras presidency) Squadron, which took up residence at Graveley with Halifaxes to represent 4 Group, while 156 Squadron retained its Wellingtons for the time-being at Warboys, drawing fresh crews from 1 Group, and 3 Group would be represented by the Stirling-equipped 7 Squadron at Oakington. In addition to the above, 109 Squadron was posted in to Wyton, where it would spend the next six months developing the Oboe blind-bombing device and marrying it to the Mosquito under the command of W/C Hal Bufton. The new force would occupy 3 Group stations, falling nominally under 3 Group administrative control and receiving its orders through that group, which was commanded by AVM Baldwin, whose tenure, which had lasted since just before the outbreak of war, was shortly to come to an end.

A "Path Finder" force was the brainchild of the former 10 Squadron commanding officer, G/C Sid Bufton, Hal's brother, and now Director of Bomber Operations at the Air Ministry. He had used his best crews at 10 Squadron to find targets by the light of flares and attract other crews by firing off a coloured Very light, and, it could be said, that the concept of target-finding and marking had been born at 10 Squadron. Once at the Air Ministry, Bufton promoted his ideas with vigour, and gained support among the other staff officers, culminating with the idea being put to Harris soon after his enthronement as Bomber Command C-in-C. Harris rejected the principle of establishing an elite target-finding and marking force, a view shared by the other group commanders with the exception of 4 Group's AVM Roddy Carr. However, once overruled by higher authority, Harris gave it his unstinting support, and his choice of the former 10 Squadron commanding officer, and still somewhat junior, G/C Don Bennett, as its commander, was both controversial and inspired, and ruffled more than a few feathers among more senior officers. Australian, Bennett, was among the most experienced aviators in the RAF, a pilot, and a Master Navigator of unparalleled experience, with many thousands of hours to his credit. He also had the recent and relevant experience as a bomber pilot through his commands of 77 and 10 Squadrons and had demonstrated his strong character when evading capture and returning from Norway after being shot down while attacking the Tirpitz in April. Despite his reserve, total lack of humour and his impatience with those whose brains operated on a lower plane than his, he would inspire in his men great affection and loyalty, along with an enormous pride in wearing the Path Finder badge. He would forge the new force into a highly effective weapon, although this would not immediately be apparent.

There is some confusion surrounding 5 Group operations on the night of the 15/16th, the group ORB recording no operations because of the weather conditions, while the 44, 50 and 207 Squadron ORBs recorded, three, four and four of their Lancasters respectively operating from Waddington and Swinderby against Düsseldorf, along with nine others from 106 Squadron at Coningsby in an overall force of 131 aircraft. The crews of F/O Chrystal, P/O Nicholson and F/Sgt Taylor took off between 00.35 and 00.38, although that of F/Sgt Taylor was omitted from the Form 541, and they were already over enemy territory by the time that the mining trio took off between 01.44 and 01.51, bound for one of the Nectarine gardens off the Frisians. The participants in the main event all reached the target area to encounter six to nine-tenths cloud at 10,000 feet and poor to modest visibility. They established their position by TR-fix confirmed by a visual confirmation on the River Rhine, or simply relied on e.t.a., and the two whose sorties were recorded carried out their attacks from 12,000 and 15,500 feet at 02.14 and 02.31. At debriefing, a number of bursts and flashes were reported, and the abiding impression was of a scattered attack, which was confirmed by local reports from Düsseldorf and its neighbour across the Rhine, Neuss, which described a light raid and no damage of note. Meanwhile, the mining trio of P/O Young and Sgts Beattie and Rickards had flown out in cloud, which, in the target area had a base at under 2,000 feet and delivered their mines from 1,500 and 2,000 feet between 03.15 and 03.34.

R5489 crashed at Branston, four miles south of Waddington, when on approach after a training sortie in the hands of Sgt Easom on the 16th, and the flight engineer and bomb-aimer lost their lives. That night was to be devoted to mining operations involving fifty-six aircraft, some representing 5 Group, despite the fact that the 5 Group ORB again denied any operational activity from its stations. Six Lancasters each were made ready by 106 and 207 Squadrons to mine the Willows, Geranium and Spinach gardens, located respectively off the Baltic ports of Sassnitz on the island of Rügen, Swinemünde, further east along the coast, and off the port of Danzig (Gdansk), which, at the time, was a German city, rather than Polish as it is today. They had a very long night ahead of them, while 44 (Rhodesia) Squadron's P/O Silcock and crew would require less than three hours to deliver their mines into the Nectarine I garden off the western Frisians. They took off at 01.56 and returned at 04.51 to report releasing their mines at 175 m.p.h., over the allotted drop site from 500 feet on a northerly heading at 03.13.

Orders were received at five 5 Group stations on the 17th to prepare for a return to Osnabrück that night as part of a 5 Group effort of thirty-two Lancasters and ten Hampdens in an overall force of 139 aircraft. The Path Finder squadrons had been expected to operate in their new role, until their commanding officers decided that they were not ready, and their debut would be delayed by twenty-four hours. At Waddington, 44 (Rhodesia) Squadron made ready eight Lancasters for the main event, and two to take the crews of P/O Young and Sgt Rickards down the Biscay coast to the Deodar garden in the mouth of the Gironde. The latter took of first, at 20.50 and 21.02, leaving the bombing element on the ground until P/O Dorehill and crew led them away at 21.55, with S/L Stewart the senior pilot on duty and last off the ground at 22.42 on his first sortie for some time. Twenty minutes out, Sgt Beattie lost the port generator that provided all electrical power, and this ended his interest in proceedings. The others pressed on to reach the target area after making a timed run from the Dümmer See, a large lake situated some twenty miles to the north-east and found three to five-tenths cloud at between 11,000 and 14,000 feet. The vertical visibility was further compromised by haze, but some were able to identify the river and railway lines, and bombing took place either on the briefed aiming point or on the built-up area generally from 9,500 to 16,000 feet between 00.02 and 00.48. Local reports confirmed a moderately destructive raid, which fell mainly into northern and north-western districts, and, thereby, built on the damage inflicted eight nights earlier. The gardeners enjoyed uneventful sorties, finding their drop zone under clear skies with horizontal visibility at up to fifteen miles, and dropped their mines as briefed from 800 and 1,000 feet at 23.50 and 00.01.

The Path Finders took to the air in anger for the first time on the 18th, when contributing thirty-one aircraft to an overall force of 118, of which twenty Lancasters and sixteen Hampdens were provided by 5 Group. They were bound for the naval port of Flensburg, situated on the eastern coast of the Schleswig-Holstein peninsula close to the border with Denmark, where the U-Boot pens were the briefed aiming point. It had been selected as a worthwhile and easy-to-locate target, but the planners had not factored in an incorrect wind forecast, which pushed the bomber stream north of the intended track and over southern Denmark. The Path Finders failed to notice, and, as a result, illuminated an area of similar coastal terrain, which led to a scattering of bombs across Danish territory up to twenty-five miles north of the frontier, and into the towns of Abenra and Sønderborg. Flensburg escaped being hit in this inauspicious operational debut of a force, which, in time, would become a highly efficient, successful and vital component in Bomber Command's armoury.

On the 19th, 5 Group was handed the task of locating and bombing a German tanker and support vessel of the Altmark class, which was reported to be off northern Spain. Seven 50 Squadron Lancasters took off in the early hours of the 20th, but were unable to locate the vessel, and all returned safely after at least eight hours aloft. That night, nine Lancasters from 44 (Rhodesia) Squadron repeated the operation, led by S/L Burnett, and also failed to locate the vessel, which, it was discovered, had put back into port. While training in the early evening of the 22nd, L7584 struck high ground some eight miles west of Thirsk in North Yorkshire and was written off, fortunately without injury to P/O Hackney and crew.

Frankfurt was selected on the 24th to host the second Path Finder-led operation, for which a force of 226 aircraft was assembled. 5 Group contributed forty-seven Lancasters, nine of them made ready at Waddington, which took off between 21.08 and 21.34 with S/L Stewart the senior pilot on duty. They headed out across The Wash on course for the Belgian coast, where P/O Wakeford and crew bombed an aerodrome at Middelkerke, west of Ostend after the communications to the rear turret failed. The remainder pressed on to find five to nine-tenths cloud in the target area at between 7,000 and 9,000 feet, with ground haze adding to the difficulties experienced by the Path Finders in locating the aiming point. The 44 (Rhodesia) Squadron crews bombed from between 7,500 and 16,500 feet, having located the target themselves by ground features, timed runs and existing fires rather than by the guidance of the Path Finders. W4105 failed to return with the experienced crew of P/O Nicholson, who had recently resumed operations after their sojourn in Africa following their ditching during a convoy patrol. It was established eventually, that the Lancaster had been homebound when crashing without survivors a dozen or so miles south-south-west of Brussels at 01.10. Opinions at debriefing would be mixed, some satisfied with the results and others not. Certainly, a number of fires had been observed across the built-up area, but no detailed assessment was possible, and no mention was made of the Path Finder contribution, which, at this early stage of its development, restricted crews to identifying and then illuminating the target. Sixteen aircraft failed to return, 7.1% of those dispatched, and among them were five Path Finders.

The third Path Finder-led operation was to be against the city of Kassel, the home to three Henschel aircraft and tank factories and other important war-industry concerns, as well as being the HQ for the military's Wehrkreis IX, and the site of a subcamp of the Dachau concentration camp, which supplied slave labour to the factories. A force of 306 aircraft was assembled on the 27th, 5 Group detailing seventy-five Lancasters and a dozen Hampdens, thirteen of the former made ready at Waddington. They took off between 21.11 and 21.35 with F/L Barlow the senior pilot on duty and lost the services of P/O Young and crew to an unserviceable rear turret soon after beginning the North Sea crossing, and P/Os Wakeford and Holland and their crews because of intercom and W/T failures shortly after reaching the Dutch coast. W/O Dainty and crew were within twenty miles of the Dutch/German frontier, when they were attacked by a Ju88, which scored multiple hits in the wings and engines with cannon and machine gun rounds and set fire to the port-central fuel tank. The bombs were jettisoned live immediately, and W4126 was nursed back to a safe landing at Martlesham Heath, where fourteen cannon shell and three machine gun holes were counted. The others continued on to the target, where they were greeted by minimal cloud and good visibility, with only ground haze between them and the aiming point. The Path Finder flares assisted greatly in enabling the crews to pick out ground detail, like a bend in the River Fulda and lakes to the south-west, and eight of the Waddington crews took advantage to deliver their cookies and incendiaries from 5,000 to 13,000 feet between 23.45 and 00.09. Sgt Rickards and crew lost their port-outer engine while homebound near Münster and overshot their landing to come to rest in a field a mile-and-a-half beyond the airfield, where R5664 was declared to be beyond economical repair. Local reports confirmed the effectiveness of the raid, which was spread across the city and destroyed 144 buildings, while causing serious damage to more than three hundred others. Among those afflicted to some extent were all three Henschel factories and a number of military establishments, and the fire services had to deal with seventy-three large blazes. However, the success was gained at the high cost of thirty-one aircraft, twenty-one of them Wellingtons, of which fifteen belonged to 1 Group. 44 (Rhodesia) Squadron posted missing the crew of P/O Suckling RNZAF in W4124, which, it was established later, had fallen to the guns of Oblt Viktor Bauer of III./NJG1, and had crashed without survivors at 00.26 some ten miles south-west of Rheine and within sight of the Dutch frontier.

A force of 159 aircraft was assembled on the 28th to send to the city of Nuremberg, deep in southern Germany, and the scene of massive Nazi Party rallies during and after Hitler's rise to power during the thirties. The Path Finders were to employ target indicators (TIs) for the first time in adapted 250lb bomb casings. 5 Group detailed sixty-three Lancasters, while also contributing seventeen Hampdens to a simultaneous raid on Saarbrücken by a force of 113 "oddments", which included 4 Group Halifaxes and new crews from other groups, but no Path Finders. 44 (Rhodesia) Squadron made ready nine Lancasters and sent them on their way from Waddington between 20.54 and 21.08 with W/C Smales the senior pilot on duty. F/Sgt Rowan-Parry and crew turned back early on because of an unserviceable mid-upper turret, leaving the others to continue the six-hundred-mile outward leg across France. Southern Germany was found to be beneath clear skies, which combined with a four-fifths moon to aid a visual identification of the city and enable the Path Finder element to exploit the conditions to deliver their TIs with great accuracy. Some of the Waddington crews pinpointed on the autobahns leading into the city and bombed from 6,000 to 14,000 feet between 00.08 and 00.45, observing many bursts and fires. There was no question in their minds as they withdrew, that they had hit the target, a belief confirmed by fires remaining visible for some seventy miles into the return flight. Local reports suggested that about a third of the force had landed bombs within the city, causing damage to the Altstadt, but that others had wasted their effort on communities up to ten miles to the north. Twenty-three aircraft failed to return, 14.5% of the force, and the Wellingtons were hit particularly hard again, losing a third of their number. During the course of another busy month, the squadron took part in nineteen operations and dispatched 104 sorties for the loss of six Lancasters, three crews and two additional crew members.

September 1942

The first half of the new month would distinguish itself through an unprecedented series of effective operations, although, it would begin ignominiously for the Path Finder Force, when posting a "black" on the night of the 1/2nd by marking the wrong town. The city of Saarbrücken had been briefed out to 231 crews, of which sixty-nine represented 5 Group, sixty-two to fly Lancasters and seven in Hampdens, a type with just two more weeks of front-line service ahead of it. 44 (Rhodesia) Squadron made ready six Lancasters, loading them with either a cookie and incendiaries or four 2,000 pounders, and dispatched them from Waddington between 23.54 and 00.09 with F/L Barlow the senior pilot on duty. All reached south-western Germany to find the target under clear skies with good visibility, and established their positions by TR, confirmed by visual identification of the River Saar and Path Finder flares. They bombed from 6,000 to 10,000 feet between 02.04 and 02.37, F/L Barlow and two other crews reporting the detonation of a cookie from another aircraft that produced a large mushroom effect with debris flying in all directions. There was no question in the minds of the crews as they retreated to the west, that this had been an outstandingly accurate attack, and some claimed to be able to see the glow of fires from up to 140 miles into the return flight. It was only later that the truth emerged, that the Path Finders had not marked Saarbrücken, but the non-industrial town of Saarlouis, situated thirteen miles to the north-west. Much to the chagrin of its inhabitants, and those in surrounding communities, the main force bombing had been particularly accurate and concentrated, and heavy damage had been inflicted.

This could have been an ill-omen for the month's efforts, but, in fact, the Command now embarked on the unprecedented run of effective operations mentioned above. It began at Karlsruhe on the night of the 2/3rd, for which a force of two hundred aircraft was made ready, the 4 Group Halifax brigade having now returned to operations following intensive training to restore confidence in the type after a period of above average losses and a series of design-flaw accidents. 5 Group put up sixty Lancasters and five Hampdens, of which eleven of the former were provided by 44 (Rhodesia) Squadron. They departed Waddington between 23.28 and 23.56 with S/L Burnett the senior pilot on duty and lost the services of P/O Day twenty miles east of Orfordness and F/O Chrystal with the Scheldt estuary in sight, both to issues with their port-inner engine. The others pressed on across the Belgian coast, and reached the target area under clear skies, Karlsruhe basking in moonlight and naked to the eyes of the bomb-aimers high above. The autobahn and the Rhine and its docks stood out clearly as a guide to the aiming point, and bombing was carried out by the 44 (Rhodesia) Squadron participants from 5,000 to 14,000 feet between 02.08 and 02.39, the city appearing to be swallowed by a sea of flames, before becoming obscured by smoke. Returning crews reported as many as two hundred fires, the glow from which remained visible for a hundred miles into the homeward journey. Post-raid reconnaissance confirmed much residential and some industrial damage, and local reports mentioned seventy-three fatalities.

When Bremen was posted as the target on the 4th, 5 Group responded with a contribution of forty-six Lancasters in an overall force of 251 aircraft. Crews were told at briefing that the Path Finders would be rolling out a new three-phase technique of a) illumination, b) visual marking and c) backing-up, which, if successful, would form the basis of Path Finder operations for the remainder of the war. Twelve 44 (Rhodesia) Squadron crews attended briefing, ten to be assigned to the Focke-Wulf aircraft factory in the Hemelingen district and two, those of W/O Wright and P/O Hackney, to attack the city. They took off between 00.11 and 00.47 with W/C Smales the senior pilot on duty, accompanied by a W/C Hooper. F/Sgt Rowan Parry and crew were at 13,000 feet over Holland and closing on the German frontier at 02.10, when they were attacked by a night-fighter, which sent cannon shells ripping through the fuselage, damaging vital equipment. The rear and dorsal turrets were rendered inoperable, leaking hydraulic oil caught alight, the bomb doors flopped open, and the intercom was knocked out, leaving them with no choice but to jettison their load and limp back to a landing at Wittering. Sgt Beattie and crew also returned early, but the details of their sortie were omitted from the Form 541. The others reached the target area to find cloudless skies and good visibility, although ground haze and smoke created challenging conditions for target identification. The bombing of the Focke-Wulf factory was carried out from 7,000 to 17,500 feet, and the town area from 15,500 and 16,000 feet, between 02.05 and 02.38. They noticed a less-intense flak defence over the city than usual, but much increased hostility as they withdrew towards the Frisian island of Norderney. F/L Barlow's W4106 collected flak damage to both wingtips but did make three passes over the target before releasing the cookie and 30lb incendiaries. Twelve aircraft failed to return from this successful operation, and debriefing reports of fires in the central districts were confirmed by a local assessment, which listed 460 dwelling houses, six large/medium industrial premises and fifteen small ones destroyed, and a further fourteen hundred buildings seriously damaged.

P/O Dorehill DFC was posted on the 5th to the Conversion Flight at the end of his tour of operations and was spared the tension of preparing for the next operation, which was to be directed at the Ruhr city of Duisburg on the night of the 6/7th. A force of 207 aircraft was assembled, which included fifty-four Lancasters and four Hampdens representing 5 Group, nine of the former provided by 44 (Rhodesia) Squadron. They departed Waddington between 01.14 and 01.27 with S/L Stewart the senior pilot on duty, and, as W/O Stott and crew overtook a Halifax over southern Holland, they had to take evasive action, when its mid-upper gunner opened fire. All reached the target area to find it partially concealed by cloud, below which, the usual industrial haze rendered ground detail indistinct. Positions were established by TR and confirmed as far as possible by visual reference, and the 44 (Rhodesia) Squadron crews attacked from 13,000 to 17,000 feet between 02.46 and 03.05, in the face of a searchlight and flak defence operating to its usual high standard. Even so, the Duisburg authorities reported the heaviest raid to date, which destroyed 114 buildings and seriously damaged more than three hundred others, and, while this was only fairly modest, it still represented something of a victory at this notoriously elusive target.

There was no pattern to the choice of targets thus far in the month, southern and north-western Germany and the Ruhr all featuring during the busy first week, and Frankfurt in south-central Germany was posted as the latest target on the 8th, for which a force of 249 aircraft was assembled. 5 Group contributed sixty-two Lancasters and nine Hampdens, the eleven participants from 44 (Rhodesia) Squadron departing Waddington between 20.30 and 20.57 with S/L Stewart the senior pilot on duty. They all reached the target area, where, according to some, the skies were clear of cloud and the visibility good, while others reported up to eight-tenths cloud at 2,000 feet and poor to moderate visibility. Another factor was the intensity of the searchlight and flak activity, which should, perhaps, have helped to guide the Path Finders to the aiming point, but, surprisingly, they failed to locate the city. Path Finder flares were in evidence, but scattered over a wide area, and it was clear that they were by no means certain of their position in relation to Frankfurt. Eight of the 44 (Rhodesia) Squadron crews established their own positions by what they could glimpse on the ground and by the dozens of searchlights fingering the darkness and bombed the primary target from 10,000 to 16,000 feet between 23.42 and 23.57, observing fires in what appeared to be the built-up area. The crews of W/O Wright and P/Os Silcock and Wakeford bombed the alternative target of Mainz, situated some twenty miles to the south-west, from 14,500 to 16,000 feet at 23.50 and 23.55. According to local reports, only a handful of bomb loads hit the intended target, and this halted the run of successes thus far in the month. The majority of bombs appeared to have fallen to the south-west of Frankfurt as far as Rüsselsheim, fifteen miles away. The Rüsselsheim authorities confirmed damage to the Opel tank works and a Michelin tyre factory, which compensated in small measure for the failure to hit the primary target.

The Path Finder Force was constantly evolving in tactics and equipment and had a new weapon in its armoury for the next operation, which was to be against the Ruhr city of Düsseldorf on the 10th. "The Pink Pansy", which weighed in at 2,800lbs, was the latest attempt to produce a genuine target indicator, and used converted 4,000lb cookie casings. A force of 479 aircraft included a contribution from the training units of 91, 92 and 93 Groups, and eighty-one Lancasters and eight Hampdens from 5 Group. 44 (Rhodesia) Squadron put up ten Lancasters, which set off from Waddington between 20.30 and 21.06 with S/L Stewart the senior pilot on duty and each carrying a cookie and incendiaries. They all reached the target area to encounter clear skies with the usual industrial haze muddying the vertical visibility, but fires were already burning to help them identify the target visually and pick out major features like a bend in the Rhine and the docks complex. The red flares were reported by some to be a little north of the main city area, and the greens to the west, while the white illuminators highlighted the more central districts. The 44 (Rhodesia) Squadron crews bombed from 12,000 to 18,000 feet between 22.15 and 22.48, observing fires to develop, and they turned away believing the attack to have been successful. P/O Hackney and crew landed to find their bombs still on board having failed to release, which was something of a surprise, as the bomb-aimer had witnessed the burst of a cookie exactly where expected. Had they realised, they would have released the load manually. Other returning crews made complimentary comments about the performance of the Path Finders and reported the glow of the fires to be visible from the Scheldt. Post-raid reconnaissance and local reports confirmed this operation to have been probably the most successful since Operation Millennium at the end of May. Other than the northern districts, all parts of the city and its neighbour, Neuss, had been hit, and 911 houses had been destroyed with a further fifteen hundred seriously damaged. In addition to the destruction also of eight public buildings, fifty-two industrial firms in the two cities sustained damage sufficient to cause a total shut down of production for varying periods. It had been an expensive victory for the Command, however, with thirty-three failures to return, of which sixteen were from the training units.

Fifteen 44 (Rhodesia) Squadron crews attended briefing on the 13th to learn that Bremen was to be their target for that night, and for the second time during the month. A force of 446 aircraft was assembled, again bolstered by aircraft and crews from the training groups, and there was a contribution from 5 Group of ninety-eight Lancasters and seven Hampdens. The 44 (Rhodesia) Squadron element departed Waddington between 22.45 and 23.54 with W/C Smales and S/L Stewart the senior pilots on duty. P/O Barley and crew turned back after about an hour with a port-outer engine issue, while P/O Stephens and crew lost their port-inner engine after it caught fire over Holland. The flames were extinguished, and they crossed the Dutch/German frontier over eight-tenths cloud intending to continue on to the target, but TR identified the town of Lingen, upon which they dropped the cookie, before turning south and releasing the incendiaries over the flare-path at Plantlünne aerodrome. The remainder reached the target area to find clear skies but considerable ground haze, which made pinpointing something of a challenge. Some major ground features, like the docks, could be identified visually, otherwise it was down to flares and fires to point the way, and the Waddington participants believed they were over the built-up area as they carried out their attacks from 11,500 to 18,000 feet between 01.20 and 01.38. A number of crews were convinced that some early arrivals had bombed at Delmenhorst, a few miles to the south-west of Bremen, and the 5 Group ORB described the Path Finder performance as unhelpful. However, the success of the operation suggested otherwise, and by far exceeded the destruction resulting from June's Thousand Bomber raid. A total of 848 houses was destroyed, and much damage was inflicted on the city's industry, including to the Lloyd Dynamo works, where two weeks production was lost, and parts of the Focke-Wulf factory were put out of action for between two and eight days. Of the twenty-one aircraft lost, fifteen belonged to the training units and one to 44 (Rhodesia) Squadron. W4169 had been homebound over central Holland, when crossing paths with the night-fighter of Oblt Manfred Meurer of III./NJG1 and crashing at 03.26 eight miles north of Apeldoorn. F/O Holland and five of his crew lost their lives, leaving the flight engineer in enemy hands.

The end of the Hampden era arrived on the following night when the naval port of Wilhelmshaven was posted as the target for 202 aircraft. Sixty-two Lancasters and four Hampdens were made ready as the 5 Group contribution, the latter from Syerston's 408 (Goose) Squadron RCAF. The nine 44 (Rhodesia) Squadron aircraft were loaded with a cookie and either 900 x 4lb or 90 x 30lb incendiaries, and eight departed Waddington between 19.59 and 20.35 with S/L Stewart the senior pilot on duty, leaving W/O Stott and crew on the ground until 21.03, presumably, because of a technical problem. This caused them to reach turning point A fifteen minutes after the briefed "time-on-target", and they decided to attack Emden as an alternative. They bombed from 17,000 feet at 22.52, but could not pinpoint the impact, which they suspected had undershot the port to the east. As they turned away, they could see a glow forty miles to the east in the sky over Wilhelmshaven, where the remaining eight Waddington crews had carried out their attacks from 13,000 to 18,500 feet between 22.11 and 22.50, with light flak bursting around them at between 15,000 and 17,000 feet. They had arrived to find clear skies over the coastal region of Jade Bay, with extreme darkness and ground haze to impede vertical visibility, but the waterline and the docks had provided an adequate pinpoint for the Path Finders to establish their position and mark accurately. It was difficult to distinguish individual bomb bursts, but the consensus was of a successful outcome, and four crews reported an enormous explosion, believed to be from an ammunition dump. It lit up the ground for five seconds and emitted flames a hundred feet into the air along with a cloud of smoke that rose to several thousand feet. Local sources confirmed that this had been the port's most destructive raid to date.

After such a run of successes, Harris had to have another go at Essen, and a force of 369 aircraft was assembled on the 16th, which again called upon the training units to supply aircraft and crews. Ninety-three Lancasters represented 5 Group, and two of the sixteen provided by 44 (Rhodesia) Squadron would be flown by crews from fellow Waddington residents, 9 Squadron, who had spent the previous five weeks under conversion training. They took off between 20.06 and 20.29 with S/L Stewart the senior pilot on duty, and all reached the target area to encounter between three and eight-tenths cloud, but generally good visibility despite the industrial haze, which could be penetrated sufficiently for some ground detail to be identified visually by the light of Path Finder flares. Even so, the overlapping boundaries of the Ruhr towns and cities made it difficult to establish positions with absolute certainty, and some of the crews dropping their bombs on e.t.a., would find, from the evidence of their bombing photos, that they had been over Bochum, Oberhausen or some other built-up expanse. Some of the Path Finder flares were estimated to be falling some twenty miles to the east of Essen, which would have put them over Dortmund and Hagen. The 44 (Rhodesia) Squadron element carried out their attacks from 15,000 to 20,000 feet between 22.06 and 22.24, seven of them over what they believed to be Essen, and the remainder over the Ruhr generally, in the face of an intense searchlight and flak response. Returning crews reported the glow of fires visible for a hundred miles into the return journey, and local sources would confirm this to be Essen's worst night of the war to date. In addition to much housing damage and more than a hundred medium and large fires, fifteen high-explosive bombs had found their way onto the Krupp complex, as did a crashing bomber loaded with incendiaries. A post-raid analysis revealed that bombs had been scattered across a large part of the Ruhr, with Bochum, Wuppertal and Herne among the hardest hit, and, until the advent of Oboe in the coming spring, such inaccuracies would remain a fact of life. It was far from a one-sided affair, and cost the Command a massive thirty-nine aircraft, 10.6% of those dispatched, nineteen of them from the training units.

If any period in the Command's gradual evolution to war-winning capability could be seen as a turning point, then, perhaps, the first half of September 1942 qualified. It can be no coincidence, that the Path Finder Force was emerging from its hesitant start, as the crews got to grips with the complexities of their demanding role, and new tactics and aids were being brought to bear against the enemy. It would be no overnight transformation, and failures would still outnumber victories for some time to come, but the encouraging signs were there, that all of the elements of technical and tactical advance were coming together, and, with other technological wizardry in the pipeline, it boded ill for Germany's industrial towns and cities.

Extensive mining operations occupied 115 aircraft on the night of the 18/19th, 5 Group supporting the effort with forty-nine Lancasters, a dozen of them representing 44 (Rhodesia) Squadron and assigned to six separate gardens, five in the western Baltic and one located off south-western France. At briefing, P/Os Hackney and Wakeford and W/O Stott were told that their destination was the Deodar garden in the Gironde estuary, while P/O Stephens was bound for Quince in Kiel Bay, P/Os Day and Silcock and Sgt Beattie for Daffodil, the southern end of The Sound (Oresund) between Copenhagen and Sweden, F/L Barlow for the distant Privet, off the port of Danzig (Gdansk), S/L Stewart for Spinach, off the port of Gdynia, and P/Os Barley and Young and Sgt Rickards for Radish in the Fehmarn Belt. They departed Waddington between 18.58 and 20.03, S/L Stewart and F/L Barlow facing a round-trip of 1,600 miles that would keep them airborne for more than nine hours.

Remarkably, it is known that all but one crew reached their respective garden area, and only P/O Young and crew were unable to establish a pinpoint in poor visibility, despite carrying out a square search. Mines were delivered from 600 to 900 feet between 22.03 and 23.59, and all but Sgt Beattie and crew returned home to report a successful night's work. W4177 disappeared into the sea, and only the body of the rear gunner came ashore for burial.

Munich was posted as one of two targets on the 19th, and would involve sixty-one 5 Group Lancasters, seven Lancasters from 83 Squadron of the Path Finders and twenty-one Stirlings from 3 Group and 7 Squadron of the Path Finders. A simultaneous operation by 118 aircraft of 1, 3 and 4 Groups would target Saarbrücken, also with Path Finder support. The two forces would follow a common route as far as Saarbrücken, leaving the 5 Group element a further 220 miles to travel to reach the Bavarian Capital, the birthplace of Nazism and a city of cultural and industrial significance. 44 (Rhodesia) Squadron was called upon to contribute just five Lancasters, which departed Waddington between 20.07 and 20.17 with S/L Burnett the senior pilot on duty. They flew out across France, entering southern Germany near Strasbourg to be greeted by clear skies and good visibility, which enabled them to identify the lakes to the south-west of the city. Most crews adopted a time-and-distance run from Lake Constance to bring them to the aiming point, which had been well-illuminated by Path Finder flares, and the cookies and 30lb incendiaries were released from 9,200 to 16,000 feet between 23.50 and 23.58. Bomb bursts were observed in the city centre, along with a large explosion to the north and numerous fires, including a large one to the south-west, and 40% of returning crews would claim to have bombed within three miles of the city centre. Saarbrücken was reported to be well-alight by crews passing by on the way home, and the Path Finders were complimented on their performance at debriefings. Bombing photos revealed that the main weight of the attack had fallen into western, southern and eastern suburbs of Munich, but there was no confirmation from local sources, and Saarbrücken had largely escaped damage after the bombing became widely scattered. Three Lancasters and three Stirlings were missing from Munich, and among them was 44 (Rhodesia) Squadron's R5554, which crashed near Maubeuge in north-eastern France, close to the Belgian frontier, killing P/O Day and three of his crew, and leaving the three survivors in enemy hands.

The squadron was notified on the 23rd, that it would be operating that night against the Baltic coastal town of Wismar and the nearby Dornier aircraft factory, as part of an all-5 Group affair involving eighty-three Lancasters. 44 (Rhodesia) Squadron made ready eleven of its own, loading them either with six 1,000 pounders with an eleven-second delay fuse, or a mixture of 4lb and 30lb incendiaries. Two-thirds of the force were assigned to the town, situated some thirty miles east of Lübeck and a third to the factory, the latter element including the crews of W/C Smales, F/O Silcock and P/O Wakeford. They departed Waddington between 22.18 and 22.43, with S/L Burnett the senior pilot on duty among those targeting the town and ran into a violent electrical storm when around a hundred miles short of Denmark's western coast. This caused many to turn back and added to a total of twenty-one early returns from all causes. Those reaching the target found ten-tenths cloud with tops at 8,000 feet and a base at 800 feet, with intense and accurate searchlight and flak activity awaiting any crews brave enough to venture so low. W/C Smales and crew enjoyed an uneventful outward flight, sinking down to between 100 and 300 feet over the Baltic, until picking up the target, situated close to the coast to the north of the town on the East Bank of the estuary. They flew along a runway on the factory airfield at zero feet on a south-easterly heading, before climbing to 50 feet to drop the 1,000 pounders at 02.10. As they raced between two balloons chased by flak, they hit the deck again, using the factory as cover, and the rear gunner reported explosions among its buildings. Their job done, they swung back round towards the coast and scraped the harbour walls as they made for the comparative safety of the sea. Within seconds, P/O Silcock released 112 x 30lb incendiaries to straddle the factory from 60 feet, and P/O Wakeford followed up seven minutes later from 200 feet. He and his crew complained about the weather on the way out but described the rainy conditions at the target as the worst of the whole operation. Those attacking the town did so from 1,500 to 4,000 feet between 01.51 and 02.19, but a hydraulics failure courtesy of flak prevented S/L Burnett from releasing his load, and he had to bring it home. P/O Hackney and crew were on track as they ran into cloud at 1,300 feet thirty miles from the target and descended to 400 feet as they emerged with the coastline ahead, only to be ensnared by searchlights, which they escaped by turning back out to sea. They followed the coastline searching for the target, but kept stumbling into searchlights and flak, and after twenty-five minutes, P/O Hackney ordered the bombs to be jettisoned. Returning crews reported fires in the town and at the Dornier factory, while local reports listed thirty-two houses and eight industrial buildings seriously damaged. Four Lancasters failed to return, and among them was the squadron's R5905, which was abandoned by the crew of Sgt Rickards over central Jutland and crashed near Ulfborg at 02.30, which suggests that they had turned back early. They all arrived safely on the ground and were captured around seventy-two hours later at Holstebro.

The squadron did not take part in the 5 Group's mining operations on the night of the 24/25th, and spent the next four nights at home, until receiving orders on the 29th to prepare seven Lancasters for mining operations that night in the Pollock and Willow gardens, situated respectively off the island of Bornholm off Sweden's southern coast, and the port of Sassnitz on Rügen. They took off between 22.43 and 23.04 with S/L Burnett leading the Pollock-bound quartet and S/L Stewart those heading for Willow, and all reached their respective target areas to encounter ten-tenths low cloud and sea fog, which prevented all but P/O Young and crew from locating their assigned drop zone at Willow. They released three mines from 800 feet at 02.32, observing all parachutes to deploy and three splashes, while S/L Stewart and P/O Wakeford planted theirs in one of the seven Silverthorn gardens in the Kattegat as an alternative. In the Bornholm area, the Lancasters were still in cloud at 250 feet, and S/L Burnett decided to bring his stores home. While heading westwards across Jutland, he came upon a train between Hjerm and Holstebro, and strafed it from 100 feet in two passes at 04.40, expending around two thousand rounds, some of which were seen to enter the locomotive and bring it to a halt enveloped in steam. F/Sgt Rowan Parry and crew found an alternative location for two of their mines in Silverthorn and brought the other home, while P/O Stephens and W/O Stott dropped theirs off Fornæs on the eastern coast of Middle Jutland. All returned safely from challenging sorties that brought the month's operational activities to a conclusion. During the course of September, the squadron took part in thirteen operations and dispatched 132 sorties for the loss of four Lancasters and crews.

October 1942

5 Group's October account opened on the 1st with news of a return to Wismar that night, for which a force of seventy-eight Lancasters was prepared, sixteen of them by 44 (Rhodesia) and 9 Squadrons at Waddington. The plan called for three-quarters of the force to attack the town, with the main square as the aiming point, while the remainder targeted the Dornier aircraft factory. 44 (Rhodesia) Squadron briefed the crews of S/L Burnett and F/L Barlow for the factory and seven others for the main element and dispatched them between 17.59 and 18.21 on what would be a round trip of some eleven hundred miles. They crossed Jutland seemingly without incident, arriving at the target area to encounter three to ten-tenths cloud with a base at between 1,500 and 7,000 feet. Poor visibility over the town was caused by heavy ground haze and an effective smoke screen, which combined with intense searchlight

glare to blot out identifying features. Brief glimpses of the coastline provided a scant reference by which to establish position, and, uncertain of their precise position, S/L Burnett and F/L Barlow flew on a further 125 miles to what they believed was Warnemünde and attacked it from 5,500 feet either side of 21.40. Meanwhile, at Wismar, bombing runs had to be carried out largely on DR, and no crew was able to establish a firm pinpoint. This led to the bombing of a number of locations along a 150-mile stretch of coastline from Wismar eastwards, and the entire undertaking proved to be a wasted effort that cost 44 (Rhodesia) Squadron the experienced crew of F/O Stephens DFC, DFM. It seems, according to the time of the loss at 21.19, that they were returning early in W4187, and came down at Skallingen, a spit of land north-west of Esbjerg, on Denmark's western coast, with fatal consequences for all on board.

The Ruhr city of Krefeld was posted as the target for a force of 188 aircraft on the 2nd, for which 5 Group contributed twenty-four Lancasters from Waddington, Coningsby and Syerston, while the rest of 5 Group stood down. 44 (Rhodesia) Squadron made ready eight Lancasters, which took off between 19.05 and 19.52 with S/L Stewart the senior pilot on duty, and all reached the western edge of the Ruhr to encounter dense industrial haze, which thwarted the Path Finders' best efforts to provide a reference for those following behind. F/L Barlow attacked an unidentified built-up area from 12,500 feet at 21.08, leaving the remainder to bomb on estimated positions on DR and isolated Path Finder flares from 8,500 to 16,000 feet between 20.40 and 21.17. Returning crews reported some scattered fires, and local sources confirmed that three streets in the northern part of the city had sustained damage, but nothing commensurate with the size of the force and the effort expended.

All heavy groups were alerted on the 5th to an operation that night against the city of Aachen, for which a force of 257 aircraft was put together, 5 Group detailing sixty-nine Lancasters, seven of them from 44 (Rhodesia) Squadron. They departed Waddington between 19.07 and 19.26 with S/L Burnett the senior pilot on duty and headed south for the Channel crossing to the French coast. P/O Barley and crew were on auto-pilot and flying in cloud at 10,000 feet over Essex, when they came under fire from the ground at 19.48. Despite firing off the colours of the day, the assault continued, and a reciprocal course was adopted as they descended to 8,000 feet, before returning to the original course. A flak shell burst directly beneath them, which knocked out the intercom system, and they turned back again to assess what further damage had been sustained, decreasing altitude again to 5,000 feet. The colours of the day were fired and ignored again, and the sortie was abandoned. P/O Miers and crew would confirm the friendly fire from the Thames estuary on their early return, after running into a severe thunderstorm some eighty miles from Waddington, through which they were unable to climb. They reached 14,000 feet without breaking into clear air, and descended to 7,000 feet to avoid icing, eventually leaving the storm behind them, and climbing to 16,000 feet at the French coast. Here, they met heavy cloud and further icing conditions, and dropped suddenly for six thousand feet, before arresting the descent and abandoning the sortie at a position some twenty-five miles inland of the coast. P/O Young was at 17,000 feet and some twenty miles from making landfall on the French coast, when he became indisposed and abandoned the sortie at 20.37. The stormy weather extended inland, which encouraged some of the force to descend for the rest of the journey to the target, Germany's most westerly city, nestling just inside the German borders with southern Holland and Belgium. On arrival in the target area, flares were visible, but up to nine-tenths cloud and poor visibility created challenging conditions, and the 44 (Rhodesia) Squadron crews of Sgt Watt, F/Sgt Rowan Parry and F/O Osborn bombed on estimated positions from 12,000 to 16,000 feet between 21.28 and 21.32. S/L Burnett and crew thought that they had attacked Aachen from 9,800 feet at 21.35, but a large flash from an unidentified source revealed two parallel rivers running north to south, which, together with the absence of flak, convinced them that they had actually bombed the Dutch city of Maastricht. Local sources would report that Aachen's southern district of Burtscheid had suffered quite extensive damage to housing and industry, and five large fires had required attention. Even so, they estimated the attack to have involved only around ten aircraft. Some bombs fell seventeen miles away onto the small Dutch town of Lutterade, and this would have consequences for the trials of the Oboe blind-bombing device in late December.

Osnabrück was posted as the target on the 6th, for which 237 aircraft were made ready, including fifty-nine Lancasters of 5 Group. 44 (Rhodesia) Squadron loaded eight of its aircraft with a cookie each and twelve SBCs of either 30lb or 4lb incendiaries and dispatched them between 19.13 and 19.28 with S/Ls Burnett and Stewart the senior pilots on duty. The Path Finders dropped flares over Makkum in Holland and the Dümmer See to the north-east of the target as route markers, and these proved to be very effective in guiding the main force in, although, inevitably, some bomb loads were released early during the twenty-mile leg between the Dümmer See and the town. Four to eight-tenths cloud lay over the town at 8,000 feet, and provided challenging conditions for accurate bombing, although opinions varied as to the quality of the visibility. The 44 (Rhodesia) Squadron crews carried out their attacks from 11,000 to 16,000 feet between 21.30 and 21.38, and much of the effort fell into the central and southern districts. Returning crew described many fires and a glow visible by some from the Dutch coast homebound, and most had confidence in the effectiveness of the raid. According to local reports, 149 houses and six industrial buildings were destroyed, 530 houses seriously damaged and more than 2,700 others slightly damaged. It was a sad night for 44 (Rhodesia) Squadron when the crews of S/L Stewart DFC and P/O Miers RAAF failed to return, and it would be some time before the Red Cross confirmed their fate. S/L Stewart and crew had failed to survive the crash of W4188 at Quakenbrück, some thirty miles north of the target, while R5903 had come down at Klosterholte, twenty miles further west, near Meppen, killing both gunners and delivering the remainder of the crew into enemy hands. P/O Miers would be repatriated a year hence after contracting tuberculosis.

Most of the following week was devoted exclusively to mining operations, and there would be little activity for 44 (Rhodesia) Squadron, other than daylight formation-flying exercises involving eight aircraft led by W/C Smales on the 8th and 9th. 5 Group launched another shot at Wismar and the Dornier factory with fifty-nine Lancasters on the night of the 12/13th, when difficult weather conditions over the sea prevented many from establishing a pinpoint on the enemy coast and forced them to navigate by DR. The town lay under six to ten-tenths cloud in a band between 1,000 and 7,000 feet, and the lack of pinpoints forced some crews to search for up to thirty minutes before bombing on estimated positions. This inevitably led to a scattered and probably ineffective attack, despite which, some returning crews reported that the factory had been left burning furiously and the flames had remained visible for seventy miles into the homeward journey.

The naval port of Kiel was posted as the target for a force of 288 aircraft on the 13th, for which 5 Group weighed in with sixty-nine Lancasters, eight of them provided by 44 (Rhodesia) Squadron and loaded with a cookie and 4lb or 30lb incendiaries. They took off between 18.32 and 19.02 with S/L Burnett the senior pilot on duty and lost the services of Sgt Easom and crew within two hours because of the failure of navigational equipment. The others reached the target area to find almost clear skies and good visibility, and red and white flares marking out the Selenter Lake, some ten miles to the east. Illuminator flares were also deployed over the town, revealing a built-up area, which the Waddington crews bombed from 15,000 to 17,000 feet between 21.15 and 21.33, most without plotting the fall. Probably half of the crews were deceived by a decoy fire site, but the rest hit the town and caused an appropriate amount of damage. Returning crews reported a much-reduced searchlight and flak defence, which was provided by the Luftwaffe, and, conscious that defensive measures attracted attention, this was a tactic employed occasionally and effectively.

A force of 289 aircraft was assembled on the 15th to send against Cologne, which had been left in peace for a considerable time, and the operation was supported by sixty-two Lancasters of 5 Group from Coningsby, Scampton, Syerston and Waddington. 44 (Rhodesia) Squadron made ready five Lancasters and sent them on their way between 19.08 and 19.25 with no senior pilots on duty. F/Sgt Elger and crew were closing on the enemy coast at Walcheren, when an engine issue caused by severe icing conditions forced them to turn back. The others pressed on across northern Belgium to be eased off track by inaccurately forecast winds and found the Rhineland Capital to be concealed beneath a layer of ten-tenths cloud. The Path Finder flares were scattered, and a large, effective decoy fire site combined with that to attract the main force away from the target. The 44 (Rhodesia) Squadron crews carried out their attacks from 15,000 to 16,500 feet between 20.53 and 21.09, observing nothing of the results, and it was left to local sources to report damage within the city to be slight and superficial.

On the 17th, the purpose behind the formation-flying training that had been causing speculation for more than a week, was revealed to crews in 5 Group briefing rooms. They learned that Operation Robinson was a daylight attack on the Schneider armaments works at Le Creusot, deep in eastern France, and the nearby Montchanin transformer station, which provided its power. Often referred to as the French "Krupp", the company belonged to the Schneider family, which had donated the famous aviation trophy bearing its name. The Schneider Trophy was initially a prize to encourage technical advances in civil aviation, but, eventually, became a speed contest for float and seaplanes competed for biannually by Britain, France, Italy and the USA. It was a massively prestigious and popular spectator event that drew crowds of up to 200,000 people. Britain claimed it outright after three consecutive wins culminating in 1931, when the revolutionary Supermarine S6B triumphed in the hands of 44 Squadron's first wartime commanding officer, W/C Boothman. Ninety-four Lancasters were to take part in the operation, which required an outward flight at low level by daylight, the attack at dusk, and a return under the cover of darkness. It was a bold plan to commit such a large force, which would be difficult to conceal, and it was only six months since the Augsburg disaster.

The plan called for eighty-eight aircraft to bomb the factory complex from as low as practicable, led by W/C Len Slee of 49 Squadron, while six others, two each from 106, 61 and 97 Squadrons, led by W/C Gibson, went for the power station in a line-astern attack. The 44 (Rhodesia) Squadron contribution amounted to nine Lancasters, which departed Waddington between 12.05 and 12.09 with S/L Burnett the senior pilot on duty. They would join up with the rest of the force over Upper Heyford, before heading for Land's End at under 1,000 feet, and, once over the sea, aim for a point just south of the Ile d'Yeu to cross the French coast midway between St Nazaire and La Rochelle at around 100 feet. Shortly before the sea crossing began, Coastal Command Whitleys had carried out a sweep to force enemy U-Boots beneath the surface and prevent them from spotting the force and transmitting a warning. For most, the three-hundred-mile low-level dash across France would be relatively uneventful, but bird strikes became a constant threat, causing injury to a number of crewmen as they smashed Perspex, while others became ingested in engines. F/O Silcock complained that the lead section was too low, which placed upon him an exhausting physical strain as he wrestled with slipstream turbulence, and others commented on bunching-up and occasional congestion, despite which, this middle leg terminated successfully at the predetermined point some forty-five miles from the target. It was at this juncture that the main force broke up to form into a fan and climb to a bombing height of between 4,500 and 7,000 feet. The target was reached at dusk under clear skies and in good visibility, and crews were able to follow a railway line directly to the heart of the factory complex, where the 44 (Rhodesia) Squadron crews bombed aa briefed between 18.09 and 18.15. Not all were able to plot the fall of their bombs, but S/L Burnett watched his five RDX 1,000 pounders fall onto a long shed, while Sgt Morris and crew observed their four 1,000 pounders and incendiaries hit the central power station on the south-eastern corner of the site. F/O Osborn and crew saw their bombs fall just short of locomotive sheds 22 and 23 and described a large volume of smoke rising through 3,000 feet to obscure the entire target area. They also complimented 49 Squadron on its leadership during the outward flight, while S/L Burnett claimed that it was the most successful operation that he had participated in. All returned safely home after a round-trip of ten hours, F/O Barley coming back on three engines after losing his port-inner to a coolant leak. At debriefing on all stations, it was unanimous that the target had been utterly devastated in return for the loss of a single 61 Squadron Lancaster from the Montchanin element, and the success prompted a message from the A-O-C 5 Group, AVM Coryton, who added to his own congratulations with similar sentiments from the Secretary of State for Air, Sir Archibald Sinclair. Unfortunately, it would be discovered later, that the damage had been less severe than first thought, and production had soon returned to normal. Another raid would be mounted against the plant eight months hence.

A new campaign, against Italian cities in support of land operations in North Africa under Operation Torch began on the night of the 22/23rd against the city-port of Genoa and the naval dockyard, where part of the Italian fleet was sheltering. It was the eve of the opening of the Battle of Alamein, which, after twelve days' fighting, would see Montgomery push Rommel's forces all the way back to Tunisia and out of the war. Ten 5 Group squadrons mustered between them 101 Lancasters, while 83 Squadron of the Path Finders contributed eleven more to take care of target marking. Twelve of the twenty-three at Waddington were made ready by 44 (Rhodesia) Squadron and took off between 17.28 and 17.47 with W/C Smales and S/L Burnett the senior pilots on duty. W/C Smales lost most of the power on his starboard-outer engine soon after take-off but elected to keep the propeller turning and carry on in an attempt to reach the target. He managed to coax W4268 to a height of 14,500 feet and not a foot more, passing south-west of Paris on the way to the wall of rock that was the Alps, which glistened under clear skies and an almost full moon. Smales somehow dragged his Lancaster over or between the peaks by applying full throttle and 2,700 revs and found the clear air and perfect visibility over Italy a joy to behold after contending with the industrial haze at German targets. The Path Finder flares could be seen by approaching main force crews from sixty miles away, and, on arriving over the city, they found the flak defence to be wildly inaccurate, while a smoke screen proved ineffective as the wind blew it straight out to sea. The crews were able to establish their positions visually on the layout of the docks and the city, and all but one of the 44 (Rhodesia) Squadron element carried out their attacks from 8,000 to 11,000 feet between 21.28 and 21.45, leaving W/C Smales to bring up the rear at 22.00. Some returning crews described the raid as a "miniature-Cologne", and local sources confirmed heavy damage in central and eastern districts, which, because of the need for fuel over bombs, had been achieved with just 180 tons of high-explosives and incendiaries, and, remarkably, without loss.

Twenty-four hours later, a force made up of elements from 3 and 4 Groups and the Path Finders attempted to follow up at Genoa, but, in cloudy conditions, attacked in error the town of Savona, thirty miles to the west. Eighty-eight 5 Group crews attended briefings on the morning of the 24th to learn that they would be undertaking the first daylight crossing of the Alps to attack the city of Milan. The city was home to many war factories, including the Isotta Fraschini luxury car works, which had been converted to military vehicle and aero engine manufacture, the Pirelli rubber works, Alfa Romeo, the Caproni aircraft plant, the Breda locomotive, armaments and aircraft works and the Innocenti machinery and vehicle factory. The operation would require an even longer flight over fighter-defended territory than the Le Creusot operation a week earlier, but it was forecast, that cloud would protect them for most of the way. 44 (Rhodesia) Squadron made ready eleven Lancasters, which departed Waddington between 12.14 and 12.40 with W/C Smales and S/L Burnett the senior pilots on duty, and headed for Selsey Bill, from where they would cross the Channel at very low level with the rest of the loose formation under a Spitfire escort. Sgt Shattock and crew were at the midpoint of the Channel when a seagull smashed through the Perspex of the bomb-aimers compartment and forced them to jettison their 4,000 pounder and turn back. Sgt Einarson and crew were just ten miles from the French coast when the guns in the rear turret became inoperable and those in the mid-upper proved to be unreliable, and this ended their interest in proceedings. Crews had been briefed to expect the cloud of a warm front awaiting them at the Normandy coast, however, to their discomfort, they saw that it had formed further inland, and they had to run the gauntlet of anti-aircraft fire as they raced over the clifftops with three hours to go to the Alps. A bank of cloud could be seen in the distance, to which the force climbed as rapidly as possible, and once reached, the crews had to plot their own individual course until rendezvousing over Lake Annecy, sixty miles short of the target. From there they formed a loose formation and lost height, until reaching the target to find eight to nine-tenths cloud with a base at 3,000 feet, but sufficient gaps through which to establish their positions visually. The marshalling yards, a seaplane base and an aerodrome were among ground features identified as the 44 (Rhodesia) Squadron crews delivered their high-explosive and incendiary payloads from 3,400 to 10,500 feet, but mostly below 6,000 feet, between 17.00 and 17.10. Some squadrons had loaded their Lancasters with a cookie, which required a minimum clearance of 4,000 feet, demonstrating the disregard for their safety of those attacking from such a low height, and even down to a few hundred feet to strafe factories and other targets of opportunity. The sun was setting ahead of them as they crossed the Alps homebound, and France passed beneath them unseen in darkness, with enemy night-fighters waiting over the coastal region as the returning bombers passed through. At debriefing, crews were enthusiastic about the effectiveness of the raid, which had cost three Lancasters, each of them shot down into the Channel. Post-raid reconnaissance revealed that the 135 tons of bombs had caused extensive damage to housing, public buildings, and a number of war-industry factories, including the Caproni aircraft works, and had also seriously affected railway communications between Italy and Germany. Local reports confirmed a figure of 441 houses destroyed or seriously damaged along with nine public buildings.

F/L Barlow was posted to 29 O.T.U., on the 26th at the end of his tour and S/L Whitehead arrived from 1654 Conversion Unit on the 27th to assume flight commander duties. During the course of the month the squadron carried out nine operations and dispatched seventy-five sorties for the loss of three Lancasters and crews.

November 1942

There would be no operations for the majority of the Command during the first week of the new month, largely as a result of the weather, and 44 (Rhodesia) Squadron was put on stand-by three times, only to be stood-down as the operations were cancelled. The first operation to take place was posted on the 6th, when Genoa was revealed at briefings to be the target for fifty-seven Lancasters of 5 Group and fifteen belonging to 83 Squadron of the Path Finders. 44 (Rhodesia) Squadron prepared a dozen aircraft and sent them on their way from Waddington between 21.24 and 21.59 with F/L Osborn the senior pilot on duty, and all reached the target after an uneventful outward flight of four hours in favourable weather conditions. The excellent visibility, along with accurate Path Finder flares, enabled them to locate the aiming point visually after identifying ground features like the breakwater, harbour and town, and they carried out their attacks from 7,000 to 12,000 feet between 01.43 and 02.16. Fires of increasing intensity were concentrated in the docks area, while a number of ships appeared to be burning in the harbour, and F/O Biggane counted a total of 116 fires across the city from his pilot's seat in W4162. Not content with his crew's part in the operation, he descended to 1,000 feet to allow his gunners to strafe Villenova aerodrome with five hundred rounds from the rear turret, fifty from the mid-upper and a hundred from the front. Crews at the tail end of the attack found its effectiveness laid out before them and described a colossal fire on a hill near the city centre. The glow from the burning city remained visible from the Alps and Nice, some eighty miles away, but, as no local report emerged, the full extent of the damage could not be assessed.

A follow-up raid on Genoa was posted on 3, 4 and 5 Group stations on the 7th, and a force of 175 aircraft assembled, which included Halifaxes, Stirlings and a handful of Wellingtons to join eighty-one Lancasters of 5 Group. The eleven 44 (Rhodesia) Squadron participants departed Waddington between 17.38 and 18.07 with S/L Whitehead the senior pilot on duty and undertaking his first sortie with the squadron. Sgt Easom and crew were flying out over Dungeness on the Kent coast at 14,000 feet, when the port-inner engine began to surge and then cut out completely, ending their sortie. P/O Young and crew crossed France at 12,000 feet without incident, until climbing in the Dijon area to 17,000 feet as they approached the foothills of the Alps. It was here that they ran into extreme icing conditions, and, with a heavy build-up on the mainplane costing them altitude, they jettisoned their load and turned for home. The others experienced the same ideal conditions as on the previous night, particularly on the far side of the Alps, and they were able to make a visual identification of the coastline, harbour and aiming point in the light of the punctual and accurately delivered Path Finder flares. A smoke screen failed to shield the city, and the flak defence seemed to give up once the bombing began, although light flak from rooftops continued to fire, even if inaccurately. The 44 (Rhodesia) Squadron crews bombed from 8,000 to 11,000 feet between 21.42 and 21.56, and, on return, reported bombs exploding in the built-up area causing numerous fires. Many crews brought home an aiming point photograph to add to those from reconnaissance flights, which confirmed the operation to have been highly successful.

The campaigns against Italy and Germany would have to run side-by-side for the time being, and, in a break from Italy, Hamburg was posted as the target on the 9th. No mention was made by the "met boys" during briefing of strong winds and ice-bearing cloud of the type that often lay in wait across the bombers' path to Germany's second city. The four heavy groups put together a force of 213 aircraft, of which, sixty-seven Lancasters were provided by 5 Group, eleven of them by 44 (Rhodesia) Squadron. They were loaded with a cookie and incendiaries each before departing Waddington between 17.55 and 18.37 with no senior pilots to lead the way. F/Sgt Elger and crew lost their wireless over the North Sea and abandoned their sortie, and Sgt Einarson lost his port-inner engine at about the same time and also turned back. This would have been as the rest of the force was about to enter the troublesome cumulonimbus cloud over the North Sea, which most negotiated successfully to reach the target area. However, on arrival they found it to be completely hidden by ten-tenths cloud with tops at 16,000 feet, which forced them to bomb on e.t.a., in the absence of Path Finder flares, but in the presence of heavy flak, particularly from naval guns, the shells from which were detonating above the bombing height. The 44 (Rhodesia) Squadron crews attacked from 11,000 to 20,000 feet between 20.24 and 21.00 but found it impossible to assess what was happening beneath the cloud. A strong wind from the north almost certainly pushed the bombing south of the intended aiming point, and this seemed to be confirmed by local reports, that many bombs had fallen into the River Elbe or into open country, and only three large fires had required attention. Fifteen aircraft failed to return, five of them belonging to 5 Group, and among these was the squadron's W4180, which crashed near Buchholz some ten miles south-west of Hamburg, killing Sgt Easom and his crew. It had been a bad night generally for 5 Group, which also registered nine early returns.

Mine-laying would occupy the ensuing two nights, and 5 Group detailed a dozen Lancasters on the 10th to send that night to the Biscay coast to the Elderberry and Furze gardens, located respectively off Bayonne and a dozen miles further south at St-Jean-de-Luz, right down on the border between France and Spain. 44 (Rhodesia) Squadron remained at home until the 13th, when orders were received at Waddington to prepare ten aircraft for an operation that night against Genoa as part of a 5 Group effort involving sixty-one Lancasters, which would act as the main force, supported by a Path Finder element comprising six Lancasters of 83 Squadron and nine Stirlings of 7 Squadron at Oakington. Nineteen of the 5 Group element were to attack the Ansaldo engineering works, which could be viewed as the Italian "Krupp", while the remainder had their own aiming point in the town. The 44 (Rhodesia) Squadron element departed Waddington between 18.06 and 18.35 with S/L Burnett the senior pilot on duty, and he had F/L Ingham beside him in the cockpit following his recent posting in from 1661 Conversion Flight. Sgt Baldwin and crew were on course for Selsey Bill for the Channel crossing, when they discovered that they were east of London heading west rather than south, and realised that their DR and P4 compasses, and, indeed, their Gee, could not be relied upon. The others pushed on across France to cross the Alps in good weather conditions that allowed the target to be identified visually from cloudless skies. Sgt Morris lost his port-outer engine after crossing the Alps but maintained altitude to reach the target. The bombing by the 44 (Rhodesia) Squadron crews was carried out from 6,000 to 10,500 feet between 21.23 and 21.50 in the face of a "beefed-up" searchlight and flak defence, and high explosive and incendiary bursts were observed right across the target area. Those plotted were found to be at least a thousand yards from the aiming point, but there was no attempt to assess the outcome through reconnaissance. Some returning crews reported the glow of fires to be visible for 130 miles into the return flight, and confidence was high that the loss-free raid had been successful.

Two days later, a force of seventy-eight aircraft was made ready to continue the assault on Genoa, and twenty-one of twenty-seven Lancasters were provided by 5 Group. 44 (Rhodesia) Squadron stayed on the ground, while those taking part enjoyed an uneventful outward flight across France, and the ten-tenths cloud to the south of the Alps stopped just short of the target to provide clear skies and moonlight. The Path Finders performed well to illuminate the aiming point, allowing it to be identified visually by a force largely untroubled by the defences. Six large fires were observed in the built-up area, and the glow was still visible from up to a hundred miles into the return journey.

Attention shifted from Genoa to the industrial powerhouse that was Turin on the 18th, when a force of seventy-seven aircraft was made ready. The city was home to Fiat's Lingotto and Mirafiori car plants, the Lancia motor works, the Arsenale army munitions factory, the Nebioli foundry and plants belonging to the Westinghouse company. The force had originally been significantly larger, but forty-two 5 Group Lancasters, including ten of the original 44 (Rhodesia) Squadron element, had been withdrawn because of doubts about the weather over their stations. The crews of S/L Burnett and F/L Osborn would represent the squadron alone and departed Waddington at 17.52 and 18.04 as part of the twenty-five-strong 5 Group effort. They arrived at the target some three-and-at-half hours later to find clear skies that left the city naked to the eyes of the bomb-aimers, who benefitted from another excellent performance by the Path Finders. The Fiat works aiming point was squarely in their bombsights as they ran in, S/L Burnett releasing a cookie and three SBCs of 8 x 30lb incendiaries from 4,900 feet at 21.48, and F/L Osborn following up two minutes later from 2,500 feet with four 1,000 pounders and thirteen SBCs of 30lb incendiaries. Many fires broke out in the city centre, and the Fiat works sustained an unspecified degree of damage, which was confirmed by bombing photos.

Following the recent run of relatively small-scale operations to Italy, the 20th brought a return to Turin with greater numbers, amounting this time to 232 aircraft, of which seventy-eight Lancasters were provided by 5 Group. 44 (Rhodesia) Squadron made ready eleven of its own and dispatched them between 18.18 and 18.50 with F/L Osborn the senior pilot on duty. It would take almost four hours to reach the target, but all from the squadron negotiated the seven-hundred-mile outward leg without incident, although F/Sgt Elger would have to contend with effective power from three engines only for almost the entire nine-hour duration of his sortie. Those arriving at the front end of the attack were able to establish their position by following the autostrada and identifying ground features in the light of flares, but, by the time that the majority of the Waddington crews arrived over the city, smoke was already drifting across it, and ground features appeared fleetingly, creating challenging conditions for target identification. Ground haze added to the difficulties, but, even so, by running in at low to medium level, some crews were able to identify the Fiat factory visually and deliver the bombs with some degree of accuracy. The 44 (Rhodesia) Squadron participants attacked mostly from 3,400 to 6,000 feet between 22.07 and 22.39, and only F/Sgt Elger remained high at 10,500 feet, knowing that he might struggle on three good engines to climb over the Alps on the way home. They left behind them massive fires raging in the city centre, with smoke rising already through 6,000 feet, and returning crews were confident in the effectiveness of their work.

Sixty-four 5 Group crews attended briefings on the 22nd, to learn that their destination that night was to be Stuttgart as part of an overall force of 222 aircraft. 44 (Rhodesia) Squadron made ready nine Lancasters, which departed Waddington between 18.40 and 18.51 with S/L Whitehead the senior pilot on duty. Located in a series of valleys, Stuttgart was always a difficult city to identify, but three hours and fifteen minutes later the first of the main force crews had Path Finder flares in their sights, illuminating the target area to apparently enable a visual identification of the aiming point. The bombs were dropped by the 44 (Rhodesia) Squadron crews from 6,000 to 12,000 feet between 21.55 and 22.34, and their bursts observed, before a safe return was made from what they described as a quiet trip with a satisfactory result. On the way home over France, Sgt Baldwin and crew descended to strafing height to attack three trains on a stretch of track between Soissons and Compiegne and marshalling yards near the latter. The front gunner expended six hundred rounds, the mid-upper eight hundred and the rear gunner one thousand, and it was a considerably lighter Lancaster that landed at Snaith at 02.52. It was soon discovered that a thin layer of cloud and ground haze had prevented the Path Finders from identifying the centre of the city, and much of the bombing had fallen onto south-western and southern districts and outlying communities up to five miles from the city centre. Local reports confirmed that a modest eighty-eight houses had been destroyed and described two bombers attacking the city centre at low level and causing extensive damage to the main railway station. 44 (Rhodesia) Squadron was represented among the ten failures to return by W4304, which disappeared without trace with the experienced crew of P/O Young.

Aircraft actually became airborne for operations on the 26th and 27th, only to be recalled immediately on receipt of a cancellation order. Instructions came through to all heavy groups on the 28th to prepare its aircraft and crews for operations that night against Turin, and, during the course of the day, a force of 228 aircraft was made ready, ninety-one of the Lancasters on 5 Group stations. *(1 Group was in the process of converting from Wellingtons to Lancasters, and 101, 103 and 460 Squadrons had begun to operate the type in the past week).* 44 (Rhodesia) Squadron made ready eleven aircraft, their bomb bays containing either a cookie and three SBCs of 30lb incendiaries, or all-incendiary loads, and launched them from Waddington between 18.31 and 19.05 with S/Ls Burnett and Whitehead the senior pilots on duty. F/Sgt Elger and crew were fifteen miles north-west of Le Havre when engine trouble ended their sortie, leaving the others to continue on across France without incident to reach the target area under clear skies, with just a little haze to mar the vertical visibility. Despite this, they were able to establish their positions by visual reference of the River Po assisted by Path Finder flares. The 44 (Rhodesia) Squadron crews bombed from 7,000 to 15,000 feet between 22.18 and 22.37, observing bursts in the town and on the Fiat works, and Sgt Morris and crew counted forty-seven fires when they were fifteen minutes into the homeward journey. Others confirmed that the city was a mass of flames and commented on a particularly large blaze in the centre and some others around the Royal Arsenal. W/C Gibson and F/L Whamond of 106 Squadron dropped the first two 8,000 pounders to fall on Italy, and all indications were that the operation had been entirely successful.

During the course of the month, the squadron took part in eight operations and dispatched seventy-seven sorties for the loss of two Lancasters and crews.

December 1942

The weather at the start of the new month restricted operations, and an unsuccessful raid on Frankfurt involving 112 aircraft on the 2nd did not include a contribution from 5 Group. Squadrons were warned of operations daily between the 2nd and 5th, but each was cancelled, and it was the 6th before an operation was posted at Waddington that would actually go ahead. 44 (Rhodesia) Squadron detailed a dozen Lancasters, while their crews were informed at briefing that Mannheim was to be their target in company with sixty-two other Lancasters of 5 Group in an overall force of 272 aircraft. They took off between 17.25 and 18.00 with S/L Whitehead the senior pilot on duty, and all reached the target, where they encountered eight to ten-tenths cloud between 4,000 and 12,000 feet, which rendered ineffective the Path Finders' efforts to mark the city with flares. A decoy site was also operating some twenty miles to the south, and this, inevitably, attracted a proportion of the bombing. Crews could bomb only on DR and e.t.a., in the case of the 44 (Rhodesia) Squadron element from 5,000 to 14,000 feet between 20.17 and 20.38. It was F/O Silcock who descended to 5,000 feet, from where the Rhine and a built-up area were visible, and he and his crew observed scattered fires and square factory buildings ablaze. Other returning crews had little of interest to report to the Intelligence Section at debriefing.

On the following night, 5 Group called for nine crews to carry out gardening duties in the Elderberry and Furze gardens off the south-western coast of France. They found up to three-tenths cloud and good visibility in the target area off Bayonne, and lights from the notoriously poor blackout at Biarritz to provide a solid reference. Lights were blazing in Spain, and a steel works at Bilboa appeared to be in full production. On the 8th, S/L Burnett concluded his tour with the squadron and was posted to 5 Group HQ. In the coming April, as 9 Squadron vacated Waddington for its new home at Bardney, he would be appointed its new commanding officer.

Notification was received on 5 Group stations on the 8th that Turin was to be the target for that night, in an operation to be conducted by a 5 Group main force of ninety-eight Lancasters, supported by thirty-five Path Finder aircraft of all types. The 44 (Rhodesia) Squadron element of fourteen departed Waddington between 17.33 and 17.55 with S/L Whitehead the senior pilot on duty and lost the services of Sgt Dening and crew early on to wireless and Gee issues. The remainder all reached the eastern side of the Alps to find clear skies and good visibility, and the city visible to the south as they approached the final turning point. Swinging towards the start of their bombing run, over to port to the east of the city, a large bend in the River Po provided a strong reference, which enabled the Path Finders to identify the aiming point and deliver their flares right on the mark. The 44 (Rhodesia) Squadron crews followed in their wake and registered that the aiming point was well-defined by two arcs of Path Finder flares, and one massive explosion a mile-and-a-half to the south-west. The bombing was carried out by the 44 (Rhodesia) Squadron crews from 7,500 to 12,000 feet between 21.10 and 21.32, and the city could be seen to be well-alight. Those arriving when the attack was already well underway reported smoke drifting across the aiming point and counted thirty to forty sizeable fires burning across the city. A huge pall of smoke was rising through 8,000 feet as the force retreated towards the Alps, and the fires would still be burning when the next bomber force arrived twenty-four hours later.

Orders came through on the 9th to prepare for another assault on Turin that night, and a dozen 44 (Rhodesia) Squadron crews attended the briefing at Waddington to learn that they would be part of a 5 Group effort of eighty-two Lancasters in an overall force of 227 aircraft. F/L Osborn was the senior pilot on duty as they took off between 17.22 and 17.50, but a faulty compass ended his interest in proceedings before leaving English airspace. The others enjoyed an uneventful outward flight and were guided the final few miles to the target by the fires still burning from the previous night. This, however, proved to be a double-edged sword, as the smoke hanging over the city created challenging conditions for the Path Finders, who failed to deliver as strong a performance this time. The raid was spread out over more than thirty minutes, during which the 44 (Rhodesia) Squadron crews attacked from 6,000 to 12,000 feet between 21.32 and 21.52. They helped to create many more fires that produced even larger volumes of smoke to obscure much of the ground from those arriving at the tail end of proceedings. Returning crews reported explosions and fires, but the consensus was of a less effective raid than that of the previous night.

For the third night in succession the torment of Turin continued, although at the hands of a reduced force of eighty-two aircraft drawn from 1 and 4 Groups and the Path Finders. They had to fight their way through severe icing conditions over France, and more than half of the force turned back before reaching the Alps. Those completing their sorties failed to inflict more than the slightest damage on the city, in what proved to be the final raid of this first Italian campaign. Sixty-eight aircraft were sent mining on the night of the 14/15th, but the twenty-three 5 Group Lancasters were recalled after an hour because of concerns about the weather for their return.

No further major operations would take place during what remained of the year, but 5 Group detailed twenty-seven Lancasters to target eight small German towns on the night of the 17/18th, seventeen for what was referred to in the 5 Group ORB as "Batter", against Soltau, some forty miles east of Bremen, and Neustadt-am-Rübenberge and Nienburg, located between Bremen to the north-west and Hannover to the south-east. A further ten Lancasters were assigned to "moling" sorties over five other towns in north-western Germany including, Cloppenburg, Diepholz and Quakenbrück, and one wonders if, in the cold light of dawn, anyone in raid planning recalled the disaster that had afflicted 57 and 214 Squadrons of 3 Group as a result of similar operations on the first night of April. Seven 44 (Rhodesia) Squadron crews were briefed for Nienburg, and three for mining duties in the Sweet Pea garden in the Kadet Channel, located between Denmark's Lolland island and the Rostock coastal region. The two elements took off together between 16.59 and 17.28, and adopted a similar course in conditions of moonlight, until separating over the western Frisians, where the bombing brigade headed inland over Holland and the gardeners continued on to the Danish coast. It was at this point that W4126 was brought down by Kriegsmarine flak and crashed at 18.45 on Texel, killing F/O McNamara and his crew. Ten-tenths cloud slid across the sky to put an end to map-reading, but Sgt Shattock and crew picked up the River Weser, and followed it at 500 feet to what they believed was Nienburg, which they attacked with two 1,000 pounders and incendiaries at 19.19. Ten minutes later and some fifteen miles west of the target, they shot up a concentration of about seven searchlights. Sgt Paige and crew broke through the cloud base at 1,500 feet, and descended to attack a built-up area, which they, too, believed to be the target, dropping three 1,000 pounders and incendiaries from 200 feet at 19.24. P/O Walker and crew found sufficient ground features to establish their position and attack Nienburg from north to south from 700 feet at 19.42, while Sgt Morris and crew failed to locate it and went for Stolzenau, some eight miles south-west of Nienburg, as an alternative. They observed their bombs to strike home from 1,000 feet at 19.34 and set course for home satisfied with their nights work. It is believed that F/Sgt Dening RAAF and crew were homebound and closing on the Ijsselmeer when ED355 was shot down by a night-fighter to crash at 20.22 onto a road near Harich in northern Holland without survivors. R5666 crashed near Bramsche on the northern side of the Mittelland Canal, but, at least, F/O Michel and four of his crew survived to fall into enemy hands, while both gunners perished.

Meanwhile, the gardeners had been contending with heavy cloud and icing conditions, which defeated Sgt Einarson and crew, who jettisoned their mines. Sgt Raymond and P/O Biggane and their crews managed to establish their positions despite the ten-tenths cloud with a base down to 800 feet and delivered their stores into the allotted locations within two minutes of each other shortly before 20.30 from 400 and 1,000 feet respectively. Nine Lancasters failed to return from these foolhardy nuisance raids, and six Stirlings and two Wellingtons were lost raiding the Opel works at Fallersleben, further to the east. Thus, a total of seventeen aircraft and crews had been sacrificed for little or no return.

Apart from isolated "moling" daylight operations, the Ruhr had been left in peace since Krefeld at the start of October, while attention had been focussed on Italian targets. Now, on the 20th, Duisburg was posted as the target, and this would mask another operation of great significance for the Command that was taking place at the same time over Holland. Although, in the event, not all would proceed according to plan, it would be a mere blip in the development of the Oboe blind-bombing device. A force of 232 aircraft was assembled for the main event, of which seventy-five were Lancasters of 5 Group, eleven of them representing 44 (Rhodesia) Squadron. They departed Waddington between 17.36 and 18.25 with S/L Whitehead the senior pilot on duty, but tragedy struck as the two resident Lancaster squadrons climbed out over the station. F/Sgt Elger's W4259 collided with W4182 of 9 Squadron, and both Lancasters plunged to the ground to crash on Canwick Road, Bracebridge Heath, two miles south of Lincoln, killing all fourteen occupants. The others would have observed the incident and pressed on across the North Sea in sombre mood, and P/O Walker and crew had reached the mid-point when electrical defects and turret issues ended their sortie. Sgt Shattock and crew got within ten miles of the Dutch coast near Haarlem, when severe ice-accretion forced them to turn back also. The remainder encountered favourable weather conditions and bright moonlight at the target, where good visibility enabled crews to peer through the slight ground haze and identify the River Rhine and the Ruhrort docks to establish a firm visual reference. Bombing was carried out by the 44 (Rhodesia) Squadron crews from 10,500 to 16,000 feet between 19.53 and 20.00, and at least fifteen fires were observed, many of them large.

Meanwhile, six 109 Squadron Oboe-equipped Mosquitos had targeted a power station at Lutterade in Holland, in a test to gauge the device's margin of error, believing the target to be free of bomb craters so as not to impair the data. Unfortunately, three of the Mosquitos suffered Oboe failure, and went on to bomb Duisburg instead, leaving W/C Hal Bufton and two other crews to deliver the bombs. What they hadn't bargained for was a whole carpet of bomb craters left over from the attack on Aachen, seventeen miles away, in October, and it proved impossible to identify those aimed by Oboe. The calibration tests would continue, however, and, come the spring, Oboe would be ready to unleash with devastating results against the Ruhr.

W/C Smales was awarded a DSO on 21st, the day on which a force of 137 aircraft was made ready for an operation that night against Munich, deep in southern Germany. As already mentioned, a few 1 Group squadrons had begun to receive Lancasters during the autumn, and would contribute in small numbers, but eighty-two of the 119 of the type made available for this operation were provided by 5 Group, and some others by the Path Finders. 44 (Rhodesia) Squadron briefed nine crews, who were in their aircraft and lined up for take-off by 17.28 and were all safely on their way by 18.02 with W/C Smales the senior pilot on duty. They pushed on across France for the long trek to the target area, which they reached after a three-and-a-half-hour outward journey, only to find it concealed beneath ten-tenths cloud with tops at a lowly 2,000 feet. The Path Finders illuminated the Ammersee to the south-west of the city, and crews carried out a time-and-distance run from there to the aiming point, the 44 (Rhodesia) Squadron crews bombing from 8,400 and 13,500 feet between 21.12 and 21.26. There were plenty of flashes below the cloud, together with the glow of fires to convince the crews that they had found the mark, but it is likely, that these came from a decoy site, as most bombing photos would reveal open country. Twelve aircraft failed to return, six of them belonging to 5 Group, and F/O Biggane DFC and his crew were among them. W4125 crashed at Bad Rappenau, north-west of Heilbronn, and only the bomb-aimer and navigator survived to fall into enemy hands.

The fourth wartime Christmas was celebrated in traditional style across the Command, and operational activity ceased until the 29th, when fourteen 5 Group Lancasters were made ready for mining duties off France's Biscay coast. The crews of F/L Ingham, P/O Walker, F/Sgt Horwood and Sgt Baldwin were briefed for the long round trip to the Deodar garden in the Gironde estuary and had to wait until after midnight before venturing out onto a snow-covered airfield to clamber into their Lancasters. They would, at least, be heading south towards slightly warmer climes as they departed Waddington offensively for the final time in the year between 01.09 and 01.47. They all reached the target area to find five to ten-tenths cloud at up to 3,000 feet and good visibility, which enabled them to deliver their mines into the allotted locations from 500 to 900 feet between 04.46 and 05.32. During the course of the month, the squadron took part in seven operations and dispatched sixty-one sorties for the loss of four Lancasters and crews.

As the New Year beckoned, a great responsibility lay on the nine operational Lancaster squadrons of 5 Group to carry the war to the enemy. There was no question that the Stirling and Mk II and V Halifaxes were inferior aircraft, and their limited availability and restricted bomb-carrying capacity meant that the Command still had to rely very much on the trusty but aging Wellington to make up the numbers if the defences were to be overwhelmed. That said, the advent of Oboe and the ground-mapping radar, H2S, would greatly enhance the Command's ability to deliver a telling blow, and 1943 would see the balance of power shift massively in the Command's favour.

Homing pigeon Billy.

This bird was released at 10.00 hours by the crew of a Waddington Hampden which had force-landed in Holland on the 21st of February 1942. Billy arrived at Waddington pigeon loft nearly 28 hours later at 13.40 hours on the 22nd of February in a state of collapse. The 11-month-old pigeon had flown 250 miles, part of it through heavy snow storms. He was awarded the animals' VC, the Dickin medal.

44 (Rhodesia) Squadron Officers 1942

Fourth row: F/O Wilkin F/O Cook, P/O Hilton
Third row: P/O Walker, P/O Mason, P/O Day, P/O Hackney, F/O Powell, P/O Fenn, P/O Miers, F/O Chrystal,   - , F/O Curtiss.
Second row: P/O Juniper, P/O Mitchell, F/L Johnson, P/O Jess, F/O Caldicott DFM, P/O Silcock, F/O Anderson, P/O Mason,   - , P/O Cowling, F/O Tate.
Front row: F/O Allen, F/O Ryan, F/L Sands, F/L Taylor DFC, F/L Locke, S/L Stewart DFC, W/C Smales DFC, G/C Lewis, S/L Burnett, S/L Nettleton VC, F/L Barlow DFC, P/O Barley, P/O Appleton, P/O Evans, F/O Wakeford.

S/L Nettleton flying in a 97 Sqn Lancaster in February 1942, checking 97 Sqn pilots' proficiency. (Many different captions accompany this photograph, but it did not serve with 44 Squadron despite the Squadron codes and subsequently went to 207 Sqn. Two features of 44 Squadron Lancasters were the smaller ID code letters and the lack of a fairing on the mid upper gun turret.)

Another view of the same flight.

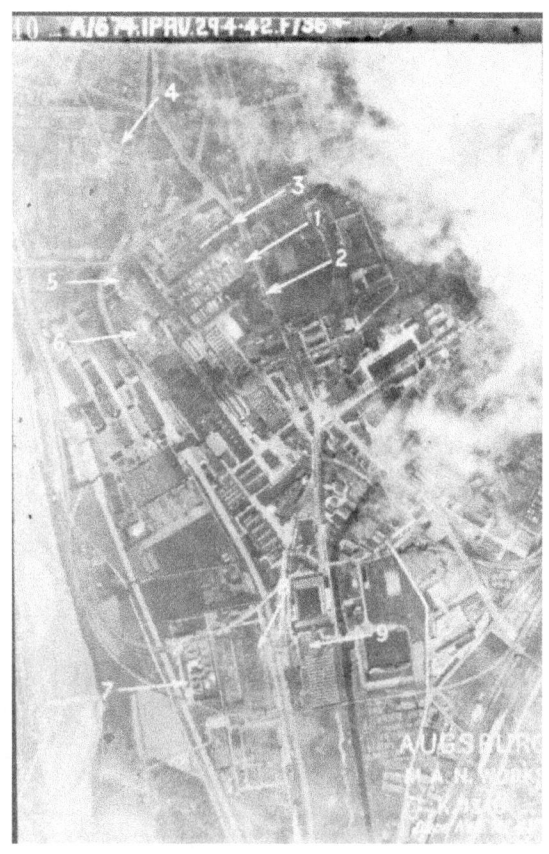

Recce photographs showing the damage done to the MAN factory in Augsburg by the low level attack led by S/L Nettleton on the 17th of April 1942.

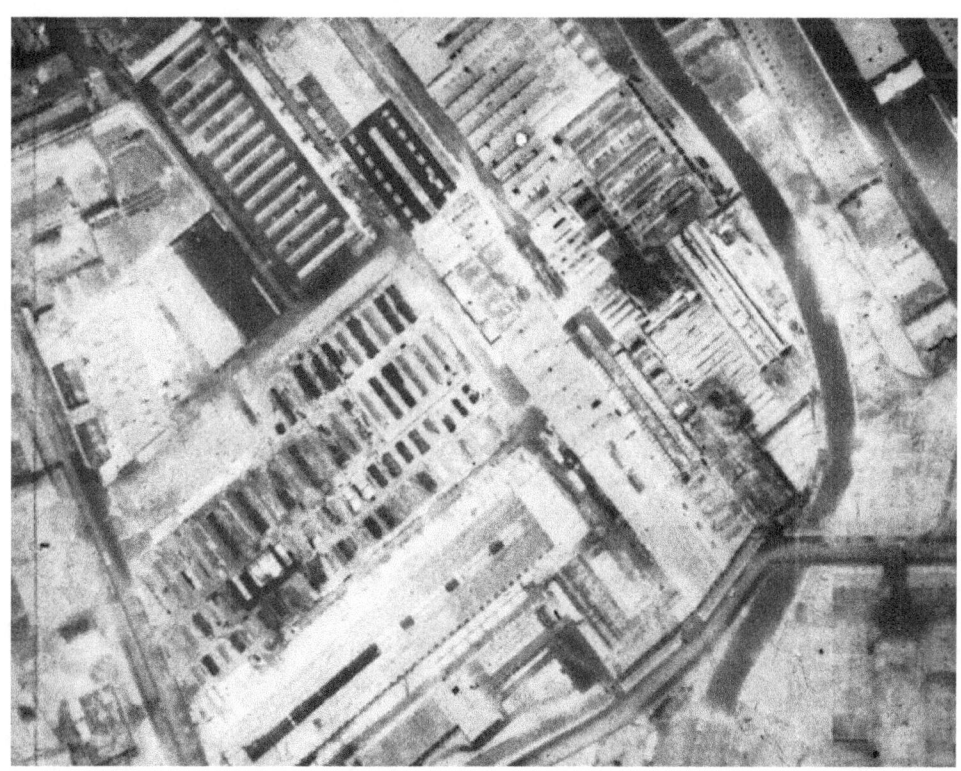

S/L Nettleton and his crew prior to the Augsburg raid.
Back Row L - R: F/Sgt Leonard Henry Mutter DFM, F/Sgt Frank Howe Harrison DFM, Sgt Donald Norman Huntley. Front Row L - R: P/O Patrick Arthur Dorehill DFM, S/L John Deering Nettleton VC, P/O D.O. Sands DFC, Flt Sgt Charles Fleming Churchill DFM

44 Sqn Lancasters

44 Sqn Lancaster L7548 KM-T lost on the Augsburg raid 17th of April 1942.

W/O Hubert Crum DFC. One of the Augsburg pilots who was shot down. He survived the crash landing and became a PoW.

W/O H V Crum's crew (in PoW camp). Back row L – R: ADE Dedman (2nd pilot), N Birkett (Nav), J Miller (MUG), B A Dowty (FE). Front: J Saunderson (W.Op), A Cobb (RG)

F/Sgt F H Harrison DFC, DFM. He flew as John Nettleton's bomb aimer on the Augsburg raid. After his time at Waddington, he flew with the Pathfinders.

Sgt R E Wing RG (F/L Sandford's crew)
Lost on Augsburg Raid

Sgt A S Morrow (W/O Lamb's crew)
Lost without trace 9th of May 1942.

F/O "Daisy/Ginger" Garwell DFC DFM
Lost on Augsburg Raid

F/O D J "Toffee" Appleton
KIA 23rd of November 1942.

Sgt Evans

F/Sgt P H H Thirkell
KIA 8th May 1942

'Home safe again' Lincoln Cathedral 1942

On right - the Saracen's Head hotel in Lincoln. A favourite haunt for aircrews.

This group sometimes flew with John Nettleton.
L – R Miles White, Roy Wilson, unknown, Roy Braines outside the Aircrew/Sergeants' Mess

44 Sqn Lancaster KM-O R545 after crashing at Gibraltar on 7th of July 1942. It ran over a piece of AAA shrapnel on the runway and burst a tyre causing the undercarriage to collapse. All of the crew escaped before the aircraft caught fire and burned out in the accident. The crew: P/O Stevens, F/O Tate, Sgt Shaddock, Sgt Stock, F/Sgt Houston, Sgt Nugent, Sgt Rowe.

F/L Ian 'Woody' Wood RAAF (AG) with his Rover. He was lost with S/L Nettleton in July 1943

P/O Denis Hartung of 44 Sqn

Three members of 44 Sqn. L – R: Sgt Hayward (FE) of P/O Silcock's crew, F/Sgt Ron Braines, Sgt Collinson (FE) of F/O Chrystal's crew.

Two 44 Sqn Flight Commanders – S/L John Nettleton VC and S/L R G Whitehead DFC. The dedication relates to F/L H R Locke, the Station Adjutant.

44 Squadron crew
L – R: F/Sgt Cole, ? , Sgt Jowers, Sgt Wiesberg, S/L Whitehead, F/O Wood, P/O Hartung.

Lancaster KM-C R5903 of 'A' Flight 44 Squadron in the summer of 1942 with her air and ground crew. This was taken just prior to a night flying test. Obviously, this Lancaster had been KM-B at some time or other. Note the fuselage windows making it an early model.

Crew of Lancaster KM-C R5903
L – R: F/O Ron Curtis (Nav), F/Sgt Paddy Copeland (W.Op), P/O Chris Chrystal (Pilot), Sgt Alan Collinson (FE), F/Sgt Dutton (MUG), F/Sgt Cole (BA), Sgt Murphy (RG).

The crew of Lancaster KM-C (Charlie) at Waddington in the summer of 1942. L -R: F/Sgt Cole (BA), F/Sgt Dutton (MUG), F/O Curtis (Nav), Sgt Collinson (FE), P/O Chrystal (Pilot), P/O 'Happy' Taylor (Pilot).

*Concentrated heavy and light flak over Bremen
13th of September 1942*

*Lancaster R5556 KM-C which would crash 13th of March 1943 while with Conversion Unit.
Note ventral turret.*

A newly arrived early Lancaster after delivery to 44 Squadron, January/February 1942. The fuselage windows were later discontinued.

A 44 Sqn Lancaster at Waddington in the summer of 1942

*Prior to take-off on Operation Robinson, the daylight raid on Le Creusot 17th October 1942.
L – R: F/O R V Allen, P/O A S Jess, F/Sgt F H Harrison DFM, S/L Gallagher DFC, S/L P Burnett,
Sgt Miller, Sgt J Bell.*

*Preparing for take off to Le Creusot 17th of October 1942
S/L F Burnett, Sgt A H Collinson, F/O R V Allen, F/O A S Jess,
F/Sgt F H Harrison DFM, Sgt A J Miller, Sgt J Bell, S/L Gallagher*

Three members of a 44 Sqn Lancaster crew in Algiers after a shuttle bombing trip on 22nd of June 1942.

Ready for Le Creusot

Harry the bomb aimer of 'Q' Queenie (W4268) of 44 Sqn. The aircraft was eventually lost over Munich on 21st December 1942.

Above and below: Wreckage of 44 Sqn Lancaster R5905 in Denmark after crash landing 24th of September 1942

Some of those who bombed Milan on 24th of October 1942.

'B' Flight of 44 Sqn on 25th October, 1942 at Waddington. Taken after the daylight raid on Milan.

P/O Vincent Giri (Rhodesian) killed on 20th of December 1942 when his Lancaster W4259 KM-D collided after take-off with 9 Sqn Lancaster W4182 also departing Waddington at the same time. Both crews died.

Crew of 44 Sqn Lancaster:

    F/S A.C.Elger

    Sgt G.D.McCready RCAF

    P/O V.N.Giri

    Sgt A.J.Easton

    Sgt R.I.Gunter

    Sgt C.Harmston

    Sgt E.Jackson

P/O V Giri

Approaching Mont.Blanc, Switzerland

Passing close to, but below the peak of Mont Blanc on 20th of November 1942 en route to Turin. Possibly another Lancaster flying above the mountain.

Part of 44 Squadron taken at Waddington in 1942.
1. Vic Allen.   2. Buck Ryan   3. Des Sands   4. F/L Taylor 5. Henry Locke (Adjutant)
6. S/L Stewart   7. W/C Smales DFC   8. F/L Barlow 9. S/L Nettleton   10. S/L Burnett 11. Bailey
12. F/L Evans   13. Unknown   14 F/O Wakeford

View of a Lancaster from the rear gunner's position

Air and Ground Crew of "Digger" when it had completed 33 raids.
Back: 2nd Sgt Brook, 3rd F/Sgt Gover, 4th F/O Barley (RNZAF), Front: 3rd Cpl Hudson

Same aircraft, different crew. "Digger" had now completed 43 raids. The ice creams denote raids carried out over Italy. Crew: 'Ging', 'Danny', 'Stinky', 'Lil', 'Lucky', 'K' and 'B'.

F/O C T Holland
KIA 13/14th of September 1942

F/O L.O. "Gunner" Halls DFC
KIA 5/6th of June 1942

F/O P A Ball DFM
KIA 4/5th August 1942

Memorial to the crew of Lancaster ED355 KM-D which crashed in Holland 17th December 1942 after being shot down. The remains of this Lancaster were discovered in 1951 during road reconstruction and this memorial was erected nearby. As well as the names of the crew, that of Jacob Corn Nagelhout, a Dutch resistance member who was born in nearby Woudsend has been appended to the stone, noting that he was killed on active service 15th of April 1945.

Crew: F/Sgt J.G.Dening RAAF,
Sgt J.A.Callan
P/O M.A.Nias
Sgt G.B.Wilkinson
Sgt L.G.Powell
Sgt W.McB J Stark RCAF
Sgt E.Croal RAAF

F/Sgt E Croal RAAF (AG) killed 17th of December 1942.

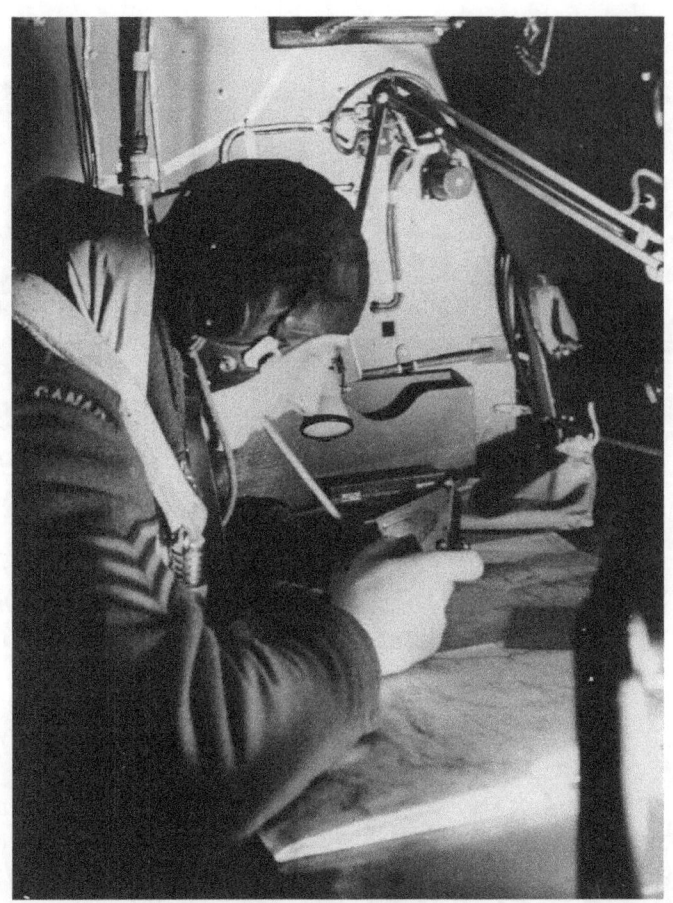
The Navigator

The Wireless Operator

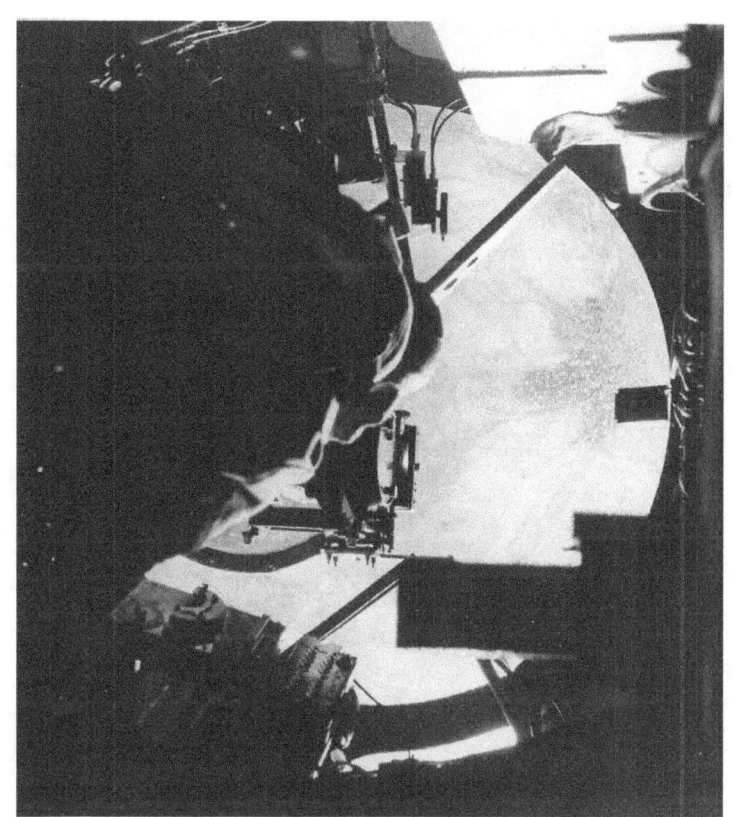

The Bomb Aimer

The Flight Engineer.

Lancaster Instrument Panel

Three of the workers. Sgt Pike centre

Cpl Pat Green, R/T Operator. She ended the war with a Mention in Despatches.

WAAF Doreen Byrne

Some of the WAAF members of the Parachute Section at Waddington. Middle of the front row is Doris Laird.

Harl Hogan (RAAF) of 44 Squadron

Parachute packer Ivy Draper

WAAF's of Waddington MT Section in 1942.

ACW 'Pip' Beck at 18, one of the first wireless operators to arrive at Waddington.

Waddington WAAFs
L – R: 'Bobby' (Telephone operator), Doris Mackintosh – Teleprinter operator, ? , ?, Pat Greene

Front of 'Pro Bono Publico' of 44 Squadron.
The light coloured bombs in the nose art denote daylight raids.

Doris Laird of the parachute packing section.

Bud Gill with the kitchen staff (the bacon and egg girls) of the Sgt's Mess

Miles White – he does not appear too impressed by the photographer!

Aircrew
Left - 'Bud' Gill, a Canadian on 44 Sqn, centre
'Slim' Cole of 420 Sqn RCAF and unknown on right.

Sgt H V Winch
KIA 27/28th August 1942

Postcards sometimes made by crews on return from a raid.

Waddington Lancaster 'Barbara Mary'

This Memorial to the crew of Lancaster ED305 of 44 Sqn in Fredericia, Denmark, was unveiled in March 2013. They were lost in the sea off Middelfart, Denmark on a 'gardening' sortie and are commemorated on the Runnymede Memorial.

The MT Section, Waddington

R5493 Walter Holland marshaller. Alf Beacon driving tractor in March 1942.

44 Sqn Lancaster W4126 KM-B at Woodford. Club House and old hangars in background.

44 Sqn Lancaster W4126 KM-B crash site 7th of December 1942. Texel Netherlands.

Testing the tyre pressure of Avro Lancaster R5540 of No 44 Squadron Conversion Flight at RAF Waddington, September 1942.

F/L T P E Barlow and his crew

44 Sqn Lancaster R5508, Waddington 1942
L-R: Sgt Miller (W.Op/AG), F/Sgt Glynn (BA), W/O F Stott DFM, (Pilot), unknown,
F/Sgt Willan (Nav), F/S Allison (W.Op), F S Braines (AG)

L. Warren-Smith (Pilot)
KIA 24/25th March 1942

Sgt E Forman (FE)
KIA 31st July/1st of August 1942

January 1943

The year began with the official formation on New Year's Day of the Canadian 6 Group, and the handing over to it of the former 4 Group stations in North Yorkshire on which its squadrons had been lodging. Eventually, all Canadian squadrons would find a home in the group, which was financed by Canada and controlled by Harris, but, initially, there were eight founder members, including 408 and 420 Squadrons, which had left 5 Group during the autumn. Further south, a continuation of the Oboe trials would occupy the first two weeks, during which 109 Squadron marked for small forces of 1 and 5 Group Lancasters at Essen on seven occasions and Duisburg once. For the first time, the cloud cover and ever-present blanket of industrial haze would have no bearing on the outcome of the raid as reliance on e.t.a., DR and Gee was cast aside in favour of Oboe, at least, that is, at targets within the device's range. Until the advent of mobile transmitter stations late in the war, Oboe would be restricted by the curvature of the earth and the altitude at which Mosquitos could fly, but this meant that the entire Ruhr lay within range of Harris's bombers. That said, the success of a raid would still rely on the ability of the Path Finders to back up the initial Oboe markers and maintain a supply of target indicators (TIs) on the aiming point.

It was for the first of these forays against Essen on the 3rd, that 5 Group detailed nineteen Lancasters, including three belonging to 44 (Rhodesia) Squadron for the crews of W/C Smales, P/O Watt and Sgt Morris. They departed Waddington between 17.18 and 17.22, each carrying a cookie and ten SBCs of 4lb incendiaries. The Path Finders dropped warning flares at various points short of the target, and red and green flares to identify the aiming point over the Krupp complex in the Borbeck district. W/C Smales described it as a new technique for high-level bombing, and the 44 (Rhodesia) Squadron trio attacked from 20,000 to 22,000 feet between 19.47 and 19.49, observing some bursts, but not their precise location. Sgt Morris reached 23,000 feet, at which altitude his controls remained light and sensitive, and he believed he could have reached higher. Even at that height, flak knocked out his mid-upper turret and compromised the oxygen supply to a number of crew positions. Much valuable information was gleaned from this second "live" trial of Oboe, the first having been mounted by a very small number of Path Finder Lancasters and Mosquitos against Düsseldorf on New Year's Eve.

S/L Nettleton VC returned to the squadron from 1661 Conversion Unit on the 4th, at the same time as the former 44 (Rhodesia) Squadron stalwart, F/L Henry Maudslay, arrived at 50 Squadron following a spell as an instructor at 1654 Conversion Unit. Since his tour with 44 Squadron, Maudslay had been involved in test flying, and had taken part in the Thousand Bomber raids in May and June 1942. Some three months hence, he would become a founder member of 617 Squadron, and serve as a flight commander under W/C Guy Gibson, only to lose his life during the epic Operation Chastise in May.

The squadron was not invited to take part in the next two forays against Essen mounted on the 4th and 7th, which involved twenty-nine 1 Group Lancasters and nineteen from 5 Group respectively, but received orders on the 8th to prepare six Lancasters for that night's Oboe trial over Duisburg, as part of an overall heavy force of thirty-eight Lancasters. This was the day on which the Path Finder Force was granted group status as 8 Group, and the stations it occupied were transferred from 3 Group. For the purpose of this book, the titles Path Finders and 8 Group are interchangeable. A further six 44 (Rhodesia) Squadron crews were briefed for mining duties in the Daffodil and Quince gardens, respectively in the southern reaches of The Sound, between Denmark and Sweden, and Kiel Bay. They took off together between 17.04 and 17.56, with W/C Smales and S/L Whitehead the senior pilots among the bombing element and F/Ls Ingham and Osborn leading the horticulturalists. It was destined to be a testing night over the western Baltic, which left F/L Osborn, F/O Silcock and F/Sgt Horwood unable to establish a pinpoint in Kiel Bay in the face of ten-tenths low cloud. Some 140 miles to the east, conditions were more favourable, and F/L Ingham was able to get beneath the 1,000-foot cloud base to deliver his mines from 600 feet at 21.27, picking up a single bullet hole in the mid-upper turret for his pains. W4176 disappeared without trace with the crew of P/O Shattock, and W4277 crashed near Abenra in southern Denmark with fatal consequences for the crew of Sgt Paige RCAF. Meanwhile, at Duisburg, five 44 (Rhodesia) Squadron crews had approached the aiming point in clear skies at 20,000 and 21,000 feet, ten thousand feet above a layer of ten-tenths cloud, which completely obscured the ground. They focussed purely on the Path Finders' red and green parachute flares to establish the position of the target, and five let their bomb loads go from 21,000 to 22,000 feet between 19.24 and 19.26 in the face of intense and accurate flak. Sgt Baldwin and crew arrived late, at 19.35, and bombed from 12,000 feet, aiming at white flares, which were on the point of fading out. No assessment of the results was possible, and flashes beneath the cloud might have been from bombs or flak batteries.

The squadron sat out the next three Essen raids on the nights of the 9/10th, 11/12th and 12/13th, involving fifty, seventy-two and fifty-five Lancasters from 1 and 5 Groups, but was invited to join in on the final raid of the current series on the 13th. Twelve of the sixty-six Lancasters were provided by 44 (Rhodesia) Squadron and took off between 16.47 and 17.27 with W/C Smales the senior pilot on duty. W/O Sanderson and crew lost the use of their radio receiver as they crossed the English coast, and jettisoned their cookie and incendiaries, leaving the others to continue on to the central Ruhr, which lay beneath seven to ten-tenths cloud with tops at 7,000 to 10,000 feet. Some crews arrived about fifteen minutes early, in the light of a moon that had waxed to half-size, and all was eerily quiet, until others started to bomb on DR seven or eight minutes before H-Hour, bringing the flak batteries to life. As had happened on previous operations, the Oboe Mosquito element experienced technical difficulties, two returning without marking, while the flares of the third failed to ignite. The Path Finder Lancaster crews took over responsibility, and the main force crews were guided to the aiming point by red warning flares, while greens and whites marked the release-point. The 44 (Rhodesia) Squadron crews bombed from 16,000 to 20,000 feet between 19.32 and 19.37, all the time under fire from a box-barrage and returned safely with nothing of interest to report at debriefing. Bombing photos showed only cloud, and it was left to local sources to report that more than a hundred buildings had been either destroyed or seriously damaged.

A new Air Ministry directive was issued on the 14th, which authorized the area bombing of the French ports providing a home for U-Boots with concrete bunkers and support facilities. A list was drawn up accordingly, headed by Lorient, and included St-Nazaire, Brest and La Pallice. As mentioned earlier, between February 1941 and January 1942, the Germans had built three giant concrete structures K1, K2 and K3 on the southernmost point of Lorient's Keroman Peninsula. They were capable of housing and servicing thirty U-Boots and providing accommodation for their crews and were impregnable to the bombs available to Bomber Command at the time. The purpose of this new campaign, therefore, was to render the town and port uninhabitable, and block or sever all road and rail communications to them. The first of the series of nine attacks on the port over the ensuing four weeks took place that very night at the hands of a force of 122 aircraft in the absence of 5 Group, and, despite accurate marking by the Path Finder element, the main force bombing was scattered and destroyed a modest 120 buildings.

5 Group's involvement with Lorient would come in February, and, in the meantime, Harris planned two operations against the "Big City", Berlin, beginning on the 16th, for which a force of 201 aircraft was made ready. This would be the first raid on Germany's capital for fourteen months and would bring with it the first use of custom-designed target indicators (TIs). The main force was to consist predominantly of 5 Group Lancasters, with others from 1 Group, while eleven Halifaxes would be included in the Path Finder element, and those reaching the target would be sharing the airspace over it with the broadcaster, Richard Dimbleby, who would be in a 106 Squadron Lancaster captained by W/C Guy Gibson. 44 (Rhodesia) Squadron detailed fourteen Lancasters, which took off between 16.18 and 16.49 with W/C Smales and S/L Nettleton the senior pilots on duty and headed for Mandø Island off the west coast of Jutland. The route would take the bomber stream across southern Jutland to the western Baltic, to follow the coastline eastwards until reaching Swinemünde, from where they would swing to the south for the run on the target. Sgt Hordon and crew had reached Rømø island, when an explosion occurred, it is believed, in the Gee-box, which caused it and other electronic devices to fail, and they had no choice but to turn back. W/C Smales and crew had progressed as far as Swinemünde, and were at 16,000 feet, when ED309 was hit by heavy flak at 19.52. A piece of shrapnel penetrated the cockpit and struck the pilot's right arm, causing a serious and painful wound. Smales ordered the bombs to be jettisoned "live" over the port and turned for home. On board as an observer was the Daily Mail Air Correspondent, who would pay tribute to Smales for his courage in bringing back his aircraft and crew in such circumstances.

The remaining twelve crews pressed on to reach the target under moonlight, with good visibility above six-tenths cloud at 10,000 feet, through which the built-up area could be seen clearly. The 44 (Rhodesia) Squadron crews mostly failed to see the red warning flares and picked up the lakes and autobahns to reach the city, and it was then that red and green TIs were seen to burst on what was assumed to be the aiming point. They dropped their cookie and incendiary bomb loads from 14,000 to 20,000 feet between 20.23 and 20.40, recognising that they were over the southern outskirts of the city, where the Tempelhof district could be identified. All returned safely to Waddington, but five of the Lancasters were handed back to their ground crews with holes in them, courtesy of the intense flak barrage. At debriefing, Sgt Calcutt and crew reported overshooting Berlin by sixty miles, before turning back and bombing blindly after the bomb-aimer's clear vision panel iced over. Others observed black smoke rising through 5,000 feet as they turned away, and many were unconvinced of the effectiveness of the raid, and this was borne out by local sources. One notable scalp was the ten-thousand-seater Deutschlandhalle, the largest covered venue in Europe, which was hosting the annual circus as the bombers approached and was efficiently emptied of people and animals with only minor injuries to a few people. Shortly afterwards, incendiaries set fire to the building and reduced it to ruins. Remarkably, only a single Lancaster failed to return from this operation, but the balance would be redressed somewhat twenty-four hours later.

170 Lancasters and seventeen Halifaxes were made ready on 1, 4, 5 and 8 Group stations for the return to Berlin that night. 44 (Rhodesia) Squadron loaded eleven of its own with a cookie and incendiaries and dispatched them from Waddington between 16.59 and 17.16 with F/L Ingham the senior pilot on duty. They would follow the same route as for twenty-four hours earlier and had a three-and-a-half hour outward flight ahead of them, stalked constantly by night-fighters once they reached western Denmark. Sgt Johnson and crew stumbled into a cone of searchlights in the Kiel area, and were bombarded by flak, some of which hit home. Unable to push through it, Sgt Johnson opted to dive towards the clearly visible docks, and released the bombs from 5,000 feet into the built-up area of the

town, where the incendiaries started a large fire, that would remain visible for fifty miles into the homeward journey. The others reached the target area to be greeted by eight to ten-tenths cloud with tops at between 10,000 and 14,000 feet, through which it was possible for most to pick out the Müggelsee to the south-east of the Capital, from where a timed run was carried out to the target. Some crews failed to see any flares, which was understandable as the Path Finders arrived thirty-seven minutes late, and so bombed on e.t.a., or DR. Some did benefit from target marking, which, sadly, was once more concentrated over the southern fringes of the city rather than over the centre. The 44 (Rhodesia) Squadron crews carried out their attacks from 15,000 to 20,500 feet between 20.30 and 21.12, and, by the latter time, some Path Finder flares were evident. Little was seen of the results of the bombing, and local reports confirmed that the operation had not been successful, and no significant damage had occurred. The disappointment was compounded by the loss of twenty-two bombers, 11.8% of those dispatched, and many of these disappeared without trace in the Baltic or North Sea, which was the fate of the squadron's ED318 with Sgt Calcutt and his crew. F/Sgt Raymond's rear gunner reported observing five parachutes as they left the target.

A force of seventy-nine Lancasters and three Mosquitos was detailed to resume the Oboe trials programme at Essen on the 21st, for which 44 (Rhodesia) Squadron briefed eight crews and dispatched them from Waddington between 17.20 and 17.26 with S/L Nettleton the senior pilot on duty. All reached the target area, noting that condensation trails were forming at 18,000 feet to advertise their presence to the German defences. There was a question as to the cloud conditions, some reporting clear skies and others ten-tenths cloud, neither of which would have mattered if the Oboe marking had worked and been visible to all. In the event, the entire Ruhr was concealed beneath thick industrial haze, which proved to be impenetrable. As far as the crews of S/L Nettleton, F/L Osborn and F/Sgts Baldwin and Horwood were concerned, there were no Path Finder markers to point the way, while F/O Silcock, W/O Sanderson, F/Sgt Raymond and Sgt Hordon relied on red Path Finder flares, and the bombs went down either on them or on e.t.a., or DR from 12,000 to 22,000 feet between 19.45 and 20.03 in the face of an intense flak barrage. Four Lancasters failed to return, and the outcome of the raid remained undetermined.

The Oboe trials programme moved to Düsseldorf on the 23rd, the huge industrial city situated some fifteen miles south-south-east of Essen. 1, 5 and 8 Groups assembled a force of eighty Lancasters and three Mosquitos, of which seven Lancasters belonging to 44 (Rhodesia) Squadron were loaded at Waddington with a cookie each and a dozen SBCs of 4lb incendiaries. They took off between 16.56 and 17.43 with S/L Whitehead the senior pilot on duty but lost the services of Sgt Hordon and crew to oxygen system failure over the North Sea. Those reaching the target area found ten-tenths cloud at 12,000 feet, heavy, accurate flak and Path Finder flares drifting towards the cloud tops. The 44 (Rhodesia) Squadron element bombed on Path Finder flares from 20,000 to 22,500 feet between 19.52 and 20.00 but saw nothing of the outcome through the cloud. Lorient had faced another assault on this night with a token Lancaster presence in a force of 121 aircraft, which inflicted further heavy damage. The fourth raid took place on the night of the 26/27th at the hands of an initial force of 157 aircraft, which attacked in poor weather conditions.

Düsseldorf was selected again as the primary target on the 27th, when the Path Finders were to use ground marking for the first time, rather than skymarking. Ground markers, which were TIs fused to burst and cascade just above the ground, could be seen through thin or partial cloud and industrial haze, and were much more reliable than the previously-employed parachute flares that drifted in the wind. However, skymarkers would remain an indispensable part of target marking techniques on nights of heavy cloud or to use in combination with ground markers. From this night onwards, Path Finder heavy aircraft would back-up the Mosquito-laid Oboe markers, to ensure that the aiming point remained marked throughout the operation. A heavy force of 124 Lancasters and thirty-three Halifaxes was made ready on 1, 4, 5 and 8 Group stations, 44 (Rhodesia) Squadron providing eleven of the Lancasters, which took off between 17.27 and 17.52 with S/L Whitehead the senior pilot on duty. F/Sgt Horwood and crew became victims of icing conditions, and, despite trying a variety of throttle settings, could not maintain height and jettisoned their load. Shortly afterwards, F/L Osborn also abandoned his sortie after failing to climb above 17,500 feet and using excessive fuel in his attempts to do so. The remaining Waddington crews pressed on to reach the target and find a thin layer of five to ten-tenths cloud at 10,000 feet, through which the red and green TIs could be seen burning on the aiming point. The 44 (Rhodesia) Squadron crews carried out their part in the proceedings from 16,000 to 21,000 feet between 20.00 and 20.12, and returned safely, impressed by the potential of ground marking, and confident that they had hit the aiming point. This was confirmed by local reports, which spoke of widespread destruction in southern districts, amounting to 456 houses, ten industrial premises and nine public buildings destroyed or seriously damaged, and many others affected to a lesser extent.

Seventy-five aircraft of 1, 4 and 6 Groups carried out the fifth attack of the series on Lorient on the night of the 29/30th. Another new blind-bombing device, the ground-mapping H2S radar, was to be employed operationally for the first time at Hamburg on the 30th, for which a force of 135 Lancasters of 1, 5 and 8 Groups would be joined by thirteen H2S-equipped Path Finder Stirlings and Halifaxes of 7 and 35 Squadrons respectively. The H2S equipment was housed in a cupola aft of the bomb bay and projected an image of the terrain onto a cathode-ray tube in the navigator's compartment. It was the job of the operator to interpret what he was seeing, and guide the pilot to the aiming point, but this was no easy task, particularly with the Mk I set, and it proved difficult to distinguish particular ground features in the jumble of images presented to him. It would take much practice and experience to master the device, but, in time, and once the Mk III set became available, it would become an indispensable tool, which, ultimately, would become standard equipment for main force as well as Path Finder aircraft. 44 (Rhodesia) Squadron made ready a dozen Lancasters loading each with a cookie and incendiaries and sent them on their way from Waddington between 23.50 and 00.36 with S/Ls Nettleton and Whitehead the senior pilots on duty. As mentioned frequently before, north-western Germany had a "gatekeeper" in the form of weather fronts, which, on this night, contained severe icing conditions and electrical storms for the bombers to negotiate as they made their way across the North Sea. The crews of Sgts Hordon and Johnson fell victim to the conditions at the mid-point of the North Sea crossing and were unable either to climb into clear air or maintain height. On return, each would report a gunner suffering the effects of frostbite. This left ten crews to fly the 44 (Rhodesia) Squadron flag over Germany's second city, where they encountered between zero and ten-tenths cloud, according to which crew report one reads, with tops at between 6,000 and 15,000 feet. They bombed onto flares or TIs from 18,000 to 21,000 feet between 03.03 and 03.21, and observed the reflections of explosions in the cloud, which led to a consensus that the operation had been effective. This was partially confirmed by local reports that mentioned seventy-one large fires, but much of the bombing fell either into the Elbe or into marshland outside of the city. This would have been disappointing to the raid planners, as Hamburg, with the nearby coastline and wide River Elbe, was an ideal target for H2S, and should have been easy to identify on the cathode-ray tubes.

W/C Smales had been undergoing treatment for his flak wound at the RAF Hospital Rauceby and was posted from the squadron at the end of the month to be succeeded by W/C Nettleton VC. During the course of the month, the squadron took part in ten operations and dispatched ninety sorties for the loss of three Lancasters and their crews.

February 1943

It was a time of honing and refining for Bomber Command, in preparation for the launching of a major campaign a month hence. February opened with the posting of Cologne as the target for an experimental operation on the 2nd, in which two marking methods were to be employed. Situated just to the south of the Ruhr, the Rhineland's capital city was within range of Oboe Mosquitos, and these were to be supplemented by Path Finder aircraft relying on H2S. A force of 159 heavies included seventy-four 5 Group Lancasters, ten of them provided by 44 (Rhodesia) Squadron, while two Path Finder Mosquitos of 109 Squadron carried the Oboe markers. The 44 (Rhodesia) Squadron element departed Waddington between 18.08 and 18.32 with F/L Ingham the senior pilot on duty, but lost the services of Sgt Johnson and crew, who had reached an impressive 23,000 feet before their starboard-outer engine failed, and severe icing compounded their challenges. The others pressed on through severe cold, which caused almost all of the guns to freeze solid but reached the target to find a layer of two to five tenths thin cloud up to 8,000 feet and patches above. This afforded good vertical visibility and a clear sight of the red and green skymarkers, even from some distance on approach to the bombing run. There was some debate as to the accuracy and concentration of the markers, which a few crews from other squadrons would report as five to ten miles to the north-west of the city, while others described them as scattered. Most of the 44 (Rhodesia) Squadron crews picked up the red and green TIs burning on the ground and had them in the bomb sight as they delivered their cookie and incendiaries from 19,000 to 21,000 feet between 21.02 and 21.15. Although few were able to observe their own bombs burst, many scattered fires were evident, the glow from which could be seen from a hundred miles into the return journey. Local reports confirmed bombs falling all over the city, but nowhere with concentration, and damage was, consequently, not commensurate with the size of the force and the effort expended. Five aircraft failed to return, and among the three missing Lancasters was W4819, which collided over southern Holland with a 102 Squadron Halifax while outbound, and crashed at 21.00, killing Sgt Hordon and his crew.

Hamburg was posted as the target on the 3rd, for which a force of 263 aircraft was made ready, unusually, with Halifaxes representing the most populous type followed by Stirlings. 5 Group contributed forty of the sixty-two Lancasters, seven of them belonging to 44 (Rhodesia) Squadron, and they departed Waddington between 18.03 and 18.25 with S/L Whitehead the senior pilot on duty. Fifteen of the 5 Group crews turned back on encountering towering cloud and severe icing conditions over the North Sea, and most of them cited frozen guns. Sgt Pennington and crew were still in cloud at 22,000 feet when they turned back, and W/O Sanderson and F/Sgt Einarson lost their bearings while enveloped in cloud and could not make up the time after establishing their positions at the Dutch coast. The four remaining squadron representatives arrived in the target area to find nine to ten-tenths cloud, which they estimated topped out at between 7,000 and 8,000 feet, while 207 Squadron crews reported the cloud to be at 17,000 to 20,000 feet. Scattered red and green Path Finder H2S-laid skymarker flares were in the bomb sights as the 44 (Rhodesia) Squadron crews bombed from 21,000 to 22,500 feet between 21.05 and 21.13, but no results were observed, and the impression was of an ineffective attack. This was confirmed by local reports, which mentioned forty-five large fires but no concentration or significant damage, and this disappointing outcome cost the Command sixteen aircraft. The losses by type made interesting reading and would reflect the trend for the remainder of the year, with the Stirlings suffering the highest numerical and percentage casualties, followed by the Halifaxes and Wellingtons, with the Lancasters clearly at the top of the food chain.

A return to Italy was posted on the 4th with Turin the target for a force of 188 aircraft, while 128 others, mostly Wellingtons, were prepared to continue the assault on Lorient. 5 Group contributed forty-eight Lancasters to the former and eight with freshman crews to the latter, 44 (Rhodesia) Squadron putting up eight Lancasters for Italy. They departed Waddington between 18.05 and 18.16 with F/Ls Ingham and Walker the senior pilots on duty and followed the usual route across France. After crossing the Alps in cloud at 21,000 feet, they found conditions on the Italian side much improved, with clear skies and excellent visibility, which facilitated a visual confirmation of the accuracy of the Path Finder TIs. An estimated one hundred searchlights were active, and the flak defence had also been "beefed-up", but was still inaccurate and in keeping with expectations at an Italian target. *(Following a raid on a German target, a bomb symbol would be painted on the forward fuselage of a bomber, but after a raid on an Italian target, the symbol would be an ice-cream cone.)* Red TIs were much in evidence in the city centre as they carried out their attacks from 9,000 to 14,000 feet between 21.44 and 21.57, and returning crews were enthusiastic about the effectiveness of their work. Local sources confirmed later that serious and widespread damage had resulted.

The seventh raid in the series on Lorient was posted on the 7th, and would be by far the largest to date, employing 323 aircraft, of which forty-three of eighty Lancasters were provided by 5 Group. It was to be conducted in two waves, an hour apart, and it was for the first wave that 44 (Rhodesia) Squadron made ready five Lancasters for freshman crews and sent them on their way shortly after 18,00. They arrived in the target area to find clear skies and ideal bombing conditions, which they exploited after making a visual identification of the aiming point confirmed by Path Finder TIs. Three of them delivered their cookie and incendiaries from 9,500 to 15,000 feet between 20.19 and 20.27 and returned to report an outstandingly destructive raid, which left a glow in the sky visible from the English coast. The second-phase element had the burning port as a beacon to draw them on, and they completed the port's destruction. Seven aircraft failed to return, including 44 (Rhodesia) Squadron's W4832, which was shot down into the sea at 20.30, killing the crew of F/Sgt Skinner. The fate of ED309 is uncertain, but it is believed that it also went into the sea, and took with it the predominantly RCAF crew of F/O Miller RCAF.

The crews of F/L Ingham and F/Sgts Morris and Raymond were called to briefing on the 8th to learn that they would be heading for the Baltic that night, F/L Ingham for the Spinach garden off the port of Gdynia, 780 miles away as the crow flies, but considerably more when routed to avoid the defences. The two NCO crews were bound for the Pollock garden, off Bornholm island to the south of the Swedish mainland, a mere 640 miles from Waddington, and all three took off together between 16.47 and 17.03. F/L Ingham reached his target area after an outward leg of almost five hours, only to find that the mines refused to release, and had to be jettisoned "live" into the briefed location from 500 feet at 21.43. Away to the north-west, the others successfully planted their vegetables from 800 and 700 feet at 20.56 and 21.37. F/Sgt Morris and crew had spent at least thirty minutes establishing their pinpoint, and were the last to land, at Bradwell Bay at 04.30, after almost eleven-and-a-half hours aloft.

Before the penultimate raid on Lorient took place, attention was switched to the important naval port of Wilhelmshaven, situated on the north-western coast of Jade Bay, some sixty miles to the west of Hamburg. A force of 177 aircraft was put together on the 11th, of which 129 were Lancasters, sixty-eight of them representing 5 Group. Seven Lancasters were made ready by 44 (Rhodesia) Squadron at Waddington, and they took off between 17.19 and 17.50 with S/L Whitehead the senior pilot on duty. The serviceability gremlins struck the crews of F/Sgt Raymond and F/O Robinson, who each had a starboard engine fail while outbound over the North Sea and had to turn back. The others reached the target area to find ten-tenths cloud with tops at around 10,000 feet, and the least reliable marking method, H2S skymarking, in progress. On the credit side, at a smaller, more compact urban target, like Wilhelmshaven, it was easier to interpret the images on the cathode-ray screens, and, on this night, great accuracy was achieved. The red and green flares were right over the aiming point as the 44 (Rhodesia) Squadron crews delivered their cookies and incendiaries from 15,000 to 20,500 between 19.59 and 20.17, but it was impossible to assess what was happening beneath the cloud until an enormous explosion took place, the glow from which lingered for ten minutes. Many crews commented on this at debriefings across the Command, and there must have been much speculation about the source, which turned out to be the naval ammunition depot at Mariensiel, situated to the south of the town. It blew itself into oblivion, devastating 120 acres and causing widespread damage in the dockyard and town.

It was back to Lorient for ten 44 (Rhodesia) Squadron crews on the 13th, who learned at briefing that they were to be part of the largest force yet sent to the port. 466 aircraft were made ready, 103 of them 5 Group Lancasters, and those representing 44 (Rhodesia) Squadron departed Waddington between 19.14 and 19.37 with S/L Nettleton the senior pilot on duty. Nettleton was still recorded in the ORB in the rank of squadron leader, but, having succeeded W/C Smales at the start of the month, had probably been elevated officially to acting wing commander rank by this time, and had taken Smales' navigator, F/L Sands DFC, into his crew. There were no early returns to deplete the squadron's impact, and, as they began the Channel crossing in the Exmouth area, both Nettleton and F/L Walker reported observing flares going down over the target as the first wave attacked. They located the target with ease in excellent visibility under clear skies, which allowed them to make a visual identification of both aiming points, the U-Boot pens on the Keroman peninsula and the town, before smoke began to drift across the area. The 44 (Rhodesia) Squadron crews bombed from 9,000 to 14,000 feet between 21.30 and 21.42 and returned safely to report massive fires right across the town and the port area.

Orders came through from 5 Group on the 14th to make ready for a return to Italy that night for a crack this time at Milan. A force of 142 Lancasters of 1, 5 and 8 Groups was assembled to carry out the attack, while 243 Halifaxes, Stirlings and Wellingtons were made ready to try their hand at Cologne. Among the eighty-nine 5 Group Lancasters were nine representing 44 (Rhodesia) Squadron, which took off from Waddington between 18.45 and 19.08 with S/L Whitehead the senior pilot on duty. Sgt Johnson and crew were struggling to maintain height and turned back when some thirty miles off the French coast. The others continued on to reach the target area after a trouble-free outward flight and were guided to the aiming point by green and red Path Finder route-marker flares. They were able to identify the aiming point visually and carried out their bombing-runs from 8,500 to 14,000 feet between 22.36 and 22.49, seven releasing all-incendiary loads and two a cookie plus incendiaries. Most loads were observed to hit the city, and many fires were reported, the glow from which remained visible for at least a hundred miles into the return journey. The operation was hailed as a success, although no local report was forthcoming to confirm or deny.

The final raid of the series on Lorient was posted on the 16th, for which another large force was made ready, this time of 377 aircraft. Of seventy-five Lancasters offered by 5 Group, eight were made ready by 44 (Rhodesia) Squadron at Waddington and took off between 18.45 and 19.07 with F/L Walker the senior pilot on duty. They were among the earlier arrivals at the target, and found clear conditions aided by an almost full moon, which enabled them to deliver their cookies and SBCs of incendiaries on red TIs onto the Keroman peninsula from 8,500 to 14,500 feet between 20.50 and 20.53. The majority of the force dropped incendiaries into the town, which, after nine attacks, 1,926 sorties and four thousand tons of bombs, was now a desolate and deserted ruin.

Preparations were put in hand on the 18th to make ready 195 aircraft for the second of four raids on Wilhelmshaven during the month. 5 Group contributed seventy-nine Lancasters, including ten belonging to 44 (Rhodesia) Squadron, which departed Waddington between 18.01 and 18.22 with F/Ls Ingham, Osborn and Walker the senior pilots on duty. All reached the target area, which was identified visually in excellent conditions, and red TIs were in the bomb sights as the 44 (Rhodesia) Squadron bomb bays were emptied from 14,000 to 20,500 feet between 20.30 and 20.41. Bombs were observed to burst and fires to spring up, and returning crews were confident that an accurate and concentrated attack had taken place. However, bombing photos revealed that the operation had been a failure, after the main weight of bombs had fallen into open country to the west of the town, and this demonstrated how easy it was to be misled by what the eye saw. Local reports admitted to a number of bombs hitting the town, causing no serious damage or casualties.

Twenty-four hours later a force of 338 aircraft set off to return to Wilhelmshaven, with Wellingtons and Halifaxes accounting for 230 of the number and Stirlings and Lancasters the rest. 5 Group dispatched thirty-three Lancasters, with only those of F/L Osborn, F/Sgt Horwood and Sgt Drysdale representing 44 (Rhodesia) Squadron. They departed Waddington between 17.58 and 18.06, and, once again, found the conditions to be excellent, with visibility that enabled crews to identify the coastline and line themselves up on the target, which was being marked by green TIs. Bombing took place from 16,000 and 16,500 feet between 20.06 and 20.10, and the bursts and fires observed in the docks area and the town left the crews with the impression that another successful raid had taken place. However, bombing photos told a different story, and revealed that the Path Finder marking had fallen to the north of the built-up area, partly through reliance upon outdated maps, which would now be replaced. Of the twelve missing aircraft five were Stirlings and represented 8.9% of those dispatched, thus confirming the type's vulnerability compared with the Lancaster and Halifax. The four missing Lancasters represented a 7.7% loss rate, while no Halifaxes failed to return, but this would prove to be a blip. During the course of the year, the food chain would become established with Lancasters firmly at the top, Halifaxes in the middle and Stirlings at the bottom, when all types operated together.

An all-Lancaster main force from 1 and 5 Groups was made ready to attack the U-Boot construction yards at Vegesack near Bremen on the 21st, with Path Finder Lancasters, Halifaxes and Stirlings to provide the marking in an overall force of 143 aircraft. Seventy-four of the Lancasters were put up by 5 Group, and eight of these departed Waddington between 18.37 and 18.56 to represent 44 (Rhodesia) Squadron with S/L Whitehead the senior pilot on duty. The squadron's excellent record of serviceability continued on this night, and all reached the target area after attempting to follow scattered route-marker flares. They were greeted by ten-tenths cloud at 3,000 feet, above which, red and green skymarker flares drifted down, also in a somewhat scattered manner and up to nine minutes late to join the TIs dimly visible burning on the ground. The 44 (Rhodesia) Squadron crews carried out their attacks from 15,000 to 20,000 feet between 20.47 and 21.05, and a considerable glow from beneath the clouds suggested a successful outcome. Bombing photos depicted only cloud, and no local report was available to provide details of damage.

115 aircraft of 6 and 8 Groups concluded the current series of raids on Wilhelmshaven on the night of the 24/25th, with indeterminate results, and the port would now be left in peace until October 1944. A major operation against Nuremberg was posted on stations across the Command on the 25th, and 5 Group responded with a maximum effort of 101 Lancasters, eleven of them made ready by 44 (Rhodesia) Squadron at Waddington. They took off between 19.25 and 20.00 with F/L Walker the senior pilot on duty, and each Lancaster carrying a cookie and SBCs of 4lb and 30lb incendiaries. They all made it to the target area, which they found to be under cloudless skies, and had to wait for the Path Finder element to turn up, some sixteen to twenty minutes after the raid was due to begin. They dropped marker flares on the approach, and the 5 Group crews carried out a time-and-distance run to the aiming point, which was marked by red and green TIs. The 44 (Rhodesia) Squadron element bombed from 8,500 to 18,000 feet between 23.21 and 23.34, and all of the indications, including what looked like an oil-depot exploding, suggested a concentrated attack, which fell predominantly in northern and western districts. This was confirmed by local reports, which mentioned damage to three hundred buildings, but also revealed that bombs had fallen onto other communities and open country up to seven miles to the north.

When Cologne was posted as the target on the 26th, 5 Group responded with ninety Lancasters, eleven of which were made ready by 44 (Rhodesia) Squadron at Waddington as part of an overall force of 427 aircraft. They took off between 18.15 and 18.47 with S/L Whitehead the senior pilot on duty, but lost Sgt Drysdale and crew to an unserviceable rear turret early on to dent the squadron's recent run of operations without "boomerangs". The others all reached the Cologne area on a night of almost perfect serviceability for the group and good vertical visibility for the bomb-aimers, some of whom were able to identify the bridges over the Rhine. It seems from some comments from other squadrons that a proportion of the force bombed before the Path Finders had a chance to mark, but, once the red and green TIs were seen on the ground, the 44 (Rhodesia) Squadron crews aimed their cookies and incendiaries at them from 15,000 to 21,000 feet between 21.19 and 21.31. Fires were reported in the city centre, as were decoys to the west of the city, and bombing photos showed fire tracks and smoke that suggested an effective raid. In fact, a large proportion of the effort had fallen to the south-west of the city, and perhaps, only a quarter had landed in the built-up area, causing much damage to housing, minor industry and public buildings.

Having dealt with Lorient under the January Directive, attention now turned upon St-Nazaire, situated further south along the Biscay coast. The force of 437 aircraft assembled on the 28th included a contribution from 5 Group of eighty-nine Lancasters, of which ten represented 44 (Rhodesia) Squadron. They departed Waddington between 18.39 and 19.05 with F/L Walker the senior pilot on duty, and all reached the target area to find clear skies and good visibility, with only a little ground haze to contend with. They bombed on red TIs from 10,000 to 18,000 feet between 21.13 and 21.38, and it was clear from the many explosions and at least forty fires burning in the docks that the port was undergoing an ordeal of destruction. W4137 suffered an undercarriage collapse on landing at 00.25, and was damaged beyond repair, although without injury to Sgt Johnson RNZAF and his crew. Post-raid reconnaissance revealed that the marking had been concentrated and the bombing accurate, and local reports confirmed that 60% of the town had been destroyed. This concluded the month's activity, during which, the squadron had taken part in fourteen operations and had dispatched 120 sorties for the loss of three Lancasters and two crews.

March 1943

March would bring with it the opening rounds of the Ruhr campaign, the first for which the Command was adequately equipped and genuinely prepared, with a predominantly four-engine bomber force to carry an increasing weight of bombs and Oboe to provide accuracy. First, however, the crews would have to negotiate operations to Germany's capital and second cities, and it was the "Big City" itself, Berlin, that opened the month's account on the 1st. A force of 302 aircraft was assembled, made up of 156 Lancasters, eighty-six Halifaxes and sixty Stirlings, 5 Group putting up a maximum effort of ninety-eight Lancasters, of which a dozen represented 44 (Rhodesia) Squadron. They departed Waddington between 18.42 and 18.56 with F/Ls Ingham and Walker the senior pilots on duty and lost the services of F/Sgt Baldwin and Sgt Johnson to engine and other mechanical breakdowns before they reached the enemy coast. The target was found to be under clear skies with only haze to impair the vertical visibility, however, reliant upon H2S, the Path Finder navigators experienced great difficulty in establishing their positions based on the images on their cathode-ray tubes over such a massive urban sprawl. This led to scattered marking, and the main weight of the attack falling into south-western districts. The 44 (Rhodesia) Squadron crews bombed from 16,000 to 20,000 feet on red and green TIs between 22.07 and 22.21, and many fires were reported, the glow from which, according to some, could be seen from two hundred miles away on the return flight. Seventeen aircraft failed to return, one, W4829, belonging to 44 (Rhodesia) Squadron, which crashed near Döberitz, some forty miles west of Berlin with no survivors from the crew of Sgt Forman. A post-raid analysis based on bombing photos revealed the attack to have been spread over an area of a hundred square miles, but, because of the increasing bomb tonnage now being carried, more damage was inflicted on the city than during any previous raid upon it. 875 buildings, mostly houses, were destroyed, and twenty factories seriously damaged, along with railway workshops in the Tempelhof district.

F/L Osborn was posted to 1661 Conversion Unit at the conclusion of his tour on the 2nd. A force of 417 aircraft was assembled to send against Hamburg on the 3rd, and eighty-nine of 149 Lancasters were provided by 5 Group, eight of them by 44 (Rhodesia) Squadron at Waddington, where each had a cookie and twelve SBCs of incendiaries winched into its cavernous thirty-three-foot-long bomb bay. They took off between 18.57 and 19.14 with F/L Walker the senior pilot on duty, and all negotiated the North Sea crossing, W/O Sanderson and crew having to descend to 10,000 feet when the rear gunner succumbed to oxygen starvation. They dropped their load onto the island of Amrum, off the west coast of the Schleswig-Holstein peninsula, at 21.07, before heading home. The others continued on to find the target basking under clear skies and in good visibility and carried out their attacks from 18,500 to 21,000 feet between 21.26 and 21.42, aided by the H2S-laid Path Finder TIs. Numerous fires were observed in the docks area along with black smoke rising to meet the bombers as they turned away. What was not appreciated, was the fact that some markers had fallen onto the town of Wedel, situated some thirteen miles downstream of the Elbe, and they had attracted perhaps the bulk of the bombs, while those hitting the primary target had caused a hundred fires that needed to be dealt with before the fire services could go to the aid of their neighbour. Ten aircraft failed to return, but there were no empty dispersals at Waddington.

On the following night, 5 Group sent six Lancasters to mine the waters of Danzig Bay and two others for similar duties in the Kattegat. The crews of W/C Nettleton and F/L Ingham were assigned to the Spinach garden off the port of Gdynia, and F/Sgt Baldwin and crew to Privet, off Danzig (Gdansk), and took off between 17.07 and 17.16, each with a round-trip of at least ten hours ahead of them. The found favourable weather conditions in the target areas and were able to plant their vegetables into the allotted locations from 500 and 800 feet between 21.51 and 22.50, before returning safely to land at Downham Market.

The decks were now cleared for the opening of the Ruhr offensive, which, over the ensuing months, would change the face of bombing and provide for the enemy an indication of the burgeoning power of the Command. This was a momentous occasion, a culmination of all that had gone before during three and a half years of Bomber Command operations. The backs-to-the-wall desperation of 1940, the tentative almost token offensives of 1941, the treading water and gradual metamorphosis under Harris in 1942, when failures still far outnumbered successes, had all been leading to this night, from which point would begin the calculated and systematic dismantling of Germany's industrial and population centres. The only shining light during these dark years had been the quality and spirit of the aircrew, and this had never faltered. It would begin on the 5th at Essen, Harris's nemesis thus far and the home of the giant armaments-producing Krupp complex occupying the Borbeck district, and, for the first time since the war began, the Command would have at its disposal a device which would negate the industrial haze protecting this city and its neighbours. The magnificent pioneering work on Oboe by W/C Hal Bufton and his crews at 109 Squadron was about to bear fruit in spectacular fashion, and the towns and cities of Germany's arsenal would suffer destruction on an unprecedented scale.

A force of 442 aircraft included ninety-seven Lancasters representing 5 Group, 44 (Rhodesia) Squadron contributing seven Lancasters bearing aloft the crews of F/L Walker in W4106, F/O Wilson in ED351, P/O Robinson in W4838, W/O Sanderson in ED305, F/Ss Horwood and Raymond in W4199 and R5729 respectively, and Sgt Pennington in W4831. They departed Waddington between 19.01 and 19.08 and were not involved in the unusually high number of early returns, although, only seven from 5 Group, which, together with those bombing alternative targets, would reduce the size of the force reaching Essen and bombing as briefed to 362 aircraft. 5 Group favoured a time-and-distance approach to the aiming point, and the 44 (Rhodesia) Squadron crews used the Path Finders' yellow route markers as the initial reference point, before exploiting the good visibility to bomb through the industrial haze onto red and green TIs from 18,000 to 20,500 feet between 21.16 and 21.25. The overwhelming impression was of a concentrated attack, which left many fires burning, and a glow in the sky reported by some to be visible from the North Sea homebound. At debriefing, F/L Walker and F/O Wilson reported terrific explosions among fires, which lit up the sky, and a pall of smoke hanging above the dull, red centre of the conflagration. Post-raid reconnaissance revealed 160 acres of devastation and damage to fifty-three buildings within the Krupp district, and the success of the operation was confirmed by local reports of 3,018 houses destroyed and more than two thousand others seriously damaged. The operation cost the Command an acceptable fourteen aircraft, and it was a most encouraging start to what would become a five-month-long offensive.

It would be a further week before round two of the Ruhr offensive was mounted, and, in the meantime, Harris turned his attention upon southern Germany, beginning with Nuremberg on the 8th. A force of 338 aircraft included 105 Lancasters of 5 Group, of which nine represented 44 (Rhodesia) Squadron, and they departed Waddington between 19.31 and 20.09 with F/L Walker the senior pilot on duty, each carrying a cookie and assorted incendiaries. Again, the squadron was not represented among the eight early returns from 5 Group, and they reached the target by following yellow route markers to find clear skies but ground haze and extreme darkness. This seemed to impede the Path Finders' ability to locate the city centre blind by H2S, and the main force crews experienced the same difficulty in identifying ground detail, allowing themselves to be guided to the aiming point by a few red and green

TIs, which appeared to lack concentration and soon burned out. The 44 (Rhodesia) Squadron crews had predominantly red TIs in the bombsights, but also a few scattered greens, and carried out their attacks from 12,000 to 16,500 feet between 23.24 and 23.54. The initial impression was of a scattered raid, but a greater concentration of fires developed, and the glow from these was reported by some to be visible for two hundred miles into the return journey. It had been an interesting trip for Sgt Gayton and crew, who had brushed wingtips with F/Sgt Brown's Lancaster while taxiing to the runway, forcing the withdrawal of both aircraft. This would have been Canadian Ken Brown's maiden operation with the squadron, but, while a spare was found for the Gayton crew, there was none for him. Sgt Gayton's ED351 was then hit over the target by incendiaries from above, fortunately, without causing crew casualties, but it would require major repairs to wings, central fuselage and both fins. Local reports confirmed the marking and bombing of Nuremberg to have been spread along a ten-mile stretch, half of it falling short of the city boundaries, while the rest destroyed six hundred buildings and damaged fourteen hundred others, including a number of important war-industry factories.

On the following day, preparations were put in hand to return to southern Germany to attack the city of Munich, situated deep in the Bavarian mountains of south-eastern Germany, a round-trip of more than 1,200 miles. A force of 264 aircraft included eighty-one Lancasters of 5 Group, of which the eight belonging to 44 (Rhodesia) Squadron were loaded with a cookie each and SBCs of incendiaries. They took off between 20.51 and 21.03, with S/L Whitehead the senior pilot on duty but lost the crew of P/O Robinson to port-outer engine failure after about an hour. The others reached the target area, where clear skies and good visibility prevailed, and the Path Finder green and white TIs could be seen to have fallen within the built-up area. F/O Wilson and crew witnessed an enormous orange explosion in a south-western district as the first Waddington arrivals began their timed runs to the aiming point from the Ammersee, and these had the TIs in the bomb sights as they released their loads from 12,000 to 16,000 feet between 00.31 and 01.00. Another huge explosion at 00.25, described by some as the largest they had experienced, lit up the sky for twenty seconds and illuminated an area of ground with a ten-mile radius, and another particularly large one occurred at 00.43. Fires were taking hold and sending a large pall of smoke rising above the city as the bomber force withdrew to the west, and F/O Wilson counted eighteen blazes in or close to the city centre. A relatively modest eight aircraft failed to return, and only two of these were from 5 Group. A post-raid analysis concluded that a strong wind had pushed the attack into the western half of the city, where 291 buildings had been destroyed and 660 severely damaged. The aero-engine assembly shop at the B.M.W factory was put out of action for six weeks, and many other industrial concerns also lost vital production.

5 Group detailed twenty Lancasters for mining sorties in the Baltic and off the Biscay coast on the 10th, and these would involve five 44 (Rhodesia) Squadron crews, all bound for northern waters. F/Sgt Baldwin and Sgts Gayton and Pennington were assigned to the Geranium garden off the port of Swinemünde, while P/O Pilgrim would target Sweat Pea II in the Kadet Channel and Sgt Smith, Willow, off the port of Sassnitz on Rügen island. They departed Waddington shortly after 18.00, and only three returned up to eight-and-a-half hours later, Sgt Pennington and F/Sgt Baldwin to report successfully delivering their stores into the briefed locations from 900 feet at 21.38 and 21.49 respectively, while F/O Pilgrim had been defeated by ten-tenths cloud and zero visibility and had jettisoned his. W4841 crashed at Sassnitz with no survivors from the crew of Sgt Gayton, and ED305 went into the sea at Middelfart, the junction of Fyn Island and the east coast of the Danish mainland, also with fatal consequences for the crew of Sgt Smith.

The trio of operations to destinations in southern Germany concluded with the highly industrial city of Stuttgart, for which a force of 314 aircraft was assembled on the 11th, 5 Group contributing ninety-six of 152 Lancasters. Seven of these were made ready by 44 (Rhodesia) Squadron at Waddington, where take-off was accomplished safely between 20.05 and 20.22 with P/O Robinson the only commissioned pilot on duty. It was to be a rare night of poor serviceability for the squadron, which began with P/O Robinson and crew losing their starboard-inner engine and having to jettison their cookie. F/Sgt Horwood and crew had reached Poix in north-eastern France when their port-outer engine caught fire, and F/Sgt Brown suffered port-inner engine failure and the overheating of the starboard-outer. The others pressed on across France to the target, where visibility was found to be excellent as the main force element arrived late to find Path Finder TIs already burning out on the ground and leaving the way clear for dummy TIs to lure the bombing away from the city centre. In this endeavour they were largely successful, although, to the bomb-aimers high above, the green TIs appeared to be legitimate, and were bombed by the remaining four 44 (Rhodesia) Squadron crews from 14,000 to 16,000 feet between 23.19 and 23.30. Most of the effort was wasted in open country, but the south-western suburbs of Vaihingen and Kaltental were hit and 118 buildings, mostly houses, were destroyed. It was a disappointing outcome, which cost eleven aircraft, only one of which was from 5 Group.

Round two of the Ruhr campaign was posted on the 12th, when 457 crews learned at briefing that Essen was once more to be their destination. 5 Group detailed ninety-five Lancasters, of which eight were made ready by 44 (Rhodesia) Squadron at Waddington and took off between 19.19 and 19.30 with S/L Whitehead the senior pilot on duty. They all reached the target to find it well marked by red and green Path Finder TIs, with only smoke to mar the visibility, and attacked from 18,000 to 20,000 feet between 21.31 and 21.46. It was clear that the bombing was accurate and mostly concentrated around the Oboe-laid TIs, and, this time, the Krupp complex found itself in the centre of the area of destruction. The defences fought back to claim twenty-three bombers, in return for which, post-raid reconnaissance confirmed another highly successful assault on this centre of war production, which, although destroying substantially fewer buildings, achieved greater concentration, and inflicted 30% more damage on Krupp than the raid of a week earlier.

On the 13th, 5 Group sent seventeen Lancasters to mine the waters in the Baltic, for which 44 (Rhodesia) Squadron made ready two of their own for the crews of F/Sgt Baldwin and W/O Sanderson and dispatched them at 20.13 bound respectively for the Pollock garden off Bornholm island and Spinach off Gdynia. They arrived in their target areas some four hours later to be confronted by a wall of fog, which prevented them from locating their briefed target areas, and backtracked to one of the Silverthorn gardens in the Kattegat, where they delivered their stores from 1,000 and 3,000 feet at 01.17 and 02.05, the latter having pinpointed on Anholt Island.

Thereafter, the weather caused a lull in operations, and it was the 22nd before orders came through to prepare for the next assault on St-Nazaire. A force of 357 aircraft was assembled, including a contribution from 5 Group of 120 Lancasters, of which fourteen were provided by 44 (Rhodesia) Squadron. They departed Waddington between 19.25 and 19.46 with W/C Nettleton and S/L Whitehead the senior pilots on duty, but lost the services of F/Sgt Brown to port-inner engine failure when five miles south of Portland Bill. The others reached the target area to find good visibility impeded only by ground haze, which did not prevent a visual identification of ground features. Red and green Path Finder TIs confirmed the location of the aiming point, and the 44 (Rhodesia) Squadron crews released their mix of high-explosives and incendiaries from 14,000 to 19,000 feet between 21.58

and 22.07. Fires were taking hold as they turned away, and, despite the recall of the Stirling element, to which fifty-five crews responded, the town and its port facilities sustained massive damage.

F/O Henry Wilson and crew were posted to the new and secret 617 Squadron on the 25th, the same day on which the former 44 Squadron pilot, S/L Henry Maudslay, was appointed one of its flight commanders. Wilson and crew would train for the attack on the Ruhr Dams under Operation Chastise, but would not take part, and Maudslay would be one of eight failing to return. Sadly, the Wilson crew were also not destined to survive the war and would be one of five out of eight crews to fail to return from a low-level attack on the Dortmund-Ems Canal near Ladbergen on the night of the 15/16th of September. F/Sgt Ken Brown and crew would also be founder members of what would become the most famous squadron in the service, when they were posted to Scampton on the 29th, but, in the meantime, they would get another two sorties under their belt, beginning on the 26th, when Duisburg was selected as the host for the third operation of the Ruhr offensive. A force of 455 aircraft was assembled, of which, ninety-four Lancasters were provided by 5 Group, ten of them made ready by 44 (Rhodesia) Squadron at Waddington. They took off between 18.32 and 18.45 with the newly promoted S/L Ingham the senior pilot on duty, having learned at briefing that marking would be by "Musical Wanganui", the code for Oboe skymarking, to be carried out by nine Mosquitos of 109 Squadron. F/Sgt Raymond and crew were soon back on the ground after an engine fire, leaving the others to press on to the target area, where they found ten-tenths cloud with tops at 10,000 feet and good visibility above. They were greeted by the Oboe release-point parachute flares, which were in the bomb sights as they dropped their cookies and incendiaries from 18,500 to 21,000 feet between 21.38 and 21.55, and a large explosion was witnessed at 21.53. What the crews couldn't know, was that five of the Oboe Mosquitos had returned early with equipment failure and a sixth had been shot down, leaving just three to deliver what could only be sparse marking. This was insufficient, and led to a scattered and ineffective attack, which, according to local reports, caused only minor damage. Fortunately, the failure cost a modest six aircraft, none of them belonging to 5 Group.

Orders were received on stations across the Command on the 27th to prepare for a trip to the "Big City" that night, and a force of 396 aircraft was duly assembled, which included 111 Lancasters from 5 Group. Fourteen of these were made ready by 44 (Rhodesia) Squadron at Waddington, and they took off between 20.25 and 20.40 with W/C Nettleton and S/Ls Ingham and Whitehead the senior pilots on duty, providing good leadership at what was among the most demanding targets. F/Sgt Shnier and crew turned back early because of hydraulics failure to the rear turret, and they were followed home by P/O Moodie and crew with an oxygen system issue. The remainder continued on to approach the city from the south-west, each carrying a cookie and SBCs of incendiaries, with the Path Finders ahead of them, again reliant upon H2S to locate the city-centre aiming point, However, the sheer size of Berlin thwarted the attempts of the H2S operators to establish their positions accurately, and this resulted in the marking of two areas at least five miles short of the centre. Crews reported three-tenths cloud at 13,000 feet and five tenths stratus at 19,000 feet with moderate to good visibility, and those from 44 (Rhodesia) Squadron bombed on red and green TIs from 16,500 to 19,500 feet between 23.00 and 23.36. From bombing altitude, the attack appeared to be effective, but local reports confirmed that the main weight of bombs had fallen between seven and seventeen miles short of the target, and 25% of those hitting the city had failed to detonate. Among nine missing aircraft was 44 (Rhodesia) Squadron's W4839, which crashed a dozen miles east-south-east of Potsdam with fatal consequences for F/Sgt Horwood and his crew.

There would be a chance to rectify the failure two nights hence, but, in the meantime, St-Nazaire would face its third heavy assault under the January Directive, for which a force of 323 aircraft was made ready on the 28th. 5 Group detailed twenty-one freshman crews, while 44 (Rhodesia) Squadron remained on the ground, and those reaching the target area encountered good visibility and red and green Oboe-laid TIs marking out the aiming point. Returning crews reported concentrated fires, and post-raid reconnaissance confirmed the accuracy and effectiveness of the raid.

On the following day, a force of 329 aircraft was assembled for the return to Berlin that night, for which 44 (Rhodesia) Squadron made ready eleven of the 106 Lancasters provided by 5 Group. They departed Waddington between 21.25 and 21.47 with S/L Ingham the senior pilot on duty, but lost F/Sgt Raymond and crew to severe icing that prevented them from climbing above 14,000 feet. They attacked a flak position at Appenrade, but no such location has been identified. They were just one of an alarming eighteen 5 Group crews to abandon their sorties for a variety of causes, leaving the remainder to reach Berlin, although doing so behind schedule with the rest of the main force because of inaccurately forecast winds. Visibility was described by most as good, which enabled them to identify the target visually, aided by red TIs burning on the ground. Bombing was carried out by the 44 (Rhodesia) Squadron crews from 18,000 to 23,000 feet between 01.04 and 01.28 and appeared to be scattered. This was confirmed later, when bombing photos revealed that most of the effort had fallen into open country south of the city, a disappointment compounded by the loss of twenty-one aircraft. This number included W4199, which crashed some twenty miles east-north-east of Berlin, killing Sgt Johnson RNZAF and his crew.

F/L Walker was posted to 27 O.T.U., on the 30th at the end of his tour. During the course of the month the squadron took part in fourteen operations and dispatched 118 sorties for the loss of five Lancasters and their crews.

April 1943

April would be the least rewarding month during the Ruhr offensive, principally, because of the number of operations directed at targets in regions of Germany beyond the range of Oboe. It began for three 5 Group squadrons with the preparation of eight Lancasters on the 2nd, to join forty-seven others to carry out the final raid on St-Nazaire, while forty-seven aircraft from other groups dealt with Lorient to bring down the curtain on the January Directive. The freshman crew of Sgt Ellis took off from Waddington at 21.11 as the sole 44 (Rhodesia) Squadron representative and approached the target a little over two hours later, too late to bomb on the green skymarkers, and the reds were of no use as they were at the same height as the Lancaster. The target was identified visually by the river and confirmed by Gee-fix and bombed from 14,000 feet at 23.22 in the face of heavy and accurate flak.

The Lancaster and Halifax stations received orders on the 3rd to prepare for an operation against Essen that night, for which the Krupp district was designated as the aiming point. They responded with forces of 225 and 113 aircraft respectively, 5 Group contributing 123 of the Lancasters, and this would be the first time that more than two hundred of the type had operated together. 44 (Rhodesia) Squadron loaded its eleven participating aircraft with a cookie and twelve SBCs of incendiaries each and dispatched them from Waddington between 19.30 and 20.03 with S/L Whitehead the senior pilot on duty. P/O Pilgrim and crew lost their intercom system over the North Sea and turned back, leaving their colleagues to cross the Dutch coast near Haarlem and uncomfortably close to the Amsterdam defences. Almost clear skies prevailed over the central Ruhr, and, because of uncertainty by the Command's meteorological section of the likely weather conditions, the Path Finders had prepared both sky and ground marking plans, which led to a degree of confusion among the main force crews as towards which they should aim their bombs. S/L Whitehead picked up the red skymarkers when a dozen miles north of the target over Dorsten, and, like the majority of the 44 (Rhodesia) Squadron crews, responded to red and green release-point flares before observing the TIs on the ground. The bombing was carried out from 15,000 to 22,000 feet between 22.02 and 22.15, and many explosions were witnessed, with fires emitting large volumes of smoke. The glow from the burning city was still visible to some from the Dutch coast homebound, and the consensus was of a successful raid. This was confirmed by bombing photographs and local reports, which spoke of widespread destruction in central and western districts, where 635 buildings had been reduced to rubble and many more seriously damaged. The searchlight and flak defence had been intense, and it became an expensive night for the Command, which registered the loss of a dozen Halifaxes and nine Lancasters. This represented 6% of those dispatched, but it was the respective loss rates of the types that was most telling, with the Halifaxes suffering 10.62% compared with 4% for the Lancasters.

The largest non-1,000 force to date of 577 aircraft was made ready on the 4th for an attack that night on the naval port of Kiel, for which 5 Group put up 112 Lancasters, nine of them representing 44 (Rhodesia) Squadron. They departed Waddington between 21.06 and 21.28 with S/L Ingham the senior pilot on duty, and all reached the target area, where they were guided towards the aiming point by yellow route marker flares, released by the Path Finder heavy brigade either side of 23.00. On arrival, Kiel was found to be concealed beneath ten-tenths cloud with good visibility above, and the cookies and incendiaries were released from estimated positions onto the glow of fires below the cloud from 15,000 to 18,000 feet between 23.28 and 23.56. It was not possible to assess the outcome, and, as bombing photos revealed only cloud, it was left to a post-raid analysis to conclude that decoy fires were operating, and probably lured away a proportion of the effort, while the strong wind caused the markers to drift, leading the remainder astray and resulting in most of the bombs missing the target altogether. According to local reports, only eleven houses were destroyed, and this was a major disappointment in view of the size of the force involved.

The Ruhr offensive continued at Duisburg on the 8th, for which a mixed force of 379 Lancasters, Wellingtons, Halifaxes and Stirlings was assembled as the heavy element, while ten Oboe Mosquitos would provide the initial marking. 5 Group was responsible for eighty-four of the Lancasters, a dozen of them belonging to 44 (Rhodesia) Squadron, which departed Waddington between 20.46 and 20.55 with S/L Ingham the senior pilot on duty and the standard Ruhr payload of a cookie and assorted 4lb and 30lb incendiaries in the bomb bays. Sgt Ellis and crew became victims of icing conditions and turned back early, while the remainder reached the western Ruhr to encounter ten-tenths cloud with tops in places as high as 20,000 feet. Such conditions completely nullified the Path Finders' attempts to mark either the route or the target, and the bombing had to be carried out on e.t.a., some crews embarking on a time-and-distance run from as far away as the Dutch coast as the last visual reference. F/O Pilgrim and crew were approaching the aiming point at 18,000 feet when a blinding flash flipped their Lancaster onto its back and sent it plunging towards the ground. They pulled out at 6,500 feet and immediately dropped their bombs onto burning incendiaries below. The other 44 (Rhodesia) Squadron crews attacked from 15,000 to 21,000 feet between 23.35 and 00.17 and had nothing of value to pass on to the Intelligence Section at debriefing. Local reports confirmed a widely scattered raid, which hit at least fifteen other Ruhr locations and destroyed just forty buildings in Duisburg.

Among nineteen missing aircraft was the squadron's ED351, which crashed near Mönchengladbach on the way home with no survivors from the crew of F/Sgt Haines.

Not content with the outcome, Harris ordered another raid twenty-four hours later, only this time, employing a much-reduced force of 104 Lancasters and five Mosquitos. 5 Group detailed seventy Lancasters, of which six represented 44 (Rhodesia) Squadron, and departed Waddington between 20.33 and 20.38 with no senior pilots on duty. There were no early returns, and they were guided to the target by red route-marker flares, and then red and green skymarkers over the aiming point, which was hidden by ten-tenths cloud with tops at 5,000 to 15,000 feet. They delivered their cookie and twelve SBCs each from 18,000 to 20,000 feet between 23.03 and 23.19, some observing a large red glow reflected in the clouds. Local reports confirmed that this was another highly scattered raid, which spread bombs over a wide area of the Ruhr and destroyed only fifty houses in Duisburg. For the second night running, 44 (Rhodesia) Squadron had an empty dispersal pan to contemplate in the cold light of dawn, and, this time, it belonged to R5898, which, it emerged later, had been shot down by a night-fighter, and had crashed near Oss in south-central Holland killing Sgt Smith and three others of the eight occupants, leaving four survivors in enemy hands.

Frankfurt was posted as the destination for 502 aircraft on the 10th, on a night when Wellingtons would represent the most populous type, demonstrating that this trusty old warhorse still had an important part to play in Bomber Command operations. 5 Group provided sixty-six of 136 Lancasters, seven of them made ready by 44 (Rhodesia) Squadron at Waddington, and they took off between 00.16 and 00.31 with S/L Peter Jennings the senior pilot on duty for the first time since arriving from SHQ Waddington. They adopted the usual route for south-central Germany across France with, on this night, ten-tenths cloud beneath them, and carried out time-and-distance runs from green route marker flares to deliver their loads from 15,000 to 20,000 feet between 02.51 and 03.14. No one saw anything other than an apparent glow of fires beneath the cloud, and bombing photos would reveal nothing, while local reports suggested that most of the bombing had missed the city altogether.

S/L Whitehead was posted to 5 Group HQ on the 12th at the conclusion of his tour, having already handed over his flight commander duties to S/L Jennings, and the former 44 (Rhodesia) Squadron flight commander, S/L Burnett, was appointed to command 9 Squadron on the same day. 208 Lancaster crews were notified on the 13th of a change of scenery for their next operation, which was to be against the docks at La Spezia on Italy's northern coast some forty miles south-east of Genoa. 5 Group detailed 124 of the Lancasters, with the remainder provided by 1 and 8 Groups, the latter also sending three Halifaxes as part of the marker force. 44 (Rhodesia) Squadron loaded a dozen of its aircraft with 1,000 pounders and SBCs of incendiaries and sent them on their way between 20.34 and 20.45 with W/C Nettleton and S/L Jennings the senior pilots on duty. Sgt Ellis and crew were southbound over Northamptonshire when they noticed a fuel leak, which would leave them with insufficient to complete their sortie, while Sgt Pennington lost the oil feed to his port-inner engine, which caught fire to end his crew's interest in proceedings. There were no further early returns, and all arrived on the Italian side of the Alps to find almost cloudless skies and only haze and smoke to mar the vertical visibility. They established their positions by visual reference of ground detail, such as rivers and the docks, confirmed by Path Finder flares, and bombing by the 44 (Rhodesia) Squadron element took place from 5,000 to 10,000 feet between 01.43 and 02.37. Three large vessels observed tied together east of the outer harbour were seen to be on fire, and the naval oil stores were targeted by some crews. By the later stages of the raid, many fires had added to the smoke obscuring the town, and a number of large explosions encouraged the crews' belief that a successful operation had taken place, which, ultimately, would be confirmed. Three aircraft from other squadrons landed on recently captured airfields in North Africa and were the first to do so before so-called "shuttle-raids" became a feature of operations to the Mediterranean region.

The busy round of non-Ruhr operations would continue at Stuttgart, for which a force of 462 aircraft was made ready on the 14th, the day on which 9 Squadron vacated Waddington to take up residence at Bardney. 5 Group detailed fifty-seven Lancasters, and five of these were made ready by 44 (Rhodesia) Squadron and loaded with a cookie and twelve SBCs of incendiaries. They took off between 22.15 and 22.24 with F/L Robinson the senior pilot on duty and lost the services of Sgt Ellis and crew to a leaking hydraulics system. F/O Moodie and crew were at 15,000 feet over north-eastern France, close to the Belgian and Luxembourg frontiers, when they were pounced upon by a night-fighter and had to jettison their bombs to aid their ultimately successful evasive action. The others approached the city from the north-east to find an absence of cloud, but haze, aggravated by smoke rising through 8,000 feet made ground detail indistinct. The aiming point was established by the green and red Path Finder TIs, and bombing was carried out by the three 44 (Rhodesia) Squadron crews from 14,500 to 16,000 feet between 01.31 and 01.57. Few crews were able to make out the impact of their own bombs and noted only a concentration of fires and considerable amounts of smoke. Post-raid reconnaissance revealed that the Path Finders had marked the centre of the city, but that a "creep-back" had developed, which had spread back along the line of approach. Creep-back was a feature of many large raids and was caused by crews bombing the first fires they came upon, rather than pushing through to the planned aiming point. It could work for or against the effectiveness of the attack, and, on this night, worked in the Command's favour by falling across the industrial district of Bad-Canstatt, before spreading further back along the line of approach onto the residential suburbs of Münster and Mühlhausen. It was here that the majority of the 393 buildings were destroyed and more than nine hundred others severely damaged.

Two major operations were planned for the 16th, the main one employing 327 Lancasters and Halifaxes to target the Skoda armaments factory at distant Pilsen in Czechoslovakia, while a force of 271 aircraft, consisting predominantly of Wellingtons and Stirlings, created a large-scale diversion at Mannheim some 240 miles to the west. 197 Lancasters and 130 Halifaxes were detailed for Pilsen, of which 102 of the former were provided by 5 Group. The plan of attack called for the Path Finders to drop route markers at the final turning point, seven miles from the target, which the crews were to then locate visually in the anticipated bright moonlight, and bomb from as low a level as practicable. It was a complicated plan that invited confusion and failure, and the outcome would question the quality of some of the briefings. 44 (Rhodesia) Squadron made ready a dozen Lancasters, loading them with either a cookie and 1,000 pounders or all-incendiary loads, before dispatching them from Waddington between 21.09 and 21.47 with S/L Jennings the senior pilot on duty. Ahead of them lay a round-trip of some 1,500 miles, which two of the squadron's crews would fail to negotiate. P/O Taylor and crew jettisoned their bombs over Germany for an undisclosed reason, while F/L Robinson and crew strayed to the south of track and into the full Munich defences. Finding themselves coned by searchlights and the target for every flak battery in the city, they were persuaded to drop their cookie, with the intention of continuing on to Pilsen to deliver the 1,000 pounders as briefed. Unfortunately, while releasing it from 9,000 feet at 00.45, the bomb-aimer allowed the 1,000 pounders to drop also, and all detonated somewhere in the eastern side of the city.

The remaining 44 (Rhodesia) Squadron participants arrived in the target area to find the forecast favourable weather conditions, with a layer of eight-tenths cloud at between 8,000 and 15,000 feet, below which, visibility was good and ground features could be made out clearly. The briefings should have made clear that the bombing was to be carried out visually from below the cloud base after making a timed run from the turning-point, which had been marked by TIs. Many 5 Group crews reported bombing from 7,000 to 10,000 feet visually and on TIs between 01.42 and 01.55, proving that they had failed to understand and comply with the instructions at briefing, and had bombed the turning point. The 44 (Rhodesia) Squadron crews made reference to yellow and green TIs and white illuminator flares, but all described difficulty in locating and identifying the factory buildings, some after spending time searching, while having to dodge searchlights and flak. They bombed from 7,000 to 8,000 feet between 01.45 and 02.00, and reported many cookies bursting in open country, and intense night-fighter activity in the Mannheim area on the way home. The details of the crew reports across the group demonstrated that they could not have related to the Skoda works. Post-raid reconnaissance revealed the truth, that, despite the claims of returning crews, no bombs had fallen within miles of the factory, and had been concentrated instead around an asylum at Dobrany, some seven miles to the south-west. This failure was compounded by the loss of thirty-six aircraft, split equally between the two types, and eighteen aircraft were also missing from the Mannheim contingent, which had, at least, achieved the destruction of 130 buildings and damage to some degree to three thousand others. The combined casualty figure of fifty-four aircraft, represented a new record for a single night.

A return to the docks at La Spezia was notified to the Lancaster squadrons of 1, 5 and 8 Groups on the 18th, and 8 Group would also contribute five Halifaxes to the overall force of 178 aircraft. The eighty-nine 5 Group Lancasters included ten representing 44 (Rhodesia) Squadron, which departed Waddington between 20.58 and 21.08 with F/L Robinson the senior pilot on duty. They all negotiated the outward flight across France and the Alps and found the weather to be ideal and visibility good in the target area, although an effective smoke screen partially obscured the town and docks until it drifted to the south to hang over the gulf. The aiming point was identified visually after a timed run from Palmaria Island to the south, and confirmed by red Path Finder TIs, on which they bombed from 5,600 to 9,000 feet between 01.51 and 02.14. The fires were becoming concentrated as they turned away and set course for home, completely satisfied with their night's work. Photo-reconnaissance revealed that the marking and bombing had missed the dockyards to the north-west but had caused extensive damage to the railway station and public buildings in the town centre.

Orders were received on the 20th to prepare for another long-range operation that night, this one against the port of Stettin, situated 640 miles away as the crow flies at the midpoint of Germany's wartime Baltic coast. 5 Group contributed ninety-one Lancasters to the force of 339 aircraft, ten of them belonging to 44 (Rhodesia) Squadron, whose crews learned at briefing that the route would take the bomber stream across the North Sea to a point north of Esbjerg on the Danish coast, before traversing Jutland to then head south-east towards the target. The distance, which was similar to that for Pilsen, dictated a slightly reduced bomb load of a cookie and SBCs of 4lb and 30lb incendiaries each, and these were lifted into the air at Waddington between 21.25 and 21.35 with F/L Haywood the senior pilot on duty. Sgt Ellis and crew reached the Danish coast before their serviceability gremlins struck again and caused their starboard-outer engine to catch fire and their auto-pilot to fail. There were targets, like Duisburg, that seemed to enjoy something of a charmed life, and managed to dodge the worst ravages of a Bomber Command attack, but Stettin was not among them, perhaps because of its location near an easily identifiable coastline. On this night, clear skies and good visibility paved the way for the Path Finders to deliver a perfect marking performance, which was exploited by the main force crews to devastating effect. The Waddington element arrived to find the city laid out before them with the river, built-up area and the docks clearly defined, and the aiming point marked by green TIs. They carried out their attacks from 11,500 to 14,000 feet between 01.08 and 01.24, and, on return, reported fires raging across the built-up area and the glow from the burning port-city visible for ninety miles into the return journey. It was thirty-six hours before a reconnaissance aircraft captured photographs of the still-burning city, and these revealed an area of one hundred acres of devastation across the centre. Local reports confirmed that thirteen industrial premises and 380 houses had been destroyed at a cost to the Command of twenty-one aircraft, four of them 5 Group Lancasters.

5 Group detailed six crews from Waddington for mining duties in the Elderberry garden off Bayonne in south-western France, and two would contain 9 Squadron crews. The 44 (Rhodesia) Squadron quartet took off between 20.50 and 21.13 with F/L Robinson the senior pilot on duty, and all reached the target area to find favourable conditions and pinpoints on the French coast at Cap Rigier and Cap Ferret and the Spanish coast at San Sebastian, from where timed runs were carried out to the release points. The mines were delivered from 600 to 1,000 feet between 01.55 and 02.21, before all but one of the 9 Squadron aircraft returned safely.

Orders on the 26th signalled a return to the Ruhr and Duisburg, for which a large force of 561 aircraft was assembled, the numbers bolstered by the inclusion of 135 Wellingtons, while 215 Lancasters represented the largest contribution by type. 5 Group was responsible for 105 of them, and 44 (Rhodesia) Squadron twelve, which departed Waddington between 00.41 and 00.53 with S/L Jennings the senior pilots on duty. They set course for the Dutch coast via the northern route to the Ruhr and reached the target area after approaching from the north-east. They found largely clear skies and good visibility and were guided to the aiming point by red and green TIs. Bombing by the Waddington element was carried out from 18,000 to 20,000 feet between 02.19 and 02.43, and gave rise to many fires, although opinions were divided as to the degree of concentration achieved. A large orange explosion was witnessed to the east of the aiming point at 02.34, but fires had not gained a hold by the time they withdrew, although black smoke was rising through 7,000 feet. Seventeen aircraft failed to return, but only one of these was from 5 Group. Post-raid reconnaissance revealed that the attack had fallen short of the city centre and had been focussed around the north-eastern districts under the line of approach, thus sparing Duisburg yet again from the full weight of a Bomber Command heavy raid. Even so, local reports confirmed the destruction of more than three hundred buildings, which represented something of a telling blow upon this target.

S/L Ingham was posted to 1661 Conversion Unit on the 27th at the conclusion of his tour, and would miss the largest mining operation of the war to date, which would involve 160 aircraft targeting the waters off the Brittany and Biscay coasts and the Frisians that night. Twenty-eight 5 Group Lancasters were detailed, just two of them representing 44 (Rhodesia) Squadron, the crews of Sgts Drysdale and Pennington departing Waddington at 20.52 and 21.09 bound for the Deodar garden in the Gironde estuary. They found clear skies and good visibility in the target area and identified Lakes Hourtain and Lacana to the west of the Gironde, before delivering their vegetables unopposed into the briefed locations from 6,000 feet at 01,12 and 01.31. The following night brought an even larger gardening effort involving 207 aircraft, of which forty-one Lancasters were provided by 5 Group, five of them by 44 (Rhodesia) Squadron. The crews of F/Os Rail and Moodie, P/O Taylor and Sgts Harding and Shearman departed Waddington between 20.48 and 20.52 bound for the Jasmine garden off the Baltic port of Warnemünde. They all reached the western Baltic, where clear skies and good visibility prevailed, and they identified the Coventer See from which to carry out a timed run to the release point. The mines were delivered into the allotted locations from 400 to 2,000 feet between 00.27 and

00.55, and, on return, F/O Rail and crew revealed that one of their wingtips had hit the sea during evasive action from flak. They were lucky, while, elsewhere, low cloud had been encountered, and the flak had proved to be troublesome, contributing to the loss of twenty-two aircraft, just one of them from 5 Group. This would be the largest-ever loss to result in a single night from mining, but, on the credit side, the number of mines delivered, 593, was also a record for one night, and would not be surpassed.

Essen was posted as the target on the 30th, as attention swung once more towards the Ruhr, and would remain upon it almost exclusively now until well into July. A force of 305 aircraft included 101 Lancasters of 5 Group, of which a dozen were loaded with a cookie and twelve SBCs each at Waddington and dispatched between 00.21 and 00.47 with the newly promoted S/L Haywood the senior pilot on duty. A layer of ice-bearing cloud lay across the bomber stream's path over the North Sea, which most crews negotiated to be greeted at the target by ten-tenths cloud with tops in places as high as 21,000 feet, and red and green Oboe-laid Wanganui flares (skymarkers) identifying the aiming point. Some crews carried out a time-and-distance run from green tracking markers, and all had some kind of flare in the bomb sight, or, at least the glow of one, as they released their loads from 17,000 to 22,000 feet between 02.57 and 03.16. Returning crews reported the glow of fires beneath the cloud and a number of large explosions, but it was impossible to determine whether or not concentration had been achieved, particularly as bombing photos showed only cloud. Post-raid reconnaissance and local reports confirmed a lack of concentration and the liberal distribution of bombs onto ten other Ruhr locations, particularly Bottrop to the north, but 189 buildings had been destroyed and 237 severely damaged in Essen, and, importantly, Krupp sites had sustained further damage. Sgt Ellis and crew failed to return in ED783, having been shot down while homebound by Hptm Wolfgang Thimmig of III./NJG1, and crashing without survivors at 03.20 eight miles east-south-east of Zwolle in north-central Holland.

During the course of the month, the squadron took part in sixteen operations and dispatched 130 sorties for the loss of three Lancasters and crews.

May 1943

May would bring a return to winning ways, with a number of outstanding successes and new records as the Ruhr offensive expanded its horizons to include targets other than Essen and Duisburg. The first of these "new" targets was Dortmund, which had been attacked many times before, but not on the scale that it was about to face on the 4th, when a force of 596 aircraft was assembled, which represented the largest non-1,000 effort to date. 5 Group made available 125 Lancasters, of which fourteen were prepared at Waddington and loaded with a cookie and twelve SBCs each, before taking off between 21.35 and 21.50 with F/L Robinson the senior pilot on duty. There were no early returns, and they pushed on across Holland to enter Germany to the north of the Ruhr and make their way to the eastern end, where they found clear skies, good visibility and only industrial and smoke haze to spoil the vertical view. Yellow Path Finder tracking skymarkers were used as the starting point for a timed run to the target, while the defences responded with many searchlight cones and intense heavy flak, and much evasive action would be required after bombing to vacate the target area intact. The initial Path Finder marking was accurately placed around the city centre, but some of the backing-up fell short, and a decoy site was also successful in luring away a proportion of the bombing. The 44 (Rhodesia) Squadron crews bombed on red or green TIs from 18,000 to 23,000 feet between 01.08 and 01.41, many leaving a gap of up to ten seconds between the release of the high explosives and incendiaries. On return, they reported many sizeable explosions, including a particularly large on at 01.12, which may have been the one reported by a 50 Squadron crew that threw flame to a height of 2,000 feet and burned for ten seconds. They also described developing fires, the glow from which could be seen, according to some, from 150 miles into the return flight. Post-raid reconnaissance revealed that approximately half of the force had bombed within three miles of the aiming point and had destroyed 1,218 buildings and seriously damaged more than two thousand others. Local reports confirmed a death toll of 693 people, which was a record from a Bomber Command attack. It was not a one-sided affair, however, and the loss of thirty-one aircraft was a foretaste of what was in store for the bomber crews operating over "Happy Valley".

During a week-long break from major operations, F/L Jack Shorthouse arrived on posting from 1660 Conversion Unit on the 10th. The lull took the Command through to the 12th, when Duisburg was posted as the target for a heavy force of 562 aircraft with ten Oboe Mosquitos to take care of the initial marking. 5 Group was responsible for 119 of the 238 Lancasters, and they would be accompanied by 142 Halifaxes, 112 Wellingtons and seventy Stirlings. Fourteen 44 (Rhodesia) Squadron Lancasters departed Waddington between 23.49 and 00.21 with S/L Haywood the senior pilot on duty, but soon lost the services of F/O Moodie and crew. Their intercom system failed as they began the North Sea crossing, but they continued on while the wireless operator attempted in vain to rectify the problem, climbing to 16,000 feet, before losing power on the port-inner engine. Still, they pressed on, reaching 19,500 feet at the Dutch coast, at which point, it was decided, that to enter the night-fighter belt with a defective aircraft was a risk too far, and they turned back. The others reached the target area guided by yellow tracking flares and found ideal bombing conditions with no cloud and good visibility, which helped the Path Finders to mark with great accuracy and focus. The main force crews were able to identify ground features and exploited the opportunity by producing a display of unusually concentrated bombing. The Waddington element released their loads onto red and green TIs from 15,000 to 22,000 feet between 02.01 and 02.31, and, at last, the attack proceeded according to plan at this elusive target, which finally succumbed to a devastating assault. Returning crews described a large explosion at 02.30, streets outlined by fire and a highly successful outcome, the best yet witnessed by some, and their impressions were confirmed by photo-reconnaissance, which revealed extensive damage in the city centre and the Ruhrort Rhine docks, the largest inland port in Germany. 1,596 buildings were totally destroyed and the Thyssen steelworks was hit, while dozens of barges and ships were sunk or damaged. However, many crews were absent from debriefing at stations across the Command, and it soon became clear that the success had been gained at a cost of thirty-four aircraft. The loss rates by type again made interesting reading and confirmed the established food chain, the Lancasters sustaining a 4.2% loss, compared with 8.9% for Wellingtons, 7.1% for Stirlings and 6.3% for Halifaxes. Such was the level of destruction that Duisburg would now be left in peace for a year.

On the following night, the squadron contributed fourteen aircraft to a 5 Group force of 124 Lancasters, which, with thirty-two other Lancasters and twelve Halifaxes of 8 Group, would attempt to rectify the recent failure at the Skoda armaments works at Pilsen. A simultaneous raid on the Ruhr city of Bochum was planned, and would involve 442 aircraft from the other groups, and, perhaps, split the defences. The Waddington element took off between 21.19 and 21.48 with W/C Nettleton and S/L Jennings the senior pilots on duty, and lost Sgt Pennington and crew to an overheating starboard-inner engine before even reaching the English coast. Soon afterwards, F/O Pilgrim also turned back because of leaking hydraulics to the rear turret, leaving the others to complete the 650-mile outward leg across France and southern Germany. They reached the target to find clear skies and good visibility, but with ground haze and a smokescreen to impair the vertical visibility. The Path Finders dropped yellow and white track markers, and red TIs with a fairly good concentration that would have been perfectly adequate over a built-up area. However, at a precision target like the Skoda works, they were too scattered to be effective. Bombing by the 44 (Rhodesia) Squadron crews was carried out from 4,000 to 11,000 feet between 01.18 and 01.33, and the impression was that most of it fell among the TIs. On his return, W/C Nettleton, who had bombed from a lowly 5,000 feet, offered the opinion, that, if the TIs had been on the target, the operation had been successful. Sadly, they were found to have missed the factory complex, and most of the bombs had fallen into open country to the north. Some compensation was gained at Bochum, where almost four hundred buildings were destroyed and seven hundred seriously damaged at a cost of twenty-four aircraft, and these were added to the nine Lancasters missing from Pilsen. 44 (Rhodesia) Squadron posted missing the crews of Sgt Olding RCAF and F/O Rail in W4305 and W4110 respectively. The latter was lost without trace, while the former was shot down outbound by Hptm Herbert Lütje of III./NJG1 and crashed at 23.59 west of the junction of the Dortmund-Ems and Mittelland canals south of Hörstel. The pilot was the sole survivor and was taken into captivity.

The above operations proved to be the last major outings for the Path Finders and main force squadrons for nine days, and, it was during this lull, that 617 Squadron entered bomber folklore with its epic attack on the Dams under Operation Chastise on the night of the 16/17th. Among those taking part was the former son of 44 Squadron, Henry Maudslay, who had been promoted at Scampton to squadron leader rank and appointed B Flight commander. He and his crew attacked the Eder Dam without success and were all killed when shot down at Emmerich on the way home. F/Sgt Ken Brown RCAF and crew were one of only two to deliver an Upkeep bomb on the Sorpe Dam, Brown displaying outstanding airmanship to bring his Lancaster and crew home safely after a successful, if, ineffective attack.

By the time that the next major operation was launched on the 23rd, the main force squadrons had undergone an expansion with the addition to many units of a third or C Flight, which, in most cases, would eventually be hived off to form the nucleus of a brand-new squadron. The giant force of 826 aircraft was the largest non-1,000 force to date and surpassed the previous record set three weeks earlier by a clear 230 aircraft. The number of available Lancasters had leapt by eighty-eight, Halifaxes by forty-eight, Stirlings by forty, and Wellingtons by forty-one, and their destination for the second time in the month was to be Dortmund. The entire Command was rested and replenished, and ready to resume the Ruhr offensive, and activity on all participating stations was hectic. 5 Group detailed a record 154 Lancasters, and fifteen of them were made ready at Waddington, where they took on board the standard Ruhr load of a cookie and twelve SBCs of incendiaries. They became airborne between 22.10 and 22.50 with S/L Haywood the senior pilot on duty, and F/L Shorthouse undertaking his first operation since joining the squadron. All reached the target area to find clear skies but considerable industrial haze, which, before the advent of Oboe, would have rendered the attack a lottery, but now, the thirteen Path Finder Mosquitos marked the centre of the city accurately, and the Path Finder heavy brigade backed-up to maintain the aiming point with red and green TIs. These could be seen from twenty miles away on approach, as could the yellow track markers assisting the early 5 Group arrivals for their time-and-distance runs. The Waddington crews bombed largely on the clusters of red and green TIs from 17,500 to 23,000 feet between 01.05 and 01.41, observing many explosions and fires, which were merging into a large area of conflagration with thick columns of black smoke rising up through 18,000 feet as the bombers turned away. Returning crews reported fierce night-fighter activity over the target and on the way home, and this was reflected in the high casualty rate of thirty-eight aircraft, the largest loss of the campaign to date. Almost half of these were Halifaxes and eight were

Lancasters, 5 Group posting missing just four crews, among which was that of Sgt Drysdale RCAF, who disappeared without trace in ED723. Post-raid reconnaissance revealed the operation to have been an outstanding success, which had hit mainly central, northern and eastern districts, where almost two thousand buildings had been destroyed, and some important war industry factories had suffered severe damage and loss of production. The scale of the success was such, that, like Duisburg, this city would remain unmolested by the heavy brigade for a year.

The Ruhr offensive continued with the posting of Düsseldorf as the target on the 25th, for which a force of 759 aircraft was assembled. 5 Group contributed 139 Lancasters, fourteen of them representing 44 (Rhodesia) Squadron, and they departed Waddington between 23.14 and 23.46 with F/Ls Barley, Robinson and Shorthouse the senior pilots on duty. There were no early returns among the Waddington element, and, on arriving at the Dutch coast, some crews were able to observe feverish activity at the target some one hundred miles and thirty minutes flying time away. It lay beneath two layers of thin cloud, and the generally poor visibility impacted the Path Finders' ability to back up the Mosquito-laid TIs to the extent that two red TIs were seen to be thirty miles apart. There were also decoy markers and dummy fire sites operating, which succeeded in causing confusion and prevented a concentration of bombing. The 5 Group crews carried out time-and-distant runs from yellow track markers, before identifying the target visually and by red and green TIs, the 44 (Rhodesia) Squadron participants bombing from 18,000 to 21,600 feet between 01.42 and 02.17. Post-raid reconnaissance and local reports confirmed that the raid had failed to achieve concentration and had developed into an "old-style" scattering of bombs across a wide area, leading to the destruction in Düsseldorf of fewer than a hundred buildings. Twenty-seven aircraft failed to return, and among them was 207 Squadron's commanding officer, W/C Parselle, who would be succeeded by 44 (Rhodesia) Squadron's S/L Jennings on the 29th.

Harris was not yet done with Essen, and the fifth visitation by the bomber force during the campaign was notified to stations on the 27th, and 518 aircraft made ready. 5 Group put up 133 Lancasters, thirteen of them from Waddington, and they were safely airborne between 22.05 and 22.51 with F/Ls Barley, Lewis and Shorthouse the senior pilots on duty. They all reached the target to be greeted by six to eight-tenths cloud with tops at 12,000 feet, with tracking flares to guide them in and Wanganui skymarkers gently descending into the cloud tops over the aiming point. The 5 Group crews carried out time-and-distance runs and bombed on white flares and red parachute markers with green stars, those from 44 (Rhodesia) Squadron doing so from 17,000 to 20,000 feet between 00.50 and 01.33. Post-raid reconnaissance revealed that much of the bombing had fallen short, but 488 buildings had been destroyed, mostly in central and northern districts, and ten nearby towns reported themselves to be victims of collateral damage. Twenty-three aircraft failed to return, and the Halifaxes again represented almost half of the casualties.

A force of 719 aircraft, including a 5 Group contribution of 129 Lancasters, was assembled on the 29th, to pitch against a new Ruhr target, the conurbation known as Wuppertal, perched on the southern rim of the Ruhr Valley east of Düsseldorf. It consisted of the towns of Barmen and Elberfeld, which were built on the proceeds of the rich coal deposits upon which they sat. The aiming point for this night's attack was the Barmen half at the eastern end, for which the 44 Squadron element of fifteen Lancasters departed Waddington between 22.22 and 23.00 with S/L Haywood the senior pilot on duty. F/L Lewis and crew had the Scheldt estuary in sight when their intercom system failed them, while F/Sgt Shnier and crew were bearing down on the Antwerp area only to be thwarted by port-outer engine failure. They swung back round to the west and attacked a last resort target, possibly the docks, at Tholen on Zeeland from 20,500 feet at 00.27. Sgt Thompson and crew also attacked a last-resort target, just west of Cologne at 01.26 after the Gee-box failed and the navigator became indisposed. The others negotiated the southern approach to the Ruhr, running the gauntlet of searchlights and flak in the Cologne and Düsseldorf corridor. They were greeted by clear skies over the southern Ruhr, with the usual industrial haze extending up to 10,000 feet, but the yellow tracking flares clearly identified the final turning-point, and, first, concentrated green and then red TIs marked out the aiming point. The 44 (Rhodesia) Squadron crews carried out their attacks with cookies and incendiaries from 18,000 to 20,000 feet between 01.00 and 01.31, and it was clear to all that something extraordinary was taking place as the built-up area beneath them became a sea of explosions and flames with smoke rising very quickly through 15,000 feet. Post-raid reconnaissance revealed this to be the most awesomely destructive raid of the campaign thus far, which devastated by fire a thousand acres, or around 80% of the built-up area, and destroyed almost four thousand houses, five of the six largest factories and more than two hundred other industrial buildings. It would be some time before the human cost could be established, but it is now accepted that 3,400 people lost their lives during this savage Saturday night. The defenders had their say also, and fought back to claim thirty-three bombers, seven of which were Lancasters, two of them having taken off from Waddington. EE123 was shot down by Oblt Manfred Meurer of I./NJG1 while homebound and crashed at 01.49 ten miles north-west of Venlo in Holland, killing F/O Holt RCAF and all but his navigator, who fell into enemy hands. W4838 was also on the way home when intercepted and shot down by a night-fighter at 04.00, to crash near Genk in Belgium. Sgt Erickson and three of his crew lost their lives, while three survivors, aided by courageous patriots, managed to retain their freedom for some weeks, before being captured.

After spending the entire war to date at Waddington, the squadron moved to Dunholme Lodge on the 31st, a station on the eastern side of the A15 opposite Scampton. As a grass airfield, it had been used as a satellite for Scampton in the Hampden days, before three hard runways were laid to accommodate the new generation of heavy bombers. It was also on this day, that 2 Group left Bomber Command to become part of the 2nd Tactical Air Force. During the course of the month, the squadron participated in seven operations and dispatched ninety-nine sorties for the loss of five Lancasters and their crews.

June 1943

There were no major operations at the start of June because of the moon period, and, although 5 Group stations were alerted on most of the first ten days, no operations actually took place. This kept the Path Finder and main force crews kicking their heels on the ground until the 11th, when Düsseldorf was briefed out to 783 crews. 5 Group was responsible for 162 of the 326 Lancasters, and fourteen of them were loaded with a cookie, four 500 pounders and ten SBCs each at Dunholme Lodge and dispatched between 22.50 and 23.48 with F/Ls Lewis, Robinson and Shorthouse the senior pilots on duty. F/O Pilgrim and crew were contending with static and lightning conditions in towering cloud as they made their way across the North Sea. When the navigator's oxygen supply failed at 21,000 feet, they were forced to jettison their load at 00.43 and turn back, reporting the cloud tops to be at 23,500 feet. The others pressed on over ten-tenths cloud, which dissipated to leave just small amounts at 2,000, 5,000 and 10,000 feet, dependent upon their time of arrival on final approach to the target. Those in the vanguard of the main force were drawn on by yellow tracking flares from 01.05, and red skymarkers with green stars at 01.16, while those a little further back in the bomber stream were guided by red and green skymarkers. They carried out time-and-distance runs to the aiming point five minutes away, noting that fires were beginning to build and join together. The Paramatta marking (ground-marking

TIs) did not seem to appear until these crews were turning away, but they were clearly visible to the crews in the rear-guard, who described a sea of flames covering a massive area and columns of smoke rising through 21,000 feet. The 44 (Rhodesia) Squadron effort was spread throughout the duration of the raid, and attacks were carried out from 18,000 to 22,500 feet between 01.25 and 02.15. All returned home to pass on their impressions to the Intelligence Section at debriefing, but not all squadrons had fared so well, and, when all aircraft had been accounted for, thirty-eight were found to be missing, a figure that equalled the heaviest loss of the offensive to date. Post-raid reconnaissance revealed an area of fire across central districts measuring eight by five kilometres, and local reports confirmed 8,882 individual fire incidents. More than seventy war-industry factories suffered a complete or partial loss of production, 140,000 people were bombed out of their homes and 1,292 lost their lives. Had it not been for an errant Oboe marker attracting a proportion of the bombing onto open country some fourteen miles to the north-east, the destruction would have been greater.

Bochum would face its second heavy visitation of the campaign on the 12th, and a force of 503 aircraft was made ready for the purpose. 5 Group contributed 165 Lancasters, of which fifteen were provided by 44 (Rhodesia) Squadron. They departed Dunholme Lodge between 22.27 and 23.10 with S/L Lynch, whose arrival was not recorded in the ORB, the senior pilot on duty, but lost F/L Shorthouse and crew to intercom and rear turret issues. Rather than waste the effort thus far expended, they bombed an aerodrome on the Frisian island of Texel from 20,000 feet at 01.05. The remaining 44 (Rhodesia) Squadron crews carried on to the target, passing over central Holland and entering Germany to the west of Münster, before turning south for a direct run on Bochum, situated between Essen to the west and Dortmund to the east. It is believed that night-fighters were waiting over Dutch airspace and the frontier region, and a number of bombers fell victim at this stage of the operation. According to the superb book, the Bomber Command War Diaries, by Martin Middlebrook and Chris Everitt, Bochum was completely covered by ten-tenths cloud, but, according to many 5 Group crew reports, they encountered three to six-tenths patchy cloud, and many described almost clear skies and good visibility. The 5 Group crews carried out time-and-distance runs from yellow tracking markers, and the 44 (Rhodesia) Squadron crews had green or red TIs in the bombsights as they let their loads go from 18,500 to 22,000 feet between 01.22 and 02.00. An electrical fault caused P/O Sharp's bombs to hang up, and the cookie was released manually from 24,000 feet near Hengelo. Despite it being released "safe", so as not to endanger Dutch civilians, it was seen to detonate on impact. Once a replacement fuse had been found and installed, some other items of ordnance were jettisoned before it blew again. Returning crews reported concentrated fires, the glow from which was visible for up to a hundred miles into the return flight. Photo-reconnaissance revealed 130 acres of devastation, backed up by local reports that 449 buildings had been destroyed and more than nine hundred severely damaged at a cost to the Command of twenty-four aircraft, at least nine of which had fallen victim to night-fighters.

Following a night's rest, the Ruhr offensive continued at Oberhausen, a major centre of oil production situated between Duisburg to the west and Essen to the east. An all-Lancaster heavy force numbering 197 aircraft contained 108 provided by 5 Group, of which eleven represented 44 (Rhodesia) Squadron. They departed Dunholme Lodge between 22.17 and 22.38 with S/L Haywood the senior pilot on duty and set course for the Scheldt estuary to bypass Antwerp on their way to the Belgian/German frontier. P/O Aldridge was soon battling issues with two engines, which forced him to turn back early, leaving the others to reach the target area to find three to ten-tenths cloud with tops in places at 18,000 feet bathed in very bright moonlight. Tracking flares were drifting above from which to make time-and-distance runs, and the 44 (Rhodesia) Squadron crews aimed at reds with green stars and white skymarkers dropped by the six Oboe Mosquitos and the backing-up 8 Group heavies. Their loads of a cookie, four 500 pounders and incendiaries went down from 19,000 to 22,000 feet between 01.21 and 01.34, in the face of intense heavy flak, which continued to chase them out of the target area into the guns of night-fighters, and between them, they accounted for seventeen Lancasters, 8.4% of the force. There were two empty dispersals at Dunholme Lodge, which should have been occupied by W4936 and W4949. The former was shot down by flak and crashed on the outskirts of the town of Weert, ten miles south-east of Eindhoven in southern Holland. There were no survivors from the crew of S/L Haywood, or, indeed, from the crew of Sgt Shearman, who fell victim to the guns of Major Günter Radusch of I./NJG1, also over southern Holland, twelve miles west of Venlo. Local reports confirmed that the Wanganui flares had been right over the city centre, where 267 buildings had been destroyed and 584 seriously damaged. S/L Watson was posted in from 1654 Conversion Unit on the 18th to fill the flight commander void created by the sad loss of S/L Haywood.

On the 16th, 1, 5 and 8 Group stations were notified that Cologne was to be the target for that night, for which a force of 202 Lancasters and ten Halifaxes was made ready. They learned at briefings that there would be no Oboe Mosquitos on hand to mark the target, as that role was to be undertaken by the Path Finder Halifax element and six Lancasters employing H2S. 5 Group detailed eighty Lancasters, of which seven at Dunholme Lodge were loaded with the usual mix of high explosives and incendiaries and dispatched between 22.05 and 22.15 with S/L Lynch the senior pilot on duty. F/L Barley climbed to 21,000 feet over the North Sea with ice forming on the inside of the cockpit Perspex, and all attempts to clear it, including the use of glycol, failed to rectify the problem. Completely blind, they were forced to turn back and descend and jettisoned the contents of the bomb bay. S/L Lynch lost a starboard engine as he crossed the English coast, and, unable to maintain height, completed the North Sea crossing to drop his bombs onto the aerodrome at Haamstede on Schouwen in the Scheldt. The remaining five arrived in the target area to find six to ten-tenths cloud, and green tracking flares from which to make a time-and-distance run to the aiming point. The Path Finders were late on target, and problems with some of the H2S sets led to sparse and scattered marking with solid white flares and reds with green stars. The 44 (Rhodesia) Squadron crews bombed from 21,000 to 23,000 feet between 01.10 and 01.15, and a number witnessed a large orange explosion at 01.08, although, generally, they were unable to assess the outcome. The impression was that a proportion of the bombing had been concentrated where intended, but that some crews had been lured away by dummy markers, and local reports, which suggested that only around a hundred aircraft had been involved, tended to support this view. Residential districts bore the brunt of the raid, and 401 houses were destroyed, with 13,000 others sustaining damage to some extent, mostly lightly, while sixteen industrial premises and nine railway stations were hit, along with public and utility buildings.

The recent successes in the Ruhr had been aided by the sheer size of the urban areas below, which all but guaranteed that the bombs would hit something useful, even after smoke had obscured the aiming point TIs. It was a different matter at a small or precision target, however, which would rapidly be enveloped in smoke from the first bombs before the rest of the attacking force had a chance to draw a bead on the aiming point. When, on the 20th, therefore, an attack was mounted under the codename Operation Bellicose against the production site of the Würzburg radar sets, which the enemy was employing very successfully to warn of and intercept Bomber Command raids, a plan was already in place to combat the problem by adopting the oft-used and still-under-development 5 Group time-and-distance method. Briefings actually took place on the day before, when crews learned that the factory was housed in the old Zeppelin sheds at Friedrichshafen, situated on the shore of Lake Constance (Bodensee) on the frontier with Switzerland, and represented a very small target. The plan was to use a designated "Master of Ceremonies" to direct the bombing, much in the manner of Gibson at the Dams, and the officer chosen was the highly experienced G/C Len Slee, the former 49 Squadron commanding officer, with the popular W/C Cosme Gomm, commanding officer of 467 Squadron RAAF, as his deputy. 5 Group was to provide the main force element of fifty-six Lancasters, five of them from 44 (Rhodesia) Squadron, with four others from 8 Group's 97 Squadron to deliver the marking for the selected crews at the head of the stream. The plan called for the Channel to be crossed at a standard altitude, before descending gradually to 10,000 feet by the time that Orleans was reached, and, thereafter, to fly at between 2,500 and 3,000 feet all the way to the Rhine. After crossing the Rhine, they were to climb to their briefed bombing height of between 5,000 and 10,000 feet for the rendezvous over the north-western shore of Lake Constance, and then circle until receiving the start signal.

The Dunholme Lodge quintet took off between 21.53 and 21.59 with F/Ls Lewis and Robinson the senior pilots on duty, and all would make it to the target on a rare night when not a single aircraft from the entire force turned back, despite encountering electrical storms and having to adjust the briefed course. That said, G/C Slee lost an engine over France, and was forced to drop back into the formation and hand over the lead to W/C Gomm, who, on arrival at the target under clear skies and in bright moonlight, became concerned about the hostility of the searchlight and light flak defences. In order to reduce the very real risk of heavy casualties, he decided to add five thousand feet to the bombing height, where, unknown to him, the wind was stronger and would push the bombing towards the north-east. The Path Finder element also had little time to climb to the new height, and this caused a slight delay in the opening of the attack. The first TI fell wide of the aiming point, but the second one was assessed by W/C Gomm to be accurate, upon which he called in the first crews, whose high explosives and incendiaries created the expected smoke and obscured the target. He decided that another TI on the aiming point might still provide a reference for some crews, but the Path Finders were driven off by the searchlights and light flak and abandoned the attempt. They were then ordered to drop flares along the shore of Lake Constance, to enable the remaining crews to begin their runs from a pre-determined landmark, fly across the lake to the opposite shore, pick up another landmark 2,000 yards from the target, and continue at a constant speed for the requisite number of seconds to cover the distance to bomb release. The 44 (Rhodesia) Squadron crews carried out their attacks on cascading green TIs from 10,000 to 12,000 feet between 02.51 and 03.08, and observed explosions and fires, some of which remained visible for eighty miles into the onward flight to landing grounds in North Africa, in what was the first official shuttle operation of the war. Post-raid reconnaissance revealed that a proportion of the bombs had hit the target, causing extensive damage, and there had been no losses among the attacking force.

While these crews were absent from England, a hectic round of four major operations to the Ruhr in the space of five nights began at Krefeld on the 21st, for which a force of 705 aircraft was assembled. 5 Group contributed ninety-two Lancasters, of which nine represented 44 (Rhodesia) Squadron, and they departed Dunholme Lodge between 22.57 and 23.50 with S/L Lynch the senior pilot on duty. There were no early returns, and all reached the target, situated a short distance to the south-west of Duisburg, and on the opposite side of the Rhine. Conditions in the target area were ideal, with small amounts of thin cloud between 6,000 and 10,000 feet and bright moonlight, which would benefit attacker and defender alike. The Path Finders delivered a near-perfect marking performance, red TIs falling in concentrated fashion to clearly identify the city centre aiming point for the main force crews. The 44 (Rhodesia) Squadron crews carried out their attacks from 19,000 to 21,500 feet between 01.36 and 02.17 and described a sea of red fire giving off masses of smoke, with one particular jet-black column rising through 18,000 feet as they turned away. All were convinced of the success of the operation, and one crew likened it to the Wuppertal-Barmen raid. There was no hint of troublesome flak or night-fighters, and yet, forty-four aircraft failed to return, the heaviest casualties of the campaign to date, and many of these were lost to the Nachtjagd. Remarkably, only three 5 Group Lancasters were among the missing, but one of these was LM330, which disappeared without trace with the eight-man crew of P/O Thompson. 35 Squadron of the Path Finders lost six of its nineteen Halifaxes. Three-quarters of the bombing photos were plotted within three miles of the aiming point, and the 2,306 tons of bombs wiped out by fire an estimated 47% of the built-up area. 5,517 houses were destroyed, the largest number to date at a single target, and more than a thousand people lost their lives.

The medium-sized town of Mülheim-an-der-Ruhr, a close neighbour of Duisburg, Oberhausen and Essen, lies around a dozen miles to the north-east of Krefeld, and it was here that the red ribbon terminated on the target maps at briefings across the Command on the 22nd. A force of 557 aircraft was prepared, of which ninety of the Lancasters were provided by 5 Group, six of them representing 44 (Rhodesia) Squadron. They departed Dunholme Lodge between 22.41 and 22.58 with F/L Shorthouse the senior pilot on duty and made their way via the Scheldt through the Cologne corridor, and arrived at the target to find small amounts of cumulostratus cloud at between 5,000 and 10,000 feet, with red and green TIs clearly visible and defining the aiming point. The 44 (Rhodesia) Squadron crews bombed from 20,000 to 22,000 feet between 01.21 and 01.35 and witnessed the development of a concentrated area of fire, which was visible from the Dutch coast homebound. Returning crews commented on the intense searchlight and flak response, and the number of night-fighters, and reported that Krefeld was still burning from the night before. Sgt Ash brought home a flak-damaged W4778, his bomb-aimer having had to release the bombs over the target manually after the electrical feed was cut, while F/L Shorthouse reported a near miss with another aircraft that crossed his path at right angles. Local reports confirmed that the town had suffered severe damage, particularly in the northern districts, where 1,135 houses had been destroyed and more than 12,000 others damaged to some extent. The road and telephone communications to Oberhausen had been cut, preventing any passage out of the town other than on foot. In fact, some of the bombing had spilled into the eastern districts of Oberhausen, which was linked to Mülheim for air-raid purposes. It was another expensive night for the Command, however, which registered the loss of thirty-five aircraft, with the Halifaxes and Stirlings representing two-thirds of them and suffering a respective loss rate of 7.7% and 11.8%.

While the Path Finder and main force units were enjoying a night off on the 23rd and girding their loins for the next round of the Ruhr offensive, fifty of the 5 Group Lancasters that had landed in North Africa following the Friedrichshafen raid, took off with two 97 Squadron Path Finder aircraft to bomb the docks at La Spezia on the way home to England. The 44 (Rhodesia) Squadron crews of F/Ls Lewis and Robinson and P/Os Pennington and Sharp took off from Blida in Algeria between 19.27 and 19.35, leaving behind F/O Moodie, whose aircraft was unserviceable, and arrived in the target area to find clear skies but hazy conditions made worse by a smoke-screen. There appeared to be a degree of confusion in getting the raid started, but a lucky hit on an oil storage facility resulted in a large explosion at 23.41 just as the main force was running-in, and most crews were able to identify the target visually, thereafter, and by red, green and white Path Finder flares. Bombing was carried out by the 44 (Rhodesia) Squadron quartet on instructions from a Master Bomber from 8,000 to 13,000 feet between 23.45 and 00.05, and all returned safely home to moan about the length of time it had taken for the raid to develop, and the poor communications with the raid controller. P/O Sharp also reported the inadvertent jettisoning of sixteen SBCs of incendiaries because of an electrical fault in the bomb-release circuitry. The authorities seemed happy to claim the destruction of the oil depot and an armaments store and declared the operation to be a success.

Having destroyed the Barmen half of Wuppertal at the end of May in one of the most devastating attacks to date, it was time to visit the same catastrophe on the western half, Elberfeld, for which a force of 630 aircraft was made ready on the 24th. 5 Group managed to support the operation with 103 Lancasters, nine of which were provided by 44 (Rhodesia) Squadron, and they departed Dunholme Lodge between 22.36 and 23.07 with W/C Nettleton the senior pilot on duty, and S/L Watson undertaking his first sortie with the squadron. Sadly, his port-outer engine caught fire at 2,800 feet as he climbed away, and he flew out to sea to jettison his bombs off Lowestoft. Sgt Ash and crew took off ten minutes late because of a wireless issue, which appeared to have been fixed, but it failed again soon afterwards, and they, too jettisoned their load. Sgt Matheson and crew were almost two hours out when they lost their starboard-outer engine and had to jettison their load at the mouth of the Western Schelde at 01.01. Each of these crews had released their cookie "safe", but all three detonated on impact with the sea. The others ran the usual gauntlet of searchlights and flak from the Cologne and Düsseldorf defence zones, the crews of which were aided by the formation of condensation trails at between 18,000 and 21,000 feet to advertise the presence of the bomber stream. There seemed to be fewer guns firing at them over the target, where small amounts of cloud with tops at 17,000 feet were insufficient to obscure the ground. The 5 Group crews carried out time-and-distant runs from yellow tracking flares until observing cascading red and green TIs, the 44 (Rhodesia) Squadron element bombing from 18,000 and 21,000 feet between 01.07 and 01.38. Those arriving at the tail end of the attack, when the built-up area was well-alight, described thick columns of smoke already passing through 19,000 feet and the glow of fires visible from the Dutch coast. Post-raid reconnaissance revealed another massively concentrated and accurate attack, which had reduced to rubble an estimated 90% of Elberfeld's built-up area, including three thousand houses and 171 industrial premises. It had also severely damaged 2,500 houses and dozens of important factory buildings, and the fact that more buildings were destroyed than damaged, provided a telling commentary on the conditions on the ground. The number of fatalities stood at around eighteen hundred, and some of the survivors might have been cheered to know that thirty-four bombers, containing 240 of their tormentors, would not be returning to England that night. Remarkably, only two of these belonged to 5 Group.

114 Lancasters were made ready on 5 Group stations on the 25th as part of an overall force of 473 aircraft, which were to attack the Ruhr city of Gelsenkirchen, where a number of synthetic oil refineries were supporting the German war effort. At Dunholme Lodge, ten Lancasters were loaded with a cookie, four 500 pounders and thirteen SBCs of incendiaries each, and were dispatched between 22.37 and 23.12 with S/Ls Lynch and Watson the senior pilots on duty. They all reached the target area to find ten-tenths stratus lying over the region with tops at 10,000 to 15,000 feet, which would not have been a problem for Oboe, had five of the twelve participating Mosquitos not suffered equipment failures. This caused tracking flares to be late and to drop in the wrong order in a somewhat scattered manner, at a time when the crews were contending with an intense flak barrage. Searchlights illuminated the cloud as those from 44 (Rhodesia) Squadron bombed on red flares with green stars from 17,000 to 21,000 feet between 01.25 and 01.54. A large explosion was witnessed at 01.43, and the glow from the target was visible from the Dutch coast, to which the returning bombers were chased by a large deployment of enemy night-fighters. Post-raid reconnaissance and local reports confirmed that the operation had failed to achieve accuracy and concentration, and, in an echo of the past, bombs had been sprayed all over the Ruhr, leaving Gelsenkirchen largely untouched. Thirty aircraft were

missing, and, this time, eight of them were from 5 Group, four alone from 106 Squadron. R5740 failed to return to Dunholme Lodge with the eight-man crew of P/O Sharp, and no clue to its fate ever emerged.

A series of three operations against Cologne would span the turn of the month and began on the night of the 28/29th, when 608 aircraft took off in the late evening to deliver what would be the Rhineland Capital's greatest ordeal of the war to date. 5 Group contributed 131 Lancasters, the 44 (Rhodesia) Squadron element of twelve departing Dunholme Lodge between 22.47 and 23.27 with S/L Watson the senior pilot on duty. The services of Sgt Wright and crew were lost to a rear turret issue when they had been outbound for an hour and forty minutes, but the remainder pressed on to the target area, where they encountered ten-tenths cloud below them at 8,000 to 10,000 feet, with good visibility above. The main force crews were unaware that five of the Oboe Mosquitos had turned back and a sixth was unable to drop its skymarkers, leaving just six to do so, and these were behind schedule by seven minutes and could manage only intermittent flares. The omens for a successful attack were not good, particularly as skymarking was the least reliable method because of drift, but, by the time the Dunholme Lodge crews arrived, they were greeted by red and white flares. S/L Watson was at the start of his bombing run with green tracking flares ahead, when his Lancaster was hit by accurate predicted flak, and the bombs were dropped into the outskirts of the city from 16,000 feet at 02.07 during the ensuing evasive action. The others carried out their attacks from 18,000 to 21,000 feet between 01.47 and 02.16 and deduced from the glow beneath the clouds and the presence of smoke rising through them that they had contributed to a successful operation. This was confirmed by post-raid reconnaissance and local reports, which provided details of forty-three industrial buildings and 6,374 others completely destroyed, and a further fifteen thousand sustaining damage to some extent. The death toll was put at 4,377, the greatest by far from a Bomber Command attack, and 230,000 others had lost their homes for varying periods. By recent standards, the figure of twenty-five missing aircraft could be considered moderate, but that was no consolation to the individual stations with empty dispersal pans. Sgt Hulbert and crew failed to return to Dunholme Lodge, having been shot down homebound by Major Günter Radusch of 1./NJG1, and crashing without survivors three miles north-east of the centre of Eindhoven. This was Radusch's second 44 (Rhodesia) Squadron victim of the month. During the course of the month the squadron participated in eleven operations and dispatched 102 sorties for the loss of five Lancasters and their crews.

July 1943

5 Group began the new month by sending a dozen Lancasters to mine the waters around the Frisians on the 1st. 44 (Rhodesia) Squadron was not called upon until the 3rd, when fifteen Lancasters were detailed as part of 5 Group's contribution of 141 to the 653-strong force assembled for the second of the raids on Cologne. The Dunholme Lodge element took off between 22.26 and 23.43 with S/L Lynch the senior pilot on duty, but lost F/Sgt Burness and crew to a defective mid-upper turret at the English coast and a starboard-outer engine issue as they approached the Dutch coast. The others pressed on in favourable conditions to reach the target, which they found clearly visible under two to three-tenths cloud at 8,000 feet and protected by many searchlight cones and a moderate flak defence. Green tracking flares guided the first wave crews to the aiming point, which the Path Finders marked with red skymarkers with green stars and red and green ground markers, achieving great accuracy and concentration, while later crews were drawn on for the final one hundred miles by the sight of the city

already burning fiercely. The 44 (Rhodesia) Squadron crews bombed on red TIs from 18,500 to 21,500 feet between 01.20 and 01.57 and reported the city to be a mass of flames, the glow from which remained visible for 170 miles into the return journey.

Some crews commented on the presence of day fighters over the target, and this was clear evidence of a new tactic being employed by the Luftwaffe. The newly formed JG300 was operating for the first time, employing the Wilde Sau (Wild Boar) tactics, which was the brainchild of former bomber pilot, Major Hans-Joachim (Hajo) Herrmann. The unit had been formed in June with borrowed standard BF109 and FW190 single-engine day fighters to operate directly over a target, seeking out bombers silhouetted against the fires and TIs. On this night, the unit would claim twelve victories, but would have to share them with the flak batteries, which claimed them also. Unaccustomed to being pursued by fighters over a target, it would take time for the bomber crews to work out what was happening, and, until they did, friendly fire would often be blamed for damage incurred by unseen causes. Post-raid reconnaissance and local reports confirmed another stunningly accurate and concentrated attack, in which twenty industrial premises and 2,200 houses had been destroyed, and 72,000 people bombed out of their homes at a cost to the Command of thirty aircraft.

The series against Cologne would be completed on the 8th by an all-Lancaster heavy force of 282 aircraft drawn from 1, 5 and 8 Groups, with six Oboe Mosquitos to carry out the initial marking. 5 Group provided 151 Lancasters, of which seventeen were made ready at Dunholme Lodge, and they took off between 22.28 and 22.57 with W/C Nettleton and S/L Watson the senior pilots on duty. Shortly after climbing out, a burning smell pervaded the forward section of W/C Nettleton's ED331, which caused sore throats, headaches and nausea among the crew forward of the main spar and forced the sortie to be abandoned. F/O Parsons and crew lost all navigation aids and the intercom as they crossed the North Sea and jettisoned their load "live" onto a defended area just inland from the enemy coast. This prompted a response from flak and a night-fighter, upon which they claimed hits as they evaded further attention. Their squadron colleagues flew through the tops of towering cumulonimbus as they made their way to the target, where ten-tenths cloud at around 10,000 feet concealed the ground from view. Sgt Whitecross and crew were almost at the south-western suburbs of the city when a flak shell detonated right underneath, persuading them that their Lancaster had sustained severe damage and that they should jettison their load, which fell from 20,000 feet onto Liblar at 01.20. Tracking flares guided the main force crews to the aiming point, but the release-point flares were late, and some crews bombed on e.t.a., before they were deployed. The 44 (Rhodesia) Squadron crews carried out their attacks from 19,000 to 23,000 feet between 01.15 and 01.32 in the face of an intense flak barrage, and a very large orange explosion was witnessed at 01.23. S/L Watson lost both outer engines to heavy flak over the target, and this knocked out the power to the turrets. They crossed the French coast homebound at around 8,000 feet relying on the inner engines and made it to a safe landing. S/L Watson praised the performance of his crew under challenging circumstances, as did F/O Pilgim his gunners for driving off the attentions of a Ju88. Post-raid reconnaissance and local reports revealed another highly successful operation, which had caused extensive damage in north-western and south-western districts, where nineteen industrial premises and 2,381 houses had been destroyed. The success cost a modest seven Lancasters, five of them from 5 Group. When the dust had settled over Cologne, the local authorities catalogued the destruction over the three raids of more than eleven thousand buildings, and a death toll of almost 5,500 people, with a further 350,000 rendered homeless.

The Ruhr campaign was winding down by the time that Gelsenkirchen was posted across Lancaster and Halifax stations as the target on the 9th, for which a heavy force of 408 aircraft was made ready supported by ten Oboe Mosquitos. A dozen 44 (Rhodesia) Squadron Lancasters were among the 112 representing 5 Group, and they departed Dunholme Lodge between 22.19 and 22.56 with S/L Lynch the senior pilot on duty. P/O Aldridge and crew turned back early because of engine issues and other malfunctions, leaving the remainder to make their way to the target above ten-tenths cloud, which stretched over the Ruhr at around 16,000 feet and topped out in places at 20,000 feet. The Path Finder skymarkers were several minutes late, partly as a result of a 50% failure rate of the Oboe equipment, while a sixth Mosquito dropped its markers ten miles to the north. The Dunholme Lodge crews timed their runs from red and green tracking flares and were over the aiming point between 01.10 and 01.42 delivering their bombs from 20,000 to 24,000 feet onto the Wanganui markers as they drifted into the cloud. Some explosions were reflected in the cloud, one particularly large one at 01.40 lighting up the area like day. However, the impression gained by those taking part was that the raid had fallen short of the recent outstanding successes, and this was confirmed by local reports. To those on the ground, it appeared that the attack had been meant for Bochum and Wattenscheid, which received more bombs than Gelsenkirchen, where limited damage occurred in southern districts.

Although two more operations to the region would be launched late in the month, Harris was already planning his next attempt to shorten the war by bombing and was buoyed by the success of the spring offensive. He could look back on the past four and a half months with genuine satisfaction at the performance of his squadrons, and, as a champion of technological innovation, take particular pride in the performance of Oboe, which had been the decisive factor. Although losses had been grievously high, and the Ruhr's reputation as "Happy Valley" well earned, its most important towns and cities had suffered catastrophic destruction. In Britain, the aircraft factories had more than kept pace with the rate of attrition, while the training units both at home and overseas were pouring eager new crews into the fray to fill the gaps. With confidence high in the ability of his Command to destroy almost any target at will, Harris prepared for his next major campaign, the erasure from the map of a prominent German city in a short, sharp series of maximum effort raids to be launched during the final week of the month.

In the meantime, 1, 5 and 8 Groups were alerted to prepare for a trip to Italy to attack the city of Turin, for which 295 Lancasters were made ready on the 12th. 5 Group put up 130 aircraft, fourteen of them representing 44 (Rhodesia) Squadron, and they departed Dunholme Lodge between 22.20 and 22.44 with W/C Nettleton the senior pilot on duty. There were no early returns, despite having to negotiate poor weather conditions over France, which included icing, and they were greeted at the target by clear skies and good visibility, and defences up to their usual poor standard, characterised by ineffective searchlights and inaccurate light flak rising to 15,000 feet. The marking was punctual, accurate and concentrated, inviting the bombing by the 44 (Rhodesia) Squadron crews to be carried out from 17,500 to 20,000 feet between 02.01 and 02.16, and a column of black smoke was observed rising through 12,000 feet as they withdrew. The return route involved a low-level circumnavigation of the Brest peninsula, and many of the thirteen missing Lancasters disappeared without trace into the sea after running into enemy night-fighters in this area. The return of W/C Nettleton was awaited with mounting tension and apprehension, until the time came when he and his seven crewmates could no longer be aloft. No trace of ED331 KM-Z or its crew was ever found, and it is presumed that it was among those finding a watery grave off the French coast. The loss of such an important figure and influence on 44 (Rhodesia) Squadron was keenly felt within the squadron and among the station staff at Dunholme Lodge, and S/L Watson had the unenviable task of stepping into the breach until a permanent successor was appointed.

W/C Williamson arrived from 106 Squadron on the 15th on promotion to acting wing commander rank, having served as a flight commander at Syerston. He would have nine days to settle in before presiding over his first operation, and would, himself, be dead a week later. Hamburg had been a regular target for the Command throughout the war to date, and had been attacked, amongst other occasions, during the final week of July in 1940, 1941 and 1942. It had been spared by the weather from hosting the first "One Thousand" bomber raid at the end of May 1942, but Harris now identified it as the ideal candidate for destruction under Operation Gomorrah, the intention of which was to cause the maximum impact to the enemy's morale in a short, sharp campaign, employing ten thousand tons of bombs. Hamburg's political status was second only to Berlin, and its value to the war effort in terms of ship and U-Boot construction and other war production was undeniable, but it suited Harris's criteria also in other respects. Its location close to a coastline aided navigation and made it accessible from the North Sea without the need to spend time over hostile territory, and its relatively short distance from the bomber stations enabled a force to approach and retreat during the few hours of darkness afforded by mid-summer. Finally, lying beyond the range of Oboe, which had proved so decisive at the Ruhr, Hamburg had the wide River Elbe to provide a solid H2S signature for the navigators high above.

The campaign would begin on the night of the 24/25th, for which a force of 791 aircraft was assembled, 143 of the Lancasters provided by 5 Group, and a dozen of these by 44 (Rhodesia) Squadron. The crews would be aided by the first operational use of "Window", tinfoil-backed strips of paper of precise length, which, when released in bundles into the airstream at a predetermined point, would drift down slowly in vast clouds to swamp the enemy night-fighter, searchlight and gun-laying radar with false returns and render it blind. The device had actually been available for a year, but its use had been vetoed in case the enemy copied it for use against Britain. It was not realized that Germany had, in fact, already developed its own version called Düppel, which it had withheld for the same reason. The Dunholme Lodge crews took off between 22.20 and 23.12 with F/L Shorthouse the senior pilot on duty but lost the services of F/O Parsons and crew to supercharger problems, which prevented them from achieving a reasonable height. At a predetermined point over the North Sea, the force began to dispense "window", beginning shortly after 00.30, and the effects appeared to be immediate as few fighters rose to meet the approaching bombers. A number of aircraft were shot down over the sea during the outward flight, two of them 103 Squadron Lancasters, but these were off course, and outside of the protection of the bomber stream, and may well have been returning early with technical difficulties.

The efficacy of "window" was made more apparent in the target area, where the crews noticed an absence of the usually efficient co-ordination between the searchlights and flak batteries, and defence appeared random and sporadic. This offered the Path Finders the opportunity to mark the target by visual reference and H2S virtually unmolested, and, although the red and green TIs were a little misplaced and scattered, they landed in sufficient numbers close to the city centre to provide the main force crews with ample opportunity to deliver a massive blow. The 44 (Rhodesia) Squadron crews were guided in by yellow tracking flares and red and green skymarkers, and delivered their loads of a cookie, four 500 pounders and thirteen SBCs of incendiaries from 18,000 to 21,300 feet onto red TIs between 01.05 and 01.44, before returning home to report a successful operation that had left part of the city ablaze with a column of smoke rising through 20,000 feet. Post-raid reconnaissance revealed that a six-mile-long creep-back had developed, which cut a swathe of destruction from the city centre along the line of approach, out across the north-western districts, and into open country, where a proportion of the bombing had been wasted. In fact, less than half of the force had bombed within three miles of the city centre during the fifty-minute-long raid, in which 2,284 tons of bombs had been delivered, but, despite that, the city had suffered a telling blow, and fifteen hundred of its inhabitants lay dead. For the Command it was an encouraging start to the campaign, particularly in the light of just twelve missing aircraft, for which "window" was largely responsible.

On the following night, and in the expectation that Hamburg would be covered by smoke, Harris switched his force to Essen, where he could take advantage of the body blow dealt to the enemy defensive system by "window". A force of 705 aircraft included 136 Lancasters of 5 Group, the twelve at Dunholme Lodge taking off between 22.04 and 22.37 with S/L Lynch the senior pilot on duty. There were seventeen early returns from the 5 Group contingent, and one of these was Sgt Rollin and crew, who had an engine cowling come loose and eventually fly away as they were on their way home after aborting their sortie. Those of 44 (Rhodesia) Squadron arriving in the target area found clear skies, with just the usual ground haze to spoil the vertical visibility, and yellow tracking flares to guide them to the aiming point, which was marked by red and green TIs. They bombed from 17,000 to 22,000 feet between 00.33 and 01.08 and reported concentrated fires around the aiming point in a one-and-a-half-square-mile area of the city. Two large, red explosions were witnessed at 00.36 and 00.39, and a column of smoke was rising through 20,000 feet as they withdrew to the west. Post-raid reconnaissance confirmed the raid to be another outstanding success against this important war materials producing city, with more than 2,800 houses destroyed, while the complex of Krupp manufacturing sites suffered its heaviest damage of the war to date. Twenty-six aircraft failed to return, just two of them from 5 Group, but 44 (Rhodesia) Squadron came through unscathed.

After a night's rest, a force of 787 aircraft was made ready for round two of Operation Gomorrah, for which 44 (Rhodesia) Squadron bombed-up and fuelled thirteen Lancasters as part of 5 Group's contribution of 155. They departed Dunholme Lodge between 22.18 and 22.56 with F/L Shorthouse the senior pilot on duty, but lost P/O Aldridge to an oxygen system issue within ninety minutes. The remainder pushed on towards Hansastadt Hamburg, crossing the coast over the Schleswig-Holstein peninsula to the north, none of them having any concept of the events that were to follow their arrival. A previously unknown and terrible phenomenon was about to present itself to the world and introduce a new word "firestorm" into the English language. A number of factors would conspire on this night to seal the fate of this great city and its hapless inhabitants in an orgy of destruction quite unprecedented in air warfare. An uncharacteristically hot and dry spell of weather had left the city a tinderbox, and the spark to ignite it came with the Path Finders' H2S-laid red and green TIs, which fell with almost total concentration some two miles to the east of the intended city-centre aiming point, and into the densely populated working-class residential districts of Hamm, Hammerbrook and Borgfeld. To compound this, the main force, which had been drawn on to the target by yellow release-point flares, bombed with rare precision and almost no creep-back, and deposited much of its 2,300 tons of bombs into this relatively compact area. The 44 (Rhodesia) Squadron crews carried out their attacks from 16,800 to 23,100 feet between 01.00 and 01.38 and observed many explosions and a sea of flames developing below. Those bombing towards the later stages of the raid observed a pall of smoke rising through 20,000 feet, and the glow of fires was reported to remain visible for up to two hundred miles into the return journey.

On the ground, individual fires began to join together to form one giant conflagration, which sucked in oxygen from surrounding areas at hurricane speeds to feed its voracious appetite. Trees were uprooted and flung bodily into the inferno, along with debris and people, and temperatures at the seat of the flames exceeded one thousand degrees Celcius. The defences were overwhelmed, and the fire service unable to pass through the rubble-strewn streets to gain access to the worst-affected areas.

Even had they done so, they could not have entered the firestorm area, and, only after all of the combustible material had been consumed, did the flames subside. By this time, there was no-one alive to rescue, and an estimated forty thousand people died on this one night alone. A mass exodus from the city, which would ultimately exceed one million people, began on the following morning, and this undoubtedly saved many from the ravages of the next raid, which would come two nights later. Seventeen aircraft failed to return, reflecting the enemy's developing response to the advantage gained by the Command through Window. No gain was ever permanent, and the balance of power would continue to shift from one side to the other for the next year. For a change, it was the Lancaster brigade that sustained the highest numerical casualties on this night of eleven, six of them belonging to 5 Group.

Bomber Command's heavy brigade stayed at home on the following night, while four Mosquitos carried out a nuisance raid on Hamburg, to ensure that the residents' sleep was disturbed. A force of 777 aircraft was put together to continue Hamburg's torment on the 29th, and, this time, 5 Group contributed 148 Lancasters, of which thirteen would represent 44 (Rhodesia) Squadron. They departed Dunholme Lodge between 22.11 and 22.54 with F/L Shorthouse the senior pilot on duty and lost the services of Sgt Whithead and crew to an issue with fuel feed to the port engines. The others continued on to reach the target, which they found under clear skies and protected only by slight ground haze. The plan was to approach from due north to hit the northern and north-eastern districts, which had, thus far, escaped serious damage, but the Path Finders strayed two miles to the east of the intended track, and dropped their markers just to the south of the already devastated firestorm area. A four-mile creep-back rescued the situation for the Command, by spreading along the line of approach into the residential districts of Wandsbek and Barmbek, and parts of Uhlenhorst and Winterhude. The 44 (Rhodesia) Squadron crews bombed on yellow, red and green TIs from 18,000 to 20,500 feet between 00.42 and 01.18, and reported smoke rising through 17,000 feet and fires visible for two hundred miles into the return journey. It was another massive blow against this proud city, but, as the defenders began to recover from the effects of "window", so the bomber losses began to creep up, and twenty-eight aircraft failed to return home on this night, five of them from 5 Group.

Before the final round of Operation Gomorrah took place, the curtain on the Ruhr offensive was brought down finally with a raid on the town of Remscheid, situated on the southern edge of the region, about six miles south of Wuppertal, where the main industries were mechanical engineering and tool-making. Up until this point, only twenty-six people had lost their lives in this town as a result of stray bombs, but it was now to face a modest force of 273 aircraft consisting of roughly equal numbers of Lancasters, Halifaxes and Stirlings with nine Oboe Mosquitos to mark out the aiming point. 5 Group put up thirty-nine Lancasters, four of which were loaded with a cookie and seventeen SBCs of various incendiaries at Dunholme Lodge and took off between 21.56 and 22.06 bearing aloft the crews of W/C Williamson on his first sortie with the squadron, F/O Hill, P/O Rogers and Sgt Holmes A'Court. They all reached the target area to find clear skies and good visibility and bombed on red TIs from 10,000 to 19,800 feet between 01.08 and 01.12, observing the burst of many cookies and a pall of smoke rising through 5,000 feet. Three 44 (Rhodesia) Squadron crews returned home with a red glow in the sky behind them, that remained visible as they crossed the enemy coast homebound and gave promise of another Ruhr town left devastated. JA895 crashed at Ratingen-Lintorf, between Mülheim-an-der-Ruhr and Düsseldorf, and there were no survivors from the crew of W/C Williamson. It would be left to a post-war bombing survey to establish that a mere 871 tons of bombs had laid waste to around 83% of Remscheid's built-up area, destroying 107 industrial buildings and 3,117 houses. Three months war production was lost, and the town's industry never recovered fully. Fifteen aircraft failed to return, and the Stirling brigade suffered 10% casualties.

During the course of the month the squadron participated in nine operations and dispatched 112 sorties for the loss of two Lancasters and two crews captained by the commanding officers.

August 1943

Briefings for the final act of Operation Gomorrah took place on the 2nd, and a force of 740 aircraft was made ready, 128 of the Lancasters provided by 5 Group. 44 (Rhodesia) Squadron detailed fourteen Lancasters, which took off between 23.05 and 23.59 with no pilots on duty above flying officer rank. The weather conditions were good initially, until 7 degrees East, where a towering bank of ice-bearing cumulonimbus cloud was encountered, which could not be circumnavigated, and stretched upwards to 20,000 feet and beyond. Upon entering it, aircraft were thrown around by violent electrical storms, and it was a hugely terrifying experience beyond anything that most crews had ever experienced, with enormous flashes of lightning, thunder, electrical discharges and instruments going haywire. F/Sgt Burness and crew were among many who simply abandoned their sorties and jettisoned their bombs over Germany or into the sea, in their case, into Jade bay from 20,000 feet at 01.40. F/O Hill and crew let their bombs go over Bremerhaven in the Weser estuary, some sixty miles short of the target, and Sgt Ransom jettisoned his somewhere in the same area after the failure of his starboard-outer engine. The remainder battled through the conditions to reach the target area, which was concealed beneath seven to ten-tenths cloud, and, while some caught a glimpse of the Elbe and isolated yellow and green Path Finder flares, the majority bombed on e.t.a., and on the glow of fires beneath the cloud and the smoke rising through it. The Dunholme Lodge crews bombed from 11,200 to 20,000 feet between 02.01 and 02.47, before returning to unanimously report an unsuccessful operation, described by some from other units as "pure hell". Little fresh damage occurred in Hamburg as bombs were sprayed over an area of a hundred miles, but that was of little consequence in view of what had gone before. The Command suffered the relatively heavy loss of thirty aircraft, and some of these had fallen victim to the weather conditions. W4778 was probably homebound when it crossed paths with Hptm Hans Joachim Jabs of IV./NJG1, who shot it down into the Waddenzee between the Dutch Frisians and the mainland, and only the bomb-aimer in Sgt Moffat's crew survived to fall into enemy hands. During the course of the four raids of Operation Gomorrah, the squadron despatched fifty-one sorties, of which forty-six bombed as briefed and just one Lancaster failed to return. (The Battle of Hamburg. Martin Middlebrook).

S/L Bowes was posted in from his flight commander role at 207 Squadron on the 3rd and was promoted to acting wing commander rank to enable him to assume command of the squadron. Italy was now teetering on the brink of capitulation, and Bomber Command was invited to help nudge it over the edge with a short offensive against its major cities. It began with elements of 1, 5 and 8 Groups making ready to attack Genoa, Milan and Turin on the 7th, and, with preparations already in hand for, perhaps, the most important operation of the war to date to be launched in ten days' time, the Turin raid was to be used to test the merits of employing a raid controller, or Master of Ceremonies, in the manner of W/C Gibson during Operation Chastise. The man selected for the job was Group Captain John Searby, currently serving as commanding officer of 83 Squadron of the Path Finders, and, before that, Gibson's successor as commanding officer of 106 Squadron. 5 Group detailed seventy-eight Lancasters divided between Genoa and Milan, and, it is believed, that all 197 aircraft reached their respective targets, after flying out in excellent weather conditions. Although the Master Bomber experiment at Turin was not entirely successful, experience was gained which would prove useful for the forthcoming Operation Hydra.

The rest of the heavy brigade remained inactive until the 9th, when a force of 457 Lancasters and Halifaxes was made ready for an operation that night against Mannheim. 44 (Rhodesia) Squadron prepared fourteen Lancasters as part of a 5 Group contribution of 143, and they departed Dunholme Lodge between 22.54 and 23.30 with S/L Watson the senior pilot on duty. After climbing out, they headed for the rendezvous point over Reading, before exiting England via Beachy Head on course for the French coast at Boulogne. There were no early returns as they made their way across Belgium on a direct track to the target, where they were greeted by a five-tenths layer of broken cloud at 4,000 feet and eight-tenths at 10,000 feet. Despite this, the visibility was fair, and the yellow skymarkers and green TIs were sufficient to provide a reference for the bomb-aimers. The 44 (Rhodesia) Squadron participants carried out their attacks from 17,500 to 21,100 feet between 01.34 and 02.03 and returned home to report a number of very large fires but a generally scattered raid. In fact, according to local reports, 1,316 buildings had been destroyed, forty-two industrial concerns had lost production, and more than fifteen hundred fires of varying sizes had required attention. Six Halifaxes and three Lancasters failed to return, two of the latter belonging to 5 Group.

Nuremberg was posted as the target on the 10th, for which a force of 653 aircraft was assembled, 128 of the Lancasters provided by 5 Group. 44 (Rhodesia) Squadron briefed twelve crews while their Lancasters were being loaded with a cookie and up to twelve SBCs of incendiaries and sufficient fuel and reserves for the 1,300-mile round-trip. Take-off was safely accomplished between 21.47 and 22.30 with S/L Lynch the senior pilot on duty, and, after climbing out and forming up, they set course for Beachy Head on the Sussex coast to follow a route similar to that of the previous night. There were no early returns to deplete the squadron's effort, and all arrived in the target area, where conditions also reflected those of twenty-four hours earlier with eight to ten-tenths cloud at 12,000 feet. The Path Finders had prepared a ground-marking plan, and there were no release-point flares to draw the head of the main force on, but the green TIs on the ground were visible to most, as were the fires for those arriving later. The Dunholme Lodge crews delivered their bombs from 17,500 to 20,000 feet between 01.08 and 01.52 and returned safely to report a good concentration of fires, the glow from which remained visible for 150 miles into the return journey. Post-raid reconnaissance and local reports confirmed that the city had sustained much housing and industrial damage in mostly central and southern districts, and a death toll of 577 people was evidence of the intensity of the bombing.

During the course of the 12th, two forces were prepared for a return to Italy that night, one of 504 Lancasters and Halifaxes to attack Milan, and the other of 152 Stirlings, Halifaxes and Lancasters to target Turin. 5 Group contributed 130 Lancasters to the former, of which eleven represented 44 (Rhodesia) Squadron, and they departed Dunholme Lodge between 21.29 and 21.45 with W/C Bowes leading the squadron for the first time, supported by S/L Watson. The route would take the bomber stream via Selsey Bill to Cabourg on the Normandy coast, and then south-east in a straight leg across central France to the northern tip of Lake Bourget, to cross the Alps and skirt southern Switzerland before the final run-in on the target. This represented a round-trip of some sixteen hundred miles, which all from 44 (Rhodesia) Squadron would complete. They arrived at the target under clear skies with just ground mist to spoil the view and bombed visually or on yellow flares and green TIs from 16,000 to 20,500 feet between 01.19 and 01.41. They observed large fires surrounding the aiming point in the city centre, and a thick column of black smoke rising through 20,000 feet as they turned away. The glow in the sky remained visible for 150 miles into the return flight, and crews were confident of success. Local reports, though short on detail, confirmed that four important war-industry factories had sustained serious damage during August, and most of it probably occurred on this night, as did the majority of the 1,174 fatalities in the city in 1943.

Milan would face two further attacks before the Command's interest in Italy ceased for good, and the first of these was posted on the 14th, for which 1, 5 and 8 Groups put together a force of 140 Lancasters. Fifty-nine of them represented 5 Group, with 44 (Rhodesia) Squadron providing six, which took off between 21.21 and 21.37 with S/L Lynch the senior pilot on duty. They all reached the target under clear skies and in good visibility aided by a brilliant moon and Path Finder route markers. The Path Finder target marking with green TIs was accurate and concentrated and was exploited by the Dunholme Lodge crews from 12,800 to 16,100 feet between 01.22 and 01.40. Many fires were seen to take hold as the force turned away, and the glow remained visible for a considerable distance into the return flight.

There was to be no respite for Milan as a force of 199 Lancasters was made ready later on the 15th for a return that night for what would be the last time over Italy for main force Lancasters. 44 (Rhodesia) Squadron provided eight of the eighty-five 5 Group Lancasters, and they took off from Dunholme Lodge between 20.22 and 20.35 with F/L Barley the senior pilot on duty. All reached the target to find clear skies, and the Path Finders guided them in with green flares over lake Bourget. Haze and smoke hung over the city from the previous night to spoil to an extent the vertical visibility, but the Path Finders marked the city-centre aiming point with green TIs, and these were bombed to good effect by seven of the 44 (Rhodesia) Squadron crews from 15,100 to 17,500 feet between 00.07 and 00.33. Enemy night-fighters were waiting over France to catch the bombers as they returned home, and, among the seven missing aircraft was that of 467 Squadron RAAF's popular commanding officer, W/C Gomm DSO, DFC, who died with all but one of his crew. The consensus of returning crews was of a concentrated attack, but no local report was forthcoming to confirm or deny. F/L Barley and crew were conspicuous by their absence at debriefing, but it wasn't long before news arrived from Blida in North Africa to confirm that they had landed there and were safe and well. They had lost one of their port engines when deep into enemy territory, and jettisoned their bombs to maintain height, before being attacked by two Ju88s and enduring twenty minutes of violent evasive action, during which the starboard-inner engine overheated, and it is believed caught fire. They would return home on the 24th.

The final raid of the war on an Italian city was carried out by 154 aircraft of 3 and 8 Groups against Turin on the following night. A successful raid was claimed at the modest cost of four aircraft, but many of the participating Stirlings were diverted on return and did not reach their home stations in time to be made ready for the night's highly important operation, for which a maximum effort had been planned. This would deplete the available number of Stirlings by sixty and heap an even greater responsibility upon the rest of the force to complete the job at the first attempt. Since the very beginning of the war, intelligence had suggested that Germany was researching into and developing rocket technology, and, although scant regard was given to the reports, photographic reconnaissance had confirmed the existence of an establishment at Peenemünde at the northern tip of the island of Usedom on the Baltic coast. The activities there were monitored through Ultra intercepts and surreptitious reconnaissance flights, and the V-1, known to the photographic interpreters at Medmenham because of its wingspan as the "Peenemünde 20", was captured on a photograph. The brilliant scientist, Dr R V Jones, had been able to gain vital information concerning the V-1's range, which would ultimately be used to feed disinformation to the enemy, largely through the double agent

"Zigzag", otherwise known as Eddie Chapman. Unfortunately, Churchill's chief scientific adviser, Professor Lindemann, or Lord Cherwell as he became, steadfastly refused to give credence to the existence and feasibility of rocket weapons and held stubbornly to his viewpoint even when presented with a photograph of a V-2 on a trailer, taken by a PRU Mosquito back in June. It required the combined urgings of Duncan Sandys and Dr Jones to persuade Churchill of the urgency to act, and Operation Hydra was planned for the first available opportunity, which occurred on the night of the 17/18th. Earlier in the day, the USAAF 8th Air Force had carried out its first deep-penetration raids into Germany to attack ball-bearing production at Schweinfurt and the Messerschmidt aircraft plant at Regensburg, and, to the shock of its leaders, had learned the harsh lesson that unescorted daylight raids in 1943 were not viable. The folks at home would not be told that sixty B17s had failed to return. It was vital that the Peenemünde installation be destroyed, and a force of 596 aircraft and crews answered the call. 5 Group contributed 117 of the 324 Lancasters, with Dunholme Lodge making ready thirteen, and the rest of the force was comprised of 218 Halifaxes and fifty-four Stirlings.

The operation had been meticulously planned to account for the three vital components of Peenemünde, the housing estate, where the scientific and technical staff lived, the factory buildings and, finally, the experimental site. Each was assigned to a specific wave of aircraft, which would attack from medium level, with the Path Finders bearing the huge responsibility of shifting the point of aim accordingly. After last minute alterations, 3 and 4 Groups were given the first mentioned, 1 Group the second, and 5 and 6 Groups the third. The whole operation was to be overseen by a Master of Ceremonies (referred to hereafter as Master Bomber), and the officer selected for this hazardous and demanding role was G/C Searby of 83 Squadron, who, as already mentioned, had stepped into Gibson's shoes at 106 Squadron after Gibson was posted out to form 617 Squadron. Searby's role was to direct the marking and bombing by VHF, and to encourage the crews to press on to the aiming point, a task requiring him to remain in the target area and within range of the defences throughout the attack. In an attempt to protect the bombers from the attentions of enemy night-fighters for as long as possible, eight Mosquitos of 139 Squadron were to carry out a spoof raid on Berlin, led by the highly experienced, and former 49 Squadron commander, G/C Len Slee. In the expectation of encountering drifting smoke as the last wave on target, the 5 Group crews were instructed to employ their oft-used time-and-distance approach to the aiming point and had practiced this over a stretch of coast near the Wainfleet bombing range at the mouth of the Wash in Lincolnshire, progressively cutting the margin of error from one thousand to three hundred yards.

The 44 (Rhodesia) Squadron element took off between 21.29 and 22.01 with W/C Bowes and S/L Watson the senior pilots on a night when many squadron commanders elected to fly, in some cases, with fatal consequences. There were no early returns to Dunholme Lodge, and the overall early-return rate was lower than normal, suggesting that crews had taken to heart the importance of the operation. The various groups made their way individually to a rendezvous point some ninety minutes flying time or three hundred miles from the English coast and sixty miles from Denmark's western coast, where they became a stream. Darkness had fallen as they crossed the North Sea, and twenty miles short of landfall over the southern tip of Fanø island, south of Esbjerg, "windowing" began, in order to simulate a standard raid on a northern or north-eastern city. Southern Denmark was traversed by the Lancaster brigade at 18,000 feet, twice the altitude required for the attack, but, worryingly, in a band of cloudless sky under a bright moon. They adopted an east-south-easterly course and began to shed altitude gradually during the 240-mile run to the target a little over an hour away, and, at the rear of the stream, the 5 Group crews focussed on the island of Rügen, the ideal starting point for their timed run to Peenemünde, which lay some fifteen miles beyond to the south-east.

The initial marking of the housing estate went awry, and some target indicators fell onto the forced workers' camp at Trassenheide, more than a mile south of the intended aiming point. Many of the 3 and 4 Group bombs fell here, inflicting grievous casualties on friendly foreign nationals, who were trapped inside their wooden barracks. Once rectified, however, the attack proceeded according to plan, and a number of important members of the technical staff were killed. The 1 Group second-wave crews encountered strong crosswinds over the narrow section of the island where the construction sheds were located, but this phase of the operation largely achieved its aims, and they were on their way home before the night-fighters arrived from Berlin, having been attracted by the glow of fires well to the north. On arrival at Rügen, the 5 Group crews began their timed run, and reached the experimental site to encounter the expected smoke, and bombed on green TIs, in the case of the 44 (Rhodesia) Squadron element, from 6,000 to 8,100 feet between 00.36 and 00.52. They and the 6 Group Halifaxes and Lancasters then ran into the night-fighters, which proceeded to take a heavy toll of bombers, both in the skies over the target, and on the route home towards Denmark. Twenty-nine of the forty missing aircraft came from this third wave, seventeen of them belonging to 5 Group and twelve to 6 Group, which represented a loss rate for the Canadians of 19.7%. The first of the 44 (Rhodesia) Squadron crews to go down was that of P/O Harding RCAF, who disappeared without trace in DV202, while on their eighth operation. W4935 crashed into the Baltic and took with it the crew of Sgt Campbell, who were on the fifth operation, and only two bodies washed ashore to be buried. JA897 was presumed to have been lost in the target area, and only the bomb-aimer in the crew of Sgt Drew survived to fall into enemy hands. It was their seventh operation. Many of the returning crews brought home aiming point photographs, despite the fact that the time-and-distance method was found to have been not entirely effective. Returning crews praised the work of the Path Finders and the Master Bomber, and post-raid reconnaissance revealed the raid to have been sufficiently effective to delay the V-2 development programme by a number of weeks, and, ultimately, to force the manufacture of secret weapons underground. The flight testing of the V-2 was eventually withdrawn eastwards into Poland, beyond the range of Harris's bombers, and, thus Peenemünde had been nullified as a threat.

Before the next campaign began, Leverkusen was posted on the 22nd as the target for a heavy force of 449 Lancasters and Halifaxes with 8 Group Oboe-Mosquitos to provide the initial marking. The aiming point was to be a factory belonging to the infamous I G Farben chemicals company, which was engaged in the development and production of synthetic oil and employed slave labour at all of its factories across Germany, including 30,000 from the Auschwitz concentration camp, where it had built a plant. One of the company's subsidiaries manufactured the Zyklon B gas used during the Holocaust to murder millions of Jewish victims. 44 (Rhodesia) Squadron made ready eleven Lancasters in a 5 Group contribution of 108, and they departed Dunholme Lodge between 21.12 and 21.43 with F/L Shorthouse the senior pilot on duty. After climbing out they headed for the Belgian coast at Knokke, to follow a well-worn route to the southern Ruhr, which would require them to pass through the searchlight and flak belt near Cologne, that was guaranteed to provide a hot welcome. By this time, they had lost the services of F/Sgt Whitecross after he became ill at around 23.00 and turned back. All of the others made it safely through the narrow searchlight and flak corridor to reach the target, where the area was blanketed by ten-tenths cloud with tops at 18,000 feet. Oboe-equipment failures forced most crews to bomb on e.t.a., in the absence of markers, until the glow of fires came to their aid as the raid developed, although a small number of crews spotted green TIs on the ground and aimed for them. Bombing was carried out by the 44 (Rhodesia) Squadron crews in the face of intense flak from 16,500 to 20,000 feet between 00.04 and 00.33, and the glow of fires and the flash of explosions was initially the only confirmation of something happening under the cloud, until a column of smoke was observed to be rising through 12,000 feet. Local reports would reveal that up to a dozen neighbouring towns had been hit, Düsseldorf suffering the destruction of 132 buildings.

Harris had long believed that the key to ultimate victory lay in the destruction of Berlin, the seat of the Nazi government and the symbol of its power. On the 23rd, orders were received on stations across the Command to prepare for a maximum effort that night against Germany's Capital City, which had not been visited by the heavy brigade since the end of March. The crews, of course, could not know that this was to be the first of an eventual nineteen raids on the "Big City", in a campaign which, with an autumn break, would drag on until the following spring. It was a campaign that would test the resolve of the crews to the absolute limit, whilst also sealing the fate of the Stirlings and the Mk II and V Halifaxes as front-line bombers. There are varying opinions concerning the true start date of what became known as the Berlin offensive or the Battle of Berlin, some commentators believing these first three operations in August and September to be the start, while others point to the sixteen raids from mid-November. However, there was little doubt in Bomber Command circles that this was it, a fact demonstrated by the comments in numerous squadron ORBs, which spoke of the "long-awaited Berlin campaign" and similar sentiments. There would be a Master Bomber on hand for this operation, and the officer chosen was Canadian W/C "Johnny" Fauquier, the tough, grizzled and popular onetime bush pilot and frequent brawler, who was enjoying his second spell as the commanding officer of 405 (Vancouver) Squadron, now of the Path Finders, and formerly of 4 Group. The route had been planned to take the bomber stream to a rendezvous point over the North Sea, before crossing the Dutch coast near Haarlem and setting a course to pass between Bremen and Hannover to bypass the southern rim of Berlin. The intention was then to turn back to approach the city from the south-east, and, after bombing, to pass out over the Baltic coast and make for the Schleswig-Holstein peninsula. Finally, seventeen Mosquitos were to precede the Path Finder and main force elements to drop route markers at key points in an attempt to keep the bomber stream on track.

A force of 727 aircraft was assembled, of which 124 Lancasters represented 5 Group, eleven of them belonging to 44 (Rhodesia) Squadron, and they departed Dunholme Lodge between 20.00 and 20.43 with S/Ls Lynch and Watson the senior pilots on duty. The route was to take the bomber stream over northern Holland to enter Germany between Meppen to the north and Osnabrück to the south, and pass to the south of Hannover to reach a position south-east of Berlin, before turning sharply to adopt a north-westerly course across the city centre. Those reaching the target area found clear skies and moonlight, but the Path Finders were unable to identify the aiming point in the centre of the city, a result of the inherent difficulties of interpreting the H2S images over such a massive urban sprawl and marked the southern outskirts instead. Many main force crews then cut the corner to approach the city from the south-west rather than south-east, and this resulted in the wastage of many bomb loads in open country and on outlying communities. The 44 (Rhodesia) Squadron crews each delivered their cookie and incendiaries visually and on red and green TIs from 18,000 to 21,000 feet between 23.47 and 00.25, doing so in the face of intense searchlight activity with moderate flak. Returning crews reported large explosions and many fires, the glow from which was visible for at least 140 miles, and a pall of smoke had already risen to meet them as they turned towards the north-west. Curiously, only a few crews commented on hearing the Master Bomber, and finding his instructions helpful. A new record of fifty-six aircraft failed to return, twenty-three Halifaxes, seventeen Lancasters and sixteen Stirlings, representing a percentage loss rate respectively of 9.1, 5.1 and 12.9, which perfectly reflected the food chain when all three types operated together. Berlin experienced a scattered raid, but because of the numbers attacking, extensive damage was caused, a little in or near the centre, but mostly in south-western residential districts and industrialized areas a little further east. 2,611 buildings were reported to have been destroyed or seriously damaged, and the death toll of 854 people was surprisingly high, caused largely, perhaps, by a failure to heed the alarms and go to the assigned shelters.

Orders were received on the 27th to prepare for an operation that night against Nuremberg, for which a force of 674 aircraft ultimately lined up for take-off in mid-evening. 5 Group contributed 140 Lancasters, the thirteen at Dunholme Lodge taking to the air between 20.58 and 21.29 with F/Ls Barley and Shorthouse the senior pilots on duty. After climbing out, they headed for the French coast, and, once there, followed the line of the frontier with Belgium until crossing into Germany south of Luxembourg on course for the target, where clear skies and intense darkness prevailed. The Path Finders had been briefed to check their H2S equipment by dropping a 1,000 pounder on Heilbronn, and some crews complied, while others, it seems, experienced technical difficulties. The initial marking was accurate, but a creep-back developed, which the backers-up and the Master Bomber could not correct, and this resulted in many bomb loads falling into open country, while others hit Nuremberg's south-eastern and eastern districts. The 44 (Rhodesia) Squadron crews aimed at green TIs from 13,000 to 21,000 feet between 00.34 and 01.12, the low height that of Sgt Smith and crew, who had lost their port-outer engine at 20,000 feet at 23.38 when halfway through the leg across France. Crews generally gained an impression of a fairly concentrated and accurate attack, which produced many fires, describing searchlights and night-fighters as numerous, and thirty-three aircraft failed to return, eleven of each type, which again confirmed the vulnerability of the Stirlings and Halifaxes when operating alongside Lancasters. The loss rate on this night was 3.1% for the Lancaster, 5% for the Halifax and 10.6% for the Stirlings.

The twin towns of Mönchengladbach and Rheydt were posted as the targets for a two-phase operation on the 30th, and it would be the first major attack for both of them. Situated some ten miles west of the centre of Düsseldorf in the south-western Ruhr, they would face an initial force of 660 aircraft of four types, in what, for the crews, was a short-penetration trip across the Dutch frontier, which would be a welcome change from the recent long slogs to eastern and southern Germany. The plan called for the first wave to hit Mönchengladbach, before a two-minute pause in the bombing allowed the Path Finders to head south to mark Rheydt. 44 (Rhodesia) Squadron made ready a dozen Lancasters as part of a 5 Group contribution of 138, and were briefed to bomb in the second wave, for which they took off between 23.34 and 00.11 with S/L Lynch the senior pilot on duty. P/O Leslie and crew were well into their take-off run, when the pilot glimpsed moving lights ahead, which he interpreted as another Lancaster, and swerved to port as the wheels came unstuck. They struggled into the air but felt a collision with an obstacle as they passed beyond the runway, and, soon afterwards, the port-inner engine began to overheat. They climbed to a safe height, jettisoned the bombs and returned to base. The others reached the target to find good visibility above the seven to ten-tenths cloud at 8,000 feet, and a near-perfect display of target-marking by Oboe delivered red and green flares to draw on the main force crews to bomb with scarcely any creep-back. The 44 (Rhodesia) Squadron element carried out their bombing runs from 18,000 to 20,000 feet between 02.02 and 02.39, and on return reported many fires, the glow from which could be seen from the Dutch coast homebound. Photo-reconnaissance confirmed a highly accurate and concentrated attack, which destroyed more than 2,300 buildings in the two towns, 171 of them of an industrial nature, along with 869 residential properties. Twenty-five aircraft failed to return, and Halifaxes narrowly sustained the highest numerical casualties. Among the missing was the former 44 (Rhodesia) Squadron pilot, S/L Cyril Anekstein, who lost his life in a Path Finder Lancaster belonging to 7 Squadron.

The month ended with preparations for the second of the Berlin operations on the night of the 31st, for which 622 aircraft were made ready, more than half of them Lancasters, 129 of them provided by 5 Group. 44 (Rhodesia) Squadron loaded nine of its own with a cookie and nine SBCs of incendiaries each and dispatched them between 20.11 and 20.33 with F/Ls Barley and Shorthouse the senior pilots on duty. The route on this night took the bomber stream on an east-south-easterly heading across Texel to a position between Hannover and Leipzig, before turning to pass to the south-east of Berlin and approach the city-centre aiming point on a north-westerly track. The return leg would involve a south-westerly course to a position south of Cologne for an exit over the French coast, but despite the attempts to outwit the enemy night-fighter controller, he would be able to predict to some extent where to concentrate his fighters. Sgt Knight abandoned his sortie at 21.37 because of a problem with his starboard-inner engine, and F/Sgt Whitecross followed suit shortly afterwards for an undisclosed reason, both jettisoning their loads "live". The remainder pressed on, and, for the first time, would report the use by the Germans of "fighter flares" to mark out the path of the bombers to and from the target. The Path Finders encountered five to six-tenths cloud in the target area, and this combined with H2S equipment failure and a spirited night-fighter response to cause the markers to be dropped well to the south of the planned aiming point. The main force crews became involved in an extensive creep-back, which would stretch some thirty miles into open country and outlying communities. The 44 (Rhodesia) Squadron crews reported up to eight-tenths thin cloud and bombed on red and green TIs from 17,500 to 20,700 feet between 23.39 and 00.02, observing many fires over a wide area. It was noted by some that two groups of green TIs were ten miles apart, and both attracted attention from the main force. F/O Parsons and crew had to fend off an enemy night-fighter, which wounded both gunners and rendered their turrets inoperable. The rear gunner remained in his turret, cut off from the intercom, while the bomb-aimer took over the mid-upper purely to keep a look-out. The outcome of the raid was a major disappointment, brought about by woefully short marking and a pronounced creep-back, and resulted in the destruction of just eighty-five houses, a figure in no way commensurate with the effort expended and the loss of forty-seven heavy bombers. The percentage loss rates made alarming reading at Bomber Command HQ, the Lancasters with an acceptable and sustainable 3%, the Halifaxes with 11.3% and the Stirlings with 16%. 44 (Rhodesia) Squadron posted missing the crew of P/O Stephenson in ED665, which crashed without survivors at Schönebeck, within the Berlin defence zone.

During the course of the month the squadron participated in twelve operations and dispatched 134 sorties for the loss of five Lancasters and their crews.

September 1943

The new month began operationally for 44 (Rhodesia) Squadron with the departure from Dunholme Lodge at 20.14 and 20.19 of the crews of P/Os Leslie and Rogers respectively, who were bound for the Nectarine I garden, situated a fraction north of due east on the other side of the North Sea. They found small amounts of scattered cloud at around 3,000 feet, and good visibility despite the absence of a moon, and homed-in on the drop zone by Gee-fix to plant their vegetables into the briefed locations from 6,000 and 5,500 feet respectively at 21.46.

Probably as a result of the heavy losses recently incurred by the Halifaxes and Stirlings, an all-Lancaster force was to conclude the current series of operations against the "Big City". 316 aircraft were made ready on the 3rd, of which 121 were provided by 5 Group, including nine by 44 (Rhodesia)

Squadron, which departed Dunholme Lodge between 19.42 and 20.11 with S/L Watson the senior pilot on duty. After rendezvousing over the North Sea, the bomber stream crossed the Dutch coast over the Den Helder peninsula, and adopted a direct course of 350 miles, which took them north of Hannover to Brandenburg, some thirty-five miles short of the target. Long, straight legs were rarely employed because of the risk of interception by the Luftwaffe, but the forecast heavy cloud with tops at 18,000 feet accompanied the stream all the way from the Dutch coast to the target area and helped to keep the enemy at bay. The Path Finders had been briefed to use H2S to navigate their way via the region's lakes to the city centre aiming point, but the cloud miraculously dispersed in time to leave clear skies and allow the Path Finders to drop ground-marking TIs rather than the less reliable skymarkers. The first TIs fell right over the aiming point, before others crept back for between two and five miles along the line of approach from the west. Fortunately, the backers up maintained the marking as the main force Lancasters came in in a single wave, and, although much of the bombing fell short of the city centre, most of it landed within the city boundaries, principally into the largely residential districts of Tiergarten, Wedding, Moabit and Charlottenburg, and the industrial Siemensstadt, where much useful damage and a loss of war production resulted. The 44 (Rhodesia) Squadron crews carried out a time-and-distance run from yellow track markers and bombed on red and green TIs from 18,000 to 20,000 feet between 23.26 and 23.39. Many fires were observed, which appeared to be merging as the bombers turned towards the north for a return route that would intentionally violate Swedish airspace. Four Mosquitos laid spoof route marker flares well away from the actual track to mislead the night-fighters, but, in the absence of the poorer performing Halifaxes and Stirlings, twenty-two Lancasters failed to return, almost 7% of those dispatched. The price paid by commanding officers and flight commanders for leading from the front was often an untimely end, to which the squadron could attest, having recently lost two commanding officers and a number of flight commanders. S/L Watson and his crew all perished when W4961 crashed outbound at Wunstorf, a town some fifteen miles north-west of Hannover, while DV155 was leaving the target area when it came down at Neuruppin to the North of Berlin, killing F/O Rundle RAAF and all but his navigator, one of four Australians in the crew, who was taken into captivity. On the following afternoon, F/L Miller and F/Os Burr and Pilgrim conducted a five-hour square search over the North Sea for downed crews in dinghies but found nothing.

Whether by design, or as a result of the losses sustained, Berlin was now shelved for the next ten weeks, while Harris sought other suitable targets, of which there were many. He would shortly begin a four-raid series against Hanover stretching over a four-week period, but, first, he focussed on southern Germany, beginning on the 5th with the twin cities of Mannheim and Ludwigshafen, which face each other from the East and West Banks respectively of the Rhine. The plan was to exploit the creep-back phenomenon that attended most large operations, by approaching the target from the west, and marking the eastern half of Mannheim, with the expectation that the bombing would spread back along the line of approach across western Mannheim and into Ludwigshafen. A force of 605 aircraft was assembled, which included 108 Lancasters of 5 Group, nine of them at Dunholme Lodge loaded with a cookie each and a variety of incendiaries packed into thirteen to eighteen SBCs. They took off between 19.46 and 20.02 with F/L Shorthouse the senior pilot on duty, and, after climbing out, set course for Beachy Head and the Channel crossing. Sgt Rollin and crew lost their entire oxygen supply within fifty-five minutes despite strenuous efforts to plug the leak, and they had to turn back. They others made it all the way in favourable weather conditions to find clear skies over the target, where the Path Finders performed at their absolute best. After first observing red and yellow markers, the 44 (Rhodesia) Squadron crews had green TIs in their bomb sights as they let their loads go from 18,000 to 20,500 feet between 23.01 and 23.29, and all reported hitting them. Those arriving towards the later stages of the raid were drawn on by the burgeoning fires fifty miles ahead, and a number of large, red explosions were observed at 23.12, 23.23 and 23.27, the last of which was followed by a purplish-red mushroom of fire. Searchlights were numerous, but the flak negligible, and it was the abundance of night-fighters that posed the greatest risk to life and limb, although most of the Dunholme Lodge crews appeared to avoid any contact. Black smoke was rising through 15,000 feet as the bombers withdrew to the west, and the glow from the burning cities was visible for 150 miles into the return journey, which thirty-four aircraft would fail to complete. Thirteen Lancasters, an equal number of Halifaxes and eight Stirlings were missing, and the percentage loss rates continued to tell the same story. 44 (Rhodesia) Squadron posted missing the crew of P/O Stiver in JA703, which crashed on the East Bank of the Rhine at Mannheim-Sandhofen, some six miles north of the city centre. Local reports confirmed that both Mannheim and Ludwigshafen had suffered catastrophic destruction, with almost two thousand fires in the latter alone, 986 of them classed as large. Mannheim's reporting system broke down completely, and little detail emerged of this raid, although it would recover in time for the next assault in less than three weeks' time.

Munich was posted as the target on the 6th, for which the squadron made ready seven Lancasters as part of the ninety-two-strong 5 Group element in an overall force of 257 Lancasters and 147 Halifaxes, the Stirling brigade made conspicuous by its absence. The Dunholme Lodge crews were airborne between 19.44 and 20.00 with no senior pilots on duty, each carrying a similar bomb load and adopting the same route as for the previous night. F/Sgt Matheson and crew had been outbound for under two hours when their starboard-outer engine caught fire and ended their sortie, leaving the others to reach the Bavarian capital city under conditions that were not ideal. The cloud varied between five and nine-tenths, although some ground features, like the River Isar, could be identified and the red, yellow and green TIs observed. The 44 (Rhodesia) Squadron crews were among those carrying out a timed run from the Ammersee, located twenty-one miles away to the south-west, and bombed from 20,000 to 21,100 feet between 23.34 and 23.59. A large number of fires was observed to be grouped around the markers, but an accurate assessment was not possible, and local reports would suggest that the attack had been scattered across southern and western districts. The searchlights were ineffective because of the cloud, but large numbers of night-fighters were again evident, and sixteen aircraft failed to return, thirteen of them Halifaxes, a percentage loss rate of 8.8, compared with 1.2 for the Lancasters.

5 Group largely left the war to the other groups for the ensuing two weeks, during which period attacks were carried out against coastal batteries at Le Portel near Boulogne under Operation Starkey, and industrial and railway targets, also in France. F/L Barley was posted to 104 O.T.U on the 13th at the conclusion of his tour. Only 617 and 619 Squadrons were in action on behalf of 5 Group, first on the night of the 15/16th, when the former sent eight Lancasters to attack the raised earthen banks of the Dortmund-Ems Canal at a point south of the twin aqueduct section near Ladbergen. Five of them failed to return, including the former 44 Squadron crew of F/L Henry Wilson, who had been founder members of 617 Squadron, and had trained for the Dams but had not taken part. On the following night, small elements from the two squadrons combined to attack the Antheor viaduct in southern France. What had been known as RAF Base Scampton since the "Base" system had been adopted in May, was redesignated 52 Base on the 16th, and still included the stations at Fiskerton and Dunholme Lodge. However, Scampton had been closed on the 1st to allow the construction of concrete runways, and, when declared operational again in the autumn of 1944, it would have been transferred to 1 Group.

It was not until the commencement of the series of raids on Hannover that 5 Group, as a whole, was roused from its slumber. The irony of such long layoffs was that airmen, despite occupying the most dangerous jobs in the fighting services, grew listless and bored when left to kick their heels, attend lectures and take part in PT, and, no doubt, cheered when the tannoys called them to briefing on the 22nd. They learned that they were to be part of a force of 711 aircraft to attack the ancient city of Hannover, situated in northern Germany midway between the Dutch frontier and Berlin. They were told that it was home to much war industry, and it was also the location of seven Nazi concentration camps, although, this was not known at the time among the Allies. According to Martin Middlebrook and Chris Everitt in Bomber Command War Diaries, the first two operations produced concentrated bombing, but mostly outside of the target, while only the third one succeeded in causing extensive damage, which, if the figures are to be believed, seem to be massively out of proportion. The author contends that the reports of the crews after the first two operations suggest strongly that the damage to Hannover was accumulative over the first three raids and did not result from just one, as will be explained in the following narrative. The telling feature is, perhaps, that no reports came out of Hannover to corroborate the testimony of the crews on the first two raids, although post-raid reconnaissance by the RAF after the second one did show that some of the bombing had fallen into open country, and the Path Finders did admit to at least one poor performance.

44 (Rhodesia) Squadron prepared a dozen Lancasters, which took off between 18.39 and 19.16 with S/Ls Lynch and Shorthouse the senior pilots on duty, before climbing out and joining up with the other 135 participants from 5 Group for the 430-mile outward leg. There were no early returns to Dunholme Lodge, and all reached the target area, where good visibility prevailed, but stronger-than-forecast winds would play their part in pushing the marking and bombing towards the south-east. The 44 (Rhodesia) Squadron crews carried out their bombing runs from 14,500 to 22,100 feet between 21.29 and 21.48, aiming at red and green TIs and dodging the intense searchlights and heavy flak, which was bursting at around 18,000 feet. Some returning crews observed a line of fires developing from west to east, with smoke rising through 14,000 feet, while others claimed that fires ran from the aiming point in a north-north-westerly direction across the city, but all were unanimous, that the raid had been highly successful, and that the glow of fires was still visible from the Dutch coast, a distance of two hundred miles. Twenty-six aircraft failed to return, twelve of them Halifaxes, which, again, sustained the highest numerical losses, and, this time, at 5.3%, even exceeded the Stirling's loss rate.

Let us now examine the claim that the main weight of bombs fell two to five miles south-south-east from the city centre, and that the operation largely failed. Firstly, two to five miles in any city means that the bombing fell within the boundaries, and, therefore, within the built-up area. Secondly, the majority of crews, if not all, reported a highly successful raid with fires right across the city, smoke rising to 14,000 feet as they left the scene and the glow visible from the Dutch coast. It is true that crews were very frequently mistaken in their belief that an attack had been successful, but the evidence on this occasion would seem to confirm their testimony. Decoy fire-sites do not produce a glow visible from a distance of two hundred miles, or sufficient volumes of smoke to reach bombing height during the short duration of a raid and be dense enough to be visible at night.

On the 23rd, and for the second time in the month, Mannheim was posted as the target for that night, and would face a force, which, at take-off, numbered 628 aircraft, 139 of them 5 Group Lancasters. Nine of these were made ready at Dunholme Lodge and took off between 18.48 and 19.04 with W/C Bowes the senior pilot on duty. There were no early returns among the 44 (Rhodesia) Squadron element, and the bomber stream pushed on across France and into southern Germany, where they encountered largely clear skies and good visibility. At the head of the stream, the Path Finders had marked out the northern districts, which had not been hit so severely during the previous operation.

The marking was accurate and concentrated, allowing the Dunholme Lodge crews to attack on red, green and yellow TIs from 18,000 to 19,500 feet between 21.49 and 22.18. Later bombing spilled over into the northern fringe of Ludwigshafen and out into the nearby towns of Oppau and Frankenthal, where much damage resulted. Returning crews reported that smoke had reached around 6,000 feet as they turned away, and that the glow of fires remained visible for 150 miles into the return journey. Thirty-two crews were absent from debriefing, and, this time, eighteen of them were in Lancasters, compared with seven each for the Halifaxes and Stirlings. This provided a somewhat topsy-turvy and unusual loss-rate of 5.7%, 3.6% and 6% respectively. Post-raid reconnaissance and local reports revealed that 927 houses and twenty industrial premises had been destroyed in Mannheim, and that the I. G. Farben factory in Ludwigshafen had sustained serious damage.

Hannover was posted as the target again on the 27th, and a force of 678 aircraft made ready. 44 (Rhodesia) Squadron answered the call with thirteen Lancasters in a 5 Group contribution of 141, and they departed Dunholme Lodge between 19.10 and 20.00 with W/C Bowes the senior pilot on duty. As they climbed out through ice-bearing cloud, F/Sgt Watts' a.s.i froze, forcing him to turn back, and, in continuing poor weather conditions over the North Sea, the same problem struck the crew of F/Sgt Barton, and they, too, aborted their sortie from near the Dutch coast. The others pressed on in the wake of the Path Finders, who were unaware that the weather forecasts on which their performance would be based, were incorrect. The result of that would be to push the marking some five miles from the city centre towards the north of the city, but, at least, the weather improved markedly over Germany to present the crews with clear skies at the target. The 44 (Rhodesia) Squadron crews delivered their cookie and 4lb and 30lb incendiaries each mostly on green TIs from 19,500 to 22,500 feet between 22.01 and 22.20, and observed many fires with smoke rising to 15,000 feet. Returning crews again reported the glow of fires visible from the Dutch coast, and confidence in the success of the operation was unanimous across the Command, giving lie to the claim that little damage resulted. Post-raid photos did reveal many bomb craters in open country, but the fire and smoke evidence did not support decoy fire-sites, and no local report was forthcoming to shed further light. The loss of thirty-eight aircraft was probably something of a shock, but, at least, common sense returned to the statistics to re-establish the status-quo after the topsy-turvy outcome of the Mannheim raid. Seventeen Halifaxes, ten Lancasters, ten Stirlings and one Wellington failed to return, giving loss-rates for the four-engine types of 9% for the Stirling, 7.3% for the Halifax and 3.2% for the Lancaster.

The month ended with an operation to Bochum in the central Ruhr on the 29th, for which 44 (Rhodesia) Squadron made ready nine Lancasters in a 5 Group effort of 111, and they were part of an overall heavy force of 343 aircraft. They departed Dunholme Lodge between 18.13 and 18.34 with no senior pilots on duty, and lost F/O Phillips and crew to engine and compass issues before they arrived at the Dutch coast. The others proceeded to the target, kept on track by two route-marker flares at 20,000 feet, and, after a two-and-a-half-hour outward flight, established their positions visually in good visibility. The Path Finders marked the aiming point with green TIs, and the bombing was carried out from 15,000 to 20,000 feet between 20.53 and 21.08 in the face of a strong searchlight and moderate flak defence. Some returning crews described the target as a mass of flames, with smoke rising rapidly to meet them, while local reports confirmed the destruction of 527 houses, with 742 others seriously damaged.

While this operation was in progress, fourteen 5 Group Lancasters were sent to the Baltic to mine the waters of the Privet I garden off distant Danzig (Gdansk). F/Sgt Matheson and crew took off at 18.13 and arrived at their destination under clear skies and in extreme darkness to deliver their mines into the briefed location from 6,000 feet at 21.59. During the course of the month, the squadron carried out nine operations and dispatched seventy-two sorties for the loss of three Lancasters and their crews.

October 1943

The start of October was a busy time for the Lancaster squadrons, which would be called upon to participate in six major operations in the first eight nights. The month's account was opened at Hagen, at the eastern end of the Ruhr on the 1st, for which a moderately sized heavy force of 243 Lancasters was drawn from 1, 5 and 8 Groups. 5 Group contributed 125 aircraft, ten of them representing 44 (Rhodesia) Squadron, and they were loaded with a cookie and up to sixteen SBCs of incendiaries each, before departing Dunholme Lodge between 18.19 and 18.34 with no senior pilots on duty. They flew out over Skegness aiming for Egmond on the Dutch coast, to then skirt the northern edge of the Ruhr as far as Werl, to the north of the now famous Möhne reservoir, from where they would turn sharply to the south-west to run in on the target. They arrived to find ten-tenths cloud with tops at 8,000 feet and red and green Oboe-laid skymarkers to aim at, and all but one of the 44 (Rhodesia) Squadron crews carried out their attacks from 18,000 to 20,500 feet between 20.58 and 21.09. Sgt Higgs and crew had strayed off track on the way out and stumbled into the defences at Amsterdam and over the Ruhr, shedding height until releasing their bombs from 10,000 feet at 21.40 at the tail end of the raid. They returned safely with the others to report a column of black smoke rising through the clouds, while their squadron colleagues described a large bluish-green explosion at 21.03, the glow of fires beneath the cloud, and an effective Path Finder performance. Sgt Smith and crew came home on three engines, unaware that their time on earth was shortly to end. Only two Lancasters failed to return, and one of them was ED348, which crashed homebound some twenty miles east of Cologne, delivering P/O Smith and three of his crew into enemy hands as the only survivors. In addition to the usual housing damage, local reports confirmed the destruction of forty-six industrial firms, among them a manufacturer of accumulator batteries for U-Boots, and this would have an impact on U-Boot production.

294 crews from 1, 5 and 8 Groups were called to briefings on the 2nd to learn that Munich was to be their target for that night. 5 Group detailed 113 Lancasters, whose crews were to adopt the time-and-distance method of bombing, and the nine at Dunholme Lodge were loaded with a cookie and ten SBCs each before taking off between 18.35 and 18.59 with F/Os Burr and West the senior pilots on duty. P/O Knight's port-inner engine cut on take-off, before picking up again, but it was the starboard-outer's fluctuating performance that persuaded him to turn back. The others set a course to the south coast to begin the Channel crossing to the Dunkerque region, before traversing France to enter Germany south of Strasbourg. They reached the target area after an outward flight of some three-and-a-half hours, and encountered cloud over the Wörthsee, situated some fifteen miles west-south-west of the centre of Munich, and the starting point for the time-and-distance run. The skies over the city were clear of cloud, but the marking was scattered and led to most of the early bombing falling into southern and south-eastern districts. The 5 Group crews were unable to establish a firm fix on the Wörthsee, and this would lead to a creep-back of up to fifteen miles along the line of approach. The 44 (Rhodesia) Squadron crews bombed on red and green TIs from 18,300 to 20,500 feet between 22.34 and 22.52, but it was not all plain-sailing and eight Lancasters were lost. JB136 crashed at Otterfing, some seventeen miles south-south-east of Munich city centre, and there were no survivors from the crew of Sgt Smith. Returning crews suggested that the raid appeared to be concentrated on the eastern side of the city, and local authorities reported that 339 buildings had been destroyed.

Kassel, the industrial city located some eighty miles to the east of the Ruhr, would receive two visits from the Command during the month, the first on the 3rd, for which a force of 547 aircraft was assembled consisting of 223 Halifaxes, 204 Lancasters and 113 Stirlings. 5 Group supported the operation with ninety-two Lancasters, of which eight were made ready at Dunholme Lodge, and they took off between 18.25 and 18.46 with S/L Lynch the senior pilot on duty. There were no early returns, and all reached the target area to find largely clear skies but thick ground haze. The Path Finder H2S "blind" markers overshot the planned aiming point, and, because of the haze and, possibly, decoy markers, the backers-up, whose job was to confirm the TIs' accuracy by visual means, were unable to correct the error. The 44 (Rhodesia) Squadron crews identified the target visually and by green TIs and bombed from 17,400 to 20,000 feet between 21.17 and 21.35, reporting on their return what appeared to be a good concentration of fires and a pall of smoke rising to meet them. In fact, the main weight of the attack had fallen onto the western suburbs, where the Henschel aircraft and tank factories and the Fieseler aircraft plant were hit, but a stray bomb load had also detonated an ammunition dump at Ihringshausen, situated close to the north-eastern suburb of Wolfsanger, which was left devastated by the blast. Twenty-four aircraft failed to return, fourteen Halifaxes, six Stirlings and four Lancasters, which gave a loss-rate of 6.3%, 3.2% and 2.9% respectively. P/O Norton RAAF and his crew were posted missing in ED433, which had crashed in the Söhrewald, six miles south-east of Kassel, killing all but the bomb-aimer, who fell into enemy hands.

The busy schedule of operations was to continue at Frankfurt on the 4th, for which a force of 406 aircraft was made ready. The American confidence in the ability of its forces to deliver daylight attacks on military and war production targets in Germany had been shaken by the high loss rates, which were not sustainable. Since the first Hannover raid, a small number of 8th Air Force B17s had been flirting with night raids alongside their RAF colleagues, and this night would bring their final involvement. 5 Group detailed ninety-five Lancasters, of which nine would represent 44 (Rhodesia) Squadron, and they departed Dunholme Lodge between 17.52 and 18.10 with F/L Hill the senior pilot on duty. They had to follow a somewhat circuitous route, which departed England over the Sussex coast and tracked across Belgium as if heading for southern Germany, before swinging to the north-east and passing to the west of Frankfurt for the final run-in of around eighty miles. This added significantly to the mileage but avoided the flak hotspots from the Dutch coast and north of the Ruhr. There were no early returns among the 44 (Rhodesia) Squadron element, and the target was reached after a four-hour outward flight, although an hour of that was generally accounted for in climbing-out and gaining height before setting course. Frankfurt was found to be clear of cloud, and the Path Finders produced a masterful marking performance to leave the city at the mercy of the main force. The 44 (Rhodesia) Squadron crews bombed on red and green TIs from 17,000 to 21,000 feet between 21.32 and 21.49 and witnessed a highly-concentrated attack taking place that left the eastern half of the city and the docks area a sea of flames. A large red explosion was observed at 21.37, which threw flames up to 3,000 feet, and smoke was rising through 8,000 feet as the bombers turned away, some crews reporting the glow from the burning city to be visible for 120 miles into the homeward leg. The success was gained at the modest cost of ten aircraft, half of which were Halifaxes.

The busy first week of the month concluded with an operation against Stuttgart, for which a force of 343 Lancasters was drawn from 1, 3, 5, 6 and 8 Groups on the 7th. A new weapon in the Command's armoury was introduced for the first time in numbers on this night with the participation of a night-fighter-communications-jamming device called "Jostle". It required a specialist operator in addition to the standard crew of seven, who, though not necessarily a German speaker, could recognise the language, and, on hearing it, jam the signals on up to three frequencies by broadcasting engine noise over them. At 101 Squadron the device was referred to as ABC or Airborne Cigar, and, once proved to be effective, ABC Lancasters would be spread through the bomber stream for all major operations, whether or not 1 Group was otherwise involved. The Lancaster would also carry a full bomb load reduced by 1,000lbs to compensate for the weight of the equipment and its operator. 5 Group put up 128 Lancasters, of which eleven were made ready at Dunholme Lodge, and they took off between 20.16 and 20.37 with W/C Bowes the senior pilot on duty. Sgt Evans and F/Sgt Lyford and their crews were coned in searchlights as they crossed over London and were subjected to heavy anti-aircraft fire. They arrived back at base early within minutes of each other at midnight, F/Sgt Lyford's Lancaster with glycol leaks affecting two engines and Sgt Evans with a dead starboard-outer, which may have been caused by the friendly fire. The others reached the target area, where ten-tenths cloud at 10,000 feet concealed the ground from view. The Path Finders employed H2S and established two areas of marking, which led to bombs falling in many parts of the city from the centre to the south-west. The 44 (Rhodesia) Squadron crews bombed from 18,500 to 20,800 feet between 00.10 and 00.20, before returning safely to report their impressions of a scattered attack, which cost a remarkably modest four aircraft. Whether or not the presence of the radio-countermeasures Lancasters was responsible could not be certain, but it was a promising start, and would lead, ultimately, to the formation of a dedicated RCM group, 100 Group, in November.

The third raid of the series on Hannover was posted on the 8th, and a force of 504 aircraft duly assembled. 5 Group contributed eighty-four Lancasters, eight of them made ready at Dunholme Lodge, and they took off between 22.35 and 22.47 with F/Os Burr and Phillips the senior pilots on duty. After climbing out, they set course for the northern tip of Texel, and all reached the target area to find largely clear skies and red and green TIs marking out the city-centre aiming point. The 44 (Rhodesia) Squadron crews bombed from 18,000 to 20,000 feet between 01.35 and 01.54, and, having arrived in the early stages of the attack, saw fires just beginning to take hold. It became clear, as they retreated westwards, that the fires were developing into a serious conflagration, but, curiously, despite the claim by some commentators that this was the one successful raid of the series, there was no mention of the glow being visible from a considerable distance, as had been the case with the first two operations. This time a local report did emerge, which described heavy damage in all districts except for those in the west, with a large area of fire engulfing the central districts. A total of 3,932 buildings was destroyed, and thirty thousand others damaged to some extent, with a death toll of 1,200 people. These statistics seem somewhat excessive for a single operation by fewer than five hundred aircraft, particularly in the absence of the kind of crew reports common to the first two raids, and this adds weight to the author's contention, that the damage was accumulative over the three operations. Twenty-seven aircraft failed to return, but there were no empty dispersals at Dunholme Lodge.

The Path Finder and main force squadrons would effectively stand down now for a period of ten days, while Mosquitos of 8 Group's Light Night Striking Force took the war to Germany. The crews were, no doubt, relieved when the lull in operations came to an end on the 18th with a call on Lancaster stations to attend briefings. The wall map revealed Hannover as the target for the fourth and last time in this series, and the crews learned that this was to be an all-Lancaster affair involving 360 aircraft. 5 Group provided 143 of them, sixteen made ready by 44 (Rhodesia) Squadron, and they departed Dunholme Lodge between 17.05 and 17.48 with S/L Shorthouse the senior pilot on duty. They made landfall over Texel and continued on an easterly track across Holland aiming for Cloppenburg, and thence Nienburg and Celle, before turning to the south-west to run in on the target close to the Misburg oil refinery. They remained unmolested by the defences until encountering a nest of night-fighters on crossing the frontier into Germany, and at least thirteen aircraft were brought down during the ensuing forty-five minutes that encompassed the approach and withdrawal phases. A layer of eight to ten-tenths cloud hung over Hannover with tops at 12,000 to 15,000 feet, and these conditions made it difficult for the Path Finders to establish the aiming point. It resulted in them dropping both sky and ground markers that lacked concentration, which would lead to a scattering of the effort. The 44 (Rhodesia) Squadron crews bombed mostly on red and green TIs or on release-point flares from 18,000 to 21,400 feet between 20.17 and 20.30, and a colossal explosion was observed at around 20.19. The strong night-fighter presence dissuaded crews from hanging around to assess the outcome further, and the impression of those returning was of a scattered attack. It was established later that most of the bombs had fallen into open country, a disappointment compounded by the loss of eighteen Lancasters. Among these was 44 (Rhodesia) Squadron's veteran R5901, which crashed at 20.36 at Bissendorf, a dozen miles or so north of Hannover, killing P/O Piper and three of his crew and delivering the three survivors into captivity. The four raids on Hannover had cost the Command 110 aircraft from 2,253 sorties, a loss rate of 4.9%, but much of the city now lay in ruins, and would receive no further attention for a year, until the oil offensive and the close proximity of the Misburg synthetic oil plant to the east would keep the region in the firing line.

The first major attack of the war on the eastern city of Leipzig was planned for the 20th, and an all-Lancaster force of 358 aircraft representing 1, 5, 6 and 8 Groups assembled. 5 Group was responsible for 140 Lancasters, and 44 (Rhodesia) Squadron fifteen, which took off from Dunholme Lodge between 17.03 and 17.31 with S/L Shorthouse the senior pilot on duty. Atrocious weather conditions were encountered outbound, with a towering front of ice-bearing cumulonimbus east of Hannover extending beyond 20,000 feet, and this persuaded many crews to turn back as engines began to falter and ice-accretion destroyed lift. F/Sgt Lyford was unable to climb into clear air, and dropped his cookie first, in the hope that it would be sufficient, and when it clearly wasn't, the rest of the load was jettisoned from 18,000 feet some twenty miles east of Hannover. P/O Higgs and crew had reached a position some twenty miles north-east of Braunschweig (Brunswick) when it became necessary to lighten their load after shedding ten thousand feet in twenty-four minutes, the first six thousand in just eight minutes. They found an aerodrome flarepath for their cookie, which they dropped from 18,500 feet at 21.29 and observed it to detonate within the airfield boundary. The others pushed on through the front to reach the target after a three-and-a-half-hour outward flight, to then encounter seven to ten-tenths cloud with tops as high as 14,000 feet. The Path Finders had been unable in the conditions to establish and mark the aiming point, leaving crews to bomb on e.t.a., on fires glimpsed through the cloud or on scattered skymarkers, the 44 (Rhodesia) Squadron element carrying out their attacks from 13,500 to 22,500 feet between 21.02 and 21.16. F/Sgt Watts RAAF and crew had to contend with a fuel shortage on the way home after flak cut a pipe, and they systematically drained each tank until it became necessary to ditch some sixty miles south-east of the Lincolnshire fishing port of Grimsby. The Lancaster, EE184, broke its back at the mid-upper turret, and the rear half sank almost immediately, to be followed fifteen minutes later by the front section. The Pilot failed to emerge from the cockpit, and the navigator fell off a wing to be carried away in the heavy swell, leaving the others in the dinghy awaiting rescue at the hands of a minesweeper three hours and ten minutes after the ditching. The remains of the pilot were eventually recovered and laid to rest in Bergen-op-Zoom war cemetery in southern Holland. Sixteen Lancasters failed to return, and those crews that did make it home were unable to offer any useful details at debriefing.

The final major operation of the month was the second one against Kassel, for which preparations were put in hand on the 22nd. A force of 569 aircraft ultimately stood ready to take off in the early evening, 133 of them 5 Group Lancasters, thirteen provided by 44 (Rhodesia) Squadron. All but one became airborne from Dunholme Lodge between 17.58 and 18.16 with F/L Hill the senior pilot on duty, but P/O Rollin failed to lift off after overshooting the runway. A navigation error threw F/O Fynn and crew behind schedule, and, by the time they had re-established their position, it was too late to continue. F/Sgt Manning and crew ran into an electrical storm over the North Sea, which affected the P4 compass, and, as the DR compass and the oxygen supply to the rear turret had already failed, they turned back early. The others pressed on across Belgium in continuing unfavourable weather conditions, which miraculously improved in the target area to leave clear skies between the bombers and the target, but ten-tenths cloud above them at 24,000 feet. At the opening of the raid, the H2S "blind" markers overshot the city-centre aiming point, leaving the success of the operation reliant upon the visual marker crews backing up, and they did not disappoint. The red and green TIs were focussed right on the aiming point, and the main force followed up with accurate and concentrated bombing with scarcely any creep-back. The 44 (Rhodesia) Squadron crews carried out their attacks from 17,800 to 21,300 feet between 20.57 and 21.18, and observed the fires just beginning to take hold as they turned away. It was after the sound of their engines had receded that the fires joined together to engulf the city in what, in some areas, developed into a firestorm, though not one as fierce as that experienced in Hamburg. The massively successful operation was achieved at a high cost of forty-three bombers, twenty-five of them Halifaxes. In Kassel, the shell-shocked inhabitants emerged from their shelters to find their city devastated and unrecognizable. After 3,600 fires had been dealt with, it would be established eventually that more than 4,300 apartment blocks containing 53,000 dwelling units had been destroyed or damaged, leaving up to 120,000 people without homes, while more than six thousand had lost their lives. 155 industrial buildings had also been destroyed or severely damaged, along with numerous schools, hospitals, churches and public buildings.

During the course of the month, the squadron participated in nine operations and dispatched ninety-nine sorties for the loss of five Lancasters, four crews and two crew members.

November 1943

November brought with it the long, dark, cloudy nights that enabled Harris to return to his main theme, the destruction of Germany's capital city. The next four months would bring the bloodiest, hardest fought air battles between Bomber Command and the Luftwaffe Nachtjagd and test the hard-pressed crews to the limit of their endurance. In a minute to Churchill on the 3rd, Harris stated, that with the participation of the American 8th Air Force, he could "wreck Berlin from end to end". He estimated that the campaign would cost the two forces between four and five hundred aircraft, but that it would cost Germany the war. This would remove the need for the kind of bloody, expensive and protracted land campaign, which he had personally witnessed during the Great War, and had prompted him to "get into the air" at the earliest opportunity. It should be remembered that this was the first time in the history of air warfare, that the means had existed to prove the theory, that an enemy could be defeated by bombing alone. It is only in the light of more recent experiences, that we have learned of the need, in a conventional conflict at least, to occupy the enemy's territory to secure submission. The Americans, however, were committed to victory on land, where film cameras could capture the glory, and would not accompany Harris to Berlin.

Düsseldorf was selected to open the month's operational account that very night, and, no doubt, while the Prime Minister was digesting Harris's epistle, a force of 589 Lancasters and Halifaxes was being prepared for action. 5 Group's contribution amounted to 147 Lancasters, of which a dozen represented 44 (Rhodesia) Squadron, and they were each loaded with a cookie and up to eighteen SBCs of various incendiaries before taking off between 16.50 and 17.18 with no senior pilots on duty. They joined the bomber stream over the North Sea and approached the south-western Ruhr after flying out over Belgium and through the concentration of fifty to sixty searchlights in the Mönchengladbach-Cologne corridor, some fifteen miles from the target. Small patches of cloud below them at 12,000 feet were drifting across the target along with smoke from the early fires, despite which, the visibility remained generally good, and the Path Finders employed both sky and ground markers to good effect to identify the aiming point in the city centre. The 44 (Rhodesia) Squadron crews bombed on red and green TIs and skymarkers from 19,000 to 22,300 feet between 19.37 and 20.01, and fires were observed to be developing on both sides of the Rhine with black smoke rising through 6,000 feet as they turned away. Eighteen aircraft failed to return, and, unusually, eleven were Lancasters and only seven Halifaxes. It was on this night, that 61 Squadron's F/L Bill Reid earned the award of a Victoria Cross for pressing on to bomb the target after his Lancaster, LM360, was severely damaged, and a number of his crew either killed or wounded. Post-raid reconnaissance revealed that central and southern districts had sustained widespread damage to industry and housing, but no report came out of Düsseldorf to provide detail.

The only serious activity for 44 (Rhodesia) Squadron thereafter, until the resumption of the Berlin campaign, was as part of a 5 and 8 Group force of 313 Lancasters, which was sent to destroy railway yards at Modane, situated in the foothills of the Alps in south-eastern France on the night of the 10/11th. 5 Group supported the operation with 136 Lancasters, of which fourteen representing 44 (Rhodesia) Squadron departed Dunholme Lodge between 20.38 and 21.07 with W/C Bowes and S/L Lynch the senior pilots on duty. Ahead of them lay an outward flight of more than 650 miles, which F/O West and crew failed to negotiate after both electrical generators malfunctioned and forced them to turn back early. The others completed the outward leg in around four-and-a-quarter hours to be rewarded by the presence of a full moon shining brightly from a cloudless sky. They pinpointed on Lake Bissorte, from where they carried out a time-and-distance run to the target, which they identified visually and by red and green TIs, before bombing from an almost uniform 15,000 feet between 01.00 and 01.14. The attack seemed to be concentrated around the markers, and fires appeared to be taking hold, while a large explosion was observed at 01.13. Returning crews were fairly confident in the quality of their night's efforts, and two hundred bombing photos revealed extensive damage to track and installations within one mile of the aiming point, and not a single aircraft had been lost.

Undaunted by the American response to his invitation to join the Berlin party, Harris would return alone, and the rocky road to the Capital was re-joined by an all-Lancaster heavy force on the night of the 18/19th, while a predominantly Halifax and Stirling contingent of 395 aircraft acted as a diversion by raiding Mannheim and Ludwigshafen three hundred miles to the south-west. The Berlin-bound crews would benefit from four Mosquitos dropping dummy fighter flares, while other Mosquitos carried out a spoof raid on Frankfurt to protect the Mannheim force. The two forces would cross the enemy coast simultaneously some 250 miles apart to confuse the enemy night-fighter controllers, and the route chosen for the Berlin brigade was via the Frisian island of Texel to a point north of Hannover, and thence to the target to pass over the centre on an east-north-easterly heading. After bombing they would return south of Berlin and Cologne, before crossing central Belgium to gain the English Channel via the French coast. An innovation for this operation was a shortening of the bomber stream to reduce the time over the target to sixteen minutes. When the first Thousand Bomber raid had taken place in May 1942, with an unprecedented twelve aircraft per minute crossing the aiming point, there was considered to be a high risk of collisions. The number had since been increased to sixteen per minute, with large raids lasting up to forty-five minutes, but, on this night, twenty-seven aircraft per minute were to pass over the aiming point.

44 (Rhodesia) Squadron made ready seventeen Lancasters as part of a 5 Group force of 182, and take-off from Dunholme Lodge was accomplished without incident between 16.58 and 17.18 with W/C Bowes and S/L Lynch the senior pilots on duty. P/O Knight lost a number of navigational aids over the North Sea, and when the oxygen supply to the rear turret and the intercom system failed, he decided to bomb the Frisian island of Vlieland, before turning back. This left sixteen others from the squadron to continue the journey to Germany's capital, over a blanket of cloud covering the whole of northern Germany. P/O John Chatterton was the son of a farming family, whose land in Lincolnshire's flat East Lindsey countryside had been commandeered by the Air Ministry to turn into the bomber station at East Kirkby, which had welcomed 57 Squadron as its first resident unit at the end of August. Chatterton had been commissioned earlier in the day and provided a detailed account of the part played by his crew during the operation. They were grateful for the red spotfire route marker dropped by the Path Finders north-east of Hannover, which confirmed that they were on track, and described the horizontal visibility as good, despite the absence of a moon. The cloud persisted all the way to the target with tops at 6,000 feet and was illuminated by searchlights as they orbited at 21.03, before carrying out their attack from 22,000 feet at 21.09. The marking was by H2S, and the other 44 (Rhodesia) Squadron participants delivered their loads mostly from 20,000 to 23,600 feet on red and green skymarkers between 20.59 and 21.21, with F/L Hill and crew the odd men out by attacking from 16,000 feet. All returned home with nothing useful to pass on to the intelligence section at debriefing, and most considered the bombing to have been scattered and probably ineffective. Local sources confirmed that there had been no concentration and confirmed the destruction of 169 houses and a number of industrial units, with many more damaged to some extent. The diversion at Mannheim was deemed to have been successful in its purpose, and caused some useful industrial damage, most seriously to the Daimler-Benz motor factory, which suffered a 90% loss of production for an unknown period. In addition to this, more than three hundred buildings were destroyed at a cost of twenty-three aircraft, while the losses from Berlin were encouragingly low at just nine.

The Lancasters stayed at home on the 19th, while 3, 4, 6 and 8 Groups combined to put 170 Halifaxes, eighty-six Stirlings and ten Mosquitos into the air for a raid on the Ruhr city of Leverkusen. They were greeted in the target area by ten-tenths cloud and an absence of marking, which was caused by equipment failure among the Oboe Mosquitos. A few green TIs were spotted some five to ten miles to the north-west of the target during the approach, but the crews were left to establish their positions on the basis of their own H2S, which, over a region as densely built-up as the Ruhr, was a challenge. As a result, the operation was a complete failure, which sprayed bombs over twenty-seven towns in the region, mostly to the north of Leverkusen.

Harris called for a maximum effort on Berlin on the 22nd, and 764 aircraft were made available, of which sixteen of 5 Group's 166 Lancasters were provided by 44 (Rhodesia) Squadron. They departed Dunholme Lodge between 16.35 and 17.04 with S/L Shorthouse the senior pilot on duty, and, after climbing out, adopted an outward route similar to that employed by the all-Lancaster force four nights earlier. This took them from Texel to a point north-west of Hannover, where a slight dogleg to port put them on a due-easterly heading directly to the target. Unlike the previous raid, however, rather than the circuitous return south of Cologne and out over the French coast, they would come home via a reciprocal route. This was based on a forecast of low cloud and fog over Germany, which would inhibit the night-fighter effort, while broken, medium-level cloud over Berlin would facilitate ground marking. An additional bonus was the availability to the Path Finders of five new H2S Mk III sets, while a new record of thirty-four aircraft per minute passing over the aiming point would be achieved by abandoning the long-standing practice of allocating aircraft types to specific waves. On this night, aircraft of all types would be spread through the bomber stream, and this was bad news for the Stirlings, which, by the very nature of their design, would be below the Lancaster and Halifax elements, and in danger of being hit by friendly bombs.

F/O Burr and crew were back home within two-and-a-half hours after failing to rectify an intercom issue, leaving the others to discover that the meteorological forecast had been inaccurate, and that the city was hidden under a blanket of ten-tenths cloud with tops at around 12,000 feet. This meant that ground marking would be largely ineffective, and that the least reliable Wanganui (skymarking) method would have to be employed. Crews ran into intense predicted flak and a mass of searchlights as they began their bombing runs, and those from 44 (Rhodesia) Squadron aimed at red and green TIs and release-point flares from 17,000 to 22,400 feet between 20.06 and 20.26. The glow of fires was observed beneath the clouds, and a very large explosion lit up the sky at 20.10. The impression was of a successful operation, but an assessment through the clouds was impossible. Post-raid reconnaissance and local reports confirmed that this attack on Berlin had been the most effective of the war to date and had caused a swathe of destruction from the city centre through the western residential districts of Tiergarten and Charlottenburg as far as the suburb town of Spandau. A number of firestorm areas were reported, and the catalogue of destruction included three thousand houses and twenty-three industrial premises. Many thousands more sustained varying degrees of damage, costing 175,000 people their homes and an estimated two thousand their lives, and, by daylight on the 23rd, the smoke had risen to almost 19,000 feet.

Twenty-six aircraft failed to return, eleven of them Lancasters, ten Halifaxes, and five Stirlings, which amounted to a loss-rate among the types respectively of 2.3%, 4.2% and 10.0%. This proved to be the final straw for Harris as far as the Stirling was concerned, which, because of its short wing design, was restricted to a low service ceiling, and by the configuration of its bomb bay to small calibre bombs. Unlike the Lancaster and Halifax, it lacked development potential, and was immediately withdrawn from future operations over Germany. It would still have an important role to play on secondary duties, however, bombing over occupied territory, mining, and, in 1944, it would replace the Halifax to become the aircraft of choice for the two SOE squadrons, 138 and 161, at Tempsford. Many of those released from Bomber Command service would find their way to 38 Group, where they would give valuable service as transports and glider-tugs for airborne landings.

A heavy force of 365 Lancasters and ten Halifaxes was made ready with some difficulty on the 23rd for a return to Berlin. Back-to-back long-range operations put a strain on those charged with the responsibility of getting the aircraft off the ground, and the Ludford Magna armourers were unable to load all nineteen 101 Squadron Lancasters with the intended weight of bombs, sending them off 2,000lb short. 5 Group detailed 141 Lancasters, of which the dozen belonging to 44 (Rhodesia) Squadron were each loaded with a cookie, and some had a 1,000 pounder along with their SBCs of incendiaries. They took off between 17.00 and 17.43 with F/Ls Hill and Phillips the senior pilots on duty, but the latter returned after an hour-and-forty minutes with an unserviceable rear turret, while the former was back on the ground after two-and-a-half- hours, having taken off late and been further delayed by a lack of power. There were eighteen 5 Group early returns among forty-six from the force as a whole, which was a further indication of the strain of back-to-back long-range operations. Another was the dumping of bombs over the North Sea by crews intending to push on to the target but wanting to gain more height. It involved largely those from 1 Group, who were shedding their cookies in protest at their A-O-C's policy of loading each Lancaster to its maximum all-up weight at the expense of altitude. The slogan "H-E-I-G-H-T spells safety" could be found on the walls of most bomber station briefing rooms at the time. The target was reached by way of the same route adopted on the previous night and was found to be covered by ten-tenths cloud with tops at between 10,000 and 15,000 feet. Guided by the glow of fires still burning beneath the clouds from the night before, and the presence of red and green TIs, the 44 (Rhodesia) Squadron crews bombed from 19,200 to 20,300 feet between 20.03 and 20.12 to contribute to another stunning blow. Returning crews described a column of smoke reaching 20,000 feet, and the glow of fires visible again from the Hannover area some 150 miles from the target. It was on this night that fake broadcasts from England caused annoyance to the night-fighter force by ordering them to land because of fog over their bases, despite which, they still had a major hand in the bringing-down of twenty Lancasters. It became a bad night for Dunholme Lodge, to which three crews failed to return. DV329 crashed at Rasdorf, well to the south of the intended return track, and only the mid-upper gunner survived from the crew of F/L Hill to be taken into captivity. LM373 came down somewhere in the Berlin area with no survivors from the crew of P/O Buckel, and LM374 was lost without trace, taking with it the crew of F/O Hanscomb. Post-raid reconnaissance and local reports confirmed that this operation had destroyed a further two thousand buildings and killed around fifteen hundred people.

After a three-night rest for most of the Lancaster crews, 443 of them were briefed on the 26th for a return to the "Big City" for the fourth attack on it since the resumption of the campaign. 5 Group detailed 161 Lancasters, fourteen of them made ready by 44 (Rhodesia) Squadron, and they departed Dunholme Lodge between 17.11 and 17.36 with F/L Phillips the senior pilot on duty. A diversionary raid on Stuttgart by a predominantly Halifax force followed the same route as those bound for Berlin, which involved an outward leg across the French coast and Belgium to a point north of Frankfurt, where they separated. An indication of the beneficial effects of the three-day lay-off was a 44% reduction in early returns by 5 Group crews compared with the previous Berlin raid. F/O Fynn and crew had to contend with the partial failure of the intercom to the rear turret, which left the rear gunner reticent to continue, while his crew colleagues were keen to complete the sortie. This created an unhealthy tension among the crew, and F/O Fynn opted to turn back. P/O Holmes A'Court's attention was occupied by engine, Gee and turret control issues, which persuaded him also to abandon his sortie. The remaining 44 (Rhodesia) Squadron crews found Berlin under clear skies, despite which, the Path Finders overshot the city centre aiming point by six or seven miles, and marked an area well to the north-west, which happened to contain many war-industry factories. The 44 (Rhodesia) Squadron crews bombed on red and green TIs from 19,500 and 22,400 feet between 21.19 and 21.30, and returning crews spoke of a mass of fires and thick smoke rising to 15,000 feet. It was learned later that thirty-eight war-industry factories had been destroyed and many others damaged, in return for the loss of twenty-eight Lancasters, many of which had fallen victim to night-fighters on the return flight.

These last three operations against Berlin undoubtedly represented the best phase of the entire campaign, and, according to local reports, the total death toll on the ground resulting from them amounted to 4,330 people, while the destruction of 8,700 apartment buildings containing more than 104,500 flats, and damage to several times that number, robbed 450,000 residents of their homes for varying lengths of time. However, Berlin was not Hamburg, where narrow streets had aided the spread of fire. Berlin was a modern city of concrete and steel with wide thoroughfares and open spaces to create natural firebreaks, and each building destroyed added to these, so that the campaign would become a bitter struggle of ever decreasing returns. During the course of the month the squadron took part in six operations and dispatched eighty-five sorties for the loss of three Lancasters and their crews.

December 1943

Berlin would continue to be the dominant theme during December, and, as November had ended, so December would begin. A heavy force of 443 aircraft stood ready to take off in the late afternoon of the 2nd, all but fifteen of them Lancasters, after the main Halifax element had been withdrawn because of fog over their Yorkshire stations. 5 Group contributed 145 Lancasters, of which thirteen represented 44 (Rhodesia) Squadron, and they departed Dunholme Lodge between 16.33 and 16.52 with S/L Shorthouse the senior pilot on duty. After climbing out, they headed for the Lincolnshire coast to rendezvous over the North Sea with the rest of the force for a straight-in-straight-out route across Holland and northern Germany with no feints or diversions. First, however, the crews had to negotiate a towering front of ice-bearing cloud over the North Sea, which would contribute to a 10% rate of early returns. 44 (Rhodesia) Squadron's F/L Phillips and crew experienced issues with all four engines misfiring, and they were back on the ground an hour-and-fifty minutes after leaving it. The others pushed through the challenging conditions, and made it to the target area, although mostly south of track after variable winds had thrown them off course and dispersed the bomber stream. They also had to contend with large numbers of enemy night-fighters that would harass the bombers all the way to the target, after the controller had been able correctly to predict it. The Path Finders were using H2S to establish their position at Stendal, but had strayed some fifteen miles south of track and mistakenly used the town of Genthin as their reference for the run-in. The 44 (Rhodesia) Squadron crews found good visibility and were drawn by release-point flares to the aiming point, where they encountered a thin layer of two to three-tenths cloud at around 5,000 feet, but up to nine-tenths between 10,000 and 12,000 feet, which the searchlights were able to pierce. They bombed on skymarkers and red and green TIs, and, where possible, ground detail like burning streets, carrying out their attacks from 17,000 to 21,300 feet between 20.15 and 20.44. They reported observing scattered fires and a number of large explosions, and some claimed the glow to be visible from 120 miles into the homeward leg. Bombing photographs suggested that the raid was only partially successful, causing useful damage in industrial districts in the west and east, but scattering the main weight of bombs over the southern districts and outlying communities to the south. It was a bad night for the bomber force, which lost forty aircraft, mostly in the target area and on the way home. Two empty dispersal pans at Dunholme Lodge should have been occupied by EE179 and JA700, which were now smouldering wrecks at Gross Kienitz, a dozen miles south of Berlin city centre, and another unidentified location near the target. There were no survivors from the crews of F/O Newell and F/O West DFM, the latter well into their second tour. Within hours, all trace of them would have been removed from the station by members of the Committee of Adjustment, and their accommodation prepared for the next occupants.

Having been spared by the weather from experiencing an effective visitation from the Command in October and exploiting the enemy expectation that Berlin would be the target again, Leipzig found itself at the end of the red tape on briefing-room wall-maps from County Durham to Cambridgeshire on the 3rd. A force of 527 aircraft was made ready, which included 103 Lancasters of 5 Group, eight of them belonging to 44 (Rhodesia) Squadron, and they departed Dunholme Lodge between 00.23 and 00.35 with F/O Mercer the senior pilot on duty. The bomber stream headed for Berlin as a feint, passing north of Hannover and Braunschweig with ten-tenths cloud beneath them and an hour's journey to Leipzig still ahead of them. Then, as they turned towards the south-east, the Mosquito element continued on to carry out a diversion at the Capital. Night-fighters had already infiltrated the stream at the Dutch coast, but the feint had the desired effect, and few night-fighters were encountered in the target area, where two layers of ten-tenths cloud prevailed with tops at around 7,000 and 15,000 feet. The Path Finders marked by H2S with green skymarkers, and the 44 (Rhodesia) Squadron crews bombed on these from 20,000 to 21,600 feet between 04.06 and 04.15, observing explosions and a strong glow beneath the clouds. The emergence through the cloud tops of black smoke suggested that an accurate and concentrated attack had taken place, and the smoke and glow remained visible for 150 miles into the return journey south-east towards the French frontier. Had many aircraft not then strayed into the Frankfurt defence zone, the losses may have been fewer, but twenty-four aircraft failed to return, fifteen of them Halifaxes. Local reports confirmed this as a highly successful operation, which had hit residential and industrial areas, and was the most destructive raid visited upon this eastern city during the war. Sadly, for the Command, it would take its revenge in time.

Thereafter, minor operations carried the Command through to mid-month, when, on the 16th, the Lancaster stations were roused to prepare 483 of the type for that night's operation to Berlin for the sixth time since the resumption of the campaign. 5 Group put up 165 aircraft, fifteen of them representing 44 (Rhodesia) Squadron, which took off between 16.20 and 16.55 with S/L Lynch the senior pilot on duty. They were to cross the Dutch coast in the region of Castricum-aan-Zee, and then head due east all the way to the target with no deviations. A three-quarter moon would rise during the long return leg over the Baltic and Denmark, but it was hoped that the very early take-off and the expectation of fog to keep the enemy night-fighters on the ground would reduce the risk of interception. Night-fighters were sent to meet the bomber stream at the Dutch coast, but the 44 (Rhodesia) Squadron crews remained unmolested and pressed on to find Berlin obscured by ten-tenths cloud with tops at around 5,000 feet. However, it could be identified by red and green skymarkers, which were bombed from 19,200 to 22,200 feet between 20.00 and 20.09. The return over Denmark passed largely without major incident, but the greatest difficulties awaited the 1, 6 and 8 Group crews as they arrived home to find their airfields covered by a blanket of dense fog. With little reserves of fuel, the tired crews began a frantic search to find somewhere to land, stumbling blindly through the murk to catch a glimpse of the ground. For many, this proved fatal, while others gave up any hope of landing, and abandoned their aircraft. Twenty-nine Lancasters and a mine-laying Stirling were thus lost, and more than 150 airmen killed in these most tragic of circumstances. To this number was added the twenty-five Lancasters failing to return from the raid, many of which were accounted for by night-fighters over Holland and Germany while outbound. Among these was DV238, which came down near Diepholz, some sixty miles north-west of Hannover, and there were no survivors from the eight occupants captained by P/O Rollin DFC. At debriefing, F/Sgt Barton's gunners claimed the destruction of a BF109, which blew up. Other crews reported the glow of fires, while others saw nothing through the cloud, and it was a local report that confirmed a moderately effective raid, which had fallen principally onto central and eastern districts, where housing suffered most.

A three-day stand-down allowed the crews to recover from the Berlin operation, and it was the 20th when all stations were notified of an operation that night to Frankfurt, for which a force of 390 Lancasters and 257 Halifaxes was assembled. 5 Group made ready 168 Lancasters, and, at Dunholme Lodge, thirteen belonging to 44 (Rhodesia) Squadron were loaded with the requisite amount of fuel and a cookie and sixteen SBCs of incendiaries each before taking off between 16.58 and 17.15 with F/L Hunter the senior pilot on duty. While the main operation was in progress, forty-four Lancasters and ten Mosquitos of 1 and 8 Groups were to carry out a diversion at Mannheim, some forty miles to the south. After climbing out, the crews set course for Southwold and the North Sea-crossing to the

Scheldt estuary, before passing north of Antwerp and flying the length of Belgium to the German frontier north of Luxembourg. The German night-fighter controller had picked up transmissions from the bomber stream as soon as it left the English coast and was able to track it all the way to the target and vector his fighters into position. Many combats took place during the outward flight, and the diversion failed to draw fighters away from the main action. The problems continued at the primary target, where the forecast clear skies failed to materialize, and the crews were greeted by four to nine-tenths cloud at between 5,000 and 10,000 feet. This allowed some of them to pick out ground features, while others fixed their positions by H2S, if so equipped, and the main force Lancaster crews simply waited for TIs on e.t.a. The Path Finders had prepared a ground-marking plan in expectation of good vertical visibility, and dropped red, green and yellow TIs, while the Germans lit a decoy fire-site five miles to the south-east of the city. Some crews described the marking as late and erratic, and those from 44 (Rhodesia) Squadron bombed on red and green TIs from 19,000 to 21,900 feet between 19.39 and 20.06. Most thought the attack to be scattered in the early stages, becoming more concentrated as it progressed, and many commented on the new cookies detonating with a brighter flash than the old ones. All but one of the 44 (Rhodesia) Squadron Lancasters returned safely to Dunholme Lodge, having contributed to a moderately successful raid, and at least one crew reported the glow of fires remaining visible for 150 miles into the return journey. DV331 crashed at Rossdorf, about six miles east of Darmstadt, and only P/O Evans and his wireless operator survived to fall into enemy hands. Any success was achieved largely as the result of the creep-back from the decoy site falling across the suburbs of Offenbach and Sachsenhausen, situated on the southern bank of the River Main. 466 houses were destroyed and more than nineteen hundred seriously damaged, despite which, the operation fell well short of its aims, and the loss of forty-one aircraft was a high price to pay. The Halifaxes suffered heavily, losing twenty-seven of their number, a loss-rate of 10.5%, compared with the Lancaster's 3.6%.

Just two more operations remained before the year ended, and both were to be directed against Germany's capital city. The first was posted on the 23rd and would involve an all-Lancaster heavy force with seven Halifaxes among the Path Finder element, and eight Mosquitos to provide a diversion. The 130 Lancasters of 5 Group included a dozen from 44 (Rhodesia) Squadron, which were loaded with a cookie and eleven SBCs each, and launched into the cold night air between 23.59 and 00.46 with F/L Wiggin the senior pilot on duty. The route to the target was somewhat circuitous and took the bomber stream in a south-easterly direction to the Scheldt estuary, before hugging the Belgian/Dutch frontier to cross into Germany south of Aachen, as if threatening Frankfurt. When a point was reached south of Leipzig, the route turned sharply towards the north and Berlin, while the Mosquito feint threatened Leipzig as the target. The vanguard of the bomber stream reached the target to find it enveloped in up to eight-tenths cloud between 5,000 and 10,000 feet. This might not have been critical had the Path Finders not suffered an unusually high failure rate of their H2S equipment, which resulted in scattered and sparse sky-marking. The 44 (Rhodesia) Squadron crews found red and green skymarker flares at which to aim their bombs from 19,000 to 21,800 feet between 04.04 and 04.25, and observed well-concentrated fires and at least four large explosions, one described as being orange and red and lasting for thirty seconds. A relatively modest sixteen Lancasters failed to return, among which was the squadron's R5669, a veteran that had spent much of the year undergoing repairs following severe damage while serving with 83 Squadron. It came down in the Hannover defence zone, and there were no survivors from the eight-man crew of P/O Knight. ED999 crashed near Diepholz, it is believed, after crossing paths with the night-fighter of Oblt Paul Zorner of I./NJG3, and the crew of Sgt Hands perished in the wreckage. A local report named the south-eastern suburbs of

Köpenick and Treptow as the areas sustaining the most damage, with 287 houses and other buildings suffering complete destruction.

The "Big City" was posted as the target again on the 29th, for what, for the Lancaster operators, would be the first of three raids on it in five nights spanning the turn of the year. A force of 712 aircraft included 163 Lancasters of 5 Group, of which nine represented 44 (Rhodesia) Squadron, and they departed Dunholme Lodge between 16.45 and 17.02 with S/L Shorthouse the senior pilot on duty. It was from this juncture that the intolerable strain on the crews of successive long-range flights in difficult weather conditions would begin to become manifest in some squadrons through the rate of early returns, which on this night reached forty-five or 6.3%. The bomber stream was routed out over the Dutch Frisian islands pointing directly for Leipzig, and, having reached a point just to the north of that city, was to turn to the north towards Berlin, while Mosquitos carried out spoof raids on Leipzig and Magdeburg. 44 (Rhodesia) Squadron was exempt from early returns, and its crews reached the target area to find ten-tenths cloud with tops at anywhere between 7,000 and 18,000 feet. Red and green Path Finder release-point flares could be seen hanging over the city, upon which they aimed their bombs from 19,500 to 21,200 feet between 20.08 and 20.19. At debriefing, crews reported a considerable red glow beneath the clouds, which remained visible for a hundred miles, and gave the impression of a concentrated and successful assault. This was not entirely borne out by local reports, which revealed that the main weight of the raid had fallen onto southern and south-eastern districts, and, also, into outlying communities to the east. 388 buildings were destroyed, although none of significance, and ten thousand people were bombed out of their homes. Eleven Lancasters and nine Halifaxes failed to return, a loss-rate of 2.4% for the former and 3.5% for the latter.

During the course of the month the squadron participated in six operations and dispatched seventy sorties for the loss of six Lancasters and their crews. It had been a testing end to a year which had brought major successes and advances in tactics, but it had also been a year of high losses, particularly among the Stirling and Halifax squadrons. While "window" had been an instant success, it had also caused the Luftwaffe to rethink and reorganise, and the night-fighter force which emerged from the ruins of the old system, was a leaner, more efficient and altogether more lethal beast than that of before. As far as the crews of Bomber Command were concerned, the New Year offered the same fare as the old one, and few would view that with relish.

44 Sqn Lancaster ED723. Lost without trace 24th of May 1943, the crew remembered on the Runnymede memorial. Crew: Sgt Drysdale RCAF, Sgt J F Lester, F/O W A Marsden, F/Sgt H W E Hyett, Sgt S Jones, Sgt A S Bushill, Sgt F A Doherty RCAF.

Sgt Hubert Morton   P/O Nicholas C Shattock

Both KIA 8/9th of January 1943 in Lancaster W4176, on a mining sortie.

Canadian Pilot F/Sgt Clifford Shnier while with 44 Sqn. He moved to 97 Sqn when the squadron moved to Dunholme Lodge and was lost with all his crew on 29th July 1943.

Sgt D G J Coombes aged 20. KIA 2nd of March 1943.

Bombing up a 44 Squadron Lancaster. Jim Hartley is in the bomb bay operating the winch while LAC's Lewis and Chapman steady the bomb. The Sergeant, a Rhodesian, appears to be arming the tail fuses on the 500lbs bombs. Possibly the Armament Officer looking on.

Lancaster KM-J ED611 on return from Peenemünde, 17/18th of August 1943. This aircraft was badly damaged – starboard outer engine U/S, turret hydraulics U/S, starboard tyre burst, starboard flaps damaged, starboard elevator damaged.
Crew: F/O D H Aldridge, Sgt T Phillips, F/Sgt D B P Heslop, Sgt T S Dellow, Sgt R W West, F/Sgt D E Welensky, Sgt T S Holmes.

A closer view of 44 Sqn Lancaster KM-J (ED611) damaged by flak during the attack on Peenemünde. It was also hit in the starboard wing, flap and tailplane.

Lancasters formating

A 44 Sqn Lancaster at Waddington. The bomb in the foreground is a 4000lb 'Cookie' or 'Blockbuster'.

The Paige Crew
Sgt M.J.Paige RCAF, Sgt J.Hutchinson, P/O A.G.Cameron, Sgt S.Wright, Sgt A.R.A.Colonna, Sgt D.B.Mogg Sgt J.H.Lightfoot. All killed 8/9th January 1943 when their Lancaster W42777 crashed in Denmark where they are all buried.

44 Sqn F/O Fred Calcutt (AG).
He was killed on the Turin raid with S/L Nettleton.
Missing his brevet for some reason.

Sgt Ronald Hordon
(KIA 2/3rd February 1943)

Believed to be the Drysdale Crew.

F/O Calcutt and P/O Eric Dudley

Three air gunners in front of the 'office'.
L – R: F/O Dennis Hartung, F/L Ian Wood, F/O Calcutt, Wood and Calcutt were both lost on the Turin raid which also took the life of S/L Nettleton.

Eric Dudley of 44 Sqn. The nose turret and bomb aimer's blister appear to be missing.

44 Air Gunners at Waddington
L – R: Dennis Hartung, ? , F/L 'Woody' Wood, P/O Eric Dudley, Front: F/O Calcutt

F/L Robinson, his crew of 44 Squadron in N. Africa and Lancaster EE184 in June 1943. The aircraft was lost on 21st of October 1943, ditching off Grimsby. Since arriving at Waddington directly from the factory on 11th of June 1943, EE184 had been in constant use, accumulating 322.45 hours.

Above and below: the Morris crew of 44 Sqn
Sgt R Twiddy (RG), Sgt T McKenna (FE), Sgt T C Somerville (WO), F/Sgt O N Morris, (Pilot), Sgt W Kilbey (Nav), Sgt H Pearce (BA), P/O E Dudley (MUG).

A 44 Sqn Lancaster at Waddington. Eric Dudley is second from the left.

P/O Eric Dudley (AG) September 1942

Copy of the passport photo carried by Eric Dudley for use on forged documents if shot down.

Sgt RAF Woods RNZAF (RG) of P/O Erickson's Crew. KIA 30th of May 1943

Waddington village square showing the Horse and Jockey pub popular with aircrew.

The RAF Waddington Engineering Wing team for the Station Sports Day in 1943. S/L E McCabe is in the centre.

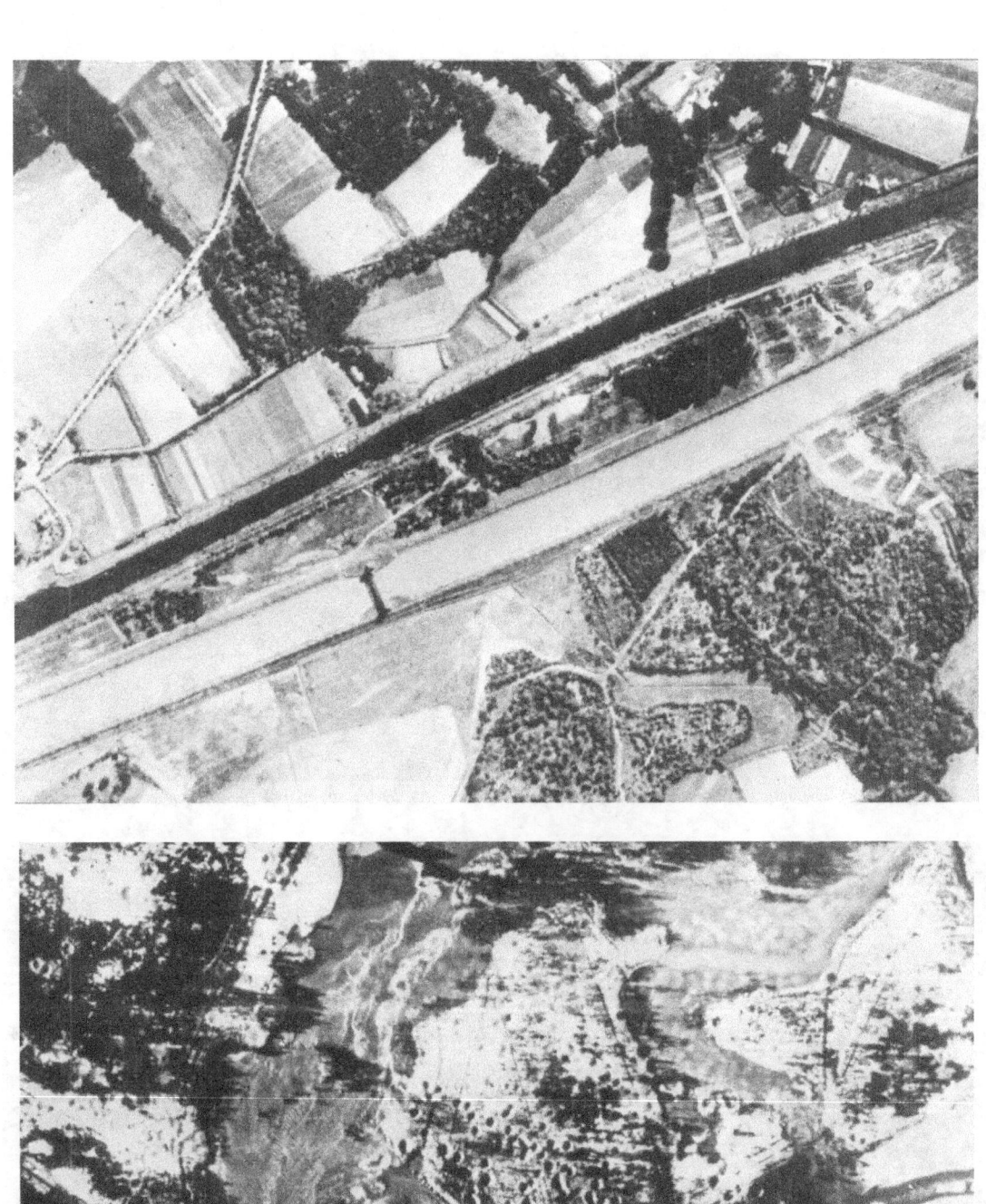

Before and after – the Dortmund Ems Canal 1943

More evidence of the determination to destroy the Dortmund Ems Canal 1943

Bill Willis (RG), Stan Letley (BA), Robert Burr (Pilot), Eddie Barnett (FE)
Dennis King (MUG), Tucker (Navigator), Roger Oswick (W.Op)

F/O Parsons and crew

Lancaster W 4839 KM-F. Lost 27th of March 1943 on Berlin raid.
Crew: F/Sgt A J Horwood, Sgt L W J Schultz, Sgt R L Cole, F/Sgt J McA Newton RCAF, Sgt F W Guild RCAF, Sgt H H Clements RCAF, Sgt G McC Sheridan. All buried in Berlin War Cemetery.

44 Sqn. F/L Shepherd and crew.
Back: Sgt E R Gray (RG), Sgt J R Jarvis (W.Op), F/Sgt J H Rignold
Front: F/O R A Horne (Nav), P/O A N Murray (BA) F/L W A Shepherd (Pilot), Sgt L G Simmons (MUG)

Flak!

Lancaster KM-O R5740 joined the Squadron July 1942 and was lost on the 26th of June 1943. Crew: P/O D M Sharp (Pilot), P/O D Maclean Struthers F/Sgt T Johnstone), Sgt R J Dash, Sgt R H W Thompson, Sgt N H Morris, Sgt E R H Griffiths, Sgt Langstaff. All are commemorated on the Runnymede Memorial. The aircraft flew 416 hours.

44 Sqn Lancaster R5740 KM-O. P/O D. M. Sharp & crew.

*F/L F M Osborne and crew back to Milan at night 14th February 1943.
Crew: Sgt Shipp, F/O E Jones, F/L Osborne, Sgt Tyrell, F/L L G Johnson,
F/Sgt Thompson, Sgt W M Batstone.*

44 Sqn Lancaster RF187 KM-P Post-war.

Flight Engineer Sgt Les Hayward DFM

44 Sqn Lancaster W4838 KM-B, May 1943.
L-R P Gretton FME, unknown, Eric Howell FME, Sgt J (Lofty) Stanford (FE), Sgt Ball/Dearman (W.Op), W/C P Jennings (Pilot), Sgt Ball/Dearman, P/O F Parker (Nav), P/O R Etheridge (MUG), Sgt R Tibbs (BA), Sgt Richards (Fitter), Bob Thrasher FMA, unknown, unknown.

Lancaster W4961 KM-S "Good health then", Dunholme Lodge 1943 – 10 operations.
L-R C E Stead (FE), J H Mallen (RG), G P Bayliss (MUG), ground crew, A J Scott (BA), K Garvey (Nav), F/L W J Lewis (Pilot), ground crew, R C Morley (W.Op)

44 Sqn Lancaster 'Miss Toronto' early 1943
L-R Mac, Vic, Nick, Cy, Maisie, Johnnie, Pop.

Lancaster PB380 KM-S, Dunholme Lodge 1943.
L-R: Vernon Southall (BA), Jock Brooks (FE), Bryn Williams (MUG), S/L P D Bird (Pilot),
Bill Willis (RG), Ross Morris (W.Op), Cyril Paul (Nav)

January 1944

The change of year was not destined to effect a change in the emphasis of operations, and this was, no doubt, a disappointment, not only to the hard-pressed crews of Bomber Command, but also to the beleaguered residents of Germany's Capital City. Proud of their status as Berliners first and Germans second, they were a hardy breed, and just like their counterparts in London during the Blitz of 1940, they would bear their trials with fortitude and humour, and would not buckle under the constant assault from above. "You may break our walls but not out hearts", proclaimed banners in the streets, and the most popular song of the day, Nach jedem Dezember kommt immer ein Mai, After every December there's always a May, was played endlessly over the airwaves, its sentiments hinting at a change in fortunes with the onset of spring. Harris allowed the Berliners little time to enjoy New Year, and, as New Year's Day dawned, plans were already in hand to continue the onslaught. Before it ended, the first of 421 Lancasters, 161 representing 5 Group, would be taking off and heading eastwards to arrive over the city as the clock showed 03.00 hours on the 2nd.

Take-off had actually been delayed because of doubts over the weather, and this meant that insufficient hours of daylight remained to allow the planned outward route over Denmark and the Baltic. Instead, the bomber stream would adopt the previously used almost direct route across Holland and northern Germany, but return, as originally planned, more circuitously, passing east of Leipzig, before racing across Germany between the Ruhr and Frankfurt and traversing Belgium to reach the Channel near the French port of Boulogne. 44 (Rhodesia) Squadron's fourteen participants took off between 23.39 and 00.13 with W/C Bowes the senior pilot on duty, and each carrying a mix of high explosives and 4lb and 30lb incendiaries. The force was gradually depleted by twenty-nine early returns, one of them, that of F/L Phillips, who arrived back at Dunholme Lodge some two hours after leaving it, citing oxygen system failure as the cause. The bomber stream covered the four-hundred-mile leg from the Dutch coast to Berlin in under two hours without once catching a glimpse of the ground through the dense cloud, and it was no different at the target, which was completely obscured by a layer of ten-tenths cloud with tops in places as high as 19,000 feet. The Path Finders had to employ skymarking (Wanganui), which was somewhat scattered, and the 44 (Rhodesia) Squadron crews aimed for these parachute flares from 20,000 to 22,000 feet between 03.06 and 03.21. They observed the glow of fires and smoke rising through the cloud tops, and W/C Bowes witnessed a huge explosion at 03.07, which lit up the clouds for three seconds, but it was impossible to assess what was happening on the ground. It was established, ultimately, that the operation had been a failure, which had scattered bombs across the southern fringes of the city, causing only minor damage, while the main weight of the attack had fallen beyond the city boundaries into wooded and open country. The disappointment was compounded by the loss of twenty-eight Lancasters, among which was W4831, which crashed some twenty miles south of Berlin city centre in the Brandenburg district, killing P/O Holmes A'Court RCAF and the other seven occupants.

During the course of the 2nd, a heavy force of 362 Lancasters and nine of the new Mk III Hercules-powered Halifaxes was made ready for a return to Berlin that night. There was snow on the ground, and many of the crews called to briefing were still tired from being late to bed following the almost-eight-hour round trip the night before. Some of these were in a mutinous frame of mind at being on the Order of Battle again so soon. 5 Group cancelled twenty-five of its intended contribution, leaving 119 to take part, nine of which belonged to 44 (Rhodesia) Squadron. The outward route crossed the

Dutch coast near Castricum and took the bomber stream to a point south-east of Bremen, followed by a dogleg to the north-west and, finally, a ninety degree change of course to the south-east in the Parchim area to leave a ninety-mile run to the target. The 44 (Rhodesia) Squadron element departed Dunholme Lodge between 23.24 and 00.08 with F/Ls Dorehill and Phillips the senior pilots on duty, and only the crew of P/O Gee was among a massive sixty early returns, 15.7% of those dispatched. They had taken off late because of a malfunctioning mid-upper turret and were unable to make up the time. Many were defeated by severe icing conditions, while others abandoned their sorties because of minor problems that might have seen them carry on had they been fully rested. The route changes worked well to throw off the night-fighters, but they would congregate in the target area after the controller correctly identified the Capital as the target forty minutes before zero-hour. Ten-tenths cloud with tops at 16,000 feet forced the bombing to take place on the red skymarkers with green stars or on the glow of fires, the 44 (Rhodesia) Squadron crews carrying out their attacks from 20,000 to 21,500 feet between 02.46 and 03.00. They reported smoke rising to 20,000 feet as they turned away, but it was not possible to make an accurate assessment of the outcome, and the impression was of an effective attack, when, in fact, it had been another failure. Bombs had been scattered across the city and destroyed just eighty-two houses for the loss of twenty-seven Lancasters, most of which had fallen victim to night-fighters in the target area.

After three trips to Berlin in five nights, the "Big City" would now be left to the Mosquitos of 8 Group's Light Night Striking Force until the final third of the month, allowing Harris to turn his attention on the 5th upon the Baltic port-city of Stettin, which had not been attacked in numbers since the previous April. It was to be another predominantly Lancaster affair, involving 348 of the type, 5 Group putting up 120 aircraft and 44 (Rhodesia) Squadron eight, and they would be accompanied by ten Path Finder Halifaxes from 35 Squadron. They took off from Dunholme Lodge between 23.38 and 00.10 with no senior pilots on duty, but each crew captained by an officer. In contrast to the seventeen early returns by 5 Group crews during the last Berlin operation, only one came home early on this night, and those continuing on found themselves in thick cloud at cruising altitude, some struggling to find a clear lane even when as high as 23,000 feet. On the plus side, they all benefitted from a Mosquito diversion at Berlin, which kept the night-fighters off the scent. Stettin was found to be partially visible through five-tenths thin cloud with tops at around 10,000 feet, and crews were able to identify some ground features before focussing on H2S-laid flares and green TIs, which the 44 (Rhodesia) Squadron crews bombed from 20,000 to 22,000 feet between 03.35 and 04.10. All returned home to provide the intelligence section with accounts of a highly accurate and concentrated attack, which seemed to leave the entire city on fire. Fourteen Lancasters and two Halifaxes failed to return, in exchange for which, post-raid reconnaissance and local reports confirmed heavy damage in central and western districts, where 504 houses and twenty industrial buildings had been destroyed, a further 1,148 houses and twenty-nine industrial buildings seriously damaged, and eight ships had been sunk in the harbour.

Following this operation, the crews of the heavy squadrons were rested until mid-month, and on the 11th, S/L Lynch and his crew were posted to 97 Squadron, formerly of 5 Group, but Path Finders since the previous April. This was one of the sideways postings during a period of high Path Finder losses, and he departed Dunholme Lodge with a well-deserved Bar to his DFC. When briefings finally took place on the 14th, there was doubtless some relief to see the red tape on the wall maps terminate some way short of Berlin. It led, in fact, to Braunschweig (Brunswick), the historic and culturally significant city situated some thirty-five miles to the east of Hannover. It had not been attacked by the Command in numbers before, and, on this night, would face a force, which, at take-off, numbered 496 Lancasters and two 35 Squadron Halifaxes. 5 Group supported the operation with 153 Lancasters, of which eleven represented 44 (Rhodesia) Squadron, and they took off between 16.32 and 17.06 with F/Ls Dorehill, Phillips and Wiggin the senior pilots on duty. After climbing out they headed towards Germany's north-western coast, where they were met by part of the enemy night-fighter response, which would harass the bomber stream all the way to the target and back. P/O Higgs and crew had been contending with engine problems as they crossed the North Sea, and, after dragging only 14,500 feet out of ED611 by the time they reached the enemy coast, they wisely turned back. Complete cloud cover at the target, in places, up to around 15,000 feet, dictated the use of red skymarkers with green stars, at which the 44 (Rhodesia) Squadron crews aimed their cookies and incendiaries from 19,000 and 21,600 feet between 19.15 and 19.26. The enemy fighters scored consistently and accounted for the majority of the thirty-eight missing Lancasters, many of which came down around Hannover. This was the fate of the squadron's veteran R5729, which crashed at 20.00 near Gieboldehausen on the north-eastern approaches to the university city of Göttingen, killing P/O Curatolo RCAF and his crew. The attack almost entirely missed the city, falling mostly onto outlying communities to the south, and was reported locally as a light raid. This would be a continuing theme in future attacks up to the autumn, as Braunschweig enjoyed something of a charmed life, leading to a belief among the populace that the surrounding villages were being targeted intentionally, in an attempt to drive the residents into the city, before a major operation destroyed it with them in it!

The Path Finders, in particular, had been taking a beating since the turn of the year, with 156 Squadron alone losing fourteen Lancasters and crews in just three operations, four and five on Berlin, and five again on Braunschweig. This was creating something of a crisis in Path Finder manpower, particularly with regard to experienced crews, and a number of sideways postings took place between the squadrons to ensure a leavening of experience in each one. One of the solutions was to take the cream from among the crews emerging from the training units, rather than wait for them to gain experience at a main force squadron.

Another lull in operations kept the crews on the ground until the 20th, when orders were received to assemble a maximum effort force for the next round of the Berlin offensive. The Halifax squadrons, which had appeared to be in hibernation since late December, were roused from their slumber, and 264 of them joined 495 Lancasters to constitute the Path Finder and main force elements, while two small Mosquito sections carried out spoof raids on Kiel and Hannover. 5 Group weighed in with 155 Lancasters, of which a dozen were made ready by 44 (Rhodesia) Squadron, and they took off between 16.22 and 16.50 with F/Ls Dorehill, Phillips and Ruddick the senior pilots on duty. It was a rare pleasure for them to be taking off in daylight, and they circled as they climbed out above Dunholme Lodge before setting course, while observing the dozens of Lancasters rising up into the dusk to join them from the neighbouring stations. They turned their snouts towards the west coast of the Schleswig-Holstein peninsula at a point opposite Kiel, rendezvousing with the other groups over the North Sea and all the time shedding individual aircraft as a hefty seventy-five crews abandoned their sorties and turned back. F/O Mercer experienced starboard-inner engine problems and jettisoned his cookie two hours after taking off as he returned home. The others made landfall over the Nordfriesland coast, before turning to the south-east on a more-or-less direct course for Berlin, and soon found themselves being hounded by night-fighters. The enemy controller had fed a proportion of his resources into the bomber stream east of Hamburg, and they would remain in contact until a point between Leipzig and Hannover on the way home, although, curiously, the 5 Group brigade saw nothing of this and would lose just a single 57 Squadron Lancaster. The two Mosquito diversions had been completely ignored by the Luftwaffe controller, who knew well in advance that Berlin was to be the target. The Path Finders arrived over the Müritzsee to the north of Berlin with a sixty-mile run-in to the aiming point, and they found this to be concealed beneath the same ten-tenths cloud that had accompanied them for the entire outward leg. The tops of the cloud lay beneath the bombers at up to 15,000 feet as the main force crews carried out their attacks on red skymarkers with green stars, those from 44 (Rhodesia) Squadron bombing from 18,500 to 23,000 feet between 19.35 and 19.52. On return, the crews commented on the lack of flak activity over Berlin and reported the glow of large fires under the cloud and smoke rising through the tops. Thirty-five aircraft failed to return, twenty-two of them Halifaxes, which represented an 8.3% casualty rate compared with 2.6% for the Lancasters. It took a little time for an assessment of the operation to be made because of continuing cloud over north-eastern Germany, by which time four further raids had been carried out. It seems from local reports that the eastern districts had received the heaviest weight of bombs in an eight-mile stretch from Weissesee in the north to Neukolln in the south, although no details of destruction emerged.

On the following day, the city of Magdeburg was posted to host its first major attack of the war. Situated some fifty miles from Braunschweig and slightly to the south of east, it was on an increasingly familiar route as far as the enemy night-fighter controllers were concerned, and within easy striking distance of the night-fighter assembly beacons. In an attempt to deceive the enemy, a small-scale diversion was planned at Berlin involving twenty-two Lancaster of 5 Group and twelve Mosquitos of 8 Group. 5 Group contributed 122 Lancasters to the main event, seven of them made ready by 44 (Rhodesia) Squadron, which were loaded with a cookie and SBCs of incendiaries each and led by F/Ls Dorehill, Ruddick and Wiggin, while P/Os Bradburn and Manning and their crews would take part in the diversion and carry a cookie and a few 1,000 and 500 pounders. They took off together between 19.41 and 20.26 and flew out over the North Sea to a point some one hundred miles off the west coast of the Schleswig-Holstein peninsula, before turning to the south-east to pass between Hamburg and Hannover. Enemy radar was able to detect H2S transmissions during night-flying tests and equipment checks, and the night-fighter controller was, thereby, always aware of an imminent heavy raid. On this night, the night-fighters were able to infiltrate the bomber stream even before the German coast was crossed, and the recently introduced "Tame Boar" night-fighter system provided a running commentary on the bomber stream's progress, enabling the fighters to latch onto it and remain in contact. The final turning-point was twenty-five miles north-east of the target, which was identified both by Path Finder markers and the bombing of twenty-seven main force aircraft. These had been driven by stronger-than-forecast winds to arrive ahead of schedule and contained crews anxious to get the job done and get out of the target area as soon as possible. They bombed using their own H2S without waiting for the TIs to go down, and, together with dummy fires, were blamed by the Path Finders as the reason for their failure to produce concentrated marking.

The conditions over Magdeburg varied according to the time of arrival, the early birds encountering seven to nine-tenths thin cloud at around 6,000 feet, while those turning up towards the end of the raid found the northern half of the city completely clear with cloud over the southern half only. The 44 (Rhodesia) Squadron crews experienced a mixture of eight-tenths cloud and relatively clear skies, and, in the face of fairly modest opposition, bombed on green TIs from 20,000 to 21,100 feet between 23.04 and 23.19, all gaining the impression that the attack was concentrated around the markers. Returning crews from other groups reported explosions and fires or their glow, and smoke beginning to rise as they turned away. A number reported a flash some twelve minutes after bombing, that lit up the clouds for seven seconds, and two large explosions at 23.15. Fires that initially seemed to be scattered, appeared to become more concentrated as the crews headed for home, and the impression was of a successful operation. While all of this was in progress, the diversionary force arrived at Berlin, some seventy miles away to the north-east, where the 44 (Rhodesia) Squadron duo found a layer of eight to ten-tenths cloud at 10,000 feet, through which they bombed from 21,000 and 22,700 feet either side of 22.55. The 5 Group ORB expressed the opinion that the diversion had succeeded in the early stages in reducing the impact of the Nachtjagd, although this was not borne out by the figures. In the absence of post-raid reconnaissance and a local report, the outcome at Magdeburg was not confirmed, and it is generally believed now that most of the bombing fell outside of the city boundaries. A record fifty-seven aircraft failed to return, thirty-five of them Halifaxes, and this provided another alarming statistic of a 15.6% loss-rate compared with 5.2% for the Lancasters. F/L Ruddick and crew failed to return in DV263, which had crashed somewhere in eastern Germany with no survivors.

The end of the month was to bring the final concerted effort to destroy Berlin and would involve three trips to this destination in the space of an unprecedented four nights. This hectic round of operations began on the 27th, after five nights of rest since the bruising experience of Magdeburg and involved an all-Lancaster heavy force of 515 aircraft. 5 Group put up a record 172, a dozen of them belonging to 44 (Rhodesia) Squadron, which departed Dunholme Lodge between 17.20 and 17.36 with F/Ls Phillips, Wiggin and Wright the senior pilots on duty. After climbing out and rendezvousing with the rest of the group, they set course on a complex route that would take the bomber stream towards the north German coast, before swinging to the south-east to enter enemy territory over the Frisians and northern Holland. Having then feinted towards central Germany, suggesting Leipzig as the target, the force was to turn north-east to a point west of Berlin, from where the final run-in would commence. The long return route passed to the west of Leipzig before turning due east to miss Frankfurt on its northern side and traverse Belgium to gain the Channel south of Boulogne. P/Os Smith and Lyford arrived back in the circuit within five minutes of each other shortly before 20.00, after both experiencing engine issues. The others pressed on towards the target, while a mining diversion off Heligoland and the dispensing of dummy fighter flares and route-markers partially succeeded in reducing the numbers of enemy night-fighters making contact. It was, therefore, a relatively intact bomber force that approached the target over ten-tenths cloud with tops at 15,000 feet. This required the Path Finders to use sky-marking, and it was the red Wanganui flares with green stars that led the 44 (Rhodesia) Squadron crews to the aiming point, where all bombed from 19,600 to 24,000 feet between 20.34 and 20.42. At debriefings, crews reported the glow of fires and the appearance of a successful raid, but no detailed assessment was forthcoming. Of course, not all would make it back to tell their stories at debriefing, and thirty-three Lancaster dispersal pans stood empty in dawn's early light. Reports from Berlin described bombs falling over a wide area, more so in the south than the north, and damage to fifty industrial premises, a number of them engaged in important war work, while twenty thousand people were bombed out of their homes. A feature of the campaign was the number of outlying communities suffering collateral damage, and, on this night, sixty-one such hamlets recorded bombs falling.

The early time-on-target had allowed crews to get a full night in bed, and they were, hopefully, fully rested, when news came through on the 28th that many of them would be returning to the "Big City" that night. A heavy force of 673 aircraft was assembled, of which 432 were Lancasters and 241 Halifaxes, 155 of the former provided by 5 Group. 44 (Rhodesia) Squadron made ready eleven Lancasters, which departed Dunholme Lodge between 23.54 and 00.36 with F/Ls Wiggin and Wright the senior pilots on duty. They were routed out over southern Denmark before turning south-east on a direct course for the target, with an almost reciprocal return and various diversionary measures to distract the night-fighter controller. Sixty-six crews turned back early, suggesting some adverse reaction to the back-to-back operations. F/O Bartlett and crew returned early because of an unserviceable receiver, while F/Sgt Barton became a victim of severe icing conditions that restricted his ability to climb and turned the Perspex opaque. He dropped his load on Sylt from 17,000 feet at 02.33, noting up to fifty searchlights and light and heavy flak coming up from the nearby mainland. Those reaching the target area encountered ten-tenths cloud, and a mixture of sky and ground-marking to aim at. The 44 (Rhodesia) Squadron crews delivered their bombs on red and green release-point flares from 19,000 to 22,000 feet between 03.27 and 03.33, some crews reporting two huge explosions at 03.18 and 03.25, the earlier one described by a 10 Squadron crew as lighting up the sky over a radius of fifty miles. Forty-six aircraft failed to return, twenty-six of them Halifaxes, as the defenders fought back to exact another heavy toll of bombers, but 44 (Rhodesia) Squadron came through unscathed. The impression gained from returning crews at debriefing was of a concentrated and effective attack, and this was partly borne-out by local reports of heavy damage in western and southern districts, where 180,000 people were bombed out of their homes. However, as had been the pattern throughout the campaign against Berlin, seventy-seven outlying communities had also been afflicted.

After a night's rest, a force of 534 aircraft was made ready on the 30th for the final operation of this concerted effort against Berlin. 5 Group offered 156 Lancasters, of which fourteen were made ready by 44 (Rhodesia) Squadron, and they took off between 16.50 and 17.04 with F/Ls Phillips and Wiggin the senior pilots on duty. After climbing out, they joined with the rest of the group to follow a route similar to that adopted two nights earlier. The bomber stream remained relatively free of harassment until approaching the target, where it was greeted by ten-tenths cloud at around 8,000 feet and the sight of Path Finder skymarking in progress. The 44 (Rhodesia) Squadron crews bombed on these from 19,400 and 22,800 feet between 20.19 and 20.33, and all commented on the smoke rising through 12,000 feet and the glow of fires beneath the cloud, which, according to some, was still visible from a hundred miles into the return flight. Thirty-two Lancasters and a single Halifax failed to make it home, among them 44 (Rhodesia) Squadron's JA843 and ND514, the fate of whose crews could not be more diverse. The former was on the bombing run at 19,500 feet, when a direct hit from a flak shell sent it falling out of control. At 13,000 feet an explosion rent the Lancaster, flinging the pilot, P/O Johnston, into space as the sole survivor. In contrast, the latter was dispatched by a night-fighter over the target, P/O Lyford RAAF remaining at the controls while his crew took to their parachutes. They all survived in enemy hands, while he perished in the wreckage, an unsung hero, whose selfless act would remain unrecognised. In return for these significant losses, and according to local reports, central and south-western districts suffered heavy damage and serious areas of fire. Other parts of the city were also hit, while many bomb loads were again scattered liberally onto outlying communities, and at least a thousand people lost their lives. 112 heavy bombers and their crews had been lost to the Command as a result of these three operations, and, with the introduction of the enemy's highly efficient Tame Boar night-fighter system based on running commentaries, the advantage had swung back in the defenders' favour.

Two further heavy raids would be directed at Berlin before the end of the winter offensive, one in February and the other in March, but they would be almost in isolation. There is no question that Germany's Capital City had been sorely afflicted by the three latest operations, but it remained a functioning city, and showed no signs of imminent collapse. During the course of the month the squadron participated in ten operations and dispatched one hundred sorties for the loss of five Lancasters and their crews.

February 1944

Bad weather during the first two weeks of February allowed the crews to draw breath and the squadrons to replenish. Harris had intended to maintain the pressure on Berlin, and would have launched a further attack, had he not been thwarted by the conditions, and as a result, the time was filled with training and mining operations. During this respite, on the 3rd, W/C Bowes relinquished his command of the squadron on posting to administrative duties with 52 Base, and was succeeded by W/C Thompson, who arrived from 1656 Conversion Unit. W/C Bowes would finish the war in command of 100 Group's 214 Squadron, flying B17 Fortresses on RCM duties.

When the Path Finder and main force squadrons next took to the air, it would be for a record-breaking effort to Berlin on the 15th, which would also be the penultimate operation of the campaign, and, indeed, of the war by Bomber Command's heavy brigade against Germany's capital city. The force of 891 aircraft represented the largest non-1,000 force to date, and, therefore, the greatest-ever to be sent against the Capital, and it would be the first time that more than five hundred Lancasters and three hundred Halifaxes had operated together. 5 Group would surpass its previous best effort by fifty Lancasters when putting 226 of them into the air, and eighteen of them would be representing 44 (Rhodesia) Squadron. The bomb bays of this huge armada would convey to Berlin the greatest-ever tonnage of bombs to any target to date, and 44 (Rhodesia) Squadron's contribution would be eighteen cookies and 1,050 x 30lb and 16,350 x 4lb incendiaries. They departed Dunholme Lodge between 17.13 and 17.35 with the recently arrived S/L Cockbain and the newly promoted S/L Hunter the senior pilots on duty, and, after joining up with the rest of the 5 Group squadrons, they set course for the western coast of Denmark, before crossing Jutland and entering Germany via the Baltic coast between Rostock and Stralsund, with a direct heading, thereafter, for the target. The return route would require the bombers to pass south of Hannover and Bremen, and cross Holland to the North Sea via Castricum. Extensive diversionary measures included a mining operation in Kiel Bay ahead of the arrival of the bombers, a raid on Frankfurt-an-Oder to the east of Berlin by a small force of 8 Group Lancasters, and Oboe Mosquitos attacking five night-fighter airfields in Holland. The force had been depleted by seventy-five early returns by the time the remainder homed in on the target, where ten-tenths cloud at around 10,000 feet concealed it from their view, but those with H2S were able to confirm their positions, while the others relied on the Path Finders' red release-point flares with green stars and red and green TIs on the ground. The 44 (Rhodesia) Squadron crews bombed on these from 20,400 to 25,000 feet between 21.15 and 21.41, and, on return, reported the markers to be highly effective and well-concentrated, and the burgeoning glow beneath the clouds convinced them that they had taken part in a successful operation. This was borne out by local reports, which confirmed that the 2,642 tons of bombs had caused extensive damage in central and south-western districts but had also spilled out into surrounding communities. A thousand houses and more than five hundred temporary wooden barracks were destroyed, and important war-industry factories in the Siemensstadt district were damaged in return for the loss to the Command of forty-three aircraft, twenty-six Lancasters, (4.6%) and seventeen Halifaxes, (5.4%). Perhaps slightly disturbing was the fact that eight of the missing Halifaxes were Mk IIIs, only one fewer than the nine Mk II/Vs.

Despite the recent heavy losses, when orders were received on the 19th to prepare for another major assault that night, this time on Leipzig, the heavy squadrons were able to offer 816 aircraft, 561 Lancasters and 255 Halifaxes. 5 Group managed 209 Lancasters and 44 (Rhodesia) Squadron eighteen, which departed Dunholme Lodge between 23.27 and 00.08 with F/Ls Dorehill, Mercer and Wiggin the senior pilots on duty. After climbing out over the station, they joined up with the others heading for the Dutch coast, where a proportion of the Luftwaffe Nachtjagd was waiting for them, while others had been drawn away by a mining diversion off Kiel. P/O Bradburn, it seems, took off without a rear gunner, and, having discovered that fact soon afterwards, turned back. Sgt Levy was unable to engage the supercharger gear because of low air pressure, and he and his crew were back home within three hours. P/O Smith and crew ran into icing conditions and jettisoned their cookie at 00.28 in order to maintain height, but continued on for a further hour, before losing an engine and releasing the rest of their load onto flak ships, which had opened fire on them. The remainder continued on, some to become embroiled in a running battle with night-fighters all the way into eastern Germany, where inaccurately forecast winds caused some aircraft to arrive at the target early. They were forced to orbit, while they waited for the Path Finders to arrive to mark the target, and the local flak batteries accounted for around twenty of these, while four others were lost through collisions. The 44 (Rhodesia) Squadron crews arrived to find ten-tenths cloud with tops at around 10,000 feet and bombed on green Wanganui flares and red and green TIs from 19,600 to 23,900 feet between 04.00 and 04.23. It seems that there was a brief period during the attack when skymarking stopped and led to some scattering of bombs, but the marker-flares were soon replenished with the arrival of more backers-up, and a considerable glow beneath the cloud remained visible for some fifty minutes into the return journey, giving the impression of a successful assault. When all of those aircraft returning home had been accounted for, there was a massive shortfall of seventy-eight, a record loss by a clear twenty-one aircraft. Forty-four Lancasters and thirty-four Halifaxes had failed to return, with a loss-rate of 7.8% and 13.3% respectively, and this prompted Harris to immediately withdraw the Mk II and V Halifaxes from further operations over Germany, which, at a stroke, removed a proportion of 4 Group's fire-power from the front line until they could be re-equipped with the Mk III variant. In the meantime, the Mk II and V operators would focus their energies for the remainder of the month on gardening duties.

Despite this depletion of available numbers, a force of 598 aircraft was made ready on the 20th for an operation that night against Stuttgart, which would be the first of three against the city over a three-week period. 5 Group contributed 176 Lancasters, sixteen of them belonging to 44 (Rhodesia) Squadron and they were each loaded with a cookie and eleven SBCs, before being dispatched between 23.35 and 00.15 with S/L Cockbain the senior pilot on duty. They made their way across the Channel to the French coast, from where the cloud remained at ten-tenths with tops at 8,000 feet all the way into southern Germany. A North Sea sweep and a diversionary raid on Munich two hours ahead of the main activity had caused the Luftwaffe to deploy its forces early, and this allowed the bomber stream to push on unmolested to the target. By the time it hove into view, the cloud had thinned to five to eight-tenths at around 6,000 feet, and the excellent visibility enabled the crews to draw a bead on the Path Finder red and green sky-markers and similar-coloured TIs on the ground. The 44 (Rhodesia) Squadron crews bombed from 21,000 to 24,100 feet between 04.00 and 04.17, observing many large fires, and, on return, there were reports that the glow from the burning city was still visible from 250 miles into the return flight. Despite some scattering of bombs, local reports described central districts and those in a quadrant from north-west to north-east suffering extensive damage, and a Bosch factory was one of the important war industry concerns to be hard-hit. In contrast to twenty-four hours earlier, a modest nine aircraft failed to return.

In an attempt to reduce the prohibitive losses of recent weeks, a new tactic was introduced for the next two operations. A force of 734 aircraft was assembled on the 24th for an operation to the centre of Germany's ball-bearing production, Schweinfurt, situated some sixty miles to the east of Frankfurt in south-central Germany. The plan called for 392 aircraft to depart their stations between 18.00 and

19.00, and to be followed into the air two hours later by 342 others in the hope of catching the night-fighters on the ground refuelling and re-arming as the second wave passed through. While this operation was in progress, extensive diversionary measures would be put in hand that involved more than three hundred other aircraft, including 179 from the training units conducting a North Sea sweep, and 110 Halifaxes and Stirlings mining in northern waters. 5 Group contributed 204 Lancasters, of which seventeen were made ready by 44 (Rhodesia) Squadron, six assigned to the first phase, and taking-off between 18.23 and 18.35 with S/L Hunter the senior pilot on duty, and eleven departing between 20.10 and 20.36 to join the second phase led by F/Ls Dorehill, Mercer and Phillips. P/O Charlesworth and crew returned early from the first phase because of a misfiring engine and navigational issues, leaving the others to reach the target and find three-tenths cloud at 3,000 to 4,000 feet, with haze spoiling the vertical visibility. The aiming point was identified by red and green TIs, and already established fires towards the south-western edge of the town as the 44 (Rhodesia) Squadron crews bombed from 21,000 to 25,000 feet between 23.06 and 23.23. Other crews over the target at this time saw no cloud, and described the visibility as excellent, enabling them to pick out the River Main as they ran in to bomb. Two columns of black smoke were observed to be rising through 5,000 feet as they turned away, and the consensus was of an effective, if, somewhat scattered attack.

Meanwhile, the second phase crews were well on their way, but F/L Phillips was forced to turn back with an unserviceable rear turret, as the remainder pressed on and picked up the glow of fires from the earlier raid at a distance of two hundred miles. The visibility in the target area remained good, despite the rising smoke, and bombing by the 44 (Rhodesia) Squadron crews took place out of almost cloudless skies onto red and green TIs from 21,300 to 23,500 feet between 01.01 and 01.16. All indications suggested an effective raid, but, unfortunately, both phases of the operation had suffered from undershooting after some Path Finder backers-up failed to press on to the aiming point. In that regard, it was a disappointing night, but an interesting feature was the loss of 50% fewer aircraft from the second wave in comparison with the first, in an overall casualty figure of thirty-three, and this suggested some merit in the tactic. 44 (Rhodesia) Squadron posted missing the crew of F/Sgt Haynes after ND525 crashed in north-eastern France during the first phase, and there were no survivors. Since the turn of the year a wind-finder system had been in use, in which selected crews monitored wind speed and direction, and passed their findings back to HQ, where the figures were collated, and any changes from the briefed conditions could be re-broadcast to the bomber stream. This had been found to be extremely useful, but, as would be discovered in the ensuing weeks, the system had its limitations.

The main operation on the following night was directed at the beautiful and culturally significant southern city of Augsburg, situated around thirty miles north-west of Munich. It was home to a major Maschinenfabrik Augsburg Nuremberg (M.A.N) diesel engine factory, which had been the target for the previously mentioned epic low-level daylight raid by 44 and 97 Squadron in April 1942. On this night, 594 aircraft were divided into two waves, and among them were 164 Lancasters of 5 Group, including sixteen representing 44 (Rhodesia) Squadron. Fourteen of these were assigned to the first phase, taking-off between 18.24 and 18.44 with F/Ls Dorehill, Mercer and Wiggin the senior pilots on duty, and just two to the second, F/L Phillips and F/O Fynn departing Dunholme Lodge at 21.28 and 21.30. P/O Chatterton turned back early on after a hydraulics feed to the rear turret left it inoperable and the gunners legs drenched in fluid. F/L Wiggin's port-outer engine began to falter forty miles inside enemy territory, forcing him to abandon all thoughts of reaching Bavaria, but he resolved to hit something of use and asked his navigator to plot a course to Dieppe on the French coast, which they bombed through ten-tenths cloud from 18,500 feet at 20.42. The rest of the first wave bomber stream flew out over Belgium with ten-tenths cloud beneath them also, but that had dissipated by the time the target drew near, and, on arrival, it was possible for crews to gain a visual reference. The Path Finders' red and green TIs were in the bomb sights as the 44 (Rhodesia) Squadron crews carried out their attacks from 21,000 to 23,000 feet between 22.39 and 22.54, and fires were beginning to take hold as they turned away. The second wave crews were drawn on by the glow in the sky from a hundred miles away and arrived to find visibility still good despite copious amounts of smoke rising through 10,000 feet, and they bombed on existing fires and red and green Wanganui flares and TIs from 21,500 and 22,000 feet at 01.15 and 01.19. The loss of twenty-one aircraft seemed to confirm the benefits of splitting the forces, and this tactic would remain an important part of Bomber Command planning for the remainder of the war. 44 (Rhodesia) Squadron posted missing F/O Bartlett and his crew in ND520, and it would not be until he and two members of his crew arrived home later in the year after evading capture, that their fate became known. They had been intercepted by the night-fighter of Hptm Ludwig Meister of III./NJG4, and, following a running battle, had abandoned the Lancaster to its fate, landing some twenty miles north of Reims. The mid-upper gunner succumbed to his wounds before help arrived, and, it is believed, that the rear gunner had been killed during the engagement. It had been a devastatingly destructive operation, in which all facets of the plan had come together in near perfect harmony, spelling disaster for this lightly defended treasure trove of culture. Its heart was torn out by blast and fire that destroyed almost three thousand houses along with buildings of outstanding historical significance, and centuries of irreplaceable culture was lost forever. There was also some industrial damage, and around ninety-thousand people were bombed out of their homes.

During the course of the month the squadron carried out five operations and dispatched eighty-five sorties for the loss of two Lancasters and their crews.

March 1944

March would bring an end to the winter campaign, but a long and bitter month would have to be endured first before any respite came from long-range forays into Germany. The crews had enjoyed a few nights off when the second raid of the series on Stuttgart was posted on the 1st, for which a force of 557 aircraft was made ready. This number included 178 Lancasters representing 5 Group, fourteen of which were provided by 44 (Rhodesia) Squadron. Take-off from Dunholme Lodge was accomplished without incident between 22.56 and 23.27 with W/C Thompson the senior pilot on duty for the first time, and there would be no early returns. They flew out over ten-tenths cloud with tops at between 12,000 and 17,000 feet, and encountered similar conditions in the target area, where the Path Finders employed a combination of sky and ground-marking. This, unfortunately, became scattered, and the bombing was directed between two main concentrations, the 44 (Rhodesia) Squadron crews carrying out their attacks on Wanganui red markers with green stars from 20,500 to 24,000 feet between 03.00 and 03.14. It was not possible to assess the accuracy of the attack, although a column of smoke had reached 25,000 feet by the end of the raid, and large fires were evident from the glow in the sky visible from up to 150 miles away. The presence of thick cloud all the way there and back made conditions difficult for enemy night-fighters, and a remarkably modest four aircraft failed to return. It was established eventually that the raid had been an outstanding success, which had caused extensive damage in central, western and northern districts, where a number of important war-industry factories, including those belonging to Bosch and Daimler-Benz, had sustained damage.

At the end of the first week, the Halifax brigade, particularly those withdrawn from operations over Germany, fired the opening salvoes of the pre-invasion campaign, the purpose of which was to dismantle by bombing thirty-seven railway centres in France, Belgium and western Germany. It began on the night of the 6/7th at Trappes marshalling yards, situated some ten miles west-south-west of Paris, and continued at Le Mans in north-western France on the following night. For most of the heavy crews, however, there was no employment following Stuttgart, until a return there in mid-month, but, in the meantime, matters were afoot at 5 Group, and had been ever since a frustrating series of operations against flying bomb launching sites conducted by 617 Squadron since December had failed to achieve the desired results. The problem had been an inability to achieve pinpoint accuracy, which was vital to destroy small, precision targets, and Oboe was just not precise enough. Accurate though Oboe undoubtedly was at an urban target, where a margin of error of 400 to 600 yards was almost pinpoint, precision targets required more. 617 Squadron had obliterated the Oboe markers, only for bombing photos to show that the targets, situated only a matter of yards away, had remained intact. W/C Cheshire and S/L Martin experimented with a dive-bombing technique, which had proved to be successful, but impracticable in a Lancaster, and Cheshire had borrowed a Mosquito for further trials. These were so promising, that the 5 Group A-O-C, AVM Cochrane, authorized a number of operations by the squadron against factory targets in France, before taking the idea to Harris. Harris approved, paving the way for 5 Group to become effectively independent of the main bomber force and begin larger-scale trials.

Orders were received at Bardney, Skellingthorpe and Waddington on the 9th to prepare eleven Lancasters each for a 5 Group attack that night against the Lioré et Olivier aircraft factory at Marignane, situated a few miles to the north of Marseilles in southern France. The area was the main pre-war hub for commercial flying boat operations, particularly for the Pan American Clipper Class flights, and the factory had been engaged in the manufacture of the LeO 45 twin-engine medium bomber for the French Air Force. They took off in mid-evening with a round-trip ahead of them of some 1,350 miles if they flew direct, and arrived in the target area under clear skies and bright moonlight that facilitated an easy identification of the factory buildings, which had been marked by red spotfires. The bombing was carried out from medium level either side of 01.30, and the high-explosives were seen to fall among the buildings, while the incendiaries appeared to be a little scattered. A large explosion was witnessed at 01.24 and a huge pall of smoke was rising through 6,000 feet as the force turned away, all to arrive home safely, most having spent more than nine hours aloft.

5 Group received orders on the 10th to prepare 102 Lancasters to form four small forces, each to attack a specific factory in France that night. The targets were the Michelin tyre factory at Clermont-Ferrand, the Bloch aircraft factory at Châteauroux, which was the first to be set up by the famed designer, Marcel Dassault, in 1935, the Morane Saulnier aircraft plant at Ossun, just north of the Pyrenese and the Ricamerie needle-bearing works at St-Etienne, the last-mentioned, the objective for sixteen Lancasters from 617 Squadron. Eleven 44 (Rhodesia) Squadron crews were briefed for Ossun along with a dozen from 49 Squadron at Fiskerton and departed Dunholme Lodge between 19.50 and 20.25 with W/C Thompson and S/L Hunter the senior pilots on duty. They all arrived in the target area to find bright moonlight, and circled, until employing flares over the town of Tarbes, a few miles to the north-east, as a rally point for the run on the aiming point. A Master of Ceremonies (Master Bomber) was on hand to direct the bombing, and, while there was some disagreement between W/C Thompson and W/C Adams of 49 Squadron, all was resolved, and the 44 (Rhodesia) Squadron crews carried out their attacks on red spotfires from 4,000 to 8,200 feet between 23.53 and 00.07, observing some buildings to disintegrate and others to catch fire. There was no opposition, and all four operations were

concluded successfully for the loss of a single Lancaster occupied by the crew of a 207 Squadron flight commander.

Now that the Mk III Halifax was becoming available in larger numbers, the Command was quickly returning to full strength, and it was a force of 863 aircraft that set out for Stuttgart in the early-evening of the 15th. This number included 206 Lancasters provided by 5 Group, fourteen of them departing Dunholme Lodge between 19.12 and 19.46 with F/Ls Dorehill, Fynn and Wiggin the senior pilots on duty. They rendezvoused with the rest of the force as they passed over Reading on their way to the south coast, and an elongated bomber stream crossed the French coast at 20,000 feet over broken cloud with clear conditions above. It maintained a course parallel with the frontiers of Belgium, Luxembourg and Germany as if heading for Switzerland, before turning towards the north-east for the run-in to the target. It was during this final leg that the night-fighters managed to infiltrate a section of the stream and score heavily, although, this was not apparent to the 44 (Rhodesia) Squadron crews. Adverse winds were responsible for the Path Finders arriving up to six minutes late to open the attack, when they employed both sky and ground-markers in the face of seven to ten-tenths cloud at between 8,000 and 15,000 feet. The Wanganui flares drifted in the wind, marking an area to the north-east of the River Neckar, while the TIs landed far apart in the north and south of the city. The 44 (Rhodesia) Squadron crews bombed on whatever markers presented themselves, mostly red TIs, from 20,200 to 23,500 feet between 23.19 and 23.33, observing a spread of fires, including two large ones ten miles apart, and smoke rising to bombing altitude. It would be established later that some of the early bombing had been accurate, but, that most of the loads had undershot and fallen into open country, a disappointment compounded by the loss, mostly to night-fighters, of thirty-seven aircraft. Among these was ND576 with the experienced crew of F/L Fynn, and the lone survival in enemy hands of the Rhodesian pilot suggests that the Lancaster broke up violently and ejected him into space, leaving the other seven occupants to perish.

From the 17th, 44 Squadron would have to share the facilities at Dunholme Lodge with 619 Squadron, which took up residence after spending a few months at Coningsby. Many operations had been mounted against Frankfurt during the preceding two years, only a small number of which had been really effective. This state of affairs was about to be rectified, however, and the first of two raids against this south-central powerhouse of industry was posted on the 18th, for which a force of 846 aircraft was made ready. 5 Group supported the operation with 212 Lancasters, seventeen of which belonged to 44 (Rhodesia) Squadron, and they were loaded at Dunholme Lodge with a cookie each and a variety of incendiaries, before taking off between 19.00 and 19.41 with S/Ls Cockbain and Hunter the senior pilots on duty. P/O Frost lost his rear turret almost immediately, and went out to sea to jettison 8,000lbs of bombs to ensure a safe landing. They touched down at 20.30 only to find the bomb bay still full. The others pressed on across France and into Germany in good weather conditions, where they encountered a layer of haze 20,000 feet thick over the target, and, according to most, no more than three-tenths cloud. This allowed the Path Finders to employ the Newhaven ground marking technique (blind marking by H2S, followed by visual backing-up), which the 44 (Rhodesia) Squadron crews exploited when carrying out their attacks on red and green TIs from 20,100 to 23,000 feet between 21.59 and 22.14. A large explosion was witnessed at 22.05, and the participants in the raid flew home confident that their efforts had been worthwhile. They had, indeed, contributed to an outstandingly successful raid, during which, 5 Group alone dropped more than one thousand tons of bombs for the first time at a single target. Local reports calculated that six thousand buildings had been destroyed or seriously damaged in predominantly eastern, central and western districts, and this was in return for the loss of twenty-two aircraft, five of which were from 5 Group. 44 (Rhodesia) Squadron posted missing another highly experienced crew, that of F/L Phillips, in LM306, which had been shot down by a night-fighter from 19,500 feet to crash some twenty-four miles east-south-east of Bonn and around fifty miles short of the target. Both gunners failed to survive, but the remainder took to their parachutes, F/L Phillips having to deploy his by hand as he fell, after the ripcord failed to do its job. All landed safely to be taken into captivity.

Frankfurt was named again on the 22nd as the target for that night, and 217 crews of 5 Group learned that they were to be part of another huge force of 816 aircraft. The sixteen participants from 44 (Rhodesia) Squadron took off between 18.43 to 19.01 with F/Ls Dorehill and Wiggin the senior pilots on duty. After climbing out above their stations and forming up, they adopted an unusual route for a target south of the Ruhr, crossing the enemy coast over Vlieland and Teschelling, before passing to the east of Osnabrück on a direct course due south for the target. There were no early returns from the 44 (Rhodesia) Squadron element, and they arrived at the target to find five to six-tenths thin, low cloud at around 4,000 feet, and Paramatta marking (blind marking by H2S) in progress. They focussed their attention on the release-point flares and red and green TIs marking out the aiming point, before bombing from 20,000 to 22,800 feet between 21.36 and 22.10. A massive rectangular area of unbroken fire was observed across the centre of the city, the glow from which could be seen for at least a hundred miles into the return flight. Returning crews reported numerous searchlights lighting up the cloud, and moderate to intense flak that reached up to the bombers' flight level. Local reports confirmed the enormity of the devastation, which was particularly severe in western districts and left this half of the city without electricity, gas and water for an extended period. More than nine hundred people lost their lives and a further 120,000 were bombed out of their homes at a cost to the Command of twenty-six Lancasters and seven Halifaxes, a loss-rate of 4.2% and 3.8% respectively. 44 (Rhodesia) Squadron was represented among the missing by ND538 and ND518, the former crashing outbound twenty-five miles east of the Luxembourg frontier and sixty miles short of the target. P/O Butt RAAF and three others lost their lives, and three survived to fall into enemy hands. The latter was heading eastwards to leave the target area, and crashed four miles east of Hanau at 22.30, killing P/O Porter RAAF and all but two of his crew, who became PoWs. It was a bad night for senior officers, 207 and 7 Squadrons losing their commanding officers, while Bardney's station commander, G/C Norman Pleasance, failed to return in a 9 Squadron Lancaster. What was about to happen over the next week and a half, however, would overshadow anything that had gone before, and would certainly not fall within what might be considered acceptable.

It was more than five weeks since the main force had last visited the Capital, and 811 aircraft were made ready on the 24th for what would be the final raid of the war by RAF heavy bombers on the "Big City". 5 Group put up 193 Lancasters, of which thirteen were made ready by 44 (Rhodesia) Squadron, and they departed Dunholme Lodge between 18.38 and 19.08 with S/L Hunter the senior pilot on duty. They had a long flight ahead of them, which would take them across the North Sea to the Danish coast near Ringkøbing and then to a point on the German Baltic coast near Rostock. When north-east of Berlin they were to adopt a south-westerly course for the bombing run, and, once clear of the defence zone homebound, dogleg to the west and then north-west to pass around Hannover on its southern and western sides, before heading for Holland and an exit via the Castricum coast. The extended outward leg provided a time-on-target of around 22.30, but an unexpected difficulty would be encountered, which would render void all of the meticulous planning. The existence of what we now know as "Jetstream" winds was unknown at the time, and the one blowing from the north with unprecedented strength on this night pushed the bomber stream south of its intended track. Navigators, who were expecting to see the northern tip of Sylt on their H2S screens, were horrified to find the southern end, which meant that they were thirty miles south of track, and about to fly over Germany rather than Denmark. The previously mentioned "wind-finder" system had been set up for precisely this eventuality, but the problem on this night was that the wind-finders refused to believe what their instruments were telling them. Winds in excess of one hundred m.p.h had never been encountered before, and, fearing that they would be disbelieved, many modified the figures downward. The same thing happened at raid control, where the figures were modified again, so that the information rebroadcast to the bomber stream bore no resemblance to the reality of the situation.

There were no early returns among the 44 (Rhodesia) Squadron element, and, by the time that the crews had reached Westerhever on the west coast of the Schleswig-Holstein peninsula, most realized that they were some distance south of track and set course for the north to try to regain the planned route and avoid the defences that would be met if they turned east over Germany. Many commented on the inaccurate wind information received during the outward journey, and having arrived in the target area, some were convinced that the Path Finders were up to ten minutes late in opening the raid. This was confirmed to some by the voice of the Master Bomber exhorting them to hurry up. Crews reported a variety of cloud conditions, from three to ten-tenths at between 6,000 and 15,000 feet, but most were able to pick out the red and green TIs on the ground, and, if not, found red Wanganui flares with green stars to guide them to the aiming point. The 44 (Rhodesia) Squadron crews confirmed their positions by H2S before bombing from 20,500 to 22,500 feet between 22.29 and 23.08 and observed what appeared to be a scattered attack in the early stages, until fires began to become more concentrated in three distinct areas, and large explosions were witnessed at 22.42 and 22.54. The defences were very active with moderate flak bursting at up to 24,000 feet, and light flak attempting to shoot out the skymarkers, but night-fighter activity was described by the 5 Group ORB as unusually quiet. There was a shock awaiting the Command as the returning aircraft landed to leave a shortfall of seventy-two, and it would be established later that two-thirds of them had fallen victim to the Ruhr flak batteries after being driven into that region's defence zone by the wind on the way home. 44 (Rhodesia) Squadron's two missing Lancasters were homebound when their end came, ND672 falling to a night-fighter attack to crash in southern Holland close to the Belgian frontier, killing P/O Hayes and all but his bomb-aimer, who evaded capture. ND565 was one of those straying over the Ruhr to be shot down by flak, coming down some seven miles north of Düsseldorf with no survivors from the eight-man crew captained by P/O Evans. Post-raid analysis revealed that the wind had also played havoc with the marking and bombing and had pushed the attack towards the south-western districts of the Capital, where most of the damage occurred, while 126 outlying communities also received bombs. 44 (Rhodesia) Squadron had been present on each of the nineteen main raids to the Capital, and the diversion there on the night of the Magdeburg debacle in January and had despatched 242 sorties for the loss of sixteen of its Lancasters, sharing with 57 Squadron the highest aircraft losses in 5 Group. The 103 men killed was the highest personnel casualty figure in the group, with a further eleven men becoming PoWs, and the percentage loss rate of 6.5% was also the highest in 5 Group. (The Berlin Raids. Martin Middlebrook).

Twenty 5 Group Lancasters were invited to take part in an attack on the extensive railway yards at Aulnoye in north-eastern France to be carried out on the evening of the 25th, while twenty-two 617 Squadron Lancasters returned to the Sigma aero-engine factory at Lyons. Although Berlin had now been consigned to the past, the winter campaign still had a week to run, and two more major operations for the crews to negotiate. The first of these was posted on the 26th and would bring a return to the old enemy of Essen that night, for which a force of 705 aircraft was made ready. 5 Group contributed 172 of the 476 Lancasters, nine of them provided by 44 (Rhodesia) Squadron, which took off between

19.30 and 19.56 with S/L Cockbain the senior pilot on duty. They climbed out over Dunholme Lodge and set course for the Dutch coast to pass north of Haarlem and Amsterdam, before swinging to the south-east on a direct run to the target. There were no early returns, and all reached the target to find it under eight to ten-tenths cloud with tops in places as high as 14,000 feet. Oboe performed well and enabled the Path Finders to mark the city with red and green TIs and Wanganui flares, which the 44 (Rhodesia) Squadron crews bombed from 19,500 and 22,500 feet between 22.00 and 22.23. They all returned safely, having been unable to assess the results of their efforts, but having gained an impression of a successful raid, based on a considerable glow beneath the clouds as they withdrew. Post-raid reconnaissance soon confirmed another outstandingly destructive operation against this once elusive target, thus continuing the remarkable run of successes here since the introduction of Oboe to main force operations a year earlier. Over seventeen hundred houses were destroyed in the attack, with dozens of war industry factories sustaining serious damage, and, on a night when the night-fighter controllers were caught off guard by the switch to the Ruhr, the success was gained for the modest loss of nine aircraft.

The period known as the Battle of Berlin, but which was better referred to as the winter campaign, was to be brought to an end on the night of the 30/31st, with a standard maximum-effort raid on Nuremberg. The plan of operation departed from normal practice in only one important respect, and this was to prove critical. It had become standard routine over the winter for 8 Group to plan operations and to employ diversions and feints to confuse the enemy night-fighter controllers. Sometimes they were successful and sometimes not, but with the night-fighter force having clearly gained the upper hand with its "Tame Boar" running commentary system, all possible means had to be adopted to protect the bomber stream. During a conference held early on the 30th, the Lancaster Group A-O-Cs expressed a preference for a 5 Group-inspired route, which would require the bomber stream to fly a long, straight leg across Belgium and Germany, to a point about fifty miles north of Nuremberg, from where the final run-in would commence. The Halifax A-O-Cs were less convinced of the benefits, and AVM Bennett, the Path Finder chief, was positively overcome by the potential dangers and predicted a disaster, only to be overruled. A force of 795 aircraft was made ready, of which 201 Lancasters were provided by 5 Group, sixteen of them representing 44 (Rhodesia) Squadron, and the crews attended briefings to be told of the route, wind conditions and the belief that a layer of cloud would conceal them from enemy night-fighters. Before take-off, a Meteorological Flight Mosquito crew radioed in to cast doubts upon the weather conditions, which they could see differed markedly from those that had been forecast. This also went unheeded, and, from around 21.45 for the next hour or so, the crews took off for the rendezvous area, and headed into a conspiracy of circumstances, which would inflict upon Bomber Command its heaviest defeat of the war.

At Dunholme Lodge, take-off took place between 21.47 and 22.24 with W/C Thompson and S/L Hunter the senior pilots on duty, and it was not long into the flight before they and the other crews began to notice some unusual features in the conditions, which included uncommonly bright moonlight, and a crystal clarity of visibility that allowed them the rare sight of other aircraft in the stream. On most nights, crews would feel themselves to be completely alone in the sky all the way to the target, until bang on schedule, TIs would be seen to fall and other aircraft would make their presence known by the turbulence of their slipstreams as they funnelled towards the aiming point. Once at cruising altitude on this night, however, they were alarmed to note that the forecast cloud was conspicuous by its absence, and, instead, lay beneath them as a white tablecloth, against which they were silhouetted like flies. Condensation trails began to form in the cold, clear air to further advertise their presence to the enemy, and the Jetstream winds, which had so adversely affected the Berlin raid a week earlier, were also present, only this time blowing from the south. As then, the wind-finder system would be unable to cope, and this would have a serious impact on the outcome of the operation. The final insult on this sad night was, that the route into Germany passed close to two night-fighter beacons, which the enemy aircraft were orbiting while awaiting their instructions, unaware initially that they were about to have the cream of Bomber Command handed to them on a plate.

The carnage began over Charleroi in Belgium, and from there to the target, the route was sign-posted by the burning wreckage on the ground of eighty Bomber Command aircraft. Among these were two from 44 (Rhodesia) Squadron, the first of them, ME629, containing the crew of P/O Frost, falling victim to the Me110 night-fighter of Lt Wilhelm Seuss of IV./NJG5, and crashing without survivors some six miles south-east of Bad Hersfeld, while still a hundred miles short of the target. ND795 had progressed further and was close to the final turning point, some twenty miles west of Coburg, when it was attacked, it is believed, by the same night-fighter, and crashed at Unteressfeld, killing P/O Charlesworth and all but the bomb-aimer, who fell into enemy hands. The wind-finder system broke down again, and those crews who either failed to detect the strength of the wind, or simply refused to believe the evidence, were driven up to fifty miles north of their intended track, and, consequently, turned towards Nuremberg from a false position. This led to more than a hundred aircraft bombing at Schweinfurt in error, which combined with the massive losses sustained before the target was reached to reduce considerably the numbers reaching the primary target. The remaining fourteen 44 (Rhodesia) Squadron crews arrived over Nuremberg to encounter eight to nine-tenths cloud with tops as high as 16,000 feet and bombed from 19,000 to 23,000 feet between 01.03 and 01.35, aiming at red and green TIs and sky-markers after confirming their positions by H2S. Many fires were observed, the glow from which, according to some reports, remained visible for 120 miles into the return journey. Ninety-five aircraft failed to return home, twenty-one of them from 5 Group, and many others were written off in landing crashes or with battle damage too severe to repair. The shock and disappointment were compounded by the fact that the strong wind had driven the marking beyond the city to the east, and Nuremberg had, consequently, escaped serious damage.

During the course of the month, the squadron participated in eight operations, and dispatched 110 sorties for the loss of eight Lancasters and their crews.

April 1944

The winter campaign had brought the Command to its low point of the war and was the only time when the morale of the crews was in question. What now lay before the hard-pressed men of Bomber Command was in marked contrast to that which had been endured over the seemingly interminable winter months. In place of the long slog to Germany on dark, often dirty nights, shorter range hops to France and Belgium in improving weather conditions would become the order of the day. However, these operations would be equally demanding in their way, and would require of the crews a greater commitment to accuracy, to avoid casualties among friendly civilians. Despite this, a decree from on high insisted that such operations were worthy of counting as just one third of a sortie towards the completion of a tour, and this flawed policy caused a degree of resentment to pervade the crew rooms. In fact, the number of sorties to complete a tour would fluctuate between this point and the end of hostilities, and time would demonstrate that operations over the Occupied countries were no less hazardous than those over Germany. Despite the horrendous losses of the winter campaign, the Command was in remarkably fine fettle to face its new challenge, with 3 Group gradually converting to Lancasters, and the much-improved Hercules powered Halifaxes equipping 4 Group and most of 6 Group. Harris was now in the enviable position of being able to achieve what had eluded his predecessor, namely, to attack multiple targets simultaneously with enough strength to be effective. Such was the hitting-power now at his disposal, he could assign targets to individual groups, to groups in tandem, or to the Command as a whole, as dictated by operational requirements. Although invasion considerations would come first, while Harris was at the helm, his favoured policy of city-busting would never be entirely shelved.

5 Group returned to operations on the 5th, with an operation involving 144 Lancasters and a Mosquito flown by W/C Cheshire of 617 Squadron. The target was the former Dewoitine aircraft factory at Toulouse in south-western France, which, under a nationalization plan in 1936 involving six aircraft companies, including Lioré et Olivier and Potez, was now operating under the name SNCASE, or Sud Est for short. Cheshire was to mark it with spotfires from low level, using the system that he was instrumental in developing, and one which would become an integral part of 5 Group operations, with refinements, from this point on. This would be Cheshire's first operational flight in a Mosquito, and the first time that he marked a target for the group, rather than just 617 Squadron. Much depended upon its success if Harris were to become sold on the idea of the low-level visual marking technique and give it his backing. At Dunholme Lodge, 44 (Rhodesia) Squadron bombed up ten Lancasters and sent them on their way between 20.29 and 20.39 with W/C Thompson the senior pilot on duty. Ahead of them lay an outward flight of more than four hours, which all of the 44 (Rhodesia) Squadron crews negotiated and arrived in time to watch Cheshire lob two red spotfires onto the roof of the factory at 00.17 during his third pass. So accurate were they, that the two 617 Squadron Lancaster backers-up were not required, and bombing took place in bright moonlight, the 44 (Rhodesia) Squadron crews delivering their loads from 9,100 to 12,000 feet between 00.13 and 00.33 and observing large fires with smoke rising through 7,000 feet. One 207 Squadron Lancaster was hit by flak over the target at 00.30 and exploded, killing all on board, and this was the only loss from an outstandingly successful operation. Within hours, Harris gave the go ahead for 5 Group to take on its own marking force, and become, in effect, an independent entity.

It would be almost two weeks before the necessary moves took place, and, in the meantime, the pre-invasion campaign got into full swing with the posting of two operations on the 9th. The Lille-Delivrance goods station in north-eastern France was assigned to 239 aircraft from 3, 4, 6 and 8 Groups, while the marshalling yards at Villeneuve-St-Georges, on the southern outskirts of Paris, were to be targeted by 225 aircraft drawn from all groups. The weather conditions were excellent, and clear skies greeted the latter force as it crossed the French coast at around 14,000 feet. The target could be identified visually, but crews aimed for the red and green TIs that had been accurately placed by the Path Finders, delivering their hardware from between 13,000 and 14,500 feet in the face of little opposition. Many bomb bursts were observed along with orange explosions, and, to those high above, the raid appeared to be highly successful. In fact, many bomb loads had fallen into adjacent residential districts, where four hundred houses had been destroyed or seriously damaged, and ninety-three people killed. This was far fewer than had died in the simultaneous operation at Lille, many miles to the north-east, where over two thousand items of rolling stock had been destroyed, and buildings and installations seriously damaged, but at a collateral cost of 456 French civilian lives. Civilian casualties would prove to be an unavoidable by-product of the campaign.

44 (Rhodesia) Squadron did not take part in the above operation but provided eight crews for that night's large minelaying effort to the Baltic area involving 103 Lancasters from 1 and 5 Groups. They

took off between 21.16 and 21.32 with S/L Cockbain the senior pilot on duty bound for the Spinach garden in Danzig Bay. They noted night-fighter activity over Denmark and the accurate Swedish flak discouraged them from straying too close to neutral airspace, and all arrived in the target area to find bright moonlight and high cirrus cloud. Visibility was perfect as they pinpointed on Hel Point for the start of their timed runs to the drop site, where they planted their vegetables as briefed from a uniform 15,000 feet between 01.31 and 01.47. Nine Lancasters failed to return, having been intercepted by night-fighters on the route home over the western coast of Denmark, and it was a reminder, that this most productive of enterprises could, on occasions, be as dangerous as operating over a city.

On the following day, Monday the 10th, a further five railway yards, four in France and one in Belgium, were posted as the targets for that night and assigned to individual groups. 5 Group was handed those at Tours in the Loire region of western France, for which 180 Lancasters were made ready, fifteen of them on the 44 (Rhodesia) Squadron dispersals at Dunholme Lodge. They took off between 22.56 and 23.28 with W/C Thompson again leading from the front and the first off the ground and set course for England's south coast and the Channel crossing. There were no early returns, and all arrived at the target to find bright moonlight and red spotfires marking the aiming point. Master Bombers were on hand to direct the two phases of the attack, the first against the western side of the yards and the second its eastern counterpart, the 44 (Rhodesia) Squadron crews attacking aiming point "A" from 6,500 to 7,500 feet, some making two passes between 01.55 and 02.55. The later stages of the second phase bombing was affected by smoke drifting across the target area and rising through 6,000 feet, persuading the Master Bomber to call a halt to bombing at 02.48, and send home any crews with bombs still on board. There were mixed opinions as to the effectiveness of the operation, some gaining the impression that the eastern half of the yards had not been touched, but others claimed the attack to have been accurate and concentrated within the yards, and two large fires were observed. Post-raid reconnaissance confirmed the success of the attack, but the Germans would round up local civilians and force them into repairing the damage to get the yards working again before long.

Aachen was a major railway centre with marshalling yards at both the western and eastern ends, but the attack planned for the night of the 11/12th was clearly designed as a city-busting exercise for which a force of 341 heavy aircraft was drawn from 1, 3, 5 and 8 Groups. 44 (Rhodesia) Squadron detailed eight Lancasters, which took off between 20.26 and 20.54 with S/L Cockbain the senior pilot on duty. The bomber stream climbed to between 18,000 and 20,000 feet by the time it reached the Belgian coast at 3 degrees east and maintained that altitude all the way to the target, where six to ten-tenths thin cloud was encountered at 7,000 to 8,000 feet. Red and green TIs identified the aiming point, and the 44 (Rhodesia) Squadron crews attacked it from 16,000 to 17,000 feet between 22.44 and 22.48, observing many bomb bursts and fires, which suggested that the attack was accurate. The crews maintained height on the way home until fifty miles from the coast, at which position they began a gentle descent to exit enemy territory at 15,000 feet or above. Reports coming out of Aachen revealed this to be the city's worst experience of the war to date, with extensive damage in central and southern districts, disruption of its transport infrastructure and a death toll of 1,525 people in return for the loss of nine Lancasters. However, post-raid reconnaissance revealed that the railway yards had not been destroyed and would require further attention.

On the 14th, the Command became officially subject to the orders coming from the Supreme Headquarters of the Allied Expeditionary Force (SHAEF), under General Dwight D Eisenhower, and would remain thus shackled until the Allied armies were sweeping towards the German frontier at the end of the summer. On the 18th, 83 and 97 Squadrons were loaned to 5 Group from the Path Finders, on what amounted to a permanent detachment, along with the Mosquito unit, 627 Squadron. The Lancaster units were to become the 5 Group heavy markers, while the Mosquitos would eventually take over the low-level marking role currently performed by 617 Squadron. This was a major coup for AVM Cochrane and 5 Group and a bitter blow to AVM Bennett, the Path Finder Chief. Relations between Cochrane and Bennett had never been cordial, but this plunged them to new depths. Both were brilliant men, Bennett, an Australian, in particular, a man of the greatest intellect, who, despite his reserve and total lack of humour, commanded the deepest respect and loyalty from his men. He and Cochrane possessed vastly different opinions on the subject of target marking, Bennett believing that a low-level method exposed the crews to unnecessary danger, while Cochrane insisted that the risks in a fast-flying Mosquito were negligible and would produce greater accuracy. Though 83 and 97 Squadrons were formerly of 5 Group, and, at that time, had undoubtedly considered themselves part of the elite, most of the current crop of crews, despite beginning their operational careers in 5 Group, had come to see 8 Group as the pinnacle, and were upset at being removed from what they considered to be an elevated status. Those that had qualified were fiercely proud to wear the Path Finder badge and enjoyed the accelerated promotion opportunities, but, happily for them, as the squadrons were only officially on loan to 5 Group, these were privileges that they would retain.

Any resentment might have been smoothed over had their reception at Coningsby been handled better, but, as the newly arrived crews tumbled out of their transports, they were summoned immediately to the briefing room, to be lectured by the 54 Base commander, Air Commodore "Bobby" Sharp. Rather than welcoming them as brothers-in-arms, he harangued them over their bad 8 Group habits, and ordered them to buckle down to learning 5 Group ways. This was an insult to experienced airmen, for whom the task of illuminating targets for 5 Group would be a piece of cake compared with the complexities of their 8 Group duties. The fact that the insult was being delivered by a pompous, self-important man with no relevant operational experience, made it doubly unpalatable. From this point on, 5 Group would be known in 8 Group circles somewhat disparagingly as the "Independent Air Force", or "The Lincolnshire Poachers".

The 5 Group target on the 18th was the marshalling yards at Juvisy, situated on the West Bank of the Seine south of Paris, which was one of four similar targets for the night. The intention had been for the new arrivals to participate, but the disgruntled commanding officers, G/C Laurie Deane of 83 Squadron and W/C Jimmy Carter of 97 Squadron, announced that they were not yet ready, and the operation would have to go ahead without them. 202 Lancasters and four Mosquitos were made ready, the latter belonging to 617 Squadron, and 8 Group would provide three Oboe Mosquitos to deliver the initial marking. 44 (Rhodesia) Squadron made ready thirteen Lancasters and dispatched them from Dunholme Lodge between 20.26 and 20.52 with F/L Higgs the senior pilot on duty. All reached the target to find clear skies and ideal bombing conditions, in which they observed W/C Cheshire's red spotfires become backed up by green TIs. Despite black smoke drifting across the aiming point and upwards from the destruction of a fuel dump at 23.32, the 44 (Rhodesia) Squadron crews were able to hit the markers from 7,000 to 11,000 between 23.32 and 23.48, and returning crews were enthusiastic about the success of the operation. This was confirmed by post-raid reconnaissance and prompted the crews to make the valid comment that, to count this operation as just one-third of a sortie was undervaluing it, a sentiment shared by all whose job involved putting their lives on the line.

Briefings on 5 Group stations on the 20th informed crews of their part in the first operation to include the three newly transferred squadrons, which was a two-phase attack on railway yards at La Chapelle, situated just to the north of Paris, while the night's main event was to be conducted by a force of 357

Lancasters and twenty-two Mosquitos drawn from 1, 3, 6 and 8 Groups against Cologne. A meticulous plan had been prepared for 5 Group, in which the phases were to be separated by an hour, each with its own specific aiming point, and 83 Squadron's W/C Deane was to be the Master Bomber with S/L Sparks his deputy. The plan called for 8 Group Mosquitos to drop cascading flares by Oboe to provide an initial reference, and for a Mosquito element from 627 Squadron to lay a Window screen ahead of the main force Lancasters. Once the target had been identified, the first members of the 83 Squadron flare force were to provide illumination for the low-level marker Mosquitos of 617 Squadron, which would mark the first aiming point with red spot fires for the main force element to aim at. The whole procedure would then be repeated at the second aiming point. At Coningsby, W/C Deane conducted the briefing, and, at its conclusion, wished the assembled throng good luck, before dismissing them, whereupon a voice from the back declared that the briefing wasn't over, and that the base and station commanders wanted their say. This had not been standard practice in 8 Group, and left Deane mystified and a little humiliated. The senior officers had only waffle to offer, but it made them feel important, while confirming the first impressions of the crews, that A/C Sharp was a self-important and irrelevant link in the chain of command.

44 (Rhodesia) Squadron made ready fourteen Lancasters as part of the overall force of 247 Lancasters of 5 Group and twenty-two Mosquitos of 5 and 8 Groups, and they departed Dunholme Lodge between 21.42 and 22.15 with S/L Cockbain the senior pilot on duty. They were assigned to the first aiming point, each loaded with a mix of 1,000 and 500 pounders and arrived at the target to find largely clear skies, good visibility and only some ground haze to mar the view. Zero hour for the opening phase was set for 00.05, but the Oboe Mosquitos were two minutes late, and some communications problems had to be ironed out before matters began to run smoothly. The 44 (Rhodesia) Squadron crews bombed from 7,000 to 11,500 feet between 00.24 and 00.47, during which a large orange explosion at 00.28 sent a column of black smoke skyward, which impaired visibility to some extent, but those attacking afterwards were able to identify a red spotfire and bomb it, observing large explosions and fires that were visible to the second phase crews as they approached. Following the second phase attack, the fires remained visible for a hundred miles into the return flight, and, at debriefing, crews expressed confidence that they had contributed to a successful operation. Post-raid reconnaissance confirmed the success of both phases of the raid, which had left the yards severely damaged for the loss of six Lancasters. Among these was 44 (Rhodesia) Squadron's ND573, which was lost without trace with the crew of F/O Skinner. A congratulatory message from A-O-C Cochrane was received on all participating stations.

The real test for the 5 Group low-level marking system would come at a heavily defended German target, for which Braunschweig was selected on the 22nd, while the rest of the Command targeted the Ruhr city of Düsseldorf. 5 Group put together a force of 238 Lancasters and seventeen Mosquitos, with ten ABC Lancasters of 1 Group's 101 Squadron to provide radio countermeasures (RCM). 44 (Rhodesia) Squadron contributed thirteen Lancasters, which took off between 22.45 and 23.24 with S/L Hunter the senior pilot on duty. F/L Hildred and crew were fifty miles from the enemy coast when the rear turret became unserviceable, and, despite attempts by the flight engineer to fix the problem, nothing could be done, and they were forced to turn back. The others reached the target area after being guided by route-markers and found six to eight-tenths thin cloud at between 8,000 and 10,000 feet, and accurate marking by the 617 Squadron Mosquito element. Despite this, the main force crews were unable to properly identify the target, a situation again compounded by communications problems between various controllers, caused by the failure of VHF and the consequent need to pass on instructions instead by W/T. This led to confusion, and many crews were forced to orbit for up to fifteen minutes before bombing. The 44 (Rhodesia) Squadron crews carried out their attacks on green TIs and red spotfires from 19,000 to 22,000 feet between 01.55 and 02.08 and returned safely to report what appeared to be a successful operation, while also complaining about the dangers of orbiting a target with aircraft heading in a variety of directions. Although some bombs did fall in the city centre, most were directed at reserve H2S-laid TIs to the south of the city, and damage was less severe than might otherwise have been.

When Munich was posted across 5 Group as the target on the 24th for another live test of the low-level visual marking method, it might have been seen as somewhat ambitious to select such a major city, that was protected by two hundred flak guns. The main operation on this night was to be conducted by a force of 637 aircraft against Karlsruhe, 150 miles to the north-west, which would help to distract the night-fighters. 234 Lancasters were made ready by 5 Group and supplemented by ten of the ABC variety from 101 Squadron, while four Mosquitos of 617 Squadron were loaded with spotfires to carry out the marking, and twelve of 627 Squadron with "window" to dispense during the final approach to the target. 44 (Rhodesia) Squadron's fifteen Lancasters took to the air between 20.33 and 21.10 with S/L Hunter the senior pilot on duty and headed for the south coast before setting course across France towards the south-east and feinting towards Italy. The 617 and 627 Squadron Mosquitos took off three hours after the heavy brigade and adopted a direct route, the latter laying a "window" screen from high level six minutes from the target, masking the arrival of the flare force that was to provide seven minutes of illumination for the 617 marker Mosquitos. 44 (Rhodesia) Squadron's excellent record of serviceability continued, as all reached the target area to encounter clear skies and good visibility. W/C Cheshire dived onto the aiming point in the face of murderous light flak, before racing away across the rooftops to safety. The main force followed hard on his heels, the 44 (Rhodesia) Squadron crews bombing on the red spotfires and green TIs from 15,000 to 21,500 feet between 01.44 and 02.00 in the face of intense searchlight and flak activity. Many fires were seen to take hold, and, as the bombers pointed their snouts back towards France to eventually pass to the north of Paris, Karlsruhe could be seen burning over to starboard. Post-raid reconnaissance and local reports confirmed the success of the raid, which left 1,104 buildings in ruins and a further thirteen hundred severely damaged. It was probably this operation that sealed the award to Cheshire of the Victoria Cross at the conclusion of his operational career of one hundred sorties.

At briefing on the 26th, sixteen 44 (Rhodesia) Squadron crews were told that Schweinfurt was to be their target that night, after the failure of the RAF to destroy it in February and the American 8th Air Force just two weeks ago. The tone was very much, "leave it to RAF Bomber Command", and, with the satisfaction of Munich still fresh in the mind, and the natural rivalry between the two forces, such attitudes were to be expected. They learned that, for this operation, 627 Squadron would act as the low-level marker force for the first time, and for a main force of 215 Lancasters, including nine from 101 Squadron to provide RCM protection. This was just one of three major operations taking place, the main event at Essen, while the railway yards at Villeneuve-St-Georges were to be targeted by a predominantly Halifax main force. The 44 (Rhodesia) Squadron crews took off between 21.03 and 21.39, with S/L Cockbain the senior pilot on duty, but lost the services of F/O Smith to starboard-inner engine failure, and they bombed harbour installations at Le Havre on the way home. The others encountered stronger-than-forecast head winds, which delayed the arrival in the target area of the heavy brigade. They found generally clear skies and good visibility, which the 627 Squadron crews failed to exploit, as their debut marking effort proved to be inaccurate. The 83 Squadron crews remarked on the lack of illumination, and those carrying hooded flares were called in a number of times to back-up. The 44 (Rhodesia) Squadron crews bombed from 14,500 to 21,000 feet between

02.22 and 02.49, aiming at red spotfires and green TIs, some following the instructions of the Master Bomber to overshoot by a thousand yards. A large white explosion was witnessed at 02.29, and many fires were reported, but, once again at this target, most of the hardware fell outside of the target area, leaving ball-bearing production more or less unscathed. Night-fighters got amongst the heavy force, and twenty-one Lancasters were shot down, a hefty 9.3%, and among them were two representing 44 (Rhodesia) Squadron. LL920 collided with ME679 of 57 Squadron, and both crashed near Oberkirchen, some thirty miles south-east of the Ruhr, and there were no survivors from the crew of F/O Oldham DFC. One man survived from the eight on board the other aircraft, which was captained by a flight commander. ME730 came down at Böblingen, twenty-five miles south-west of Heilbronn, killing F/Sgt Kewley RNZAF and all but two of his crew, who fell into enemy hands.

5 Group made preparations on the 28th to send a force of eighty-eight Lancasters and four Mosquitos to attack the Alfred Nobel Dynamit A G explosives works at St-Médard-en-Jalles, situated in a wood on the north-western outskirts of Bordeaux in south-western France. A further fifty-one Lancasters and four Mosquitos would head in the opposite direction to target an aircraft maintenance facility at the Kjeller Flyfabrikk, some ten miles north-east of Oslo, which had been occupied by the Germans since April 1940 and was used by Junkers, Daimler-Benz and BMW. This was the destination for fourteen 44 (Rhodesia) Squadron Lancasters, which departed Dunholme Lodge between 20.55 and 21.29 with W/C Thompson and S/L Hunter the senior pilots on duty. They all arrived in the target area to find clear skies and excellent visibility, and identified the target by H2S, confirmed by yellow TIs at the start of the bombing run and flares and red spotfires on the aiming point. A two-thousand-yard correction was broadcast to compensate for a poor marking performance, and the 44 (Rhodesia) Squadron crews carried out their attacks from 5,000 to 7,000 feet between 01.32 and 01.49, many making more than one pass to take in a number of aiming points. Explosions were observed on the airfield and runway, and among barrack buildings and some of the sheds, and an ammunition dump went up at 01.40. On return, W/C Thompson was scathing about the quality of marking and control, and the amount of smoke given off by too many hooded flares. Meanwhile, the attack near Bordeaux had also been spoiled by smoke and haze from a wood burning nearby, and only twenty-six aircraft had bombed before the Master Bomber called a halt.

The operation was rescheduled for the following night, when the Michelin tyre factory at Clermont-Ferrand was added to the target list and 44 (Rhodesia) Squadron stayed at home. Sixty-eight Lancasters were assigned to the explosives works and fifty-four to the tyre factory, with five 627 Squadron Mosquitos at each to provide the low-level marking. The aiming point was identified both visually and by red spotfires and red and green TIs, which could be seen burning between factory buildings, and returning crews were filled with enthusiasm at the explosions that had ripped the site apart, some commenting that it was the most destructive attack they had taken part in. Post-raid reconnaissance confirmed that both targets had been severely damaged with a massive loss of production. During the course of the month the squadron participated in ten operations and dispatched 152 sorties for the loss of two Lancasters and crews.

May 1944

Seventeen 44 (Rhodesia) Squadron crews were called to briefing at Dunholme Lodge on the 1st, to learn that they would be going to southern France that night to attack the Poudrerie explosives works. They would be part of two 5 Group forces totalling 131 Lancasters and eight Mosquitos targeting the city, the other to attack a SNCASE aircraft assembly factory at Saint-Martin-du-Touch, a western suburb of Toulouse. A third 5 Group force of forty-six Lancasters and four Mosquitos would be sent against an aircraft repair workshop at Tours in western France. The 44 (Rhodesia) Squadron crews took off between 21.16 and 21.43 with S/L Hunter the senior pilot on duty and employed Gee for the first part of the outward flight until it was jammed, relying thereafter on good navigation, green track markers provided by the Path Finders, and H2S. They all reached the target to find moonlight, clear skies and excellent visibility, with flares and red spotfires marking out the aiming point, and carried out their attacks from 6,000 to 9,600 feet between 01.36 and 01.45 in accordance with the instructions of the Master Bomber. F/Sgt Baxter and crew made three runs across the target over a forty-five-minute period, but found the spotfires completely obscured by thick smoke, and brought their bombs home. The attack was clearly focussed on the aiming point, where many bomb bursts were observed, and the glow of the burning site remained visible for a hundred miles into the return journey. All crews returned to their respective stations confident of a successful outcome, and post-raid reconnaissance revealed all three factories to have been heavily damaged.

Briefings took place on 1 and 5 Group stations on the 3rd, for what would become a highly contentious operation that night against a Panzer training camp and transport depot at Mailly-le-Camp, situated some seventy-five miles east of Paris in north-eastern France. The units based there posed a potential threat to Allied forces as the invasion unfolded and needed to be eliminated. The events of the operation proved to be so controversial, that recriminations abound to this day concerning the 5 Group leadership provided by W/Cs Cheshire and Deane. Although the grudges by 1 Group aircrew against them can be understood in the light of what happened, they are unjust, and based on emotion and incorrect information, and it is worthwhile to examine the conduct of the operation in some detail. W/C Cheshire was appointed as marker leader, and was piloting one of four 617 Squadron Mosquitos, while 83 Squadron's commanding officer, W/C Deane, was overall raid controller, with S/L Sparks as Deputy. Deane and Cheshire attended separate briefings, and neither seemed aware of the complete plan, particularly the role of the 1 Group Special Duties Flight from Binbrook, which was assigned to mark its own specific aiming point for an element of the 1 Group force.

The thirteen 44 (Rhodesia) Squadron participants became airborne between 21.38 and 22.07 with S/L Hunter the senior pilot on duty, and all reached the target area to find clear skies, moonlight and excellent bombing conditions, but confusion already beginning to influence events. 617 Squadron's W/C Cheshire and S/L Shannon were in position before midnight, and, as the first flares from the 83 and 97 Squadron Lancasters illuminated the target below, Cheshire released his two red spot fires onto the first aiming point at 00.00½ from 1,500 feet. Shannon backed them up from 400 feet five and a half minutes later, and, as far as Cheshire was concerned, the operation was bang on schedule at this stage. A 97 Squadron Lancaster also laid markers accurately, to ensure a constant focal point, and Cheshire passed instructions to Deane to call the bombers in. It was at this stage of the operation that matters began to go awry. A communications problem arose, when a commercial radio station, believed to be an American forces network, jammed the VHF frequencies in use. Deane called in the 5 Group element, elated that everything was proceeding according to plan, but nothing happened. He checked with his wireless operator that the instructions had been transmitted, and called up S/L Sparks, who was also mystified by the lack of bombing. A few crews from 9, 207 and 467 Squadrons had heard the call to bomb, and did so, but, for most, the instructions were swamped by the interference. The 44 (Rhodesia) Squadron crews realised that R/T was jammed, and S/L Hunter and seven others bombed from 5,000 to 8,000 feet between 00.11 and 00.17 when they saw others doing so, with smoke already beginning to drift across the target area. W/C Deane then attempted to control the operation by W/T, which also failed.

Post raid reports are contradictory, and it is impossible to establish an accurate course of events, particularly when Deane and Cheshire's understanding of the exact time of zero hour differed by five minutes. Remarkably, it also seems, that Deane was unaware that there were two marking points, or three, if one includes 1 Group's Special Duties Flight. Cheshire, initially at least, appeared happy with the early stages of the attack, and described the bombing as concentrated and accurate. It seems certain, however, that many minutes had passed between the dropping of Cheshire's markers and the first main force bombs falling, during which period, Deane was coming to terms with the fact, that his instructions were not getting through. A plausible scenario is, that in the absence of instructions, and with red spot fires clearly visible in the target, some crews opted to bomb, and others followed suit. These would have been predominantly from 5 Group, but as the 1 Group crews became increasingly agitated at having to wait in bright moonlight, with evidence of enemy night-fighters all around, some of them inevitably joined in.

Now a new problem was arising. Smoke from these first salvoes was obliterating the entire camp, and Cheshire had to decide whether or not to send in Fawke and Kearns to mark the second aiming point. His feeling, and that of Deane, as it later transpired, was, that it was unnecessary. The volume of bombs still to fall into the relatively compact area of the target would ensure destruction of the entire site. By 00.16, the first phase of bombing should have been completed, leaving a clear run for Fawke and Kearns across the target, however, the majority of 5 Group crews were still on their bombing run, a fact unknown to Cheshire, who asked Deane for a pause in the bombing, while the two Mosquitos went in. As far as Cheshire was concerned, there was no response from Deane, who would, anyway, have been confused by mention of a second aiming point. In the event, Deane's deputy, S/L Sparks, eventually found a channel free of interference, and did, in fact, transmit an instruction to halt the bombing, both by W/T and R/T, and some crews reported hearing something. While utter chaos reigned, Kearns and Fawke dived in among the falling cookies at 00.23 and 00.25 respectively, to mark the second aiming point on the western edge of the camp. At 2,000 feet, they were lucky to survive the turbulence created by the exploding 4,000 pounders, when 4,000 feet was considered to be a minimum safe height. They were not entirely happy with their work, but F/O Edwards of 97 Squadron dropped a stick of markers precisely on the mark, and S/L Sparks was then able to call the 1 Group main force in along with any from 5 Group with bombs still on board. Among these were the remaining 44 (Rhodesia) Squadron crews who attacked from 5,000 to 8,000 feet between 00.27 and 00.35. Meanwhile, the night fighters continued to create havoc among the Lancasters, as they milled around in the target area, and, as burning aircraft were seen to fall all around, some 1 Group crews succumbed to their anxiety and frustration. In a rare breakdown of R/T discipline, they let fly with comments of an uncomplimentary nature, many of which were intended for, and, indeed, heard by Deane.

Despite the problems, the operation was a major success, which destroyed 80% of the camp's buildings, and 102 vehicles, of which thirty-seven were tanks, while over two hundred men were killed. Forty-two Lancasters failed to return, however, two thirds of them from 1 Group, and 50 Squadron was 5 Group's most afflicted unit with four Lancasters and crews unaccounted for. 44 (Rhodesia) Squadron posted missing the crew of P/O Nolan RAAF in veteran Lancaster EE185, which was probably a victim of one of the Nachtjagd's most successful pilots, Hptm Martin Drewes of III./NJG1. It came down without survivors at 01.18 near Dreux, twenty-five miles west of Paris, at a time when it should have been around 120 miles further to the east and may have been returning early. At debriefing, S/L Blome-Jones of 207 Squadron described the situation as a complete shambles and chaos, the controller as inefficient and the discipline of some crews as bad. Others voiced the opinion that this was a trip worthy of more than one-third of a sortie. On the following day, an inquest into the conduct of the raid revealed that the wireless transmitter in Deane's Lancaster had been sufficiently off frequency to allow the interference from the American network to mask the transmission of instructions and prevent the call to bomb from reaching the main force crews. The 1 Group A-O-C, AVM Rice, decided he would not participate in further operations organized by 5 Group, which was probably not a blow to Cochrane, who was confident that his group did not need back-up.

On the 6th, 1 and 5 Groups were invited to send a modest force each to attack ammunition dumps in France, 5 Group detailing sixty-four Lancasters and four Mosquitos for a site at Louailles, situated some four miles south-east of the town of Sable-sur-Sarthe, south-west of Le-Mans. Clear skies and excellent visibility provided ideal conditions, and a Master Bomber was on hand to direct the attack, which resulted in numerous bomb flashes that lit up the long storage sheds. Two enormous explosions were each followed by a large mushroom of smoke rising through 3,000 feet as the force withdrew. Dunholme Lodge sat this one out but was alerted on the 7th to prepare for its part in five small-scale operations to be mounted against airfields, ammunition dumps and a coastal battery in support of the coming invasion. 5 Group was involved in two raids, the airfield at Tours and an ammunition dump at Salbris, some sixty miles to the east, and it was for the latter that 44 (Rhodesia) Squadron made ready a dozen Lancasters. An additional Lancaster was loaded with mines for P/O Richards and crew to deliver to the Nectarine I garden off the western Frisians, for which they set off at 19.36. The bombing brigade took off between 21.35 and 22.07 with W/C Thompson and S/Ls Cockbain and Hunter the senior pilots on duty on what turned out to be another night of perfect conditions. They headed south to pass by Reading on their way to Selsey Bill for the Channel crossing, intending to make landfall at Cabourg before setting course for the target. They lost the services of P/O Davey and crew when the mid-upper gunner reported sick just thirty-five miles into the outward flight, leaving the others to continue on with Gee working perfectly all the way out, and, with twenty miles horizontal visibility under bright moonlight, the red spotfires were observed well in advance of arrival at the aiming point. ND741 crashed at 00.30 at Herbilly, within sight of the western bank of the River Loire and some thirty miles short of the target, and only the flight engineer in S/L Hunter's crew survived to fall into enemy hands. Some of the others, by this time, were on their bombing runs, and, between 00.28 and 00.31, all carried out their attacks from 6,000 to 8,000 feet, and observed large, vivid explosions and a column of smoke rising through 11,000 feet as they withdrew. Post-raid reconnaissance confirmed that both targets had been bombed accurately and effectively to leave them severely damaged. Meanwhile, P/O Richards and crew had successfully delivered their mines unopposed from 4,000 feet at 23.30 and returned safely from an uneventful sortie.

Another small-scale operation was mounted by the group on the 8th against the airfield and seaplane base at Lanveoc-Poulmic, located on the northern side of the peninsula forming the southern boundary of the L'Elorn estuary opposite Brest. A force of fifty-eight Lancasters and six Mosquitos identified the target easily by the coastline and layout of the hangars, which they left on fire along with other buildings and the entire site enveloped in smoke. The night of the 9/10th brought attacks on seven coastal batteries in the Pas-de-Calais by four hundred aircraft. The purpose of these operations was to confirm in the mind of the enemy the belief that the Allied invasion forces would land at Calais, and right up to D-Day itself, the coastal region between Gravelines to the east of the port and Berck-sur-Mer to the south-west, would be subjected to constant bombardment. 5 Group, meanwhile, prepared fifty-six Lancasters and eight Mosquitos to attack two factories, the Gnome & Rhône aero-engine works and the Goodrich tyre factory at Gennevilliers in northern Paris, while a second force of thirty-nine Lancasters and four Mosquitos targeted a small ball-bearing factory at Annecy, situated in south-eastern France close to the frontiers with Switzerland and Italy. 44 (Rhodesia) Squadron made ready a dozen Lancasters for Paris, and they departed Dunholme Lodge between 22.04 and 22.30 with F/L Hildred the senior pilot on duty. They rendezvoused with the other squadrons over Reading, before beginning the Channel crossing at Shoreham-on-Sea and making landfall on the French coast near Dieppe. Moonlight and clear skies enabled them to map read after Gee was jammed at the French coast, and H2S proved useful as they closed on Paris. Yellow TIs and red spotfires identified the aiming point, and the bombing by the 44 (Rhodesia) Squadron crews proceeded from 7,250 to 9,200 feet between 00.33 and 00.40. Local sources confirmed damage to the target, but, also, collateral damage that killed twenty-seven French civilians and injured more than a hundred. ND515 was among five missing Lancasters, and was established later to have crashed in France with no survivors from the crew of F/O Bradburn DFC. Post-raid reconnaissance confirmed the Annecy site also to have been severely damaged.

Five railway targets were selected for attention on the night of the 10/11th, among them the marshalling yards at Lille for 5 Group. Bomb bursts were seen across the tracks, and two large explosions were observed to confirm a successful assault on this important hub linking north-eastern France with Belgium. Night-fighters were out in force, and most of the night's casualties resulted from this operation, from which a dozen Lancasters failed to return. 5 Group put together a force of 190 Lancasters and eight Mosquitos on the 11th, to target a military camp at Bourg-Leopold in north-eastern Belgium, for which 44 (Rhodesia) Squadron made ready sixteen Lancasters. They departed Dunholme Lodge between 22.04 and 22.36 with S/L Cockbain the senior pilot on duty, and all reached the target to find hazy conditions and a little thin cloud at around 10,000 feet, despite which, they would be able to identify ground detail in the form of buildings and huts in the light of illuminating flares. Three Oboe Mosquitos were on hand to deliver the initial marking, but inaccurately forecast winds caused the 83 Squadron element to arrive late, by which time the main force crews had begun to orbit to await instructions. A communications problem prevented some crews from hearing the Master Bomber's broadcasts, but the aiming point could be seen to be marked by red spotfires and green TIs. From the Master Bomber's perspective, the initial Oboe marker had been visible only to a few crews, and quickly burned out, and so he called for another Mosquito to drop a red spot fire onto the aiming point. Before this was accomplished, however, the main force began to bomb, and F/L Hildred and six other 44 (Rhodesia) Squadron crews were among ninety-four to release their loads, doing so from 14,500 and 16,750 feet between 00.22 and 00.28. As smoke began to obscure the ground, the Master Bomber, S/L Mitchell, quickly became uncomfortable about the close proximity of civilian residential property, and called a halt to the bombing at 00.35, before sending the rest of the force home, some of them after circling for more than twenty minutes. S/L Cockbain and seven others from the squadron retained their bombs, while F/Sgts Binien and Oswald dropped theirs on the marshalling yards at Hasselt.

Minor operations occupied elements of the Command, thereafter, until the 19th, when the station teleprinters worked overtime dispensing the details of five operations that night targeting marshalling yards, two on coastal batteries and one against a radar station. 5 Group detailed 225 Lancasters, 112 to be sent to Amiens with eight Mosquitos, and 113 for Tours with four Mosquitos, the 44 (Rhodesia) Squadron element of sixteen assigned to the former. They departed Dunholme Lodge between 22.47 and 23.24 with W/C Thompson the senior pilot on duty, before setting course for north-eastern France via Hastings and Dieppe, and finding the target shrouded in a layer of eight to ten-tenths cloud between 6,000 and 11,000 feet. The aiming point was identified by red spotfires, but when checked on H2S, these appeared to be up to five miles from where they should have been. 207 Squadron's F/O Smart and crew were on the bombing run at 7,000 feet when they collided with another Lancaster and sustained considerable damage but managed to deliver part of their bomb load at 01.26 and make it home to a safe landing at Manston. It is quite possible that the other Lancaster was ND689 of 44 (Rhodesia) Squadron, which was the only failure to return and is known to have crashed in the general target area, killing five of the occupants and delivering P/O Hobbs and two others into enemy hands. Thirty-seven aircraft had bombed when instructions came through by W/T at 01.25 to terminate the attack and return home, by which time, W/C Thompson and three other 44 (Rhodesia) Squadron crews had already carried out their attacks from 5,000 to 7,500 feet between 01.20 and 01.23. The others either jettisoned their loads on the way home across the Channel or brought them back. The Tours raid had been directed at the marshalling yards in the centre of the city, which required great precision on the part of the marker and main forces, both of which performed magnificently to leave the target severely damaged without causing collateral damage.

For the first time in a year, Duisburg was posted as the target for a heavy raid on the 21st, for which a force of 510 Lancasters was drawn from 1, 3, 5 and 8 Groups. They would be supported by twenty-two Mosquitos, and, while this operation was in progress, seventy Lancasters, including some from 5 Group, and thirty-seven Halifaxes would undertake gardening duties in the Nectarines and Rosemary gardens around the Frisians and off Heligoland, and in the Forget-me-not, Silverthorn and Quince gardens in the Kattegat and Kiel Bay regions of the Baltic. 44 (Rhodesia) Squadron would support both operations, assigning five Lancasters to the main event and eleven to the gardening effort, and it was the latter which departed Dunholme Lodge first, between 21.48 and 22.09 with F/Ls Hildred and Stephenson the senior pilots on duty. Those bound for the Ruhr took off between 22.30 and 22.54 led by F/L White, having been told at briefing to adhere to the plan for the outward route, which involved a few aircraft from 3 Group gaining height as they adopted a north-westerly course as far as Sleaford, so as not to cross into enemy radar cover earlier than necessary. The groups would rendezvous at 18,000 feet over the North Sea at 3 degrees east to cross the enemy coast via the western Frisians at 20,000 feet and climb to 22,000 or 23,000 feet, before increasing speed for the run across the target. All of the 44 (Rhodesia) Squadron participants reached the Ruhr, which they found to be concealed beneath ten-tenths cloud with tops at between 11,000 and 20,000 feet, into which the red Wanganui markers with-yellow-stars fell almost before they could be seen. A number of crews commented on the data provided by the wind-finder system to be inaccurate, and this made it a challenge to establish positions. The 44 (Rhodesia) Squadron crews used the explosion of cookies, the glow of fires and the evidence of intense flak as references and bombed from 18,500 to 21,500 feet between 01.18 and 01.29, before returning home with little useful information to report. The loss of twenty-nine Lancasters was a reminder to the Command that the Ruhr remained a dangerous destination, although most of the missing had come down onto Dutch and Belgian soil or into the sea homebound, after falling victim to night-fighters. Martin Drewes of III./NJG1 alone accounted for at least three Lancasters. 44 (Rhodesia) Squadron's ND976 crashed in Belgium, killing P/O Dunn RAAF and three of his crew, leaving two in enemy hands and one to be spirited away by the Resistance. Returning crews were not enthusiastic about the outcome, and post-raid reconnaissance confirmed that a modest 350 buildings had been destroyed in the southern half of Duisburg, and 665 others had been seriously damaged. While this operation had been in progress, the gardeners had encountered up to eight-tenths cloud in the western Baltic, through which they had planted their six vegetables each into the allotted positions from 14,000 to 15,000 feet between 00.56 and 01.24.

Just like Duisburg, Dortmund was posted on the 22nd to host its first large-scale visit from the Command for a year and would face an all-Lancaster heavy force of 361 aircraft drawn from 1, 3, 6 and 8 Groups. While this operation was in progress, 220 Lancasters of 5 Group and five from 101 Squadron were to target Braunschweig, which, thus far, had evaded severe damage at the hands of the Command. 44 (Rhodesia) Squadron made ready fourteen Lancasters, which departed Dunholme Lodge between 22.23 and 22.49 with W/C Thompson displaying outstanding leadership qualities by continuing to lead from the front. P/O Stockwell and crew experienced a number of issues as they began the North Sea crossing but were compelled by two failed generators and Gee and H2S failure, ultimately, to admit defeat. The others pressed on through the clearly evident night-fighter activity from the Dutch coast all the way to the target and negotiated the patches of ten-tenths cloud over northern Germany, and intense searchlight activity as they passed between Bremen and Osnabrück. The forecast at briefings had suggested clear skies over Braunschweig, but, in fact, the marker force encountered four to seven-tenths drifting cloud with tops up to 7,000 feet. Although highly effective in the right weather conditions, the 5 Group low-level visual marking method could easily be rendered ineffective by cloud cover. The blind heavy markers dropped skymarkers by H2S, while the 627 Squadron Mosquito element went in at low level to release red spotfires. Some crews described "hopeless confusion" with flares and incendiaries spread over a distance, and many had to rely on their own H2S to establish their position. Some found a complete absence of marking and orbited for up to fifteen minutes until a few green TIs appeared, and bombing by the 44 (Rhodesia) Squadron element took place on these or on incendiary fires from 19,000 to 22,000 feet between 01.18 and 01.42. Considerable interference over R/T communications added to the problems, and, although the Master Bomber could be heard in discussions with his Deputies, no instructions were received from him, and the attack lacked cohesion. Post-raid reconnaissance confirmed that most of the bombing had fallen onto outlying communities, confirming in the minds of the residents that this was an intentional ploy by the Command. It was a relatively expensive failure that cost thirteen Lancasters, although none belonging to 44 (Rhodesia) Squadron.

The main operation on the 24th would involve 442 aircraft in an attack on two marshalling yards at Aachen, Aachen-West and Rothe-Erde in the east. As the most westerly city in Germany, sitting on the frontiers of both Holland and Belgium, it was a major link in the railway network that would be a route for reinforcements to the Normandy battle front. Other operations on this night would be directed at coastal batteries in the Pas-de-Calais and war-industry factories in Holland and Belgium. 5 Group detailed forty-four Lancasters to attack the Ford motor works in Antwerp, and fifty-nine for the Philips electronics factory at Eindhoven in southern Holland, while Dunholme Lodge remained off the Order of Battle. Those bound for Eindhoven were more than an hour into the outward journey when the Master Bomber sent them home by W/T, presumably after a Met Flight Mosquito crew had found poor visibility in the target area. There were no such difficulties at Antwerp, where the target was identified by illuminating flares, a yellow TI and red spotfires, despite which, post-raid reconnaissance revealed the factory to be intact.

Three of sixteen 44 (Rhodesia) Squadron Lancasters had taken off for Stuttgart on the 25th, before the operation was cancelled, and they were recalled. The night of the 26/27th was devoted to minor operations, including mining off the Occupied coasts by forty-two aircraft including six representing 44 (Rhodesia) Squadron. They were divided between Nectarine I off the western Frisians and one of the Silverthorn gardens in the Kattegat off the eastern coast of Jutland. With further to travel, the latter trio departed Dunholme Lodge first between 22.36 and 22.43 with F/L Stephenson the senior pilot on duty and were followed into the night between 23.09 and 23.15 by the others, led by F/L Dobson. Both elements found favourable conditions, with ten-tenths cloud over the Baltic, but good visibility and a light sky, and positions were established on Sjaelland Point by H2S before the mines were delivered from 10,000 feet between 01.15 and 01.21. Almost cloudless conditions over the North Sea also revealed a lighter than normal night sky, and the mines were dropped unopposed from 4,000 to 6,000 feet between 00.27 and 00.32.

The night of the 27/28th was to be one of feverish activity, which would generate more than eleven hundred sorties, reflecting the close proximity of the invasion, now just ten days away. The largest operation would bring a return to the military camp at Bourg Leopold in Belgium, the previous attack on which, two weeks earlier, had been abandoned part-way through. There was also a repeat of the Aachen attack of the 24th, which had failed to destroy the Rothe-Erde marshalling yards at the eastern end of the city and needed further attention. 5 Group was not involved in either of the above, and, instead, prepared forces of one hundred Lancasters and four Mosquitos and seventy-eight Lancasters and five Mosquitos respectively to target marshalling yards and workshops at Nantes and the aerodrome at Rennes, situated some fifty miles apart in north-western France. The group would also support operations against coastal batteries, of which there were five on this night, including one at Morsalines, situated on the eastern seaboard of the Cherbourg peninsula, some ten miles north of what, during the forthcoming Operation Overlord, would be the Americans' Utah landing ground. This was the target for eighteen 44 (Rhodesia) Squadron Lancasters, which departed Dunholme Lodge between 22.23 and 23.01 with the newly promoted S/L Hildred the senior pilot on duty. All reached the target area on Gee-fix to find seven tenths cloud at 3,000 to 4,000 feet, but fair visibility and the aiming point identified by flares, red spotfires and green TIs. The 44 (Rhodesia) Squadron participants carried out their attacks from 5,000 to 7,000 feet between 00.55 and 01.15 in accordance with the instructions of a Master Bomber and observed the bombing to be concentrated around the markers. Cloud and smoke obscured much of the detail, but the consensus was, that if the markers had been accurate, the target had been hit.

On the 28th, 181 Lancasters and twenty Mosquitos continued the attacks on coastal batteries overlooking the Normandy beaches, which, a week hence, would be the scene of Operation Overlord. Dunholme Lodge was not called into action on this night, or on the following two nights, and it was on the 31st when the next operational orders were received to prepare for further operations that night against coastal batteries covering the Normandy beaches. 5 Group was to send a force of eighty-two Lancasters and four Mosquitos to attack a railway junction at Saumur in the Loire Valley, and another of sixty-eight Lancasters to a coastal battery at Maisy, overlooking what would the Americans' Omaha Beach. It was for the latter that 44 (Rhodesia) Squadron prepared a dozen Lancasters, which took off between 22.52 and 23.09 with W/C Thompson and S/L Cockbain the senior pilots on duty. They had to pass through a belt of storm-bearing clouds as they flew from base to Reading, and the foul weather continued as they crossed the coast at Selsey Bill to start the Channel crossing. The leading crews were within seven miles of the French coast when they were recalled by W/T and diverted to Westcott in Buckinghamshire, where, at 02.53, a fully-loaded ME794 ran off the end of the runway, crossed the A41 and was wrecked. F/Sgt Oswald and crew extricated themselves and walked away, and at 03.30, a large explosion tore the Lancaster asunder and killed a Flying Control officer who had attended the scene. A few miles away at Oakley, ND698 also come to grief on landing in the hands of F/Sgt Canty RAAF and crew at 03.17, and they, too, walked away from the wreckage before it was consumed by fire. The reprieve for both crews would prove to be temporary. During the course of the month the squadron carried out thirteen operations and dispatched 153 sorties for the loss of seven Lancasters and five crews.

June 1944

June would be a hectic month making great demands on the crews. The bombing of coastal batteries was to be the priority during the first few days of the month leading up to D-Day, but 5 Group would open its account by returning to Saumur to attack a second railway junction on the 1st. The day dawned cloudy and cold, and these conditions would persist throughout the first week of the month, causing concern among the invasion planners. 44 (Rhodesia) Squadron remained at home, while fifty-eight Lancasters took off in the late evening to find ten-tenths cloud covering the route out to within twenty miles of the town, where it dispersed completely to leave clear skies and good visibility under a three-quarter moon. The flare force was almost superfluous in the conditions, but the first wave was called in by the Master Bomber, W/C Jeudwine, to release from 15,000 feet at 01.08, and the first red spot fire from an Oboe Mosquito fell bang on the aiming point two minutes later. Smoke became a problem as it drifted across the area to obscure the spotfire that was still burning, and a green TI was dropped to maintain the aiming point. Apart from a few scattered sticks to the north, and on an island in the Loire to the south, the attack seemed to be accurate. Returning crews reported little opposition, fires in the yards and a large explosion at 01.35, and the success of the raid was confirmed by photographic reconnaissance, which showed severe damage to the track.

Fifteen 44 (Rhodesia) Squadron crews were among those called to briefing at Dunholme Lodge on the 2nd, when they were told that they would be joining forty-six other Lancasters of the group to maintain the invasion deception by attacking a coastal battery at Wimereux, situated south-west of Calais. They took off between 23.41 and 00.10 with F/Ls Dobson and Stephenson the senior pilots on duty, and all reached the French coast to encounter the most unfavourable weather conditions including ten-tenths cloud at 10,000 feet. The glow of red TIs greeted their arrival, but the Master Bomber was uncomfortable with the conditions and sent the force home after only F/L Stephenson, F/O Hough and F/Sgt Binien had released their bombs from 17,000 to 20,000 feet between 01.40 and 01.42. The outcome, in terms of damage, was unimportant, as long as it reinforced in the mind of the enemy, that Calais was to be the destination of the expected invasion force. The Squadron remained off the Order of Battle thereafter until D-Day Eve, while ninety-six Lancasters of the group carried out an operation on the 3rd against a listening station at Ferme-d'Urville, situated on the Cherbourg peninsula to the west of the port, a target which had escaped damage when attacked by Halifaxes two nights earlier. The bombing was focussed within a five-hundred-yard radius of the aiming point and was confirmed by post-raid reconnaissance to have obliterated the site.

Orders came through on the 4th to prepare for attacks that night on coastal batteries, three in the Pas-de-Calais to maintain the deception, and the one at Maisy, overlooking the Utah and Omaha beaches. 259 aircraft of 1, 4, 5, 6 and 8 Groups were made ready, the majority for the deception targets, while fifty-two of the Lancasters, all representing 5 Group, were assigned to Maisy. 44 (Rhodesia) Squadron was not involved in these pre-dawn attacks, which took place through ten-tenths cloud with a base at around 4,000 feet. This necessitated the use of Oboe skymarkers, and positions were confirmed by Gee-fix and a faint red glow, before the bombing was carried out from just above the cloud tops. It was impossible to assess the outcome, and similar cloudy conditions had thwarted two of the three attempts in the Pas-de-Calais.

The night of the 5/6th was D-Day Eve, and, during the course of the night, a record number of 1,211 sorties would be flown against coastal defences and in support and diversionary operations. Sixteen 44 (Rhodesia) Squadron crews attended briefing at Dunholme Lodge, where no direct reference was made to the invasion, but, unusually, they were given strict altitudes at which to fly, and were told not to jettison bombs over the sea. They learned also that they would be among more than a thousand aircraft targeting ten heavy gun batteries along the Normandy coast, and that their specific objective was at La Pernelle, some three miles north of the recently attacked Morsalines battery, which, although not disclosed to them, was close to Utah Beach. The plan called for 5 Group to provide 122 Lancasters and four Mosquitos for this site, and 115 Lancasters and four Mosquitos for a second target at Saint-Pierre-du-Mont, which was the closest to Omaha Beach. 83 Squadron would provide the illumination and the marking for the former, while 97 Squadron took care of business at the latter, led by W/C Jimmy Carter. 44 (Rhodesia) Squadron loaded its Lancasters with a mixture of 1,000 and 500 pounders and launched them from Dunholme Lodge between 01.27 and 01.55 with W/C Thompson the senior pilot on duty. They all arrived in the target area to find a layer of ten-tenths cloud with a base at around 7,000 feet and tops at 12,000 feet, with broken cloud below, through which the glow of the red and green TIs and red spotfires could be seen. The bombing was carried out by twelve of the 44 (Rhodesia) Squadron crews from 6,000 (F/L Stephenson) to 12,000 feet between 03.37 and 04.03, while four others still had their bombs on board when the master Bomber called a halt to proceedings and sent them home. Any homeward-bound crews looking down through the occasional gaps in the clouds were rewarded by the incredible sight of the greatest armada in history, ploughing its way sedately southwards towards the French coast. A total of five thousand tons of bombs was dropped during the night, and this was a new record. Only seven aircraft failed to return from these operations, three of them from Sainte-Pierre, including the one containing 97 Squadron's W/C Carter and seven highly experienced crewmen, all but one of whom held either a DFC or DFM.

As the beachheads were being established during the course of the 6th, preparations were put in hand to support the ground forces by attacking nine road and railway communications centres through which the enemy could bring reinforcements. 5 Group was assigned to two targets, Argentan supply depot and railway centre located some thirty miles south-east of Caen, and a road bridge in Caen itself, for which forces of 112 Lancasters and six Mosquitos and 120 Lancasters and four Mosquitos respectively were assembled. 44 (Rhodesia) Squadron made ready sixteen Lancasters for the latter, and they departed Dunholme Lodge between 00.18 and 00.54 with W/C Thompson and S/Ls Cockbain and Hildred the senior pilots on duty. They had been preceded into the air at 22.25 and 22.28 by the crews of F/L Stephenson and F/O Merrick, who were bound on mining sorties for the Jellyfish garden off Brest. The main element began the Channel crossing at Bridport and headed for the Channel Islands before turning sharply to the east to cross the Cherbourg peninsula. All reached the target area to find ten-tenths cloud with a base at 5,000 to 6,000 feet, below which, 627 Squadron Mosquitos ran in at low-level to drop red spotfires, which were then supplemented by red TIs from the heavy marker element. The 44 (Rhodesia) Squadron crews attacked the aiming point from below the cloud base from 3,000 to 5,000 feet between 02.38 and 02.52, in accordance with the Master Bomber's instructions, and were able to clearly pick out the river, marshalling yards and town detail. Six Lancasters failed to return from the Caen raid, largely as the result of the need for the force to orbit while the markers were assessed. 44 (Rhodesia) Squadron's ND519 went into the sea off Douvres, taking with it the crew of F/L Stratis DFC, and only three bodies were recovered for a local burial. Meanwhile, the gardening duo had successfully fulfilled their brief by planting their vegetables from 14,000 feet at 00.59 and 01.08.

Four railway targets were earmarked for attention by a force of 337 aircraft on the 7th, while elements of 5 Group were being prepared to join forces with 1 and 8 Groups to attack a six-way road junction at Balleroy, situated fifteen miles west of Caen on the approach to the Foret-de-Cerisy, where it was believed the enemy was concealing a fuel dump and tank units. 44 (Rhodesia) Squadron was not involved in the operation, which took place in conditions of ten-tenths cloud with a base at 8,000 to 10,000 feet with haze below. The initial Oboe markers appeared to be accurate and on time, but another marker fell simultaneously some five miles to the south-west and attracted some bomb loads. The Master Bomber quickly gained control of the situation and directed the bombing to the correct marker, which was pounded by concentrated bombing. Dense clouds of black smoke and one particularly large explosion were evidence of a successful outcome, during which the gunners in the crew of the 207 Squadron commanding officer shot down three enemy fighters in a twenty-minute period.

The night of the 8/9th was devoted to the disruption of railway communications, for which 483 aircraft were detailed and assigned to five centres. Orders were received at Dunholme Lodge for 44 (Rhodesia) Squadron to prepare a dozen Lancasters as part of a 5 Group force of fifty-four Lancasters and four Mosquitos assigned to railway installations at Pontabault, while a second force of ninety-seven Lancasters and four Mosquitos attended to a similar objective at Rennes in Brittany, thirty miles to the south-west. 617 Squadron would also operate on this night to deliver the very first Barnes Wallis-designed 12,000lb Tallboy earthquake bombs against the railway tunnel at Saumur. The 44 (Rhodesia) Squadron element took off between 22.15 and 22.38 with S/L Cockbain the senior pilot on duty, having been preceded into the air between 22.03 and 22.08 by four crews bound for the Cinnamon garden off the port of La Pallice. All of the bombing brigade reached the target area to encounter up to six-tenths stratocumulus at 6,000 feet and a layer at 2,000 feet, and the first attempt to mark was cancelled with yellow TIs. The second attempt with red spotfires and TIs was successful, and the bombing took place in accordance with the instructions of the Master Bomber from 1,800 to 6,000 feet between 00.44 and 00.56. Returning crews reported concentrated bombing on or near the markers, and the operation was deemed to have been successful. While this operation was in progress, S/L Hildred, F/L Stephenson and F/Os Balsdon and Merrick had flown through challenging weather conditions to reach France's Biscay coast, and had delivered their mines from 8,000 to 15,000 feet between 01.56 and 02.04.

401 aircraft from 1, 4, 6 and 8 Groups were detailed on the 9th to target airfields in the battle area, while 5 Group concentrated on a railway junction at Etampes, south of Paris. 108 Lancasters and four Mosquitos were to take part, sixteen of them representing 44 (Rhodesia) Squadron, which departed Dunholme Lodge between 21.38 and 22.07 with W/C Thompson and S/L Hildred the senior pilots on duty. Those reaching the target found eight to ten-tenths cloud with a base at 8,000 feet, and patches of two to three-tenths lower down at 4,000 feet, but this had had no effect on the marking with red spotfires, backed up with green and yellow TIs and illumination flares. Some crews thought that they had picked up a recall signal, and others a message at around midnight to orbit, until being called in to bomb. The 44 (Rhodesia) Squadron participants carried out their attacks from 5,000 to 7,000 feet between 00.12 and 00.20, two crews after the Master Bomber had called an end to bombing at 00.17. It appeared to be a successful operation, which cost six Lancasters, including 44 (Rhodesia) Squadron's NN697, which was shot down by a night-fighter to crash at Morigny-Champigny, on the north-eastern edge of the target with no survivors from the crew of F/O Balsdon. On return, P/O Richards and crew claimed the destruction of a BF109. Photo-reconnaissance confirmed that all tracks

had been cut for a distance of four hundred yards to the north-east of the junction, but it revealed also that the town had sustained collateral damage, which caused many civilian casualties.

5 Group detailed 108 Lancasters and four Mosquitos on the 10th and briefed the crews for an attack on a railway junction at Orleans, situated some thirty miles south-west of Paris. 44 (Rhodesia) Squadron was not involved in this operation, which took place under clear skies and in good visibility and appeared to be successful. The campaign against communications targets continued on the 12th at six locations, including Caen and Poitiers, for which 5 Group detailed forces of 109 Lancasters and four Mosquitos and 112 Lancasters and four Mosquitos respectively. 44 (Rhodesia) Squadron made ready fifteen Lancasters to take part at the former, where road bridges were the specific targets, and they departed Dunholme Lodge between 23.47 and 00.17 with S/Ls Cockbain and Hildred the senior pilots on duty. All reached the Caen area, where they encountered six to ten-tenths cloud with tops at between 4,000 and 6,000 feet, which provided difficult conditions in which to spot the TIs on the ground. A strict timing was imposed for the duration of the attack, and ten 44 (Rhodesia) Squadron crews delivered their loads from 5,000 to 10,000 feet between 02.22 and 02.30, before the Master Bomber called a halt and sent more than thirty Lancasters home without bombing. In contrast, clear conditions attended the raid on Poitiers, and photo-reconnaissance revealed the Paris to Bordeaux line to have been cut in seven places. A new oil campaign began on this night, prosecuted by 286 Lancasters and seventeen Mosquitos of 1, 3 and 8 Groups, whose target was the Nordstern (Gelsenberg A G) plant at Gelsenkirchen. Such was the accuracy of the attack, that all production of vital aviation fuel was halted for a number of weeks at a cost to the Germans of a thousand tons per day.

The 14th brought the Command's first daylight operation since the departure of 2 Group twelve months earlier. The target was Le Havre, from where the enemy's E-Boats and other fast, light marine craft were posing a threat to Allied shipping supplying the Normandy beachheads. The two-phase operation was conducted by predominantly 1 and 3 Groups with 617 Squadron representing 5 Group and took place in the evening under the umbrella of a fighter escort. The attack was highly successful, and few craft survived the onslaught. Other operations on this night were directed against railway installations at three locations in France, while elements of 4, 5 and 8 Groups attended to enemy troop and vehicle concentrations at Aunay-sur-Odon and Évrecy near Caen. 5 Group assembled a force of 214 Lancasters and five Mosquitos for the former, of which fourteen of 44 (Rhodesia) Squadron departed Dunholme Lodge between 22.10 and 22.45 with W/C Thompson the senior pilot on duty. The weather was generally clear with some low cloud, but this did not hamper the marking process, which proceeded punctually and accurately. W/C Jeudwine was the Master Bomber, with 83 Squadron's W/C Joe Northrop as Deputy, and the latter made four passes over the target, at 00.30 at 8,000 feet, 00.41 at 10,000 feet, and at 00.54 and 01.00 at 11,000 feet, dropping clusters of flares on the first two, green TIs on the third and red TIs on the fourth. The 44 (Rhodesia) Squadron crews bombed the above-mentioned TIs from 6,000 to 10,000 feet between 00.36 and 00.58, observing what appeared to be a concentrated attack that produced numerous fires and much black smoke.

A force of 297 aircraft from 1, 4, 5, 6 and 8 Groups was assembled on the 15th to try to do to Boulogne what had been done to Le Havre twenty-four hours earlier. It was again left to 617 Squadron to represent 5 Group, and the operation was concluded with equal success. While this was in progress, 5 Group dispatched 110 Lancasters and four Mosquitos to deal with a fuel dump at Châtellerault, situated between Tours and Poitiers in western France. 44 (Rhodesia) Squadron was not involved in the operation, which took place under clear skies and in good visibility, after which, post-raid reconnaissance confirmed that eight out of thirty-five individual fuel storage sites within the target had been destroyed.

Plans were put in hand on the 16th to launch 829 sorties that night against a number of targets. Just three days earlier, the first V-1 flying bombs had landed on London, and this prompted a response in the form of a second new campaign to open during the month against the revolutionary weapon's launching and storage sites in the Pas-de-Calais. Four targets were earmarked for attention, 5 Group assigned to a storage site at Beauvoir, located some twenty miles inland from Berck-sur-Mer. The large storage sites, many in various stages of construction, were referred to in Bomber Command parlance as "constructional works", while others, called "ski sites", were small buildings with a distinctive "J" shape from which the name was derived, and were attached to launching ramps. 112 Lancasters were detailed, seventeen of them representing 44 (Rhodesia) Squadron, which departed Dunholme Lodge between 22.48 and 23.22 with W/C Thompson the senior pilot on duty. They all reached the target area to find nine to ten-tenths cloud with tops at 6,000 to 8,000 feet and bombed on the faint glow of red Oboe markers from 10,000 to 13,000 feet between 00.40 and 00.49. It was impossible to assess the outcome, which left crews with little to pass on to the Intelligence Section at debriefing.

The oil campaign continued on this night in the hands of 1, 4, 6 and 8 Groups at Sterkrade-Holten, a district of Oberhausen in the Ruhr, but cloudy conditions caused the bombing to be scattered, and there was little impact on production. With the exception of 617 Squadron, 5 Group remained inactive for the next few days, leaving the "specialists" to attack constructional works at Watten and Wizernes with Tallboys in daylight on the 19th and 20th. Cloudy conditions affected accuracy at the former and caused the latter to be aborted so as not to waste the precious, highly-engineered and inordinately expensive Tallboys.

5 Group had to wait until Mid-Summer's Night, the 21st, before becoming involved in the oil offensive, and was handed two targets to attack simultaneously. A force of 120 Lancasters and six Mosquitos was assembled for the refinery at Wesseling, south of Cologne, and 120 Lancasters and four Mosquitos for the Scholven-Buer plant in Gelsenkirchen, both with a sprinkling of ABC Lancasters of 101 Squadron for RCM duties, and the latter including a number of Oboe Mosquitos. 44 (Rhodesia) Squadron made ready sixteen Lancasters for Wesseling, and they departed Dunholme Lodge between 22.55 and 23.27 with S/L Cockbain the senior pilot on duty, before heading into the greatest disaster to befall 5 Group in the war. They made landfall on the enemy coast in the Western Schelde and crossed Belgium to enter Germany south of Aachen. S/L Cockbain had the target in sight ahead, and could see red and green TIs going down, when a night-fighter attacked and inflicted severe damage to the starboard wing and control surfaces. The control column jammed in a forward position, causing the Lancaster to dive out of control, upon which the bomb load was jettisoned from 8,000 feet at 01.42 and the crew ordered to abandon the Lancaster. Three crew members complied, and their parachutes were seen to deploy, while three others remained on board with S/L Cockbain as he attempted to regain control. By jamming his feet against the instrument panel, he managed to pull out of the dive, rescinded the bale-out order and asked his bomb-aimer to take over the navigation. They cleared the enemy coast via Westkapelle, and made it all the way back to base, where S/L Cockbain credited his crew's part in their safe return.

Meanwhile, 350 miles to the south-east, the others had arrived in the target area, having observed many combats since the coast and expecting to find clear skies. Instead of this, they encountered up to ten-tenths low cloud at 2,500 to 4,000 feet, which was the Achilles Heel in the otherwise highly-effective 5 Group low-level marking method, and it meant that it was impossible for the Mosquito crews to do their job. Faced with this situation, the Master Bomber, W/C James "Willie" Tait, ordered a blind attack, forcing the Lancaster crews to bomb on their own H2S or on the red and green TIs dropped by 83 Squadron also on H2S. The 44 (Rhodesia) Squadron crews bombed from 17,000 to 20,000 feet between 01.40 and 01.50 in the face of heavy predicted flak, F/L White reporting a large explosion as he ran in on the aiming point at 01.46, which caused an extensive red glow in the cloud, and another was witnessed at 01.51. P/O Mitchell had not bombed when the Master Bomber sent him home in a flak-damaged LM192, which turned out to be one of only ten to return to Dunholme Lodge from this operation. After the war, a secret German report would suggest a 40% loss of production at the site, but this was probably of very short duration as the limited number of casualties on the ground pointed to a scattered and largely ineffective raid. Whatever the degree of success, it was gained at the high cost of thirty-seven Lancasters, a massive 28%, and all but two of them belonged to 5 Group Squadrons. 44, 49, 57 and 619 Squadrons each lost six Lancasters, although one from 57 Squadron ditched off the English coast and the crew was rescued, while 207 and 630 Squadrons each had five empty dispersal pans to contemplate in the cold light of dawn.

An analysis concluded that the Wesseling force had been hacked to pieces by night-fighters benefitting from the excellent visibility above the cloud, and it was 44 (Rhodesia) Squadron's worst loss of the war, surpassing even the Augsburg raid of April 1942. It is not possible to determine the sequence of losses, as the outward and inbound routes each crossed Belgium and Holland, but the likelihood is, that most were on their way to the target when their end came. ME804 was a night-fighter victim and crashed on the south-western outskirts of Genk, with no survivors from the eight-man crew of P/O Richards. LM434 came down near Lanklaar, ten miles to the east-north-east almost on the Dutch border, killing P/O Scholtz RCAF and his Canadian bomb-aimer, and leaving four others in enemy hands and one on the run, ultimately to evade capture. LM592 was a little further north on the Dutch side of the frontier with Belgium when it fell to a night-fighter, killing P/O Canty and his crew. P/O Wood RNZAF and crew were in LL938, and were a polyglot of Dominion and Allied nationalities, made up of three members of the RAF, and one each from the RAAF, RCAF and USAAF. The pilot and three others perished in the crash at Nederweert in Holland, and three joined the growing number of 44 (Rhodesia) Squadron crew members in captivity. The wreckage of ND552 was found close to that of LM434 and produced no survivors from the crew of F/O Smith. There were no survivors either from the crew of P/O Baxter in ND973, which was another night-fighter victim and crashed some three miles south-east of Roermond in Holland.

Similar conditions had thwarted any chance of low-level marking at Scholven-Buer, but the preliminary Mosquito-borne Oboe markers had been backed up by red and green TIs from 97 Squadron Lancasters, and the glow from these was observed dimly through the cloud. The crews aimed for these, but it was impossible to assess the outcome, and the operation cost eight 5 Group aircraft, most falling to the night-fighters waiting to greet them as they crossed Holland outbound. A secret German report would suggest a 20% loss of production for a limited period.

While more than four hundred aircraft of 3, 4, 6 and 8 Groups targeted four flying-bomb sites on the 23rd, 1 and 5 Groups were sent respectively against railway yards at Saintes and Limoges in western France. Ninety-seven Lancasters and four Mosquitos were detailed for the latter, and they found clear skies and good visibility in the target area, in which ground features like the River Vienne and the railway sidings stood out prominently. Red spotfires and green TIs marked out the aiming point, and a number of large explosions were observed with much smoke. Another very large explosion was witnessed by some crews when one hundred miles into the return flight at 02.46, and post-raid reconnaissance would confirm a highly accurate and concentrated attack.

617 Squadron had attempted to continue the Tallboy assault on the constructional works at Wizernes in daylight on the 22nd, but the attack had been abandoned in the face of ten-tenths low cloud. The squadron returned the bombs to store and brought them back to France on the 24th to score a number of direct hits. Fifteen 44 (Rhodesia) Squadron crews were called to briefing on the 24th to learn of their part in a busy night of operations involving more than seven hundred aircraft targeting seven flying-bomb sites. 5 Group was assigned to Pommeréval and Prouville, situated respectively some fifteen miles south-east of Dieppe, and east of Abbeville, and detailed 103 Lancasters and four Mosquitos for each. The 52 Base squadrons from Dunholme Lodge and Fiskerton were among those assigned to the former, and the 44 (Rhodesia) Squadron participants took off between 22.11 and 22.35 with S/L Hildred the senior pilot on duty. All reached the target area to be greeted by the favourable conditions of clear skies and twenty-mile visibility, and W/C Tait was again on hand in the role of Master Bomber to watch the Oboe marker go down on time at 23.50. He assessed that it was five hundred yards south of the aiming point and directed the flare force to illuminate another one that was much closer, before sending in the low-level Mosquitos. The main force Lancasters followed close on their heels and delivered concentrated bombing around the aiming point, which the 44 (Rhodesia) Squadron crews identified by green TIs. They delivered their bombs from 6,500 to 8,500 feet between 00.04 and 00.16, observing the bursts to be concentrated within a few hundred yards of them. There was little defence from the ground, but night-fighters were evident, and four Lancasters failed to return, two of them belonging to 44 (Rhodesia) Squadron. ME628 crashed at Bellencombre some fifteen miles south of Dieppe, killing F/Sgt Oswald and three of his crew and delivering one into enemy hands, while leaving two on the run, ultimately, thanks to the courage of the Resistance, to evade capture. ND751 came down a little further north, sadly, with no survivors from the crew of P/O Aiken RCAF.

At Prouville, the preliminary Oboe Mosquito was punctual, but the subsequent marking was hampered by intense searchlight activity working in co-operation with flak and night-fighters, and bombing was delayed while the aiming point was positively identified and marked. It took until all of the illuminator flares had been expended before the low-level Mosquitos dropped red spotfires and the heavy brigade from 97 Squadron backed up with red and green TIs. The bombing was controlled by the Master Bomber, but the impression was of a somewhat haphazard attack that lacked concentration and cost thirteen Lancasters, possibly as a result of the delay in opening the attack.

More than seven hundred aircraft were detailed for operations against six flying-bomb sites on the 27th, while two railway yards would occupy the attention of other elements. There were two targets for 5 Group, a flying-bomb site at Marquise, situated some five miles inland from Cap Gris-Nez, and railway yards at Vitry-le-Francois south-east of Reims. 44 (Rhodesia) Squadron contributed fifteen Lancasters to the force of eighty-six assigned to the former, and they departed Dunholme Lodge between 22.50 and 23.20 with F/Ls Dobson, Merrick and White the senior pilots on duty. There were no early returns, and the outward flight was completed within seventy-five minutes under clear skies and in good visibility. The marking was punctual and accurate, and the 44 (Rhodesia) Squadron crews delivered their eleven 1,000 and four 500 pounders each onto red TIs from 16,000 to 19,000 feet between 00.50 and 00.54 before returning to report a successful operation. F/L Merrick and crew were absent from debriefing, and it was only after the body of the rear gunner found its way to the Frisian island of Terschelling many months later, that the fate of ME743 became clear.

The 103 Lancasters and four Mosquitos assigned to the Vitry marshalling yards were greeted at the target by varying amounts of cloud, reported as between zero and seven-tenths at around 7,000 feet, but the visibility was good, and the aiming point was clearly marked by red spot fires and green TIs. Not all had bombed when the Master Bomber called a halt and ordered crews with bombs still aboard to take them home, after smoke obscured the aiming point. There were no further operations for 44 (Rhodesia) Squadron in a month that had brought thirteen operations generating 173 sorties for the loss of eleven Lancasters and their crews.

July 1944

The new month began as June had ended, with flying-bomb sites providing employment for over three hundred aircraft on both the 1st and 2nd. It was the 4th before the Independent Air Force was invited to re-enter the fray, when it was called upon to attack a V-Weapon storage site in caves at St-Leu-d'Esserent, some thirty miles north of Paris. The caves had originally been used for growing mushrooms, and they were protected by some twenty-five feet of clay and soft limestone, to say nothing of the anti-aircraft defences brought in by the Germans. There is some confusion concerning the timing of the operation, which involved not only seventeen Lancasters, a Mustang and a Mosquito from 617 Squadron, but also 211 other Lancasters and eleven Mosquitos from 5 Group, with three ABC Lancasters to provide RCM cover and three Path Finder Oboe Mosquitos to carry out the marking of an initial reference-point. Some accounts suggest that 617 Squadron attacked early in the evening, and was followed by the group later on, when, in fact, both elements took off at the same time. There were actually two aiming points, the road and railway communications to the area dump for the main force, and the tunnel complex at Creil, a settlement located three miles north-east of St Leu, for 617 Squadron and fourteen Lancasters of 44 (Rhodesia) Squadron, which took off between 23.00 and 23.40 with F/Ls Dobson and White the senior pilots on duty. Only P/O Ibbotson and crew returned early with an engine issue, leaving the others to press on and reach the target area under clear skies and in good visibility, which was of equal assistance to the night-fighters. There were no searchlights, but the expected volume of flak was thrown up as the two elements ran across their respective aiming points, the 44 (Rhodesia) Squadron crews carrying out their attacks with 1,000 and 500 pounders from 14,000 to 18,000 feet between 01.36 and 01.41. Night-fighters pounced on the bombers over the target and on the route home, and thirteen Lancasters failed to return, one of them belonging to 44 (Rhodesia) Squadron. ME699 crashed close to the target with fatal consequences for P/O Young RAAF and five others, while two escaped with their lives and managed to retain their freedom. Post-raid reconnaissance revealed that a large area of subsidence had blocked the side entrance to the caves at St-Leu and that the road and railway links had been cut over a distance of four hundred yards.

On the 6th, over five hundred aircraft were engaged on operations against V-Weapons targets, and 617 Squadron was assigned to a V-3 super-gun site at Mimoyecques. Originally planned as one of two sites near Cap Gris Nez containing twenty-five barrels each, which were angled at 50 degrees and aimed at London, test failures and delays meant that a single three-barrel shaft stretching a hundred metres into the limestone hill, five miles from the coast and 103 miles from its target, was all that existed at the time. Each fifteen-metre-long smooth-bore barrel, which was designed on the multiple-charge principle to progressively boost the acceleration of the one-ton projectile as it travelled towards the muzzle, was to be capable of pounding London at the rate of hundreds per day without let-up. It was protected by a concrete slab thirty meters wide and five-and-a-half meters thick, which was correctly believed by the designers to be impregnable to conventional bombs. It had been attacked on a number of occasions without success, but 617 Squadron scored direct hits with Tallboys, and provisional reconnaissance revealed four deep craters in the immediate target area, one causing a large corner of the concrete slab to collapse. The extent of the damage underground would not be apparent to the planners at Bomber Command, but the shafts and tunnels had been rendered unusable and would remain so. Although Cheshire did not know it, this was to be his final operation, not only with 617 Squadron, but also of the war in Europe.

The authorities were not convinced that the site at St-Leu-d'Esserent had received terminal damage and scheduled another attack on it for the late evening of the 7th. Before the operation got under way, more than 450 aircraft from 1, 4, 6 and 8 Groups had carried out the first major operation in support of the Canadian 1st and British 2nd Armies, which were trying to break out of Caen. The target had been changed from German-fortified villages to an area of open ground north of Caen, where almost 2,300 tons of bombs was dropped somewhat ineffectively, and, ultimately, that decision proved to be counter-productive by causing damage to the northern suburbs of the city rather than to German forces. 5 Group detailed 208 Lancasters and fifteen Mosquitos for St-Leu, the 44 (Rhodesia) Squadron element of eighteen departing Dunholme Lodge between 22.10 and 22.50 with W/C Thompson the senior pilot on duty. They arrived in the target area to find medium-level cloud, which prevented the moonlight from providing illumination, although, below the cloud level, the visibility was good. The Master Bomber was the former 207 Squadron officer, W/C Ed Porter, and he oversaw the delivery of the Oboe yellow TI at 01.06, which was followed by the first stick of flares four minutes later. The first red spot fire went down at 01.08, a hundred yards south of the aiming point, but in line with the direction of the bombing run and backing-up by red and green TIs continued until 01.13. The marking was assessed as sufficiently accurate to call in the main force at 01.15, and the 44 (Rhodesia) Squadron crews dropped their loads of eleven 1,000 and four 500 pounders from 10,500 to 15,000 feet between 01.14 and 01.25. The Master Bomber's VHF was indistinct, so 83 Squadron's S/L Egging assumed control, and sent the force home at 01.25. Twenty-nine Lancasters and two Mosquitos failed to return after night-fighters got amongst them, and this represented 14% of the force. It was another sobering night for Dunholme Lodge, after three 44 (Rhodesia) Squadron Lancasters and one from 619 Squadron were absent from their dispersals. LM631 was some fifteen miles from the French coast at Dieppe when it crashed at Lucy at 01.30, killing P/O Gowing and his flight engineer, who may have stayed at the controls while the rest of the crew baled out. If so, their sacrifice saved their five crew mates, who were spirited away by the local Resistance to retain their freedom. ME859 came down further to the east at Equennes-Eramcourt, and there were no survivors from the crew of P/O Graaff. ME634 was homebound to the west of Beauvais when fire from a night-fighter killed F/L Carnegie at the controls and left his crew with no choice but to take to their parachutes. The Lancaster crashed at 02.00 at St-Germer-de-Fly, while the crew floated down, three into the arms of the enemy and three to be picked up by the Resistance. One of those captured had been severely injured after leaving the aircraft, and he succumbed soon afterwards. Photo-reconnaissance revealed that both ends of the tunnel complex had collapsed, as had a section in the middle, and the approach road and rail links had been heavily cratered and blocked.

There was no immediate opportunity for the afflicted squadrons, particularly 106 and 207, which had lost five crews each, to "get back on the horse", and there must have been a sombre air, while the populations of RAF Metheringham and Spilsby each came to terms with the loss of thirty-five familiar faces in one night. A special congratulatory message arrived on the participating stations from A-O-C, AVM Sir Ralph Cochrane, who considered it the finest effort by the group to successfully press home the attack in the face of the fiercest opposition. Operations were posted on 5 Group stations on the 10th and 11th, and then cancelled, before the 12th, when fifteen 44 (Rhodesia) Squadron crews were called to briefing to be given the details about that night's operation against railway installations at Culmont-Chalindrey in eastern France. Two aiming points were planned, at the western and eastern ends, for which a force of 157 Lancasters and four Mosquitos was made ready. While this operation was in progress, another by elements of 1 Group further south at a railway junction at Revigny would, hopefully, help to dilute the night-fighter response. The 44 (Rhodesia) Squadron crews departed Dunholme Lodge between 21.37 and 22.03 with F/L Dobson the senior pilot on duty and headed for Bridport to begin the Channel crossing as far as the Channel Islands, before turning east-south-east to pass south of Paris to reach the target. F/O Lewis and crew were unable to access all of their fuel because of a jammed transfer cock and brought their bombs home. The others flew out over eight-tenths low cloud until shortly before reaching the target area, where the conditions improved to provide clear skies, and, promisingly, no sign of defensive activity from the ground. The controller at the eastern aiming point experienced VHF communications problems, which delayed that part of the attack, and eventually the entire force was directed to the western aiming point. The 44 (Rhodesia) Squadron crews delivered their eight 1,000 and two or three 500 pounders each onto two red spotfires from 5,000 to 8,000 feet between 01.51 and 02.11, and explosions were observed, followed by fires that remained visible for fifty miles into the return flight. The high proportion of delayed action fuses in use prevented an immediate assessment of results, but post-raid reconnaissance would confirm an effective operation. LM638 was homebound, when in collision with a 576 Squadron Lancaster, which had strayed south of track while returning from Revigny. F/O Arnold RCAF and his crew had time to abandon the Lancaster, which crashed at around 02.00 at Auberive, some fifteen miles west of the target, and the pilot and four others evaded capture. Sadly, only the two gunners survived from the 1 Group Lancaster.

A dozen 44 (Rhodesia) Squadron crews were detailed to operate on the 14th and were informed at briefing that their target was to be the huge marshalling yards at Villeneuve-St-Georges, situated on the southern rim of Paris. They would be part of a force of 111 Lancasters, six Mosquitos and an American twin-engine P38 Lightning containing the Master Bomber, W/C Jeudwine. They departed Dunholme Lodge between 21.49 and 22.15 led by F/L Dobson and followed a similar route to that of forty-eight hours earlier. W/C Jeudwine was having compass trouble, and would arrive on target twelve minutes late, so contacted his Deputy, 83 Squadron's W/C Joe Northrop, to take matters in hand. A large amount of cloud lay over the target area with a base at 5,000 feet, but clear conditions below enabled Joe to identify the aiming point and he judged the Oboe marker to be within fifty yards of it. He called in the 5 Group marker force, which lobbed the TIs within the confines of the yards, and the operation appeared to be proceeding smoothly and precisely according to plan. The 44 (Rhodesia) Squadron crews bombed on red and green TIs from 5,000 to 10,000 feet between 01.36 and 01.55, and most of it hit the yards, while a proportion also fell outside to the east. Meanwhile, 1 Group had returned to Revigny, but had been thwarted by ground haze, which forced the Master Bomber to abandon the attack before any bombing could take place. Seven Lancasters were lost for no gain, and it would fall to 5 Group to finish the job a few nights hence at great expense.

Flying-bomb sites and railways dominated the target list on the 15th, and 5 Group was handed a railway junction at Nevers, a city on the North Bank of the Loire in central France. 44 (Rhodesia) Squadron contributed eight Lancasters to the force of 104, which was accompanied by four Mosquitos to carry out the low-level marking. They departed Dunholme Lodge between 22.18 and 22.25 with S/L Hildred the senior pilot on duty and were followed into the air between 22.32 and 22.37 by six others for mining duties in the Silverthorn III and Pumpkin gardens in the western Baltic, led by W/C Thompson and S/L White. The bombing element all reached the target after an outward flight of more than three-and-a-half hours to find clear skies and a little haze. The marker force exploited the favourable conditions to mark promptly and accurately, and the 44 (Rhodesia) Squadron crews delivered their nine 1,000 and four 500 pounders each onto a red spotfire and green TIs from 3,800 (S/L Hildred) to 6,000 feet between 01.58 and 02.14. The entire force was carrying delayed-action ordnance, and no immediate assessment could be made, but a large explosion suggested, perhaps, that an ammunition train or dump had been hit. Meanwhile, the gardening element had reached their target area, four employing Sjaellands Point as the starting point for their timed run, while W/C Thompson chose Ebeltoft, and all delivered their mines into the briefed locations from 8,000 feet between 01.22 and 01.24. F/O Hough and crew failed to return in PB206 and were lost without trace. Photographic reconnaissance later in the day revealed that the Nevers site had been all but obliterated, and there was much damage to rolling stock.

Fourteen 44 (Rhodesia) Squadron crews were called to briefing at midnight on the 17/18th to learn of their part in a tactical support operation to be carried out at dawn by a force of 942 aircraft, of which 201 of the Lancasters were to be provided by 5 Group. It was the start of the ground forces' Operation Goodwood, which was Montgomery's plan for a decisive breakout into wider France as a prelude to the march towards the German frontier. The aiming points were five enemy-held villages to the east of Caen, Colombelles, Mondeville, Sannerville, Cagny and Manneville, all of which stood in the path of the advancing British 2nd Army. The 44 (Rhodesia) Squadron element departed Dunholme Lodge between 03.49 and 04.16 with W/C Thompson the senior pilot on duty, and all reached the target area to find their aiming point, the Mondeville steel works, which the Germans had converted into a strongly defended fortress, already marked by red and yellow TIs, but about to be swallowed up and obscured by drifting smoke. Bombing took place from 6,000 to 10,000 feet between 05.45 and 06.11 in accordance with instructions from the Master Bomber, and, as far as could be determined, fell accurately onto the markers. ND517 was shot down in the target area, delivering F/O Cuthbert and five of his crew into enemy hands, while the nineteen-year-old mid-upper gunner lost his life. The RAF dropped five thousand tons of bombs to good effect onto the two German divisions in just half an hour, and the Americans followed up with a further two thousand tons.

Operations were not done for the day, and, that night, following two failed attempts by 1 Group to cut a railway junction at Revigny at a combined cost of seventeen Lancasters, the job was handed to a 5 Group element of 109 Lancasters, four Mosquitos and a P38 Lightning containing the Master Bomber, W/C Jeudwine. It was to be a busy night of operations, which included another railway and two oil targets, along with support and diversionary activities involving a total of 972 sorties. 44 (Rhodesia) Squadron remained at home while 619 Squadron represented Dunholme Lodge and would lose five Lancasters with just three survivors between them. They crossed the French coast near Dieppe and passed through an intense searchlight belt some twenty miles inland, while being harried all the way into eastern France by night-fighters, which had been fed into the stream shortly after it entered enemy airspace. In just forty-five minutes, sixteen Lancasters fell victim to night-fighters and one to flak, before the survivors reached the target to find clear skies, but haze obscuring ground detail. This target continued to present problems, beginning with the first wave of flares, delivered at about 01.30, which were too far to the east. More flares were ordered, and the bombing was put back by five minutes, while Wanganui markers were dropped by Mosquito, and the situation was assessed. The whole attack seemed chaotic, and the use of many delayed-action bombs meant that it was difficult to see what was happening on the ground. Photo-reconnaissance revealed, that the operation had been successful in cutting the railway link to the battle front, but had cost twenty-four Lancasters, almost 22% of those dispatched. *(For a full and highly detailed account of the three Revigny raids read the amazing book, Massacre over the Marne, by Oliver Clutton-Brock.)*

5 Group crews stood-by on the 19th for a possible daylight operation, and it was evening before orders came through to prepare for an attack on a flying-bomb storage site at Thiverny, situated just to the north of St-Leu-d'Esserent. A force of 103 Lancasters and two Mosquitos was detailed, fifteen of the former provided by 44 (Rhodesia) Squadron, and they departed Dunholme Lodge between 19.10 and 19.30 with S/L Hildred the senior pilot on duty. The attack was to take place in daylight under the protection of a Spitfire escort, which was picked up at the south coast. All from the squadron reached the target in fine weather conditions, but with ground haze making it difficult to identify the aiming point. Late preliminary marking by the Path Finder element and communications problems between the Master Bomber and his Deputy added to the frustrations and led to most crews having to orbit for five minutes before bombing visually in the face of moderate to intense heavy flak bursting as high as 18,000 feet. The 44 (Rhodesia) Squadron element carried out their attacks from 14,000 to 18,000 feet between 21.29 and 21.36 and returned safely to make their reports. Post-raid reconnaissance revealed some loose bombing, but sufficient aiming point photographs were brought back to suggest a successful outcome, and there had been no losses.

Railway yards and a triangle junction at Courtrai (Kortrijk) in Belgium provided the targets for a joint effort by 1, 5 and 8 Groups on the 20th, for which 44 (Rhodesia) Squadron contributed sixteen Lancasters to the 5 Group force of 190 Lancasters and five Mosquitos. They departed Dunholme Lodge between 22.48 and 23.19 with W/C Thompson and S/L White the senior pilots on duty, and all reached the target area to find it free of cloud, but slightly obscured by ground haze. The Oboe marking was well-placed in the marshalling yards, and backed up by green TIs, onto which the squadron participants delivered their eleven 1,000 and four 500 pounders each from 10,000 to 14,000 feet between 00.56 and 01.07. They returned home safely to report a large orange explosion at 00.57 and a successful outcome, which was confirmed by post-raid reconnaissance that revealed both aiming points to have been obliterated in return for the loss of nine Lancasters.

Following two nights at home for 5 Group and a two-month break from city-busting, Harris sanctioned a major raid on the naval port of Kiel on the 23rd, for which a force of 629 aircraft was made ready. 44 (Rhodesia) Squadron did not contribute to the 5 Group force of ninety-nine Lancasters, which headed for the rendezvous point to form up behind an elaborate "Mandrel" jamming screen laid on by 100 Group, before setting course for Denmark's western coast. *(In November 1943, 100 Group had been formed to take over the Radio Countermeasures (RCM) role, which had been the preserve of 101 Squadron since its introduction a number of months earlier. 101 Squadron, however, would remain in 1 Group and continue to provide RCM for the remainder of the war.)* When they arrived unexpectedly and with complete surprise in Kiel airspace, they rendered the enemy night-fighter controller confused and unable to bring his night-fighter resources to bear. Kiel was covered by a nine to ten-tenths veil of thin cloud with tops at 4,000 feet, and a skymarking plan was put into action, which enabled the main force to bomb on the glow, first of the flares, and then of fires. It was not possible to determine the outcome, but the glow of fires remained visible for a hundred miles into the return journey, which suggested an effective raid. This was confirmed by local reports, which conceded that this had been the town's most destructive raid of the war and had inflicted heavy damage on the port and shipyards and cut off water supplies for three days and gas for three weeks. Many delayed-action bombs had been dropped, and these continued to cause problems for some time.

5 Group divided its forces on the 24th to enable it to support the first of a three-raid series in five nights on the city of Stuttgart, and an oil refinery and fuel dump at Donges. Situated on the North Bank of the Loire to the east of St Nazaire, this target had been attacked successfully by elements of 6 and 8

Groups on the previous night, but clearly required further attention. The group detailed ninety-nine Lancasters for southern Germany in an overall force of 614, while 104 Lancasters and four Mosquitos were made ready for western France, with five 8 Group Mosquitos in attendance. 44 (Rhodesia) Squadron, having missed the Kiel raid, had sixteen fully rested crews to support the Stuttgart operation, and they departed Dunholme Lodge between 21.32 and 21.50 with S/L White the senior pilot on duty. They all reached the target area to find nine to ten-tenths cloud cover with tops at 4,000 to 7,000 feet, which required the employment of Wanganui flares (skymarking) to mark the aiming point. The 44 (Rhodesia) Squadron crews bombed on the red glow on the cloud base from 17,000 to 20,500 feet between 01.50 and 02.00 in accordance with the instructions of the Master Bomber, and set course for home fairly satisfied with the outcome, although it was impossible to make an accurate assessment. At debriefings across the Command, crews reported a glow of fires covering an area of perhaps five square miles, which remained visible for eighty miles into the return journey. No local report came out of Stuttgart for this night, but it had been a successful and destructive raid, although gained at a cost of seventeen Lancasters and four Halifaxes.

5 Group split its forces again on the 25th to support the second of the raids on Stuttgart with eighty-three Lancasters, and a daylight attack on an aerodrome and signals depot at Saint-Cyr involving ninety-four Lancasters and six Mosquitos. *(There are at least four locations called Saint-Cyr, and it is believed that the one targeted on this night was in the Ile-de-France to the west of Paris.)* 44 (Rhodesia) Squadron briefed seventeen crews for Stuttgart, which departed Dunholme Lodge between 21.03 and 21.37 with F/Ls Belasco and Dobson the senior pilots on duty and headed for landfall on the French coast between Fecamp and Dieppe. F/O Mitchell and crew lost their starboard-outer engine over France, and, unable to maintain height on three, turned back and jettisoned their 2,000 pounder and six 500lb J-cluster bombs. F/L Belasco and crew were passing to the east of Paris when attacked by a night-fighter, which dived down onto them and inflicted damage on both turrets. Two other night-fighters joined in to chase the Lancaster as it turned towards the north and sought out medium to low-level cloud in which to hide. The pursuit lasted until Caen, at which point the assailants were lost and the bomb load jettisoned. The others, meanwhile, had entered Germany north of Strasbourg accompanied by layers of cloud, which, over the target, was at five to ten-tenths with tops in places as high as 20,000 feet. There was haze below the cloud level to create further challenges for the marker force, and the red and green TIs appeared to the main force crews to be somewhat scattered. Bombing by the 44 (Rhodesia) Squadron crews took place from 17,000 to 21,000 feet between 01.57 and 02.12, but it was impossible to assess the outcome, and there was little optimism at debriefings that a successful operation had taken place. In fact, this was probably the most destructive of the three raids in this current series, but it would be only after the third one that cumulative reports came out of the city to confirm much destruction and heavy casualties. Post-raid reconnaissance revealed a successful attack at the Saint-Cyr site, which had left all of the buildings severely damaged.

The hectic round of operations continued for 5 Group on the 26th with preparations for an attack on two aiming points in the marshalling yards at Givors, situated on the West Bank of the River Rhône in south-east-central France. 178 Lancasters and nine Mosquitos were made ready, seventeen of the former by 44 (Rhodesia) Squadron, and they departed Dunholme Lodge between 21.01 and 21.39 with S/L Hildred the senior pilot on duty, and a round-trip of eleven hundred miles ahead of them. Bad weather had been anticipated, but the conditions during the outward leg over France were even worse than forecast with icing and electrical storms, and fourteen aircraft turned back. There were no 44 (Rhodesia) Squadron crews among these as they covered the almost five-hour outward flight to reach the target and be greeted by severe weather conditions in the form of rain, thunderstorms and lightning.

The cloud was down to around 7,000 feet with poor visibility below, and the flare force made a number of runs across the target between 01.42 and 02.07, and orbited in between, awaiting instructions. There were occasional glimpses of the ground, but the Master Bomber was experiencing great difficulty in getting Mosquito TIs onto the two aiming points. Eventually, one of the Deputies managed to put a green TI onto the southern aiming point, and the main force began to bomb at around 02.00. The 44 (Rhodesia) Squadron crews carried out their attacks from 5,500 to 8,000 feet between 02.12 and 02.21, using the light from flares and aiming at green TIs, all in accordance with instructions. They could offer little to the Intelligence Section at debriefing, where the crew of F/O McKechnie was conspicuous by its absence. They had borrowed Lancaster PB346 from 619 Squadron, and all perished when it crashed in flames three miles north-north-west of the small town of Montrevault in north-western France while homebound. Post-raid reconnaissance revealed that the attack at Givors had fulfilled its aims in closing the tracks to the north of the junction and damaging the locomotive depot in the yards.

The night of the 28/29th would prove to be busy, eventful and expensive, as the Command prepared for major operations against Stuttgart and Hamburg and a number of smaller undertakings involving a total of 1,126 aircraft. The final raid of the series on Stuttgart was to be an all-Lancaster affair of 494 aircraft drawn from 1, 3, 5 and 8 Groups, while 307 Lancasters and Halifaxes of 1, 6 and 8 Groups carried out the annual last-week-of-July attack on Hamburg, a year and a day after the devastating firestorm of Operation Gomorrah. 5 Group put up 176 Lancasters, fourteen of them made ready by 44 (Rhodesia) Squadron, and they were each loaded with a 2,000 pounder and thirteen or fourteen 500lb J cluster bombs. They departed Dunholme Lodge between 21.46 and 22.13 with F/Ls Belasco and Dobson the senior pilots on duty and joined other elements of the force over Reading. They made landfall on the French coast south of Fécamp, by which time F/L Belasco and crew had been forced to turn back with an unserviceable mid-upper turret. The others flew across France in bright moonlight above the cloud layer, but the lack of the forecast medium cloud at 18,000 feet exposed them to the night-fighter hordes that had infiltrated the bomber stream as it closed on the target. It was the Luftwaffe's Nachtjagd that would gain the upper hand on this night, but the 44 (Rhodesia) Squadron crews must have been in a section of the bomber stream that remained unmolested, as none reported seeing a night-fighter. There was a layer of up to ten-tenths thin cloud over the city, with tops in places at around 10,000 feet, and the Path Finders initially employed skymarker flares (Wanganui), and then green TIs, at which the 44 (Rhodesia) Squadron crews aimed their bombs from 16,000 to 18,000 feet between 01.56 and 02.04. LM171 and PB266 both came down at 02.30, the former on the outskirts of the town of Haiterbach, twenty-five miles south-west of Stuttgart, killing the two gunners and delivering P/O Gale and the rest of his crew into enemy hands. The latter crashed at Stuttgart-Wangen, a south-eastern suburb, killing F/O Duncan RAAF and both gunners, and leaving three members of the crew in enemy hands and one on the run, remarkably, ultimately, to retain his freedom. Thirty-nine Lancasters failed to return, fourteen of them from 5 Group, and night-fighters also caught the Hamburg force on its way home, bringing down a further twenty-two aircraft to raise the night's casualty figure to sixty-one aircraft. Although it was difficult to make an accurate assessment of this final Stuttgart raid, the series had severely damaged the city, leaving its central districts devastated, with most of its public and cultural buildings in ruins, and 1,171 of its inhabitants dead.

A dozen 44 (Rhodesia) Squadron crews were briefed and put on stand-by at Dunholme Lodge late on the 29th in anticipation of an early-morning tactical support operation in the Villers Bocage-Caumont region of the Normandy battle area south-west of Caen. They were to be part of an overall force of 692 aircraft to attack six enemy positions facing predominantly American forces, and they took off for their aiming point at Cahagnes between 05.55 and 06.23 with S/L Hildred the senior pilot on duty. They approached the target over ten-tenths cloud with tops at 5,000 feet and a base at 3,500 feet and were five minutes from the bombing run at 07.59, when the Master Bomber sent them home with their bombs.

5 Group prepared for two daylight operations on the 31st, one of them an evening attack on a flying bomb storage tunnel at Rilly-la-Montagne, some five miles south of Reims, for which a force of ninety-seven Lancasters and three Mosquitos was assembled, that included sixteen Lancasters of 617 Squadron, led by its recently appointed successor to Cheshire, W/C James "Willie" Tait. Tait was well-known to 5 Group crews as a member of the Master Bomber fraternity at Coningsby, but had spent most of his long operational career in 4 Group, and was among the most experienced pilots in the entire Command. A second operation was to be directed at locomotive facilities and marshalling yards at Joigny-la-Roche, situated north of Auxerre and some ninety miles south east of Paris. A force of 127 Lancasters and four Mosquitos was drawn from 1 and 5 Groups with 44 (Rhodesia) Squadron supporting it with thirteen Lancasters that departed Dunholme Lodge between 17.18 and 17.40 with S/L Hildred the senior pilot on duty. They made their way south to rendezvous with the rest of the two forces, 83 Squadron forming into two vics, one at 15,000 and the other at 18,000 feet, to lead the Rilly force to the target under a fighter escort. Meanwhile, the Joigny-la-Roche force had arrived in the target area, also with a fighter escort, to find no more than three-tenths cloud with tops at 7,000 feet, and good enough visibility to enable a visual identification of the aiming point. The marking was concentrated, as was the bombing onto the red TIs, and, with one exception, the 44 (Rhodesia) Squadron crews delivered their eleven 1,000 and four 500 pounders each from 12,000 to 15,000 feet between 20.26 and 20.30. F/O Davey and crew were on their bombing run when the bomb-firing switch jammed to prevent the bomb-aimer from releasing the load, and, having been told not to orbit, brought their load home. Post-raid reconnaissance confirmed both operations to have been successful for the loss of a single Lancaster from Joigny and two from Rilly, one of the latter containing the 617 Squadron crew of F/L Bill Reid VC, who survived with one of his crew after their Lancaster had been hit by bombs from above.

During the course of the month, the squadron carried out fifteen operations and dispatched 207 sorties for the loss of ten Lancasters and their crews.

August 1944

August would bring an end to the flying bomb offensive, and also see a return to major night operations against industrial Germany. Flying bomb sites were to dominate the first half of the month, however, and sites would be targeted in daylight on each of the first six days. It began with 777 aircraft being committed to operations against numerous flying bomb-related sites on the afternoon of the 1st, although there were serious doubts about the weather conditions, which were poor over England. 5 Group's targets were at La Breteque, situated in Normandy, some ten miles east-south-east of Rouen, Mont Candon, a mile or two south-west of Dieppe, and Siracourt, located some thirty miles east of the coastal town of Berck-sur-Mer. Forces of fifty-three Lancasters, fifty-nine Lancasters and a Lightning and Mosquito and sixty-seven Lancasters and four Mosquitos respectively were made ready, the first and last-mentioned supported by 44 (Rhodesia) Squadron with seven and six Lancasters. Those bound for Siracourt departed Dunholme Lodge between 14.54 and 15.17 with S/L Hildred the senior pilot on duty, and they were followed into the air between 16.25 and 16.51 by the La Breteque element led by

F/L Belasco. They joined forces with the others of their respective formations as they made their way towards the south and lost the cloud as they began the Channel crossing, only for it to build again to nine to ten-tenths stratocumulus with tops at between 2,000 and 5,000 feet over the Pas-de-Calais region. One Lancaster bombed at La Breteque, before the Master Bomber called a halt to proceedings, and the other two attacks were abandoned before any bombing took place. It was a similar story for the other groups, and, in total, only seventy-nine aircraft bombed.

On the following afternoon, 5 Group contributed 194 Lancasters, two Mosquitos and a P38 Lightning to operations by 394 aircraft against one flying bomb launching and three supply sites. Ninety-four Lancasters and two Mosquitos were assigned to a storage site at Trossy-St-Maximin, situated north of Paris and close to St-Leu d'Esserent, and a hundred Lancasters and the P38 to the Bois-de-Cassan facility. 44 (Rhodesia) Squadron loaded fourteen Lancasters with a mix of 1,000 and 500 pounders destined for the former, some with a delay fuse of up to thirty-six hours and dispatched them from Dunholme Lodge between 14.18 and 14.36 with F/L Newmarch the senior pilot on duty. Some from other squadrons complained that the leaders flew too fast, and there were comments about excessive weaving, but all from 44 (Rhodesia) Squadron reached the target area to find three to seven-tenths patchy cloud. The Oboe proximity markers went down on time, and were backed up with TIs, and, once the bombing started, the defences opened up with accurate flak that caused damage to twenty-seven aircraft. Despite that, most of the formation passed over the aiming point and plastered it, the 44 (Rhodesia) Squadron crews from 15,000 to 18,000 feet between 17.00 and 17.05. Post-raid reconnaissance revealed many new craters, a large rectangular building stripped of its roof and sides, and the southern end of two road-over-rail bridges demolished. At Bois-de-Cassan, there was three to five-tenths patchy cloud over the target, but few saw the Oboe proximity markers go down, and most bombed on visual reference. The lead aircraft turned suddenly at the last moment and caused a number of those following to overshoot the aiming point, causing their bombs to fall wide of the mark. Post-raid reconnaissance revealed fresh damage with many new craters.

Despite the effectiveness of the operation, the Trossy-St-Maximin site was included among targets for more than eleven hundred aircraft on the following day. The 1 and 5 Group crews were told at briefing, that the importance of the site to the Third Reich demanded that no building be left intact, and one or two may have escaped damage during the previous day's attack. 187 Lancasters, one Mosquito and the P38 Lightning were made ready as 5 Group's contribution to the operation, the thirteen 44 (Rhodesia) Squadron participants departing Dunholme Lodge between 11.32 and 11.58 with F/Ls Belasco and Newmarch the senior pilots on duty. Each Lancaster was loaded with a dozen 1,000 pounders and four of 500lbs, all of which reached the target area intact. The 5 Group element was to attack about fifteen minutes after 1 Group, and, as they reached the target, smoke could be seen rising to 8,000 feet, and this, combined with a fierce flak defence, presented the crews with challenging conditions. The 44 (Rhodesia) Squadron element bombed from 15,000 to 16,000 feet between 14.31 and 14.33, doing so by visual reference under instruction from the Master Bomber, having been prevented by the smoke from seeing the markers. Many aircraft returned to their respective stations bearing flak damage, although the 44 (Rhodesia) Squadron crews were more concerned about the dense concentration of aircraft over the aiming point, which was dangerous and led to a scattering of bombs. F/O Freestone's PB192 provided evidence of damage caused by a bomb from above. Photo-reconnaissance was unable to confirm that the site had been obliterated, and it would need to be attacked again on the following day, a job that would be handed to 6 Group, while most of 5 Group stayed at home.

The 5th dawned bright and clear, and brilliant sunshine glinted off the Perspex of fifteen 44 (Rhodesia) Squadron Lancasters as they took off from Dunholme Lodge between 10.45 and 11.17 bound for familiar airspace over St-Leu-d'Esserent with F/L Newmarch the senior pilot on duty. They were part of a 5 Group force of 189 Lancasters and one Mosquito, which represented about 25% of the effort by 4, 5, 6 and 8 Groups against two flying-bomb sites, the other in the Forét-de-Nieppe, close to the Belgian frontier. It was an almost intact force that homed in on the target to find it partly protected by up to six-tenths patchy cloud with tops at about 12,000 feet. This prevented the Master Bomber from picking up the aiming point until thirty seconds from it, which meant a very late course change to bring the bombers into position. This was achieved, however, although smoke and cloud hid the markers from view, and most crews picked up the aiming point by means of ground features. They ran through a spirited flak defence, the 44 (Rhodesia) Squadron crews bombing from 15,500 feet between 13.32 and 13.35. Returning crews reported a fairly concentrated attack, which PRU photos seemed to confirm with views of fresh damage, and heavily cratered approaches.

The squadron detailed thirteen crews for operations on the morning of the 6th, and they were in their Lancasters before 09.00 to carry out the checks before departing for another swipe at the flying-bomb launching site at Bois-de-Cassan in the L'Isle-Adam, a few miles to the south-west of St-Leu. They were part of a 5 Group force of ninety-nine Lancasters and the P38 Lightning and took off between 09.33 and 09.58 with S/L White the senior pilot on duty. They made their way south to join up with the rest of the formation, with 83 Squadron's G/C Deane the Master Bomber and F/L Drinkall acting as his deputy. Deane began to experience problems with his navigation homing equipment as he crossed the English coast outbound and decided to hand over to F/L Drinkall while remaining with the formation. When about forty miles inland of the French coast, a large cumulus cloud barred the way up to 20,000 feet, and F/L Drinkall communicated his intention to take the force below it, descending to 16,000 feet. G/C Deane warned him not to go below 15,000, and advised him not to enter the cloud, but to turn to starboard. However, they were immediately enveloped in cloud, and G/C Deane did his best to hang on to F/L Drinkall's tail as he continued to descend, and the two eventually became separated. Emerging on the other side of the cloud, Deane saw a large formation in the distance, and followed it. Passing through the cloud had caused the formation to become widely scattered, and it could not be reformed. Only thirty-eight aircraft bombed after picking up the aiming point visually, among them the 44 (Rhodesia) Squadron crews of F/Os Anning, Lade and Oxborrow, who carried out their attacks from 12,000 and 14,750 feet between 12.16 and 12.21. Fifty-eight crews were unable to bomb, but still had to contend with a fierce flak and fighter defence. Three Lancasters failed to return, and among them was that of F/L Drinkall and crew, who failed to survive. Photo-reconnaissance revealed some fresh damage to the eastern side of the target, but two large buildings on the main roadway immediately south of the aiming point remained intact, and further operations would be required.

Other than night flying tests (NFTs), there was little activity during the day on the 7th, the first time during the month that no daylight operations had been mounted. It was from teatime onwards that the feverish activity began, to prepare 1,019 aircraft for attacks on five enemy positions facing Allied ground forces in the Normandy battle area. The aiming point for 179 Lancasters and one Mosquito from 5 Group was the fortified village of Secqueville, situated some fifteen miles east of Le Havre. Sixteen 44 (Rhodesia) Squadron Lancasters departed Dunholme Lodge between 21.19 and 21.44 with F/L Newmarch the senior pilot on duty, and joined up with the others as they travelled south. The target could be seen by the approaching bombers to be under clear skies, although haze shrouded ground detail to an extent, and star shells were fired from the ground to illuminate the aiming point.

This enabled the Path Finder aircraft to drop red TIs onto it for the main force crews to aim at, and the first phase of bombing proceeded according to plan in concentrated fashion, lasting fifteen minutes. Ten of the 44 (Rhodesia) Squadron crews carried out their attacks from 6,000 to 9,000 feet between 23.22 and 23.25, and it was then that smoke began to obscure the markers, and the Master Bomber called a halt to proceedings before the remaining six from 44 (Rhodesia) Squadron had bombed.

A rare day off for 5 Group on the 8th was over, when the four 44 (Rhodesia) Squadron crews of S/L White, F/L Dobson and F/Os Davey and Stockwell departed Dunholme Lodge between 00.48 and 00.54 on the 9th bound for the Deodar garden in the Gironde estuary. It was approaching 04.00 when they established their positions by H2S and pinpointed on Pointe-de-Grave on the western side of the estuary, before making timed runs of between 3¾ and eleven miles to deliver their stores from 9,500 feet between 04.03 and 04.19. The 9th was also operation-free until late afternoon, when briefings took place for that night's operation against an oil storage dump in the Forét-de-Châtellerault, situated south of Tours in western France. It was to be predominantly a 5 Group show involving 171 Lancasters and fourteen Mosquitos, but with five 101 Squadron Lancasters to provide RCM cover. 44 (Rhodesia) Squadron dispatched a dozen Lancasters between 20.33 and 20.55 with F/Ls Dobson and Newmarch the senior pilots on duty, all of which arrived in the target area under clear skies. However, the presence of considerable ground haze created poor visibility for the marker crews attempting to identify the two aiming points, and the flares dropped by the first two waves of the marker force were scattered, prompting the Mosquito marker leader to drop a Wanganui flare as a guide to the third flare-force crews. This meant that some crews had to orbit for up to twenty minutes before the Master Bomber was satisfied that the green TIs were in the right spot and called in the main force. They produced accurate bombing, resulting in three large explosions and volumes of black smoke, which, within five minutes, completely obscured the aiming point. A pause in the bombing was called, before it recommenced, until the lack of a verifiable marker compelled the Master Bomber to call a halt. All of the 44 (Rhodesia) Squadron crews carried out an attack from 5,000 to 8,000 feet between 00.03 and 00.12 and returned home safely to make their reports.

The mighty Gironde estuary, situated on France's Biscay coast, narrows as it leads inland towards the south-east, before dividing to become the Garonne River to the west and the Dordogne to the east. Its banks and islands were home to a number of important oil production and storage sites at Pauillac, Blaye, Bec-d'Ambe and Bordeaux, and the region was a frequent destination for gardening activities. Bordeaux itself was a vitally important port to the enemy, contained U-Boot pens and was heavily defended along the entire length of the waterway. Orders were received on 52, 54 and 55 Base stations at teatime on the 10th to prepare sixty-two Lancasters and five Mosquitos to bomb oil storage facilities at Bordeaux, and 44 (Rhodesia) Squadron responded with eight of its own, which departed Dunholme Lodge between 18.38 and 19.07 with S/L White the senior pilot on duty. They headed towards the south, joining up with the other elements, which included nine Lancasters from 83 Squadron to act as the flare and marker force. The flight out was in daylight, which enabled the Deputy Master Bomber to recognise that the formation had become somewhat disorganized. There were about twenty main force aircraft ahead of the flare force, and the remainder behind it to starboard, but they were catching up, and veering further and further to starboard, until they were some ten to twenty miles off track. Fortunately, the situation rectified itself, and the force arrived in the target area to find clear skies with a little ground haze. As they ran in on the aiming point, a limited amount of heavy flak began to burst at 16,000 to 18,000 feet, while the considerable light flak fell short, and neither proved to be troublesome. Within thirty seconds of the flares illuminating the ground, the TIs were burning close to the aiming point, and the 44 (Rhodesia) Squadron crews bombed from 16,000 to 18,000 feet between 22.31 and 22.42. Returning crews were confident of a successful attack, but, as few explosions were observed, it was difficult to accurately assess the outcome.

On the 11th, while 617 Squadron took care of the U-Boot pens at La Pallice, thirty-nine other Lancasters and two Mosquitos from 5 Group attacked a similar target at Bordeaux under the protection of six Mosquitos of 100 Group. For the evening operation, 5 Group was switched to communications targets at Givors, located about twenty miles to the south of Lyon in south-east-central France. There were to be two aiming points, the town's marshalling yards to the north, and a railway junction to the south, and 44 (Rhodesia) Squadron's sixteen-strong element was assigned to the former in an overall force of 175 Lancasters and ten Mosquitos. They departed Dunholme Lodge between 20.12 and 20.52 with F/Ls Dobson and Newmarch the senior pilots on duty, and all arrived in the target area to find clear skies and a little haze, favourable conditions, which the seemingly usual organized chaos of contradictory or confusing instruction via VHF and W/T threatened to waste. Unaccountably, the 5 Group ORB described the W/T control as excellent and the VHF R/T as good. Permission to bomb was not received until 01.12, by which time some crews had been forced to spend fifteen minutes orbiting three times, while the Master Bomber and his Deputy discussed the accuracy of the markers. Despite the wrinkles, both aiming points were well-illuminated and marked, and the bombing was concentrated in the correct place. The 44 (Rhodesia) Squadron crews confirmed their positions by Gee and H2S-fix before carrying out their attacks on red TIs in accordance with the Master Bomber's instructions from 5,700 to 9,000 feet between 01.09 and 01.24. They all returned to home airspace critical of some aspects of the raid, but confident that it had been concluded successfully. Photo-reconnaissance revealed heavy damage to both aiming points, with the ground badly-cratered and many tracks severed, and the middle span of the railway bridge over the River Rhône was revealed to have received a direct hit.

The main operation on the 12th was an experiment to gauge the ability of main force crews to locate and attack an urban target on the strength of their own H2S equipment in the absence of a Path Finder element. This resulted from the huge volume of operations generated by the four concurrent campaigns, each of which called upon the finite resources of 8 Group, compelling it, in the short term at least, to spread itself more and more thinly. The conclusion of the flying-bomb campaign at the end of the month, together with the end of tactical support for the ground forces, would remove the pressure, and the planned independence of 3 Group through the G-H bombing system from the autumn would solve the problem altogether. In the meantime, however, no one knew what demands might be made of the Command, and it would be useful to see what main force crews could do when left to their own devices. The target was to be Braunschweig, for which a force of 379 aircraft was assembled, seventy-two of the Lancasters provided by 5 Group. 44 (Rhodesia) Squadron made ready ten Lancasters, which departed Dunholme Lodge between 21.03 and 21.13 with F/L Dobson the senior pilot on duty. It was a night of heavy Bomber Command activity at numerous locations involving more than eleven hundred sorties. A second large operation over Germany was directed at the Opel motor factory at Rüsselsheim two hundred miles to the south, and involved 297 aircraft, but, as events were to prove, this would not weaken the enemy night-fighter defences, and powerful elements of the Nachtjagd were waiting for the Braunschweig force as it crossed the German coast at around 18,000 feet. Night-fighter flares were in evidence from then until the coast was crossed again on the way home, and it would prove to be an expensive night for the Command as a whole. The Brunswick force made its way eastwards under clear skies, before encountering nine to ten-tenths thin cloud in the target area with tops at 7,000 feet. This was not a problem, as the whole purpose of the operation was to locate and bomb the target blind by H2S. The 44 (Rhodesia) Squadron element bombed from 19,000 to 22,000 feet between 00.04 and 00.08 and observed the glow of fires beneath the cloud. Some of the bombing did, indeed, hit Brunswick, but there was no concentration, and many outlying towns also reported bombs falling. Twenty-seven aircraft failed to return from this operation and a further twenty from a disappointing tilt at the Opel factory, demonstrating that the Nachtjagd still had sufficient resources to effectively divide its strength.

While the above was in progress, a "rush job" called upon the services of 144 crews to attack German troop concentrations and a road junction north of Falaise. 5 Group supported the attack with twenty-five Lancasters, the crews of which found a blanket of ten-tenths stratus cloud with tops at 2,000 feet, through which the green TIs were clearly visible and bombed. Post-raid reconnaissance confirmed that the area around the junction was heavily cratered and the roads leading from it were mostly blocked.

Later, on the 13th, 5 Group notified 617 Squadron to prepare aircraft for an attack on the U-Boot pens and a cruiser at Brest, and fifteen Lancasters from 53 Base to target an oil storage depot at Bordeaux. The main activity during the afternoon of the 14th was an operation in support of Canadian divisions in the Falaise area, which involved 805 aircraft targeting seven enemy troop positions. 5 Group took part, by sending sixty-one Lancasters to the village of Quesnay, where accurate bombing left the village in ruins. Master Bombers were on hand to control the bombing at each aiming point because of the close proximity of the opposing armies, but, despite the most stringent efforts to avoid friendly fire incidents, some bombs did fall into a quarry occupied by Canadian troops, killing thirteen men, injuring fifty-three others and destroying a large number of vehicles.

5 Group had actually begun the day with an attack by elements of 617 and 9 Squadrons on the derelict French cruiser Gueydon at berth at Brest, which, it was believed, the enemy might sink strategically along with other ships in the harbour, to render it unusable if liberated. In the evening, 128 Lancasters and two Mosquitos were made ready to send back to Brest for another go at the Gueydon, a tanker and a hulk, and among those taking part were eighteen crews from 44 (Rhodesia) Squadron, who departed Dunholme Lodge between 17.47 and 18.24 with S/L White the senior pilot on duty. They arrived over the port to find clear skies and excellent visibility, but also a fierce flak defence, and a number of aircraft would return bearing the scars of battle. The 44 (Rhodesia) Squadron crews bombed from 14,500 to 16,250 feet between 20.21 and 20.34, and a number of direct hits were observed on both vessels, with smoke issuing out of the tanker. Just two Lancasters failed to return, and one of them was the squadron's PD222, which crashed close to the target, killing F/O Gilchrist RCAF and four of his crew, two of them fellow Canadians and one a member of the RAAF. The RAF flight engineer and Canadian mid-upper gunner survived and were soon back in England, the former to have flak-splinter wounds tended to in hospital. Photo-reconnaissance revealed that the tanker had settled on the bottom, and the cruiser had suffered a similar fate with its decks now awash.

In preparation for his new night offensive against Germany, Harris called for operations against enemy night-fighter airfields in Holland and Belgium. In response, a list of nine such targets was prepared for attention by daylight on the 15th, and they would involve a thousand aircraft. 5 Group was handed Deelen in central Holland and Gilze-Rijen in the south, and prepared forces of ninety-four Lancasters and five Mosquitos for the former and 103 Lancasters, four Mosquitos and the P38 Lightning flown by S/L "Count" Ciano for the latter. 44 (Rhodesia) Squadron was assigned to Deelen and dispatched eighteen Lancasters between 09.30 and 10.06 with S/L White the senior pilot on duty. They found the target under clear skies in excellent visibility and were able to identify the aiming point visually. The Lancasters were each loaded with eleven 1,000 and four 500 pounders, which the 44 (Rhodesia)

Squadron crews dropped onto yellow TIs almost as one from 14,000 to 16,300 feet between 12.11 and 12.13, in accordance with instructions from the Master Bomber. Many bomb bursts were observed on the aerodrome, and post-raid reconnaissance confirmed 230 craters on the runways and damage to hangars and other buildings.

The new offensive began with simultaneous attacks on Stettin and Kiel on the night of the 16/17th, 5 Group contributing 145 aircraft to the overall all-Lancaster force of 461 assigned to the former. 44 (Rhodesia) Squadron made ready eight Lancasters for the main event and six to join twenty-four others for mining duties in the geranium garden off the Baltic port of Swinemünde, some thirty miles to the north. It was the latter which departed Dunholme Lodge first, between 20.51 and 21.17, with S/L White the senior pilot on duty, and they were followed into the air between 21.24 and 21.32 by the bombing element, each captained by a pilot of flying officer rank. F/Sgt Binien and crew turned back from a position some ninety miles off Flamborough Head after losing their port-outer engine, while F/O Stockwell and crew had reached Jutland by the time that their starboard-outer let them down, and this reduced the gardening element by two. It took some three-and-a-half hours for the two sections to reach the target area, where the bombing brigade was greeted by up to nine-tenths high cloud with a base at 18,000 to 20,000 feet and sufficient breaks to register clear visibility below. Concentrated red and green TIs could be seen marking out the aiming point, and the 44 (Rhodesia) Squadron crews bombed these from 16,500 to 20,000 feet between 01.00 and 01.21, and reported fires taking hold. Not all returning crews were confident about the outcome, some suggesting the raid had been scattered, when, in fact, it had been highly successful, destroying fifteen hundred houses, numerous industrial premises, and sinking five ships in the harbour, while seriously damaging eight more. The four gardeners delivered their mines as briefed from 200 to 500 feet between 01.16 and 01.25 and returned safely. The attack on Kiel had been less successful but had caused extensive damage in the docks area and among the shipbuilding yards, while wasting much of the effort outside of the town to the north-west.

Seventeen 44 (Rhodesia) Squadron crews were called to briefing early on the 18th to be told of that morning's operation against two flying-bomb dumps in the Forét-de-L'Isle Adam, north of Paris. 158 Lancasters, six Mosquitos and the P38 Lightning were to be involved, with 83 Squadron leading, and providing the back-up marking on the heels of the low-level Mosquitos at the two aiming points in the east and west. The 44 (Rhodesia) Squadron element departed Dunholme Lodge between 11.20 and 12.01 with F/L Dobson the senior pilot on duty, and each Lancaster carrying ten 1,000 and three or four 500 pounders. They headed south in squadron formation to rendezvous with the rest of the force and pick up the fighter escort, and, when over the mid-point of the Channel at 13.15, sixty or seventy American Liberators passed across the bows of the gaggle, heading east a thousand feet higher, prompting the lead Lancaster to change course. This may have been the cause of comments by some crews on return, that not all had observed station keeping as set out at briefing, a situation that would result in aircraft bombing out of the planned sequence and on wrong headings. The last to take off had been the crew of F/O Lewis, some twenty-two minutes late, and, unable to make up the time, they abandoned their sortie at the French coast. On arrival in the target area, the others encountered five to seven-tenths cloud with tops at around 8,000 feet, which hampered identification of both aiming points, and instructions were issued to not bomb unless a clear view of the target had been established. Some were able to pick out the aiming points assisted by smoke markers, and the 44 (Rhodesia) Squadron crews bombed almost as one from 10,500 to 11,500 feet between 14.09 and 14.11, observing a number of bursts. Bombing photos suggested that the attack had overshot to the north, and this was confirmed later by PRU pictures.

53 Base was called into action on the 19th to provide fifty-two Lancasters for an attack on La Pallice, situated on the Biscay coast to the north of the Gironde estuary, and reached the target area to find six to nine-tenths cloud hanging over the western aiming point, and seven to eight-tenths over the eastern one, with tops at 15,000 feet. This created challenging conditions in which to identify the targets, made more so by intense light flak, but crews claimed to have done so visually before carrying out their attacks. This was the first day of a spell of wet, cloudy and, sometimes, windy weather, which would last for the next week, and, apart from a number of small-scale operations, 5 Group remained largely on the ground.

Major operations resumed on the 25th, when preparations were put in hand to make ready more than nine hundred aircraft to launch against three targets, Rüsselsheim and nearby Darmstadt in southern Germany, and the port of Brest, while a further four hundred would be engaged in a variety of smaller endeavours. The largest operation was to be the all-Lancaster affair involving 461 aircraft from 1, 3, 6 and 8 Groups in a return to the Opel motor works, while 334 others attended to eight coastal batteries around Brest. 5 Group was assigned to Darmstadt, a university city and centre of scientific research and development, and one of a few almost virgin targets considered to be worthy of attention. 5 Group assembled a force of 191 Lancasters and six Mosquitos, eighteen of the former made ready by 44 (Rhodesia) Squadron, and they departed Dunholme Lodge between 20.17 and 20.59 with S/L Millington the senior pilot on duty, following his posting-in from 49 Squadron on the 16th. The Master Bomber was one of five crews to return early, leaving his two Deputies from 83 Squadron, F/L Meggeson DFC and S/L Williams DFC to step into the breach, and 44 (Rhodesia) Squadron's F/O Freestone was among the "boomerangs", after a fuel leak developed.

The target area was found to be free of cloud, and some ground haze was present, but this was not responsible for matters going awry early on. VHF communication proved to be weak, which made it difficult for the Deputy Master Bombers to pass on instructions, and five aircraft dropped flares at 01.05, which turned out to be too far to the west, and the low-level Mosquitos reported at 01.07, that they were unable to find the aiming point. H-hour was pushed back to 01.22, although bombing actually began at 01.19, and, soon after, someone left their VHF on transmit, creating a noise that drowned out all voice communications, at the same time that W/T became jammed. One of the Deputies was heard indistinctly instructing the crews to "bomb on the box" (H2S), and then he and the other Deputy were shot down. The main force crews did their best to comply, among them fifteen of those from 44 (Rhodesia) Squadron, who were over the target at 5,000 (F/L Dobson) to 10,000 feet between 01.19 and 01.45 and described a widely scattered attack. On their way to Darmstadt, F/O Lewis and crew came upon Rüsselsheim, fifteen miles to the north-west, which was under attack from the other groups, and they unloaded the contents of their bomb bay there from 7,800 feet at 01.18. The lack of marking persuaded some of the force to seek alternative targets, and S/L Millington found a built-up area between Mannheim and Mainz, probably Worms, and bombed it from 9,000 feet at 01.34.

The German port of Königsberg, now Kaliningrad in Lithuania, is located on the eastern side of the Bay of Danzig and was being used by the enemy to supply its eastern front. It lay some 860 miles in a straight line from the bomber stations surrounding Lincoln, which increased to a round trip of 1,900 miles when the routing across Denmark was taken into account. This made it the most distant location ever targeted by the Command and was exceeded only by SOE flights to Poland. Such a distance required sacrificing bombs for fuel, and it was a reduced load of a single 2,000 pounder and twelve 500lb J cluster bombs that was loaded into each of 44 (Rhodesia) Squadron's thirteen Lancasters, which were part of an overall heavy force of 174. Having been briefed for this target twice before without going, there was some doubt as to whether or not this one would go ahead, but it did, and the first of the 44 (Rhodesia) Squadron Lancasters began to roll at Dunholme Lodge at 19.51 to be followed by the others over the ensuing forty-six minutes with F/L Newmarch the senior pilot on duty. Accompanying the force to the target area would be ten Lancasters carrying mines for delivery into the Tangerine garden, the sea-lanes off Pillau at the entrance to the estuary serving Königsberg. Four of these crews, those of S/L White, F/L Dobson and F/Os Anning and Stockwell, took off among the main body between 20.23 and 20.36. Ahead of them lay a ten-hour marathon, which all from 44 (Rhodesia) Squadron would complete. When they arrived in the target area almost five hours later, after flying through electrical storms and icing conditions over Denmark, the skies were clear and the visibility good, and they were greeted by around a hundred searchlights and an intense flak defence. The flare force went in at 14,000 to 15,000 feet between 01.05 and 01.12, to be followed minutes later by the heavy markers at a lower level. The 44 (Rhodesia) Squadron crews identified the aiming point by red TIs and bombed them from 7,000 and 8,000 feet between 01.18 and 01.23. F/O Hart had been forced to take evasive action after being twice coned during the approach to the target and ended up at 1,500 feet, and he was unable to regain sufficient altitude before the Master Bomber issued the order to cease bombing at 01.24. Returning crews were fairly enthusiastic about the outcome, reporting punctual marking, concentrated bombing and fires that could be seen, according to some, from 250 miles into the return journey. Photo-reconnaissance revealed that the main weight of the attack had fallen into the town's north-eastern districts, where fire had ripped through many building blocks at a cost of just four Lancasters. However, the job was not yet done, and a second operation would have to be mounted. Three of the gardeners returned to report delivering their mines successfully from 10,000 to 12,000 feet between 01.13 and 01.24, but the crew of S/L White was absent from debriefing. News eventually arrived via the Red Cross that NE138 had disappeared into the sea in the target area, and that only S/L White had survived to be taken into captivity.

The final operations in the long-running flying-bomb campaign were conducted by small Oboe-led forces against twelve sites on the 28th, and Allied ground forces took control of the Pas-de-Calais a few days later. It was clear, that a decisive blow had not been delivered on Königsberg, and, at 17.30 on the 29th, briefings took place on the participating 5 Group stations for the return. Sixteen 44 (Rhodesia) Squadron crews learned that they were to be part of a 5 Group force of 189 Lancasters, while the crews of F/L Dobson and F/O Stockwell were to be among ten crews assigned to the Tangerine garden. They took off together between 19.58 and 20.37, each of the bombing brigade Lancasters captained by a pilot of flying officer rank, and, because of the extreme range, they again carried between them only 480 tons of bombs to deliver onto four aiming points. The bomber stream made its way across the North Sea and Denmark and reached the target to encounter eight to ten-tenths cloud with a base at around 10,000 feet. The Master Bomber, W/C Woodroffe, one of 5 Group's most experienced raid controllers, having decided on a visual attack, instructed the first flare force wave to drop below the cloud, and kept the spearhead of the main force circling for twenty minutes before the marking began. The later arrivals could see the markers going down as they approached for what was a complex plan of attack that proceeded with the first flares going down at around 01.05 and continuing at regular intervals thereafter. At 01.24, the third flare force wave was instructed to illuminate the red spot fire, and a minute later an instruction was given to overshoot by 400 yards to the east of the aiming point. At 01.26, a marker aircraft was told to run over the red marker and overshoot by 300 yards, while, at 01.27, another was ordered to overshoot by 600 yards east of the aiming point, before the visual backers-up were sent to track over the reds and greens and overshoot by 300 yards. The flare force was invited to go home at 01.30, and, at 01.34, the visual marker crews were instructed first to back up the greens by 600 yards on a westerly heading, and, two minutes later, the concentrations of reds and greens. The 44 (Rhodesia) Squadron crews identified the target by the red and green TIs and searchlight concentrations and confirmed their positions by H2S before bombing from 9,000 to 10,500 feet between 01.34 and 01.51. F/O Lade and crew had been ordered to begin orbiting to port, when they were coned by searchlights and hit by flak, which caused a fire in the starboard-inner engine and damaged the port-outer. They lost height to 1,200 feet, where they jettisoned the incendiaries, before climbing back up to 5,000 feet to dump the 2,000 pounder. They would make it home to a landing at the emergency strip at Carnaby in Yorkshire. The Master Bomber called a halt to bombing at 01.52 and sent the crews home, where the absence of four 50 Squadron Lancasters at Skellingthorpe prompted a scathing review of W/C Woodroffe's performance, blaming his stubbornness for the high casualty rate of fifteen Lancasters, 7.9% of those dispatched. They maintained that the backers-up had confirmed the marking to be accurate, despite which, he kept some crews orbiting for up to forty minutes. Post-raid reconnaissance confirmed that the operation had been an outstanding success, which destroyed over 40% of the town's residential and 20% of its industrial buildings.

The flying-bomb campaign may now have ended, but a new one against V-2 rocket storage and launching sites began on the 31st with raids on nine suspected locations in northern France. 5 Group sent three forces of forty-nine, forty-six and fifty-two Lancasters with two Mosquitos each to respectively target sites at Auchy-les-Hesdin, Rollancourt and Bergueneuse, all situated some twenty miles inland from the coast at Berck-sur-Mer. 52 Base was assigned to the first-mentioned, for which 44 (Rhodesia) Squadron made ready sixteen Lancasters and dispatched them from Dunholme Lodge between 15.43 and 16.08 with every pilot of flying officer rank. All reached the target area to find five to eight-tenths cloud with a base at 6,000 feet and tops as high as 18,000 feet, out of which issued occasional heavy rain showers. The force was told to orbit until the cloud bank moved away to allow the Mosquitos to drop smoke markers, which failed to ignite. The Master Bomber directed the bombing to be carried out visually, and the 44 (Rhodesia) Squadron crews complied from 10,000 to 12,750 feet between 18.08 and 18.18, and a large explosion was witnessed at 18.10. The operation appeared to be a little scattered, but largely successful, as were those at the other sites. This concluded a month of feverish and record activity for most heavy squadrons, during which 44 (Rhodesia) Squadron took part in twenty-three operations and dispatched 270 sorties for the loss of two Lancasters and their crews.

September 1944

The destructive power of the Command was now almost beyond belief. Each of its heavy bomber groups was capable of laying waste to a German town and city at one go, and, from now until the end of the war, this would be demonstrated in awesome and horrific fashion. Much of the Command's effort during the new month would be directed towards the liberation of the three French ports remaining in enemy hands, but operations began for 5 Group, according to most sources, with an attack on shipping at Brest on the 2nd, for which sixty-seven Lancasters were detailed from 55 Base. However, the 44 (Rhodesia) Squadron ORB asserts that sixteen of its Lancasters took off from Dunholme Lodge between 10.52 and 11.28 on the 1st bound for Brest with S/L Millington the senior pilot on duty, and that no operation was undertaken by the squadron on the 2nd. One must assume an error on the part of the squadron scribe, and that the details of the squadron's part in the Brest operation relate to the 2nd. F/O Evans lost his starboard-inner engine as he flew south and was forced to turn back. The others had to negotiate thunderstorms on the way out, and, on arrival in the target area, initially found a layer of five to seven-tenths cumulus cloud between 2,000 and 9,000 feet affording a range of visibilities between good and poor. However, as the cloud appeared to be drifting away, they were ordered to orbit until the aiming point could be identified visually. The bombing was carried out unopposed, by the 44 (Rhodesia) Squadron element from 11,000 to 12,000 feet between 14.38 and 15.03, and was observed to straddle the quays, in which vessels were berthed. Post-raid reconnaissance revealed damage to a number of the vessels, and additional destruction within the town.

Preparations were put in hand on the following morning to launch attacks on six Luftwaffe-occupied aerodromes in southern Holland. A total of 675 aircraft were to be involved, 5 Group detailing 103 Lancasters and two Mosquitos for its target at Deelen, 44 (Rhodesia) Squadron dispatching seventeen Lancasters between 14.54 and 15.29 with no senior pilots on duty. All reached the target area without incident, although cloud on the way out had created challenging conditions for formation-keeping. Over enemy territory they encountered varying amounts of cloud up to nine-tenths with tops at 7,000 feet and orbited while they awaited gaps through which to identify the aiming point visually. The marking was assessed to be accurate, and thirteen of the 44 (Rhodesia) Squadron crews bombed from 13,500 to 16,000 feet between 17.31 and 17.40 in the face of a spirited flak defence from the airfield. F/O Lade's bombing computer let him down, and three crews were unable to identify the aiming point through the cloud, prompting F/O Slade to criticise the use of smoke-puffs as inadequate for the purpose and suggest that TIs would have been more effective. There were no losses, and returning crews were relatively confident that they had fulfilled their brief, although it would be the 6th before photo-reconnaissance provided a partial cover of the target area and revealed at least sixty craters around runway intersections and taxiways.

Most of 5 Group remained at home over the ensuing five days, while enemy strong-points in and around Le Havre received daylight visitations from other elements of the Command on the 5th, 6th, 8th and 9th. These operations took place during a spell of unhelpful weather conditions, and the attacks of the 8th and 9th were not fully pressed home. Mönchengladbach was posted as the target for 113 Lancasters and fourteen Mosquitos on the 9th, for which operation briefings took place at 01.30. The nineteen 44 (Rhodesia) Squadron crews learned that they were to attack the centre of this town, which, with Operation Market Garden looming, was expected soon to be within striking distance of the advancing Allied forces. They would have to wait until the early hours of the 10th before departing Dunholme Lodge between 02.36 and 03.17 with no senior pilots on duty, and the former 44 (Rhodesia) Squadron pilot, S/L Belasco, now a flight commander, leading the 207 Squadron element. There would be no early returns as they made their way via Ostend to the target on the heels of the flare forces, which had started a little early at 05.05 and had continued until 05.14, at which point they were sent home. The main force was called in to attack under clear skies and in good visibility, the 44 (Rhodesia) Squadron crews identifying the aiming point by means of red TIs, which they bombed from 15,000 to 15,700 feet between 05.18 and 05.26. A number of large explosions occurred at 05.21 and 05.23, and a heavy pall of smoke was rising to meet the crews as they turned away to observe the glow of fires from the Dutch coast up to eighty miles away. There were no losses, and photo-reconnaissance confirmed the claims of the crews, revealing a highly successful raid, which had left the town centre in ruins.

A further attack on German positions around Le Havre was carried out on the 10th and involved almost a thousand aircraft, 5 Group supporting the effort with 108 Lancasters and two Mosquitos, including ten from 44 (Rhodesia) Squadron, which departed Dunholme Lodge between 15.26 and 15.48 with

S/L Millington the senior pilot on duty. There were no early returns, and the crews were greeted at the French coast by clear skies and just a little ground haze, which enabled them to identify the target visually. F/O Croker's bomb-aimer found that he had a defective bomb sight and could not carry out an attack, leaving the others to release their bombs onto red TIs from 10,000 to 11,000 feet between 17.21 and 17.27. There was no opposition, and, by the time that they turned back, the area had become enveloped in smoke. The 11th would bring the final attacks on the environs of the port, and would involve 218 aircraft drawn from 4, 5, 6 and 8 Groups. 5 Group contributed ninety-three Lancasters from 53, 54 and 55 Bases, which arrived in the target area under clear skies with slight haze just after dawn, and located their aiming points, to the north and south of the outer defences, each of which was named after a car manufacturer. Initially, there were no markers on the Cadillac north aiming point, and nothing was heard from the Master Bomber, which left the crews to their own devices. Photo-reconnaissance confirmed accurate and concentrated bombing, and, within hours of this operation, the German garrison surrendered to British forces.

Many of the crews involved in the morning activity, found themselves on the Order of Battle and back in the briefing room later in the day to learn of their part in 5 Group's return to Darmstadt, which had escaped serious damage at its hands during the last week of August. A force of 221 Lancasters and fourteen Mosquitos was made ready, and the 44 (Rhodesia) Squadron element of nineteen departed Dunholme Lodge between 20.40 and 21.19 with F/L Newmarch and the newly promoted F/L Anning, the senior pilots on duty. They began the Channel crossing at Beachy Head, aiming for the French coast near Berck-sur-Mer, before traversing France to enter Germany in the Strasbourg area and turning north to the target. They arrived to find the skies over southern Germany clear of cloud, and, despite some ground haze, good visibility prevailing as the flare force went in at 17,000 feet at 23.52, homing in on a green Mosquito-laid TI. The Master bomber seemed satisfied with the illumination, and required no further flares, leaving the backers-up to drop their TIs over the ensuing four minutes, before being sent home at 23.59. The main force followed up with extreme accuracy and concentration, the 44 (Rhodesia) Squadron crews bombing on red and green TIs from 15,000 to 16,000 feet between 23.59 and 00.11. The city centre became engulfed in flames, which spread outwards to consume large parts of the built-up area, and the glow, according to some, could be seen from the French coast, 250 miles away. The conditions had been ideal for the 5 Group marking method, and photo-reconnaissance confirmed the main weight of the attack to have fallen in the central and surrounding districts to the south and east. It was learned after the war, that the attack had resulted in a genuine firestorm, only the third to be recorded after Hamburg and Kassel in 1943, although a number of local ones may have occurred in other cities like Berlin and Stuttgart. More than twelve thousand people died in the inferno, and a further seventy thousand, 60% of a total population of 120,000, were made homeless. The operation cost the group twelve Lancasters, among which were 44 (Rhodesia) Squadron's LL965 and PB535, the former crashing some seven miles north-west of Worms at 23.30 with the target just a few miles ahead, and there were no survivors from the crew of F/O Westgate. The latter was homebound and just south of Worms when it came down at 01.30, killing F/O Lade RAAF and the rest of his crew, which included three other members of the RAAF.

Orders were received on 5 Group stations on the 12th to prepare for a return to southern Germany that night, this time to target Stuttgart. Eighteen 44 (Rhodesia) Squadron crews attended the briefing at Dunholme Lodge and learned that they were to be part of a force of 195 Lancasters and fourteen Mosquitos, which would be accompanied by nine ABC Lancasters from 1 Group's 101 Squadron. A simultaneous operation by 378 Lancasters and nine Mosquitos of 1, 3 and 8 Groups would take place at Frankfurt, a hundred miles to the north. The 44 (Rhodesia) Squadron element took off between

18.35 and 19.11 with F/Ls Anning, Davey and Oxborrow the senior pilots on duty, and joined the bomber stream as they headed south to adopt a course similar to that of twenty-four hours earlier. They mostly enjoyed an uneventful flight across France to Stuttgart, which was found to be under clear skies with moderate visibility and ground haze, and, therefore, ideal conditions for the low-level markers. The marking and backing up was very accurate, and the main force bombing concentrated upon the city centre, with a slight tendency to creep back towards the north-eastern district of Bad Canstatt and beyond into Feuerbach. The 44 (Rhodesia) Squadron crews bombed on red TIs from 16,000 to 17,000 feet between 23.11 and 23.17, and all but one returned safely to report a successful operation. A huge explosion was reported at 23.25, which lasted for about five seconds, and, when a PRU aircraft photographed the city on the following morning, the entire centre was obscured by the smoke from numerous and widespread fires. Only four Lancasters were missing from this operation, among them 44 (Rhodesia) Squadron's PB189, which crashed at 23.45 onto a goods station within the city, killing F/L Oxborrow DFC and the seven other occupants. Local reports from Stuttgart described the central districts as "erased", and it seems that a firestorm erupted in northern and west-central districts, wiping them from the map. Almost twelve hundred people lost their lives, the highest death toll ever in this much-bombed city.

Other than the first of 617 Squadron's three attacks on Tirpitz on the 15th, launched from Yagodnik in Russia, 5 Group undertook no further operations until the morning of the 17th, when contributing to a total of 762 aircraft assembled to attack troop positions at seven locations around the port of Boulogne. The raids would be staggered over a four-hour period and benefit from a 5 Group effort of 195 Lancasters and four Mosquitos, twenty of the former representing 44 (Rhodesia) Squadron and departing Dunholme Lodge between 06.49 and 07.25 with S/L Bird the senior pilot on duty. He had been posted in two days earlier from 51 Base at Swinderby, which was responsible for crew conversion. The 44 and 619 Squadron elements were part of the first wave of aircraft to attack one of two aiming points assigned to 5 Group and were an hour ahead of the second wave. They found clear skies with good visibility and no opposition, and saw red TIs marking out the aiming point. The Master Bomber's instructions were a little indistinct, but sufficient to direct the bombing, and twelve of the 44 (Rhodesia) Squadron crews delivered their eleven 1,000 and four 500 pounders each from 8,000 to 9,000 feet between 08.36 and 08.46. Eight were either orbiting or on their bombing run when the Master Bomber halted the attack at 08.45, and they either took their bombs home or jettisoned them. The following waves completed the job, although some crews were hampered by drifting smoke, and a total of three thousand tons of bombs was sufficient to pave the way for Allied ground forces to move in shortly afterwards to accept the surrender of the German garrison. This left only Calais of the major French ports still under enemy occupation.

5 Group stations received orders on the 18th to prepare for an operation that night against the port of Bremerhaven, located on the East Bank at the mouth of the River Weser, some thirty miles north of Bremen. It was to be a classic 5 Group-style attack, employing the low-level visual marking method and involved 206 Lancasters and seven Mosquitos. At Dunholme Lodge, 44 (Rhodesia) Squadron loaded fifteen Lancasters with a mix of 2,000 pounders and 500lb J cluster bombs plus incendiaries and sent them off between 17.54 and 18.22 with S/L Millington the senior pilot on duty, and they were followed immediately into the air by the crews of F/Ls Anning and Freestone and F/Os Poole and Slade, bound for the Yams garden in Jade Bay and the Weser estuary. There were no early returns from either element, allowing the squadron to arrive intact in the target area to find favourable weather conditions and good visibility. The bombing brigade ran in on the aiming point at medium level to release their loads onto red TIs from 13,600 to 16,500 feet between 20.55 and 21.10, mostly in

accordance with the Master Bomber's instructions. A number of huge explosions were witnessed at 21.02 and 21.07, and, as they headed out of the target area, they could see many large fires spreading throughout the built-up area, the glow from which remained visible for at least 150 miles. Meanwhile, the gardeners had established their positions by H2S, aided by the light of flares from the nearby raid, and delivered their mines into the briefed locations from 11,800 feet between 20.54 and 20.58. Post-raid reconnaissance revealed that this first major attack on the port, carried out by what, at the time, could be considered to be a modest force, had devasted the built-up areas north and south of the harbour entrance, wiping out installations and warehousing, and only the most northerly and southerly suburbs had escaped complete destruction. Local reports produced a figure of 2,670 buildings reduced to rubble and thirty-thousand people bombed out of their homes, all at the modest cost to 5 Group of a single Lancaster and a Mosquito.

Nineteen 44 (Rhodesia) Squadron crews assembled for briefing at Dunholme Lodge on the 19th and learned that they were to be part of a predominantly 5 Group attack on the twin towns of Mönchengladbach and Rheydt. This represented a shallow penetration into Germany, just ten minutes from the Dutch border, and, therefore, a short round trip of four-and-a-half to five hours, followed by a night in bed. 217 Lancasters and ten Mosquitos were made ready, along with ten ABC Lancasters from 101 Squadron, and the 44 (Rhodesia) Squadron participants took off between 18.38 and 19.08 with F/Ls Anning, Freestone and Newmarch the senior pilots on duty, each Lancaster carrying a 2,000 pounder and eleven 500lb J cluster bombs. The Master Bomber for the operation was W/C Guy Gibson VC, DSO, DFC, who had been agitating to get back into the war before it was over to ensure that his service did not end in a backwater, while others gained the glory by being in at the death. Gibson was a warrior, and the war had brought out of him qualities, which, in peacetime, may have lain dormant. War had also given him a direction, and he revelled in the company of fellow operational types, particularly those of the officer class. Having been torn away from the operational scene following the success of the Dams operation, his purpose had gone, and he had become listless, frustrated and discontented. His time in the operational wilderness had not, however, deprived him of his arrogance and self-belief, and, when the opportunity to fly as Master Bomber on the coming raid presented itself, he grabbed it. He was driven the three miles from Coningsby to Woodhall Spa to collect his 627 Squadron Mosquito, which, for whatever reason, he rejected, and swapped with F/L Mallender, causing a degree of resentment. Gibson had already set the tone for the evening by rejecting the advice of W/C Charles Owen, who had been Master Bomber at this target ten nights earlier. Owen had advised him to leave the target by a south-westerly route, and cross north-eastern France to the coast, and also to observe orders to remain above 10,000 feet. Gibson insisted that he would fly home via a direct route across Holland at low level and would not be dissuaded. He took off ahead of the 627 Squadron element at 19.51, to meet up with the main force over the target, where two aiming points were to be marked.

Some crews reported icing clouds at around 9,000 feet as they made their way to the target over Belgium at around 9,000 feet, and chose to keep below, before climbing fast to 15,000 feet as the cloud dispersed. The marking was complex, with a green marker to be dropped on a factory in a western district of Mönchengladbach, and a yellow marker on railway yards in the north, while a red marker was to be placed on railway yards in Rheydt, two miles to the south. It would have been a demanding plan even for an experienced Master Bomber, which Gibson was not, but, even so, his instructions were heard clearly. All seemed to be going to plan, with accurate and punctual marking for the green and yellow forces, but late, though accurate marking for the red force, and some of the red force crews were diverted to the green aiming point. The 44 (Rhodesia) Squadron crews were assigned to the green force, and identified it by flares and TIs, before bombing from 13,100 to 15,500 feet between 21.40 and 21.56, observing the target to be well ablaze with the glow visible for at least a hundred miles into the return flight. Post-raid reconnaissance confirmed a highly destructive attack on both towns for the loss of four Lancasters and a Mosquito. Gibson had returned low over Holland, just as he said he would, and crashed on the outskirts of Steenbergen in south-western Holland, with fatal consequences for him, and Coningsby's recently appointed station navigation officer, S/L James Warwick.

It was now time to turn attention upon Calais as the final port still under enemy occupation. Only one 5 Group Lancaster was involved in the first round of attacks on enemy positions on the 20th, after which, the group remained inactive until the 23rd. Orders came through on that morning to prepare 136 Lancasters and five Mosquitos for an attack that night on the aqueduct section of the Dortmund-Ems Canal south of Ladbergen. It was the scene of a disaster for 617 Squadron in September 1943, when five of eight crews had failed to return. An element from 617 Squadron would be on scene also on this night, to open the attack with Tallboys, to which the raised banks containing the waterway were particularly vulnerable. Germany's canal system was a vital component in the transport network and facilitated the import of raw materials and the export of finished goods to support the war effort. Its wide thoroughfares allowed the passage of large barges, and, as the slack in Germany's war production was taken up during 1944, traffic was being pushed through at increasing levels. While this operation was in progress, a second 5 Group force of 108 Lancasters, four Mosquitos and the P38 Lightning would hit the Handorf night-fighter airfield some ten miles to the south to prevent it from interfering. The main operation on this night, however, would be conducted by 549 aircraft from 1, 3, 4 and 8 Groups seventy miles to the south-west at Neuss, situated across the Rhine opposite Düsseldorf, and this, hopefully, might help to split the enemy defences.

44 (Rhodesia) Squadron prepared nineteen Lancasters to attack Handorf aerodrome, and they departed Dunholme Lodge between 18.30 and 19.08 with S/L Bird the senior pilot on duty. All reached the target area to encounter a layer of ten-tenths cloud between 8,000 and 9,500 feet, but with good visibility beneath. The Master Bomber found himself unable to direct the attack, and experienced great difficulty in communicating the fact to his Deputy because of intense interference on VHF. Identification and marking of the aiming points proved to be difficult, and only two green TIs could be seen by a few crews. There would be complaints later that there was no control, and some crews orbited and remained in the target area for up to thirty-five minutes before bombing either on green TIs at Handorf or on yellows at Münster, which was selected as the last-resort target. Nine 44 (Rhodesia) Squadron crews carried out their attacks on Handorf from 16,000 to 18,000 feet between 21.49 and 22.14, while seven, including that of S/L Bird, were unable to establish a pinpoint and those of F/Ls Anning and Dobson and F/O Coventry bombed Münster. Fourteen Lancasters failed to return after the Canal-Busters were badly mauled by night-fighters on the way home, but post-raid reconnaissance revealed that breaches in both branches of the canal, probably caused by Tallboys, had left a six-mile stretch drained and unnavigable. It also revealed no new damage at Handorf, where only twenty-two aircraft had bombed.

The second of the series of raids on enemy positions around Calais was mounted by 188 aircraft on the 24th, for which 5 Group detailed thirty Lancasters from the 53 Base stations of Skellingthorpe and Waddington. In the event, only 126 aircraft bombed, eight of them from 5 Group, and they attacked either on a reference provided by Oboe skymarkers or came below the cloud base to bomb visually. At such a height, they were sitting ducks for the heavy and light flak batteries, which accounted for seven Lancasters and a Halifax. It was a similar story on the following day, when only a third of more than eight hundred aircraft were able to deliver their bombs, before the Master Bomber called a halt to proceedings in the face of low cloud. The campaign continued on the 26th, with two separate raids against seven enemy positions around Cap Gris Nez and nearer Calais involving more than seven hundred aircraft. This time the conditions were favourable, and bombing was observed to be concentrated around the aiming points.

On the afternoon of the 26th, nineteen 44 (Rhodesia) Squadron crews attended briefing, and learned that the night's operation was to be against the city of Karlsruhe in southern Germany, for which 216 Lancasters of 5 Group were made ready, along with ten of the ABC variety from 101 Squadron and eleven Mosquitos. It was to be a two-phase attack with a two-hour gap between, and the 52, 53 and 55 Base elements assigned to the second phase. This meant a late take-off, and it was between 00.15 and 01.15 that the 44 (Rhodesia) Squadron crews departed Dunholme Lodge with S/L Millington the senior pilot on duty. They flew out over France with ten-tenths cloud beneath them, which persisted all the way to the target, but thinned to a narrow band with the base estimated to be at between 6,000 and 7,000 feet. The plan was to bomb through the cloud on H2S, guided by Wanganui flares, and some approaching crews observed a red TI cascade above the cloud at 03.54. The 44 (Rhodesia) Squadron crews focused on the glow of red and green TIs and bombed them from 12,750 and 15,500 feet between 04.00 and 04.07 in accordance with the instructions of the Master Bomber. All returned safely to report what appeared to be a city in flames and the glow of fires visible for up to 150 miles into the return journey. There were no plottable bombing photos, but reconnaissance confirmed that the attack had been spread throughout the city and had left a large part of it devastated.

As the crews returned to their stations after 07.00, elements of 1, 3, 4 and 8 Groups were preparing to leave theirs for a further attack on the Calais area. On arrival, the Master Bomber ordered the 340-strong force to come below the cloud base to bomb visually, and another successful operation ensued. Later that day, seventeen 44 (Rhodesia) Squadron crews attended briefing for an operation that night against Kaiserslautern, an historic city on the edge of the Palatinate Forest, some thirty miles west of Mannheim. It would be the first major attack of the war on this location, for which a force of 217 Lancasters, including ten from 101 Squadron, and ten Mosquitos, was made ready. The 44 (Rhodesia) Squadron Lancasters were loaded with 2,000 pounders, 500lb J cluster bombs and 4lb incendiaries, which they lifted into the air between 21.01 and 22.07 with F/Ls Dobson and Freestone the senior pilots on duty. Clear skies over England gave way to a build-up of cloud over the Channel, and, from the French coast to near the target, they encountered ten-tenths cumulus with a base at 2,800 feet. The target was partially covered by a thin layer of five to eight-tenths cloud with tops at 3,000 feet, with a further layer at 6,000 to 7,000 feet. The marking with red and green TIs was punctual and accurate, and a green TI visible in the centre of the town became the objective for the main force crews in accordance with the Master Bomber's instructions at 00.58. The 44 (Rhodesia) Squadron crews attacked from 4,000 to 5,500 feet between 01.00 and 01.08 and observed the bombing to be concentrated. Two yellow explosions were seen at 01.02, and fires were beginning to take hold as the force retreated towards the west. Reconnaissance revealed massive damage within the city, caused by more than nine hundred tons of bombs, and an estimated 36% of the built-up area was reduced to ruins.

The final raids on German positions around Calais were carried out by 490 aircraft of 1, 3, 6 and 8 Groups on the 28th, and the garrison surrendered to Canadian forces shortly thereafter. The squadron changed address for the final time during the war on the 30th, when moving to Spilsby, which, together with East Kirkby and Strubby, constituted 55 Base. 207 Squadron had been the sole occupants for the past year and would now have to share the facilities with the new arrivals. Dunholme Lodge was taken out of the front line, and 52 Base would be disbanded within two days. During the course of the month the squadron participated in thirteen operations and dispatched 212 sorties for the loss of three Lancasters and their crews.

October 1944

A theme running throughout October would be a campaign against the island of Walcheren in the Scheldt estuary, where heavy gun emplacements were barring the approaches to the much-needed port of Antwerp some forty miles upstream. Attempts to bomb these positions in September had proved unsuccessful, and it was decided to flood the land, both to inundate the batteries, and to render the terrain difficult to defend when the ground forces moved in. 252 Lancasters were drawn from 1, 5 and 8 Groups and made ready on the 3rd to attack the seawalls at Westkapelle, the most westerly point of the island. 5 Group contributed 128 Lancasters, allotted to four of eight waves of thirty aircraft each, with the Tallboy-carrying 617 Squadron Lancasters standing off to be called in only if required. A breach was opened by the fifth wave, which was extended by those following behind, and the flood waters had reached the town by the time the last Lancasters turned for home. 44 (Rhodesia) Squadron had not been invited to take part, and it was the 4th when orders were received to prepare three Lancasters for mining duties in the Silverthorn III garden in the Kattegat as part of a seventeen-strong 5 Group force. The crews of F/O Evans and F/Ls Anning and Dobson departed Spilsby between 17.24 and 17.28 bound for Sejerø Bay off the north-western coast of Denmark's Sjælland island, and F/Ls Anning and Dobson reached the target area to find good visibility and varying amounts of cloud between zero and eight-tenths. They encountered no opposition and delivered their six vegetables each from 12,000 feet within four minutes of each other either side of 21.00. PB235 failed to return with the crew of F/O Evans, who died with four others, it is believed, after abandoning the Lancaster, which crashed on Sams island, some twenty miles from the drop zone. The likelihood is, that they came down in the cold waters of the Baltic and drowned, three of them to be recovered for burial, while the two survivors were taken into captivity.

5 Group's first major outing of the month was posted on the 5th and was a daylight attempt to bomb the port of Wilhelmshaven through ten-tenths cloud on H2S. A force of 227 Lancasters, one Mosquito and the P38 Lightning was assembled with 44 (Rhodesia) Squadron providing eighteen aircraft, which set out from Spilsby between 08.04 and 08.20 with S/L Millington the senior pilot on duty. Whether or not it was part of the plan, the controller led the force around the northern side of Heligoland, before heading for Jade Bay, where they found the forecast layer of ten-tenths cloud between 3,000 and 5,000 feet with good visibility above. The 44 (Rhodesia) Squadron crews established their positions by H2S-fix or by observing others and delivered their ten 1,000 pounders and four 500lb J cluster bombs each from 15,000 to 18,000 feet between 11.03 and 11.08. No results were observed, and there was no possibility of making an assessment, but the impression of a scattered attack was confirmed later when photo-reconnaissance became possible.

From this point until the end of the war, German towns and cities were to be subjected to a new and terrible bomber offensive, beginning with a second Ruhr campaign, which was to open at Dortmund, and for which a 3, 6 and 8 Group force of 523 aircraft was made ready on the 6th. 5 Group, meanwhile, had its own target, and prepared 237 Lancasters and seven Mosquitos for what would prove to be the thirty-second and final raid of the war on the city of Bremen. 44 (Rhodesia) Squadron loaded seventeen Lancasters with a mixture of high explosives and incendiaries and dispatched them from Spilsby between 17.12 and 17.52 with F/L Davey the senior pilot on duty. Having climbed out and set course, they left the cloud behind and headed into crystal clear skies over the North Sea with a three-quarter moon. F/O Lewis and crew were some forty miles north of the central Frisians when their port-outer engine failed and ended their sortie. The others found the target area to be free of cloud, which was ideal for the 5 Group low-level marking method, and the conditions handed the hapless city on a plate to the bombers. The 44 (Rhodesia) Squadron crews carried out their attacks in the face of many searchlights and the usual flak response and aimed for the red and green TIs from 18,000 to 19,500 feet between 20.25 and 20.31. They turned away from a city in flames, the glow from which remained visible for a hundred miles and more. The success of the operation was confirmed by post-raid reconnaissance and local reports, which described a huge area of fire, and catalogued the destruction of more than 4,800 houses and apartment blocks, and severe damage to war industry factories, all achieved at the modest cost of five aircraft. Now that the focus of operations had moved from France to Germany, the number of sorties to complete a tour had been reduced from thirty-five to thirty-three, and this meant an unexpected bonus to some, who found themselves suddenly declared tour-expired.

Following the failure of Operation Market Garden, the German frontier towns of Cleves (Kleve) and Emmerich were earmarked for attention by daylight on the 7th. Five miles apart and separated by the Rhine, both would suffer massive damage at the hands of large forces from 1, 3, 4 and 8 Groups. 5 Group, meanwhile, was to return to Walcheren, to target the seawalls near Flushing, and made ready 121 Lancasters and three Mosquitos, fourteen of the former representing 44 (Rhodesia) Squadron. They took off between 12.06 and 12.18 with S/L Bird the senior pilot on duty, and all reached the target area to identify the two aiming points visually and by red TIs. The 44 (Rhodesia) Squadron crews delivered their fourteen 1,000 pounders each in two runs between five and twelve minutes apart from 5,000 to 8,500 feet between 13.41 and 13.57. Many of the bombs carried by other squadrons contained a thirty-minute delay fuse, while others detonated on impact, and the dyke was already beginning to crumble as the bombers headed home, where confirmation of a successful outcome would catch up with them.

Focus remained on the Scheldt defences, and the gun battery at Fort Frederik Hendrik near Breskens on the East Scheldt was targeted by elements of 1 and 8 Groups on the 11th, while 115 Lancasters from 5 Group were assigned to others near Flushing on the North Bank of the West Scheldt. At the same time, sixty-one Lancasters and two Mosquitos from the group were to attempt to breach the seawalls at Veere, situated on the eastern side of Walcheren opposite Westkapelle. 44 (Rhodesia) Squadron contributed fourteen Lancasters to Veere, and they departed Spilsby between 13.11 and 13.36 with S/L Bird the senior pilot on duty. F/O Sutherland and crew lost their hydraulics as they crossed the English coast, but pressed on with the intention of using the emergency air bottle to lower the bomb doors. They were orbiting north of the target awaiting their turn to run in with the undercarriage having flopped down through the lack of hydraulic pressure, and then found that no air bottle was on board, and they could not open the bomb doors. On arrival at their respective targets, the other crews encountered varying amounts of cloud between two and seven-tenths with tops at 4,000 to 5,000 feet, and the 44 (Rhodesia) Squadron crews carried out their attacks from 4,000 to 7,000 feet between 14.49 and 15.01. Post-raid reconnaissance revealed an area of flooding of 800 x 250 yards at Veere, but no new damage to the gun positions.

The 14th brought the postings of F/Ls Anning and Dobson and their crews to 617 Squadron after impressing during their time with 44 (Rhodesia) squadron, and both would survive the war. This was also the day on which were fired the opening salvoes of Operation Hurricane, a terrifying demonstration to the enemy of the overwhelming superiority of the Allied air forces ranged against it. Bomber Command ordered a maximum effort from all but 5 Group to attack Duisburg, for which 1,013 Lancasters, Halifaxes and Mosquitos answered the call. The American 8th Air Force would also be in business on this day, targeting the Cologne area further south with 1,250 bombers escorted by 749 fighters. The RAF force took off at first light, picked up its own fighter escort, and delivered 4,500 tons of high-explosives and incendiaries into Duisburg shortly after breakfast time, causing unimaginable destruction. That night, similar numbers returned to press home the point about superiority, bringing the total weight of bombs over the two raids to 9,000 tons from 2,018 sorties in fewer than twenty-four hours. The only involvement by 5 Group were single sorties by a Lancaster and a Mosquito to conduct a photo-reconnaissance of the operation.

However, 5 Group took advantage of the evening activity over the Ruhr to return to Braunschweig, the scene of quite a number of unsatisfactory previous attempts to land a really telling blow. A force of 232 Lancasters and eight Mosquitos was made ready, of which seventeen of the former were provided by 44 (Rhodesia) Squadron. They departed Spilsby in the wake of the 207 Squadron element between 22.56 and 23.11 with S/L Bird the senior pilot on duty, and all reached the target area to find conditions ideal for low-level marking. Approaching the target at 18,000 feet from the south-west over Hallendorf and Salzgitter, the latter the home to the Reichswerke Hermann Göring steelworks, crews had to run the gauntlet of searchlight cones and heavy flak for the three minutes it took to pass through. They were greeted by clear skies and good visibility, which facilitated accurate marking with red and green TIs by the heavy brigade, and, although the early stages of bombing tended to undershoot, the Master Bomber quickly brought it back on track, calling for crews to overshoot by up to nineteen seconds. The 44 (Rhodesia) Squadron contingent passed over the aiming point at 17,250 to 18,000 feet between 02.30 and 02.36 and delivered their loads accurately to contribute to a highly effective raid. 83 Squadron's F/O Price complained that main force crews were jettisoning incendiaries all the way back as far as the Rhine, and thereby illuminating the track for any stalking night fighters. In the event, only a single Lancaster failed to return from what was, indeed, confirmed to be an outstanding result, which had wiped out the entire centre of this historic city, and visited damage on almost every district.

On the following night, 5 Group sent five Lancasters to mine the waters of the Silverthorn garden in the Kattegat region of the western Baltic. Two 207 Squadron crews represented Spilsby, and both failed to return. Stubborn resistance by the occupiers on Walcheren demanded further operations against the seawalls at Westkapelle, for which 5 Group detailed forty-seven Lancasters and three Mosquitos on the 17th. 44 (Rhodesia) Squadron loaded each of five Lancasters with fourteen 1,000 pounders fitted with delay fuses of varying lengths and dispatched them from Spilsby between 12.59 and 13.14 with no senior pilots on duty. They arrived at the target to find favourable conditions, and four bombed within seconds of each other at 14.01 from 5,500 to 5,700 feet, leaving F/O Daggett and crew to bring up the rear at 14.06. They returned safely home with an aiming point photo each, while a reconnaissance aircraft remained over the target from 14.55 to 15.10 to record the delayed-action bomb blasts, but the photos would reveal no extension to the breach in the dyke.

Following a night off, twenty 44 (Rhodesia) Squadron crews joined eighteen from 207 Squadron in the Spilsby briefing room on the 19th, to receive details of the 5 Group operation that night against Nuremberg, while 560 aircraft from the other groups plied their trade at Stuttgart, some ninety miles to the south-west. A new record 5 Group force of 263 Lancasters and seven Mosquitos stood ready in the early evening, and the 44 (Rhodesia) Squadron element began taking off at 17.10, each bearing aloft a 2,000 pounder and twelve 500lb J Cluster bombs. They were all safely airborne within fourteen minutes, with F/Ls Davey and Heath the senior pilots on duty, but the former lost his starboard-inner engine, and was back on the ground after two hours. As F/O Kelly climbed away, an escape hatch cover broke away at 800 feet, leaving him uncertain as to what to do next. He circled the airfield while the wireless operator sought instructions with an Aldis lamp, but on receiving no response, it was decided to continue with the sortie. At 15,000 feet, F/O Kelly began to experience back pain, and by the time they had reached the French coast, this had become severe and was followed by nausea. The bomb-aimer took over the controls for an hour, gradually reducing altitude until they were safely out of the bomber stream and could turn back, at which point, the mid-upper gunner reported the failure of his oxygen supply. Still unwell, F/O Kelly took over the controls again, and brought the Lancaster back to a safe landing. As far as the others were concerned, the outward flight across France was uneventful, and they found the target to be covered by a wedge of eight to ten-tenths cloud between 3,000 and 10,000 feet, with poor visibility below. The marker force laid down flares and backed them up with others along with red and green TIs, which were observed to be somewhat scattered, and bombing had to take place on their glow seen through the cloud. The 44 (Rhodesia) Squadron crews carried out their attacks from 16,500 to 19,900 feet between 20.56 and 21.04 in accordance with the Master Bomber's instructions, before returning home uncertain as to the outcome. The impression given by the glow of fires was of an effective attack, but post-raid reconnaissance revealed the bombing to have fallen not on the intended city centre aiming point, but predominantly into the more industrial southern districts, where almost four hundred houses were destroyed, along with forty-one industrial buildings.

It was back to Walcheren on the 23rd for 112 Lancasters of 5 Group, this time to target the coastal battery at Flushing. The Spilsby squadrons loaded six Lancasters each with fourteen 1,000 pounders, the 44 Squadron (Rhodesia) element taking off between 15.10 and 15.14 with no senior pilots on duty. They were greeted at the target by eight to ten-tenths cloud with a base at between 3,000 and 5,000 feet, and poor visibility below caused by haze and rain. The force was led in on what appeared to be a decent approach but was ordered to "orbit port" as the lead crews experienced great difficulty in identifying their respective aiming points. A second run was no more revealing, even for those crews who ventured down as low as 2,000 feet, and twenty would still have their bombs on board when ordered to go home. Five of the 44 (Rhodesia) Squadron crews carried out their attacks from 4,000 to 4,500 feet between 16.29 and 16.31 and were among eighty-eight crews to do so. LM645 failed to return, having been brought down in the target area, and there were no survivors from the crew of F/O Russell. Post-raid reconnaissance revealed evidence of seventy bomb bursts, including four near-misses, and the destruction of a number of buildings on the site.

That evening, a new record force of 1,055 aircraft was sent against Essen as part of the Hurricane "message", and dropped 4,538 tons of bombs, more than 90% of which was high explosive. This number was achieved without 5 Group, which took the night off, and committed only twenty-five Lancasters to gardening duties in northern waters on the following night. 44 (Rhodesia) Squadron briefed the crews of F/Ls Freestone and Heath and F/Os Hart and Sutherland for the Yew Tree garden, which was between the mainland of North Jutland and Læso island in the northern Kattegat. They took off between 17.04 and 17.28 and reached the target area to find ten-tenths very low cloud with tops at between 2,000 and 6,000 feet. They established their positions by H2S-fix and delivered their six mines each from 7,000 and 10,000 feet between 21.46 and 21.49, before returning safely from uneventful sorties. Essen was pounded again by more than seven hundred aircraft in daylight on the 25th, after which it ceased to be an important source of war production. Operation Hurricane moved on to Cologne on the 28th, when two districts east of the centre were totally devastated by more than seven hundred aircraft.

5 Group occupied the day with the preparation of a force of 237 Lancasters and seven Mosquitos for an operation that night against the U-Boot pens at Bergen in Norway. 44 (Rhodesia) Squadron made ready eighteen Lancasters and dispatched them between 22.04 and 23.08 with F/Ls Davey, Freestone and Heath the senior pilots on duty. There were only two early returns from the entire force, which reached the target area after a three-and-a-half-hour outward flight, having battled their way through electrical storms. They had been told to expect clear conditions, although some doubts had been expressed about the forecast, and these were confirmed when the force was met by eight-to ten-tenths cloud between 4,000 and 14,000 feet, which obscured the aiming point. This would not have been a problem over Germany, but the risk to Norwegian civilians was uppermost in the mind of the Master Bomber as he pondered his options before calling for the main force to descend. Even then, most were unable to pick out any markers, and the situation was exacerbated by intermittent VHF reception, which persuaded 83 Squadron's F/L Cornish to fly up and down the coast acting as a communications link between the Master Bomber and the main force. The flare force contingent did what they could from between 12,500 and 15,000 feet, and the main force supporters flew as low as 4,500 feet, without being able to identify the target. The operation was abandoned after only forty-seven aircraft had bombed, and the entire 44 (Rhodesia) Squadron element was sent home with their loads intact, parts of which would be jettisoned on the way.

The final operations against Walcheren were undertaken by 5 Group on the 30th, when two forces of fifty-one Lancasters and four Mosquitos each were sent against coastal batteries at Westkapelle and Flushing. 44 (Rhodesia) Squadron contributed eight Lancasters to the Westkapelle attack, and they departed Spilsby in the wake of the 207 Squadron element between 10.39 and 10.44 with no senior pilots on duty. They ran into four to seven-tenths cloud at 6,000 feet over the target, despite which, visibility was good, and the aiming point was identified visually and marked by red TIs. Some of these became buried in the dunes and were partially concealed, leading to a little overshooting, but the 44 (Rhodesia) Squadron crews were able to deliver their loads accurately from 3,400 to 3,600 feet between 12.01 and 12.06. Ground forces went in on the following day, and a week of heavy fighting preceded the island's capture. Even then, the clearing of mines from the approaches to Antwerp kept the port out of commission for a further three weeks. On the evening of the 30th, nine hundred aircraft returned to Cologne, and almost five hundred went back again twenty-four hours later to complete the destruction of the Rhineland Capital. During the course of the month the squadron carried out twelve operations and dispatched 144 sorties for the loss of two Lancasters and their crews.

November 1944

The new month began with a daylight operation on the afternoon of the 1st, against the Meerbeck synthetic oil plant at Moers/Homberg, on the West Bank of the Rhine facing Duisburg. 44 (Rhodesia) Squadron briefed eighteen crews as part of an overall 5 Group force of 226 Lancasters and two Mosquitos, which were to be joined by fourteen 8 Group Mosquitos to provide the Oboe marking. They took off from Spilsby between 13.31 and 13.44 with S/L Bird the senior pilot on duty, and, as events turned out, were fortunate to precede 207 Squadron's twenty Lancasters into the air. All proceeded as planned until PD290 EM-N swerved out of control and careered off the runway to plough into 429 Squadron Halifax, MZ424, which, along with a number of others from the Canadian Squadron, was parked by the control tower after being diverted on return from Cologne. The incident prevented the six remaining 207 Squadron Lancasters from taking-off to join up with the rest of the force, which reached the target to find it completely obscured by cloud with tops at between 6,000 and 9,000 feet. Wanganui flares from earlier arrivals were well-scattered over a circle with a ten-mile radius, prompting a backer-up from 83 Squadron to drop a yellow TI over the built-up area, in the hope of attracting some bombing. The problem seemed to be, that crews at the head of the stream had seen no markers or were past them by the time that they became evident and had taken their bombs home. Some 44 (Rhodesia) Squadron crews caught a glimpse of the target area through a chink in the cloud, while others carried out a time-and-distance run from the last visual pinpoint, before aiming at red skymarkers to deliver their fourteen 1,000 pounders each from 16,000 to 17,000 feet between 16.08 and 16.12. F/O Worrall saw only what he thought were three red verey flares, and, in the knowledge that Allied ground forces were in the vicinity of the West Bank of the Rhine, opted to retain his bombs. The attackers had faced an intense flak response, and 44 (Rhodesia) Squadron's LM650 was hit, mortally wounding the pilot, F/O Haworth, who succumbed within five minutes, and injuring the flight engineer. The bomb-aimer, F/Sgt Walters, took over the controls and brought the Lancaster and crew back to English airspace, where the pilot was attached to a parachute and dropped out, followed by the rest of the crew. The flight engineer failed to survive, while the others landed safely and the Lancaster crashed at 17.45 near Battle, in what is now East Sussex. F/Sgt Walters was awarded the Conspicuous Gallantry Medal, which would be gazetted on the 19th. Homberg already had an evil reputation as a flak hotspot, and there was plenty of work for the ground crews at Spilsby to repair damaged engines and patch holes. At debriefing many crews reported difficulty in hearing the Master Bomber, after his VHF transmissions became jammed by someone in another aircraft leaving the transmit button on. Ultimately, the conditions rendered the whole attack ineffective, and, although 159 crews released their bombs, it is unlikely that any hit the intended target.

Düsseldorf's turn to face a massive force came on the 2nd, when 992 aircraft were made ready for what would prove to be the final major raid of the war on this much-bombed city. 5 Group put up 187 Lancasters for this rare experience for the "Lincolnshire Poachers" to operate with the rest of the Command. The 44 (Rhodesia) Squadron element of eighteen took off between 16.19 and 16.46 with S/L Newmarch the senior pilot on duty but lost the services of F/O Jetson and crew when their Gee failed as they climbed out. They were above cloud at the time and could not see the rest of the squadron, which they had intended to follow, and, by the time that they had descended to below the cloud base, they were twenty minutes behind and too late to continue. The others arrived at the target to find clear skies, moonlight and only ground haze to slightly mar the vertical visibility. The moonlight nullified the searchlights ringing the city, but, of greater concern, was the heavy flak bursting at 17,000 to 20,000 feet. The main force crews found the aiming point to be well illuminated and marked with red and green TIs, onto which each of the 44 (Rhodesia) Squadron participants dropped a cookie, six 1,000 pounders and six 500 pounders from 17,000 to 21,000 feet between 19.15 and 19.35. Returning crews reported fires beginning to take hold and smoke rising to 2,000 feet as they turned away and were confident of a successful raid. This was confirmed by post-raid reconnaissance, which revealed that the northern half of the city had received the main weight of bombs, and that five thousand houses had been destroyed or seriously damaged.

The continuing campaign against Ruhr cities would be prosecuted by 749 aircraft at Bochum on the 4th, while 5 Group renewed its acquaintance with the Dortmund-Ems Canal, which had been repaired following the successful breaching of its banks near Ladbergen in September. Now that Germany's railways were being pounded, the Dortmund-Ems and the nearby Mittelland Canal, took on a greater significance as vital components in the transportation system, particularly with regard to the movement of raw materials to and from the Ruhr region. A force of 168 Lancasters and two Mosquitos contained thirteen 44 (Rhodesia) Squadron aircraft, which took off between 17.36 and 17.54 with F/L Davey the senior pilot on duty. They were headed for the familiar aqueduct section of the canal near Ladbergen and hoped to sneak in under cover of the main operation sixty miles to the south, and, hopefully, avoid the attentions of night-fighters. The first marker aircraft of 83 Squadron arrived at the target at 19.19, after making a GPI run (ground position indicated) by means of H2S from Münster and encountered clear skies with ground haze. A blind-dropped green TI burst on the canal bank four hundred yards short of the aiming point, and the flare force went in between 19.20 and 19.28. Red TIs were observed to fall between the two aqueducts, after which, the Master Bomber cancelled the third wave of flares and sent them all home to leave the way clear for the main force. The first bombs tended to overshoot, but, thereafter, the main force produced an accurate and concentrated attack, the 44 (Rhodesia) Squadron crews bombing from 10,000 to 13,000 feet between 19.31 and 19.36. Among three missing Lancasters was PB192, from which F/O Allwood and four of his crew parachuted into the arms of the enemy, while both gunners failed to survive. Photo-reconnaissance confirmed that both branches of the canal had been breached and drained, leaving barges stranded and the waterway unnavigable.

To capitalize on the success, an attack was planned for the 6th against the Mittelland Canal at Gravenhorst, a point about a mile north of Das Nasse Dreieck, the "Wet Triangle" at Bergeshövede. This is a triangular basin, where the two waterways converge about ten miles north of Ladbergen, before the Dortmund-Ems continues on to the west, and the Mittelland north and then to the east. It was in this basin that the lives of S/L Allesbrook and the other seven members of his 617 Squadron crew had ended in September 1943. It was a 5 Group show involving 239 Lancasters and seven Mosquitos, sixteen of the former representing 44 (Rhodesia) Squadron. They departed Spilsby between 16.14 and 16.54 with F/Ls Davey and Heath and the newly promoted Capt Hirschfeld of the South African Air Force the senior pilots on duty, and all reached the target area to find clear skies but haze up to around 4,000 feet affecting the visibility. The Master Bomber called in the flare force, despite which, the low-level Mosquito markers experienced great difficulty in identifying the aiming point. A single Mosquito eventually did deliver its target indicator accurately onto the aiming point, where it fell into the water and was extinguished. The Master Bomber called a halt to proceedings after thirty-one aircraft had bombed, and the 44 (Rhodesia) Squadron participants jettisoned the delayed-action 1,000 pounders, before setting course for home and encountering not only night-fighter activity, but also very challenging weather conditions of electrical storms and low cloud. Ten Lancasters failed to return, but all from 44 (Rhodesia) Squadron landed safely.

Earlier on the 6th, a series of raids on Ruhr oil refineries had begun with a heavy area attack at Gelsenkirchen, and this was followed by smaller-scale operations at Homberg on the 8th, Wanne-Eickel on the 9th and Castrop-Rauxel on the morning of the 11th. A change in leadership at 44 (Rhodesia) Squadron saw W/C Thompson DSO, DFC, AFC depart for HQ 7 Group on the 9th, to be succeeded on promotion by W/C Newmarch. Fifteen 44 (Rhodesia) Squadron crews joined seventeen from 207 Squadron in the Spilsby briefing room to learn that they would shortly be attacking the Rhenania-Ossag synthetic oil refinery at Harburg, situated on the South Bank of the Elbe opposite Hamburg. 237 Lancasters and eight Mosquitos were to take part in another all-5 Group show, while elements of 1 and 8 Groups targeted a similar plant at Dortmund. Most of the Spilsby Lancasters were loaded with a cookie, six 1,000 and five 500 pounders, while a few would carry fourteen Nº14 cluster bombs with their cookie. Another early evening take-off had the 44 (Rhodesia) Squadron element airborne between 16.28 and 16.43 with F/L Richardson and Capt Hirschfeld leading the way. There were no early returns to Spilsby, and the 44 (Rhodesia) squadron element reached the target area to find largely clear conditions, with only a thin layer of stratus at 8,000 feet and another at 17,000 to 18,000 feet between them and the aiming point. This they identified either by H2S or red and green TIs, before delivering their loads from 16,000 to 19,000 feet between 19.20 and 19.30. The defenders threw up a heavy flak barrage, which reached as high as 23,000 feet, but there were no Spilsby Lancasters among the seven that failed to return. As the homebound F/O Caryer and crew joined the crowded Spilsby circuit in LM648, they collided with PB428 of 207 Squadron, and both aircraft plunged to earth with no survivors. In a sombre atmosphere at debriefing, crews reported a large explosion at 19.28, followed by an oil fire, and local reports would confirm that heavy damage had been inflicted upon the town's residential and industrial districts.

The 16th was devoted to the destruction of the three small towns of Heinsberg, Jülich and Düren, located respectively in an arc from north to east of Aachen, and close to the German lines upon which the American ground forces were advancing. A total of 1,188 aircraft was involved, and 1, 5 and 8 Groups provided the heavy bombing and marking force of 485 Lancasters for the last-mentioned. 44 (Rhodesia) Squadron contributed eighteen aircraft to the 5 Group effort of 214, and they took off from Spilsby between 12.36 and 12.49 with F/Ls Hayler and Richardson the senior pilots on duty, and each carrying eleven 1,000 and four 500 pounders. They flew to the target over ten-tenths cloud, which cleared to three-tenths stratus above 6,000 feet as they approached the aiming point in the final wave of the attack. They bombed in accordance with the instructions of the Master Bomber from 10,000 to 13,000 feet between 15.35 and 15.42, and observed smoke rising through 9,000 feet as they turned for home, confident in the success of the attack. All of the Spilsby crews claimed to have hit the target, but most of the photos were unplottable because of the smoke covering the area. The operation was a complete success at a cost of just three aircraft, and post-raid reconnaissance confirmed that the town had been all-but erased from the map, and local reports gave a death toll in excess of three thousand inhabitants. In the event, unfavourable ground conditions prevented the American advance from succeeding.

Nineteen 44 (Rhodesia) Squadron crews joined eighteen from 207 Squadron in the Spilsby briefing room on the 21st, to be told, that they were going back to the Mittelland Canal on a night of multiple operations involving 1,345 sorties. Three operations, each by 270 aircraft, were to be directed at railway yards at Aschaffenburg, situated about twenty miles south-east of Frankfurt, and oil plants at Castrop-Rauxel and Sterkrade in the Ruhr. 5 Group prepared two forces of 137 and 123 Lancasters respectively, with Mosquito support, for the Mittelland and Dortmund-Ems Canals, while a whole host of minor operations would complete the Order of Battle. The Spilsby squadrons were assigned to the former at Gravenhorst, for which the 44 (Rhodesia) Squadron element took off between 17.34 and 18.11 led by recently promoted pilots of flight lieutenant rank and Capt Hirschfeld. Having taken off last and behind schedule, F/O Fugger and crew cut corners on the route to make up time and would arrive at the target with the rest of the squadron. They encountered a layer of six to ten-tenths cloud in the target area between 4,000 and 8,000 feet, which did not inhibit the accuracy of the marking, but the instructions of the Master Bomber caused some confusion, a situation exacerbated by a week VHF signal. At first, he ordered the crews to come below the cloud base, to which some responded, before he changed his mind and told them to return to the briefed bombing height. This led to bombing heights among the 44 (Rhodesia) Squadron participants ranging from 4,000 to 9,500 feet. He issued instructions to aim for the more southerly of two red TIs, and they complied as best they could between

21.02 to 21.19, observing what appeared to be a good concentration of bomb bursts. F/L Mangos and F/Os Hart and Wood joined in at Ladbergen after failing to recognize their primary target because of smoke and a lack of TIs and delivered their attacks from 3,000 to 8,250 feet between 20.58 and 21.05. Post-raid reconnaissance revealed that the Mittelland Canal had been breached over a distance of fifty feet on the western bank, south of the road bridge, and this had left a thirty-mile stretch of the waterway drained with fifty-nine barges stranded in one small section.

Reconnaissance at Ladbergen revealed success also, showing the left-hand channel, which was the only one repaired since the last attack, to have been breached again where it crossed the River Glane, which had been unable to cope with the volume of water released, leading to extensive flooding on both sides of the canal. The two operations were concluded for the loss of just two 49 Squadron Lancasters. The Germans recognized that repairing the canals was an open invitation to Bomber Command to return, but so vital were they to the transportation system, that they could not be abandoned. The answer was to complete repairs, but to leave the sections drained and apparently still under repair, until sufficient traffic had built up to push through in one night. They would then be flooded and re-emptied to dupe RAF reconnaissance flights and maintain the deception.

On the following night, 5 Group dispatched 171 Lancasters and seven Mosquitos to attack the U-Boot pens at Trondheim in Norway, a distance of more than eight hundred miles. 44 (Rhodesia) Squadron launched ten Lancasters into the air between 15.47 and 16.02 with F/L Hayler and Capt Hirschfeld the senior pilots on duty, and they joined a dozen others from 207 Squadron as they flew north. F/L Hayler was forced to turn back after three hours when his port-inner engine failed, leaving him with little chance of reaching the target on time or of achieving the necessary bombing altitude. The others arrived in the target area to find clear skies and excellent visibility, only to be thwarted by an effective smoke screen that prevented the marker force from finding the aiming point, and the Master Bomber had no option but to send the force home.

5 Group mounted a rare daylight mining operation on the 23rd, for which fourteen Lancasters were made ready, four of them representing 44 (Rhodesia) Squadron. The destination for F/Ls Lewis and Sutherland and F/Os Hart and Wood was the Young Eglantine garden in the Elbe Estuary, for which they departed Spilsby between 04.46 and 04.49, and flew out over ten-tenths cloud with tops up to 12,500 feet. F/L Lewis was two hours out over the North Sea when his H2S failed, forcing him to turn back. The others arrived in the target area, where they established positions on H2S before carrying out timed runs to deliver their six vegetables each unopposed from 13,000 feet between 06.37 and 06.42.

The weather was mainly responsible for curtailing operations over the next few days until the 26th, when briefings took place on 5 Group stations at 20.00. The seventeen attending 44 (Rhodesia) Squadron crews learned that Munich was to be their target for an all-5 Group affair involving 270 Lancasters and eight Mosquitos, which represented a maximum effort. They departed Spilsby between 23.36 and 00.09 with S/L Bird the senior pilot on duty, and each carrying a 1,000 pounder and thirteen Nº4 J-cluster bombs. Forming up and climbing to operational altitude was a time-consuming business, and it would be five hours before the target was reached. There were no early returns among the 44 (Rhodesia) Squadron participants, which found the target area under clear skies with good visibility and confirmed their positions by means of H2S. Aside from one errant red TI, the low-level Mosquito marking was accurate, and the Master Bomber ensured that the crews focused upon the reds and greens on and close to the planned aiming point. The 44 (Rhodesia) Squadron crews bombed from 16,000 to

17,500 feet between 05.00 and 05.08 and returned safely to praise the quality of the route and target marking and the concentration of the attack. The last-mentioned was confirmed by post-raid reconnaissance and a local report that singled out railway installations as being particularly hard-hit.

This was the final operation of the month for 5 Group, but among others taking place before the end was an attack by 1 and 8 Groups on Freiburg in southern Germany. It was a minor railway centre within thirty-five miles of advancing American and French ground forces and was thought to be harbouring large numbers of enemy soldiers. The force of over 330 Lancasters delivered 1,900 tons of bombs, missing the railway yards, but destroying two thousand houses and killing over two thousand inhabitants. During the course of the month, the squadron took part in ten operations and dispatched 148 sorties for the loss of three Lancasters, two crews and two other airmen.

December 1944

There were no operations for 5 Group for the first three nights of the new month, largely because of the weather, and, in the meantime, 1, 4, 6 and 8 Groups pounded the Ruhr town of Hagen on the night of the 2/3rd. Worthwhile targets were becoming more and more scarce at a time when the Command was at its most powerful, and this final period of the war would bring the most devastating attacks to date on the German homeland. When the Spilsby squadrons returned to action in the early evening of the 4th, it was to provide nineteen Lancasters each as part of a 5 Group force of 282 of the type and ten Mosquitos. Their target was the town of Heilbronn, situated thirty miles due north of Stuttgart, which had the River Neckar and a north-south rail link running through it, but, otherwise, had no genuine strategic importance, and would not have been expecting to be attacked. The main operation on this night was actually by 535 aircraft of 1, 6 and 8 Groups at Karlsruhe, some fifty-six miles west-south-west of Heilbronn, and the concentration of aircraft in this area would be certain to bring out the night-fighters. The 44 (Rhodesia) Squadron element took off between 16.15 and 16.42 with a handful of pilots of flight lieutenant rank leading the way, and each carrying a cookie and either five 1,000 pounders or twelve SBCs of 4lb incendiaries. There were no early returns as they made their way across France in good conditions to find three to five-tenths thin stratus over the target at around 12,000 feet, through which some crews were able to pick out the Neckar. The aiming points were the marshalling yards and the town, which were illuminated by the flare force ahead of the low-level Mosquitos' run to drop red TIs for the visual markers to back up. The marshalling yards were marked with yellows, which the main force element was unable to distinguish in the burgeoning fires, and this persuaded them to focus on the red and green TIs in the city itself instead. The 44 (Rhodesia) Squadron crews attacked from 12,000 to 13,000 feet between 19.29 and 19.34, adding to the general destruction, and, as the force retreated westwards into electrical storms, 82% of the city's built-up area was in the process of being destroyed by what probably amounted to a firestorm. The post-war British Bombing Survey estimated 351 acres of destruction, and a death toll of at least seven thousand people. It cost 5 Group twelve aircraft, four of which had departed Spilsby in the late afternoon. The fate of the two missing 44 (Rhodesia) Squadron Lancasters demonstrated the diverse fortunes of war, the entire crew of F/O Dann surviving the loss of PB751 to fall into enemy hands, while Capt Hirschfeld SAAF and his crew all perished when PD373 fell victim to a night-fighter and crashed eleven miles south-south-west of Heilbronn city centre.

The town of Giessen was 5 Group's objective on a night of heavy Bomber Command activity on the 6/7th. Other operations centred on the oil refinery at Leuna (Merseburg) in the east, which was the target for 475 Lancasters of 1, 3 and 8 Groups, while 450 aircraft from predominantly 4 and 6 Groups attacked railway installations at Osnabrück in the north. 44 (Rhodesia) Squadron briefed eighteen crews as part of an overall 5 Group heavy force of 255 Lancasters, while their aircraft were being loaded with a cookie and thirteen SBCs of 4lb incendiaries. They departed Spilsby between 16.54 and 17.15 with F/Ls Davey and Sutherland the senior pilots on duty and set course for their destination some eighty-five miles south-east of Cologne in west-central Germany, and thirty-five miles north of Frankfurt. The main force crews had been assigned to two aiming points, two-thirds of them to the town, and the remainder to the marshalling yards, and those arriving in the target area found up to eight-tenths thin cloud and good visibility. F/Sgt Spencer and crew were not among them, having lost their Gee and a.s.i before the pilot became unwell and turned back. The flare force began illuminating three minutes early and to the west of the target, but the Mosquito-laid red TIs fell close to the aiming point and the Master Bomber ensured that they were backed up by greens. The 44 (Rhodesia) Squadron crews bombed from 11,300 to 12,200 feet between 20.15 and 20.25, and all returned safely to report another successful raid, which would be confirmed by reconnaissance photographs.

The Urft Dam was one of a number of similar structures in the beautiful Eifel region of western Germany, close to the Belgian frontier. There was a fear that the enemy might strategically release flood water to hamper the American advance into Germany, and it was decided to attempt to breach the dam, to allow any excess water to drain away. The first of a number of attacks on the region took place on the 3rd at Heimbach, the small town nestling against the northern reaches of the reservoir, but the 1 and 8 Group force failed to identify it, and no bombs fell. On the following day, a small 8 Group effort against the dam was unsuccessful, as was a 3 Group attack on the nearby Schwammenauel Dam on the 5th. The job was handed to 5 Group on the 8th, for which a force of 205 Lancasters was made ready, fourteen of them by 44 (Rhodesia) Squadron, while nineteen from 617 Squadron would be carrying Tallboys. The 44 (Rhodesia) Squadron element departed Spilsby in a snow shower between 08.37 and 08.50 with no senior pilots on duty and was greeted at the target by six to nine-tenths cloud at between 6,000 and 8,000 feet and moderate visibility. Most made multiple runs across the target area seeking out the dam, but four crews failed to identify the aiming point through the cloud and withheld their bombs. The remaining ten carried out their attacks from 8,000 to 9,800 feet between 10.55 and 11.14, and, after 129 aircraft had bombed, the Master Bomber called a halt and sent the force home. Poor weather conditions over Lincolnshire demanded a diversion, and the Spilsby crews put down at Thorney Island on the south coast, from where they straggled back up to the north on the following day.

The conditions had prevented any assessment of results, which meant that another attempt on the dam would be necessary, and preparations were put in hand on the 10th to return with a force of 217 Lancasters. 44 (Rhodesia) Squadron launched fourteen aircraft at around 04.30 on a cold and frosty morning, but the entire force was recalled before it reached the English coast. 233 Lancasters and a Mosquito were scheduled to take off in the early morning of the 11th to join five 8 Group Mosquitos at the target, but take-off was postponed until midday, when the fifteen 44 (Rhodesia) Squadron participants departed Spilsby between 12.14 and 12.28 with F/Ls Mangos, Richardson and Sargent the senior pilots on duty. F/L Mangos and crew turned back at 13.50 after instrument failure ended their interest in proceedings, leaving the others to encounter icing conditions at the French coast, and find that the weather in the target area was hardly an improvement on the previous day. Up to nine-tenths cloud with tops at 8,000 feet made life difficult for the Master Bomber, who tried to bring the crews down below the cloud base, some complying, while others were able to identify the aiming point through a four-mile-long gap. Nine of the 44 (Rhodesia) Squadron crews attacked from 8,000 to

10,000 feet between 14.50 and 15.02, while five others responded to the Master Bomber's "Dewdrop" instruction to cease bombing and go home. Post-raid reconnaissance revealed a number of hits on the dam, and cratering all around, but no actual breach had occurred.

The squadron was put on standby to operate twice on the 14th, but, ultimately, only the crews of F/L Sutherland and F/O Daggett were called upon, taking off at 15.27 and 15.32 respectively for gardening duties in one of the Silverthorn gardens of the Kattegat. The drop zone lay between the east coast of North Jutland and the north-western tip of Sjaelland Island, an area covered by ten-tenths cloud between 2,000 and 8,000 feet. Positions were established by H2S and the vegetables delivered into the briefed locations from 15,000 feet at 18.41 and 18.44.

The main operation on the night of the 15/16th was directed at Ludwigshafen in southern Germany, home to a number of I G Farben factories, which were using slave workers in the production of synthetic oil. The attack by 327 Lancasters and fourteen Mosquitos of 1, 6 and 8 Groups landed 450 high explosive bombs and incendiaries in the Ludwigshafen plant, causing massive damage and fires, and was the greatest setback to production during the war. Further north, the Oppau factory ceased production completely for an extended period, and five other industrial concerns also sustained severe damage, as did some residential areas. It was on the 16th that German ground forces began a new offensive in the Ardennes, in an attempt to break through the American lines and reach the port of Antwerp in what would become known as the Battle of the Bulge.

Munich had become something of a 5 Group preserve during the year, and a further operation against it was planned for the night of the 17/18th, which would turn out to be another night of heavy Bomber Command activity. The main raid was to be by more than five hundred aircraft, predominantly of 4 and 6 Groups, on Duisburg, while 1 Group targeted Ulm with over three hundred Lancasters, leaving 5 Group to send 280 Lancasters some seventy miles beyond to the Bavarian Capital City. 44 (Rhodesia) Squadron briefed eighteen crews, while their Lancasters were being prepared for the 1,300-mile round-trip, and they departed Spilsby hot on the heels of the 207 Squadron contingent between 16.13 and 16.24 with W/C Newmarch the senior pilot on duty for the first time since his elevation to squadron commander. It turned out to be a night of poor serviceability for the Spilsby squadrons, when F/Os Barlow, Walker and Worrall and three from 207 Squadron returned early with a variety of technical issues, leaving the others to cross the French coast near Berck-sur-Mer, and reach the target to find generally clear skies and good visibility. It had become standard practice for some main force crews to act as supporters for the flare force at the head of the attack to "beef up" the numbers, and to retain their bombs for a second pass with the main force. F/L Gallivan and crew were among these, before rejoining the main force, only to find that their bombs refused to release and had to be brought home. The remaining 44 (Rhodesia) Squadron crews bombed on red and green TIs from 13,200 to 15,000 feet between 19.57 and 20.10 in accordance with the instructions of the Master Bomber, who declared himself satisfied with the results. The resultant fires were visible from a hundred miles into the return journey, and, while, as usual, no local report was available to confirm or deny, the Command claimed severe and widespread damage to the city.

On the following night, it was the turn of the distant Baltic port of Gdynia to play host to 5 Group, for which 44 (Rhodesia) Squadron put up a dozen Lancasters in an overall force of 236 of the type. The intention was to catch elements of the German fleet at anchor, in particular the Lützow, and also to destroy harbour installations, as well as cause damage within the town. *(The original Lützow was actually never completed and was sold to the Russian navy in 1940 as a hull minus superstructure.*

The pocket battleship, Deutschland, was renamed Lützow, to avoid humiliation for the nation should she be lost in battle.) While this operation was in progress, fourteen other Lancasters of the group were to sneak in under cover of the main activity to deliver mines to the Privet and Spinach gardens in Danzig (Gdansk) Bay. 44 (Rhodesia) Squadron supported this undertaking with the crews of F/Os Daggett, Hart and Wood, who were assigned to Privet, and the two elements departed Spilsby together between 16.30 and 17.04 with F/L Hayler the senior pilot on duty. F/O Thomson and crew turned back after around two hours when the navigator became unwell, for which petrol fumes were blamed. The others pressed on to reach the target area after an outward flight of almost five hours and found clear skies and good visibility. As was usually the practice, the initial identification was by H2S, but the harbour and town could be picked out visually until a smoke screen was activated. The illumination and marking proceeded according to plan, and the 44 (Rhodesia) Squadron crews delivered their eight 1,000 pounders on red and green TIs from 11,000 to 14,000 feet between 21.54 and 22.07 in accordance with the Master Bomber's instructions, and, in the face of intense light flak. The smoke screen eventually obscured the Lützow, and crews with bombs still to deliver turned their attention to the port area and town. It was not possible to make an accurate assessment of results, but bomb bursts were seen across the docks and quaysides. Reconnaissance photos confirmed that damage had been inflicted upon shipping, port installations and residential property in the waterfront districts, at a cost of four Lancasters, two of them from 207 Squadron. Meanwhile, the gardeners were experiencing some difficulties in identifying the drop zone by H2S, and F/O Wood and crew ended up jettisoning their stores, while F/O Daggett and crew released theirs from 15,000 feet at 22.07, probably after pinpointing on Point Hel. F/O Hart and crew noted that the attack on Gdynia appeared to be going well as they delivered their mines on their second run from 15,000 feet at 22.25, having employed both H2S and a visual reference to establish their position.

Thick fog kept the crews on the ground on the 20th, and threatened to do so also on the 21st, but an operation was called on the basis, that the weather over Scotland after midnight would be clear for returning aircraft, even if Lincolnshire remained fogbound. Most of the Spilsby crews had been forced to remain at Kelstern since returning from Gdynia, and it was lunchtime on the 21st before they straggled back to Spilsby. Eleven 44 (Rhodesia) Squadron Lancasters were detailed for the 5 Group operation that night, and briefings took place while the ground crews did their best to get the aircraft ready in time. In briefing rooms across southern and south-eastern Lincolnshire, crews learned that their target would require them to retrace their recent steps to Germany's eastern Baltic region, although the I G Farben-owned Wintershall oil refinery at Politz, situated less than ten miles north of the port of Stettin, was some two hundred miles short of their trip to Gdynia. *(This location is often wrongly spelled Pölitz, which is a town in Germany's Schleswig-Holstein region at the western end of the Baltic.)* A force of 207 Lancasters and a single Mosquito was assembled, and, unusually, it included an element from 617 Squadron carrying Tallboys. The 44 (Rhodesia) Squadron contingent departed Spilsby between 17.02 and 17.29 with F/Ls Hayler, Mangos and Sutherland the senior pilots on duty, each crew sitting on a cookie and twelve 500 pounders. F/Os Walker and Kennedy turned back with engine issues, while F/O Craig and crew had been forced to transfer to a spare aircraft and had taken off late. They attempted to make up time, but, ultimately, decided it was a futile gesture and abandoned their sortie. The others reached the target, many after cutting corners to keep up with the stream, and found clear skies with ground haze, which may have been a smoke screen. This important war-industry asset was protected by around fifty searchlights, and heavy flak accompanied the Lancasters as they ran in on the aiming point. The markers fell some two thousand yards north-north-west of the plant, a situation recognized by the Master Bomber, but he was unable to persuade the backers-up to shift the point of aim accordingly, and most of the bombing would miss the mark. The 44 (Rhodesia) Squadron element bombed on red and green TIs from 15,500 to 19,000 feet between 22.04 and 22.20 and observed most of the bomb bursts to be around the markers. Fires remained visible for almost a hundred miles into the return journey, but the plant had not been destroyed, and it would be necessary to mount further raids.

The final wartime Christmas period was celebrated on 5 Group stations undisturbed by operational activity between the 22nd and Boxing Day, which was not the case for some other groups. The peace came to an end on the 26th, when crews from all groups were roused from any resulting stupor to attend briefings for operations against enemy troop positions at St Vith in Belgium. The German advance towards Antwerp had run out of steam after its earlier successes, and starved of fuel and ammunition, it was now attempting to withdraw back into Germany. 5 Group contributed twenty-six Lancasters to the force of 296 aircraft for the first joint operation since October. The seven 44 (Rhodesia) Squadron participants departed Spilsby between 13.04 and 13.30 with F/Ls Gallivan and Mangos the senior pilots on duty, those at the tail end instructed to make up twenty minutes by cutting corners. F/Sgt Spencer and crew crossed the sea at 1,000 feet intending to make landfall between Ostend and Dunkerque but strayed too close to the latter and their Lancaster was hit by light flak and machine-gun fire. The port-outer engine was knocked out and a large hole appeared in the port wing, which, together with other damage, left no choice other than to jettison the bombs and go home. The others found the target to be under clear skies with good visibility and could identify the aiming point visually and by a red TI. When this became obscured by smoke, the Master Bomber ordered the crews to descend to 10,000 feet and bomb the upwind edge of the smoke. The 44 (Rhodesia) Squadron crews carried out their attacks from 10,000 to 13,750 feet between 15.32 and 15.35, some on green TIs, and observed the attack to be well concentrated. A number of crews reported a four-engine bomber going down but not crashing, and five parachutes were observed.

On the 28th, the experienced 44 (Rhodesia) Squadron crews of F/L Sutherland and F/Os Coventry, Daggett and Plenderleith were told that they would be part of a 5 Group force of sixty-seven Lancasters targeting shipping, specifically the cruiser Köln, at Horten in Oslo Fjord. They departed Spilsby between 19.34 and 19.40 but lost the services of F/O Plenderleith and crew after their port-outer engine caught fire soon after take-off. The others reached the target area after an outward flight of four-and-a-half hours and found the skies to be relatively clear and the visibility good. However, a thin layer of alto-cumulus cloud at between 15,000 and 20,000 feet reduced the brightness of the moonlight and cast deceptive shadows on the water to prevent a clear identification of the target. The aiming point was marked by Wanganui flares, but most crews followed the Master Bomber's instructions after establishing their own reference point. A patch of light flak to the north-east of the harbour mole was thought to be concealing a large naval unit, and this area was marked and bombed. Some crews would claim to have attacked a large vessel moving from this area in a southerly direction, and other shipping in the harbour, all in the face of intense shipboard and shore-based light flak. The 44 (Rhodesia) Squadron trio orbited, until bombing from 6,250 to 7,250 feet between 23.44 and 23.54, two of them making two passes, but claimed no direct hits and the operation produced inconclusive results.

The 29th dawned fine and frosty, and two 44 (Rhodesia) Squadron crews had time for lunch before being briefed for mining sorties in the Onion garden in Oslo harbour in concert with nine others from 5 Group. F/O Wood and F/L Hayler took off at 15.44 and 15.50 and arrived in the target area some three hours later to find clear skies below 12,000 feet and excellent visibility. They established their positions by H2S before delivering their mines into the briefed locations from 12,000 feet at 18.50 and 18.59. The squadron carried out its final bombing operation of the year in the early hours of the 31st, when sending eleven Lancasters as part of a 5 Group force of 154 of the type to attack an enemy supply line at Houffalize in the Ardennes region of Belgium. They took off between 02.21 and 02.37, with F/Ls Gallivan and Mangos the senior pilots on duty and found the target area under five to seven-tenths stratus cloud at 5,000 to 6,000 feet, with another layer of eight-tenths with tops at 9,000 feet, all of which made identification very difficult. The marking was punctual and accurate, but the red TIs were observed only by a proportion of the crews who chanced upon a gap in the clouds directly over the aiming point. F/L Mangos and F/Os Dalton and Gardiner withheld their bombs after failing to establish a firm aiming point, while F/O Daggett's bomb sight failed at the critical moment, and this left seven 44 (Rhodesia) Squadron participants to bomb from 9,500 to 12,000 feet between 05.01 and 05.13. A number of crews in the force descended to below the cloud base and confirmed that the bombing was concentrated around the markers, but it would be deemed necessary to revisit this objective within a short time.

It was dusk when F/O Wood and F/L Hayler took off at 16.20 and 16.22 to head for the Yew Tree garden, the channel between Læsø Island and the east coast of North Jutland. They picked up a pinpoint at Frederikshavn on the mainland coast and carried out timed runs at 15,000 feet to deposit their mines into the allotted locations at 20.24, before returning home safely to wrap up a very successful, if, testing year for the squadron. During the course of the month the squadron conducted fourteen operations and dispatched 137 sorties for the loss of two Lancasters and their crews. The New Year beckoned with the scent of victory in the air, however, any thoughts that the enemy defences were spent were misplaced, and even though they were unable to protect the entire Reich, they would continue to provide stubborn opposition for a further three months.

44 Sqn Lancaster R5729 KM-A
Lancaster R5729 in a dispersal at Dunholme Lodge before setting out on a night raid to Berlin. This veteran aircraft had taken part in more than 70 operations with the squadron since joining it in 1942. It was finally shot down with the loss of its entire crew, during a raid on Brunswick on the night of 14/15th of January, 1944. Crew: P/O L Curatolo RCAF, Sgt G Williams, (FE), Sgt P Hughes (Nav), F/Sgt T Whitely (W.Op), F/Sgt David Mullin RCAF (BA), Sgt S Weldon (MUG), Sgt G Armitt (RG).

Lancaster R5729 side view.

Above and below: John Chatterton and his aircrew and groundcrew prior to night flying test 18th of April 1944 with ND578 KM-Y on dispersal at Dunholme Lodge.

F/L John Chatterton and aircrew prior to operation to Juvisy 18th of April 1944, plus extra 1st dickey Nav. Crew: Sgt F Letts, F/O D J Reyland, F/Sgt WH Barker, Sgt J Mitchie, Sgt WHR Champion, Sgt J R Davidson, F/Sgt R Riddoch.

F/L Chatterton and Rear Gunner Sgt Jock Davidson prior Juvisy.

P/O J Chatterton's official end of tour photo April 1944 at Dunholme Lodge. The original bomb aimer Pete Lees was lost in November 1944 when flying with another crew. His replacement Mansel Scott, had finished his tour and left by the time this photo was taken. Crew: Sgt F Letts, F/O D J Reyland, F/Sgt WH Barker, Sgt J Mitchie, Sgt WHR Champion, Sgt J R Davidson.

*44 Squadron Dance Band
K B Beard, Des Thomas, George Auty, A W Paples, Harry Minting.*

Dunholme Lodge – 3rd June 1944
Prime Minister of Southern Rhodesia, Godfrey Huggins.
Air Commodore S Pope, G/C Butler, W/C F W Thompson

'Sky Floosie' after having carried out 78 operations. The lighter coloured bombs denote daylight raids. The bowser was presented to the Squadron by the African employees of the Shabani Mine in Southern Rhodesia.

44 Sqn Dunholme Lodge 1944

'Sky Floosie' Crew: F/O B Slade RCAF (Pilot), F/Sgt John Crammond (FE), F/Sgt S Henderson RCAF (Nav), F/O Shute RCAF (from USA), Sgt F Bishop (W.Op), Sgt J Beechey (MUG), Sgt Don Spankie RCAF.

F/Sgt John Crammond

'Sky Floosie' Crews
Back: Cpl Ernie Bradford, Ernie Dickens (both bowser drivers), rigger,
2 Rhodesian ground crew, electrician ground crew. Front: 2 flight mechanics, unknown.

44 Sqn Lancaster ME699 KM-T. P/O W.A. Young. Five crew KIA, two evaded 5th of July 1944.

44 Sqn Lancaster ND514 KM-C. 31st January 1944. A number of different crews have been identified as the subjects of this photograph. It is believed to be that of P/O Lyford, who lost his life as the result of a night-fighter attack, leaving his crew to fall into enemy hands.

44 Sqn Lancaster ND578 KM-Y, 121 Operations.

Lancaster ND578 KM-Y and crews 1944

Lancaster ND578 KM-Y and crews 1944

44 Sqn Lancaster KM-C – 81 operations

Crew of A-Able 44 Sqn, Spilsby 1944-45
Back L-R: Jack Hardy (BA), 'Jock' Spence (MUG), Cyril Crooks (FE), Joe Ward (RG),
Front L-R: Norman Roberts (W/Op.), Ken Walker (Pilot), Al Turner (Nav)

*44 Sqn Lancaster ME859 KM-S. P/O D. Graaff & crew all KIA 8th of July 1944.
Crew: P/O D Graaff (Pilot), Sgt L Critchley (FE), F/O V Purvis DFC (Nav),
F/Sgt F Gibberson (BA), F/O J Hodge (W.Op), W/O R B Groves (MUG), W/O A Holland (RG)*

*Lancaster LM654 KM-L, October 1944 on completion of their first tour.
Back L-R: Ron Valentine (BA), ground crew, F/L Stew Anning (Pilot), ground crew, John 'Tuck'
Slater (W.Op). Front L-R: 'Kiwi' Cardwell (Nav), 2 ground crew, Fred Snedker (FE)*

Lancaster NE138 KM-Z, Dunholme Lodge, damaged after Wesseling raid 20/21st of June 1944. Survivors after that raid L-R Colin H McKenzie (BA), S/L Steve Cockbain (Pilot), J Stuart Dean (RG), Walter Faraday (FE)

January 1945

The final year of the war began with a flourish, as the Luftwaffe launched its ill-conceived and, ultimately, ill-fated Operation Bodenplatte (Baseplate) at first light on New Year's Day. The intention to destroy the Allied air forces on the ground at the recently liberated airfields in France, Holland and Belgium was only modestly realized, and it cost the German day fighter force around 250 aircraft. Many of the pilots were killed, wounded or fell into Allied hands, and it was a setback from which the Tagjagd would never fully recover, while the Allies could make good their losses within hours from their enormous stockpiles.

5 Group was also active that morning, having roused the crews early from their beds to attend briefings for an attack on the recently repaired Dortmund-Ems Canal near Ladbergen, for which 102 Lancasters and two Mosquitos were made ready. 44 (Rhodesia) Squadron loaded ten Lancasters with the appropriate canal-busting ironware, namely a cookie and thirteen 1,000 pounders, some with delayed-action fuses, and dispatched them between 07.40 and 08.15 with S/L Bird the senior pilot on duty. He had taken off late after transferring to a spare aircraft and would be unable to make up the time before reaching enemy territory. The 54 Base squadrons from Coningsby and Metheringham fell in line behind 83 Squadron, with the 55 Base squadrons from East Kirkby, Spilsby and Strubby about three miles further back, and a third section, made up of 53 Base units from Waddington, Skellingthorpe and Bardney some twenty miles to the rear. The last-mentioned were allowed to catch up, putting the force two minutes behind schedule at point C, over the North Sea. It was between points C and D that the fighter escort was expected to join them, and, although it was not immediately apparent, it did eventually put in an appearance. F/L Gallivan and crew turned back within two hours because of an engine issue, leaving the others to maintain their positions in the gaggle, which held together fairly well, although the controller would complain later that the legs were too short to keep the gaggle tight, and some aircraft were seen to break formation. When about eight minutes from the target, smoke from a Mosquito-laid red TI could be seen, which was assessed as being on the southern tip of the island between the two branches of the canal. It was clearly visible to all crews, who were able to home in on it without difficulty. A six-gun flak battery greeted their arrival with accurate salvoes, but this did not inhibit the bombing runs, and the 44 (Rhodesia) Squadron crews carried out their attacks from 10,000 and 11,000 feet in a three-minute slot from 11.16. On return, a number of crews complained that the gaggle was too tight and put crews at risk from "friendly" bombs. The impression was of an effective operation, the use of delay fuses having prevented an immediate assessment of the results, but photo-reconnaissance revealed later, that the canal had been breached again and the surrounding fields had become flooded.

Operations for the day were not yet done for 5 Group, which now had an appointment with the Mittelland Canal at Gravenhorst, for which 152 Lancasters and five Mosquitos were made ready. 44 (Rhodesia) Squadron dispatched the crews of F/Os Parkin, Plenderleith and Gardiner between 17.01 and 17.03, and all reached the target area to find that the clear conditions enjoyed during the morning raid nearby, had persisted, and so accurate were the initial TIs and illumination, delivered visually or by H2S, that the third flare force was not required and was sent home. The main force was called in ahead of H-Hour at around 19.10, and the 44 (Rhodesia) Squadron element bombed on red TIs from 11,000, 12,000 and 20,000 feet at 19.13 and 19.14. One of the perils of operating on New Year's Day was the risk of falling victim to trigger-happy American flak gunners, who had been spooked by the

German raids at dawn, and now fired at anything that moved, and a number of RAF aircraft and crews would be lost in such "friendly fire" incidents. The employment of predominantly delayed-action bombs again prevented an immediate assessment of results, but a highly successful operation was confirmed later by photo-reconnaissance.

5 Group remained on the ground when Nuremberg and Ludwigshafen were raided by large forces on the night of the 2/3rd, and both operations were hugely destructive. A controversial attack was planned against the small French town of Royan in the early hours of the 5th, in response to requests from Free French forces, which were laying siege. Situated on the east bank at the mouth of the Gironde Estuary, it was occupied by a German garrison, and was in the way of an advance towards the port of Bordeaux. The inhabitants had been offered an opportunity by the German garrison commander to evacuate the area, but around two thousand had declined, and would suffer the consequences. 1, 5 and 8 Groups put together a force of 347 Lancasters and seven Mosquitos, of which fourteen of the former represented 44 (Rhodesia) Squadron. They departed Spilsby between 00.53 and 01.33 with S/L Bird the senior pilot on duty, each carrying a cookie and sixteen 500 pounders. They were in the first of two waves heading for the unsuspecting target, separated by one hour, and it was approaching 04.00 as they lined up for the bombing run in cloudless skies and excellent visibility. The start of the attack was delayed for two minutes to allow misplaced markers to be corrected, but a red TI went down at 04.01 very close to the aiming point, and another fell in the middle of the town, near the beach, at which point, the Master Bomber called in the main force. The 44 (Rhodesia) Squadron crews carried out their attacks from 9,500 to 10,000 feet onto Path Finder markers between 04.04 and 04.14, and witnessed a yellow oil fire at 04.08, which began to emit volumes of black smoke. This was just one of a number of large explosions created by the first phase of bombing, and the resultant fires would act as a beacon to the 1 Group force following behind. F/O Walker returned with his bomb load intact after it failed to release on his first pass over the aiming point and the bomb-aimer forgot to reset for the second one, by which time, the Master Bomber had called a halt. The attack destroyed about 85% of the town, and between five and eight hundred people lost their lives. In the event, the town was not taken, and it would be mid-April before the garrison surrendered.

5 Group was not involved in a major attack on Hannover by more than 650 aircraft on the night of the 5/6th, the first on this northern city since the series in the autumn of 1943. However, a rushed battle order came through to 5 Group stations at 18.30, which would lead to another late briefing and take-off for 131 crews, and it was actually between 00.03 and 00.47 on the 6th that nine 44 (Rhodesia) Squadron crews departed Spilsby bound for a German supply column trapped at Houffalize in the Belgian Ardennes. F/Ls Gallivan and Sargent were the senior pilots on duty as they made their way south on a clear night above low cloud, which, over the target, formed thin layers of eight to ten-tenths cover between 4,000 and 10,000 feet. The marker force crews were able to identify the aiming point visually, and the first red Mosquito-laid TIs were seen to go down close together, followed by greens at H-3. They were backed up to leave a compact group of reds and greens visible by their glow through the clouds, and the Master Bomber, who was circling at 10,000 feet, called in the main force to bomb. Seven of the 44 (Rhodesia) Squadron crews complied from 9,250 to 11,250 feet between 03.03 and 03.09, while F/Os Walker and Plenderleith were among around a third of the force to retain their bombs in accordance with instructions at briefing, if they failed to identify the aiming point. Afterwards, one of the marker crews descended to 3,500 feet between the cloud layers, where they saw two large columns of smoke, the source of which could not be identified. Post-raid reconnaissance confirmed that the target had been bombed with great accuracy, and the success had been gained for the loss of two Lancasters.

Later in the day, 5 Group detailed thirteen Lancaster for mining duties in the Spinach garden off Gdynia and seven for Privet off Danzig. 44 (Rhodesia) Squadron dispatched the crews of F/O Coventry and F/L Mangos to the former at 16.14 and 16.23 respectively, and they had reached Denmark when F/O Coventry's H2S failed, forcing him and his crew to turn back. F/L Mangos and crew reached the target area to find a layer of ten-tenths cloud with good visibility above and delivered their five mines from 17,000 feet at 20.33, having established their position by H2S. They undertook the return journey with an unserviceable rear turret.

A major operation against Munich was planned for the 7th, for which a two-wave force of 645 aircraft was drawn from all five of the Lancaster-equipped groups. 5 Group, which was unused to sharing this target, would lead the way with 213 Lancasters and three Mosquitos, leaving the second wave to follow on two hours later, the tanks of the heavy brigade containing sufficient fuel for a nine-hour round-trip. The 44 (Rhodesia) Squadron element of sixteen Lancasters departed Spilsby as dusk was descending between 16.38 and 17.02, with W/C Newmarch the senior pilot on duty. F/Sgt Spencer and crew lost an engine on each wing and jettisoned their bombs before landing at Juvincourt in north-eastern France, leaving the others to find broken medium-level cloud at 14,000 feet above the target, with haze or thin cloud below. By this time, the Master Bomber had made a visual identification of the aiming point and sent the first two primary blind markers in to deliver their TIs at the same time thirty seconds ahead of the planned opening of the attack. The flare force went in immediately afterwards, and illuminated the city very effectively, allowing ground detail to be identified. Red TIs went down west and east of the River Isar, bracketing the aiming point, and the Master Bomber ordered the backers up to drop their TIs between the reds, after which, the next batch of flares formed a circle around the aiming point. The main force was then called in, and the 44 (Rhodesia) Squadron participants delivered their loads accurately within the specified area from 15,150 to 19,750 feet between 20.30 and 20.40. F/O Thomson and crew overshot the target, blaming inaccurately forecast winds, and were too late to make a second pass. The cookie was jettisoned "live" over the target, and the rest of the load brought home. The city was seen to be burning well as the force withdrew, and the glow of fires could be seen from up to 130 miles away. Two hours after the 5 Group attack, in what would become an established pattern, the 1, 3, 6 and 8 Group force arrived to complete the destruction of the central and some industrial districts, and this proved to be the final large-scale attack of the war on Munich.

With the exception of 617 Squadron, 5 Group remained on the ground for the ensuing six days, with snow-clearing providing exercise for all capable of wielding a shovel. The crews were, therefore, no doubt relieved to be called to briefing on the 13th, when they learned that 5 Group would be operating alone against the Wintershall oil refinery at Politz near Stettin. The plant had sustained damage in the previous attack in December, but production had not been halted, and a force of 218 Lancasters and seven Mosquitos was assembled for the return, of which seventeen of the former were provided by 44 (Rhodesia) Squadron. Another dusk departure saw them taking off between 16.24 and 16.52 with the recently posted-in S/L Ferguson the senior pilot on duty for the first time. F/O Worrall's navigator complained of stomach pains as they crossed the North Sea at 1,500 feet in accordance with instructions to not climb until approaching the Danish coast at 19.30. They flew on for thirty minutes to see if his condition improved, which it did not, and they turned back from a position some two hundred miles out. The others arrived in the target area on time to find clear skies with slight haze, by which time the blind marker crews had identified the target by means of H2S and delivered their green TIs in a line approaching the target shortly after 22.00. The illuminators then dropped their flares, which caused ground detail to stand out, highlighted by the snow on the ground. A blind-bombing attack had been planned, but, because of the excellence of the conditions, Mosquitos were able to go in at low level. The main force was called in, and the 44 (Rhodesia) Squadron crews bombed from 14,000 to 16,750 feet between 22.16 and 22.27 to help seal the fate of the plant. Photographic reconnaissance confirmed that the site had been severely damaged, and Bomber Command claimed it to be in ruins.

Oil targets would continue to dominate during the remainder of the month, and a two-phase attack was planned for the following night against the refinery at Leuna, near Merseburg in eastern Germany, as previously mentioned, one of many similar sites situated in an arc from north to south to the west of Leipzig. The first phase would be carried out by 5 Group, which detailed 210 Lancasters and nine Mosquitos, fourteen of the former contributed by 44 (Rhodesia) Squadron. They took off from Spilsby between 16.07 and 16.26 with S/L Ferguson the senior pilot on duty and headed for the Sussex coast near Brighton to begin the Channel crossing for the southern approach to eastern Germany. They reached the target area to find clear skies but poor vertical visibility due to a layer of haze, which, in the event, was no hindrance to the primary blind markers, whose job was to establish their position over the aiming point by means of H2S. They delivered their TIs from 18,000 feet, after which, the first element of the flare force went in. The Master Bomber called for ground marking only, which was carried out by the low-level Mosquito element, and, by 20.50, he was satisfied and sent the marker aircraft home. The main force produced what appeared to be concentrated bombing, the 44 (Rhodesia) Squadron crews dropping their loads of a cookie and nine 500 pounders each onto red and green TIs from 14,250 to 16,750 feet between 21.02 and 21.11, doing so with a fourteen-second overshoot in accordance with the Master Bomber's instructions. Returning crews reported explosions and smoke rising upwards as they turned for home and left behind a beacon for the second wave of 363 Lancasters and five Mosquitos of 1, 6 and 8 Groups following three hours behind. They would add to the massive destruction, which effectively put the plant out of action for the remainder of the war.

Three oil plants were selected for attention on the night of the 16/17th, at Zeitz, near Liepzig, Wanne-Eickel in the Ruhr, and Brux in north-western Czechoslovakia (now Most in the Czech Republic), some 140 miles due south of Berlin. It was for the last-mentioned that fourteen 44 (Rhodesia) Squadron crews were briefed as part of a 5 Group force of 224 Lancasters and six Mosquitos, which would be accompanied by seven 101 Squadron ABC Lancasters performing RCM duties. They were each carrying a cookie and nine 500 pounders for what would be a nine-hour round-trip and departed Spilsby between 17.48 and 18.14 with S/L Ferguson the senior pilot on duty. There were ten early returns from the force, and among them was the crew of F/O Peterswald, who had been contending with a number of instrument and control issues as they traversed France and were within twenty miles of the German frontier west of Saarbrücken when they turned back. The others reached the target area to encounter nine to ten-tenths low cloud with tops at 3,000 feet, which interfered with the low-level marking system. The four primary blind markers identified the target by means of H2S, and dropped green TIs, and they were followed by the first illuminators, who also relied on H2S to deliver their flares. It seems that a number of Mosquitos managed to get below the cloud base to put red TIs onto the aiming point and reported that the greens were among the oil tanks. However, the reds were not generally visible through the clouds, and the Master Bomber called for skymarking, while informing flare force 3 that it would not be required. The 44 (Rhodesia) Squadron participants bombed either on the glow of the red TIs or on the cascading greens from 14,000 to 16,500 feet between 22.32 and 22.39, and observed many explosions and large columns of thick, black smoke emerging through the cloud tops. Photo-reconnaissance would confirm, that massive damage had been inflicted upon the plant, and a severe setback delivered to the enemy's oil production.

There would be no further operations for 5 Group during the month, although a number would be posted before being cancelled. The squadron spent the period inducting new crews, attending lectures, training, and, during the last few days, clearing snow from the runways. During the course of the month the squadron operated on nine occasions and dispatched ninety-nine sorties without loss.

February 1945

The weather at the start of February provided difficult conditions for marking and bombing, particularly for 5 Group, and a number of operations would struggle to achieve their aims in the face of thick, low cloud and strong winds. 5 Group was back in harness immediately at the start of the new month following the long lay-off, and 271 Lancaster and eleven Mosquito crews were called to briefings on all 5 Group stations on the 1st to learn that their target was to be the marshalling yards in the town of Siegen, situated some fifty miles east of Cologne. This was a 5 Group show, and was one of three major operations planned for the night, the others, by larger forces, taking place at Ludwigshafen and Mainz further into southern Germany. A high wind during the night had helped to clear some of the snow, and the nineteen 44 (Rhodesia) Squadron Lancasters took off without incident between 16.03 and 16.18 with S/L Ferguson the senior pilot on duty, and each carrying either twelve 1,000 pounders or a cookie and sixteen 500 pounders. They all reached the target area shortly after 19.00 and encountered ten-tenths cloud between 3,000 and 7,000 feet, which caused problems for the flare and marker force, some of which were finding it difficult to obtain a clear H2S image on their screens. Eventually, one of the primary blind markers ran in and dropped green TIs at 19.05 from 15,000 feet, and their glow was visible through the clouds. This prompted the first flares, followed by an attempt to mark at low-level with red TIs, which were not visible through the clouds, and, when the Master Bomber called for skymarking at 19.10, the remaining illuminators were superfluous to requirements and were sent home. The bombing phase was put back by four minutes until 19.20, forcing crews to either orbit or dogleg to waste time if they were still on approach, and then instructions were issued to aim at the skymarkers, which were being driven by the strong wind across the intended aiming point and beyond the target. The glow of red target indicators was faintly visible through the clouds, but this was most likely a decoy fire site prepared by the Germans. It attracted many bomb loads, perhaps some from the 44 (Rhodesia) Squadron participants, who bombed from 8,000 to 12,000 feet between 19.20 and 19.37, contributing to what became a widely scattered raid. Much of the bombing fell into open and wooded country, and, although the railway station sustained damage, the marshalling yards escaped.

The next briefing revealed the bad news that a tour of operations was to be increased again to thirty-six sorties. Sixteen 44 (Rhodesia) Squadron crews were in attendance at 15.00 on a drizzly afternoon on the 2nd, to be told further, that the night's operation was to be against Karlsruhe in southern Germany. This was to be another 5 Group effort involving 250 Lancasters and eleven Mosquitos, and was again, only one of three major operations taking place. Wiesbaden was to receive its one and only major raid of the war at the hands of almost five hundred aircraft, while a 320-strong predominantly Halifax force dealt with an oil plant at Wanne-Eickel in the Ruhr. The 44 (Rhodesia) Squadron element departed Spilsby between 19.43 and 20.21 with S/L Bird the senior pilot on duty and headed for the assembly point over Reading. The winds turned out to be lighter than forecast, and this caused a change in route, which now took the force directly from Reading to the target, straddling the Franco-Belgian frontier all the way to Germany, where they encountered heavy cloud between 3,000 and 15,000 feet. The flare force arrived over the target at 17,500 to 18,500 feet between 23.03 and 23.28 and tried to perform their assigned tasks in difficult conditions, some with malfunctioning H2S boxes. The Mosquitos tried to establish an aiming point, but the illumination was not getting through to the ground, and, even had they dropped red TIs, it is unlikely that they would have been visible. At 23.11, the Master Bomber called for skymarking and sent the Mosquitos and remaining illuminators home. S/L Bird crossed the aiming point first as a supporter for the flare force, and, after completing a square orbit, arrived too late to bomb and brought his load home. The other 44 (Rhodesia) Squadron crews bombed on the glow of markers, as instructed by the Master Bomber, from 14,000 to 16,900 feet between 23.19 and 23.25, and all but two returned safely. This final raid of the war on Karlsruhe was a complete failure, and cost fourteen Lancasters, four of them from 189 Squadron, and PA195 and SW251 from 44 (Rhodesia) Squadron. Both crashed somewhere in southern Germany, taking with them to their deaths the crews of F/O Worrall and F/L Gallivan respectively, the first to be lost in 1945.

While the frontier towns of Goch and Cleves were being pounded by the other groups on the night of the 7/8th ahead of the advancing British XXX Corps, 5 Group returned to the Dortmund-Ems Canal with 177 Lancasters and eleven Mosquitos, the former carrying delayed action bombs. 44 (Rhodesia) Squadron made ready ten Lancasters for the main operation and three others for the crews of F/Ls Daggett and Wood and F/O Craig for mining duties in the Forget-me-not garden in Kiel harbour. The latter departed Spilsby first between 19.24 and 19.26, leaving the bombing brigade to follow them into the air later, between 21.02 and 21.09, led by F/L Sutherland. They all reached the target area to find seven to ten-tenths cloud between 6,000 and 9,000 feet, and, in accordance with the Master Bomber's instructions, delivered their twelve or fourteen 1,000 pounders from 9,250 to 11,500 feet between 23.59 and 00.09 onto what were believed to be accurate TIs observed through gaps in the cloud. It turned out to be a rare unsuccessful attack on this target, photographic reconnaissance revealing that the bombs had fallen into fields and had failed to cause any breach. Meanwhile, F/L Daggett and crew had turned back from Odense Fjord on Denmark's Fyn Island after losing their starboard-outer engine, leaving the remaining two gardeners to deliver their six mines each into the briefed locations from 15,000 feet at 22.43 and 22.54.

Seventeen 44 (Rhodesia) Squadron crews found themselves being briefed on the following day for another long round-trip to the Wintershall oil refinery at Politz, as part of a 5 Group force of 227 Lancasters and seven Mosquitos. They were to act as the first wave in a two-phase attack, which would be completed two hours later by 248 Lancasters from 1 and 8 Groups. They took off between 16.49 and 17.15 with F/Ls Mangos, Sutherland and Wood the senior pilots on duty. The blind markers and the flare force crews went in at 13,000 to 14,500 feet between 21.03 and 21.15 to carry out their assigned tasks in the face of an ineffective smoke screen, but, more seriously, also fierce night-fighter activity on approach to and over the target. The main force reached the target area to find clear skies and excellent visibility, and the 44 (Rhodesia) Squadron crews identified ground detail in the light of the illuminating flares before delivering their loads onto red TIs in accordance with the Master Bomber's instructions from 9,000 to 12,000 feet between 21.15 and 21.28. A number of crews reported up to six explosions and smoke rising through 3,000 feet as they turned away to the west, confident in the quality of their work. On return, F/O Young and crew reported that they had begun to fall behind schedule between turning points B and C and had cut corners in an attempt to catch up. Gee was found to be too weak to be of use, and the DR Compass led them astray to the extent that they overshot the target and saw it behind them to the west. As they closed on it at 21.30, the Master Bomber called a halt, thus wasting the effort expended in what would be an eight-hour twenty-minute round trip. The squadron commander magnanimously declared a completed sortie for all except the navigator. Ten Lancasters failed to arrive back in home airspace, and among them was 44 (Rhodesia) Squadron's ME299 with the long-serving crew of F/L Mangos RNZAF, from which the bomb-aimer and flight engineer escaped with their lives to be taken into captivity.

Briefings took place on the 13th for the first round of Operation Thunderclap, the Churchill inspired offensive against Germany's eastern cities, which was devised partly to act in support of the advancing Russians, and also as a demonstration to Stalin of RAF air power, should he turn against the Allies after the war. The historic and culturally significant city of Dresden was selected to open the offensive in another two-phase affair, with a 5 Group force of 246 Lancasters and nine Mosquitos leading the way, to be followed three hours later by 529 Lancasters of 1, 3, 6 and 8 Groups. It had proved to be a successful policy thus far, with the 5 Group low-level marking system and main force attacks providing a beacon for the second force, and should it be required on this night, 8 Group would provide any necessary marking for phase two from high level. The 44 (Rhodesia) Squadron contingent of fifteen Lancasters took off between 18.01 and 18.17 with W/C Newmarch the senior pilot on duty and had absolutely no concept of the ramifications of the operation, both in terms of its outcome on the ground, and its hysterical aftermath. Dresden was Germany's seventh largest city, and its largest remaining relatively unbombed built-up area, which, according to American sources, contained more than a hundred factories and fifty thousand workers contributing to the war effort. It was also an important railway hub, to the extent that the marshalling yards had been attacked twice in late 1944 by the USAAF.

The heavy force was two hours out when W/C Maurice Smith of 54 Base, the Master Bomber for the 5 Group attack, lifted off the Woodhall Spa runway at a few minutes before 20.00 hours in Mosquito KB401 AZ-E, a 627 Squadron aircraft on loan, and he was followed away by eight others from 627 Squadron. F/L Plenderleith and crew had to contend with a lack of power from the starboard-outer engine, and they abandoned their sortie after little more than an hour. The heavy brigade and the Mosquitos arrived in the target area at the same time to encounter three layers of cloud, between 3,000 and 5,000 feet, 6,000 to 8,000 feet and 15,000 to 16,000 feet, but otherwise good visibility. The first primary blind marker delivered green TIs from 15,000 feet at 22.03, and was followed in by the flare force, which lit the way for the low-level Mosquitos. The main force Lancasters were carrying eight hundred tons of bombs, those from 44 (Rhodesia) Squadron in the form either of a cookie and twelve 500 pounders or one 2,000 pounder and fourteen cluster bombs, and these were delivered from 13,500 to 15,000 feet between 22.13 and 22.20 onto the glow of red TIs in accordance with the Master Bomber's instructions. As far as the crews were concerned this was no different from any other attack, and the fires visible for a hundred miles into the return journey nothing out of the ordinary.

By the time the second force of 1, 3, 6 and 8 Group Lancasters arrived over Dresden three hours after 5 Group, the skies had cleared, and the fires created by the earlier attack provided the expected beacon. A further eighteen hundred tons of bombs rained down onto the historic and beautiful old city, setting off the same chain of events that had devastated parts of Hamburg in July 1943, and a number of other cities since. Dresden's population had been swelled by masses of refugees fleeing from the eastern front, and many were engulfed in the ensuing firestorm. On the following morning, three hundred American bombers carried out a separate attack under the umbrella of a fighter escort and completed the destruction. There were claims that RAF aircraft had strafed the streets and open spaces to increase the level of terror, and such accusations abound in the city to this day. In fact, American fighters were responsible, and were trying to add to the general confusion and chaos. Initial propaganda-inspired reports from the Office of the Propaganda Minister, Joseph Goebbels, falsely claimed a death toll of 250,000 people, but an accurate figure of twenty-five thousand has been settled upon since.

The destruction of Dresden has been used by some in this country also as a weapon with which to denigrate Bomber Command and Harris, and label them as war criminals. Curiously, no accusations have been levelled at the Americans. It should also be understood that Harris had no interest in attacking Dresden, and had to be nagged by Chief-of-the-Air-Staff Portal to fulfil Churchill's wishes. The aircrew simply did the job asked of them, and Dresden was no different from any other attack on a city. The death toll at Hamburg was much higher, and yet, there has been no similar outcry. The legacy of this operation served to deny Harris and the men under his Command their due recognition for the massive part they played in the ultimate victory, and only in recent times has a monument been erected in Green Park in London and a campaign clasp awarded, sadly, far too late for the majority. Churchill, with his eyes set on a peacetime election, betrayed Harris and the Command in a typical politically motivated U-turn, in which he accused Harris of bombing solely for the purpose of inflicting terror. In the post-war honours, Harris was the only commander in the field to be omitted.

Round two of Thunderclap was planned for the following night, when Chemnitz was posted as the target for 717 aircraft drawn from 1, 3, 4, 6 and 8 Groups, while 224 Lancasters and eight Mosquitos of 5 Group targeted an oil refinery in the small town of Rositz, situated twenty-five miles due south of Leipzig and thirty miles north-west of Chemnitz. A dozen 44 (Rhodesia) Squadron Lancasters were made ready, and they all became safely airborne between 16.45 and 17.13 with S/L Ferguson the senior pilot on duty. The others pushed on across Germany to be greeted by six to ten-tenths thin cloud in the target area in two layers, one at 6,000 to 8,000 feet, and the other at 10,000 to 12,000 feet, but the primary blind marker made a good run on H2S at 15,000 feet at 20.48 to drop green TIs, and the illuminators followed up between 20.51 and 20.58 from a similar height. The main force crews arriving on time carried out support runs with the marker element, before being called in to bomb at 21.07, the 44 (Rhodesia) Squadron crews releasing their cookie and nine 500 pounders each onto red and green TIs, or on their glow, from 6,000 to 10,950 feet between 21.02 and 21.11. F/O Dalton arrived too late to support the flare force as intended, and while on his bombing run was attacked by a FW190, which he managed to shake off. Before he could release the bombs, however, the Master Bomber called a halt, leaving Dalton and his crew to fly directly to Chemnitz to add their bombs to that raid. Three or four large fires were evident in the oil plant, and black smoke was rising through 5,000 feet as the force turned away. It was established afterwards, that the southern part of the oil plant had been damaged, but it would be necessary to return to finish the job. The Chemnitz raid had been compromised by adverse weather conditions, and it would be March before success was achieved against this target.

F/L Daggett and crew took off at 16.55 on the 15th to join seven others from 5 Group on mining sorties in the Silverthorn III garden in the Kattegat. They encountered ten-tenths cloud with tops at between 2,000 and 12,000 feet, through which six mines were delivered by H2S from 14,000 feet at 20.06. An oil refinery at Böhlen was posted as the target on the 19th for a 5 Group force of 264 Lancasters and six Mosquitos. It was another of the collection of similar plants in the Leipzig area and some ten miles north of Rositz, for which 44 (Rhodesia) Squadron dispatched eighteen Lancasters in a late take-off between 23.43 and 00.05 with F/L Hayler the senior pilot on duty. They all completed the three-and-a-half-hour flight out and would meet up with the later-departing Mosquito element at the target, which included the Master Bomber for the occasion, 54 Base's W/C Benjamin, who was flying the same

Mosquito used by W/C Smith at Dresden six nights earlier. They encountered ten-tenths cloud over the target in two layers at 5,000 to 8,000 feet and 10,000 to 14,000 feet, and this would introduce a challenging element to the operation. The illuminators went in at around 15,000 feet between 04.05 and 04.13, and the VHF chatter suggested that a Mosquito had been able to mark a factory building with a red TI, and that that had been backed up. The main force was called in, before W/C Benjamin's VHF was suddenly cut off, and his Deputy took over. It would be established later, that the Master Bomber's Mosquito had been shot down by flak, and that W/C Benjamin DFC & Bar had died alongside his navigator. The 44 (Rhodesia) Squadron crews carried out their attacks in accordance with confusing instructions, doing so from 9,000 to 13,000 feet between 04.16 and 04.31, and aiming mostly at the glow in the cloud of red and green TIs. Post-raid reconnaissance revealed only superficial damage to the site, which would have to be attacked again.

The following night, the 20th, proved to be a busy one, with more than five hundred Lancasters targeting Dortmund, while 268 Halifaxes from 4 and 6 Groups provided the heavy elements for raids on Rhenania-Ossag oil refineries in Düsseldorf and Monheim. 5 Group, meanwhile, prepared itself for a further attempt on the Mittelland Canal at Gravenhorst, for which ten 44 (Rhodesia) Squadron crews were briefed as part of an overall force of 154 Lancasters and eleven Mosquitos. They departed Spilsby between 21.38 and 21.59 with F/L Daggett the senior pilot on duty, and all reached the target area to find ten-tenths cloud between them and the aiming point. The primary blind marker succeeded in delivering two green TIs by H2S from 12,000 feet at 00.53, and they fell on the starboard side of the canal. After the flare force went in, the Mosquito element descended to 400 feet, but could not identify the aiming point, and, just before H-Hour, the Master Bomber sent the markers home, to be followed almost immediately by the main force as he abandoned the operation.

The operation was rescheduled for twenty-four hours later, when Duisburg and Worms were also to be attacked by heavy forces of 362 and 349 aircraft respectively. 5 Group detailed 165 Lancasters and twelve Mosquitos, and, among those attending the briefing at Coningsby was G/C Evans-Evans, the station commander, who would be taking the bulk of the 83 Squadron commanding officer's highly experienced crew with him. Evans-Evans was 43 and a larger-than-life character, who had commanded 115 Squadron for a spell earlier in the war during its Wellington era and had never lost the enthusiasm to be "one of the boys" and take part in operations. A number of years of good living had widened his girth, and it must have been a struggle to fit into the cramped confines of a Lancaster cockpit. The thirteen 44 (Rhodesia) Squadron participants took off between 16.59 and 17.07 with F/Ls Hayler, Shephard and Symons the senior pilots on duty, and reached the target area to find moonlight beaming down from clear skies with some ground haze. One of the primary blind markers was able to deliver his green TIs, doing so two minutes late because of a change in the wind, and they fell about a mile south of the aiming point, quite close to the Wet Triangle meeting point of the Mittelland and Dortmund-Ems Canals. After the flare force had done its job, the Mosquitos delivered their red TIs, which were backed up successfully, before the main force was called in at 20.25. The 44 (Rhodesia) Squadron crews released their loads of thirteen 1,000 pounders each from 8,000 to 11,000 feet between 20.34 and 20.41, but could not assess the outcome because of the use of long-delay fuses. The presence of night-fighters was clearly evident by the number of combats taking place, and among nine missing Lancasters was the one belonging to 83 Squadron containing G/C Evans-Evans and seven others. Only the rear gunner survived, and, among those killed was the twenty-two-year-old navigator, S/L Wishart DSO, DFC & Bar, who had completed sixty-one operations in Lancasters with 97 Squadron and eighteen in Mosquitos as navigator to Master Bombers. G/C Ingham was left deeply saddened by the loss of his crew.

Spilsby was not involved in the 5 Group operation by seventy-four Lancasters to bomb what was believed to be a U-Boot base at Horten in Oslo Fjord on the night of the 23/24th. Whether or not a U-Boot base existed is uncertain, but no shipping was seen by the crews, and a local report described heavy damage in the port area and a shipyard, and the sinking of a tanker and floating crane. While that was in progress, F/Os Barlow and Dives were to join eight other Lancasters from the group to sneak in under cover of the main event to mine the waters of the Onion garden in Oslo harbour, a little further north. They departed Spilsby at 17.22 and 17.25 and reached the target area to find clear skies and good visibility, before planting their vegetables into the briefed locations from 13,500 feet at 20.46 and 21.53 respectively. On return, they reported smoke climbing through 8,000 feet over Horten, and large fires visible for eighty miles into the return journey.

A daylight attack on the Dortmund-Ems Canal was planned for the afternoon of the 24th, and would involve 166 Lancasters and five Mosquitos, eighteen of the former provided by 617 Squadron with Tallboys on board, while 44 (Rhodesia) Squadron contributed thirteen, each loaded with fourteen 1,000 pounders. They departed Spilsby between 14.06 and 14.23 with F/Ls Hayler and Symons the senior pilots on duty, and reached the target to encounter ten-tenths cloud with tops at between 4,000 and 9,000 feet, at which point, the Master Bomber abandoned the operation and sent the force home with its bombs. During the course of the month, the squadron carried out thirteen operations, including those aborted, and dispatched 156 sorties for the loss of three Lancasters and their crews.

March 1945

The new month would see the Command bludgeon its way across Germany, concentrating on oil, rail and road targets, along with the few towns still boasting a built-up area. Mannheim was raided for the last time in numbers by a large force from 1, 6 and 8 Groups on the 1st, while 5 Group remained at home. Later, on the 2nd, Cologne was pounded for the final time, first by a force of seven hundred aircraft, which inflicted huge destruction across the city, particularly west of the Rhine, and, later, by a 3 Group force, of which only fifteen bombed because of a faulty G-H station in England. The city ceased to function, thereafter, and was still paralyzed when American forces marched in four days later. Just when it seemed that German resistance to air attack might end, March would prove that the defenders were still capable of mounting a challenge, even though they were stretched beyond their capacity to protect every corner of the Reich.

5 Group opened its March account with a return to the Ladbergen aqueduct section of the Dortmund-Ems Canal on the evening of the 3rd, for which 212 Lancasters and ten Mosquitos were made ready. Thirteen 44 (Rhodesia) Squadron crews attended briefing, and they departed Spilsby between 18.38 and 18.49 with W/C Newmarch the senior pilot on duty, each with thirteen 1,000 pounders beneath their feet. They were followed into the air between 17.22 and 17.34 by the crews of F/Os Dives and Barlow and F/L Wood, who were bound for the Onion garden in Oslo harbour. By the time that F/L Richardson and crew reached the Brussels area, they were experiencing navigation problems through faulty equipment and an inability to obtain a firm radar-fix. After eventually establishing their position, it was discovered that the DR compass could not be relied upon, and, as it was now too late to continue to the target, they turned back. The others encountered eight to ten-tenths cloud in the target area at between 3,500 and 6,000 feet, and it was noted that the defences had been strengthened since the last

attack and were throwing up a curtain of intense light flak as high as 15,000 feet. H2S allowed the two 83 Squadron primary blind markers to locate the canal and deliver their green TIs from 14,000 feet at 21.47 and 21.49, and the first illuminators went in a minute later to light the way for the Mosquitos, after which, a large red glow could be seen through the clouds. At 21.59 the Master Bomber called in the main force to bomb on the glow or on sight of the TIs through gaps in the thin cloud, and the 44 (Rhodesia) Squadron crews complied from 8,000 to 10,000 feet between 22.01 and 22.05, contributing to the breaching of both branches, which rendered the waterway unnavigable and out of action for the remainder of the war. Meanwhile, the gardeners had found clear skies and good visibility over Oslo Fjord, and delivered their mines into the briefed locations from 10,000 feet between 20.51 and 21.05.

The Luftwaffe mounted Operation Gisella on this night, sending some two hundred intruders to catch the bombers as they prepared to land, and they succeeded in shooting down twenty for the loss of three of their own. The Spilsby crews were diverted to safer areas on their return, and F/O Ryan RAAF and crew were warned of the dangers in a "Bograt 15 mins" signal as they approached base at 00.36, and again with "Bograt 10 mins" at 00.54. Shortly afterwards, ME442 crashed among trees in Grannington Park on the Brocklesby Estate near Grimsby, killing all on board.

Seventeen 44 (Rhodesia) Squadron crews attended briefing on the 5th, to learn that 5 Group would be sending 248 Lancasters and ten Mosquitos back to Böhlen for another crack at the synthetic oil refinery. A simultaneous operation by a Thunderclap force of 760 aircraft would attempt to redress the recent failure at Chemnitz, some thirty-five miles to the south. Take-off from Spilsby was completed by the 44 (Rhodesia) Squadron crews without incident between 17.00 and 17.12 with S/L Bird the senior pilot on duty, and all reached the target area to encounter ten-tenths cloud in layers between 2,000 and 11,000 feet. Uncertainty concerning the prevailing conditions on arrival led to the preparation of two marking plans, low-level and skymarking, and the lead primary blind marker made his first run at 14,000 feet to drop green TIs at 21.40. He did not see them burst because of the cloud but thought that the illuminator flares were well-placed. Some of the Coningsby crews had H2S difficulties, and not all were able to pinpoint on Leipzig for the run-in. This meant that they were unsure of their position, and, when the Master Bomber called for Wanganui flares at 21.45, they withheld them, rather than risk dropping them inaccurately and attracting some of the bombing. A large explosion was witnessed at 21.50, and, three minutes later, Wanganui flares were observed by the approaching main force crews. Fourteen of the 44 (Rhodesia) Squadron crews delivered their cookie and eleven 500 pounders each from 10,750 to 13,250 feet between 21.52 and 22.02, observing another large explosion at 21.57. The Master Bomber called a halt at 22.01 and sent everyone home, leaving evidence of fires and smoke behind them. F/Os Fugger and Morgans failed to identify the aiming point and decided not to bomb indiscriminately. Four Lancasters failed to return, and among them was LM654 with the crew of F/O Peterswald RAAF, six of whom fell into enemy hands, while the mid-upper gunner managed to evade a similar fate. Post-raid reconnaissance revealed extensive damage to the coal-drying plant, and some hits in other areas of the site, but it was still not a knockout blow. Meanwhile, the Thunderclap force had succeeded in inflicting severe fire damage in central and southern districts of Chemnitz.

The target posted on 5 Group stations on the 6th was the town and port area of Sassnitz, located on the Baltic island of Rügen, about thirty miles north of Peenemünde. This was a region with memories of heavy casualties sustained by 5 Group in August 1943. The two-fold purpose of the operation was to destroy the port installations and facilities and sink shipping to render it unusable as a refuge for escaping Kriegsmarine units. 150 Lancasters and seven Mosquitos were made ready, eleven of the former by 44 (Rhodesia) Squadron, which also loaded four others with mines destined for the Willow garden on the approaches to Sassnitz. They departed Spilsby together between 18.14 and 18.45 with W/C Newmarch the senior pilot on duty, and all reached the target area to find five to nine-tenths drifting cloud with tops up to 8,000 feet. An 83 Squadron blind marker made a run at 22.50 to drop green TIs over the port from 12,000 feet, and the flare force maintained illumination of the town and outer harbour for the next twenty-five minutes. Apart from a short break, when cloud slid across the aiming point, the markers remained visible to the main force crews, and those from 44 (Rhodesia) Squadron bombed on red TIs from 8,500 to 9,750 feet between 23.00 and 23.11, some after orbiting to await a clear view of the ground. F/O Young and crew found themselves to be east of the target at 22.54, and headed in that direction with all possible speed, observing bombing activity at H+18, which ceased two minutes later and left them to return empty-handed. F/Sgt Spencer and crew experienced similar difficulties with navigation and found themselves at one point near Gothenburg in Sweden, before arriving at the target at 23.23, only to be unable to pick out the aiming point through the cloud. Three large ships were identified in the harbour, and these were attacked, and, according to post-raid reconnaissance, sunk. There was also extensive damage in the northern part of the town. Meanwhile, F/Ls Hayler and Wood and F/Os Barlow and Dives had encountered five to seven-tenths cloud with tops at 9,000 feet and dropped their six mines each into the allotted location in the harbour from 13,000 feet between 23.02 and 23.17. Just one Lancaster failed to return from Sassnitz, and that was the squadron's NG396, which crashed in the Baltic, and took with it the crew of F/O Boyle RCAF.

It was back to the oil campaign for 5 Group on the following night, for an attack on an oil refinery at Harburg, south of Hamburg, for which a force of 234 Lancasters and seven Mosquitos was made ready. They would not be alone over Germany, however, as more than a thousand other aircraft would be engaged against similar targets at Dessau and Hemmingstedt and in minor and support operations. 44 (Rhodesia) Squadron provided thirteen Lancasters, which took off between 18.21 and 18.44 with S/L Ferguson the senior pilot on duty. F/O Davies turned back after his port-inner engine lost power on take-off and had to be feathered. The others arrived over the target to find eight-tenths thin cloud and red and yellow target indicators clearly visible, which they bombed in accordance with the Master Bomber's instructions with a seven-second overshoot from 11,000 to 12,750 feet between 21.59 and 22.05. Bomb bursts were clearly seen, along with explosions and black smoke rising through 10,000 feet, and all but two from 44 (Rhodesia) Squadron returned safely to Spilsby, confident in the success of the operation. PB417 and NN768 failed to make it back with the others, and it appears that the former came down in Allied territory, it is believed in France, and the crew of F/O Morgans was described as "safe". The precise fate of the latter is also uncertain, and, while six members of the crew were taken into captivity, the pilot, twenty-year-old F/O Jetson RAAF, is commemorated on the Runnymede memorial. 5 Group crews distinguished themselves on this night by claiming the destruction of seven enemy fighters. Post-raid reconnaissance confirmed further damage to this previously attacked target, with oil storage tanks taking the most hits, and revealed that a rubber factory had also been severely damaged.

An all-time record was set on the 11th, when 1,079 aircraft, the largest Bomber Command force ever for a single target, was assembled to attack Essen for the last time. 5 Group contributed 199 Lancasters and a single Mosquito, 44 (Rhodesia) Squadron loading fourteen Lancasters with a cookie and sixteen 500 pounders each and dispatching them between 12.04 and 12.12 with S/L Ferguson the senior pilot on duty. The city was covered by ten-tenths cloud with tops at 6,000 feet, which required the Path Finder element to employ skymarkers in the form of red and blue smoke puffs, and these were bombed by the 44 (Rhodesia) Squadron crews from 15,000 to 18,500 feet between 15.17 and 15.21. More than

4,600 tons of bombs were dropped into the already ravaged city and former industrial powerhouse and left it with smoke rising through 10,000 feet as the force turned away. It would still be in a state of paralysis when the American ground forces captured it unopposed on the 10th of April. Operations were not yet over for the 11th, as 5 Group sent eleven Lancasters that night to mine the approaches to Oslo harbour in the Onion III garden. F/L Daggett and F/O Barlow departed Spilsby at 17.50 and found the target area to be under clear skies with good visibility. They identified the drop zone by H2S, before making timed runs to deliver their stores from 12,000 feet, F/O Barlow at 21.24, short of the intended release point because of a misunderstanding with the bomb-aimer, and F/L Daggett in the correct location at 21.32.

A little over twenty-four hours later, the short-lived record was surpassed by the departure from their stations in the early afternoon of 1,108 aircraft, which had Dortmund as their destination. This time 5 Group provided 211 Lancasters, fifteen of them from 44 (Rhodesia) Squadron, which departed Spilsby between 13.22 and 13.43 led by F/Ls Shephard and Simons, and each carrying a cookie and sixteen 500 pounders. F/O Thomson was heading south over Cambridgeshire when his port-outer engine began to surge and then emit white smoke, at which point he decided to turn back. The other 44 (Rhodesia) Squadron crews found the Ruhr still under a blanket of ten-tenths cloud, this time with tops at 6,000 feet. The Path Finders marked the target with green and blue smoke puffs, and the main force was directed by the Master Bomber to aim for the blues, an order complied with by the 44 (Rhodesia) Squadron crews from 13,000 to 16,800 feet between 16.52 and 16.56. Returning crews spoke of brown smoke climbing through the clouds to 8,000 feet from the northern end of the city, and also a ring of smoke encircling the area. In fact, the smoke was so dense, that it remained visible for 120 miles into the return flight. A new record of 4,800 tons of bombs was delivered, and photo-reconnaissance revealed that the central and southern districts of the city had received the greatest weight and had been left in chaos with all industry silenced permanently and railway tracks torn up.

The Group's next objective was the Wintershall oil refinery at Lützkendorf, another site to the west of Leipzig and south-west of Leuna in the Geiseltal. *(Lützkendorf no longer exists on a map of Germany and is now known as either Mücheln or Krumpa)*. The briefing of 244 Lancaster and eleven Mosquito crews took place on the 14th, sixteen of the former representing 44 (Rhodesia) Squadron, and they departed Spilsby between 17.00 and 17.10 with six pilots of flight lieutenant rank leading the way. They headed out over the Wash and the bulge of East Anglia en-route to the Scheldt Estuary, but F/L Allen's port-inner engine cut, and they returned to the Wash to jettison their load. The remaining Lancasters crossed Belgium to swing south of Cologne, before pointing their snouts to the east for the long leg to the target. They were met on arrival by conditions described variously as ten-tenths cloud, no cloud, thin layer of cloud, thin banks of stratus with tops at 12,000 feet, a little medium cloud, poor visibility and good visibility, but there was unanimity with regard to the haze. Ahead, the primary blind markers could be seen delivering their green TIs at 21.49, followed by the illuminators immediately afterwards between 21.51 and 22.00 to drop flares and bombs. Finally, the low-level Mosquitos did their job to accurately mark the aiming point before the main force was called in, the 44 (Rhodesia) Squadron participants bombing on red and green TIs in accordance with the Master Bomber's instructions from 8,000 to 11000 feet between 22.01 and 22.12. Returning crews claimed an accurate attack, reporting explosions and fires, and thick black smoke drifting across the plant and ascending through 7,000 feet, which rendered impossible a detailed assessment. Night-fighters were very much in evidence over the target and during the return flight, but the 44 (Rhodesia) Squadron crews managed to evade contact and were diverted on return. Eighteen Lancasters failed to return, 7.4% of those dispatched, and post-raid reconnaissance revealed a partially successful operation, which meant that a further visit would be required.

Twelve 44 (Rhodesia) Squadron crews assembled in the briefing room at 14.00 on the 16th, to learn that they were to attack the virgin target of Würzburg, a small city on the River Main, situated some sixty miles south-east of Frankfurt in southern Germany. While this operation was in progress, a similar-sized force, drawn from 1 and 8 Groups, would be delivering the final attack of the war on Nuremberg, fifty miles to the south-east. A 5 Group force of 225 Lancasters and eleven Mosquitos was made ready for an early-evening take-off, and the 44 (Rhodesia) Squadron element got away between 17.37 and 18.08 with S/L Ferguson the senior pilot on duty. Eighteen minutes after leaving the ground at 17.43, ND869 crashed into the sea off Skegness and took with it to their deaths the crew of F/L Shephard, whose body was recovered along with that of the rear gunner. The other crews all reached the target area to find clear skies with ground haze, and the marking and flare forces having carried out their assigned tasks between 21.25 and 21.34. When the main force crews followed up to exploit the favourable bombing conditions, the 44 (Rhodesia) Squadron crews found red and yellow target indicators marking the aiming point and complied with the Master Bomber's call for a sixteen-second overshoot, to deliver their loads of a cookie and incendiaries each from 10,000 to 11,500 feet between 21.32 and 21.38. They returned to Spilsby without incident to report a successful operation but had to wait for the reconnaissance reports to discover the extent of the destruction. The bombing had lasted just seventeen minutes, during which period 1,127 tons of bombs had fallen into the historic old cathedral city, destroying an estimated 89% of the built-up area and killing four to five thousand people. The Nuremberg operation had also been highly destructive, but had cost 1 Group twenty-four Lancasters, thus proving, that the enemy defences were not yet spent and could still give the Command a bloody nose.

There was still business to attend to at the Böhlen oil refinery, and 5 Group prepared a force of 236 Lancasters and eleven Mosquitos on the 20th, to deal what was hoped to be the knockout blow. Briefings began at 20.00, and, at Spilsby, was attended by sixteen 44 (Rhodesia) Squadron crews, with S/L Bird the most senior pilot present. Thirteen were to participate in the main event, while S/L Bird and F/Ls Daggett and Jory took part in a small-scale diversionary raid on Halle, situated some twenty miles to the north-west of Leipzig. They took off together between 23.25 and 23.44, each carrying a cookie and eleven 500 pounders, and set out on the now familiar path to eastern Germany, where conditions in the target area were fairly good, with three to six-tenths cloud topping out at 6,000 to 8,000 feet. The bomber stream arrived early because of stronger-than-forecast winds, and the main force had to orbit while the first primary blind marker delivered green TIs at 03.33. They fell 750 yards south of the plant, to be followed at H-16 by a yellow TI bursting two miles short of the target. A cluster of illuminator flares ignited ahead, revealing that a smoke screen had been activated and was generating much smoke to create difficulties for the Mosquito low-level markers, despite which, they deposited red TIs on the button, and the main force was called in. A few dummy TIs attracted a number of bomb loads, but the 44 (Rhodesia) Squadron crews complied with the instructions of the Master Bomber to bomb on specific reds and yellows from 11,000 to 12,400 feet between 03.44 and 03.54. The main weight of the attack was concentrated around the target, and numerous explosions were witnessed, as was smoke rising through 5,000 feet as they turned away. Meanwhile, the trio of 44 (Rhodesia) Squadron participants over Halle delivered their loads from 15,600 to 16,000 feet between 03.43 and 03.45 and may have helped to reduce losses from the main event. F/O Hennessy and crew experienced a total hang-up over the target, caused by the bomb-release master switch, which prevented an immediate jettison while still over the aiming point. They were going round again when the Master Bomber called a halt and sent them home. As they headed out of the target area, they were intercepted by a night-fighter, which they evaded after managing to finally dump their bombs. The operation put the oil plant out of action, and it was still idle when American forces moved in a few weeks later.

It was after 22.00 on the 21st that 151 Lancaster and eight Mosquito crews of 5 Group were informed that the Deutsche Erdölwerke synthetic oil refinery at Hamburg was to be their target that night. 44 (Rhodesia) Squadron loaded fourteen Lancasters with a cookie and sixteen 500 pounders each and sent then into the air between 01.21 and 01.33 with S/L Ferguson the senior pilot on duty. F/O Thomson and crew were more than an hour out when the hydraulic feed to the rear turret burst and persuaded them to turn back. F/L Simons and crew were some thirty miles north of the eastern Frisians when the port-outer engine failed, and, in trying to maintain height, the others began to overheat, ending their sortie also. The others pinpointed on the Danish coast to approach the target from the north, and found thin stratus cloud at around 2,000 feet, through which the primary blind marker dropped green TIs on H2S from 14,000 feet at 03.55. The first illuminators went in thirty seconds later and continued to light up the aiming point until 04.01, by which time the Mosquitos had marked, allowing the main force to be called in at 04.05. The 44 (Rhodesia) Squadron crews bombed from 15,000 to 17,750 feet between 04.01 and 04.14, observing many fires and a large explosion at 04.11, that produced red flame and black smoke. Another was reported at 04.16, and it was clear to the homebound crews that the attack had been successful, a fact confirmed by post-raid reconnaissance, which revealed that twenty storage tanks had been destroyed. The operation cost just four Lancasters, among them 44 (Rhodesia) Squadron's PB251, which was brought down by flak to crash at 04.30 some eight miles east-south-east of Heide on the Schleswig-Holstein peninsula, with no survivors from the crew of F/O Hennessy.

The Spilsby squadrons were not involved in 5 Group's operations against railway bridges at Nienburg and Bremen on the 22nd and 23rd, but they were called to briefing on the afternoon of the 23rd to learn of their part in a raid that night on the town of Wesel. This had the misfortune to lie close to the Rhine and in the path of advancing British ground forces, which, since the 16th of February, had caused it to be systematically reduced to rubble by repeated air attacks, and now had one final onslaught to face, having already endured one by 3 Group earlier in the day. 195 Lancasters and eleven Mosquitos were made ready, the dozen representing 44 (Rhodesia) Squadron departing Spilsby between 19.25 and 19.33 with F/Ls Allan, Daggett and Simons the senior pilots on duty, most carrying thirteen 1,000 pounders and a single 500 pounder. The crews found the target under clear skies with slight ground haze and were able to identify it visually. The aiming point was well-marked by red and green TIs, which were bombed from 8,000 to 12,000 feet between 22.33 and 22.37 in accordance with the Master Bomber's instructions. It was noticed, that, despite the Master Bomber ending the attack at H+8, bombing had continued. Post-raid reconnaissance confirmed the effectiveness of the raid, which left only 3% of Wesel's buildings standing, and, after the war, it would claim justifiably to be the most completely destroyed town in Germany.

During the course of the month the squadron took part in fourteen operations and dispatched 161 sorties for the loss of eight Lancasters, seven complete crews and four members of another. Thus, was concluded an unhappy month for the squadron, but fewer than four weeks of operations remained ahead of the crews before the bombing war finally came to an end.

April 1945

A change of leadership at 44 (Rhodesia) Squadron brough W/C Flett to the helm to succeed W/C Newmarch. There would be a gentle introduction to April for 5 Group, and it was not until the 4th that the "Independent Air Force" was called into action. The operation was against what was believed to be a military barracks at Nordhausen, situated in the Harz Mountains between Hannover to the north-west and Leipzig to the south-east. The site was actually a pair of enormous parallel tunnels under the Kohnstein Hill, which had been developed originally by the BASF Company to mine gypsum between 1917 and 1934. Following the destruction of Peenemünde, smaller tunnels had been created as a link between them to form a horizontal ladder effect, and the site turned over to the Mittelwerk GmbH (Gesellschaft mit beschrenkter Haftung, or Limited Company) for the manufacture of V-2 rockets and other secret projects. The "barracks" were part of the Mittelwerk-Dora forced workers camp, where inmates existed under the most horrendous conditions and brutal treatment, while they were starved, worked to death or simply executed by an increasingly desperate regime seeking to change the course of the war. It had been attacked on the previous day by 1 Group, and would now face an initial 5 Group force of 243 Lancasters, which were to be divided between the barracks and the town, ninety-three to the former and 150 to the latter. The twenty representing 44 (Rhodesia) Squadron were assigned to the former, and each of their Lancasters was loaded with a cookie and sixteen 500 pounders. They departed Spilsby between 05.57 and 06.33 with seven pilots of flight lieutenant rank leading the way but lost the services of F/L Allan to engine issues after ninety minutes. The others arrived at the target to encounter five-to-seven-tenths cloud with tops as high as 7,000 feet and were able to identify the target visually until smoke began to obscure the barracks, at which point, those still with bombs were redirected to the town. With the exception of F/O Spencer and crew, the 44 (Rhodesia) Squadron element bombed the barracks from 13,000 to 16,000 feet between 09.14 to 09.18, and, although some of the early bombing of the town was seen to undershoot, the Master Bomber corrected this by calling for a five-second overshoot, and, thereafter, the markers were soon obscured by smoke. F/O Spencer and crew attacked the town from 13,800 feet at 09.15 and returned safely with the rest of the squadron. At debriefing, the crews were able to report a concentrated attack on both aiming points, claiming severe damage, but, tragically and inevitably, heavy casualties were suffered by the unfortunate slave workers.

The only sizeable effort on the night of the 7/8th was by 175 Lancasters and eleven Mosquitos of 5 Group, which had a benzol plant at Molbis, near Leipzig, as their target. Situated south of the city, and less than two miles east of Böhlen, it was becoming a familiar destination for 5 Group via a well-trodden route across Belgium to pass south of Cologne. 44 (Rhodesia) Squadron made ready fifteen Lancasters, which departed Spilsby between 18.25 and 18.38 with F/Ls Allan, Daggett, Jory and Simons the senior pilots on duty, but lost F/O Gardiner to a rear turret issue after two hours. The others found themselves delayed by wrongly forecast head winds, and would reach the target area, although, not necessarily in time to participate in the attack. Two 83 Squadron primary blind markers formed the tip of the spear, and identified Zeitz on H2S, before making the ten-mile north-easterly run from there to the target. Green TIs were released from 15,000 feet at 22.48, and the flare force followed up between 22.50 and 22.57 to enable the low-level Mosquitos to drop red and green TIs among the chimneys of the plant. The following main force crews were greeted by clear skies with ground haze, or, perhaps, a smoke screen in operation, but the highly accurate and visible marking was an invitation for the main force to plaster it with high explosives. In the event, only seven of the 44 (Rhodesia) Squadron element bombed the primary target on red and green TIs from 11,500 to 14,000 feet between 23.07 and 23.14, while four others, who were still short of the aiming point when the Master Bomber called "Cease bombing", at 23.11, attacked last resort objectives like searchlight and flak concentrations. Three others brought their loads home from what photo-reconnaissance confirmed was a complete success, which ended all production at the plant.

Two major operations were scheduled for the 8th, the larger one involving 440 aircraft from 4, 6 and 8 Groups to be directed against Hamburg's shipyards, where the new Type XXI U-Boots were under construction. 5 Group, meanwhile, would take on the Lützkendorf refinery, following a failed attempt on the 4th by 1 and 8 Groups to conclusively end production at the site. A force of 231 Lancasters and eleven Mosquitos was put together, of which the twenty 44 (Rhodesia) Squadron participants departed Spilsby between 17.58 and 18.26 with a whole host of pilots of flight lieutenant rank leading the way. They all reached the target area, where conditions were as they had been twenty-four hours earlier, with clear skies and either ground haze or generated smoke. The primary blind markers ran in at 14,000 feet at 22.33 to deliver green TIs, and the illuminators followed between 22.35 and 22.42, after which, the main force was called in. The 44 (Rhodesia) Squadron crews attacked in accordance with the Master Bomber's instructions to bomb the southerly red and yellow TIs after an eleven second overshoot. They ran in at 11,200 to 14,000 feet between 22.45 and 22.52, and all returned safely to diversion airfields, confident that it would not be necessary to return to that particular target. They described their experiences to the Intelligence Section at debriefing, reporting many explosions, including a large one at 22.47, which was surpassed in size by another one two minutes later, and flames were said to have reached up to 3,000 feet. The complete destruction of the site was confirmed by photo-reconnaissance, and the plant would remain out of action for what remained of the war. Earlier in the day, the length of a tour had been reduced from thirty-six to thirty-three sorties, and those with that number already under their belt, would, no doubt, get drunk in celebration that night.

The squadron sat out a modest 5 Group raid on oil storage tanks and U-Boot pens at Hamburg in daylight on the 9th, and, when eleven of its crews were called to briefing on the 10th, it was to discover that they would be going back to the Leipzig area for the third successive operation, this time to hit a stretch of railway track linked to the Wahren marshalling yards, situated to the north-west of the city. A larger operation on this night, involving more than three hundred aircraft from 1 and 8 Groups, was to be directed at the Plauen marshalling yards to the south-west of Dresden, and the two forces would adopt a similar route until shortly before reaching Leipzig. 5 Group contributed all seventy-six Lancasters for Leipzig and eleven Mosquitos, with 8 Group providing the other eight Oboe Mosquitos, which, now that mobile Oboe stations had been set up on the Continent, could operate over the whole of Germany. The 44 (Rhodesia) Squadron element of eleven took off between 18.25 and 18.48 with F/L Simons the senior pilot on duty and each carrying eleven 1,000 pounders. F/L Simons and crew were soon on their way home with electrical system failure and a fire in the fuse box, leaving the others to reach the target area to find clear skies and excellent conditions for bombing. There were many ineffective searchlights, but flak was light, probably because of a heavy night-fighter presence. The Oboe Mosquitos dropped green TIs as a reference for the 83 Squadron crews, which provided the illumination between 22.51 and 22.57 for the low-level Mosquito element. They placed their red TIs accurately onto the aiming point, before the main force bombed the southernmost red TI in accordance with the Master Bomber's instructions. The 44 (Rhodesia) Squadron element carried out their attacks from 11,700 to 13,800 feet between 22.59 and 23.03, and all but one returned home to make their reports. ND631 crashed somewhere in north-eastern Germany, almost certainly on the way home, killing the experienced F/O Kennedy and six of his crew, and delivering the single survivor into enemy hands. Photographic-reconnaissance would confirm serious damage to the eastern half of the targeted stretch of track.

A major attack on Kiel by elements of 3, 6 and 8 Groups was planned for the night of the 13/14th, while 5 Group took advantage of that activity to send eighteen Lancasters to lay mines in the Forget-me-not garden in Kiel harbour. F/L Simons and F/Os Craig, Irving and Parkin departed Spilsby shortly after 20.30, and F/O Craig and crew were some sixty miles short of the Danish coast when an unserviceable rear turret forced an early return. The remaining trio encountered six to ten-tenths stratus with tops up to 7,000 feet, through which they delivered their vegetables by H2S from 10,450 to 10,900 feet between 23.23 and 23.39.

5 Group was used to being handed the most distant targets, and, as the final days of the bombing war approached, it found itself facing three long-range trips on consecutive nights, all to railway targets. The first of these was at Pilsen in Czechoslovakia, for which a force of 222 Lancasters and eleven Mosquitos was made ready. The fourteen 44 (Rhodesia) Squadron crews attended briefing in the early evening and made their way to the runway at around 23.30 with W/C Flett the senior pilot on duty for the first time. F/L Allan swung off the runway, as did a 207 Squadron Lancaster, and both were scrubbed from the operation, leaving twenty-seven Lancasters to depart Spilsby between 23.24 and 00.10. F/L Webster and crew lost their hydraulics system on take-off, and headed for the jettison area, while F/L Konschel and crew had reached deep into enemy territory and had the Czech frontier in sight when their port-outer engine cut at 03.25 and the starboard-outer began to overheat. The bombs were jettisoned, and having fallen well behind schedule, they decided to cut across to the planned return route, where they hoped to slot into the homebound bomber stream for protection. The others, meanwhile, found clear skies in the target area and only slight haze, and, ahead, watched the first primary blind marker deliver green TIs at 03.38, before the flare forces followed between 03.51 and 03.56. The main force was called in at 03.58, and the 44 (Rhodesia) Squadron participants bombed from 13,600 to 16,000 feet between 03.58 and 04.10, aiming at the north-westerly red and yellow TIs with an eight-second overshoot in accordance with the Master Bomber's instructions. Returning crews reported a large explosion at 04.00, followed by oily smoke, and it was concluded that the raid had been successful. W/C Flett and crew had experienced a frustrating first operation, after reaching the target as a supporter for the flare force at H-13. As they repositioned for the bombing run, they lost the Master Bomber's transmissions, and then the bombs hung-up during the second pass across the aiming point. They left the target at H+5, still unable to dislodge the bombs, and had to bring them home.

There was good news to celebrate on the 17th, when the length of a tour was reduced yet again to thirty sorties, releasing many crews to contemplate a long future. Among those benefitting was S/L Belasco of 207 Squadron and formerly of 44 (Rhodesia) Squadron. That evening, the target posted for ninety 5 Group Lancasters and eleven Mosquitos was the marshalling yards at Cham, on Germany's border with Czechoslovakia, for which seventeen 44 (Rhodesia) Squadron crews were briefed. They departed Spilsby between 23.44 and 00.17 with no senior pilots on duty, and the Lancasters loaded with a mixture of 1,000 and 500 pounders. It took more than four hours to reach the target area, where they were greeted by clear skies with slight ground haze. The primary blind marker dropped the first green TIs on H2S from 14,000 feet at 03.47, and the flare forces went in between 03.51 and 03.54 to light the way for the Mosquito low-level markers. Their efforts were seen to be very concentrated, but the use of delay-fused bombs meant that no immediate assessment would be possible. The 44 (Rhodesia) Squadron crews bombed in accordance with the Master Bomber's instructions from 9,000 to 11,000 feet, and they were over the aiming point to bomb the north-westerly red TIs between 03.59 and 04.05. Photo-reconnaissance later confirmed that tracks had been torn up and rolling stock damaged, and it was another success for the group.

5 Group was not involved when a force of over nine hundred aircraft reduced the island of Heligoland to the appearance of a cratered moonscape on the 18th, and the Spilsby squadrons also sat out a raid that night by 113 Lancasters and ten Mosquitos of the group that put out of action the railway yards at Komotau (now Chomutov), also in Czechoslovakia, which proved to be the last raid in the communications offensive, begun more than a year earlier. Spilsby was not called into action again until the 23rd, when 5 Group sent 148 Lancasters to attack the railway yards and port area of Flensburg on the eastern coast of the Schleswig-Holstein peninsula. The twelve 44 (Rhodesia) Squadron crews departed Spilsby between 15.02 and 15.22 with F/Ls McKay and Webster the senior pilots on duty and reached the target area to encounter ten-tenths cloud with tops at 4,500 feet, which persuaded the Master Bomber to send the force home with their bomb loads intact.

5 Group operated for the final time on the 25th, with an operation in the morning against the SS barracks at Hitler's Eaglesnest retreat at Berchtesgaden in the Bavarian mountains, and later that night on an oil refinery at Tonsberg in Norway. 5 Group supported the former with eighty-eight Lancasters and a single Mosquito in an overall 1, 5 and 8 Group force of 359 Lancaster and sixteen Mosquitos. The eight 44 (Rhodesia) Squadron participants departed Spilsby in the wake of the 207 Squadron element between 04.20 and 04.35 with W/C Flett the senior pilot on duty. All arrived in the target area to find clear skies, despite which, it proved difficult to identify the barracks in the absence of visible markers, and the Master Bomber's instructions were not getting through. However, a nearby lake and the town stood out clearly, and six of the 44 (Rhodesia) Squadron element were able to establish their position before carrying out their attacks from 15,200 and 16,000 feet between 08.59 and 09.03. F/Os Craig and Maltas brought their bombs home after failing to identify the aiming point. When F/L Webster and crew touched down at Spilsby at 13.06, they had the honour to bring to a close 44 (Rhodesia) Squadron's sixty-eight-month-long period of offensive action, spanning the first day of the war to the end of strategic bombing. It was difficult to assess the accuracy of this operation, but it appeared to be effective, and no local report emerged to provide clarity.

During the course of this final month of the bombing war, 44 (Rhodesia) Squadron took part in nine operations and dispatched 121 sorties for the loss of a single Lancaster and its crew. The very first sorties in support of Operation Exodus, the repatriation of prisoners of war, were launched later on the 26th, when forty-two Lancasters from 5 Group were dispatched to an unnamed continental airfield, which may have been Melsbroek in Belgium. W/C Flett headed a contingent of eight 44 (Rhodesia) Squadron Lancasters to Brussels on the 2nd of May for PoW repatriation duties. The squadron would continue to support Operation Exodus, but there is no mention of participation in Operation Manna, the supply of food to the starving Dutch people still under occupation, which began during the final few days of April and continued until the cessation of hostilities on the 8th of May.

44 (Rhodesia) Squadron has one of the finest wartime records of service in Bomber Command. It was one of only two squadrons to serve the Command without a break from the first day of the war to the last, and, although it detached aircraft for short periods to Coastal Command, the squadron as a whole was never withdrawn from the Order of Battle. It was also the only squadron to serve exclusively in 5 Group from start to finish without a break. It enjoyed the distinction of introducing the Lancaster to operational service and had two commanding officers who wore the Victoria Cross. It was not a lucky squadron, and suffered the heaviest Lancaster losses, both in numbers and percentage, in the Group and the Command, the heaviest overall losses in 5 Group, and equal third highest losses overall in the Command.

Lancaster ND578 KM-Y. Spilsby. January 1945.

44 Sqn A Flight, Spilsby, early 1945.
Back L-R: Sgt E Grey (RG), Sgt L Simmons (MUG), F/Sgt Jim A Bignald (W.Op), F/O A Murray (BA), F/L W A 'Shep' Shephard (Pilot),
Front L-R: Ray Jagger, Eric Howell, Walter Smith

Crew of KM-C PA256 at Spilsby
Groundcrew – Eric Howell -Ron Exell

44 Sqn Crew from Lancaster PB417 KM-R.
P/O P.W.B. Morgans & crew safe after aircraft lost 7th of March 1945.

Post-war photograph of F/L John Chatterton but still in 44 Sqn.

Lancaster KM-V May 1945.
L-R: F/Sgt R Bilsland (Nav), F/O D Irving RAAF (Pilot), F/L W Cooper (BA), Sgt W Simpson (RG), Sgt H T West (FE), F/Sgt F Groenewald Rhodesian (MUG), F, Sgt R Brandli RAAF (W.Op)

Crew of Sgt Valentine Barford (Nav),
The rest of the crew are thought to be: F/Sgt G S Graham (Pilot), Sgt Hemshall (FE), Sgt E Howard (BA), F/Sgt R Haynes (W.Op) Sgt J Wark (MUG), Sgt W H Pelwer.

In Memoriam

44 (Rhodesia) Squadron

MOTTO **FULMINA REGIS IUSTA** (The king's thunderbolts are righteous)   Code **KM**

Stations

WADDINGTON	16.06.37. to 31.05.43.
DUNHOLME LODGE	31.05.43. to 30.09.44.
SPILSBY	30.09.44. to 21.07.45.

Commanding Officers

WING COMMANDER J N BOOTHMAN	24.04.39. to 08.12.39.
WING COMMANDER W J M ACKERMAN	15.12.39. to 12.03.40.
WING COMMANDER D W REID	12.03.40. to 12.03.41.
WING COMMANDER S T MISSELBROOK DSO	20.03.41. to 13.12.41.
WING COMMANDER R A B LEAROYD VC	19.12.41. to 08.05.42.
WING COMMANDER P W LYNCH-BLOSSE DFC	08.05.42. to 10.05.42.
WING COMMANDER K P SMALES DSO DFC	10.05.42. to 01.03.43.
WING COMMANDER J D NETTLETON VC	02.03.43. to 13.07.43.
WING COMMANDER E A WILLIAMSON	15.07.43. to 01.08.43.
WING COMMANDER R L BOWES	03.08.43. to 03.02.44.
WING COMMANDER F W THOMPSON DFC AFC	03.02.44. to 09.11.44.
WING COMMANDER R A NEWMARCH	09.11.44. to 01.04.45.
WING COMMANDER S E FLETT	01.04.45. to 12.06.45.

Aircraft

HAMPDEN	02.39. to	12.41.
LANCASTER I/III	12.41. to	05.47

Operational Record

OPERATIONS	SORTIES	AIRCRAFT LOSSES	% LOSSES
637	6405	192	3.0

CATEGORY OF OPERATIONS

BOMBING	MINING	OTHER
518	108	11

HAMPDENS

OPERATIONS	SORTIES	AIRCRAFT LOSSES	% LOSSES
338	2043	43	2.1

CATEGORY OF OPERATIONS

BOMBING	MINING	OTHER
246	81	11

LANCASTERS

OPERATIONS	SORTIES	AIRCRAFT LOSSES	% LOSSES
299	4362	149	3.4

CATEGORY OF OPERATIONS

BOMBING	MINING
272	27

Aircraft Histories

HAMPDEN.	**To December 1941.**
L4042	From 16 OTU.
L4074 KM-O	From 50 Squadron. To 25 OTU.
L4085 KM-A	Ditched off Aberystwyth on return from mining sortie 1.8.40.
L4086	To 49 Squadron via 14 OTU.
L4087	FTR from mining sortie 19/20.7.40.
L4088	FTR from mining sortie 21/22.4.40.
L4089	Shot down by Spitfires off Berwick on return from reconnaissance sortie to Norway 21.12.39.
L4090	Shot down by Spitfires off Berwick on return from reconnaissance sortie to Norway 21.12.39.
L4091	To 16 OTU.
L4098 KM-J	Crashed on landing at Waddington during training 2.5.40.
L4099	From 50 Squadron. FTR Kristiansand Norway 12.4.40.
L4100	To 106 Squadron.
L4102	FTR from reconnaissance sortie to the Elbe Estuary 25/26.3.40.
L4115	From 61 Squadron. To 16 OTU.
L4153	Force-landed near Grimsby on return from patrol 27.2.40.
L4154	Force-landed near Colchester on return from Berlin 20/21.10.40.
L4168	From 7 Squadron. To 50 Squadron and back. To 16 OTU.
L4171	FTR from operation to a communications target 23/24.5.40.
L4178	From 106 Squadron. To 144 Squadron.
P1152	To 50 Squadron.
P1173	FTR Kristiansand Norway 12.4.40.
P1187	To 420 Squadron RCAF.
P1322	From 106 Squadron. To 25 OTU.
P1324	Force-landed in Northamptonshire on return from mining sortie 2.10.40.
P1325	FTR from targets in the Pas de Calais area 11/12.6.40.
P1331	Crash-landed at Waddington on return from patrol 23/24.4.40.
P1338	FTR Bremerhaven 11/12.9.40.
P1339	To 1 AAS.
P1340	Crashed near Harwich on return from Emmerich 3/4.6.40.
P2077 KM-H	FTR Bernburg 13/14.8.40.
P2087 KM-M	FTR Krefeld 6/7.9.40.
P2121	FTR Antwerp 17/18.9.40.
P2122	To 144 Squadron after conversion for use as torpedo bomber.
P2123	Ditched off Norfolk on return from Berlin 1.9.40.
P2137	FTR Berlin 20/21.10.40.
P2142	To 16 OTU.
P4285 KM-U	From 50 Squadron. Crashed on approach to Coningsby on return from Kassel 9.9.41.
P4286	From 50 Squadron. FTR Breda 14/15.5.40.

P4290 KM-B	Ditched off Suffolk on return from Stettin 5/6.9.40.
P4310	FTR Soest 12/13.6.41.
P4352	FTR from mining sortie 3/4.7.40.
P4353	Crashed on take-off from Waddington for air-test 25.8.40.
P4371	FTR Calais 10/11.9.40.
P4372	FTR Gelsenkirchen 29/30.8.40.
P4373	To 25 OTU.
P4374 KM-J	Crashed on landing at Radlett during ferry flight 2.9.40.
P4375	FTR Hamburg 28/29.7.40.
P4393	Crashed on landing at Waddington following ferry flight 9.7.40.
P4400	From 25 OTU. To 420 Squadron RCAF.
P4406 KM-K	FTR from mining sortie 27/28.7.41.
P4414	To 106 Squadron.
P4415	To 1 AAS.
P5321	From 7 AAU. To 408 Squadron RCAF.
P5332	From 7 AAU. To 420 Squadron RCAF.
X2898	From 83 Squadron. To 16 OTU.
X2910	FTR Berlin 14/15.10.40.
X2913	FTR Bremerhaven 11/12.9.40.
X2916	To 25 OTU.
X2917 KM-D/R	Crashed in Norfolk when bound for Calais 6.8.41.
X2918	FTR Cologne 10/11.3.41.
X2921 KM-Z	From 106 Squadron. Crashed soon after take-off from Waddington when bound for a mining sortie 7.9.41.
X2965	FTR Cologne 1/2.10.40.
X2966	Force-landed on Sutton-on-Sea beach on return from Le Havre 29.11.40.
X2982 KM-Z	Crash-landed in Yorkshire on return from Mannheim 13.5.41.
X2995	Crashed soon after take-off from Waddington when bound for Hamburg 14.11.40.
X2996	FTR Berlin 14/15.11.40.
X2997	Crashed on landing at Waddington on return from Merseburg 17.10.40.
X2999	FTR Berlin 17/18.4.41.
X3008	Crashed on landing at Bircham Newton on return from Hamburg 17.11.40.
X3023	Crashed in Norfolk on return from Lützkendorf 20.11.40.
X3025 KM-Q	Hit by AE157 of 50 Squadron on the ground at Waddington and damaged beyond repair 3.9.41.
X3026	To 1 TTU after conversion for use as torpedo bomber.
X3049	FTR from mining sortie 10/11.12.40.
X3057	To 49 Squadron.
X3061	From 83 Squadron. To 420 Squadron RCAF.
X3142	To 16 OTU.
X3149 KM-B	To 420 Squadron RCAF.
X3150	To 455 Squadron RAAF after conversion for use as torpedo bomber.
AD726	FTR Cologne 31.8/1.9.41.
AD727	To 61 Squadron.

AD747 KM-G	Crashed in Shropshire during ferry flight 19.6.41.
AD755	Crashed in Lincolnshire following early return from Cologne 31.7.41.
AD758	From 106 Squadron. To 408 Squadron RCAF.
AD829	From 83 Squadron. To 455 Squadron RAAF.
AD840 KM-E	FTR Hamm 8/9.7.41.
AD847	Crash-landed near West Raynham on return from Hamburg 27.4.41.
AD855	From 106 Squadron. To 420 Squadron RCAF.
AD864	FTR Hamburg 2/3.5.41.
AD868 KM-R	From 61 Squadron. FTR Brest 17/18.12.41.
AD869 KM-U	To 420 Squadron RCAF.
AD899	FTR from mining sortie 8/9.4.41.
AD904	Crashed in Shropshire during ferry flight 19.6.41.
AD913 KM-K	Abandoned over Surrey on return from Frankfurt 3.9.41.
AD915 KM-T	To 420 Squadron RCAF.
AD917 KM-P	Crashed near Waddington while in transit 28.8.41.
AD920	To 144 Squadron after conversion for use as torpedo bomber.
AD930 KM-I	Crashed on approach to Waddington on return from Hamburg 16.9.41.
AD933 KM-E	Crash-landed in Worcestershire on return from Düsseldorf 28.11.41.
AD939 KM-N	Collided with a Spitfire near Waddington during training 31.8.41.
AD962 KM-A	FTR Brest 24.7.41.
AD966 KM-R	Crashed in Lincolnshire during training 1.8.41.
AD968 KM-S	To 420 Squadron RCAF.
AD975 KM-J	FTR Cologne 13/14.10.41.
AD981 KM-A	Ditched off Cromer on return from Rostock 12.9.41.
AD982	To 408 Squadron RCAF.
AD983 KM-M	Crashed in Lincoln on return from mining sortie 22.7.41.
AE127	FTR Soest 12/13.6.41.
AE128 KM-M	From 144 Squadron. To 455 Squadron RAAF.
AE129	Crashed in Lincolnshire following early return from mining sortie 14.6.41.
AE130 KM-O	To 455 Squadron RAAF after conversion for use as torpedo bomber.
AE152 KM-J/R	FTR Berlin 2/3.9.41.
AE153	FTR Hamm 8/9.7.41.
AE186	From 61 Squadron. To 420 Squadron RCAF.
AE192	To 408 Squadron RCAF.
AE196	From 408 Squadron RCAF. FTR from mining sortie 13.12.41.
AE201	To 455 Squadron RAAF after conversion for use as torpedo bomber.
AE202 KM-K	From 61 Squadron. To 420 Squadron RCAF.
AE218 KM-W	To 50 Squadron.
AE239	FTR Düsseldorf 16/17.8.41.
AE242	To 455 Squadron RAAF.
AE254 KM-W	FTR Berlin 2/3.9.41.
AE257 KM-X	FTR Bremen 21/22.10.41.
AE258	To 420 Squadron RCAF.
AE260	To 420 Squadron RCAF.
AE290	From 61 Squadron. FTR Le Havre 23/24.10.41.
AE298	To 420 Squadron RCAF.

AE313 KM-C	FTR Frankfurt 2/3.9.41.
AE377	FTR Dunkerque 8/9.11.41.
AE379	To 420 Squadron RCAF.
AE382 KM-A	FTR Dunkerque 10/11.10.41.
AE384	To 420 Squadron RCAF.
AE385	To 420 Squadron RCAF.
AE390	To 420 Squadron RCAF.
AE393	To 420 Squadron RCAF.
AE398	Crashed near Coltishall while training 26.10.41.
AE399	To 420 Squadron RCAF.
AE428	To 50 Squadron.
AE430	To 455 Squadron RAAF.
AT128	To 420 Squadron RCAF.
AT130	To 420 Squadron RCAF.
AT132	To 420 Squadron RCAF.
AT134	To 420 Squadron RCAF.
AT135	To 420 Squadron RCAF.
AT136	To 420 Squadron RCAF.
AT144	To 420 Squadron RCAF.

MANCHESTER.   **December 1941 to June 1942.**

L7382 KM-N	From 83 Squadron. Training only. To 6AGS.
L7385	Training only. To 207 Squadron.
L7401	From 408 Squadron RCAF. Training only. To 61 Squadron.
L7415	From 408 Squadron RCAF. Training only. To 61 Squadron.
L7425	From 97 Squadron. Training only. To 61 Squadron.
L7430 KM-N-	From 25 OTU. Conversion Flt only. To 1654 CU.
L7453	From 83 Squadron. Training only. To 61 Squadron.
L7477	Training only. To 61 Squadron.
L7480 KM-A-	From 207 Squadron. To 1661 CU.
L7481	From 25 OTU. Conversion Flt only. To 1661 CU.
R5790	From 83 Squadron. Conversion Flt only. To 1661 CU.

LANCASTER.   **From December 1941.**

BT308	From Ringway. Familiarisation/training only. To 97 Squadron.
L7530	No operations. To 207 Squadron.
L7531	No operations. To 97 Squadron.
L7532	To 97 Squadron.
L7533 KM-K/J	FTR Warnemünde 8/9.5.42.
L7534 KM-F	To 50 Squadron via 44 Squadron Conversion Flight July 42.
L7536 KM-H	FTR Augsburg, Sgt Rhodes, 17.4.42.
L7537 KM-L	FTR Düsseldorf 31.7/1.8.42.
L7538 KM-B	To 97 Squadron and back. Crashed on landing at Waddington while training 20.2.42.
L7539 KM-G	To 61 Squadron.

L7540	To 83 Squadron.
L7541 KM-O/U	To 1660 CU.
L7542	Crash-landed at Skellingthorpe during training 7.2.42.
L7543	To 207 Squadron.
L7544	Training only. To 207 Squadron.
L7545 KM-R	To 1654 CU.
L7546 KM-J	First off on the squadron's first Lancaster operation flown by S/L Nettleton 3.3.42. To 207 Squadron.
L7547 KM-D	To 207 Squadron.
L7548 KM-T	FTR Augsburg, W/O Crum, 17.4.42.
L7549 KM-Q	To 44 Squadron Conversion Flight. Crashed 22.4.42.
L7565 KM-V	FTR Augsburg, W/O Beckett, 17.4.42.
L7566	To 83 Squadron.
L7567 KM-C	To 49 Squadron.
L7568 KM-W	Crashed on landing at Waddington while training 10.7.42. To 83 Squadron.
L7569 KM-U	From 97 Squadron. To 106 Squadron.
L7576 KM-E-	From 97 Squadron. To 1660 Conversion Flt via 44 Squadron Conversion Flt.
L7581 KM-R	Crashed on take-off from Waddington for air-test 20.5.42.
L7584 KM-S	To 44 Squadron Conversion Flt. Crashed in Yorkshire while training 22.8.42.
R5484 KM-K	No operations. To 83 Squadron.
R5489 KM-X	Crashed on approach to Waddington while training 16.8.42.
R5491	To 61 Squadron.
R5492 KM-M	To 106 Squadron.
R5493 KM-M	FTR from mining sortie 24/25.3.42 and was the first operational loss of a Lancaster.
R5494 KM-O	To OADU.
R5495	To 97 Squadron.
R5496	To 97 Squadron.
R5497	To 97 Squadron.
R5506 KM-P	FTR Augsburg, F/L Sandford 17.4.42.
R5508 KM-B	S/L Nettleton's aircraft for Augsburg 17.4.42. for which he was awarded a VC. To 97 Squadron Conversion Flight.
R5510 KM-A	FTR Augsburg, F/O Garwell, 17.4.42.
R5514	To 156 Squadron.
R5515 KM-A	Crash-landed at Waddington while training 6.6.42.
R5516 KM-F	FTR Essen 5/6.6.42.
R5542	To 83 Squadron via 44 Squadron Conversion Flight.
R5547	From 207 Squadron. To 1654 CU.
R5554 KM-Q	FTR Munich 19/20.9.42.
R5555 KM-P	FTR Warnemünde 8/9.5.42.
R5556 KM-C	To 1661 CU.
R5557 KM-G	FTR Warnemünde 8/9.5.42.
R5568 KM-T	FTR Warnemünde 8/9.5.42.
R5603 KM-D	FTR Essen 4/5.8.42.
R5624 KM-P	To 1661CU.
R5631 KM-J	To 106 Squadron Conversion Flight.

R5664 KM-R	To OADU and back. Crashed while landing at Waddington on return from Kassel 28.8.42.
R5665 KM-A	To 106 Squadron.
R5666 KM-F	FTR Nienburg 17/18.12.42.
R5669 KM-Z	From 83 Squadron. FTR Berlin 23/24.12.43.
R5685	From 50 Squadron. Training only. Returned to 50 Squadron.
R5697 KM-H/R	To 106 Squadron.
R5726	From 50 Squadron. To 100 Squadron.
R5727	To Canada as pattern aircraft November 1942.
R5729 KM-A	FTR Brunswick 14/15.1.44.
R5732 KM-G	Crashed at Waddington following early return from Mainz 12.8.42.
R5733 KM-P	From 50 Squadron. To 1654 CU.
R5740 KM-O	FTR Gelsenkirchen 25/26.6.43.
R5744	Completed 21 operations. To 9 Squadron.
R5842	From 61 Squadron. To 49 Squadron Conversion Flt May 1942.
R5846 KM-X-	From 61 Squadron. To 1661 CU.
R5858 KM-G	Ditched during Atlantic patrol 14.6.42.
R5862 KM-V	To 1660 CU.
R5863	No operations. To 207 Squadron.
R5898 KM-G	From 49 Squadron. FTR Duisburg 9/10.4.43.
R5901 KM-X	From 106 Squadron. FTR Hannover 18/19.10.43.
R5903 KM-C/R	FTR Osnabrück 6/7.10.42.
R5905 KM-R	FTR Wismar 23/24.9.42.
W4105 KM-K/X	FTR Frankfurt 24/25.8.42.
W4106 KM-T	Crash-landed at Waddington while training 23.3.43.
W4110 KM-K	FTR Pilsen 13/14.5.43.
W4124 KM-D	FTR Kassel 27/28.8.42.
W4125 KM-Q	FTR Munich 21/22.12.42.
W4126 KM-B	From 44 Squadron Conversion Flight. FTR Nienburg 17/18.12.42.
W4135	From 50 Squadron. No operations. To 97 Squadron.
W4136	To 61 Squadron via 44 Squadron Conversion Flight.
W4137 KM-L	From 44 Squadron Conversion Flight. Crashed on landing at Waddington on return from St-Nazaire 1.3.43.
W4162 KM-Y	Completed 17 operations. To 83 Squadron.
W4169 KM-S	FTR Bremen 13/14.9.42.
W4176 KM-X	FTR from mining sortie 8/9.1.43.
W4177 KM-W	FTR from mining sortie 18/19.9.42.
W4180 KM-D	FTR Hamburg 9/10.11.42.
W4187 KM-S	FTR Wismar 1/2.10.42.
W4188 KM-G	FTR Osnabrück 6/7.10.42.
W4199 KM-H	FTR Berlin 29/30.3.43.
W4259 KM-P	From 44 Squadron Conversion Flight. Collided with W4182 (9 Squadron) over Lincoln when bound for Duisburg 20.12.42.
W4266	From 50 Squadron. No operations. Returned to 50 Squadron.
W4267	From 50 Squadron. Crashed in Norfolk 27.1.43.
W4268 KM-Q	To 622 Squadron via 1654 CU.
W4277 KM-S	FTR from mining sortie 8/9.1.43.

W4304 KM-C		FTR Stuttgart 22/23.11.42.
W4305 KM-J/G		FTR Pilsen 13/14.5.43.
W4778 KM-T		From 106 Squadron. FTR Hamburg 2/3.8.43.
W4819 KM-G		From 9 Squadron. FTR Cologne 2/3.2.43.
W4829 KM-V		From 9 Squadron. FTR Berlin 1/2.3.43.
W4831 KM-C		From 9 Squadron. FTR Berlin 1/2.1.44. (aircraft's 13th Berlin sortie).
W4832 KM-U		FTR Lorient 7/8.2.43.
W4838 KM-B		FTR Wuppertal 29/30.5.43.
W4839 KM-B/F/S		FTR Berlin 27/28.3.43.
W4841 KM-W		FTR from mining sortie 10/11.3.43.
W4933 KM-Y		From 156 Squadron. To 50 Squadron.
W4935 KM-M		FTR Peenemünde 17/18.8.43.
W4936 KM-W		FTR Oberhausen 14/15.6.43.
W4949 KM-H		FTR Oberhausen 14/15.6.43.
W4961 KM-S		FTR Berlin 3/4.9.43.
DV155 KM-G		From 617 Squadron. FTR Berlin 3/4.9.43.
DV166 KM-B		From 49 Squadron. To 1669 CU.
DV202 KM-Z		FTR Peenemünde 17/18.8.43.
DV238 KM-M		From 49 Squadron. FTR Berlin 16/17.12.43.
DV263 KM-M		FTR Magdeburg 21/22.1.44.
DV283 KM-W		To 101 Squadron.
DV286		From 207 Squadron. To 300 Squadron.
DV329 KM-W		FTR Berlin 23/24.11.43.
DV331 KM-T/Z		FTR Frankfurt 20/21.12.43.
DV384 KM-A/V		To 50 Squadron.
ED305 KM-G/S		From 467 Squadron RAAF. To 617 Squadron on loan. FTR from mining sortie 10/11.3.43.
ED307 KM-R		FTR Cologne 28/29.6.43.
ED309 KM-S		From 50 Squadron. FTR Lorient 7/8.2.43.
ED314 KM-M		To 61 Squadron.
ED315		No operations. To 460 Squadron RAAF.
ED318 KM-X		FTR Berlin 17/18.1.43.
ED331 KM-Z		FTR Turin 12/13.7.43. whilst being flown by W/C Nettleton VC.
ED348 KM-M		From 57 Squadron. FTR Hagen 1/2.10.43.
ED351 KM-Y		FTR Duisburg 8/9.4.43.
ED355 KM-D		FTR Nienburg 17/18.12.42.
ED433 KM-V		From 101 Squadron. FTR Kassel 3/4.10.43.
ED611 KM-J		To 463 Squadron RAAF.
ED665 KM-L		FTR Berlin 31.8/1.9.43.
ED716 KM-F		To 550 Squadron.
ED723 KM-U		FTR Dortmund 23/24.5.43.
ED735 KM-K		To 617 Squadron.
ED783 KM-F		FTR Essen 30.4/1.5.43.
ED869 KM-G		From 97 Squadron. To 5 LFS.
ED999 KM-X		From 49 Squadron. FTR Berlin 23/24.12.43.
EE123 KM-K		FTR Wuppertal 29/30.5.43.
EE179 KM-B		From 97 Squadron. FTR Berlin 2/3.12.43.

EE184 KM-B		Ditched in the North Sea on return from Leipzig 20/21.10.43.
EE185 KM-K/A		To 617 Squadron on loan. Returned to 44 Squadron. FTR Mailly-le-Camp 3/4.5.44. Flew 13 operations to Berlin.
HK616		From 622 Squadron.
HK623		From 622 Squadron. To 38 Maintenance Unit.
JA684 KM-Q		To 5 LFS.
JA700 KM-P		FTR Berlin 2/3.12.43.
JA703 KM-W		To 617 Squadron on loan. Returned to 44 Squadron. FTR Mannheim 5/6.9.43.
JA843 KM-O		FTR Berlin 30/31.1.44.
JA895 KM-H		FTR Remscheid 30/31.7.43.
JA897 KM-F/H		FTR Peenemünde 17/18.8.43.
JA903		From 5 LFS. To 75 (NZ) Squadron.
JB136 KM-T		FTR Munich 2/3.10.43.
LL885		From 622 Squadron.
LL920 KM-V		FTR Schweinfurt 26/27.4.44.
LL938 KM-S		FTR Wesseling 21/22.6.44.
LL965 KM-C/V		FTR Darmstadt 11/12.9.44.
LM170 KM-E		To 1668 CU.
LM171 KM-R		FTR Stuttgart 28/29.7.44.
LM192 KM-K		To BCIS 12.44.
LM306 KM-L		From 49 Squadron. FTR Frankfurt 18/19.3.44. Flew 11 Berlin operations.
LM330 KM-Q		FTR Krefeld 21/22.6.43.
LM373 KM-V		FTR Berlin 23/24.11.43.
LM374 KM-S		FTR Berlin 23/24.11.43.
LM434 KM-F		FTR Wesseling 21/22.6.44.
LM592 KM-Q		FTR Wesseling 21/22.6.44.
LM625 KM-H		
LM631 KM-W		FTR St-Leu-d'Esserent 7/8.7.44.
LM638 KM-P		FTR Culmont-Chalindrey 12/13.7.44.
LM639		To Flight Refuelling Ltd. 7.10.44.
LM645 KM-P		FTR Walcheren 23.10.44.
LM648 KM-K		From 49 Squadron. Collided with PB428 (207 Squadron) in the circuit returning from Harburg 11/12.11.44.
LM650 KM-T		Crashed in Sussex on return from Homberg 1.11.44.
LM654 KM-L		FTR Böhlen 5/6.3.45.
LM655 KM-C		
ME299 KM-E		FTR Pölitz 8/9.2.45.
ME394 KM-X		
ME442 KM-V		Shot down by an intruder over Lincolnshire on return from the Dortmund-Ems Canal at Ladbergen 4.3.45.
ME550		
ME571 KM-P		To 463 Squadron RAAF.
ME573 KM-S		To 463 Squadron RAAF.
ME574 KM-W/P		Crashed on landing at Dunholme Lodge while training 7.1.44.
ME628 KM-V		FTR Pommerval 24/25.6.44.
ME629 KM-R		FTR Nuremberg 30/31.3.44.
ME634 KM-P		FTR St-Leu-d'Esserent 7/8.7.44.

ME672 KM-A	FTR Berlin 24/25.3.44.	
ME694 KM-L	FTR Stuttgart 25/26.7.44.	
ME699 KM-T	FTR St-Leu-d'Esserent 4/5.7.44.	
ME730 KM-R	FTR Schweinfurt 26/27.4.44.	
ME743 KM-G	FTR Marquise 27/28.6.44.	
ME791 KM-K	Crashed near Nottingham on return from training flight 11.6.44.	
ME794 KM-V	Destroyed in landing at Westcott on return from Maisy Palaiseau 1.6.44.	
ME804 KM-O	FTR Wesseling 21/22.6.44.	
ME844	From 15 Squadron.	
ME859 KM-S	FTR St-Leu-d'Esserent 7/8.7.44.	
ND496 KM-A	From 7 Squadron. To 75 (NZ) Squadron.	
ND514 KM-C	FTR Berlin 30/31.1.44.	
ND515 KM-Z/E	FTR Gennevilliers 9/10.5.44.	
ND517 KM-U	FTR Colombelles 18.7.44.	
ND518 KM-C/D	FTR Frankfurt 22/23.3.44.	
ND519 KM-E	FTR Caen 6/7.6.44.	
ND520 KM-A	FTR Augsburg 25/26.2.44.	
ND525 KM-Q	FTR Schweinfurt 24/25.2.44.	
ND538 KM-T	FTR Frankfurt 22/23.3.44.	
ND552 KM-X	FTR Wesseling 21/22.6.44.	
ND565 KM-C	FTR Berlin 24/25.3.44.	
ND566 KM-O	FTR Stuttgart 1/2.3.44.	
ND573 KM-S	FTR La Chapelle 20/21.4.44.	
ND574 KM-G	To Flight Refuelling Ltd.	
ND576 KM-M	FTR Stuttgart 15/16.3.44.	
ND578 KM-Y		
ND631 KM-B	To 617 Squadron. Returned to 44 Squadron. FTR Leipzig 10/11.4.45.	
ND689/G KM-G/O	FTR Amiens 19/20.5.44.	
ND698/G KM-Q	Crashed on landing at Oakley on return from Maisy Palaiseau 1.6.44	
ND741 KM-K	FTR Salbris 7/8.5.44.	
ND751 KM-J	FTR Pommerval 24/25.6.44.	
ND795 KM-C	FTR Nuremberg 30/31.3.44.	
ND843	To Flight Refuelling Ltd.	
ND869 KM-M	Ditched in the sea off Skegness when bound for Würzburg 16.3.45.	
ND973 KM-A	FTR Wesseling 21/22.6.44.	
ND974 KM-P	From 83 Squadron.	
ND976/G KM-R	FTR Duisburg 21/22.5.44.	
NE138 KM-Z	FTR mining 26/27.8.44.	
NF991 KM-D		
NG195 KM-C		
NG396 KM-G	From 1661 CU. FTR Sassnitz 6/7.3.45.	
NG397	From 1661 CU.	
NG415 KM-F		
NN697 KM-R	FTR Etampes 9/10.6.44.	
NN765	From 1661 CU. To 57 Squadron.	
NN768 KM-K	From 619 Squadron. FTR Harburg 7/8.3.45.	

PA195 KM-V	From 1661 CU. FTR Karlsruhe 2/3.2.45.	
PA256 KM-C		
PA276		
PB182	To 83 Squadron.	
PB189 KM-A	FTR Stuttgart 12/13.9.44.	
PB190 KM-J		
PB192 KM-F	FTR Ladbergen 4/5.11.44.	
PB205	To 619 Squadron.	
PB206 KM-Q	FTR from mining sortie 15/16.7.44.	
PB235 KM-C	FTR from mining sortie 4/5.10.44.	
PB251 KM-O	FTR Hamburg 21/22.3.45.	
PB266 KM-S	FTR Stuttgart 28/29.7.44.	
PB283 KM-K	To 1661 CU.	
PB346	To 619 Squadron.	
PB360	From 49 Squadron. To 57 Squadron.	
PB380 KM-S	To 75 (NZ) Squadron.	
PB417 KM-R	FTR Harburg 7/8.3.45.	
PB424 KM-X	To 75 (NZ) Squadron.	
PB534 KM-Q		
PB535 KM-Z	FTR Darmstadt 11/12.9.44.	
PB732	To 189 Squadron.	
PB733	To 1661 CU.	
PB743	To 189 Squadron.	
PB751 KM-G	From 619 Squadron. FTR Heilbronn 4/5.12.44.	
PB818 KM-C	From 195 Squadron.	
PB819 KM-K	From 622 Squadron.	
PB869	To 1661 CU.	
PD222 KM-U	FTR Brest 14.8.44.	
PD225	From 622 Squadron.	
PD228 KM-A	From 622 Squadron.	
PD366	From 622 Squadron.	
PD372 KM-Z		
PD373 KM-X	FTR Heilbronn 4/5.12.44.	
PD381	From 207 Squadron.	
PD422 KM-T	To 75 (NZ) Squadron.	
RA603		
RE131 KM-E		
RE132 KM-G		
RF203		
RF206		
RF210 KM-O		
RF234	To 619 Squadron.	
RF238		
RF240		
RF265		
SW251 KM-X	FTR Karlsruhe 2/3.2.45.	

HEAVIEST SINGLE LOSS.

21/22.06.44. Wesseling. 6 Lancasters FTR.

44 (Rhodesia) Squadron Roll of Honour

Hampden crews

Date	Aircraft	Operation	Rank	Name
21.12.39.	L4090	Reconnaissance	LAC	Gibbin T
25.03.40.	L4102	Reconnaissance	Sgt	Williams S A
			Sgt	Jones A R
			Sgt	Cross R W
			A/C1	Chapman A C
12.04.40.	L4099	Kristiansand	F/O	Taylor W G
			Sgt	Tonkiss J R
			Sgt	Ison W J
			Cpl	Brown H D
	P1173	Kristiansand	F/O	Robson H W
			P/O	Johnstone K J A
			Cpl	Evans J H
			Cpl	Evans W H G
14/15.05.40.	P4286	Breda	F/O	Ashfield L J
			P/O	Crawley C D
			Sgt	McKinlay F W
			Cpl	Preston F
23/24.05.40.	L4171	Communications	S/L	Johnson C E
			P/O	Barker D C
			Sgt	Collins H G
			Cpl	Crook W
03/04.06.40.	P1340	Emmerich	P/O	Roots R W
			Sgt	Kendrew A G
			Sgt	Connell S P
11/12.06.40.	P1325	La Fere/Laon	F/Sgt	Sumpster C L
			Sgt	Jeffrey W
			Sgt	Sandall J F
			Sgt	Simpson J
03/04.07.40.	P4352	Gardening	P/O	Todd D A
			Sgt	Apperson E T
			Sgt	Baird A
			F/L	Bull W S
19/20.07.40.	L4087	Gardening	Sgt	Farrands E L
			Sgt	Nixon P D
			Sgt	Miller R T
			P/O	Green B
28/29.07.40.	P4375	Hamburg	S/L	Macintyre J G
01.08.40.	L4085	Gardening	Sgt	Farmer E D
			Sgt	Wood C E
29/30.08.40.	P4372	Gelsenkirchen	P/O	Dunkels C O
06/07.09.40.	P2087	Krefeld	Sgt	Bell W
			Sgt	Bracegirdle J RNZAF
10/11.09.40.	P4371	Calais	F/L	Rogers D J
			Sgt	Brading R J
			Sgt	Westhorp B N
			Sgt	Lacey H G
11/12.09.40.	P1338	Bremerhaven	F/L	Smythe T L S
			P/O	Wise S C
			Sgt	Jones W H
			F/O	Coombes W F E

	X2913	Bremerhaven	P/O	Stewart D E
			Sgt	Joyce D A
			Sgt	Goodwill W
			Sgt	Hobson G J
17/18.09.40.	P2121	Antwerp	Sgt	Henderson T V
			P/O	Goode R G
			Sgt	Angus J H
			Sgt	Sugden J
01/02.10.40.	X2965	Cologne	Sgt	Day H
			Sgt	Tomlinson J
			Sgt	Devlin G J
			Sgt	Sillett E R
14/15.10.40.	X2910	Berlin	Sgt	Burt L J
			Sgt	Windle D
			Sgt	Baldwin J
			P/O	Carrell R M
20/21.10.40.	P2137	Berlin	Sgt	Hartop C W
			Sgt	Stubbs C V
			Sgt	Bennett R G
			Sgt	Milbourne R L
13/14.11.40.	X2995	Hamburg	P/O	Miller K L
			Sgt	Pewsey D
			Sgt	Egar E
14/15.11.40.	X2996	Berlin	F/O	Perkins R D
			Sgt	Maybury J G W
			Sgt	Green J D
			Sgt	Hawksby T W
20.11.40.	X3023	Lützkendorf	Sgt	Ottaway J L F
			P/O	Kerr A R
			Sgt	Elliott S F
08/09.04.41.	AD899	Gardening	P/O	Curley J G
			P/O	Laverack E T
			Sgt	Ashurst F
			Sgt	Campbell K S
17/18.04.41.	X2999	Berlin	F/Sgt	Sneeston J N
			Sgt	Brundish E N
			Sgt	Taylor J M
			Sgt	Mulford J W
02/03.05.41.	AD864	Hamburg	P/O	Jeff J E P
			P/O	Tripp H U A
			Sgt	Leaper R J
			Sgt	Egar E
09.05.41.		Active service	Sgt	Vigar J
12/13.06.41.	P4310	Soest	F/Sgt	Mercer C T C
			Sgt	Main R K
			F/Sgt	Kossick A
			Sgt	Park J R
	AE127	Soest	Sgt	Wardrop J
13/14.06.41.	AE129	Brest	Sgt	Saunders S P C
			Sgt	Miller J R
			Sgt	Greenaway R
			Sgt	Dickson T J
19.06 41.	AD904	Ferry	Sgt	Greig C F
			Sgt	Walshe J O
			Sgt	Boardman T K

Date	Aircraft	Target	Rank	Name
08/09.07.41.	AD840	Hamm	Sgt	Wilson A W
			Sgt	Soutar L A
			F/Sgt	Lytle S J
			Sgt	Mackenzie H D
	AE153	Hamm	F/Sgt	Tyler E D
			Sgt	Livis M RCAF
			F/Sgt	Betts K G
			Sgt	Black F W
22.07.41.	AD983	Gardening	Sgt	Bruce D M
			Sgt	Relyea W R B RCAF
			Sgt	Connolly J A
			Sgt	Lynch P J
24.07.41.	AD962	Brest	P/O	Grant J M RCAF
27/28.07.41.	P4406	Gardening	Sgt	Gammon P C
			Sgt	Winchester B
			F/Sgt	Slater G R
			Sgt	Whittaker N H
01.08.41.	AD966	Air test	Sgt	Le Blanc Smith G M
			Sgt	Dodds G D RCAF
			Sgt	Forsythe A
			A/C1	Jeffcote T B
			A/C1	Clark A D
06.08.41.	X2917	Calais	Sgt	Bradbury C S
			Sgt	McQuade W A RCAF
			F/Sgt	Yeomans S D
			Sgt	Howe D H
16/17.08.41.	AE239	Düsseldorf	Sgt	Armstrong J G
			Sgt	Morley C R RCAF
			Sgt	Flint J
			Sgt	Edwards S C
28.08.41.	AD917	Transit	Sgt	Mallen S
			Sgt	Windsor E A
31.08.41.	AD939	Training	P/O	Owen P R
			Sgt	Forbes D G
			A/C2	Prest F B
31/01.09.41.	AD726	Cologne	Sgt	Harvey S A
			Sgt	Taylor H A RCAF
			F/Sgt	Phillips J E
			Sgt	Hayes R K
02/03.09.41.	AD913	Frankfurt	Sgt	Stephens J
	AE313	Frankfurt	Sgt	de Brath D N N
			Sgt	Cole R L
	AE152	Berlin	P/O	Thompson E A W
			P/O	Cook H J RCAF
			Sgt	Dyer E
			Sgt	McBeth W
	AE254	Berlin	Sgt	Robertson L A
			Sgt	Unwin H N
			F/Sgt	Turner H B
			Sgt	Riddell T P A
07.09.41.	X2921	Gardening	Sgt	Watt A A
			Sgt	Newcombe J R
			Sgt	Wimbush A D
			Sgt	Cox E S
16.09.41.	AD930	Hamburg	Sgt	Cox R L
			F/Sgt	Barry J

Date	Aircraft	Target	Rank	Name
13/14.10.41.	AD975	Cologne	Sgt	Owen E
			F/Sgt	Edmondson G H RCAF
			Sgt	Shearer G
			Sgt	Ramsay G R
21/22.10.41.	AE257	Bremen	P/O	Budd W H
			P/O	Schafheitlin D RCAF
			Sgt	Austin W E
			Sgt	Hughes M J
23/24.10.41.	AE290	Le Havre	Sgt	Bell P H
			Sgt	Holmes K A
			Sgt	Atkinson R H
			Sgt	Laing A T
08/09.11.41.	AE377	Dunkerque	P/O	Frost W J
			P/O	Smith F L
			Sgt	Copsey T
			P/O	Lindsay J
13.12.41.	AE196	Gardening	W/C	Misselbrook S T
			Sgt	Gumbley A H G RNZAF
			Sgt	Leggett L D
			F/O	Jeffcoat H J
17/18.12.41.	AD868	Brest	P/O	Kaschula T L
			Sgt	Henderson J G
			Sgt	Wade E
			Sgt	Hall K E

Lancaster crews

Date	Aircraft	Target	Rank	Name
24/25.03.42.	R5493	Gardening	F/Sgt	Warren-Smith L
			Sgt	Marston R A
			Sgt	Murdock A F
			Sgt	Clifford C E W RAAF
			Sgt	Boyd J
			Sgt	Cluff E B
			Sgt	Flower W H
			F/Sgt	Davidson J McN
17.04.42.	L7536	Augsburg	Sgt	Rhodes G T
			Sgt	Baxter L H RNZAF
			Sgt	Daly B I J
			Sgt	Merricks C L
			Sgt	Wynton J A
			F/Sgt	Edwards G A
			F/Sgt	Gill H V
	L7565	Augsburg	W/O	Beckett J F
			Sgt	Moss B D
			F/Sgt	Ross A E RCAF
			Sgt	Seagoe B G
			Sgt	Hackett J H
			Sgt	Trustram R L
			Sgt	Harrison A J

	R5506	Augsburg	F/L	Sandford R R
			P/O	Peall H A P
			F/O	Gerrie A
			Sgt	Hadgraft G W J
			Sgt	Venter P J
			F/Sgt	Law L
			Sgt	Wing R E
	R5510	Augsburg	F/Sgt	Flux R J
			F/Sgt	McAlpine D H RCAF
			Sgt	Edwards I
08/09.05.42.	L7533	Warnemünde	W/O	Lamb N P J
			P/O	Gardiner P
			Sgt	Morrow A S
			Sgt	Webster L R
			F/Sgt	Hunt C R D
			Sgt	Evans K
			Sgt	Holeman R
			Sgt	Jones R H
	R5555	Warnemünde	W/C	Lynch-Blosse P W
			P/O	MacKay D G
			P/O	Beatson R V RNZAF
			F/L	McClure C S C
			P/O	Sommerville J McF W
			Sgt	Gower J B
			P/O	McLaren D G
			F/Sgt	Rogers J
	R5557	Warnemünde	W/O	Jones P O
			Sgt	Evans L E
			Sgt	Drennan J C
			P/O	MacDonald M H D RCAF
			F/Sgt	Thirkell P H H
			Sgt	Miller J H
			F/Sgt	Ship C H
			F/Sgt	Bolus A H
	R5568	Warnemünde	F/O	MacLagan G
			P/O	Sturgess H J S
			P/O	Belton F W
			Sgt	Crane W McD
			Sgt	Oliver R D
			Sgt	Nesbitt B L
			Sgt	Hough G W
05/06.06.42.	R5516	Essen	F/O	Halls L O
			P/O	Ransom R M
			Sgt	Bloomfield J A
			Sgt	Croft A B
			Sgt	Gottlieb A I
			Sgt	Melhado L S
			Sgt	Jones H
31/01.08.42.	L7537	Düsseldorf	F/Sgt	Tetley N
			Sgt	Forman E
			Sgt	Macmahon J M
			Sgt	Egan E B RCAF
			F/Sgt	Kelly G
			Sgt	Rix P
			Sgt	Gardner C N

Date	Aircraft	Target	Rank	Name
04/05.08.42.	R5603	Essen	F/O	Ball P A
			P/O	Marshall G P
			P/O	MacQueen I A J RCAF
			Sgt	Scott W D
			F/Sgt	Bentley J H
			F/Sgt	Firman G A RCAF
			F/Sgt	Williams A E
16.08.42.	R5489	Training	Sgt	Fletcher J
			Sgt	Pullinger D RNZAF
24/25.08.42.	W4105	Frankfurt	P/O	Nicholson D F
			P/O	Beaumont L M RCAF
			P/O	McDonald G C RCAF
			P/O	Rickard J M
			Sgt	Holland J V
			F/Sgt	Hagger F
			F/Sgt	Page R G
27/28.08.42.	W4124	Kassel	F/O	Suckling R H RNZAF
			Sgt	Bickers T
			Sgt	Rowbottom M
			Sgt	Allen E C
			Sgt	Winch H V
			Sgt	Johnson A E
			Sgt	Christie A F RCAF
13/14.09.42.	W4169	Bremen	F/O	Holland C T
			Sgt	Williams R E
			Sgt	Huntley D N
			Sgt	Fiddler G L RCAF
			F/O	Lovegrove C H
			Sgt	Murphy P C
18/19.09.42.	W4177	Gardening	Sgt	Beattie J
			Sgt	Cliffe J
			Sgt	Locke J R
			Sgt	Bentley A F
			Sgt	Walters F
			Sgt	Wrigley A K
			Sgt	Drinkwater J W RCAF
19/20.09.42.	R5554	Munich	P/O	Day W H
			Sgt	McGough C
			F/Sgt	Glynn M J
			Sgt	Burford U E T
01/02.10.42.	W4187	Wismar	F/O	Stephens J D V S
			Sgt	Dowden N E
			F/O	Tate J E
			F/Sgt	Hereford P
			Sgt	Williamson R E W
			F/Sgt	Nugent C G RCAF
			F/Sgt	Rowe H R
06/07.10.42.	R5903	Osnabrück	Sgt	Burke J
			Sgt	Gadson R B
	W4188	Osnabrück	S/L	Stewart I A
			Sgt	Shepherd C D
			F/O	Ryan P H RNZAF
			F/Sgt	Leyshon C H R
			P/O	Williams C H
			P/O	Corrie J E
			F/Sgt	Mutter L H

Date	Aircraft	Target	Rank	Name
09/10.11.42.	W4180	Hamburg	Sgt	Easom R
			Sgt	Cusden V H
			F/Sgt	Fox L H
			Sgt	Obbard J
			Sgt	Gruber R I
			Sgt	Lee V J
			Sgt	Shepperson O R
22/23.11.42.	W4304	Stuttgart	P/O	Young S R
			Sgt	Weymouth C A
			F/O	Appleton D J
			Sgt	Page W K D
			Sgt	Waters E A RNZAF
			Sgt	Brock T W
			F/Sgt	Tough J G R RCAF
17/18.12.42.	R5666	Nienburg	F/Sgt	Kingshorn J
			Sgt	Sheppard W G
	W4126	Nienburg	F/O	McNamara L G L
			F/O	McCleery R N RCAF
			F/O	Loree J W RCAF
			Sgt	MacLeod K R
			Sgt	Beckett G
			Sgt	Jones G W
	ED355	Nienburg	F/Sgt	Dening J G RAAF
20/21.12.42.	W4259	Duisburg	F/Sgt	Elger A C
			Sgt	McCready G D RCAF
			P/O	Giri V N
			Sgt	Easton A J
			Sgt	Gunter R I
			Sgt	Harmston C
			Sgt	Jackson E
21/22.12.42.	W4125	Munich	F/O	Biggane D F H
			Sgt	Imrie W
			Sgt	Read K N RCAF
			Sgt	Cook R
			Sgt	Pont H C
08/09.01.43.	W4176	Gardening	P/O	Shattock N C
			F/Sgt	Barrett W
			Sgt	Stack E F RAAF
			Sgt	Crowley M J
			F/Sgt	Morton H W H
			Sgt	Bell J A M
			Sgt	Gladwish R E
	W4277	Gardening	Sgt	Paige M J RCAF
			Sgt	Hutchinson J
			P/O	Cameron A G
			Sgt	Wright S
			Sgt	Colonna A R A
			Sgt	Mogg D B
			Sgt	Lightfoot J H
17/18.01.43.	ED318	Berlin	Sgt	Calcutt R
			Sgt	Mitchell C P
			Sgt	Allen D S
			Sgt	Perkins R D
			Sgt	Fenton R C
			Sgt	Bradbury R D
			Sgt	Lawrence V

Date	Aircraft	Target	Rank	Name
02/03.02.43.	W4819	Cologne	Sgt	Horden R
			Sgt	Traill I C
			Sgt	Copp P B
			Sgt	Cox L
			Sgt	Lawrence E C RCAF
			Sgt	Checketts F R W
			Sgt	Harrold E G
07/08.02.43.	W4832	Lorient	F/Sgt	Skinner D
			Sgt	Hunter J
			Sgt	Waddell H T RAAF
			Sgt	Vincent G T
			Sgt	Knight A RAAF
			Sgt	Howells A
			Sgt	Walton R
	ED309	Lorient	F/O	Millar J W RCAF
			Sgt	Drury R W RCAF
			F/Sgt	Perkins K M RCAF
			Sgt	Curtis L H
			Sgt	Black H G RCAF
			Sgt	Scrimgeour W W RCAF
			Sgt	Bond A L
01/02.03.43.	W4829	Berlin	Sgt	Forman B F
			Sgt	Farmer L
			Sgt	Coombes D G J
			Sgt	Holleron L J
			Sgt	Toft W E
			Sgt	Little J
			Sgt	Brown B F RCAF
10/11.03.43.	W4841	Gardening	Sgt	Gayton J D
			Sgt	Kirkup R D
			Sgt	Burgess W C
			Sgt	Quick L A
			Sgt	Miller D H RCAF
			Sgt	Taylor A J
			Sgt	Allen G
	ED305	Gardening	Sgt	Smith B T C
			Sgt	Black G R RCAF
			F/O	Carr R H
			Sgt	Cook C H D
			Sgt	Love G S
			Sgt	Brown C V
			Sgt	Healey A
27/28.03.43.	W4839	Berlin	F/Sgt	Horwood A J
			Sgt	Schultz L W J
			Sgt	Cole R L
			F/Sgt	Newton J McA RCAF
			Sgt	Guild F W RCAF
			Sgt	Clements H H RCAF
			Sgt	Sheridan G McC
29/30.03.43.	W4199	Berlin	Sgt	Johnson K J RNZAF
			Sgt	Shipp W H
			P/O	Leng I F
			Sgt	Edmonds R A
			Sgt	Somerville T C
			Sgt	Marlin C G L
			Sgt	Twiddy R

Date	Aircraft	Target	Rank	Name
08/09.04.43.	ED351	Duisburg	F/Sgt	Haines I C
			Sgt	Richardson S
			Sgt	Asbury R A
			Sgt	Prince R G
			Sgt	Ward F G
			Sgt	Strandberg E RCAF
			Sgt	Yeo L J
09/10.04.43.	R5898	Duisburg	Sgt	Smith W
			P/O	Salt J H
			Sgt	Nash L J
			Sgt	Dixon S
30/01.05.43.	ED783	Essen	Sgt	Ellis L J
			Sgt	Le Page R L
			F/O	Rollings W A RCAF
			Sgt	Browne J B
			Sgt	Ellis H C
			Sgt	Williams R
			Sgt	McClellan S S
13/14.05.43.	W4110	Pilsen	F/O	Rail W D
			Sgt	Underwood N K
			Sgt	Bromwich A T C
			Sgt	Digby W C
			Sgt	Boardman R C
			Sgt	Walker R S A
			Sgt	Batty G
	W4305	Pilsen	Sgt	Stephens P
			Sgt	Orchard E L
			Sgt	Dewey R
			Sgt	Taylor N E
			Sgt	Cram D
			Sgt	O'Halloran W E RCAF
23/24.05.43.	ED723	Dortmund	Sgt	Drysdale J L RCAF
			Sgt	Lester J F
			F/O	Marsden W A
			F/Sgt	Hyett H W E
			Sgt	Jones S
			Sgt	Bushill A S
			Sgt	Doherty F A RCAF
29/30.05.43.	W4838	Wuppertal	Sgt	Erickson D W
			Sgt	Chadfield G E
			Sgt	Thompson E A
			Sgt	Woods R A F RNZAF
	EE123	Wuppertal	F/O	Holt P G RCAF
			Sgt	Tucker I
			Sgt	McColl D
			Sgt	Young W
			Sgt	Stoddart R T
			Sgt	Robinson H
14/15.06.43.	W4936	Oberhausen	S/L	Haywood G B
			Sgt	Foot R G
			F/O	Kirby R
			Sgt	Boardman R
			Sgt	Rivers R W
			Sgt	Brand R C H
			Sgt	Armstrong J H

	W4949	Oberhausen	Sgt	Shearman P J
			F/Sgt	Pugh E L
			Sgt	Ballamy N L
			F/O	Richards F M
			Sgt	Card B W
			Sgt	Zedy G C A
			Sgt	Akeister C W
21/22.06.43.	LM330	Krefeld	P/O	Thompson H C
			P/O	Welsh L S
			Sgt	McGrath L R
			Sgt	Mindel S D
			Sgt	Harrison L A
			Sgt	England N N
			Sgt	Metcalfe N
			Sgt	Arlow J H
25/26.06.43.	R5740	Gelsenkirchen	P/O	Sharp D M
			P/O	Struthers D MacL
			F/Sgt	Johnstone T
			Sgt	Dash R J
			Sgt	Thompson R H W
			Sgt	Morris N H
			Sgt	Griffiths E R H
			Sgt	Langstaff K W
28/29.06.43.	ED307	Cologne	Sgt	Hulbert C V L R
			Sgt	Lewis D M
			Sgt	Sykes J A
			Sgt	Tooth A
			Sgt	Jones T R
			Sgt	Denney G A
			Sgt	Galligan P J RAAF
12/13.07.43.	ED331	Turin	W/C	Nettleton J D
			F/O	Ludlow A R
			Sgt	Money J E
			Sgt	Seager D E A
			F/O	Juniper K S
			F/L	Cramp D
			F/L	Wood I M RAAF
			F/O	Calcutt F I
30/31.07.43.	JA895	Remscheid	W/C	Williamson E A
			Sgt	Pugh L S
			Sgt	Turner F T
			P/O	Timmins R A
			Sgt	Jordan R M
			Sgt	Jones G G
			Sgt	MacRae D H C
02/03.08.43.	W4778	Hamburg	Sgt	Moffatt A R
			Sgt	Croft L G
			F/O	Kirkham F R RCAF
			Sgt	King S A
			Sgt	Fincham R E
			Sgt	Sewell W A

17/18.08.43.	W4935	Peenemünde	Sgt	Campbell R McM
			Sgt	Watkins J G
			F/O	Popperwell L G
			Sgt	Thompson A H
			Sgt	Graham J
			Sgt	MacAninch H C
			Sgt	Philip W
	DV202	Peenemünde	P/O	Harding R C RCAF
			Sgt	Weston T N
			F/Sgt	Prendergast L
			Sgt	McDermott L F
			Sgt	Quance W H
			F/Sgt	Pynisky P RCAF
			F/Sgt	Shaw S
	JA897	Peenemünde	Sgt	Drew W J
			Sgt	Reid J D McG
			Sgt	Rudkin S I
			Sgt	Jopling J T
			Sgt	James T H R
			Sgt	Bassett J H
31/01.09.43.	ED665	Berlin	P/O	Stephenson G N
			Sgt	Robertson J A
			P/O	More E G RCAF
			F/Sgt	Smith A R
			W/O2	Betts D RCAF
			F/Sgt	Hopkin S D
			Sgt	Beggs W J
03/04.09.43.	W4961	Berlin	S/L	Watson R G
			Sgt	Edwards A W F
			Sgt	Tyreman N A
			Sgt	Smith E J
			Sgt	Reynolds J A G
			Sgt	James C G
			Sgt	Gilbey K
	DV155	Berlin	F/O	Rundle S T J RAAF
			Sgt	Crow P
			Sgt	Bellman N E RAAF
			Sgt	Gregory R T RAAF
			Sgt	Caudell W E
			Sgt	Findlay W
05/06.09.43.	JA703	Mannheim	P/O	Stiver D E
			Sgt	Edwards C B
			Sgt	McNair A
			F/O	Quinton L F RCAF
			Sgt	Chaplin K W
			Sgt	Mosey E
			Sgt	Davies D E
01/02.10 43.	ED348	Hagen	Sgt	Bennett M O D
			Sgt	Dobson J
			Sgt	Meakin G S

Date	Aircraft	Target	Rank	Name
02/03.10.43.	JB136	Munich	Sgt	Smith B C
			Sgt	Kemp G S
			P/O	Linford J V
			Sgt	Taylor A B
			Sgt	Hopkinson C
			Sgt	McMullin H
			Sgt	Watt K
03/04.10.43.	ED433	Kassel	P/O	Norton H G RAAF
			Sgt	Stevens J H
			Sgt	Stait S D
			Sgt	Greenfield E E
			Sgt	Whalley W A
			Sgt	Martin R G
18/19.10.44.	R5901	Hannover	P/O	Piper H C G
			Sgt	Emson J W
			Sgt	Thomas H H
			Sgt	Austin H
20/21.10.43.	EE184	Leipzig	P/O	Watts R H RAAF
			Sgt	Connor J N
23/24.11.43.	DV329	Berlin	F/L	Hill C E
			F/O	Wright E G
			P/O	Marsden J
			F/O	Nunn C W
			Sgt	Myerscough T
			Sgt	Ledsham R
	LM373	Berlin	P/O	Buckel W
			Sgt	Ambrose E
			F/Sgt	Beebe J
			Sgt	Lees P M
			Sgt	O'Brien G J
			Sgt	Taylor J
			Sgt	Hardy M H RAAF
	LM374	Berlin	F/O	Hanscomb C K
			Sgt	Langley C C
			P/O	Whitticks H J
			F/O	Laxton C S
			Sgt	Reeves A
			Sgt	Seaman A A M
			Sgt	Strickland R C RCAF
02/03.12.43.	EE179	Berlin	F/O	Newell W F
			Sgt	Currie W B
			F/O	Dell F A
			F/O	Rosser T
			Sgt	Jones R W
			P/O	Kay G H RCAF
			Sgt	Johnson W P
	JA700	Berlin	F/O	West G A
			Sgt	Woodley A
			P/O	Cox F G
			F/O	Hazell A W
			Sgt	Corrie C C
			F/Sgt	Clayton H L
			F/Sgt	Smith W J

Date	Aircraft	Target	Rank	Name
16/17.12.43.	DV238	Berlin	P/O	Rollin D A
			F/Sgt	Moodie A T
			Sgt	Blackmore J C
			P/O	Melia T B
			Sgt	Tocher E J
			Sgt	Chew B
			Sgt	Standing R
20/21.12.43.	DV331	Frankfurt	Sgt	Tuppen P J A
			F/O	Burrell R
			P/O	Blake F J
			Sgt	Davies W D R
			Sgt	Thomas H P
23/24.12.43.	R5669	Berlin	P/O	Knight T H
			Sgt	Blackley E J
			Sgt	Cooper K T
			Sgt	Symonds D J
			Sgt	Yeatman A R C
			Sgt	Birchall E
			Sgt	Tutt G B
			Sgt	Whitney S W
	ED999	Berlin	Sgt	Hands R L
			Sgt	Bowles H
			Sgt	Wilde J A
			Sgt	Coombe A P
			Sgt	Phillips G E
			Sgt	Beech K A
			Sgt	Burgess C
01/02.01.44.	W4831	Berlin	P/O	Holmes A'Court W A RCAF
			Sgt	Dickinson R
			P/O	Woods J W
			F/O	Baker R B
			F/O	Blaha O D
			Sgt	Kidley R A
			W/O2	Myers T W RCAF
			Sgt	Norton H A
07.01.44.	ME574	Training	Sgt	Welch W H
14/15.01.44.	R5729	Brunswick	P/O	Curatolo L RCAF
			Sgt	Williams G H
			Sgt	Hughes P R
			F/Sgt	Mullin D S RCAF
			Sgt	Whiteley T
			Sgt	Weldon S H
			Sgt	Armitt G RAAF
21/22.01.44.	DV263	Magdeburg	F/L	Ruddick J
			Sgt	Ferguson D A
			Sgt	Mirams D C
			Sgt	Duggan D C
			Sgt	Balaam E
			F/Sgt	Proctor E W
			F/Sgt	O'Connell R J

Date	Aircraft	Target	Rank	Name
30/31.01.44.	JA843	Berlin	Sgt	Parker G R
			F/Sgt	Gow C H
			F/Sgt	Wareham S J
			Sgt	MacDonald J W
			Sgt	Macrae F
			Sgt	Jones T M
	ND514	Berlin	P/O	Lyford N J RAAF
24/25.02.44.	ND525	Schweinfurt	F/Sgt	Haynes G T
			Sgt	Bennett V
			F/Sgt	Halliday G R S
			F/Sgt	Bergland N RCAF
			Sgt	Weddle G A
			Sgt	Openshaw R
			Sgt	Nicolson G P
25/26.02.44.	ND520	Augsburg	Sgt	Swingler J A
			Sgt	Cowley T B
01/02.03.44.	ND566	Stuttgart	Sgt	Campbell J McL
15/16.03.44.	ND576	Stuttgart	F/O	Berrington J R
			Sgt	Orme D D
			Sgt	Adder M
			Sgt	Clark G
			Sgt	Johnson R
			Sgt	Jack W C
			Sgt	Sagar J
18/19.03.44.	LM306	Frankfurt	F/Sgt	Curtis D
			W/O	Dowling T E RAAF
22/23.03.44.	ND518	Frankfurt	P/O	Porter J H RAAF
			P/O	Davies H N
			F/Sgt	Barclay J
			Sgt	Holmes W
			Sgt	Bowen H J
	ND538	Frankfurt	F/O	Butt R E RAAF
			Sgt	Donald G
			Sgt	Shaw J
			F/Sgt	Spurden G C
24/25.03.44.	ME672	Berlin	P/O	Hayes B M
			Sgt	Ella J M
			Sgt	Wellfare R H
			Sgt	Walker W K
			Sgt	Radcliffe K L RCAF
			Sgt	Perrie W G
	ND565	Berlin	P/O	Evans A
			F/Sgt	Terrell A G
			Sgt	Evans C J
			F/O	Garland G F
			F/Sgt	Hatton P J
			Sgt	Myles A P
			Sgt	Burnard M E RCAF
			Sgt	Miller K V
30/31.03.44.	ME629	Nuremberg	P/O	Frost C A
			Sgt	Stanton F
			F/Sgt	Ashton T
			F/O	Devon H A
			Sgt	Johnson A J
			Sgt	Carr J H
			Sgt	Hamlin J

	ND795	Nuremberg	P/O	Charlesworth T G W
			Sgt	Jeffery K A
			F/Sgt	Hill R P G
			Sgt	Percival S
			Sgt	Scott G W
			Sgt	Evans L J
20/21.04.44.	ND573	La Chapelle	F/O	Skinner G A
			Sgt	Farmer A
			Sgt	Freeman W T
			Sgt	Prewer D
			Sgt	Ward T D
			Sgt	Scott J Y
			Sgt	Singfield W G
26/27.04.44.	LL920	Schweinfurt	F/O	Oldham G W
			Sgt	Walker F B
			F/Sgt	McKerrow J A
			F/O	Petts L W
			Sgt	Williams W F
			Sgt	Frame R D
			Sgt	Whittles G W
	ME730	Schweinfurt	F/Sgt	Kewley W E RNZAF
			Sgt	Booth D
			Sgt	Webber M J
			Sgt	Lees G D RCAF
			Sgt	Rutzki J RCAF
03/04.05.44.	EE185	Mailly-le-Camp	P/O	Nolan A W RAAF
			Sgt	Charlton E H
			F/Sgt	Milton K B
			F/O	Blake E G RNZAF
			Sgt	Boreham C J
			Sgt	Cook R D
			Sgt	Higgins P
07/08.05.44.	ND741	Salbris	S/L	Hunter C H
			F/O	Greenwood A
			F/O	Willis G K RCAF
			P/O	Salmon F A
			P/O	Alexander R C
			P/O	Miles G R
09/10.05.44.	ND515	Gennevilliers	F/O	Bradburn J
			Sgt	Jones A H
			P/O	Norman G H
			P/O	Gillard G P
			Sgt	Woolley C L
			F/L	Mortimer G E
			P/O	Clarke A G
19/20.05.44.	ND689	Amiens	F/O	Barber R J RCAF
			F/Sgt	Fenwick T P
			W/O2	Scott D J RCAF
			Sgt	Garnsey J E
			P/O	Ingram S B
21/22.05.44.	ND976	Duisburg	P/O	Dunn L W RAAF
			Sgt	Southern J
			Sgt	MacFadyen C
			Sgt	Thomas I B

Date	Aircraft	Target	Rank	Name
06/07.06.44.	ND519	Caen	F/L	Stratis W A
			Sgt	Haly R F E
			F/O	Greenfield G C A
			F/Sgt	Hawkes E P
			F/Sgt	Knight G H RAAF
			Sgt	Roe E J
			Sgt	Page H P
09/10.06.44.	NN697	Etampes	F/O	Balsdon D E
			Sgt	Death L F
			F/O	Clubb F J RAAF
			F/Sgt	Walters R S L
			P/O	White P B RAAF
			Sgt	Burns G J
			Sgt	O'Neill E L RCAF
21/22.06.44.	LL938	Wesseling	P/O	Wood R RNZAF
			F/Sgt	Leonard A M RCAF
			T/Sgt	Martin A E USAAF
			Sgt	McKenzie V
	ME804	Wesseling	P/O	Richards T B
			Sgt	Thompson H V D
			F/Sgt	Fazackerley R
			Sgt	Wright G L
			F/Sgt	Buckby J A
			Sgt	Pursglove H R
			F/Sgt	Spinks W E RCAF
			Sgt	Greenfield H M
	LM434	Wesseling	P/O	Scholtz N J W RCAF
			F/Sgt	Willson J C RCAF
	LM592	Wesseling	P/O	Canty E A RAAF
			Sgt	Clay R E
			F/O	Vowles J R RAAF
			Sgt	Norris E
			P/O	Crook W M
			Sgt	Scott E G
			Sgt	McCoy L J P RAAF
	ND552	Wesseling	F/O	Smith N J RAAF
			Sgt	Barber J D
			F/O	Calder T S
			F/Sgt	Steele M W
			Sgt	Bozier L H
			Sgt	Blackie D
			Sgt	Brett R W
	ND973	Wesseling	P/O	Baxter G
			Sgt	Betterton D
			W/O2	Rutherford B A M RCAF
			W/O2	Young S RCAF
			W/O	Scholes K
			F/Sgt	Taylor D A RCAF
			Sgt	Whitfield D R R L
24/25.06.44.	ME628	Pommerval	F/Sgt	Oswald R
			W/O	Richardson A J
			Sgt	Hutchinson L J H
			Sgt	Sargent R H
	ND751	Pommerval	P/O	Aiken D E RCAF
			Sgt	Lewarne H A

			W/O2	Riddoch R A RCAF
			F/Sgt	Simmons A M RCAF
			Sgt	Rawson F S
			Sgt	Hare J
			Sgt	Lewis J
27/28.06.44.	ME743	Marquise	F/L	Merrick F X
			Sgt	Carling R D J C
			F/O	Poulter J
			F/O	Bartlett R N RCAF
			Sgt	Dickinson C
			Sgt	Warll H P RCAF
			Sgt	Thomas J W
04/05.07.44.	ME699	St-Leu-d'Esserent	P/O	Young W A RAAF
			F/O	Wareham F E
			F/O	Braathen H RCAF
			Sgt	Jackson T L
			Sgt	Rennie W W RCAF
			Sgt	Houseman R
07/08.07.44.	ME634	St-Leu-d'Esserent	F/L	Carnegie R F
	ME859	St-Leu-d'Esserent	P/O	Graaf D
			Sgt	Critchley L A
			F/O	Purvis V D
			F/Sgt	Gibberson F H
			F/O	Hodge J S
			W/O	Groves R B RAAF
			W/O	Holland A
	LM631	St-Leu-d'Esserent	P/O	Gowing K J
			Sgt	McDonald R J
15/16.07.44.	PB206	Gardening	F/O	Hough W J
			Sgt	Hoare H D
			F/Sgt	Priestley L
			F/Sgt	Singer J H RCAF
			Sgt	Nichols H W
			Sgt	Andersen P RCAF
			Sgt	King E C
18.07.44.	ND517	Mondeville	Sgt	Burroughs K D
25/26.07.44.	ME694	Stuttgart	F/Sgt	Whitehead T W
26/27.07.44.	PB346	Givors	F/O	McKechnie D N
			Sgt	Barker A
			Sgt	Little W R RCAF
			Sgt	Dean R G
			Sgt	Williams R A
			Sgt	Courtenay E J
			Sgt	Craven A
28/29.07.44.	LM171	Stuttgart	Sgt	Marshall R
			Sgt	Fardoe T E
	PB266	Stuttgart	F/O	Duncan A J RAAF
			F/Sgt	Hennessy F E
			F/Sgt	Walker G A
14.08.44.	PD222	Brest	F/O	Gilchrist H G RCAF
			F/Sgt	Maguire D J
			F/O	McAulay M RCAF
			F/O	Mercer R W RAAF
			F/Sgt	McLeod J M RCAF

Date	Aircraft	Target	Rank	Name
26/27.08.44.	NE138	Gardening	Sgt	Rickeard A J
			P/O	Jones R C M
			F/Sgt	Jenkins T E
			F/O	Marston L F A
			F/Sgt	Burnett W McG H
			F/Sgt	Watts D H
11/12.09.44.	LL965	Darmstadt	F/O	Westgate E
			Sgt	Fisher R A
			F/Sgt	Taylor W
			F/Sgt	Thompson W H
			Sgt	Randall R W
			Sgt	Murphy J C
			Sgt	Gee H
	PB535	Darmstadt	F/O	Lade D S RAAF
			F/Sgt	Starkie T
			W/O	Alcock T L RAAF
			F/O	McCallum J A W
			Sgt	Benjamin M
			F/Sgt	Conquest H J RAAF
			F/O	Hourigan I P RAAF
12/13.09.44.	PB189	Stuttgart	F/L	Oxborrow J E P
			F/O	Macgregor J R
			Sgt	Cotter D A
			F/Sgt	Hamilton D A C
			F/Sgt	Murphy F A
			Sgt	Mitchell N
			Sgt	Penton D
			Sgt	Halliwell J F C
04/05.10.44.	PB235	Gardening	F/O	Evans N J
			Sgt	Snoxell D A P
			F/Sgt	Hunter K
			F/Sgt	Harper J D
			Sgt	Cahill D
23.10.44.	LM645	Walcheren	F/O	Russell H A S
			Sgt	Leeming C
			W/O	Towill C E
			Sgt	Dennett T A
			W/O	Abraham R G
			Sgt	Morley J
			Sgt	Campbell E
01.11.44.	LM650	Homberg	F/O	Haworth J H T
			Sgt	Seiler F M
04/05.11.44.	PB192	Dortmund-Ems Canal	Sgt	Beckley M G
			Sgt	Farley E R
11/12.11.44.	LM648	Harburg	F/O	Caryer P A C
			Sgt	Driscoll R D
			F/O	Grassie C R RCAF
			F/O	Arnett D S
			F/Sgt	Mitchell D L RAAF
			Sgt	Keen D
			Sgt	Routledge J

Date	Aircraft	Target	Rank	Name
04/05.12.44.	PD373	Heilbronn	Capt	Hirschfeld G W SAAF
			Sgt	Lorrain A D
			F/O	Yorke P
			F/O	Murphy D E RAAF
			F/Sgt	Jones H S RAAF
			Sgt	Storr J
			Sgt	Mitchell J
02/03.02.45.	PA195	Karlsruhe	F/O	Worrall C
			Sgt	Wilson W J
			Sgt	Fuller J R
			F/Sgt	Clements J A
			F/Sgt	Watt J
			Sgt	Judd J E
			F/Sgt	Maidment G E
	SW251	Karlsruhe	F/L	Gallivan T E RCAF
			Sgt	Balloch A
			F/O	Armstrong O W RCAF
			F/Sgt	Beaumont L H RCAF
			Sgt	Bowden S J
			F/Sgt	Dufresne E C RCAF
			F/Sgt	Johnson D W RCAF
08/09.02.45.	ME299	Politz	F/L	Mangos K RNZAF
			F/Sgt	Finlayson D D
			F/L	Bingham K R
			Sgt	James W J
			Sgt	Jones M
04.03.45.	ME442	Ladbergen	F/O	Ryan J J F RAAF
			Sgt	Jarman T H
			F/Sgt	Russell R R
			F/Sgt	Terry H J
			Sgt	Birch H
			Sgt	Payne H
			Sgt	Rogan W H
06/07.03.45.	NG396	Sassnitz	F/O	Boyle B F RCAF
			Sgt	Thornton W C
			F/Sgt	Pickup J
			F/Sgt	Turner W J C
			F/Sgt	Doggart T W
			F/Sgt	Smith J C
			Sgt	Hance C J
07/08.03.45.	NN768	Harburg	F/O	Jetson E T RAAF
16/17.03.45.	ND869	Würzburg	F/L	Shephard W H
			Sgt	Beauchamp A W
			F/Sgt	Allan J
			F/Sgt	Judge R B
			Sgt	Brown D F
			Sgt	Snape R D
			Sgt	Mitchell R F G
21/22.03.45.	PB251	Hamburg	F/O	Hennessy B F
			Sgt	Boothman A
			Sgt	Davies D H
			F/Sgt	Kay K
			Sgt	Lyons J
			Sgt	White G A
			Sgt	Richards H

10/11.04.45.	ND631	Leipzig	F/O	Kennedy P W
			P/O	Woodhouse G C R
			Sgt	Olson E P P
			W/O2	Turner A F D RCAF
			F/Sgt	Short J E
			F/Sgt	McBurney C
			F/Sgt	Bull A E

Key to Abbreviations

A&AEE	Aeroplane and Armaments Experimental Establishment.
AA	Anti-Aircraft fire.
AACU	Anti-Aircraft Cooperation Unit.
AAS	Air Armament School.
AASF	Advance Air Striking Force.
AAU	Aircraft Assembly Unit.
ACM	Air Chief Marshal.
ACSEA	Air Command South-East Asia.
AFDU	Air Fighting Development Unit.
AFEE	Airborne Forces Experimental Unit.
AFTDU	Airborne Forces Tactical Development Unit.
AGS	Air Gunners School.
AMDP	Air Members for Development and Production.
AOC	Air Officer Commanding.
AOS	Air Observers School.
ASRTU	Air-Sea Rescue Training Unit.
ATTDU	Air Transport Tactical Development Unit.
AVM	Air Vice-Marshal.
BAT	Beam Approach Training.
BCBS	Bomber Command Bombing School.
BCDU	Bomber Command Development Unit.
BCFU	Bomber Command Film Unit.
BCIS	Bomber Command Instructors School.
BDU	Bombing Development Unit.
BSTU	Bomber Support Training Unit.
CF	Conversion Flight.
CFS	Central Flying School.
CGS	Central Gunnery School.
C-in-C	Commander in Chief.
CNS	Central Navigation School.
CO	Commanding Officer.
CRD	Controller of Research and Development.
CU	Conversion Unit.
DGRD	Director General for Research and Development.
EAAS	Empire Air Armament School.
EANS	Empire Air Navigation School.
ECDU	Electronic Countermeasures Development Unit.
ECFS	Empire Central Flying School.
ETPS	Empire Test Pilots School.
F/L	Flight Lieutenant.
Flt	Flight.
F/O	Flying Officer.
FPP	Ferry Pilots School.

F/S	Flight Sergeant.
FTR	Failed to Return.
FTU	Ferry Training Unit.
G/C	Group Captain.
Gp	Group.
HCU	Heavy Conversion Unit.
HGCU	Heavy Glider Conversion Unit.
LFS	Lancaster Finishing School.
MAC	Mediterranean Air Command.
MTU	Mosquito Training Unit.
MU	Maintenance Unit.
NTU	Navigation Training Unit.
OADU	Overseas Aircraft Delivery Unit.
OAPU	Overseas Aircraft Preparation Unit.
OTU	Operational Training Unit.
P/O	Pilot Officer.
PTS	Parachute Training School.
RAE	Royal Aircraft Establishment.
SGR	School of General Reconnaissance.
Sgt	Sergeant.
SHAEF	Supreme Headquarters Allied Expeditionary Force.
SIU	Signals Intelligence Unit.
S/L	Squadron Leader.
SOC	Struck off Charge.
SOE	Special Operations Executive.
Sqn	Squadron.
TF	Training Flight.
TFU	Telecommunications Flying Unit.
W/C	Wing Commander.
Wg	Wing.
WIDU	Wireless Intelligence Development Unit.
W/O	Warrant Officer.

Notes

Notes